# TEACHING CHILDREN TO BE LITERATE

# TEACHING CHILDREN TO BE LITERATE

## A REFLECTIVE APPROACH

### Anthony V. Manzo

University of Missouri–Kansas City

### Ula C. Manzo

Central Missouri State University

**Harcourt Brace College Publishers**

Fort Worth   Philadelphia   San Diego   New York   Orlando   Austin   San Antonio
Toronto   Montreal   London   Sydney   Tokyo

| Publisher | Ted Buchholz |
| --- | --- |
| Acquisitions Editor | Jo-Anne Weaver |
| Developmental Editor | Tracy Napper |
| Project Editor | Annelies Schlickenrieder |
| Production Manager | Jane Tyndall Ponceti |
| Art Director | Sue Hart |
| Picture Editor | Lili Weiner |
| Cover Photographer | Will Crocker |

ISBN: 0-15-300560-2
Library of Congress Catalog Card Number: 93-80671

Address for Editorial Correspondence: Harcourt Brace College Publishers, 301 Commerce Street, Suite 3700, Fort Worth, TX 76102.

Address for Orders: Harcourt Brace & Company, 6277 Sea Harbor Drive, Orlando, FL 32887. 1-800-782-4479, or 1-800-433-0001 (in Florida).

Printed in the United States of America

5 6 7 8 9 0 1 2 3   039   9 8 7 6 5 4 3 2

To our youngest—Byron, Nathan, Kate, Kristin, Claire-Marie, and (in press)—and to yours . . .

## ABOUT THE AUTHORS

Anthony Manzo is the 1993 recipient of the William S. Gray Citation of Merit of the International Reading Association, a lifetime award for significant research and impact on the field of literacy education. Professor Manzo has authored and co-authored several articles and books, and an innovative new informal reading–thinking inventory. Currently he directs the Center for Studies in Higher Order Literacy at the University of Missouri at Kansas City.

Ula Manzo has taught at the elementary, secondary, and college levels. She has been a central office administrator in an urban school system. She has authored and co-authored several articles, books, and an innovative new informal reading–thinking inventory. Currently she teaches at Central Missouri State University.

The Manzos have co-authored *Literacy Disorders: Holistic Diagnosis and Remediation*, 1993, and *The Informal Reading–Thinking Inventory* (with Michael McKenna; available fall 1994), both published by Harcourt Brace College Publishers.

# PREFACE

Most children welcome the opportunity to become literate with the same enthusiasm that early humans embraced the opportunity to learn how to make fire. They will give you their attention, work with you, and even practice and innovate on their own. Almost anyone who knows how to read and write can share these gifts with these children. For some children, however, becoming literate is a bit more difficult. The reasons for these difficulties are many and complex. The attempt to have *all* children become literate has led to many theories and proposals. This book tells about many of those theories and proposals, and what research and practice have revealed about their efficacy. It is written primarily for the preservice elementary school classroom teacher. The book is designed not merely to inform but to teach: to provide a resource that can be used again and again to discover and rediscover professional information and direction for guiding the efforts of *all* children to become literate.

This book is based on three practical assumptions. The first is that teacher education should begin by involving prospective teachers in examining and defining the philosophy and goals that will guide their efforts and choice of teaching methods. The second is that teachers need to be prepared to work in a variety of possible settings, and need to select approaches and methods that are best suited to varied grade levels and student characteristics. The third is that teachers need to build familiarity with the research literature of the field, since the subjective experiences and wisdom of teachers needs to be anchored, wherever possible, in a more objective framework that combines and complements the art, craft, and science of professional education.

Based on these assumptions, one of the objectives of this book is to prepare teachers for a rewarding career in literacy education as we know it today, while also equipping them with the background knowledge, will, and wisdom to be active participants in meeting tomorrow's challenges. These objectives are consistent with the teacher's role as a rational "guardian of the past and trustee of the future." Within this tradition, this textbook offers the following:

- a broad understanding of current literacy approaches, methods, and materials
- an emphasis on the role of literacy education in promoting the spirit of democratic life
- varied perspectives, to engage preservice teachers in examining their own views, and their individual inclinations, talents, and possible areas of need
- a good deal of encouragement and assistance in how to be a reflective and inventive teacher

Within this framework, this book addresses timely issues such as the following:

- addressing the *whole* child, rather than a narrow focus on skills
- meeting the needs of children from diverse, multicultural backgrounds
- providing for children with special learning needs
- accessing appropriate applications of computer technology

- using a variety of traditional and recent approaches to literacy assessment, including portfolio collection
- incorporating the rich array of children's literature to enhance literacy instruction
- empowering children to influence their environment, rather than simply being influenced by it
- promoting higher-order reading and thinking from the earliest glimmerings of interest in being literate

Any effort to address such a wide array of contemporary concerns is bound to result in more material than any single instructor might find suitable for one course, though not more than each and every teacher-in-training will come to need. You may wish to be selective in what is emphasized in a typical term of study. A variety of features are built into the text to aid in organizing and selecting topics for emphasis. These include the following:

- *Graphic Overviews* of "where you are" in the journey through the book, which will help focus reading and thinking in each chapter
- *Quotations* that serve as organizing concept(s) for each chapter
- *Reflective Inquiries and Activities* at the end of each chapter that attempt to stimulate relevant thoughts, provide hands-on experiences, and stimulate fresh insights
- *Graphic Summaries* of "where you've been" in each chapter
- *Appendixes* to provide details that are too extensive for inclusion in the chapters
- *Citations* that are extensive enough to serve as an ongoing resource for building educators as well as teachers
- *Instructor's Manual* with test questions available

Beyond learning about literacy instruction through the use of this textbook, we trust that you will find things to smile at as you read, as we did as we wrote. The education of children, while a serious business, can also be uplifting and even amusing.

The authors wish to extend special thanks to five research assistants: Fengfang Lu, Siriwan Ratanakarn, Brenda Anderson, Robert Kahn, and Karen Garber. Also thanks to Acquisitions Editor Jo-Anne Weaver, Developmental Editor Tracy Napper, and the Harcourt Brace production team, Annelies Schlickenrieder, Jane Ponceti, and Sue Hart.

We also appreciate the feedback given us from the following reviewers: Richard Burnett, University of Missouri-St. Louis; Judith Cassady, Bowling Green State University; Bruce Gutknecht, University of North Florida; Barbara Guzzetti, Arizona State University; June Knafle, University of Illinois at Chicago; Gary Negin, California State University, San Bernardino; Grace Nunn, Eastern Illinois University; Donna Ogle, National-Louis University; Edward Paradis, University of Wyoming; Taffy Raphael, Michigan State University; Robert Rickelman, University of North Carolina, Charlotte; Robert Schwartz, Oakland University; Barbara Walker, Eastern Montana College; and Karen Wood, University of North Carolina, Charlotte.

Anthony V. Manzo
Ula C. Manzo

# CONTENTS

# TEACHING
# CHILDREN
# TO BE LITERATE

From your parents you learn love and laughter and how to put one foot in front of the other. But when books are opened you discover that you have wings.

Helen Hayes

# PART 1

# LITERACY AND LITERACY PROVIDERS

### CHAPTER 1

# LITERACY AND
# THE READING PROCESS

**2 Influential
Teachers**

**3 Emergent
Reading & Writing**

**4 Reading
Aloud**

**1 The Reading
Process**

## **W**here You Are

Reading is a complex act, no matter what one's ability. It has proven to be easy for some to learn, and mysteriously difficult for others. Despite its challenges, educators now are aiming higher than merely teaching children to read. We now say that we must teach children to be literate—to read, to think, to speak, and to write. This new demand, however, may not be a new burden: the additional parts make the whole more complete, more real, and more engaging. Take the first step now by moving toward a new understanding of literacy from three perspectives: that of children, of teachers, and of reading theorists.

**5
Reading
& Responding**

**6
Word
Recognition**

**7
Vocabulary**

**8
Improving Basic
Comprehension**

**9
Constructive
Reading**

**10
Content Area
Reading**

**11
Children with
Special Needs**

**12
Literacy
Assessment**

**13 The Classroom
& School Literacy Program**

We never know how high we are
till we are called to rise;
and then, if we are true to plan,
our statures touch the skies.
Emily Dickinson

## THE "NEW" LITERACY

In the current age of information, the term *literacy* has gathered some broad and metaphoric meanings. There is talk of "computer literacy," "scientific literacy," and even "media literacy." For the past hundred years, the term was most often used in the context of "functional literacy," or the ability to read and write well enough to handle the demands of daily life. This was a suitable and perhaps appropriate objective of public elementary education up to the early part of the twentieth century. Now, as we stand ready to enter the next century, educators are beginning to move beyond the basic goals of combating illiteracy and toward the broader goals of promoting a new literacy level. For educators, this new literacy means:

- Teaching children not merely to read, but also to write, speak, listen, and think in ways that enhance understanding of basic concepts and subject area knowledge
- Teaching children to use oral and written language in ways that enhance personal social growth and adjustment
- Ensuring that appropriate opportunities for literacy development are extended to all children
- Participating in the ongoing quest to better understand how children become literate, in this fuller sense, and how we can help them to do so

This last point does not mean that everyone should be expected to become a researcher or pioneer. It *does* mean that everyone needs to be educated sufficiently to cheer on the efforts of pioneering thinkers. It also means that every person should be educated to avoid superstition, overcome unsupported personal biases, and be open to alternative possibilities. This is done, in literate societies, through the schools and the home. It is done by conveying what we think we know, through telling and through modeling, and through urging children to read, write, question, and reflect on what they believe and do.

This new view of literacy is so much more encompassing than earlier views that several authorities are suggesting that it be called something different. The term *critical literacy,* for example, is gaining in popularity. Shannon (1990) defines critical literacy as "people using literacy to understand themselves, to make connections between their lives and the operations of the social structure, . . . to participate in control of their lives, . . . and to discuss democracy as a means to social justice rather than an end in itself" (pp. 156–157). By any name, teaching children to be literate means more, and involves more, than merely teaching them to read. This heightened goal has profound implications for the role and stature of elementary school teachers in modern society (O'Brien, 1992). While it adds to teachers' responsibilities, it also adds to the respect that is accorded to those who teach the young.

The remainder of this text is the story of how teachers, schools, and communities are trying to reach this goal by elevating "reading" instruction to include more opportunities and inducements to read and become lifelong learners. The story begins with a child's and a teacher's view of *learning to read* and then explains how these views align with theoretical perspectives on the reading process.

## INITIAL PERSPECTIVES ON LEARNING AND TEACHING READING

Tradition suggests that a basic text should first define its terms and introduce the theoretical foundations of a topic. In the case of *reading,* however, anyone doing it already has a pretty good idea of what it is, so it seems logical to delay technical definitions and distinctions momentarily and to address reading from the more human perspective of how it is seen and experienced by children and teachers. To start from this perspective seems especially appropriate, since the real subject of the text is not a philosophical treatment of what reading *is,* but how it is *learned* and how it might best be *taught.*

From the perspective of teaching and learning, the questions that become most influential are those that address the learner's background, preparation, and expectations, and the understandings, duties, and obligations of the teacher. Hence, the initial topic explored is that of how reading is encountered by children as they sit hoping to learn to do it, and experienced by teachers meeting them hoping to be successful in helping them do it.

⅂⊗+⊔∪ób⅃ ⅂⅂≠×⊗⊥⊥: + ×⊏∪∨⊔'⊥ Ʒ⊗⅂⊥Ʒ⊗×∧∪⋓⊗

The unusual symbols above are meant to give you a quick glimpse of what a child might feel on first opening a book in any early stage of learning how to read. Just as you open this text with high motivation to get on with learning how to teach reading, children generally approach learning to read with high levels of motivation and will to learn. Nonetheless, the basic "decoding" task of translating letter groups into words can be quite daunting. To remind parents and teachers of just *how* difficult this decoding component of reading can be, McKee (1948) invented the novel alphabet used in the heading above. Viewing decoding from the child's perspective helps us to understand why many children think that decoding *is* reading, and reminds us of the importance of providing instruction designed to emphasize reading as a meaning-making process. Figure 1.1 contains a key to translating these novel "letters" into our familiar alphabet and provides a translation of the heading above.

Imagine reading a passage written in McKee's alphabet. Tedious? Interesting? Challenging? Now imagine what you would need to do to be able to easily read an entire page of text written in this novel alphabet without referring to a conversion chart. Imagine how this task might be complicated if you were not permitted to speak to the children around you, or if you were very shy, or very active, or from a non-English speaking family, or if your family hadn't shared some of the mysteries and delights of reading with you. This scenario only begins to approximate what some children feel when they first set about the business of learning to read. Conversely, assume that you have been part of a planned and well-thought-out program

**FIGURE 1.1**  **Novel and Conventional Orthography**

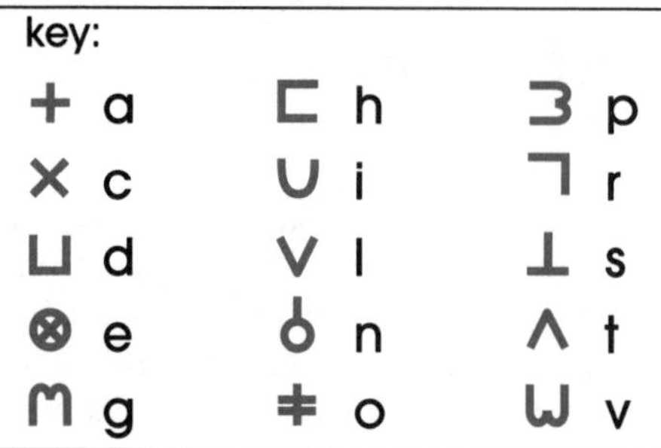

key:

| | | | | | |
|---|---|---|---|---|---|
| + | a | ⊏ | h | Ǝ | p |
| ✕ | c | ∪ | i | ˥ | r |
| ⊔ | d | ∨ | l | ⊥ | s |
| ⊗ | e | ȯ | n | ∧ | t |
| ⋔ | g | ∓ | o | ⨆ | v |

[1]Heading translation:
Reading Process: A Child's Perspective

to reduce the challenge of initial reading—one which introduced you to books as a young child and perhaps even exposed you to the alphabet, many of its sounds, and several words you could recognize at sight before you entered school. Would reading then be a snap? Not really. Remember, although there are only 26 symbols in our alphabet, these are used in various ways to represent approximately 44 to 46 sounds and to code over 80,000 root words, many of which have unconventional pronunciations; combinations and variations may reach three times this number. Furthermore, the most frequently used of these words do not even follow the rules of sound–symbol relationships that children are taught to rely on. For example, the bump on your face should be *noze,* but it's spelled *nose.* The opposite of your left side should be your *rite,* but it's spelled *right.* The first woman in your life should be *muther,* but in every schoolbook she's *mother.* There is a growing body of research to suggest that there are no definable boundaries even to the simplest of letter sounds (Yopp, 1992). Researchers recorded the syllable /di/ on tape and then replayed it over and over again while cutting off a bit of the syllable each time until they could get down to a pure /d/ sound. What they wound up with was something that could only be described as a chirping sound with no resemblance to normal speech (Gleitman & Rozin, 1973). See Figure 1.2 for a comparison of the process of beginning reading with the process of fluent reading.

Adding to the complexity and challenge of learning to read is the extremely high level of importance placed on reading in the early grades. Success is expected, and while most children *do* succeed, failure occurs too often. And when it does, it can be disastrous to a child's self-esteem, personal motivation, and actual ability to make normal academic progress. Most children know that the main reason they are going to school is to learn how to read. Should they fail in this task, they begin, even at this early age, to view themselves as failures in life as well.

**FIGURE 1.2** **Comparison of Beginning Reading with Fluent Reading**

In initial stages, the child's attention is *focused* on studying pictures, and the "look" of reading, rather than on decoding letter combinations into spoken words. There also is awareness of the general meaning of the material, based on the pictures.

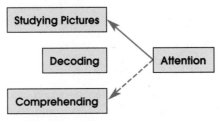

As the child acquires knowledge of letters and sounds, attention is focused on decoding the words, with secondary awareness of the pictures and the general meaning of the words.

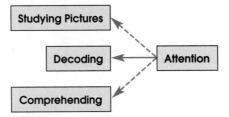

When decoding becomes automatic, attention is focused on comprehension, with only secondary attention needed to decoding and information from pictures.

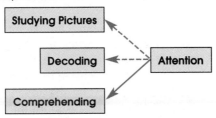

Eventually, the reader can focus on any set of cues whenever it seems to contribute most to the overall meaning.

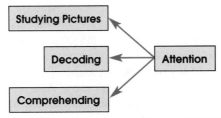

*Adapted from Samuels, Schermer, & Reinking, 1982, pp. 131 & 133.*

Considering the difficulty of the task and the amount of pressure that is placed upon children to succeed, it is something of a wonder that most children do learn to read, that many come to enjoy it, and that some few even look forward to writing in this peculiar code for others to read. It appears that children's thirst to find and make meaning is, for the most part, greater than the obstacles of mastering the task. Some children, however, have difficulties with the decoding and/or thinking aspects of reading, and these difficulties pose a considerable test of our professional knowledge, skill, and humanity. This brings us to the teacher's perspective on reading.

## READING PROCESS: A TEACHER'S PERSPECTIVE

Judging by the criticisms leveled at teachers and teaching, it must be one of the best kept secrets in contemporary life that *teaching really works.* Benjamin Bloom, a prominent educator, points out that one can get a "glimpse of the great power of pedagogy" when reflecting on the fact that every day millions of students are taught ideas such as the theory of relativity and DNA genetic coding that but a generation ago only a few could understand (1976). Teachers know that teaching "works," but tend to feel a bit uneasy about accepting praise; most teachers know that teaching is not an exact science, but a blend of art and technology. In spite of all that is known and is being learned about the teaching–learning process, some aspects of it remain a mystery.

Research has informed us about some practices that work and some that do not. But too often researchers have neglected to examine whether a particular practice may work for certain students and not for others. As a result, we have tended to neglect even the most obvious social/emotional dimensions of teaching and learning that most parents or grandparents, from their loving perspectives, expect us to take into consideration.

Fortunately, fresh approaches to research are beginning to demystify reading by encouraging teachers and researchers to tell the story of their trials and efforts, especially with less proficient learners, in more human terms. This trend is evident in almost every new issue of current journals in the field. For example, Wayne Otto, who writes a regular column on research for the *Journal of Reading,* suggests that the educational researcher's legitimate role is more that of effective storyteller than data-bound scientist (1990). Not surprisingly, this more humanistic approach can generate some refreshing new hypotheses about teaching and learning. A personal research story comes to mind that is especially relevant here.

The first author came to a surprising insight while using McKee's novel alphabet in a demonstration lesson with children. It took some years to refine the insight into a working hypothesis, but what finally emerged was the idea that this novel alphabet might offer a useful way to sidestep some of the emotional barriers influencing the performance of seriously disabled readers. Accordingly, with the help of three graduate assistants, we conducted a study in which four children who had been diagnosed as dyslexic were taught to read using McKee's alphabet. Theoretically, it should have been much more difficult for them to master this new alphabet than the traditional one to which they had years of exposure, both incidentally and in formal instruction. Nonetheless, they learned to read it at a rate that exceeded that of their tutors (Manzo, 1977a, 1985). The children in the study didn't realize it, but they had convinced themselves that they could not learn to read. They were "programmed" to fail whenever they saw the familiar alphabet. When the familiar alphabet was replaced with the novel one, and they were told that children like themselves were able to learn to read easily using this new alphabet, the emotional short circuit was removed and their real ability to learn was released. They were not only *able* to learn to translate symbols into words, but they did so at an astonishing rate. This story/study illustrates five important themes that characterize the view taken in this text toward literacy research and reading instruction:

- Good teaching is directed toward *children,* not toward the act of reading.
- Teaching reading to *all* children is a challenge that requires considerable professional knowledge and skill.
- Teaching also means watching children, listening to children, and being a child advocate.
- A restructured situation can be an ideal way for teachers to reach new insights, and for children to overcome prior negative experiences and raise their expectations for themselves.
- More research needs to come from real teaching situations that center on the practical problems faced by students and teachers.

Having defined this larger context, it is necessary to take a closer look at some of the definitions and issues that are involved in the "reading act." This basic technical information will help you to read, understand, evaluate, and give voice to your own evolving approach to reading instruction. It also will help you sort through and solve several of the challenges that you will face in real classrooms with real children.

## THE READING ACT: PROCESS AND PRODUCT

The act of reading is said to be composed of two parts: the process and the product. The "process" refers to the functions, or operations, that one goes through in deriving meaning, whereas the "product"—or more appropriately "products"— refers to the actual information and insights reached as a result of reading.

Reading is said to be a "black box" operation, meaning that it occurs between the ears, out of sight. It cannot be directly observed, and thus it is difficult to diagnose and correct difficulties that may arise. Most of what is known about the reading process has been inferred from study of its *products* (like interpreting shadows on the wall), including oral reading performance and the ability to answer questions after reading. Recognition of this dilemma has led literacy specialists to conclude that: (a) we must use methods of teaching that reveal more about the process; and (b) whenever possible, children should be trained to be more reflective about their own reading so that they may more fully participate in monitoring and "fixing" reading difficulties as these occur. There is a growing sense that the reading process may differ in the way that it occurs and unfolds for different individuals, and in the way it functions at different stages of human development. For example, some highly impulsive youngsters may follow a different pattern than less impulsive kids in using word analysis rules. And an individual child, as a function of typical development, will come to rely more on context as an older and more skilled reader than when he or she was younger and less fluent in anticipating the word that might come next in a sentence. Consider now a working definition of reading, and then some of the more popular perspectives, or theoretical models, of the process.

## DEFINITIONS OF READING

Harris and Sipay offer this uncluttered, traditionalist definition of reading: "Reading is the *meaningful* interpretation of written language" (1990, p. 10). Others have tended to define reading in ways that reflect the perspective of their research or school of thought. For example:

- Anderson, a cognitive psychologist, has popularized the view that reading is a process of *constructing* meaning from written text (Anderson et al., 1985).
- Perfetti, a linguist, sees reading in more instrumental terms, referring to it as thinking guided by print (1986).
- Goodman, a linguist and educational humanist, tends to see reading more as a natural extension of language process, but with some special benefits. Language, he says, enables us to share experience, learn from others, and to plan and work together. Written language expands this process to those who are not present, those who have died, and those yet to be born (Goodman, Bird, & Goodman, 1991).

There is merit in each of these definitions, for these perspectives and more come into play at different times. Reading is a *tool,* and its definition is influenced by the reader's purpose and the demands of the situation. Trying to define reading in terms of one single function is like trying to define a hammer merely as something used for striking nails. Hammers also are used to pry *out* nails, to shape metal, to force things that don't quite fit, and even to crack nuts. Imagination and situation interact to define the function of a tool.

From the point of view of reading as a function of the whole child, our simplified definition is: *reading is comprehending, interpreting, and applying textual material.* This definition implies that reading involves more than, and extends further than, the printed page. The reader brings a great deal of information and experience *to* the page and extends comprehension beyond the information and perspective presented *on* the page. Some of the components involved in this process are discussed next.

## COMPONENTS OF LITERACY

The components of literacy are described here in three categories: text-specific, integrated language arts, and personal/cognitive. While these categories are not necessarily mutually exclusive, they are offered here to help you form a conceptual foundation for understanding various aspects of full literacy and the instructional decisions that you will need to make to attend to these. Much of the language used here is liberally borrowed from Durkin's classic text in elementary reading (revised, 1989).

## Text-Specific Components

Text-specific components of literacy include those understandings and abilities that permit the child to "decode" a printed message into its spoken language equivalent and to comprehend its meaning as its author intended. These include:

1. Understanding what is meant by a "word" and where one word ends and another begins
2. Understanding what is meant by a sound *within* a word
3. Understanding that English words are read in a left-to-right progression and that lines on a page are read from top to bottom
4. Ability to recognize many words readily in print
5. Ability to decode—or work out the pronunciation of—most other words in the child's listening and speaking vocabularies
6. Ability to arrive at an appropriate meaning for a word within the context in which it is presented
7. Ability to make both text-based and knowledge-based inferences
8. Ability to distinguish between literal and figurative meanings of words, phrases, and sentences
9. Ability to make connections of words within and between sentences (as in recognizing a stream of interrelated actions and between certain pronouns with their appropriate noun referents)
10. Ability to connect words and meanings to the larger context of one's own life and times, toward the end of better understanding and transferring learning and insights back and forth between print and life circumstances

## Integrated Language Arts Components

This category includes the other language arts of writing, listening, and speaking, and the relationships of these to reading. It reflects the perspective that the language arts function together as the receptive and expressive channels for thinking. These components include:

1. A growing *expressive* vocabulary of words used in speaking and writing
2. Familiarity with increasingly complex language forms, and the ability to apply this in writing, speaking, and listening, as well as in reading
3. An expanding knowledge of allusions and background information that forms the basis of oral and written communication in various subject areas
4. Progress toward legible handwriting and adequately accurate spelling, as appropriate for age and grade level

5. A growing appreciation for literature as art and an inclination to read for recreation and pleasure

### Personal/Cognitive Components

Personal/cognitive components of literacy are all those things readers need to do to go beyond literal comprehension to make reasonable interpretations and to evaluate and apply what is read. Items in this category are drawn largely from the "critical literacy" research of Gray and Rogers (1956), who described various aspects of "reading maturity" in their studies of adults, and from the writers' studies of children's and adolescents' "progress toward reading maturity" (Casale, 1982; Manzo & Casale, 1981; Manzo & Manzo, 1990). Elements in this category include:

1. An inclination and ability to think abstractly
2. An interest in acquiring a rich fund of general information
3. An ability to speak and write clearly and reflectively
4. The inclination and ability to deal with ambiguities and to reach critical judgments
5. The inclination and ability to think constructively and creatively
6. An effort to engage in personal self-examination
7. An ongoing effort to understand larger structures and ideas, such as basic life forces, societal demands, and historical movements

In order to conceptualize the early stages of literacy acquisition, it is useful to get a sense of the age and grade levels at which these things typically could be expected to occur. Curriculum design, testing, and instruction are based on these expectations. Of course, *individuals* may vary widely from these norms, but it is difficult to note variations without knowledge of what is "typical" at a given age and grade level. These stages, which we have detailed from preschool to postschool years (Manzo & Manzo, 1990), should look familiar to you and should conform to your personal experiences and your knowledge of others. Our focus here is the stages of *reading* acquisition, since this is the emphasis of this book.

## STAGES OF READING ACQUISITION

**Early Childhood (prenatal–age 3)**   Even before birth, much of what the child will find easy or difficult to do and to learn is being decided by genetic codes and quality of prenatal care. For example, there are distinct areas of the brain that govern language facility, including the ease with which a child will learn phonics, spelling, and oral reading. Apart from these mechanical aspects of reading, however, every infant can be taught to cherish reading when the language he or she is taught includes labels that focus attention toward books, words, and letters, and when they see that "significant others" use books for their personal enjoyment and social bonding. In such an environment, even children who cannot yet speak can be seen carrying a favorite book to an adult and even turning the pages while the parent or older sibling reads aloud. The combination of being held and being read to tells the child that we think reading is natural and valued. When the child is reinforced for inviting a willing parent to read aloud to him or her, the value of reading is strengthened as the child links it with the power to influence his or her environment—one of the most basic of human survival drives. Through early and continuous positive experiences, reading is established as part of the child's mental agenda, or the things he or she will see, care about, and acquire.

**Preschool to Primary Grades (ages 4–8)**  Most children have established the concept that print has meaning. In this stage, they are learning individual speech sounds (or phonemes) and how to decode letters into sounds and sounds into words. They also are mastering other very basic concepts (e.g., small –medium–large) and acquiring vocabulary at a rate that will be unparalleled in subsequent grades. Thinking, however, is largely egocentric and focused around self and home. Toward the end of this period a great deal of personal effort goes into trying to be "good" and obeying stated rules.

**Middle Grades 4–6 (ages 9–12)**  Most children have mastered the fundamentals of word attack strategies, recognition of high frequency vocabulary, and most basic language patterns. Their reading tends to move from one area to another as their funds of knowledge continue to grow. Thinking begins to change dramatically. At first very concrete, it moves quickly to more refined forms of categorization, generalization, and abstraction. Most youngsters begin to transfer learning from one context to another. This ability springs from a primitive form of abstract thinking that the eminent child psychologist Jean Piaget calls "conservation." The concept of conservation involves the realization that things may change in form though not in substance—physically, a piece of clay is the same weight whether in the shape of a ball or a platter; verbally, something may be said in several different ways, including figuratively, and have essentially the same meaning. At this stage, children's reasoning tends to focus on the real world around them. From a social perspective, children continue to abide by adult rules, although the peer group plays an increasingly influential role in shaping values, self-image, and behavior. This period also marks the onset of "metacognition," or awareness of one's own thinking, and the inclination and ability to self-monitor and self-correct reading.

**Grades 7–10 (ages 13–16)**  Reading patterns and behaviors are equal to the requirements of most school-like textual materials, although guidance and assistance often may be required. Peer influence and rapid hormonal and other physical changes tend to disrupt and distract from school and home. Ironically, thinking sharpens as the teen mind struggles to understand the role of the self in the social group. Critical-evaluative thinking, however, remains relatively primitive because it is uninformed by knowledge gained from experience and is subject to distortion by a growing desire to become more of a "rule maker" than a "rule abider."

**Grades 10 – College (ages 17–25)**  Comprehension, vocabulary, and study habits grow and are honed in direct relationship to career interests and social and educational opportunities. Without specific training, thinking and general knowledge are analogous to those of the 9–11 age group, though at a higher level. Thinking is generally effective and well-informed, though somewhat two-dimensional. The rapid changes and tough choices of adolescence have given way to slower changes and more binding, and therefore stabilizing, choices. This process can easily continue for ten or more years in contemporary societies where entrance into responsible adult life is delayed by the demands of higher levels of education and greater financial "start-up" costs. Forced delays in ability to accept the responsibilities of adult life can impede development of realistic views of society and world forces. Ironically, this creates a need for even more education. Continuing education for adults is justified in these times on the grounds that society itself is volatile. Even the best trained and educated can, and likely will, be displaced vocationally during a normal lifetime.

**Postschooling (ages 26 and older)**    Reading grows insightful and is routinely applied to a wide range of human affairs. Life experiences round out formal education. Some previous notions are validated and others dispelled, but mostly there is a growing sense that life is composed of paradoxes and that quality of life means reading, writing, and doing things that are meaningful, creditable, and, ideally, durable.

School reading programs generally try to parallel these stages. The earliest grades are mostly devoted to teaching youngsters to read and form basic concepts, the middle grades to teaching them how to use strategies for independent reading and thinking in increasingly more challenging materials, and the higher grades to challenging them to learn from reading and to think beyond the boundaries of a text. Classroom instruction addresses and includes each previous and each subsequent stage. At one time, these stages tended to occur in rather segmented form. It is now thought, however, that children can be guided through these stages most naturally when their interests, tastes, and other needs are drawn upon to engage them in authentic, meaningful reading, writing, listening, and speaking.

From this background, it now is possible to better understand and follow some slightly more theoretical perspectives on the reading process. These are frequently referred to as *models* of reading. A model, in this context, is a symbolic representation of one's understanding of the parts of a process and the ways in which these parts interrelate.

## MODELS OF READING

Models are constructed from varying levels of evidence, experience, and speculation. Models of the reading process differ in significant ways and have important implications for how we teach and evaluate student progress in reading (Singer, 1985). Ruth Strang, one of the early authorities in the field of reading, was fond of pointing out that what children did in "reading" was directly related to the teacher's vision of the process and its purpose. If the teacher saw reading as a decoding process, children came to be adept decoders. If the teacher saw reading as literal comprehension, children gained skill in answering literal questions. If the teacher saw reading as analyzing and appreciating literature, children's reading achievements reflected this view. There are several additional reasons why a teacher ought to have a sound background of knowledge about the reading process:

- It saves teachers from adopting unexamined beliefs and practices that are antithetical to reflective teaching.
- It is the conceptual basis for the business of teaching, and competent people know their business.
- It helps teachers to clarify and refine what they personally believe about the reading process, and hence about the teaching of reading.
- It offers teachers a framework for understanding, categorizing, and evaluating new ideas about reading strategies and practices.
- It helps teachers to select procedures for personal mastery and provides a rational basis for supporting these decisions.
- It helps teachers to consider points of view other than their own and to understand the rational basis for these.

Most views of the reading process can be sorted into one of the three categories that are frequently described as bottom-up, top-down, or interactive. The next section describes these three popular concept terms and then offers a practical and concrete way to sort out the varying views on reading.

## BOTTOM-UP MODELS

*Bottom-up models* of the reading process are said to be "text-driven." These models emphasize reading as a process of *getting* meaning from the printed page. This is accomplished, according to these models, through sequential mastery of a series of "reading subskills." The first step is accurate visual perception and recognition of letters, then of sounds, then of words, and eventually of sentence and passage meaning. Children tend to be seen as "blank slates" on introduction to reading. Direct instruction, frequent mastery testing, and follow-up reteaching are advocated as the means of promoting subskill mastery that will eventually lead to attaining overall competency and higher-level critical analysis (Gough & Cosky, 1977; LaBerge & Samuels, 1974). Accordingly, at early grade levels bottom-up approaches tend to have a heavy code, or phonics emphasis, and assume that appropriate comprehension will follow. Not unexpectedly, these reading programs have tended to produce greater decoding gains in the first three grades and fewer cases of serious remedial readers than some approaches based on top-down models (Juel & Roper-Schneider, 1985).

To summarize, in bottom-up models:

- Reading *is seen as* the process of accurately decoding an author's writing through efficient use of a sequence of subskills.
- Reading *is taught by* first identifying the necessary subskill sequence, directly teaching each successive subskill, and reteaching any unmastered subskills as

necessary. There is a strong emphasis on mastery of the phonic elements of word decoding.

- Reading *progress is evaluated* by frequent testing for mastery of each subskill.

## TOP-DOWN MODELS

*Top-down models* of the reading process tend to be "meaning-driven." The reader is said to begin with prior knowledge and actively to compare what is read to what is already understood. Top-down models tend to de-emphasize subskills and literal understanding and to focus on building background information and personal responding (Goodman, 1970, 1984; Smith, 1978). Children are seen as emergent language learners, who enter school with a wealth of knowledge, skill, and experience with language. In general those who hold to this position believe less in formal or direct instruction and more in the power of immersion in a literate environment. Skills are expected to be acquired incidentally as a result of real and extensive experiences with reading and writing. The general lack of emphasis on skills mastery is also evident in the way reading assessment is approached by top-down enthusiasts. Students' oral reading, for example, is evaluated not in terms of decoding accuracy but in terms of meaning accuracy. Decoding errors are called "miscues" and are considered simply to be mismatches between the student's active attempt to construct meaning and the literal message coded in the passage.

In comparison with bottom-up models, top-down models can be summarized as follows:

- Reading *is seen as* a process of predicting meaning based on prior knowledge and experience, and then verifying and correcting predictions as the author's message is translated.
- Reading *is taught by* providing meaningful text and emphasizing the relationship between the child's prior experience and information on the printed page. Phonic elements of decoding are taught, for the most part, incidentally as students encounter words in print.
- Reading *progress is evaluated by* assessment of the child's ability to derive appropriate meaning from print, not from mere accuracy in decoding and oral reading.

## INTERACTIVE MODELS

*Interactive models* are more like top-down models than bottom-up, but are considered to be a synthesis of the two. It is important to note that the word "interactive" in this model refers to the reader's inner dialogue with him or herself. It is not meant to suggest that the reader interacts in any real sense with the author or that the print is responsive. Hayes (1990) has made it clear that any other interpretation misses the point and gives the impression that the author somehow talks back, or that readers are invited to build their own meaning for what is read, totally free of the intentions of the author and the constraints of the words. Interactive models place heavy emphasis on building a fund of knowledge and an interest in reading.

Preparing to guide literacy development

They differ from top-down models, however, in that they do not discount the importance of a code emphasis, particularly at early grade levels. Interactive models of reading acknowledge that reading can only have a top-down structure when the reader is able to decode the words and is familiar with the material. Where this is not true, reading becomes a bottom-up process as the reader attempts to build sufficient meaning from what is being read to construct a conceptual basis for continuing to read, respond, and comprehend (Rumelhart, 1977). Hence, reading approaches based on interactive models of reading tend to include more direct skill instruction than top-down approaches. They do not, however, advocate an emphasis on the diagnosis and teaching of subskills in isolation from meaningful contexts. Proponents of interactive models have become increasingly interested in developing new "process-based" formats for testing the reader's personal strategies, or means of monitoring and fixing reading problems as they occur, rather than merely testing mastery of a series of subskills.

A summary of interactive models illustrates their similarity to and difference from top-down models:

- Reading *is seen as* a process of predicting meaning based on prior knowledge and experience, and then verifying and correcting predictions as the author's message is carefully translated.
- Reading *is taught by* meaningful text, relating text to the child's prior experiences, and providing as much direct instruction as is needed to provide children with the necessary strategies for independently monitoring and fixing typical problems with decoding, verifying, and reformulating predictions of the author's message.
- Reading *progress is evaluated* by assessing the child's ability to derive appropriate meaning from print and by his or her flexible use of appropriate reading strategies—which is often determined by having the youngster think aloud as she or he encounters various decoding and comprehension challenges.

Most reading specialists tend to endorse interactive models of reading (Pearson & Fielding, 1991). We have found it useful in instructional planning to further distinguish between the *reconstructive* and the *constructive* aspects of interactive models. *Reconstructive* reading, or *understanding* the author's message, and *constructive* reading, or *personalizing* and building on the author's message, do not necessarily occur in this order. Clearly, comprehending must to *some* extent precede personalization; however, the process of personalizing information often can contribute to initial comprehension.

## RECONSTRUCTIVE/CONSTRUCTIVE ASPECTS OF INTERACTIVE READING

Pearson and Fielding (1991) noted that *all* reading is essentially reconstructive. This conclusion is another way of making the point that the printed word is static and unalterable, and that it is the reader who must act on the print to re-create meaning. The reconstructive/constructive view of interactive reading says that in early developmental phases of reading it is quite natural for the child to be preoccupied with decoding print into familiar language and concepts, but that the teacher need not be similarly preoccupied lest reading be reduced to its least significance. For anyone first learning to read, it is difficult to move beyond the reconstructive aspects of the process even with the simplest of reading materials. Even as skilled readers we sometimes are thrown back into this reconstructive mode when we encounter a difficult word (think back to how you felt when you encountered McKee's alphabet at the beginning of this chapter), an unfamiliar style, or a new concept.

Beyond decoding, reconstructing the author's meaning is a process of lining up the author's intended referents and meanings with our prior knowledge and experiences. As we become more fluent at decoding and translating the author's message, or "reading the lines," we tend to become more able and inclined to search for other meanings "between" and "beyond the lines." We do this by asking ourselves questions about the relevance and value of what is being said, the possible motives of the author for saying it, and "real-life" applications of the message. This constructive process leads to growth in knowledge and in the ability to perceive, comprehend, and learn even more.

The reconstructive/constructive model supports the need to teach *both* word attack skills *and* the means to engage in the constructive reflection that leads one beyond the author's intended message. This two-phase view of the reading process reminds us that reading is a thinking and feeling process, and therefore, one that can be strengthened or weakened by personal internal responding. This realization lends support to the argument that reading instruction must incorporate consideration for the affective as well as the cognitive development of the child.

It is important to note that the reconstructive/constructive model says that the process can take place in an "A–B" sequence, as assumed in a bottom-up model where the reader first decodes the message, then interprets its literal meaning, and finally moves to analysis, evaluation, and personal responses. But it also is quite natural, and even desirable under certain circumstances, for reading instruction to occur in a "B–A" sequence, as top-down models describe: the reader is encouraged to begin with a prediction or a reaction and then to read to verify or alter this position. Needless to say, some poor readers are overly reactive to what they read. They try to construct meaning from minimal information and clues (Stanovitch, 1986a). They lunge beyond the lines before they have achieved basic understanding of the lines. However, even more proficient readers sometimes begin with a prediction that is more in the form of a predisposition, or even an objection to what the reader thinks the material will say. When the predisposition is "overly potent," as Thorndike (1917) referred to it a long time ago, it can distort accuracy and comprehension and even dampen motivation to read. This is one reason why it is important to teach and model objectivity in reading. It seems to be human nature to read and understand what we agree with and *already* understand, and to misinterpret or avoid facts and arguments that we do not understand or that are contrary to our attitudes and beliefs. In other words, predictions driven by overly heightened emotions can have a negative effect on comprehension, even when the material does not contradict what the reader believes (Lipson, 1982; Swafford, 1991; Waern, 1977b). The teacher who remains aware of the reconstructive/constructive interaction taking place during reading will better be able to dispel over-reactions that distort meaning or intentionally arouse some optimal level of emotion when the students see the material as irrelevant.

In sum, the reconstructive/constructive model of reading reflects a whole-child view of literacy. Instruction based on this model cannot address the act of reading, or even reading and language development, alone: Reading activates the whole child, reading affects the whole child; therefore, reading needs to be taught to the *whole child.* Since this whole-child approach is basic to the remainder of the text, this seems a good time to digress briefly to explain what it should be taken to mean in this context.

## THEORETICAL MODELS APPLIED TO A WHOLE-CHILD APPROACH

Teaching the "whole child" means many things. It means, for example, that the *curriculum* is child-centered (Searfoss & Readence, 1989). More importantly, a whole-child approach requires that teachers make a conscious attempt to rise above the tendency to think and act as if every child were the same. Naturally, there are certain characteristics that most of us share. That's how we can know and empathize with one another. However, our differences can be significant. For example, to the impulsive child, a wonderful *long* story is much more captivating if it is read/told as a wonderful *short* story. If you are thinking that you will teach every child to love wonderful *long* stories, you are tipping toward "behaviorism"— or the belief that each individual is merely a "blank slate" awaiting the mark of experience, training, and instruction.

Teaching the whole child means helping each child to find and come to grips with his or her physical/emotional self. It means avoiding the supposition that *every* child can be taught to do what *we* can do. Working to overcome this supposition is almost a definition of charity, maturity, and professionalism. The remainder of this text is best understood as promoting progress toward reading *maturity,* more than toward mere reading *competence.* It is for this reason that the text is called

*Teaching Children to Be Literate* rather than *Teaching Children to Read.* The difference between doing the one and doing the other challenges teachers to be more reflective, and consequently, more effective and probably more respected than teachers and programs that are willing to settle for less.

**W**here You've Been

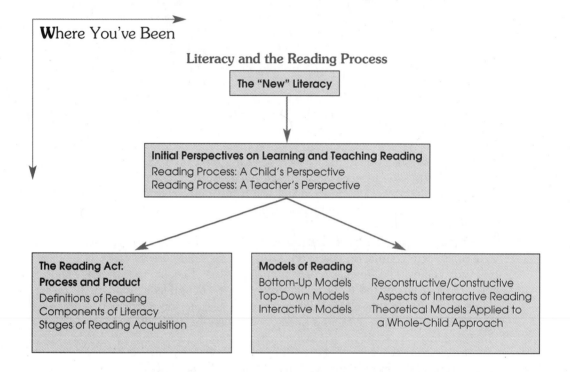

Literacy and the Reading Process

The "New" Literacy

Initial Perspectives on Learning and Teaching Reading
Reading Process: A Child's Perspective
Reading Process: A Teacher's Perspective

The Reading Act:
Process and Product
Definitions of Reading
Components of Literacy
Stages of Reading Acquisition

Models of Reading
Bottom-Up Models       Reconstructive/Constructive
Top-Down Models          Aspects of Interactive Reading
Interactive Models        Theoretical Models Applied to
                                    a Whole-Child Approach

Where You're Going

The next chapter considers how one may refine and develop professional skill as a teacher and serve as an advocate for children and for literacy. The chapter then presents a handy list of some popular overarching principles of teaching that are applicable to teaching reading and promoting full literacy. It also critiques the various schools of thought that have developed around the teaching of reading. The purpose of this presentation, at this stage in your professional development, is not to have you choose one school of thought, but to open your mind to some of the possible ways to sort out and interpret the vast amount of information on literacy education that you are likely to encounter.

### Reflective Inquiries and Activities

1.  Try to explain (or write) to a parent about why the reading curriculum for your class now is aimed at building "critical literacy," rather than mere reading competence.

2.  From your experiences as a student, describe classroom scenarios that seem to illustrate the differences between bottom-up, top-down, and interactive models of reading. Discuss and compare your scenarios with one another.

3.  Write a percentage value in for each category representing the way you think you probably were (a) taught to read and (b) learned to read (or typically read):

    (a)  How you were taught:

    _____% + _____% + _____% = 100%
    Bottom-up    Top-down    Interactive

    (b)  How you learned, or typically read:

    _____% + _____% + _____% = 100%
    Bottom-up    Top-down    Interactive

4.  Becoming literate is a lifelong process. Given the opportunity to receive additional instruction today, which of the things listed would you personally like to learn to do better? Mark each on a scale of: 1 = least to 5 = most.

    _____ a.  word attack
    _____ b.  syllabication and spelling
    _____ c.  rapid word recognition
    _____ d.  vocabulary enrichment
    _____ e.  factual comprehension
    _____ f.  inferential comprehension
    _____ g.  critical reading
    _____ h.  creative/constructive reading
    _____ i.  rate of reading
    _____ j.  discussing and explaining
    _____ k.  summary writing
    _____ l.  critique writing
    _____ m.  notetaking
    _____ n.  studying
    _____ o.  reducing disruptive emotional responding
    _____ p.  study of children's literature
    _____ q.  study of adult literature
    _____ r.  study of nonfiction topics in science and math
    _____ s.  study of nonfiction topics in social studies
    _____ t.  reading for longer durations
    _____ u.  reading for pleasure
    _____ v.  others:_____

5.  If you have done some of the previous exercises, you probably have had your childhood memories and adult feelings stirred regarding the teaching of reading and some closely related topics. Begin a list now of: (a) things that you would

do for or with children to help them become literate; (b) things you would *avoid* doing because you think them ineffective or countereffective; (c) stretching a bit further, things you might do to help teachers become better prepared to teach and promote literacy if you were in charge of teacher education.

| a) Things to Do for Children | b) Things to Avoid Doing | c) Things to Do for Prospective Teachers |
|---|---|---|
| • | • | • |
| • | • | • |
| • | • | • |
| • | • | • |
| • | • | • |

You should feel informationally, conceptually, and affectively ready to tackle Chapter 2.

# 2 LITERACY PROVIDERS: PRINCIPLES AND BELIEFS OF INFLUENTIAL TEACHERS

**2** Influential Teachers

**1** The Reading Process

**3** Emergent Reading & Writing

**4** Reading Aloud

**5** Reading & Responding

**6** Word Recognition

**7** Vocabulary

**8** Improving Basic Comprehension

**9** Constructive Reading

**10** Content Area Reading

**11** Children with Special Needs

**12** Literacy Assessment

**13** The Classroom & School Literacy Program

**W**here You Are

This chapter opens with a discussion of teacher empowerment as a backdrop for introducing a set of general principles for becoming an influential teacher. The chapter then describes the six most common beliefs, or approaches, that underlie the teaching of reading and related language arts.

*The role of the teacher is to inform, model, guide, observe, correct, and encourage.*

Lev Vygotsky (1962)

## TEACHER EMPOWERMENT

With teaching and schools assailed as they are from all quarters today, you might wonder if you are choosing the right profession. There are good reasons to think that you are. According to management and business guru Peter Drucker (1990),[1] education is the future. The twenty-first century, he notes, arrived twenty years early. Already we have seen the demise of communism, which Drucker describes as false selflessness, and the softening of capitalism, or total selfishness. Modern people are coming to value quality of life over inflated incomes and pressurized living. There is a growing emphasis on having a satisfying career, a respect for basic life values, and an educated mind. From these observations, Drucker predicts that in the future, "power" will be defined in terms of merit and personal achievements rather than status symbols, money, and connections. This conclusion means that the next great changes in our society will be in education. The most important of these changes, from a career point of view, will be the level of professionalism that will be required of educators. Instead of the old saying, "Those who can, do; those who can't, teach," in the future you should expect to hear, "Those who can, teach!"

A strong movement toward strengthening the professionalism of the teaching profession is already well under way. This movement, referred to as *teacher empowerment,* is a strong thread running through contemporary education (Burnett, 1991; Carr & Williams, 1991; Levesque & Prosser, 1991). Teacher empowerment is more than a "buzz word"; it is an honest recognition of the fact that schools are not succeeding as well as they should, and that it is *teachers*—not curriculum, technology, school structure, or any combination of these—who have the greatest potential for influencing student progress. This potential is only realized, however, when teachers understand and assume their role in its fullest measure. What is an "empowered" teacher, then, and how do you get there from here?

For the moment, we will define "empowerment" as *the ability and the freedom to make decisions and to influence people and policies. Ability,* in this context, refers to the combination of knowledge, skills, and inclination that permits one to act in an informed, confident, and assertive manner. *Freedom* means the power and the will to act in this way. History tells us that power is never easily given; it must be won. The process of winning power, however, need not involve a *power struggle.* Most often, it simply means amassing the knowledge, energy, and commitment to provide a needed service in an admirable way.

Three attributes of a group often cause society to render to it the power to lead. These are *vision, responsibility,* and *personal appeal.* These qualities are detected in small ways, such as in having an enlightened perspective, or in reflecting one's sense of responsibility and personal confidence in the workplace. For example, a story is told of the architect Frank Lloyd Wright, who was observing construction at the South American site of a church he had designed. Walking among the stonecutters, he paused to ask one of the workers what he was doing. With a puzzled look,

---

[1] From a Financial News Network interview with Drucker, June 11, 1990.

the worker answered that he was "cutting stones." This perfunctory answer prompted Wright to ask another worker the same question. This worker answered that he was "supporting his wife and children." This slightly more elevated sense of work led the architect to question a third worker. This man paused briefly, then looked up at the stranger and replied, "I'm helping Frank Lloyd Wright to build a magnificent cathedral."

Each of these workers was shaping stones, but they had very different personal perceptions of their tasks. The first two had reduced themselves and their peers to drones, while the third clearly was a valuable asset who could be trusted to think and act within the spirit of the larger effort. In a similar way, many teachers rise above merely teaching children to read and strive toward the larger goal of teaching children to be literate.

Professors Levesque and Prosser (1991) undertook to discover the roots of this kind of personal empowerment among teachers. To do so, they identified and told the stories of teachers who had acquired this special form of confidence. In analyzing these stories, they learned that empowerment began with rejecting the role of the drone. One teacher said that it began for her "when she realized that she wanted answers," and that the chief source of answers was to be found in conferring with her silent and visible partners in the form of authors, colleagues, and, yes, students. These interactions, she said, caused her to reflect and realize that she could "do something" (p. 15). Empowerment, she further noted, seemed to come with "involvement" or willingness to give help to others, including colleagues, students, friends, and less fortunate others.

Burnett (1991) offers this bit of advice for teacher empowerment: Teach as if your students were paying clients who "if not empowered [themselves] as a result of their interaction with you and among themselves, would simply walk off" (p. 12). There is a profound and slightly awesome message in this practical bit of advice. After you have listened to all that others have to say about how to teach effectively, ask yourself whether your students would continue to return for their next lesson based on what you did that day. This is the kind of question that leads reflective, empowered teachers to become "action researchers."

*Action research* simply is research conducted by a teacher in his or her own classroom by identifying a problem, systematically implementing a possible solution, collecting and analyzing the resulting information, and making decisions about the extent to which the problem was resolved. The role of action researcher strengthens teachers' credibility as initiators as well as implementers of professional expertise. Literacy specialists now are articulating a strong link between teacher empowerment and action research (Clyde & Condon, 1992; Santa, 1988). Short (1990), for example, calls a classroom a "community of inquiry."

Four basic steps for conducting action research have been suggested by Cochran-Smith and Lytle (1990):

1. Reconnaissance: Observe some classroom situation or problem that can be measured or counted.

2. Planning: Review the professional literature and/or talk to school or university authorities about possible solutions or plans that could result in measurable changes in things that are observable or countable.

3. Acting: Conduct the planned intervention, or remedy, and collect and record your data.

4. Reflecting: Consider what happened by trying to answer some specific questions, such as: What do the observations say about pupil learning or attitudes? What patterns or trends may be revealed in the data? What other ideas or possibilities has this investigation triggered, or what suggestions for how to approach subsequent classes?

The "reflecting" stage is the critical point in all research (Carr & Williams, 1991). Research is supposed to evoke fresh insights. It is supposed to result not merely in more information but in greater wisdom.

One means of growing in wisdom is for the teacher to record some of her or his efforts and experiences and potentially to share these with others through a faculty interest group. We have adapted a format from a business school to this purpose. It is called a SEAR. It asks the teacher to describe a Situation, Event, Action, and Result. See Box 2.1 for one teacher's creative solution to the problem of not having the inclination herself to respond to an overly energetic journal writer.

Most major professional journals in education now have a section set aside for such anecdotal and action-research accounts. For a handy volume on the subject,

---

**BOX 2.1**    **A SEAR Solution**

| | |
|---|---|
| SITUATION | This SEAR was devised in the context of a fourth-grade creative writing class and homeroom. The creative writing class involved an English module and journal writing.<br>Call words: *creative writing, rapport, communication, establishing relationships* |
| EVENT | Christina was a fairly quiet, capable, productive student who loved writing in her journal. She did not limit herself just to the assigned material, but wrote in her journal nearly daily, like a diary. I *loved* her enthusiasm, but I could not keep up with the comments, editing, and encouragement she needed. I found myself bringing her journal home, and it would invariably find its way to the bottom of my stack, under the rest of my workload. |
| ACTION | I commented to my husband about my guilty feelings of not always being able to read Christina's journal in a timely fashion and the inability to always write her back. My husband, who is a teacher at the high school level, expressed an interest in reading her journal. Christina was very receptive. She had met my husband; in fact, he had taught my homeroom a few times. |
| RESULT | Even though I continued to give Christina feedback, my husband and she established a wonderful rapport through her journal and other creative writing. At awards night, Christina received a writing award, and my husband was there to congratulate her. |

| Teacher Name: | Lori Stevens | Address: | 1815 S. Jefferson; Kearney, MO 64060 |
|---|---|---|---|
| Solicited by: | Lori Stevens | Phone: | 1-816-635-4114 |

see *Teachers are Researchers: Reflection and Action* (Patterson, Santa, Short, Smith, eds., 1993, published by the International Reading Association).

In summary, the empowered teacher is a reflective teacher who sees beyond the daily objectives of the reading curriculum to larger literacy goals. Further, the reflective teacher is, by nature, inclined to action research because the process of reflection invites teachers to scrutinize their own instructional decisions and to take greater charge of instructional operations (Bracey, 1987; Sharan & Sharan, 1987). Teacher educators are realizing, however, that this level of empowerment is not attained without corresponding obligations and responsibilities. Where once it may have sufficed for a teacher to know and be able to implement specific methodologies, reflective teaching requires a sound grasp of the theoretical principles of teaching and learning that underlie specific methods and approaches. Reflective teaching means adapting and adjusting procedures and materials to attain the best "fit" for particular students. In order to adapt and adjust something effectively, one needs to know precisely what it is made to do and how it does it.

Another important element of empowerment is the willingness to take responsibility for potentially dangerous matters. The most respected and highly rewarded professions tend to be those that assume responsibility for some "substance" that is powerful and potentially dangerous. In the case of doctors, it is chemicals called medicine that can either save or further endanger life. In the case of lawyers, it is knowledge of legal precedents that can win or lose their clients' influence, money, or even their constitutional rights. For teachers, the powerful and potentially dangerous "substance" is the minds and hearts of children. Their impact may not be as clear and immediate as that of doctors and lawyers, but teachers can play a large role in shaping the future course of children, influencing national trends, and influencing our own profession's level of influence and leverage. When teachers act as advocates for children, rather than adversaries, they help youngsters to better self-understanding while winning those children as lifelong voters for quality education. Advocacy does not mean rendering to kids whatever their whims would be; on the contrary, it means the kind of "tough love" that comes from holding them to high standards. Youngsters tend to respect authority that is fair, helpful, and challenging.

This respect was evident from the earliest research on what youngsters most value in teachers done by Frank Hart in 1934, when teaching was one of the most highly respected of professions. In a sample of 10,000 students, the five most frequently listed qualities admired in teachers were:

1. Helpful with schoolwork, explains lessons and assignments clearly, and uses examples
2. Cheerful, has a sense of humor, can take a joke
3. Human, friendly, companionable
4. Makes work interesting
5. Strict, has control of class, commands respect

The cover illustration from an early professional education journal, shown on page 28 seems to embody the spirit of this list of qualities.

The "ideal" teacher: then and now

Today, more than sixty years later and after seemingly enormous changes in the nature of schooling and the technology of teaching, similar studies have almost identical results. Clearly, students want teachers who can impart knowledge, but who also are willing and able to take responsibility for more than the mere transmission of information. Students appreciate the teacher who sees them as people, can show them why knowledge is interesting and useful, and whose social-psychological maturity provides students with a respectable model for dealing with youthful self-doubts, perplexing questions, and recovery from misguided deeds. This expectation can be awesome, particularly for the novice teacher who is feeling his or her own way. However, research is quite clear about the potential influence of the *teacher,* regardless of methods, materials, or other variables, on student learning and perceptions.

Public awareness of this influence seems to be on the rise. In film, television, and magazines, and even children's books, teachers are once again being portrayed as people to be admired for their personal as well as their professional qualities. The importance of this perception cannot be overstated, for one of the more powerful ways of promoting literacy is to have children see valued and influential people with books and pencils in hand.

For a recent example of teachers in books, see *Billy and the Bad Teacher* (Clements, 1992). In it, Billy, a perfect fourth-grader, makes a list of things he dislikes about his teacher. However, when he starts to think about what a teacher *should* be like, he discovers that Mr. Adams, even with his little quirks, already does the things Billy thinks are important, such as: reading aloud *every single day*, giving time for free writing after lunch, and knowing how to make even fractions fun—all good examples of practices that can make a difference in children's lives and learning.

## THE TEACHER DIFFERENCE

Where literacy education is concerned, the effect of the individual teacher was dramatically illustrated in the "First-Grade Studies." Technically known as the Cooperative Research Program in First-Grade Reading Instruction, the First-Grade Studies were sponsored by the U.S. Office of Education in the mid to late 1960s. The research involved twenty-seven individual projects, structured to determine if there was one approach to initial reading instruction that was superior to all others (Bond & Dykstra, 1967).

The relevance of these studies to the topic of teacher effectiveness can be summarized as follows: No *single* approach to beginning reading instruction was shown to be conclusively better than all others; however, there were noticeable trends. For example, many individual *classes* within the various treatment groups made significantly greater gains than the group as a whole. This finding was attributed to the "teacher effect" (Bond and Dykstra, 1967). In other words, the effect of the teacher alone can exceed the effect of any particular method or set of materials.

For a time this finding had a dampening effect on methods comparison research. However, it eventually was realized that what the outcome of the First-Grade Studies really *meant* was that there were some teacher behaviors and practices that simply were more powerful than the particular reading methods and materials compared in those studies. This finding ushered in the still-continuing period of "naturalistic" research. Naturalistic research begins by identifying teachers and schools that clearly are "effective." Information about these teachers and schools is collected and compared, or "correlated," to similar information about other teachers and schools to determine what the effective ones do that is different. Not surprisingly, many of the behaviors and practices identified as most effective turned out to be the practice of "old-fashioned" principles of good teaching and learning that had been overlooked in some of the early methods and materials research studies. These basic practices and their underlying principles deserve particular attention in a text on the teaching of reading and related language arts. The teacher who understands and applies these practices is very likely to be one who will make a difference, no matter what kind of situation or program he or she steps into.

## BEING AN INFLUENTIAL TEACHER

*What we learn is what we do; knowledge must be operative, not just figurative.*

*Piaget*

Many states and school districts are implementing or moving toward policies that hold teachers accountable for student learning. As summarized in the quotation above, teachers must be more than knowledgeable; they must effectively translate knowledge into action. While this is a formidable task, it is not one that a teacher must undertake alone. A great deal of the existing knowledge about teaching and learning already has been translated into recommended practice. In the next section, you will find a listing of effective teaching practices—knowledge translated into action. In reviewing this list, you should find that the practices described are entirely achievable by anyone choosing to acquire and implement them. Note, however, that the remainder of this text, if not the rest of a career, could be spent in acquiring poise and ease in weaving these practices into daily routines.

## EFFECTIVE TEACHING PRACTICES

This section could be called a general "grammar of teaching." It provides a listing of the most basic practices of effective teaching with brief explanations. These "grammatical" elements underlie most of the approaches and methods advocated in the remainder of this text. The first element focuses on the role of the teacher as a motivator.

1. **Remember to Engage Student Attention**    "Academic engaged time" has been found to be one of the most reliable predictors of achievement in reading and learning in school (Fisher et al., 1978). It refers simply to the total proportion of time the child is observed to be actually engaged in academic pursuits. The term "academic engaged time" was coined to distinguish this concept and the techniques used to measure it from an earlier concept known as "time on task," which often was based on rather superficial measures of children's behaviors. To maximize academic engaged time, every lesson should include some form of motivational introduction. This may be elaborate, as in conducting a relevant simulation activity prior to reading, or attention-getting, as in putting on a train engineer's cap to read *The Little Engine That Could,* or it may be as nonchalant as simply asking youngsters what they know about Paul Revere before reading Robert Lawson's *Mr. Revere and I.* A very natural form of academic engagement tends to occur when instruction is based on involving children in authentic activities such as actually writing a letter instead of practicing writing one.

2. **Quicken the Pace of Instruction**    The reasons are not fully understood yet, but the evidence is clear: When the *pace* of teaching is quickened, more is covered and more is learned by students at all levels of ability (Carroll, 1963; Chang & Raths, 1971; Paulsen & Macken, 1978). This principle has been found to apply to a wide range of learning outcomes, from number of new words learned to number of books covered (Anderson, Evertson, & Brophy, 1979; Barr, 1973–74). It even has been shown to be true in highly conceptual subjects such as mathematics and science (Comber & Keeves, 1973; Good, Grouws, & Beckerman, 1978; Walker & Schaffarzick, 1974). The reasons for this are not yet known but may well involve the way faster-paced instruction quickens the heartbeat, changes the sometimes lumbering mood

of school, and, hence, heightens attention. The additional information that is covered when moving quickly may contribute to more effective concept formation. A faster pace also provides time for more repetitions—a frequently overlooked and important point developed next.

3. **Repeat Important Information**   Repetition increases the quality of academic engaged time. It does this by increasing the probability that something misunderstood or just plain *missed* the first time will be heard the second time and acquired by the third or fourth time. As suggested above, repetition need not slow down instruction. When the overall pace of a lesson is quickened, more *new* information as well as more *repetitions* can be compressed into the same period of time. One way to achieve necessary repetitions, other than constant teacher restatement, is to ask students to restate in their own words something they have just heard or read. This practice also has the benefit of keeping students alert to when they might be asked to do this, rather than becoming conditioned, and possibly lulled, into waiting for the teacher to provide the needed repetitions. Another technique is occasional recitation, or simple question-and-answer, lessons that are recognized for what they are: needed drill, not unlike physical conditioning, designed to get the student ready for a big game—such as a test or a presentation. A third use of repetition that is well documented is to have students engage in "repeated readings" (Koskinen & Blum, 1986; Samuels, 1979) until they become fluent in recognition of new words.

4. **Provide Spaced Practice**   One of the most common and durable findings from learning laboratory research is that students at all levels benefit more from spaced or "distributed" practice, as it is known technically, than from an equal or even greater amount of time spent in "massed" or longer duration practice. Further, Rosenshine (1986) has found that effective teachers provide for independent practice and for weekly and monthly reviews. Despite the long history and replication of this principle, it has been our experience in reviewing teachers' lesson plans and actual observations of many reading and language arts classes that it is seldom used effectively in those situations where it would be appropriate. In practical terms, this usually means doing something as simple as taking a 40-minute lesson and dividing it into three lessons of 25 minutes, 10 minutes, and 5 minutes, spaced over the day, and, ideally, with the addition of a 5-minute review periodically over the ensuing days. The distribution of practice, or recitation and discussion, in this way also provides meaningful opportunities to consider the various aspects of an idea or utility of a learning strategy in different contexts, hence advancing the next major point.

5. **Focus Teaching at the Child's "Instructional Level"**   This is another way of saying that children generally should be taught at the level at which they cannot quite work independently but at which they can learn with proper scaffolding, or support and guidance (Betts, 1946). In other terms, this level has been referred to by the Russian theorist, Lev Vygotsky (1962,

1978) as the "zone of proximal development"—or the immediate next step forward in mental development (Camperell, 1982; Goodman, 1992a,b).

6. **Teach Toward Independence**   The key to teaching toward student independence is to provide for the gradual *release of responsibility* to the student for his or her own learning (Pearson & Fielding, 1991). This typically is achieved through *instructional scaffolding* and the subsequent *fading* of this type of structural support. Instructional *scaffolds* are any reasonable means of supporting students' initial attempts to read and learn on their own, such as marginal notes, listening before reading, and guiding questions. These supports then are removed or *faded* in stages until the student becomes self-directed, self-teaching, and self-reliant. Through this process, the teacher essentially is a "thinking coach," helping students to become "strategic learners and problem solvers" (Gaskins, 1988, p. 35).

7. **Teach Students to Transfer Learning to New Contexts**   Transfer of learning is best promoted in three ways: by providing students with a concept base for what they are being asked to master; by asking strategic questions that require students to make specific connections between the new information and the contexts in which applications are expected; and, finally, by teaching in the actual context that students are expected to master, such as teaching reading and writing through reading and writing.

8. **Use Teacher-Directed as Well as Incidental Learning Approaches**   Some of the attention that has been given in recent times to the teacher as a reflective inquirer and a subjective force in instructional decision making has been misinterpreted to mean that the teacher should not use published teaching strategies. In fact, reflective inquiry should include the option of the teacher selecting and using many of the carefully honed and tested direct methods of teaching that have been developed through the field's collective experience and research. To do otherwise is to recklessly sever the field from its knowledge base (Camperell, 1982). Direct instruction typically is characterized by a prescribed set of steps. Often the teacher is asked to really take charge, even to the point of telling students what they are going to learn, how they are going to learn it, why they are going to learn it, and when they have learned it (Gaskins, 1988; Pearson & Fielding, 1991). While this may sound authoritarian, it also can be reassuring and efficient. It also has been found that most types of learning occur best under these conditions (Rosenshine & Stevens, 1984). This has been found to be true at every socioeconomic level, in every grade, and for bright as well as for remedial level students (Soar, 1973; Solomon & Kendall, 1979; Stallings & Kashowitz, 1974). These findings may be related to the fact that direct instruction contains several of the most rudimentary aspects of effective instruction.

9. **Select Methods of Teaching That Contain the Rudiments of Quality Instruction**   The rudiments of quality instruction tend to include the following features: a statement of objective, guided practice, feedback and correc-

"Whew!" She sure fights illiteracy wherever she finds it."

tions, independent practice (Rosenshine & Stevens, 1984), weekly and monthly reviews (Rosenshine, 1986), and liberal use of modeling and reciprocity (Manzo, 1969a; Manzo & Manzo, 1993; Palincsar & Brown, 1984). For now, consider "modeling" to simply mean "demonstrating," and "reciprocity" to mean giving students an opportunity to gently "poke back" and influence the direction of instruction.

10. **"Teach Up"**    This is the term Estes (1990) uses to remind teachers that we shouldn't shy away from trying to explain a complex concept, or to ask the tough questions. Ruddell and associates (1989, 1990) in a longitudinal study of influential teachers at the primary level found that one of the chief characteristics of such teachers was the habit of raising higher-order questions. Collins-Block (1991) confirmed and extended these findings to the upper elementary and middle grade levels.

11. **Use Three Forms of "Conversation" That Characterize Successful Teaching**    At the center of most interactions with students is the teacher's intention to accomplish one or more of three basic objectives: to inform, or impart knowledge or strategy; to become better informed of student needs; and/or to motivate and provide nurturance to students' social-emotional growth and development. To achieve these goals, artful teachers tend to rely on three forms of conversation (Manzo & Manzo, 1993) that can be referred to as:

- instructional conversations    interactions structured to impart knowledge and strategies for acquiring knowledge

- diagnostic dialogues
  whole class or one-on-one interactions structured to discover specific sources of inhibition to student learning

- therapeutic talks
  small group or one-on-one interactions structured to bring students to a better understanding and regulation of themselves

Application of the general term *conversation* to each of these types of student–teacher interaction was suggested by Tharp & Gallimore (1989a). This terminology is particularly appropriate, since it suggests a certain amount of respectful give and take between the teacher and students, and reminds us that we should spend more time "talking with" rather than "talking to" students.

12. **Use Cooperative, Collaborative, and Competitive Teaching and Learning Approaches**  In the real world, we are seldom asked to undertake projects and problems in a solitary way (Richardson & Morgan, 1990; Vaughan & Estes, 1986). There is a growing, though frankly not totally unchallenged, body of research that indicates that aspects of learning are enhanced by cooperative practices (Johnson & Johnson, 1987; Larson & Dansereau, 1986; Wood, 1987). However, there are certain values in well-thought-out cooperative approaches that tend to exceed immediate academic learning outcomes. Such approaches tend to reach out and up to what Dewey referred to, over ninety years ago, as *spirit of service,* and learning how to work in *self-directed* but *harmonious* ways. There is, too, a subtle but important shift taking place in cooperative learning to include collaborative learning. Collaboration refers to all parties, including the teacher, being mutually involved in negotiating objectives as well as means, rather than merely "cooperating" with an initiating authority. Interestingly, the interest in collaborative approaches is arising from teachers themselves, who often are asked by university researchers to "cooperate" in studies and such that tend to represent the researcher's agenda but not necessarily that of the teachers. Collaboration often means some trade-offs to satisfy the needs of the participating members, either immediately or at a later date. By any name, cooperative or collaborative, the result often is a more relaxed classroom atmosphere and a reduction in the immature behaviors that tend to accompany a pervasively boss-to-subordinate relationship (Gentile & McMillan, 1987). The methodologies presented ahead are built on, or contain options for, several levels and types of cooperative and collaborative relationships among youngsters, of children with their teachers, of teachers with one another, and of teachers and children with parents and community resources. Having said this, let's not fall prey to overlooking one of the basic *Lessons of History* so well spoken in Will and Ariel Durant's book by that title: Every system must sooner or later rely upon some form of personal profit to stir

individuals and groups to be productive; the first biological lesson of history is that life is competition, and competition is not only the life of trade, it is the trade of life (1969). Where schooling is concerned, this truism must be preserved so youngsters can learn how to be resilient, that is, to bounce back from mistakes and the inevitability of coming in somewhere between second and last in most competitions. This can be done, in many cases, through inter-group competitions so that the benefits of cooperation within teams is preserved, even while the potential benefits of competition are being permitted to operate.

**13.** **Teach so that *You* Can Continue to Learn**  It is a widely acknowledged fact that we tend to *learn* what we *do,* more than we *do* what we *learn.* The one way to continue to learn and grow as a teacher is to select and use methods that cause one to learn by doing. Such methods are called *heuristics.* A heuristic teaching method is one that changes the way students and teachers typically interact with one another and, consequently, is likely to effect positive changes. It does this by evoking behaviors and responses that encourage self-exploration and insights on the part of both students and teachers (Manzo & Manzo, 1985, 1990a, 1993; Marzano, 1991). Heuristics are based on a principle of learning by doing rather than merely by being told what to do. In a manner of speaking, all professions are based on learning by doing, including law and medicine. Given the proper mind set, almost any experience can serve as a heuristic—or opportunity to draw insights from hands-on doing. However, this is most likely to occur when professionals think of their teaching efforts and experiences as being mini-experiments that need to be reconsidered in more reflective moments, and, where possible, shared and critiqued with others. This is the essential basis for our picture of the teacher as an "action researcher." Research in this context doesn't necessarily mean careful measurement and elaborate statistical analysis; rather, it tends to mean something much less distracting and far more self-examining. The heuristic methods recommended ahead are the structural mechanisms, or means by which to promote "reflective inquiry," and self-directed career-long growth. Since this concept may be new to you, some elaboration seems in order.

The idea of heuristic teaching is a fresh idea that is over 2500 years old. Heuristic teaching is most often exemplified in the unusual approach taken by the great philosophers such as Socrates when they answered a question with a question or a series of questions. Notice that when they did this, they intentionally altered conversation slightly, and most teaching. Their objective, of course, was to help their students to think for themselves, to learn how to learn, not merely to acquire what was being served up.

The approach advocated here is very similar but for the fact that it is, as suggested earlier, focused on *self*-discovery in the teacher as well as in the student. To that extent, it might more correctly be called a "double heuristic." By any name, the idea is to excite and ignite a more intensive level of engagement and self-awareness in the teacher as well as the student. For convenience at this early stage of acquiring this concept, we suggest that you substitute the phrases "structural change" and "guidelines for doing and learning" each time you see the word heuristic. You will see many examples ahead in the text of this idea in action. You might also try the action research suggestion at the end of the chapter to get a more tangible sense of a teaching heuristic in operation.

14. **Teach the Whole Child**   This principle, introduced in Chapter 1, is one of the guiding themes of this text. It serves as a reminder that instruction needs to be addressed to *more* than the cognitive domain. While it once was assumed that learning took place merely in the top one-eighth of an inch of cerebral cortex, modern neurophysiology is confirming the good sense impression that there are many other aspects of the central nervous system that are involved and can be effectively drawn upon to enhance human learning. Several methods and practices described ahead should give you a practical sense of what it means to involve the often-overlooked affective domain and the rarely mentioned sensorimotor, or physical domain that plays so great a role in early infant and child development (Ceprano, 1981; Dreher, 1990; Manzo & Manzo, 1993; Piaget, 1963). The sensorimotor domain typically is accessed through physical gesturing or acting out.

15. **Do Something Joyful!**   There is a chemistry to joy that can raise hope and convert school into a place where life is lived and experienced, not merely as a staging area for a future life. There is no hard data of which we are aware to support this proposition, but that may be because it is part of everyone's common experience. Studies of teachers that students perceive as influential from as far back as the 1934 Hart study previously cited have most always included reference to the importance of a teacher having a sense of humor. Guzzetti (1990) found that teachers who were inclined to try the role of raconteur, or wry wit, awoke greater interest and comprehension in their students. Joyfulness, however, does not require the teacher to be a comedian, quick wit, or raconteur, desirable as this might be; it simply means keeping an upbeat perspective and a caring attitude, and being willing to try to do some things that may not come so naturally. Of course, children will differ somewhat on what they find to be clever or joyful, but it is likely to include things as large and as subtle as the following: listening to the teacher read a rousing or touching story; reading joke books and humorous tales; having learning tasks translated into games that provide opportunity for social interaction as well as academic practice; and showing genuine interest in what kids do. One simple way to communicate genuine interest is to intentionally open your eyes wide when children speak to you; you will find that doing this will naturally increase your attention, uplift your spirit, and bring your face to a slow smile. This bit of advice is gleaned from a relatively new field of study, called "social psychology."

While these fifteen overarching principles of teaching and learning are hardly an exhaustive list, they do represent some of the more important deductions of the last hundred years of research and classroom experience at all levels of education. Consider now the basic approaches to teaching reading or the schools of thought that tend to dominate this area of education. Some of these approaches tend to be more hospitable hosts to the previously mentioned overarching principles than others.

The philosophical approach that you come to teach under will not always be a free choice, since some schools, school districts, or states may make that decision for you. However, as the teachers in the First-Grade Studies showed, no one can, or should, completely control how a teacher operates. The idea that teachers can always make a difference, in some personal way, is at the very heart of the profession.

## APPROACHES TO TEACHING READING

The schools of thought that constitute the most popular approaches to reading are largely the products of influential teachers and scholars. Understanding these approaches is rather like learning a new word. Each approach, like any word, has complex and evolving meanings, depending on who is using it, and in what context. Nonetheless, as with words, there is something basic about an approach that needs to be grasped before you are able to move toward deeper understanding.

To aid your comprehension of these basic approaches, you will find statements that tell of: (a) their historical and philosophical underpinnings; (b) their assumptions regarding the role of teachers and the needs of children; and (c) their perspective on the nature of the "reading process."

The most popular approaches tend to have more in common than may be apparent. They tend to agree, for example, that in order to read effectively, one needs, somehow, to learn to decode words from print and acquire a considerable sight word vocabulary, *and* to build a rich meaning vocabulary and related fund of knowledge with which to comprehend, *and* to think clearly about the significance and application of what has been read. Further, most approaches, no matter which direction they begin from, at least give lip service to the fact that children need to be *literate* rather than merely *skilled,* and that most youngsters need to be taught how to write, listen, and speak as well as read effectively. Many approaches also, at least in some nominal way, believe in objectives such as fostering personal-social growth and adjustment, since it now is indisputable that these influence the way children think and what they come to do with what they read and learn. The difference among these approaches, then, is not so much in what they acknowledge to be important, but in their priorities and, therefore, in what they are genuinely willing to do toward those ends.

Put another way, most differences about what should be done to teach reading effectively tend to stem from different emphases on which are the more critical objectives and just how these best should be met. This section attempts to describe the major positions that tend to be taken and the practices most often advocated within each context. The following positions are described:

Heritage Approach
Basal (Eclectic) Approach
Basal-Supplement Approach
Mastery Teaching Approach
Whole Language Approach
New Eclecticism Approach

## HERITAGE APPROACH

The heritage model is basically concerned with transmitting the values and traditions of the culture (Farrell, 1991). In the distant past, teachers would have taught reading from the Bible, and more recently from the "Great Books" of Western thought. Two of the more popular modern proponents of this approach are Alan Bloom (1987) and E. D. Hirsch, Jr. (1987). They basically hold to the traditional proposition that reading is taught in order to impart a sense of (Western) *cultural literacy* and a shared relevant background of information (or schema) by all who would call themselves "literate" in Anglo-American-European society.

Hence, their interest is not so much in the teaching of reading as in the content represented. Nonetheless, this essentially conservative—some would say reactionary—position, with its emphasis on the development of the intellect along classical Western lines and values, has become linked to a methodology that could be called "intensive phonics." This connection is made not so much by the heritage proponents as by strong advocates for phonics instruction who seem to share their conservatism and other such background factors.

There are no popular commercial programs on the market that offer the heritage model as a total reading package today. The closest commercial offerings are the "Great Books" program and a book by Hirsch listing a few hundred things that he believes everyone can and should know. A few years back, the Lippincott Linguistic Readers did attempt to produce a unified program of this type, but without much popular success. You will find, as you read ahead, that the heritage model was well incorporated into early basals that used unaltered quality literature as the content for reading instruction. In a sense, history has come full circle with the emphasis now placed on literature by whole language proponents, although this latter approach shares little else with the earlier heritage model.

## BASAL (ECLECTIC) APPROACH

From an historical perspective, it was Professor William H. McGuffey of the University of Virginia who set the stage for today's basal reading instruction when he presented the educational world with his brainchild known as *McGuffey's Eclectic Readers* in 1840 (Auckerman, 1981). The term *eclectic,* at that time, referred to the wide array of literature that was represented in this prebasal reader series. Instructions to the teacher consisted of only two pages of explanation and suggestions. Today the term *eclectic* refers to the varied approaches to teaching represented in basals and basal-supplemental approaches that contain extensive pages of directions and recommendations to teachers.

By the 1870s, early reader series took on the familiar occupations of the nineteenth century, stressing articulation and oratorical speech, and a heavy influence on morality. England's Victorian period was fully felt even here in "the breakaway colony." Graham Crackers, for example, were originally created and marketed by a Doctor Graham as a wholesome foodstuff that would keep children *morally correct* as well as *physically regular*.

Despite strong competition from *Monroe's Readers* (1872) and *Ward's Rational Method in Reading* (1894), *McGuffy's Eclectic Readers* survived. This was largely due to their being carried westward to new settlements along with the Bible and copies of *Pilgrim's Progress*. Most schoolmasters considered this array of books to constitute everything a youngster would need to know to be literate, morally straight, and acculturated. This Basal Heritage Model seemed to be part of the new nation's way of giving itself both a cultural heritage and a new and unifying identity. It should be noted, however, that this was a time of worldwide revolution in accepting print media as a source of pleasure and recreation. It was the time of publication and initial popularization of Carlo Collodi's *Pinocchio* (1882), Johanna Spyri's *Heidi* (1880–81), Jules Verne's *20,000 Leagues Under the Sea* (1870), Louisa May Alcott's *Little Women* (1868), and Mark Twain's *The Adventures of Tom Sawyer* (1876). While not considered to be "educational" at the time, these and many other books that emerged during this time would eventually find their way to acceptability and even status as "classics" in the nation's libraries and schools.

Some time later came the first strong phonics push. The 1912 *Beacon Readers* (named for Ginn & Company's offices on Beacon Street in Boston where many publishing houses still are located) was among the first to use extensive phonics methods, including the use of diacritical markings to help beginning readers to decode and pronounce new words (an idea found to be ineffective by Fry in one of the First-Grade Studies). Some basals went even further and offered full pronunciation guides that were more difficult to master than the standard alphabetic system. For example, the most popular story-starter might be written as: 'wən(t)s ə- pon'ə 'tīm.

Recognizing the popularity of Ginn's *Beacon Readers,* Scott Foresman soon published *The Elson Readers* (circa 1915). It was the revision of this series, authored by William S. Gray, that initiated the form and format of basal readers from that time forward (Goodman et al., 1988). It was in Gray's basal series that the familiar "Dick and Jane" made their appearance on the American reading scene. This basal's immediate popularity established Scott Foresman as the leader in the industry from the 1940s through the 1960s. Competing basal series authored by other leaders in the field, such as Emmett Betts, Donald Durrell, and David Russell, followed with a string of books built around similar nuclear families whose relationships, pets, and activities were the content of the stories from preprimary to sixth-grade levels. Story characters almost always took trips to the zoo, the airport, the fire station, and, of course, to grandfather's farm (Auckerman, 1981).

In Catholic school versions, the children were named Joseph and Mary, and regularly prayed and attended church.

In all of these basals, no one was anything other than white, women never held jobs, and no one was disabled, ill, or ever died. Increasingly, basals of the 1970s, 1980s, and 1990s began to reflect better ethnic and male/female balance in a variety of roles, as well as a host of other contemporary influences: e.g., inclusion of the disabled, seniors, urban/suburban and rural settings, representation of different geographic regions, more balanced literary genres—especially humor, science fiction, mystery, and biographical vignettes of contemporary people. Basals have, in effect, returned to the concern for literary quality that was inherent in the McGuffey Readers, although some would argue that they fail to do so each time they alter ("dumb-down") text to meet the presumed needs of novice readers (Goodman et al., 1988).

From a philosophical and educational point of view, most basals through the 1980s have been built on two fundamental assumptions:

- Teaching children to read is the most important function of the elementary school.

- Kindergarten to grade 3 is a time to learn how to read; grades 4–6 is a period of practice and consolidation where reading speed, study-type reading, critical reading, and related language arts are acquired; grade 7–onward is a period when reading is done largely to learn content, to become conversant with adult literature, and to strengthen and extend concepts.

The Basal-Eclectic system offers a wide array of books: some to be read *to* children and others to be read *by* children as their basic practice material. Additionally, they provide optional materials ranging from inflatable letters to the much-maligned exercise sheets. Basals typically extend from the preprimary to middle school levels, though some go to ninth-grade level.

The core materials of the basal system have been:

- A series of graded books written with, or altered to, a controlled vocabulary, and sentences that increase in length, linguistic complexity, and density at each grade level

- A "scope and sequence" plan (introduced by David Russell) that details the skills that should be taught, and the order in which they should best unfold to conform to logic and knowledge of normal child development

The term "basal" was meant to connote that once the teacher identified the level at which students were reading, she could place them in a book that was at their *instructional level,* and that the combination of reading at one's instructional level, while receiving *sequential skills instruction,* would come together with normal childhood development to promote systematic progress to each higher level of proficiency.

In recognition of the different levels of reading ability that exist in a typical heterogeneously grouped class, books and exercise materials were provided to accommodate three to five groups of youngsters. The expectation was that some lessons

## Basal Teacher's Manual

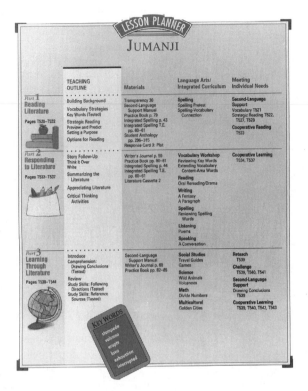

*Source: Treasury of Literature,* Teacher's Edition, Harcourt Brace Jovanovich (1993). Used by permission.

or stories would be done by the entire class, but that most lessons and reading would be conducted in small groups of students with similar reading levels. Although these reading groups typically were not called "high," "medium," and "low," students were quite aware of their ranking; thus, the popular satirical allusion to "eagles," "sparrows," and "crows."

Basal programs provided a good deal of assistance to teachers in the form of lesson formats, including suggested activities and recommended questions. They also provided their own batteries of assessment tests and even forms for record keeping and notifying parents of pupil progress.

As suggested above, today's basals are called "eclectic" because they tend to use a wide array of teaching methods (see photo above). This is done mostly by adding options, but rarely by eliminating any. Hence, the typical comprehensive basal has been criticized as being amoeba-like: It incorporates just about everything that every buyer might want, irrespective of whether it conforms to any unifying philosophical view.

The most common thread that still runs through most basals is an approach to teaching word deciphering that is called *analytic* phonics. This approach combines whole word instruction, phonics practice, and some study of phonics rules. Teaching is directed toward helping youngsters to analyze enough of a word's phonetic characteristics, along with the context in which it occurs, to recognize it as one that already is in their listening–speaking vocabularies.

To accommodate the concerns of some of the more phonics-oriented groups, some basal programs also offer a more explicit form of phonics instruction, often called *synthetic,* or *intensive* phonics. This approach stresses the teaching of phonics rules, but takes "sounding-out" a step further to include figuring out how a word might be said when it is encountered out of context, or is *not* in the student's listening–speaking vocabulary, and even includes applying phonics rules to "nonsense" or non-words.

The most serious criticism of basals have been leveled at:

- The stilted quality of the stories, which are composed according to the publisher's pattern and lack the appeal of quality children's literature
- The reduced challenge in comprehension and word recognition that results from controlling vocabulary and sentence length
- The difficulty of managing three to five small groups working in different materials in a single classroom
- A tendency to offer three units of activity per class session that rarely are related to one another—a reading selection, worksheets, and phonics drill

Most current basals, as previously noted, are trying to shake this skills-based image as they strive to be more "literature-based" (see Harcourt Brace Jovanovich's *Treasury of Literature* series as an example). A few programs also have made significant progress away from routine grouping toward an emphasis on whole-class and cooperative learning.

As a rule, basal-reading programs have not paid much attention to the other language arts: writing, speaking, listening, and thinking. This lack set the stage for the establishment of the basal-supplement approach.

## BASAL-SUPPLEMENT APPROACH

The basal-supplement approach essentially is a basal reading program that is augmented with one or more commercial programs and/or materials developed by the school or the school district. The supplements might include any combination of the following:

- Additional phonics training material
- Supplemental trade books—fiction and nonfiction literature in complete book form
- Supplemental anthologies and comprehension exercises
- Spelling programs
- Writing and related language arts supplements
- Computer-assisted materials
- Thinking skills programs and activities

## SUPPLEMENTS

### Integrated Spelling

Write-in workbooks with motivating activities, suggestions, and assessment. (Teacher's Editions available separately.)

### Big Book Literature Cassette Collection

Delightful recordings of Big Book stories.

### Laserdisc (Grades 1—8)

Features dynamic full-motion videos and still images that build concepts, illustrate key vocabulary, and stimulate critical thinking—all accessed easily by bar codes. A Teacher's Guide with bar codes is provided, and bar code stickers are available separately to be placed at point-of-use in the *Student Anthology Teacher's Editions.*

### Reading Software

Offers engaging classroom software programs with activities that reinforce vocabulary, comprehension, and thinking skills. Each package includes a Teacher's Guide.

- Handwriting programs and activities
- Materials for children with special needs (e.g., Learning Disabled, Limited English Proficiency, etc.)

The key concept underlying the basal-supplemental classroom is the belief that a basal program is necessary to provide continuity to the school reading program, but that it should be augmented with the best language arts supplements that a school committee can identify (see photos on preceding page). Specifically, the basal-supplement philosophy maintains that:

- The basal permits children in any school or district to share a common cultural experience with children elsewhere in the country.
- The basal provides instructional alignment from grade to grade and across schools in a district (and even across districts and states).
- The basal offers a structured management system that is guided by the curriculum.

The basal-supplement approach also permits schools to meet newer concerns without undergoing curriculum upheaval. For example, by the late 1960s, the growing sense of the cultural diversity in the country increased criticism of the white middle class orientation of the basals and engendered several basal-supplements attempting to represent that multicultural diversity in the reading selections and the illustrations in books offered to children. The basal industry, sensing that this was an honest concern, as well as a threat to their market share, moved quickly to respond to the felt need. Initially, they did so in some patronizing ways, such as coloring children in existing basals brown and yellow, and later with literature from and about different nations and cultures within the American scene. However, basal programs survived this initial criticism largely because publishers were able to "hit" the market quickly with trade books and other supplementary material that contained more realistic portrayals of ethnic children and urban life. In more recent times both basals and supplements have expanded their concern to include the literature of many nations, peoples, and subcultures within the larger culture (such as native Americans, Spanish-surnamed, etc.).

The basal-supplement approach slowly is becoming more of an integrated reading–language arts program. Several different schools of thought are housed under this general category. Consider now another belief system that first challenged basals to be even more sequential and management-oriented, but now is largely incorporated within them.

## Mastery Teaching Approach

Most basal programs were influenced by the "skills mastery" orientation that was popular in the field of reading into the early 1970s. This essentially bottom-up approach begins with a meticulously articulated scope and sequence of skills and accompanying behaviors. The assumption is that each sequential skill must be mastered before the student is able to move to the next slightly more difficult one. Instruction is defined as a cycle of: teach, test, reteach those who have not reached mastery, and then test again.

These systems were heavily influenced by two movements in education: B. F. Skinner's[1] brand of behaviorism and Benjamin Bloom's (1971) concepts of mastery learning. Behaviorism was based on the proposition that individual learning could be reduced to a set of definable behaviors that could be trained into most anyone, largely through use of "behavior reinforcement schedules" that controlled rewards and thereby conditioned "appropriate" responding. Mastery learning was based on the humanistic proposition that most people (75% by one estimate) could achieve as well as the best students if educators could identify and teach to the specific cognitive and affective "entry characteristics" necessary for successful learning (Bloom, Hastings, & Madaus, 1971). This was an especially compelling notion to educators who were struggling to help African Americans to overcome the negative effects of slavery, followed by segregation and poverty.

These early efforts continue to exist today in several diverse forms: as coordinated skills-management systems in many basal reader programs (Otto, Wolf, & Elderidge, 1984); as an assessment model with "performance indicators" (Paris et al., 1992—see Appendix D); and in a highly structured program known as DISTAR (Engleman & Brener, 1983). DISTAR, an acronym for Direct Instructional System Teaching and Reading, is a commercial program that provides actual scripts for teachers. These scripts include the exact words to say and things to do to lead lessons that provide quick pacing, multiple repetitions, and rote training. It was designed to be "teacher-proof."

Not surprisingly, many teachers find it tedious and claim that it reduces them to teaching machines. However, it sometimes gets the job done. Several studies have shown this program to have positive short- and long-term effects in inner city schools (Becker, 1977; Beck & McCaslin, 1978; Meyer, Gersten, & Gutkin, 1983). The program's effectiveness tends to be attributed to the fact that it is highly task-oriented. Its successful results, however, may be related to aspects of the program that are not popularly known. The program, for example, typically involves extensive teacher training, supervision, daily technical assistance, and extensive parental involvement. While these factors do not negate the positive results, they do suggest that future comparison studies need to take these factors into consideration. Furthermore, there is some contrary evidence even among children for whom it was claimed to be best suited. For example, DISTAR did not prove to be of any significant consequence in helping "48 perceptually impaired" children when compared with a traditional basal program (Kuder, 1990). In other words, it is no panacea for learning and reading disabled children, but it has proven to be a reasonable option for some children. It should be noted, however, that at least two studies have shown that explicit letter and sound training (phonemic segmentation) is more effective when used in combination with story material derived from children's natural language than when used in more isolated skills-oriented programs such as DISTAR (Sawyer, 1988; Uhry & Shepherd, 1993). Further, there are several arguments against mastery learning that go beyond outcomes measured by tests. One is its assumption that if a little drill is good, a lot is much better—an

[1] Read *Walden II* for a look into the future as he saw it.

approach that has been called "drill and kill" (Goodman, 1992a). Another is the belief that mastery learning is too bottom-up in its assumption that if skills are acquired first, concepts will somehow follow. Finally, mastery learning simply is at odds with American traditions of individualism and high regard for critical thinking. We have been hard pressed to find a teacher who has used it who isn't happy to leave it. Nonetheless, DISTAR appears to have some valid uses, particularly as a transitional program for children with certain severe learning deficits or behavioral problems (Slavin & Yampolsky, 1991).

The Whole Language Approach, discussed next, claims to be the antithesis of mastery learning. It is covered in great detail, since it seems to be the "Zeitgeist"— or spirit of our time. It also has been recognized as a quasi-political movement (Edelsky, 1992).

## WHOLE LANGUAGE APPROACH

The most frequent question asked about whole language is, what is it? The cover graphic of one journal defined it as follows:

> *Whole language* (n.) A theoretical position about how language learning occurs. The tenets of the theory involve the belief that: 1. language is learned through actual use, 2. that reading and writing are best learned through the use of authentic (unaltered) texts, and 3. that learning is best achieved through direct engagement and personal experience.
>
> *Illinois Reading Council Journal, 20* (2), cover.

This definition is useful both for what it says and for what it doesn't say. From an historical perspective, whole language seems to have theoretical roots in humanistic philosophy. Humanism is a cultural and intellectual movement dating back to the Renaissance. It is concerned with the interests, needs, and welfare of human beings, more so than abstract principles of good and bad. From a school-based perspective, it places a strong emphasis on the humanities, such as music, art, and literature, and advocates for an integrated reading–language arts curriculum. This movement toward a more humanistic and integrated educational system lost favor in the industrial period, from about 1860 to the 1930s. During this period, school was designed largely to teach one how to "fit in" and how to handle tough times— which everyone was taught to expect. Words like "pluck" and "gumption" were popularized to build self-sufficient, though not self-actualized, children. Reading, writing, history, geography, arithmetic, and proper comportment were taught in a segmented, rote learning manner. This period of unfettered capitalism and child labor was slowly pushed out by a more child-centered curriculum.

A string of people from Maria Montessori, the Italian pediatrician who worked with Rome's underprivileged children, to developmental psychologist Jean Piaget, contributed to the growing sense that children were not merely "little adults" in training to assume socially defined roles, but individuals with unique talents and potential. Following in this tradition, in today's public schools parents demand the best for themselves and for their children. In response, educators have begun to offer a more integrated curriculum—one offering a far better balance of concern for children, respect for parent needs, and a growing realization of the need for some form of "ethical–moral" education and community and family support systems. The transition to the current form of whole language seems to have begun in earnest about 35 years ago. Veatch (1959) and Allen and Allen (1969) were among the earliest and staunchest advocates of teaching reading through a whole language, or an "integrated language arts" approach, as it was then known. In a recent textbook, *Pathways to Literacy,* Sampson, Allen, and Sampson (1991) describe the essential nature of an integrated reading–language arts curriculum that closely resembles today's whole language movement. The following points, paraphrased from that text, provide a solid basis for understanding contemporary whole language:

- Reading, writing, spelling, listening, and speaking should not be taught as separate skills, but as opportunities to learn that are encountered in a meaning-centered curriculum (p. 4).
- Language Arts instruction in a meaning-centered curriculum proceeds best when it follows natural language learning as experienced by the "cognitive field position"—a holistic perspective based on the learner's interacting with the environment, more so than isolated teaching and training (pp. 5–7).

It is only in recent years that this basic theme really has come to be known as a "whole language" approach. In the late 1960s, it was known as "psycholinguistics," reflecting the background and training of its chief spokesman, Kenneth Goodman. As a student of language, Goodman proposed that reading practices should be firmly grounded in the psychology of language development. More recently, Yetta Goodman has emphasized that whole language is more a philosophy than a set of practices (1989). Others, such as Burnett (1991), claim that the whole language philosophy was thoroughly described earlier and specifically by Kohl in a book simply called *Reading: How To* (1973). Still others have observed that it was the brainchild of Jeannette Veatch, who, beginning in the early 1960s, advocated for essentially the same propositions (Veatch, Sawicki, Elliott, Flake, Blakey, 1979). Today Veatch is most remembered for her advocacy of an aspect of whole language that she called "Individualized Reading" (c.f., Veatch, 1985), a program in which children self-select books, read them independently, and "conference" with the teacher.

Thus while the basic theme and the practices of integrated language arts and individualized reading have had supporters for many years, the current whole language form has many more "converts." This is in part due to the winning ways and convincing approach of several advocates (Clyde & Condon, 1992; Edelsky, 1992; Goodman, Bird, & Goodman, 1991; Harste, Burke & Woodward, 1984; Shannon, 1989; Smith, 1973, 1982, 1985; Watson, 1991; Weaver, 1993). Watson's contribution has been particularly appreciated by teachers. She organized one of the first support groups for sharing useful tips and mutual help, called Teachers Applying Whole Language, or TAWL (Salzer, 1991).

Clearly, however, it is the artistry of Kenneth Goodman that is most responsible for the current popularity of whole language. For example, compare below how Goodman's presentation of how language (i.e., reading, writing, speaking, and listening) is best learned with the very similar ideas of Allen (1991–92), who by any account also is a master communicator.

Language is learned best when:

- It's real and natural.
- It's whole.
- It's sensible.
- It's interesting.
- It's relevant.
- It belongs to the learner.
- It's part of a real event.
- It has social utility.
- It has purpose for the learner.
- The learner chooses to use it.
- It's accessible to the learner.
- The learner has power to use it.

Despite such compelling rhetoric, a growing number of authorities are finding "holes" in whole language, as Vail (1989) put it. A sample of these criticisms (Burnett, 1990; Groff, 1991; Hoffman, 1992; Kameenui & Shannon, 1988; Manzo & Manzo, 1993; McKenna, Robinson, & Miller, 1990; Thompson, 1992) are summarized below. Consider a point to be consensual unless otherwise noted.

- Whole language claims to be a philosophy, but it sometimes acts more like an ideology (Hoffman, 1992; Thompson, 1992).
- It tends to be a "top-down" approach with only slight provision for those individuals whose innate learning style is more "sequential" and rule-guided than "simultaneous" or intuitive and meaning-driven.
- It is based on the belief that isolated word study is actually detrimental to meaningful reading, "when several comprehensive reviews of empirical studies have concluded that reading instruction programs that stress word recognition inevitably produce significantly higher levels of reading ability than those that do not" (Groff, 1991, p. 27).
- Most whole language instruction is based on an "incidental" learning model, or a teach-it-if-and-when-it-comes-up basis. While it is true that youngsters who learn to read "naturally" at home before even entering school tend to learn in this way, they also tend to be weak in oral reading (Clay, 1975). More importantly, direct instructional models, as noted earlier in the chapter, have proven more effective for all students at all levels of schooling (Rosenshine & Stevens, 1984), particularly so for poor and minority children (Delpit, 1988; Stahl & Miller, 1989; Stice & Bertrand, 1990).
- The emphasis on reading "meaningful narratives" with words containing inconsistent symbol-to-sound patterns can make it unnecessarily difficult to apply and practice word analysis strategies.
- Whole language approaches tend to be language- and story-centered; therefore, children who are not highly verbal or fiction-oriented, such as those who gravitate toward science and technology, can be inadvertently penalized (Delpit, 1988; Manzo & Manzo, 1993; Thompson, 1992).

- There are few defined methods for teaching, and those few that are defined do not seem to differ significantly from previous choices (Thompson, 1992).
- Whole language probably places too much emphasis on the subjective observations and judgments of teachers under "in-flight" conditions, rather than on validated instructional methods and some potentially useful materials.
- Whole language seems to be beset with too many "don't's"; for example, it has taken strong stands against phonics, direct instruction, drill, behavioral psychology, standardized testing, and especially basals: "basal readers . . . are *bad* for kids, and . . . they don't need them" (Goodman, 1992b, p. 362).
- Definitions of whole language can be distractingly vague (Thompson, 1992).
- More than not being able to provide *empirical* support for whole language, enthusiasts have tended to avoid the obligation to do so (McKenna, Robinson, & Miller, 1990). Goodman himself has stated that he prefers to keep arguments for whole language based on philosophy rather than evidence because, he proposes, traditional research methods are inadequate to deal with innovations that are leaping ahead of research, rather than attempting to follow it (1992b).
- Contrary to its stated intentions, whole language may *not* be whole child (Delpit, 1988; Manzo & Manzo, 1993). The "immersion" message is based on the possibly misguided belief that a literate environment is enough to raise a literate child. This is analogous to saying that you need only surround kids with a rich musical environment and they will (incidentally) come to appreciate music and to learn how to play an instrument.
- The rhetoric of whole language proponents can be strident and intolerant of others who hold alternate positions (Hoffman, 1992).

In short, the whole language movement can be somewhat more harsh and disenfranchising than its otherwise humanistic and highly language-oriented proponents seem to realize. It also is notable that most reading professionals acknowledge several of the basic elements of whole language philosophy. For example, you will see ahead in the text how considerable credit is given to the whole language philosophy's emphases on:

- Whole book reading
- Writing—from earliest years
- Writing across the curriculum
- Avoidance of "drill and kill" exercises
- Immersion in a literate environment
- The social nature of learning
- Talk about teachers as well as students (Stiles, 1992)

What you will *not* find in the pages ahead is a denial of the value of direct teaching, nor of *all* forms of drill, under all circumstances. Instead, you will see an attempt to identify relevant experimental research on all sides of these issues. For example, DeFord (1986) compared the reading and writing of children in a *skills-based* classroom, a *phonics* classroom, and a *whole language* classroom. She found that in the skills and phonics classrooms, where language was more restricted, children's progress in writing also was inhibited. Most authorities on writing are struggling to develop research designs that will permit the further documentation of this kind of experimental evidence (Linn, Baker, & Dunbar, in press; Shearer, 1992). The next school of thought also emphasizes the need to document theory with evidence. In doing so, it seems to represent an evolution toward a more intelligent form of eclecticism.

## New Eclecticism Approach

Oddly, there is no agreed-upon name for what may be the most widely held philosophy in modern literacy education. The lack of a formal name probably is due to the fact that this school of thought does not have many "don't's." It is more inclusive than exclusive. It has no chief spokesperson, and there are many variations. It is only for purposes of discussion that we have dubbed this class of philosophies as the "New Eclecticism" (Manzo & Manzo, 1993). The term "new" here is *not* meant to suggest that it has never existed before, but rather that it is something that is always in the act of becoming. This means being open to each new or felt need and responsible development in education. This willingness to accept and incorporate new and reformed ideas is seen as part of an ongoing effort to keep a balance and yet meet the needs of any given time. Hence, the New Eclecticism is more pragmatic than ideological. It has led some, such as Wood and Mateja (1983), to freely adapt secondary level strategies to the elementary school, while the more common practice was the reverse—extending elementary school strategies upward to secondary levels. In a similarly eclectic vein, many of the widely used methods texts in the field carry a wide and workable array of methodologies (e.g., Tierney et al.'s 1991, *Reading Strategies and Practices,* and Walker's 1993 *Diagnostic Teaching of Reading*). In the context of such eclecticism, whole language is most acceptable as a needed recovery from overemphasis on mastery learning and certain forms of basal commercialism. However, to deny that some children may have needs which we do not address, whether it be for immersion or direct instructional approaches, is to deny them equal opportunity for appropriate instruction.

The newest part of the New Eclecticism is the sense that it is part of a worldwide openness among thinking people to bring down the walls that may be artificially dividing us, to rise above our own ego-, ethnic-cultural needs, and to see other's efforts as honest experiments in a collective attempt to find better ways to do anything and everything. To that extent, it clearly is inspired by the breakup of the USSR and the growing realization that even American democracy and capitalism need to continue to be examined and fine-tuned if the basic tenets are to survive and flourish.

What then are the tenets of some of the New Eclectic philosophies as these relate to literacy and learning? It seems that those individuals who would be most at home under this umbrella also would be comfortable with these tenets:

1.  Teachers should seek creative solutions to conflicting ideas rather than simply choosing one or the other or looking for a safe middle ground.
2.  Wherever possible, teaching approaches should be supported by cross-verifying research and experience in natural school settings.

3. Decisions should be guided by a holistic philosophy that puts children first, including those who are different from ourselves.

4. There is a need, beginning at the elementary level, to further emphasize content and concept mastery and thinking, particularly critical–creative thinking.

5. To maintain a standard of quality in the profession, teachers should know and use the knowledge base of the field, including tested and published instructional strategies.

6. Effective instructional delivery needs to be broad-based; that is, it should address cognitive, affective, and sensorimotor domains and take full advantage of incidental and direct instruction.

7. The purpose of schooling is the education of the *whole* child, and hence each segment of the curriculum is responsible, to some reasonable and pragmatic extent, for the advancement of other segments of the curriculum.

8. Collaboration and cooperation among different perspectives, and among professionals from classrooms to universities, is essential to working out the most effective and efficient ways of accomplishing all of the above.

You will see many examples ahead of how this problem-identification and problem-solving orientation can pay off in some very satisfactory ways. Consider now how two leading literacy educators conceptualize this "new eclecticism."

Searfoss and Readence (1989) have summarized their *child-centered eclectic* literacy program as including these six points:

1. Reflects instruction by teachers who understand how children use language, especially reading

2. Creates a learning environment that accepts prior knowledge and language ability of children

3. Guides learning through success-oriented, direct teaching

4. Requires that children actively participate in their learning, thus sharing in the responsibility for the success of the program

5. Provides professionally planned and organized reading instruction, integrated with oral language and writing

6. Assesses progress in learning to read (in a variety of ways)

The authors' own perspective on the New Eclecticism is similar to that of Searfoss and Readance, but it takes a stronger stance on the value of direct teaching, on the need to promote higher-level thinking, and on the need to stress the child's responsibility for his or her own learning. This last point is important if the teacher is to avoid what Caputo (1987) characterized as excessive child-centeredness, where no one is *ever* corrected for being just plain wrong in their comprehension or interpretation of text. In this same vein, the New Eclecticism, as we see it, is also open to all possible ways to teach, and especially to traditional approaches that may well contain some wisdom or reflect some deep-felt needs of students and teachers. It is in this way that the New Eclecticism avoids *disempowering* teachers by turning them into dinosaurs with each new discovery or emphasis. Its goal is to sustain prior training and experience and to build on it. So, for example, when

Troyer and Yopp (1990) found that many veteran teachers did not know what was meant by "phonemic awareness" or "emergent literacy"—two popular new themes—they simply moved to close this gap by identifying methods that met this need, and by drawing attention to some of the practices of those teachers that already were within the scope of these newer objectives. Reutzel and Cooter (1992) refer to this as the spirit of "building bridges rather than walls" (p. 3).

## GETTING STARTED

The old Chinese adage that *every great journey begins with a single step* is appropriate to consider here. More appropriate, however, is the observation of the eminent psychologist and educator Jerome Bruner (1978), who said that all learning (and as teachers we are lifelong learners) takes something to *get it started*, something to *keep it going* and something to *keep it on target*. In the matter of becoming a great teacher, the following steps are recommended:

1. Begin to identify your basic perspective from those presented thus far (see exercise number one ahead for ideas).

2. Acquire a sound knowledge base. Those teachers who possess high levels of knowledge about reading have been found to exhibit the traits most associated with providing successful reading instruction (Conley, 1984).

3. Identify a few methods that you will use as catalysts, or vehicles, to teach with and also to learn better how to teach. In the text these are referred to as "heuristic," or self-discovery methods.

4. Provide as much "scaffolding," or support, to yourself in pursuing new skills as you would to a student. For example, some teachers-in-training have made themselves notes that are printed large enough to serve as desktop "prompters" of the methods they are trying to refine and internalize. (Pilots use these to get 747 jumbo jets off the ground, as do television talk show hosts who deal with time constraints, unexpected events, and interruptions that make their situation not unlike the contemporary classroom.)

5. Give yourself time to master a new method or approach before passing judgment on it or on yourself. Whenever we try anything new, our performance is diminished at first by the distraction of trying to remember just what to do and by other performance pressures.

6. If possible, tape your early efforts and compare them with your later ones. Both you and the class will look and sound sharper in subsequent efforts.

7. Monitor your progress on a point scale. George suggests that teachers use this simple scale to rate themselves on both their level of knowledge and level of use, after viewing videotapes for each teaching strategy they wish to master:

   1 = non-use

   2 = mechanical use

3 = routine use

4 = refined (i.e., reflective) use
   *In George, Moley, & Ogle (1992).*

These suggestions may appear to be somewhat mechanical. However, their purpose is to direct your attention to some of the more technical aspects of becoming a great teacher and to initiate related conversation with peers and professors. It is this type of interaction that supports an ongoing developmental process for the teacher who is a student of teaching as well as a teacher of students.

## **W**here You've Been

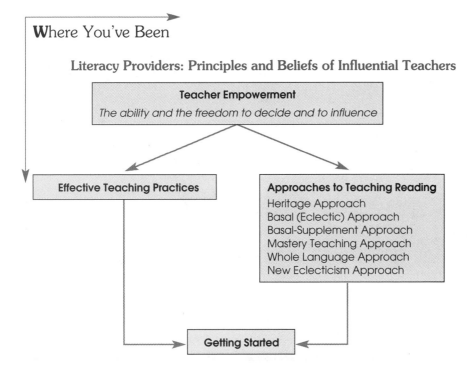

**Literacy Providers: Principles and Beliefs of Influential Teachers**

**Teacher Empowerment**
*The ability and the freedom to decide and to influence*

**Effective Teaching Practices**

**Approaches to Teaching Reading**
Heritage Approach
Basal (Eclectic) Approach
Basal-Supplement Approach
Mastery Teaching Approach
Whole Language Approach
New Eclecticism Approach

**Getting Started**

## **W**here You're Going

The next section of the book helps to further lay a foundation for **reflective inquiry**. The first chapter in this section tells what we have learned as a profession about "emergent reading and writing," or the development of literacy from infancy to the primary grades.

### *Reflective Inquiries and Activities*

1.  Write up a SEAR suggested to you by a cooperating teacher or from your own experience. Share it with classmates. To maximize the value of this interaction, add space for "Comments" suggested during discussion that extend the SEAR idea. For example, in Box 2.1, the reporting teacher's husband, also a teacher, took over the job of interacting with the overly prolific journal writer. A possible comment in response to this SEAR might be, "I wonder if interested parents and community volunteers might not become readers and responders to students' journal writing and other creative writing activities."

2.  Consider each of the Effective Teaching Principles listed on pages 30–36. Express your level of support for and belief in each of these on a 5-point scale: 1 (low) to 5 (high). If you are a visual learner, you might display your current profile. Assemble all items you marked 5 next to one another on a bottom line, then put those marked 4 above them, then the 3s, 2s, and 1s (see illustration below). Color coding will make comparisons with others easier. These can also be expressed on a simple bar graph.

**Illustration #1**

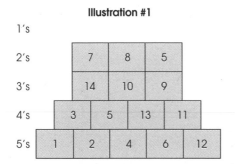

**Illustration #2**

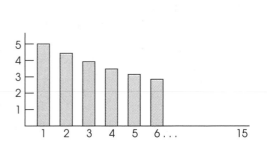

Reflective Inquires and Activities

3.  Consider each of the major belief systems listed on pages 38–52. Again, express your level of comfort with each on a 5-point scale: 1 (low) to 5 (high). Display and discuss with other students.

4.  Are you aware of any apparent contradictions between your responses to the Effective Teaching Principles on pages 30–36 and your own beliefs? Try to express these contradictions in a few sentences. Review your response several times during the term. Looking at things repeatedly in different lights is a traditional way to convert knowledge into wisdom.

5.  Keep a professional journal. Begin immediately, as a preservice teacher, by keeping a weekly record of information and ideas that seem most meaningful to you and your personal reflections on what you are hearing and reading.

> *People who keep journals live life twice. Having written something down gives the opportunity to go back to it over and over, to remember and relive the experience.*
>
> Jessamyn West

6.  Keep an upbeat perspective. Teaching is serious business, but if you take your-self too seriously, you will diminish your ability to do it well. Professor Irene Allen (1991–92) tells teachers that one way to keep yourself loose is to record and share the humorous things that happen when you teach or observe classes. Here are three examples from journal entries of her student teachers:

    *Amanda had read the story* Clifford, the Small Red Puppy *to her first-grade group. She had finished the story and had asked a few questions to be sure the pupils understood the story. One of the questions she asked was, "When did Clifford stop growing?" One little boy piped up with, "At the end of the book."*

    *Kim always left the classroom when the first-graders left for lunch. One day as she was leaving, the children moaned and asked her if she had to go. She decided to be honest with them and said, "Yes, I have to go because I have classes to attend also." One little girl, Julie, came up to her with eyes as wide as saucers. She looked up at Kim and said, "You mean you're not a grown-up?"*

    *Lisa worked with a reading group of about six students. She read to them at a round table and had them sitting close so they could hear her and see the pictures. After reading the story, she asked them to "scoot their chairs* out *so they'd have room to write." At that moment, she looked down at the material which she was about to pass out, and when she looked up the pupils were all sitting about ten feet from the table, looking slightly puzzled.*

7.  Informal-Action-Research Project: Prepare a group of youngsters to read pas-sages with and without the charge to read to recall *everything* in an assign-ment. Evaluate the quality and quantity of their recalls. Ask yourself questions such as these to aid reflection and insight:

    (a) Was the point of this lesson apparent in students' responses (that is, did students seem to exert greater control over their learning outcomes)?

    (b) If it was not apparent, what might I do next to amplify and underscore that point—give a test on the material(?); discuss what should have been learned after the experience(?); share with them what has been learned by others from such an experience(?); share, too, what they will learn *before* the experience(?); a combination of these(?).

    Check your findings against the points made and the research available on the Guiding Reading Procedure covered in the chapter on reading com-prehension. (This is a good readiness or schema-building activity for better understanding and learning from that chapter.)

8.  Consciously try to add new precepts to guide your teaching to those listed in this chapter. Draw from many sources, such as your classmates, your instruc-tor, or a supervising teacher. One of the most insightful accounts we have seen of a principle of teaching was in a *Time* magazine story of how a gentle cow-boy works patiently with untrained horses rather than trying to dominate and "break 'em." You will find other such sources in the pages ahead.

# PART II

# FOUNDATIONS OF LITERACY

# 3 EMERGENT READING AND WRITING: EARLY CHILDHOOD TO PRIMARY GRADES

**2** Influential Teachers

**1** The Reading Process

**4** Reading Aloud

**3** Emergent Reading & Writing

## Where You Are

Many educators once believed that children were developmentally unable to learn to read prior to about six and a half years of age. Experience and research have led to the realization that children begin to learn the foundational concepts of literacy from their earliest years—perhaps their earliest months of life. This chapter lays out aspects of this "emergent literacy." It describes teaching practices that are appropriate to preschool and primary grades, and the role of the parent—every child's first teacher.

**5** Reading & Responding

**6** Word Recognition

**7** Vocabulary

**8** Improving Basic Comprehension

**9** Constructive Reading

**10** Content Area Reading

**11** Children with Special Needs

**12** Literacy Assessment

**13** The Classroom & School Literacy Program

*It takes the whole village to raise a child.*

African Proverb

# WHEN ARE CHILDREN "READY" TO READ?

## EARLY RESEARCH

For nearly thirty years it was held that the best time to begin formal instruction in reading was 6.5 years of age. This conclusion was based largely on the findings of a famous study conducted in the upper middle class community of Winnetka, Illinois, by Mabel Vogel Morphett and Carleton Washburne (1931). After a time, however, reports began to surface that approximately one percent of children were entering school already able to read. These reports led to several "early reader" studies (e.g., Durkin, 1966) and set the stage for current research and views which now are collected under the name "emergent literacy." Since most of these studies were centered on what was taking place in the home, much of what is being done to facilitate the emergence of literacy is based on observations in homes where children learned to read without any "apparent" direct instruction (Strickland & Morrow, 1988).

Elizabeth Sulzby says that the term "emergent literacy" addresses what young children learn about reading, writing, and print prior to entering school (1991). However, Sulzby (1989) notes that, for some, it may be more broadly defined to include reading and writing behaviors that not only precede, but are the *beginnings* of conventional literacy instruction. Simply put, emergent literacy is concerned with facilitating or incidentally beginning the teaching of reading at a very early age.

Since emergent literacy addresses the period between birth and the time children are formally taught to read and write, it necessarily is concerned with the influence of parents, community, and early childhood education programs. Fortunately, in a time of gloom and excessive criticism of public schooling, early childhood education remains a worldwide success story—an incubator for fresh discoveries and innovations, and therefore an area of which elementary school teachers need to be knowledgeable.

## *SHOULD* CHILDREN BE ENCOURAGED TO READ EARLY?

The teaching of reading and writing together at an early age is growing in popularity once again, but it is not without its skeptics. In fact there is some evidence of a countertrend to re-establish play and socialization as the priority of pre and even primary schooling.

Questions that often arise when the idea of reading at an early age is discussed include, "Why bother?"—and secondly, "Might it be detrimental?" The reasons for beginning reading early when placed side-by-side with the reasons for not doing so give the appearance that it is a close call as to whether it is a wise thing to do. In fact, it can be very wise or very foolish depending more on precisely *what* is done, *why* it is done, and most importantly *how it is done* than on whether it *is* done.

To clarify, Lapp and Flood (1992) offer four traditional criticisms and rebuttals, to which we have added two others for your consideration. The discussion centers on early reading, but is meant also to address the popular trend to combine early reading with writing.

The lesson in all this seems to be to proceed with reflection and caution. Be enthusiastic about reading and writing, and teach whatever a child may have inter-

| CRITICISM | REBUTTAL |
|---|---|
| 1. Early reading can hurt the child's vision. | There is no evidence to support this. Children merely lack familiarity with nearpoint tasks—those closer than 14 inches from the eyes. In fact, most children are able to color, draw, and even write by 4 to 5 years of age without evidence of eye strain. |
| 2. Parents often feel obliged to help, but they are not qualified and can be too emotionally involved. They may push children beyond their capacities and could make them dread reading. | This is true, but there are many things parents can do that can be invitational, fun, and emotionally bonding. |
| 3. Those who read early will be bored in school. | Boredom will ensue if children are made to start over again. This need not happen. They can move ahead and even learn by helping others in a classroom designed to create a community of readers. |
| 4. Childhood should be for play, not formal instruction. | Reading can be fun, and the child's will and inclinations can be used to guide how much is taught and when. |
| 5. What's the hurry? A 4- or 5-year-old has no pressing needs for textual information: the world around him or her is filled with enough questions, wonders, and pleasures. | True enough, but reading, even at this tender age, can add to wonder and pleasure—it can be the source of some answers and of new questions. And 4- and 5-year-olds have some of the same informational needs as older children—``What does the TV guide say is on now?'' ``What does this comic strip say?'' and so on. |
| 6. Successful preschool reading, especially when it was the object of overzealous parents, can lead to big disappointments if it gives a child a misimpression that he or she is much brighter than classmates who came to school unable to read. | There is no easy rebuttal to this argument. Even children who are enthusiastic about reading, but otherwise of average or lesser ability, will have fallen from a high place as others learn to read and then pass them by. Facing, rather than denying this problem, will lead to solutions. |

est to learn, but don't be misled into thinking that early reading needs to be systematically taught and pursued to win the battle for universal literacy or to establish an individual's social superiority. The best justification for beginning reading early is where there is reason to believe that the child will not benefit by waiting or will benefit in some needed way by the early start. One place where early reading efforts often are justified is among children from lower socioeconomic circumstances. Efforts to teach them to read early are less likely to create a disparity with their "true" abilities than to provide compensation and correction from depressed circumstances.

# FOUNDATIONS OF EMERGENT LITERACY

Sulzby and Teale (1991) have suggested three ideas that underlie research and practices in emergent literacy. These are listed below, along with two additional ideas that may help you to form a sound concept of this stage of literacy development.

1. The child is innately predisposed to learn language (Chomsky, 1965), and reading and writing are natural extensions of language acquisition.

2. Children's language acquisition and interest in extending language to include reading and writing is determined in large measure by the nature of their interactions with their environments. This idea was originated by Jean Piaget, the pioneer developmental psychologist, who showed that certain innate aptitudes and abilities would be substantially advanced in an environment that urged, more so than merely permitted, their "construction."

3. To urge language and literacy development, adults essentially need only to provide a print-rich environment and to interact with children in ways that draw attention to print and print artifacts (Robinson & Dixon, 1991). The actions of adults and children in such an environment will promote incidental and deliberate development of literacy growth, much as it does of language. For example, when a parent looks at a "bottle" on the floor and says to the child, "The bottle fell down," the parent is incidentally teaching language. When the parent shows the child the bottle falling and says, "Fall down!"—which usually is followed by a sharper "No!" to begin to tell the child not to knock it over intentionally, the parent is deliberately teaching language and appropriate behavior. The child's early association of language with being a "cause" or "force" for manipulating the environment taps into and reinforces a great natural source of human motivation—to control one's environment and, hence, destiny. In a print-rich setting, this identical process is expanded to include reading signs and labels and to writing notes and letters. In this way, the parent says, "This can be done," *and* it is proper and life-enhancing to do so.

4. Efforts to understand and guide emergent literacy should be sensitive to other aspects of childhood development. The things children are asked to engage in should be developmentally appropriate. For example, a good deal of research indicates that young children like poetry that has rhythm, rhyme, humor, straightforward content, and familiar narrative structures—such as the poetry of Prelutsky and Silverstein—and tend to *dislike* poems that contain excessive visual imagery or figurative language (Kutiper and Wilson, 1993). In other words, children tend to prefer poems that align with childhood developmental processes rather than those with "literary merit," as judged by adult standards.

5. Emergent literacy is a period of early learning which, when properly nurtured, can strengthen teaching and learning throughout schooling. In this nascent, or formative stage, the child builds personal *categories of information,* called "schemata", (plural for "schema"), that form the basis for subsequent learning.

Let's look more closely at this intriguing notion of emergent literacy. It is one that primary school teachers understand profoundly from their experiences with

FIGURE
**3.1** **Illustration of Schema Theory**

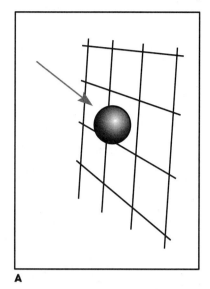

A

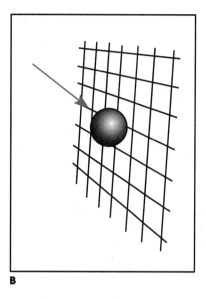

B

The incoming information is more likely to be "caught" (perceived and remembered) by the well-developed schema represented in illustration B than in the less well-developed schema represented in illustration A.

small children, but that most other teachers, even those who have raised their own children, need to carefully reflect upon.

## SCHEMA THEORY

*Schema* (Flavell, 1981) can be defined as a personal framework of information about a topic. It can be thought of, metaphorically, as a kind of "net" in which each thread is a bit of information that contributes to the pattern of the whole. The more threads of information a person has about a topic, the more finely woven is the "net." The more finely woven the net is, in turn, determines how capable it is of "catching" new bits of information related to the topic (see Figure 3.1). In other words, schema theory simply says that learning will occur most easily when the learner has at least a *basic* conceptual framework of prior knowledge about the topic, and learning will be most *difficult* where there is little prior knowledge or appropriate concept basis.

Recalling an appropriate schema also permits the reader to make inferences that enhance comprehension. In a story sequence about golf, for example, when the word "ball" is mentioned, the reader pictures a ball that looks quite different from a baseball or a basketball, even though the author doesn't explicitly describe the golf ball.

As applied to the act of reading, it is in the emergent literacy period that children are forming basic concepts about books and print that will one day develop into much more elaborate schemata. They learn, for example, that there can be a relationship between pictures and spoken words; they begin to form a sense of "story" in which a sequence of events has a recognizable beginning, middle, and end; they relate this sense of story to the left-to-right sequence of pages in storybooks, and so on. These first steps toward *creating* schemata where none had existed are known as *early learning.*

## EARLY LEARNING

The most challenging stage of learning is the point at which the learner must somehow acquire *new* concepts or processes for which she or he has little if any prior knowledge or experience. The eminent psychologist D. O. Hebb referred to this point in learning as "early learning" (1949).

The difficulty of "early learning" at any age was first demonstrated by a German physician (Selden, 1932, as reported in Hebb, 1949). Selden seized a unique opportunity to discover whether early learning was a different *kind* of learning—as he hypothesized—than subsequent learning. Selden was able to work with several adults who had been blind from birth, but whose vision was to be restored by the (then) new process of removing cataracts from the lenses of their eyes. Despite their visual impairment, these adults seemed to have most other basic concepts in place. They could read braille, and they could identify most common objects by touch. Nonetheless, when their vision was restored, it took many weeks of practice before they were able to *visually* identify squares, circles, triangles, spheres, and cubes when presented with these in either two- or three-dimensional form. Incredibly, there were some patients who, despite being able to easily recognize a cube of sugar in a hand could not identify it in a slightly different context, as when it was hanging from a thread (Dember, 1965). One patient whom Selden called "exceptionally intelligent" could not identify all five faces on certain pictures for as long as *two years* following the operation that restored his sight. Further evidence of the difficulty of early learning was established in a series of studies with chimpanzees that were raised in total darkness (Riesen, 1949, 1950). When the animals were brought into the light, some were unable, for their entire adult lives, to handle tasks that required visual distinctions.

The point is that early learning is *much* more complex than one might assume. More importantly, as Selden had hypothesized, it appears to be different in *kind,* as well as in degree, from later learning. Early learning is that first abstract mental leap toward creating a new schema. For example, multiplying numbers involves creation of a new schema that is built on much of the same basic information used in a schema for adding and subtracting numbers, but requires a significant reorganization of this information. Some children do not develop a functional schema for multiplication for several years after its introduction. For them, the early learning period is much longer and needs to be treated with much more care and attention than our curriculum guides and sequence charts would suggest. If such children were nurtured more carefully and wisely during this extended early learning stage, there is a good chance that they would not only learn multiplication but that they would attain the formal operational level of thinking and the schema-enriched

Laying the foundations for lifelong literacy

framework needed to quickly master division and to continue to learn mathematics thereafter.

The early learning stages of reading also pose difficulties. Gates, one of the founders of modern reading instruction, discovered that children who were able to detect even very slight distinctions in objects and pictures had *no* similar ability to detect distinctions in letters and words. His studies led him to conclude that "success in reading and spelling is dependent upon training in clearly perceiving significant features of *words,* rather than objects or pictures" (as cited in Sherk, 1967, p. 12). In other words, even though children could do "adding" and "subtracting," they couldn't do the seemingly related task of "multiplication" (or beginning reading).

It isn't easy to say precisely what this finding means in terms of reading instruction, probably because it means different things for different children. At the least, however, it suggests that overcoming early learning deficiencies requires early exposure to the specific desired task, not to some task that might appear to be similar. If you want someone to learn to hit a pitched ball, it is wise to have them start by hitting one off a tee, and then have them hit one thrown to them underhand. However, it would *not* be very productive to have them practice graceful swinging, or weight lifting to build the upper body for hitting the "long" ball. In more reading-related terms, it is wise to expose children early and continuously to books and to oral reading rather than to seemingly related tasks involving discriminating between and among symbols with the expectation that this might carry over to distinguishing between and among letters.

## EMERGENT LITERACY VERSUS "READING READINESS"

Those with strong interests in emergent literacy distinguish it from previous views of this phase in the child's development. They point out that until the late 1950s the preformal stage of reading was viewed as a time of "maturation or neural ripening" that simply needed to be permitted to happen and was not greatly influenced by instruction or guidance. By the 1960s, the more widely accepted view of this stage was referred to as "prereading" or "reading readiness." In this view there was a sequence of skills that children must master before they could profit from actual reading instruction. It was thought, further, that these skills could be identified and that they could be taught, thus making children "ready" to read at an earlier age. As a result, reading readiness programs were designed to accompany most basal reading series. These programs reflected the mistaken impression that learning to read required mastery of a series of skills that were only marginally related to actual reading. Therefore, these programs stressed nonprint visual–perceptual training materials that had no significant relationship to making meaning from print or to reading for meaning.

The concept of emergent literacy differs from that of reading readiness in that emergent literacy does not support spending unnecessary time and effort on visual–perceptual training; rather, it stresses reading as a meaning-making, language, and social process that also involves emergent writing. In earlier times, little thought and attention were given to the role of early writing, a topic discussed in some detail ahead in this chapter and throughout the text. First, however, consider some of the important language and social concepts that influence success in learning to read and write.

## LANGUAGE AND CONCEPTS AFFECTING EARLY READING AND WRITING

It has been clear for some time that at least four general categories of factors play an important role in early success in learning to read and write:

- Aspects of aptitude, or specific intelligence
- Family orientation toward literacy
- Experiences with and knowledge of print
- Individual maturation and childhood maturation

Where the first two factors are present, the third tends to follow without much prompting. When the first two are less positive, the third—experiences with and knowledge of print—becomes most important and often needs to be explicitly addressed. This is important to realize since it suggests that no matter how limited one's general and even specific verbal aptitude may be, or even how nonliterary the family orientation might be, it is possible and necessary to provide appropriate experiences that can raise almost any child's probability of experiencing success in learning to read and write. To do this effectively, however, it is necessary to know what kinds of experiences with and knowledge of print appear to have the strongest influence on early reading and writing success.

There are, depending upon how one counts, six to eight concepts about print that tend to be useful in planning appropriate or "facilitating reading [and writing] experiences" (George, 1975) for children. Each of these concepts is briefly defined below. To make these concepts more concrete, they are accompanied by a description of how researchers usually measure a child's familiarity with that factor, and the findings of a recent study by Robinson and Dixon (1991) in which they tested the extent to which preschoolers' familiarity with these print concepts tends to differ according to socioeconomic status. The children in the study were 4-year-olds enrolled either in a Head Start program for those at the poverty level or in tuition-based preschools.

**Letter Naming,** or knowledge of and ability to identify letters of the alphabet. This ability can be measured simply by presenting lower case letters individually on $3 \times 5$ cards. The process can then be repeated with capital letters. A third score can be derived by awarding an extra point for all letters properly named in lower and upper case print. It was on this factor that middle socioeconomic status (SES) youngsters differed most from their lower SES peers. Middle SES preschoolers know three times as many letter names as low SES youngsters (Robinson & Dixon, 1991).

**Letter Sounds,** or knowledge of and ability to identify and say an appropriate sound for each letter, again in lower and/or upper case. Children who know letter sounds at a young age have a greater probability of success in early reading. However, children who do not know letter sounds early do *not* necessarily have a *lower* probability of early success. On the average, low SES youngsters know fewer than one letter sound, whereas middle SES youngsters know nearly two (Robinson & Dixon, 1991). This small difference is significant because it suggests that low SES youngsters are in the difficult "early learning" stage, whereas middle SES children have formed a schema for letters and sounds and have learned one or two solid examples to build on. Hence, they are past the biggest obstacle to subsequent learning.

**Invented Spellings,** or a child's inclination and ability to "write" a word in some way so as to be able to "read" it back. One popular way to assess this ability is to read seven items to the child—these items can be words, phrases, or short sentences—first asking the child to "write down on paper anything that will help you remember these items." The differences among low and middle SES preschoolers on this factor are small (25% vs. 30%). This may be because even middle SES preschoolers seldom are encouraged to "write," and therefore their prior experiences related to this factor are much like those of lower SES children. Differences on this factor increase significantly, however, once children have had some formal schooling (Robinson & Dixon, 1991).

**Syllable and Phoneme Words,** or combining syllables and phonemes (or sound parts) into words. This may be tested simply by asking the child to identify a word that is spoken in two isolated syllables (ze-bra; el-bow; ba-by) or isolated sounds (/ch/ai/r; ph/o/ne). This task usually is preceded by a demonstration and a practice effort to help make the nature of the task clear. Lower and middle SES preschoolers differ significantly on their ability to perform this task. With syllables, low SES children scored 60 percent and middle SES 90 percent; with phonemes, the differences were 3 percent and 9 percent, respectively (Robinson & Dixon, 1991). Note that the phonemic task was much more difficult for both groups: it closely resembles the mature decoding process.

**Environmental Print** refers to a child's concept of symbols that are part of common experiences. It is thought to be a natural precursor of concepts of letters and print (Goodman, 1986; Harste, Burke, & Woodward, 1984). Environmental print often is measured by showing children color photographs and asking them to tell what each "is," or says, and where it says what it says. Pictures typically are of logos and signs and familiar objects with words on them, such as a McDonald's sign, a Coca-Cola glass, a box of crayons, or a stop sign (Christie, 1992). Low and high SES youngsters do not differ significantly on the ability to "read" environmental print (Robinson & Dixon, 1991). This may be because children are reading the context rather than the print, or object (Mason, 1980), or simply because both groups of children have about equal exposure to these objects and conditions.

**Literacy Objects and Functions** refers to certain objects and functions that are specifically tied to reading and writing. Assessment typically involves showing students either the objects or vivid pictures of these and asking what they are and what people do with them. Typical items might include: a telephone book, map, newspaper, menu, receipt, and checkbook. On the average, low SES children could identify about 22 percent of these as compared with 38 percent for middle SES children. Children also differed in the ways they explained "functions," or what people do with such things (Robinson & Dixon, 1991). Both objects and functions appear to be useful items for predicting and teaching toward emergent literacy needs.

**Readable Print** refers to the ability to distinguish between words and non-words. This is assessed by asking children to look at groups of letters or scribbles or numbers and tell whether each grouping is "a word that big people read" or not (e.g., I, FFF, 64M2J). Oddly, no significant differences were noted between low and middle SES children on this task; both recognized about 60 percent of choices as words or nonwords (Robinson & Dixon, 1991). No reasonable explanation for this has yet been offered in the literature on emergent literacy.

Conclusions drawn from the research of Robinson and Dixon parallel those of several other researchers, such as Clay (1975), but also challenge some contrary previous findings. For example, their findings challenge some popular beliefs in reporting that:

- *Naturally occurring* environmental print (signs and logos) probably *does not* play a critical role in early literacy development.
- The *mere presence* of literacy artifacts (newspapers, magazines, etc.) in the home *is not* a good predictor of eventual reading success.

However, in support of previous findings, Robinson and Dixon conclude that:

- Knowledge of letter names and the interactions of children with others about literacy artifacts *is* important and productive in becoming literate.
- At least in the early stages of literacy, children who use "invented" spellings rather than conventionally "correct" spellings are at no disadvantage in learning to read and may be at an advantage in learning to write. (This, of course, makes infinite sense, since we wouldn't prevent children from talking until they could pronounce every word correctly and in proper grammatical form.)

We take these findings to mean that incidental learning does not tend to occur without three essential elements noted by Bruner (1970): (1) something to get it started—such as someone pointing out and labeling environmental print ("Oh, here's the men's room. The letters m-e-n on the sign say *mmm-en*."); (2) some-

**FIGURE
3.2**

thing to keep it going—such as consistent reminders to look for known elements of print ("Do you see any other door signs in this hall?"); and (3) something to keep it from being random—such as gentle directing away from nonexamples ("No, those are not 'words' on the side of that building, but someone did spray-paint something there that may be some kind of message.").

To complete the picture of emergent literacy, we now shall take a closer look at the topic of emergent writing. In particular, we will take up the question of whether and to what degree schools and parents should condone or even operate preschool or emergent reading and writing programs.

To understand the options and the practices in the emergence of writing in children, it is useful to know a bit about the emergence of writing in literate societies.

## BRIEF HISTORY OF THE READING–WRITING CONNECTION

Bloomer and Norlander (1989) have compiled an interesting report of the historical development of the reading–writing connection. The slice of the story that follows is largely the result of their documentary research.

Reading and writing developed more or less simultaneously. The graphic form of our current alphabet is customarily attributed to the Romans. It was the Phonecians, however, who were among the first to successfully discard pictures and represent words by the distinctive marks we now call letters. It appears that this first code was made up almost exclusively of what we would today call consonants, since these letters represented the most distinctive speech sounds.

Early teaching methods, from the tenth through the nineteenth centuries, appear to have occurred in a three-pronged approach that was believed to roughly parallel the evolution of the alphabet system. Students were taught oral reading, elocution (proper pronunciation), and writing in an integrated fashion, though largely to the exclusion of silent reading. Each of these components was believed to teach and reinforce the other. This system continues to work fairly well in French, German, and Spanish since these are phonetically regular languages. However, in the English-speaking world we have kept phonetically untranscribable and unpronounceable words from Anglo-Saxon, Celtic, and French origins. These words have one form when they are spoken and another form when written. For example, *night* for *nite, knee* for *nee.* Much of the confusion between writing and speaking can be traced to the period from about 1400 to about 1750—the time referred to by linguists as the period of the "Great Vowel Shifts." It was at this time that vowels began to assume the schwa sound (represented by the symbol ə, and pronounced "uh" (as the /a/ in *a-bout*), a single sound that any vowel may make. This made oral language much more fluent, but it also added to the difficulty of learning to decode and to spell, particularly since it tends to be the most commonly used words that no longer follow phonetic rules for sound–symbol correspondence.

By the mid 1950s, it was generally acknowledged that the irregular nature of the modern English language should be taken into consideration in teaching beginning reading. This was done largely through basal reader programs that taught a core list of frequently occurring but irregularly spelled words as "sight words" simply through drill and practice. In Chapter 6 on word recognition you will read more about how this approach led to what Chall called the "great debate" about the relative value of phonics versus sight word instruction (Chall, 1967, 1983a).

The phonetic irregularity of our language has also had a strong impact on our approach to teaching beginning writing. For the most part, it was simply assumed that there could be *no* attempt to teach writing until children had mastered the rudiments of reading. After all, how could children write words they could not yet read? Recent research into the nature of beginning writing, however, indicates that there are dimensions of the emergent writing process that are more important than accurate spelling.

## EMERGENT WRITING

The meaning of the term "writing" varies, as do all words, with the context in which it is used. Writing can mean handwriting, composition, or the dictation of a story by one person to another.

Historically, "writing" instruction has emphasized three elements:

- Letter formation and other mechanical aspects of writing
- Children dictating experiences and stories to the teacher who recorded these for them to "read"
- Basal-type stories dictated to children, who were expected to write these down to sharpen their spontaneous transfer of oral language back to code with good handwriting, spelling, and punctuation skills

Today, the emphasis is placed on encouraging children to write for themselves and to compose in order to communicate with others. Learning to write is seen as an emergent process occurring in roughly five stages:

## A Window on the Emergence of Written Expression

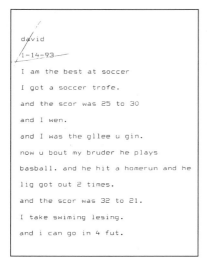

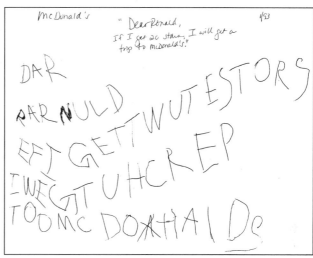

- Scribbling
- Drawing
- Nonphonetic lettering
- Phonetic (but not conventionally "correct") spelling
- Conventional spelling

Nonphonetic lettering and phonetic spelling are referred to above as "invented spelling." Because of the large number of English words that have nonphonetic spellings, and the large number of phonics/spelling rules and their exceptions ("*i* before *e* except after *c*"—as in *receive* and *deceive,* but what about *sufficient?*), the invented spelling stage is now understood to be an important bridge from emergent to full literacy.

The topic of spelling is more fully discussed in the chapter on word recognition and analysis. We shall now turn to reading and writing activities for preschool and kindergarten. Note, as you read, how these are fashioned to develop children's concepts about print and to generate interest in and commitment to joining the literacy club—one of the most prestigious groups one could aspire to, and one that we as teachers are mandated to see opened to all.

## PRESCHOOL AND PRIMARY READING–WRITING ACTIVITIES

Reading and writing activities are right for preschool and kindergarten when they concurrently meet one or more of the other basic needs of children at this stage of development, such as security, identity, and belonging. Here now are some specific examples of how concepts and positive feelings about print can be engendered.

## LETTERS: INFORMATION THROUGH PRINT

To introduce children to print while building belonging and identity, send a letter to the home before school begins, addressed to the child, inviting him or her to come and visit on a specific day and time. Ask that they bring along a parent, grandparent, or older sibling, or, if no one else is available, a neighborhood friend who attends the school. Invite an upper class student to help show the youngsters around. This is best done in the spring in anticipation of fall entry. See "A Letter to Sara," below.

### A Letter to Sara

April 2, 1992

Dear Sara,

We heard that you will be coming to school here soon. We are looking forward to meeting you.

Please come and visit us on Friday, June 1, at 1:00 P.M. Bring your parent, grandparent, or an older friend. We will have cookies and juice, and show you around the building.

Please have someone help you to write back and tell us if you are coming, and who will be coming with you.

You may have some drawings, letters, or words that you have written. If you like, you may bring these with you, and we will keep them here for you until school begins.

We will meet in the front hallway on Friday. We hope to see you then.

Sincerely,

*Marge Wright*

Mrs. Marge Wright
Kindergarten Teacher

With such a letter, the child's first contact with school is established through the written word. It invites early evidence of the ability to write and draw which can be collected for students' personal portfolios as soon as they arrive at school. To help busy parents, a preprinted, stamped response card may be enclosed instead of requesting a written response. The card should simply require a check for those planning to attend, a space for the name of the accompanying adult or older child, and a space for the child's first name. Space can be provided for children or parents to ask questions they would like brought up at the time of the visit. A phone number for call-ins should be included for those parents who may not be disposed to write an answer or may be late to respond. A follow-up letter should be sent within 10 days to confirm appointments that have been made and to remind those you have not heard from to reconsider the offer.

The letter writing theme can be extended on the day of the meeting. With the help of a few parents, the children can be divided into pairs and helped to dictate a short note to a partner. Encourage something simple like an exchange of addresses and phone numbers. In this way, each child would have a writing experience in their first contact with school and would go home knowing at least one other child by name. Each child will take home tangible evidence that he or she is on the road to becoming literate and of belonging to a special and secure place away from home. If the teacher has the slightest reason to believe that a parent might be illiterate, she should invite children wishing to do so to meet with her for this activity.

*Sample dictated note:*

*Dear Claire Marie,*
*I live at 212 Bard Road. It's near the 7–11 store. My phone number is 236-2478.*
*I hope you will call me sometime.*

*Kristin*

This simple letter writing activity can be used to initiate a classroom mailbox and provide direct and incidental instruction in letter writing. For a useful resource, see Loreen Leedy's *Messages in the Mailbox (or) How to Write a Letter* (1991).

The next suggestion takes print concepts and experience with early reading an immediate step further.

## DISTINGUISHING FEATURES

A key print concept in learning to read is to begin to realize and then discern how words are different from one another in some distinguishable ways. This is especially true of "twin" words that must be encountered in context to be told apart—like *read* which is pronounced differently in present or past tense.

A whimsical but effective way to impart the *concept* of the distinguishing feature of each word also helps to build children's basic sense of belonging and identity. Simply take, or make, two medium-sized picture frames. Have a child hold one up to his or her face and ask the class to describe all that they see (see Figure 3.3). The teacher helps by adding some keener and gentler observations in a parenthetical way, rather than by asking questions. Children are likely to say things such as: "Jackson has dark skin." "He has curly hair." "He has *eyebrows*" (teacher adds: "that look like they are smiling"). "He has two ears" (teacher adds: "two *medium-sized* ears"). "His eyes are large, and *happy looking*" (The children are getting the idea of adding modifiers!). They add, "Jackson has a *square-top* hair cut."

Have Jackson pass the picture frame on and continue describing other youngsters. When you get to two similarly structured faces, try to elicit statements that key in on distinguishing features (see Figure 3.4). The teacher might also add something like, "Our description of Asa sounds a lot like our description of Jackson. I wonder what we can say that would help someone tell them apart?" Students might offer that Asa's face is a little wider than Jackson's, to which the teacher might add, "He seems to be doing a lot of thinking." Questions and comments worded in this way naturally invite participation, whereas asking, "How are Jackson and Asa different?" tends to impart a sense of nonconversational teaching, and even of testing, and adds unnecessary tension at this impressionable stage of early learning.

**FIGURE 3.3**

The teacher may need to be quick on her feet to add compliments where observations may be interpreted negatively. Preselecting the youngsters whose faces will be compared usually takes the edge off this activity until youngsters learn a little poise and diplomacy—valuable assets in oral language and social–emotional development. In general kids tend to like this activity so much that teachers may divide the class into small groups, each with a frame, until each face has been described.

To transfer this training to its target of reading words, merely place the frame around several letters or words from a story dictated by the children previously written on the board or made up on oak tag to fit inside the frame. At this stage, it shouldn't matter whether the children know these words or not, merely that they try to describe them.

Again, the teacher can incidentally begin to teach other print concepts by parenthetical comments to the children's conversational observations about the oversized word. In looking at the word below, for example, children might say:

> **DRIVE**

**FIGURE
3.4**

"Those are letters," to which the teacher might add, "yes, letters that say a word." Asked to describe any of the letters, a student might offer that "the first letter is a line with a big belly," to which the teacher might add, "and the *second* letter also has a straight downward *line.*" With this conversational prompt, the teacher signals the idea that words are read left-to-right, that words are made up largely of straight lines and curves, and that through attention to such details, words can be distinguished from one another. Further, the teacher is incidentally modeling the more elaborative language of print (Pinnell & Jaggar, 1991).

## TEACHING THE ALPHABET

There are two considerations in teaching the alphabet. One is related to graphic similarities and the other to a rather odd debate about what should be taught *first*.

Regarding graphic similarities, it is useful to know that there are four groups of letters that tend to produce confusion (Dunn-Rankin, 1968), and therefore should not be taught at the same time:

1. e, a, s, c, o
2. b, d, p, and o, g, h
3. f, l, t, k, i, and h when combined
4. n, m, u, and h and r

**FIGURE 3.5**

Marie Clay (1991) points out some other frequent confusions from her classroom experiences and research: y and k; and I, i, l, L, and 1. This latter confusion is attested to by kindergarten teacher Judith Kezlan, who tells of her student who proudly spelled "ball" as "b/a/eleven."

The second issue involves a debate that has endured for years over whether the alphabet should be taught first by the letter names or by their sounds. The reflective teacher will wish to know that the research tends slightly to favor teaching the sounds over the letter names (c.f., Ehri, 1983). However, the instruments used in the research have also tended to overlook one basic utilitarian reason for teaching letter names, namely, the simple convenience of being able to talk about the letters without making odd, isolated sounds. The research also overlooks the fact that learning the names adds only 26 additional word names to a child's vocabulary, and children have an almost infinite capacity to learn new words. So it would not seem to constitute any additional drag on their learning to be taught both names and sounds. It is notable that there are many ways to teach both effectively and in ways that children seem to enjoy.

One company, for example, sells letters that are inflatable "huggables" whose names are A, B, C, and so on, and who have children who are a, b, c. The inventive teacher might make these letters with the help of children and parents. There also are letter cards that can be made or purchased that display the letter, a picture, and an appropriate letter sound (see Figure 3.5). Cards such as these have been successfully used for generations. The missionary Frank Laubauch, founder of the Laubauch Literacy Foundation, used similar cards as part of his "each-one-teach-one" program that brought literacy to the sub-Sahara region of Africa at the turn of the century.

To update this tradition, and simultaneously teach labeling and sounds, try this variation. Find pictures to illustrate the initial sound of each of the 21 consonants of the alphabet and two pictures each for the long and short vowel sounds. Label the pictures in amusing ways, using names of children in the class where possible, as illustrated in Figure 3.6. You will find many opportunities to reinforce these associations in planned and incidental ways. For example, children can be urged to tell stories, or be told stories about the characters, by name, with selected traits being emphasized to underscore associations:

**FIGURE 3.6**

**Barry Bored**

B   b

**Corey Cat**

C   c

**David Dog**

D   d

**Adrian Ape**

Ā   ā

**Alice Apple**

Ă   ă

D̲avid D̲og [picture] snapped at C̲orey C̲at [picture].

A̲drian A̲pe [picture] said, "Stop!"—but B̲arry

B̲ored [picture] was not amused.

Our personal favorite way of introducing and reinforcing the alphabet is largely incidental and literature-based. It involves reading the folktale *Gunnywolf* to children and having them chime in on the part where the little girl sings the alphabet song to the Gunnywolf, with the effect of soothing him to sleep (p. 76). By three years of age many children will already know some, if not all, of the alphabet song and many of the letters from preschool, family coaching and television viewing. But they also are likely to have acquired some misunderstandings (as with the child mentioned earlier who spelled "ball" "b - a - eleven") that will need to be identified and corrected by a teacher attuned to these possibilities.

ABC books to be treasured can be found at garage sales and flea markets (Bohning, 1991a), and new ones are being printed all the time. To further build familiarity with the alphabet and print concepts, use "Environmental Print Strategies"

**Sample Alphabet Book:**
*The Gunnywolf*

'abcdefghijklmnopqrstuvwxyz," sang the Little Girl
... a tiny voice.

"Little Girl!" said the Gunnywolf.
"Sing that good, sweet song to me."

"M
M
N
A
B,"
sang the Gunnywolf,
and he fell sound asleep.

The Little Girl ran away as fast as she could.
Pit-a-pat, pit-a-pat, pit-a-pat, pit-a-pat!

(Christie, 1992), such as "label and switch." Simply attach readable cards to various items in the classroom: "chalkboard," "bulletin board," "desk." Then involve children in discussions about the labeled objects and areas of the room. To add a more explicit instructional value, discuss the distinguishing and contrasting features of the labels. This kind of labeling can be used throughout the day to build children's awareness of environmental print. For example, Christie (1992) suggests that during clean-up time, the teacher might say, "Look, that sign says 'Big Blocks,' so put those blocks there" (p. 123). For another variation, once children have become accustomed to the labels, initiate a weekly challenge by switching the labels around. When someone notices, bring it to everyone's attention and say that they can expect this to happen on "Wacky Wednesdays," and that they will need to put the labels right again before the next day. Activities such as these clearly counter the low predictive value of environmental print found by Robinson and Dixon (1991), by using print in a more instructive way than just having it "there."

The next writing activity, the Language Experience Story, serves a very special function in guiding children's emergent literacy. It is perhaps the most fundamental means of imparting the concept that *print is spoken language written down.*

## THE LANGUAGE EXPERIENCE STORY

The Language Experience Story, sometimes called the dictated story, is created by the teacher recording the children's account of an actual experience or of something that has been read to them. It is done in an active, experiential way that closely resembles the way children characteristically learn. The teacher begins by prompting children to think of how the story should begin. For example, "Let's write a story about our nature walk. How should our story start?" The children's story is written in large print on chart paper. It is recorded exactly as the children speak it, so that they recognize *their own words and language patterns* in print. In guiding the children's story dictation, the teacher incidentally teaches many of the basic story elements, such as beginning–middle–end, interesting description, and characterization. Writing the children's story also offers many opportunities to incidentally teach children about elements of written language, such as the use of punctuation, quotation marks, and other conventions that make print clear and lively. After the story is written, the teacher uses it for any combination of activities such as the following:

- The teacher rereads the story, pointing to each word while reading.
- The teacher points to and reads one sentence from the story, asks children to repeat that sentence, and then points to random words in the sentence for children to read.
- The story is used for practice in letter recognition: "Let's see if you are learning your letters. Say the letter's *name* when I point to it in the story." Or, for recall of letter sounds: "I will point to a letter. You say the *sound* the letter makes in the word." Or, "Tell me the letters in the story that you know by name and sound" (underline all that are known in a bright color).
- Each child copies the entire story and then draws a picture to illustrate it.
- The children copy each sentence on a strip of paper, practice putting the sentences in order, and read the sentences in sequence and in mixed-up order.
- The children copy "new" words from the story on cards, which may be hole-punched and kept on a ring for independent practice.

Through activities such as these, the Language Experience Story is used as the basis for both incidental and direct instruction in many of the basic print concepts discussed above, as well as for additional elements of word recognition and analysis.

**FIGURE 3.7**

## How to Make an Accordion Book

This lesson format was designed to teach children to write stories modeled on a basic story pattern. It is written in "accordion book" form, using a sheet of 11" × 17" construction paper, first folded lengthwise, then into accordion form, as shown below:

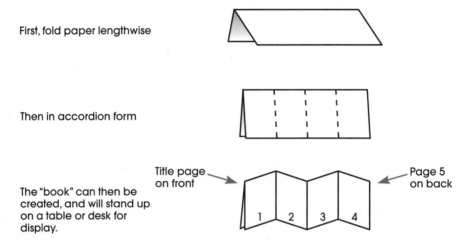

First, fold paper lengthwise

Then in accordion form

The "book" can then be created, and will stand up on a table or desk for display.

Title page on front

Page 5 on back

1  2  3  4

Page 1 tells **"who"** the story is about; page 2 tells what the main character **"wanted"**; page 3 tells what problem is encountered—the **"but"**; page 4 tells how the main character attempts to deal with the problem—the **"so"**; and page 5 tells how the problem is resolved—the **"then."**

## BRIDGING TO INDEPENDENT WRITING: WHO/WANTED/BUT/SO/THEN PATTERN BOOKS

The Language Experience Story approach also provides an ideal instructional bridge from the most basic writing pattern of simple listing, to stories with a recognizable beginning, middle and end, and to even more advanced patterns. New writing patterns can be modeled and discussed through the Language Experience Story as an introduction to independent writing practice activities.

Price and Fearson, second-grade teachers in Red Oak, Texas, use the Language Experience Story to introduce what they call the "who/wanted/but/so/then" pattern. They then have children create their own illustrated "accordion book" stories, where the folded pages provide an additional reminder to include each component of the pattern. When folded, the completed story looks like a book; when extended, it makes an attractive standing display. See Figure 3.7 for directions for constructing the who/wanted/but/so/then accordion book, and for an illustration by second-grader Blake C.

## A Second-Grader's Who/Wanted/But/So/Then Story

cover

page 1—"who"

page 2—"wanted"

page 3—"but"

page 4—"so"

page 5—"then"

*Lesson format and sample story thanks to Elizabeth Price and Gloria Fearson, second-grade teachers at Red Oak Elementary School, Red Oak, TX.*

## CLASS-WRITTEN BIG BOOKS

"Big Books" are simply children's books reproduced in an oversized format (Holdaway, 1972). They were created as a way to enable teachers to share an intimate reading experience with a group of children. A big book can be shared with a group the way an ordinary book can be shared with a single child.

Most basal reading programs now come with Big Books (see below). Linda Karges-Bone (1992) suggests that teachers should create their own Big Books. These can be assembled from children's writings, dictated stories, and other expressive works. Children enjoy seeing their own work combined into something tangible and lasting. One teacher-made Big Book of this type that we have seen in an elementary school was called "How We Helped." It included each child's dictated and illustrated story of a time when he or she had tried to "help," and how it had turned

Big Books for shared reading experiences

out: usually funny, sometimes well, but occasionally disastrous, as when one child warmed up his gerbil, forgotten on the side porch overnight, in the microwave.

### STICK-ON STORYBOOKS

The DLM publishing company offers a number of picture books that come with removable ruled stick-on paper. The child affixes the ruled paper beneath the pictures on each page of a book and writes his or her own story. The child's "story pages" can then be removed and stored, while the book is used by another child with new strips of stick-on paper. The classroom teacher can easily make similar materials from discarded books or use stick-on paper with any picture book.

Let's return now to the topic of teaching children to read, since the pleasure children take in reading is one of the major stimulants for writing. Reading also gives children something to say and subtly imparts the techniques of saying it so that others will wish to read it.

### PRINT RECORDS IMPORTANT INFORMATION, AND WONDER RELEASES IT

The teacher should wonder aloud about all manner of things that easily available print can quickly answer. Gestures as simple as these build an orientation toward and respect for the sheer utility and friendliness of print.

"I wonder how many crayons are in a box? Let's just read the box and see." (This can be followed by a count to see if there is the correct number in the box.)

"I wonder what this color is called? It's a little red and a little purple. Let's see what it says on the crayon. Oh, it's called magenta!"

The same basic wonder and search for information can be extended into quick reviews of anything previously taught, even the alphabet. To review the alphabet, merely print a new word on the board and ask the children to say each letter. Then guide their analysis of the particular word by grouping the letters for them. For example, in the word ma-gen-ta, ask or tell them to try to pronounce the first two letter sounds, then the next three, then the last two. Responses will be a bit awkward at first, but early efforts to learn how to decipher letters into sounds are bound to be a bit awkward and lumpy. One wonderful teacher we have observed breaks the mild tension of early and awkward trials by joking, laughing, and "kibitzing" with the children about their early efforts. Feedback and encouragement are key means of expressing the art of teaching. Try something natural and characteristic of yourself, since it is something that needs to be done many times each day.

The same basic strategy used for introducing and reinforcing word attack can be extended into a comprehension lesson simply by raising a question that is answered by a block of print that can be read to the children.

> "I wonder what all this writing is on this bottle of aspirin? Let's see if we can figure it out." *(Read aloud and discuss.)*

> "I wonder if the child who fell in the well will be OK? Should I read the news story to you that tells about it?" *(Read aloud and discuss.)*

To further reinforce word learning, to teach writing, and to impart such humanistic feelings as empathy and caring, the teacher can build on the news story cited above by suggesting that the class write a letter to the child or the parents involved. The letter can express deep sympathy where all did not turn out well or relief and joy where it did. In either case, the real situation permits the teacher to quietly use print to teach important values and to promote personal-social growth and adjustment—both critical elements in human development and in making genuine progress toward becoming literate.

On a slightly more formal note, we shall turn now to a more difficult challenge than learning the alphabet by name or sound or that print is speech written down. Let's look at the challenge of having children learn to hear and *differentiate* sounds in our alphabetic system. This is the "phonemic segmentation" task you will recall that Robinson and Dixon (1991) found to be extremely difficult for both low and middle SES children in their early efforts to learn to read. Phonemic awareness can be thought of as one element in what could be called "emergent phonics."

## PHONEMIC AWARENESS (EMERGENT PHONICS)

The relationship between phonemic awareness and reading in an alphabetic orthography such as ours is a significant predictor of reading success, even when intelligence and SES are taken into account (Goldstein, 1976; Zifcak, 1977). Phonemic awareness, you will recall, means being able to recognize the definable boundaries of a series of letter sounds when they appear alongside one another in a word: /c/a/t/. To be unable to do this, or to do so poorly, clearly is a considerable disadvantage in sounding out words and in spelling them. It is, you may recall from Chapter 1, an extremely difficult thing to do. When researchers tried to *actually* separate a /d/ sound from a spoken word, by taperecording a spoken word containing the /d/ sound and then clipping the tape down until they could isolate the /d/ sound, they were unsuccessful. In every case they would come up *not* with the "pure" sound of /d/ but with a strange chirping sound (Gleitman & Rozin, 1973). In other words, children need to learn, somehow, to hear and identify "representations of representations"; that is, to deal with two levels of abstraction: the representation of a "d" for the sound of /d/ when we say /d/ alone, and then the odd way(s) it might actually sound when combined with other letters in the context of a spoken word. In short, says Hallie Yopp, "phonemes are abstract units of speech" (1992, p. 696).

This realization has led to speculation on whether phonemic awareness arrives at some point as a product of maturation of our innate ability to learn language. However, the research clearly indicates that it can be taught (Ball & Blachman, 1991; Hohn & Ehri, 1983; Marsh & Mineo, 1977; Yopp & Troyer, 1992). How this training subsequently affects reading progress also has been investigated. Results indicate that children so trained between the ages of 4–6 showed considerable progress on both reading and spelling (Bradley & Bryant, 1983; Lundberg, Frost, & Petersen, 1988).

Yopp and associates (1985, 1988; with Ivers, 1988; with Troyer, 1992) have devised several ways to improve phonemic awareness. They categorize these activities as follows:

- Sound matching
- Sound isolation
- Sound blending
- Sound addition or substitution
- Sound segmentation

Most of these activities are game-like, since they are for very young children.

**Sound Matching**    A sound is identified, perhaps from a picture shown to the children. Notice that they need not know the names of the letters since only the sound will be stressed. The teacher shows a picture of a dog and then initiates a song sung to the music for *"Jimmie Cracked Corn and I Don't Care."* The song asks the children to think of another word that begins with the same sound:

Who has a /d/ word to share with us?
Who has a /d/ word to share with us?
Who has a /d/ word to share with us?
It must start with the /d/ sound!

The words contributed by the children then are incorporated into the song:

*Dog* is a word that starts with /d/
*Dog* is a word that starts with /d/
*Dog* is a word that starts with /d/
*Dog* starts with the /d/ sound.

**Sound Isolation**   This reverses the previous task. Children are given a word and asked to identify a sound in either the beginning, middle, or end of the word. A song is used once again. A single sound may be emphasized throughout the entire song, or each verse may change the sound. Lyrics are sung to "Old McDonald Had a Farm."

initial sound:

What's the sound that starts these words:
*Turtle, time, and teeth?*
(wait for a response from the children)
/t/ is the sound that starts these words:
*Turtle, time, and teeth.*
With a /t/, /t/ here, and a /t/, /t/ there.
Here a /t/, there a /t/, everywhere a /t/, /t/.
/t/ is the sound that starts these words:
*Turtle, time, and teeth!*

What's the sound that starts these words:
*Chicken, chin,* and *cheek?*
(wait for a response)
/ch/ is the sound that starts these words:
*Chicken, chin,* and *cheek.*
With a /ch/, /ch/ here, and a /ch/, /ch/ there,
Here a /ch/, there a /ch/, everywhere a /ch/, /ch/.
/ch/ is the sound that starts these words:
*Chicken, chin,* and *cheek!*

medial sound:

What's the sound in the middle of these words:
*Leaf* and *deep* and *meat?*
(wait for a response)
/ee/ is the sound in the middle of these words:
*Leaf* and *deep* and *meat.*
With an /ee/, /ee/, here, and an /ee/, /ee/ there,
Here an /ee/, there an /ee/, everywhere an /ee/, /ee/.
/ee/ is the sound in the middle of these words:
*Leaf* and *deep* and *meat.*

final sound:

What's the sound at the end of these words:
*Duck* and *cake* and *beak?*
(wait for a response)
/k/ is the sound at the end of these words:
*Duck* and *cake* and *beak.*
With a /k/, /k/ here, and a /k/, /k/ there,
Here a /k/, there a /k/, everywhere a /k/, /k/.
/k/ is the sound at the end of these words:
*Duck* and *cake* and *beak!*

**Sound Blending**   Typically, the act of blending involves making each successive phonetic sound repeatedly until a known word in the child's speaking and listening vocabulary is recognized. In the context of "prereading," it is a simpler aural activity of recognizing the word from an accurate, but segmented representation. Hence, the child may not even see the word, but merely hear the teacher say "/k/a/t/," to which the child should respond /cat/.

Yopp and Troyer (1992) recommend a little game that builds and sustains interest called "What Am I Thinking Of?" To provide a further clue, a class of things is identified. If the class was animals, the teacher would say "/k/ow/" or "/d/u/k/." Aural blending also can be done to the tune of the song, "If You're Happy and You Know It, Clap Your Hands."

> If you think you know this word, shout it out!
> If you think you know this word, shout it out!
> If you think you know this word,
> Then tell me what you've heard,
> If you think you know this word, shout it out!
> (Teacher says a segmented word such as /k/a/t/,
> and children respond by saying the blended word.)

**Sound Addition or Substitution**   Again, with no graphic representation of the letters necessarily in sight, this activity typically requires a child to hear and then add or substitute a sound of the alphabet to further build familiarity with its phonemic or sound boundaries. Yopp (1992) offers these activities for sound addition or substitution.

- Ask children to select a sound for the day, say /t/. Then say every name spoken that day by substituting a /t/ for its actual first letter: "Teter" for Peter, "Tilly" for Billy, "Tarry" for Harry.
- Again, using a song, such as "Old McDonald Had A Farm," the refrain "Ee-igh, ee, igh, oh" may be sung as "Bee-bigh, bee-bigh, boh!" or "Wee-wigh, wee-wigh, woh!"

**Sound Segmentation**   Segmentation is the most difficult phonemic task to perform (Robinson & Dixon, 1992; Yopp, 1988). It involves isolating sounds in spoken words. Here are some formats recommended for informally teaching phonemic segmentation:

- The simplest is to just repeat the initial sound of words in familiar songs, such as "When the m-moon shines; over the c-cowshed" or "P-P-P-Pop! Goes the weasel!"
- This same iteration can be done with children's names: "M-m-m-m-Mark," "B-b-b-b-b-Betsy." (A reflective teacher might choose to skip this exercise if there is a particularly sensitive stutterer in the class.)
- The highest level of difficulty involves separating sounds with words in between and then reconnecting them, such as in this song sung to the tune of "Twinkle, Twinkle, Little Star":

Listen, listen
To my word
Then tell me all the sounds you heard: *race*
(slowly)
/r/ is one sound
/a/ is two
/s/ is the last in *race*
It's true.
Listen, listen
To my word
Then tell me all the sounds you heard: *coat*
(slowly)
/k/ is one sound
/o/ is two
/t/ is the last in *coat*
It's true.
Thanks for listening
To my words
And telling all the sounds you heard!

There is some evidence to suggest that having the visual symbols of the alphabet present, at least in the second semester of kindergarten, results in greater gains in phonemic awareness (Hohn & Ehri, 1983).

Yopp (1992) recommends these additional "good sense" guidelines when using activities such as those described above.

1. Avoid drills and rote memorization. The experiences should be playful and engender positive feelings toward learning.
2. Conduct activities in group settings that encourage social interactions and language play.
3. Activities should be conducted so as to stimulate curiosity, and all responses at this tender stage of learning should be welcomed enthusiastically.
4. The teacher should allow for individual differences, particularly with activities such as phonemic awareness, which research has shown to vary greatly among children, especially at this young age.
5. Be sure that the tone of the activities is not evaluative, although you can collect informal diagnostic information from your observations of the children.

## PARENTS AND LITERACY

The education of a child is *not* synonymous with the schooling of a child. Education requires the cooperation and support of family, friends, and neighbors. It is said that "it takes the whole village to raise a child." Many churches, fraternal organizations, and even corporations are putting more money, time, and effort into supporting this belief than ever before. While it is true that the greatest influence on a child's disposition toward reading and learning is environmentally and genetically transferred from parents, grandparents, and even uncles and aunts, it also takes a healthy neighborhood and supportive society to solidify the goals of literacy. This support can become circular, since healthy neighborhoods and functional societies are the products of literacy as well. Schools that help parents to raise literate children are contributing to the goals of building a functional and democratic society. R. Taylor (1992) has provided us with a wonderful account of the way this circle of literacy can support and be supported by families and communities in his ethnographic reports of life and literacy in Iceland. Many of the methods presented in chapters ahead, such as Reader's Theatre, are part of family life on this lush, green island (early mapmakers misnamed Iceland as Greenland, and vice versa).

The discussion that follows is addressed in large measure to the role of parents, but should be taken to include grandparents, other relatives, guardians, and concerned neighbors. It is only within the modern age that the formerly significant contributions of other relatives have been diminished. In earlier times, when people lived for longer periods in familiar neighborhoods, relatives and, indeed, friends and neighbors were all part of an integral system that supported and monitored child development and education.

Today much of this hidden faculty has been disbanded by the nature of contemporary life. It should be no surprise that it is now, when parents have the least support from these other sources, that the need has grown to be the greatest.

## TEACHERS HELPING PARENTS HELPING CHILDREN

Parents are their children's first and most influential teachers (Curry, 1992; France & Meeks, 1987). Movement back to parents helping children is taking shape in some sharp and gentle ways. Arkansas, for example, actually has passed a law that says parents can be fined for failing to attend a parent-teacher conference. The ideas represented here are of a gentler variety. They are based on the proposition that parents can be overtaxed and in need of relief, not further obligation and guilt. These ideas should be taken as suggestions that teachers can make to parents and as help that can be brought to parents.

### One Don't and Some Do's

Before we list these "do's," there is one important *don't* to consider. *Please don't* give children assignments that *require* parents to shop for certain items or be at a certain place at a certain time. Many children come from one-parent homes or homes where both parents work. Parents often are stretched to their limits, if not beyond. Don't give parents homework! Now, here are some possible *do's* to consider.

- *Do* be a parent helper: Build a file of resources that you can share with parents. For example, assemble a *Kids' Videos* list for home viewing. Talk to your home video store operators. There are wonderful tapes for children on topics from how to use the telephone to dealing with a hospital stay. One study with junior high students showed that two-thirds of students permitted to choose a book to

## Information on Television for Families

ABC Community Relations; ABC-TV; 1330 Avenue of the Americas; New York, NY 10019-5402

CBS Television Reading Program; 51 West 52 Street; New York, NY 10019-6010

NBC Parent Participation Workshops; Teachers Guide to Television; 699 Madison Avenue; New York, NY 10021

Action for Children's Television; 46 Austin Street; Newtonville, MA 02160

Parent-Teacher's Association; 700 N. Rush Street; Chicago, IL 60611

Prime-Time; 120 LaSalle Street; Chicago, IL 60603

National Council for Children and Television; 20 Nassau Street; Princeton, NJ 08540

read selected one related to a television program they had seen (Hamilton, 1976). There now are book tie-in programs sponsored by all three major networks. For more information on how to make television work for a family write to the stations and organizations listed in Box 3.1.

- In a similar vein, develop a list of recommended books for parents and children to read together at home. The school librarian or the children's librarian at the public library often will have resources to assist you in this project. Remember to include nonfiction as well as fiction in the list. For an excellent book on this topic that also includes tips for making TV work for a family see: Arthea J. S. Reed (1988), *Comics to Classics* (International Reading Association; 800 Barksdale Road; Newark, DE 19714). See also the section of the next chapter on "Selecting New Books" for children.

### MegaSkills®

The next set of ideas for working with parents comes from Dorothy Rich (as reported in Rosow, 1991). Rich stresses teaching children what she calls "MegaSkills®," referring to ten overarching ingredients of the traditional American ethic and the keys to success in life and learning. These are described as follows:

*Confidence*—feeling able to do it

*Motivation*—wanting to do it

*Effort*—being willing to work *hard*

*Responsibility*—doing what's right

*Initiative*—moving into action

*Perseverance*—completing what you start ("winners get up one more time than they fall down")

*Caring*—showing concern for others

*Teamwork*—working with others

*Common sense*—using good judgment

*Problem solving*—putting what you know and what you can do into action

There are those who would argue that these skills represent the white, Anglo-Saxon, Protestant culture and need *not* be taught to *every* child in a pluralistic society such as ours. Rosow (1991) argues that this is short-sighted in that it keeps the secrets of success from the "have-nots," whereas the children of the literate elite can count on their parents to fill in the blanks the school may have missed. It is the parents and children of the disenfranchised who may most need to be informed and trained in delivering this "class" privilege to their children. Of course, there is room for other ingredients and for greater or lesser stress on those listed. However, it could be disastrous to overlook any one of them, since they are basic to life in a democratic, capitalistic, and highly technical society. There is little chance that any parent or other pressure group will take exception to these core values if respect is also shown for other less "success"-oriented but deeply held values, such as tolerance, open-mindedness, patience, integrity, and individual courage.

### Parent Focus Groups

This next idea for working with parents is one that also will help you to grow in professional knowledge and wisdom as an educator. It involves inviting parents of children with related needs or interests to occasional meetings, or focus groups, for an hour or two of "investigative conversation." In these meetings teachers and parents discuss how they or others they know have successfully or unsuccessfully tried to deal with the specific reading or child-rearing issue under discussion. Investigative conversation of this type helps both teachers and parents to discover what they need and expect and to appreciate alternate perspectives on the issue.

Parent focus groups should be done with the principal's explicit approval, and ideally should include other teachers, counselors, and guest consultants. Topics of focus may vary. Popular focus sessions include: The Difficult Child, Sibling Rivalry, Improving Word Attack, Building Vocabulary, Reading to Children, Helping with Homework, and even Report Cards. Recently, in fact, schools have begun to attempt to make report cards more facilitative of parent-teacher interactions (Afflerback, 1993). See Box 3.2 for an example of a proposed report card format that stresses reading behaviors of two types: engagement and strategy use.

The goal of building basic reading skills is an ideal vehicle for schools to incidentally help parents and society to build character and inculcate desired values in children. In an article written for parents, Knafle (1989) wisely points out that it is quite easy and natural for parents to learn about and to shape the thoughts and values of children when discussing fictional stories and characters. Such conversations often can be diagnostic, instructional, and therapeutically enriching for parents and children. Story discussion also can diffuse some of the resentment that arises when parents attempt to directly question or advise youngsters. One parent tells us that she likes to use the example of *The Cat in the Hat* to talk to her children about what they should *never* do when their parents are not home. Such discussions also permit children to reciprocally interact with and influence their parents' sometimes excessive fears as well.

When using Parent Focus Groups, remember that the information gained from parents can be just as valuable as the information that you, especially if you are a

## Proposed Reading Report Card Format

*Engaged Reading Activities*

\_\_\_\_ Chooses reading during independent class time
\_\_\_\_ Reads a variety of texts on a variety of topics
\_\_\_\_ Borrows books from the school library
\_\_\_\_ Shares books with teacher and classmates
\_\_\_\_ Understands the value of reading as a tool
\_\_\_\_ Understands the value of reading as recreation
\_\_\_\_ Reads with enthusiasm

*Strategy Use When Reading*

\_\_\_\_ Sets purposes for reading
\_\_\_\_ Adjusts rate of reading to reflect task and goals
\_\_\_\_ Uses flexible strategies to decode unfamiliar words
\_\_\_\_ Predicts and monitors meaning
\_\_\_\_ Summarizes text effectively
\_\_\_\_ Searches for text information needed to perform specific tasks
\_\_\_\_ Exhibits metacognitive ability; reflects on what is read
\_\_\_\_ Reads fluently

*Afflerbach (1993), p. 461.*

young teacher, can initially provide to them. This is a good thing to keep in mind so that you do not come off as sounding like a "know-it-all." The parents that you are speaking to, at the very least, have children and adult life experiences, and are often as well or better educated than most young teachers. This may be humbling, but it is true. It is best to treat parents as you would have them treat you. In fact, treat them as you would have your teachers treat your parents or grandparents, whose knowledge and wisdom you probably respect. See Box 3.3 for an example of what can come out of mutual respect and an investigative, child-centered outlook. It is from our personal experience as parents and professional educators.

### Fostering Family Literacy

Let's turn now to some ideas that are more specifically related to actually fostering reading in the home. Fortunately, most parents are very interested in their child's progress in reading and are quite willing to help at home when it does not detract from their other obligations. Parental involvement, in some form, is vital since it now is clear that merely "having books and other reading materials present in the home does not necessarily ensure that children will use them" (Ollila & Mayfield, 1992, p. 18). To this end, many school districts have assembled materials to give parents ideas for reading with their children. One such booklet by Charles, Njegovan, Triplett, and Asberry (1990–1991) is illustrated with children's drawings and offers these pointers to parents to "help your child with reading while at home":

BOX
3.3 **Investigative Outlook: "Your Child Has a Reading Problem"**

In a traditional basal classroom, a young teacher placed our son in a low reading group for much of the first half of fourth grade before we even discovered as much. We visited with her on a parent-teacher day. Another veteran teacher was present, obviously along to support her and verify the need from their joint perspective and contact with our son.

We told them then that we were puzzled by the placement and her recommendation that he should receive additional tutoring in reading. He was, after all, raised in a very literate home, and could often be found reading *Time* magazine for his own information and amusement.

In any case, we were willing to hear more about why they were so convinced that he needed help with reading. As it turned out, they based it on his poor oral reading in class, particularly when he had to verify an answer given by reading a section of text aloud. We asked if they had verified their observations with an informal Reading Inventory (the IRI is discussed in a later chapter) or with information from available standardized test scores. They answered that his poor reading was evident, and that it would be to us, if we would just listen to him read orally.

Ula went a step further and gave him an informal reading inventory. This involves having the student read word lists and paragraphs orally and answer comprehension questions about each paragraph. The student then listens to additional passages that are read aloud and are followed by more comprehension questions. Sure enough, when reading aloud, he made lots of clumsy "errors" in oral reading. However, his comprehension when reading and being read to was three or four years above his grade level. A subsequent check of the standardized test scores at the school supported this finding. It had taken some time, but from this point we were able to move toward several professional understandings from which we and his teachers profited.

In brief, they are as follows. Having been immersed in what, today, would be called a "whole language" environment, Anthony tended to use reading well for getting meaning and in discussion and thought, but he really still did need some additional work on basic word attack skills. Additionally, with our interest piqued, we have learned that there is growing evidence from research in neurophysiology that oral reading is located in a very discrete portion of the brain, and that some few youngsters will have problems in oral production and fluency that they do not have when reading silently. Oddly, Anthony also seemed to be developing a previously nonexistent speech problem from trying to read orally. In due course he began to find the resources within himself to improve his own oral reading, largely due to an instinctive socialization process that causes most of us to subconsciously monitor, improve, and shape ourselves to expectations. He more or less tutored himself, as it were.

From this experience, the teachers said that they learned to check their files and to cross-verify classroom observations with test data. We, in turn, were re-awakened to the need for some direct instruction in reading to supplement the benefits of a literacy-rich environment and to be more aware of the growing literature on the role of neurophysiology in reading and learning. The latter led us to construct a Primer on the Brain in reading and learning, available in a recent text on diagnosis and remediation (see Manzo & Manzo, 1993).

- Pick a time to read every night.
- Go to the library and pick books you want to read.
- Take a book to read while you are waiting for appointments, the bus, etc.
- Pick favorite books to read over and over again.
- Take turns reading sentences out of the book.

## Sample Pages from a Child-Illustrated Booklet of Tips on Helping Children Read

Take turns reading sentences out of the book.

Take turns describing your favorite character in the book.

- Take turns describing your favorite character in the book.
- Ask your child to read her favorite part of the book.
- Read the story to your child, then ask him a question.
- Read a story and write a new ending to the story.
- Ask the child to tell the story in her own words.
- Draw pictures of your favorite part of the book.
- Pick a sentence that your child likes, and ask him why he likes it.
- Make a poster about your reading—look through old magazines with your child to choose pictures that show what the books you read are about. Cut and paste the pictures on a large piece of paper.

Charles and associates listed each of these pointers on a separate page and added a student drawing to illustrate each one. The result was a fun and useful booklet that was distributed to parents throughout the district (see sample pages above).

Others have offered additional suggestions for fostering family literacy. When combined with the suggestions of Charles and associates above, this makes for a very complete record of what teachers and parents can do to help raise literate children. The following suggestions include a particular sensitivity to children from lower SES and non-English speaking homes.

- Make our classrooms examples of "print-rich environments" by providing plenty of books, magazines, posters, and notes.
- Communicate with parents in clear language. Find speakers of their languages when they are not proficient in English.
- Invite parents to story times or other literacy events and help them to enjoy these occasions with their children. Use the opportunity to help parents understand that good (open-ended) questions are designed to stimulate thought, not extract correctness.
- Tell parents about local library story hours and services and invite the librarian to meet them.

- Teach parents how to identify "good book" features such as language forms that permit children to predict what words or ideas will come next, Caldecott and Newbery Medalists awards, and their own children's recognition and delight over books made familiar at school (Rosow, 1991).

Sanborn (1991) summarizes additional ideas for working with parents that are particularly well suited to greater public exposure of the good things that are happening in schools. These suggestions were collected by Sanborn at an in-service workshop by a former president of the International Reading Association, Patricia Koppman:

- When planning parent workshops or meetings, consider having them three times during the day (7:30 A.M., noon, and 7:00 P.M.) so that all parents are given the opportunity to attend.
- Deliver a "copyready" ad promoting reading and/or parents helping children with reading to your local newspaper. Ask them to print it whenever they have space available.
- Hold "Make and Take" parents' meetings at which the parents make books and/or gameboards that they can use with children at home.
- To boost attendance at a parent workshop, involve children in a staged program held in conjunction with the workshop.
- Conduct a parent workshop that stresses the following points: (1) spend time with your child; (2) look for strengths in your child; (3) talk *with* your child, not at him or her; (4) listen to your child; (5) read to your child; (6) control the TV.
- Distribute a printed "oversized bookmark" with nursery rhymes, the address of the local library, and a "Reading Begins at Home" message through social workers, clinics, doctors' offices, etc. Placemats with the same type of message could be distributed to local restaurants.
- Provide collections of used books to homeless shelters and shelters for abused families.
- Develop programs with local public libraries.
- Encourage parents to take their children on trips. Even a short trip on the bus or subway will excite curiosity and interest in the world around us. Conduct a workshop on local points of interest parents can visit with their children. Provide background information that parents can share with their children.
- Encourage parents to guide their children to better movie-going and to selection of television programs that will provide worthwhile information as well as entertainment.
- Encourage parents to set aside a regular time for homework and give the child a definite place to work.
- Help parents to understand the importance of accepting their child as he or she is. Parents should encourage the child to improve, but avoid negative comparisons with a sister, brother, or friend.
- Recommend ongoing sources of information to parents that will keep literacy and learning in the forefront of their busy lives, in a nonstressful way. See Box 3.4 (p. 94–95) for some excellent sources, largely compiled from Susan

Mandel Glazer (1990) and an earlier article by Sandra McCormick (1977) that stressed choosing books to read to preschool children.

For additional professional information, consult Lloyd Ollila and Margie Mayfield (1992) in the second edition of *What Research Has to Say About Reading Instruction* (Eds., Samuels & Farstrup, 1992). The Ollila and Mayfield chapter cites over 150 studies done primarily in the U.S. and Great Britain that support the value of parental involvement in beginning reading programs. For details on how parents can help children in inner city situations, see the Parents Encouraging Pupils (PEP) Program, designed and tested by Shuck, Ulsh, and Platt (1983). However, consider too that PEP can be a palindrome to mean Pupils Encouraging Parents—the next idea offered for your consideration.

## INFLUENTIAL CHILDREN

In addition to helping parents to help children, there is the promising prospect that teachers can help children to help their parents and other children in the home and in their communities. Many children who come to school able to read, as noted earlier, are able to do so because other *influential children* have taught them (Durkin, 1966). In most cases, it is an older sibling or cousin who undertakes the role of teacher. The fact that children can be a positive influence on home and community is becoming clearer with the increased popularity of practices such as: (1) environmental or ecological studies in which information is collected by observing children and families in natural settings, rather than through structured inventories and tests; (2) the movement toward "ecological" approaches to fostering learning in remedial-level youngsters (Indrisano, 1982); and (3) the whole language concept of incidentally teaching reading as an extension of social and language learning. While each of these practices is based on children being nurtured by the environment, also implicit in each is the potential for children to be an influential force for improving home life and, consequently, their own situations. Though physically small, children can, like the tiny plankton in the ocean, have a significant impact on the ecology of their homes and communities. To intentionally strengthen and influence children is to potentially strengthen and influence all those with whom they come in contact. Studies by Whitehurst and associates (1988a, b) provide some empirical support for this proposition. They found that even very young children, when invited to *discuss* things their parents read to them, soon led the discussion well past literal and interpretive levels and into higher-order realms of evaluative and conjectural thinking with their comments and questions. Here are some "starter" ideas and activities to consider for empowering children to bring literacy home in ways that can be uplifting and contagious:

- Help children practice reading a short piece until it can be done so well that they can take it home to read for the *enjoyment* of their families.
- Work through some typical home-life situations with children that may be stressful, such as "Getting off to School in the Morning." Discuss and even simulate things that influential children can do to reduce the stress often associated with this day-setting event so that it is more pleasant for all.

---

**BOX 3.4**

## Literacy Support Sources for Parents and Professionals

### Information Sources

Family Literacy Center
2805 E. 10th Street
Bloomington, IN 47408-2698
(812) 855-5847

Dorothy Rich, President
Home and School Institute
Special Projects Office
1201 16th Street, N.W.
Washington, DC 20036
(202) 466-3633

Parents' Choices
Box 185
Newton, MA 02168
(617) 965-5913

Reading Is Fundamental
P.O. Box 23444
Washington, DC 20026
This foundation gives away books to needy parents and offers wonderful guidelines and steps for combining the efforts of schools and parents. Carmelita Williams of Norfolk State University (Norfolk, VA) operates a model program for Afro-American minorities that welcomes inquiries and guests.

### Recommended Reading for Parents

- *A Parent's Guide to Children's Reading*, 5th ed. Nancy Larrick. Bantam Books, 1982
- *Bibliography of Books for Children*. Sylvia Sunderlin. Association for Childhood Education International, 1989
- *Eyeopeners! How to Choose and Use Children's Books About Real People, Places, and Things*. Beverly Kobrin. Viking, 1988
- *The Difficult Child*. Stanley Turecki & Leslie Tonner. Bantam, 1989
- *Growing Up Happy*. Bob Keeshan. Doubleday, 1989
- *What Do You Really Want for Your Children?* Wayne W. Dyer, Avon, 1986
- *Your Baby and Child from Birth to Five*. Penelope Leach. Knopf, 1978

### Resources from International Reading Association for Parents' Books:

*Children, Parents and Reading*. Mary M. Beohnlein & Beth H. Hagar (#341)
*Magazines for Children*. Donald R. Stoll, ed. (#153)

---

- Read and write experience stories about these discussions. Here are some topics that contain problem spots in parent–child relations that influential children can be taught to manage better. We call these the "Where-Is's." They typically arise in the last tense moments as children and parents prepare to go off to school and work. Ask children to tell about when these questions arise and what happens when they do not have satisfactory answers.

  - Where is your homework?
  - Where is your lunch?
  - Where are your glasses?
  - Where are your shoes?

Or worse, when the *child* asks, "Mom, where is my homework/lunch/glasses/shoes???"

**BOX 3.4 cont'd**

*The New Read-Aloud Handbook.* Jim Trelease (#637)
*Young Children and Picture Books: Literature from Infancy to Six.* Mary Renck Jalongo (#634)

**Parent Booklets:**

*Beginning Literacy and Your Child.* Steven B. Silvern & Linda R. Silvern (#164)
*Creating Readers and Writers.* Susan Mandel Glazer (#165)
*Helping Your Child Become a Reader.* Nancy L. Roser (#161)
*How Can I Prepare my Young Child for Reading?* Paula C. Crinnell (#163)
*You Can Encourage Your High School Student to Read.* Jamie Myers (#162)
*You Can Help Your Young Child with Writing.* Marcia Baghban (#160)

**Parent Brochures**

IRA has available ten brochures covering a variety of topics pertaining to ways in which parents can help children of all ages become readers. To receive single copies of all ten brochures, send a self-addressed envelope stamped with first class postage for three ounces to Parent Brochures at the address below. The brochures are available in bulk quantities also, and ordering information appears in each brochure.

International Reading Association
800 Barksdale Road
PO Box 8139
Newark, DE 19714
(302) 731-1600

**Children's Choices**

Children's Choices is a yearly list of books that children identify as their favorites. To receive a single copy, send a self-addressed envelope stamped with first class postage for four ounces to Children's Choices at the International Reading Association address listed above.

**Video**

*Read to Me,* produced by the Idaho Literacy Project (distributed by IRA—address above)

- Plan a few parent–child functions, such as picnics in the park, that permit parents to meet one another. Hold a brief outdoor program of dramatic and humorous readings by you and the children. Increasingly, people seem to be feeling isolated by living in communities that are different from the ones they grew up in. School-based activities help to bring parents and teachers together through children in ways that build community spirit and natural support networks.

- Read books and stories that highlight their potential to be positively influential. See, for example: *Kids with Courage* (Lewis, 1992) and *Kid Stories* (Delisle, 1991). These books even contain guided questions, activities, and resources designed to get kids positively and sensibly involved in actively "doing good," more so than in the more passive gesture of "being good."

- Encourage children to think creatively, inventively, and constructively as well as critically. Often, this takes little more than parents and teachers remembering to

## From *The Twisted Witch and Other Spooky Riddles*

Why did the monster
eat the caboose?

The locomotive told
him to "choo, choo."

Why do witches scratch?

Because there's always
an "itch" in a "witch."

What did the police-
man say when a black
widow spider ran down
his back?

How does a witch tell
time?

What happens to a fast
witch on a slow broom?

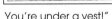

You're under a vest!"

She looks at her witch
watch.

She flies off the handle.

ask for it, even to the extent of asking children to help us overcome some of the inhibitions that sometimes snuff out curiosity, exploration, and invention: "Can anyone think of some way to encourage Curious George to keep being curious, but not *too* curious?" With most of our instincts causing us to be followers, children educated to be creative problem-solvers can be a vital influence on families and communities in need of inventive alternatives to the growing incidence of violence, frustration, and despair.

- Read books to children and have children read books that make for interesting and amusing dinner conversation. Have children show and tell their jokes at home. One favorite of children and parents are joke books, such as David Adler's *The Twisted Witch and Other Spooky Riddles* (1985).

- Combine reading/language arts efforts with those of other disciplines. For example, physical education and health teachers often have wonderful anecdotal accounts of youngsters who have saved lives with CPR, the Heimlich maneuver, and the prompt and effective use of "911."

- Encourage children to be influential by "playing school" at home, as elaborated in the next section.

## LET'S PLAY SCHOOL!

Invite some upper grade children to "play school" with the kindergartners. In an important study elaborated upon in the next chapter, Labbo and Teale (1990) have shown that even weaker readers in the upper grades make good teachers and improve in their own reading by helping younger students to read. The impact of this idea was amplified when the weaker upper grade readers were given separate lessons in how to best teach younger children and particularly in how to read aloud to the younger children.

To facilitate school-play, assemble "Play School" kits and develop a checkout system permitting children to take the kits home. Kits can include any logical combination of the following:

- A small chalkboard
- Alphabet cards with matching pictures
- Several nonprint and large print trade books
- Blank cards to write favorite words and names on
- Word cards containing high-frequency words
- Cards with whole words on the front side and matching pictures on the back side
- Envelopes and note paper for writing letters (you could include a few stick-on "pretend" stamps or even a real stamp or two for real letters)

PTAs and other volunteer groups can be asked to help assemble kits for children to take home. When children play school outside of school, they are extending their engaged time on task with reading, as well as increasing their orientation toward literacy as an integral part of their lives.

The previously noted findings reported by Durkin (1966) and Whitehurst and associates (1988 a, b) strongly suggest that children who assume this orientation actually can make a difference in the literacy levels of their homes and communities. We probably overlook the power of children to influence change because conversation tends to be directed toward them merely as targets, or objects to be reached.

Ironically, parents have been telling us for generations about how some children have severely disrupted their lives while other children have brought solace to them. Every teacher knows this as well. An entire semester can be diminished or enhanced by the behavior and attitudes of just a few students. Children clearly have more power to influence home, life, and community than we tend to give them credit for. We need to think more about how to channel this power. Throughout the remainder of this text, you will find additional examples and recommendations related to helping to channel children's potential to be agents of positive change in their homes and communities.

**W**here You've Been

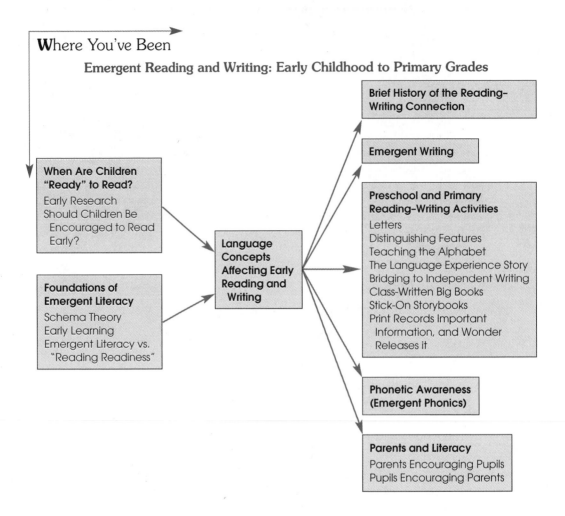

**Emergent Reading and Writing: Early Childhood to Primary Grades**

**When Are Children "Ready" to Read?**

Early Research
Should Children Be
  Encouraged to Read
  Early?

**Foundations of Emergent Literacy**

Schema Theory
Early Learning
Emergent Literacy vs.
  "Reading Readiness"

**Language Concepts Affecting Early Reading and Writing**

**Brief History of the Reading–Writing Connection**

**Emergent Writing**

**Preschool and Primary Reading–Writing Activities**

Letters
Distinguishing Features
Teaching the Alphabet
The Language Experience Story
Bridging to Independent Writing
Class-Written Big Books
Stick-On Storybooks
Print Records Important
  Information, and Wonder
  Releases it

**Phonetic Awareness (Emergent Phonics)**

**Parents and Literacy**

Parents Encouraging Pupils
Pupils Encouraging Parents

**W**here You're Going

The next chapter is more of a refreshing pause than a big step ahead. It focuses on one of the most important yet simple actions that an adult can take with children: to read to them and to pass on the tradition of doing so for others.

### Reflective Inquiries and Activities

1.  Write a letter (not necessarily to actually mail) to one of your former teachers about something you wished he or she had done, had not done, or had better understood about you, your reading, and your learning when you were in school. Since you probably will try not to make this same mistake as a teacher yourself, arrange to share letters with other classmates so that you may learn from each other.

2.  Which of the emergent literacy ideas presented in the chapter seem to appeal most to you as a teacher, and then as a probable parent? Share these with classmates to get different perspectives.

3.  How do you feel at this point about the way you would most likely balance your class in terms of incidental and direct instruction? Is your view any different now than when you first considered this question?

4.  Observe children in a situation where emergent literacy behaviors can be seen and understood for their significance in helping children to become literate. For example, observe children in a preschool where a Big Book has been introduced for the first time. Ask children if they would like to "read" for you.

5.  Try some high-level problem solving. Go back to the section on "Language Concepts Affecting Early Reading" and review the findings of Robinson and Dixon's study (1991). Two factors, environmental print and readable print, were found to be *insignificant* as predictors of reading success when low, middle, and high SES students were compared. What questions would you raise about these findings? How or why do you suppose these counter-intuitive results were found? Do these findings suggest to you that these two domains are not useful or productive areas for concentrating instruction? (Should you wish or need to do so, you can write to or otherwise contact these two researchers at Drake University, Des Moines, Iowa.)

6.  If you are looking for a topic for a course paper, consider the topic of "Influential Children" in the last section of this chapter. You might try to put together a program to teach children to be more active agents for promoting literacy in school, at home, and in their neighborhoods. For further ideas on this topic, think back to some instances or anecdotes from your own life that illustrate your own or other children's power to influence home or school life. Try especially to remember positive influences on interests in reading and learning. You might also wish to refer to some sections ahead in this text for more ideas about how children can be influential. See especially the "Community of Language" approach to vocabulary enrichment, the Cultural-Academic Trivia game, the Reader Response Exchange system, Peer Tutoring, teaching children to think creatively, and "Enabling Questions."

# 4 READING ALOUD, LISTENING, AND SPEAKING

**2** Influential Teachers

**3** Emergent Reading & Writing

**4** Reading Aloud

**1** The Reading Process

## Where You Are

Overshadowed for years by more "modern-sounding" ideas, oral reading is making a strong comeback in the eyes of teachers, parents, and researchers. This chapter describes the benefits of oral reading, as well as some potential hazards to avoid. It highlights the benefits of oral reading to listening and speaking, warns against overemphasizing passive listening, and provides some strategies for improving voice and diction.

**5** Reading & Responding

**6** Word Recognition

**7** Vocabulary

**8** Improving Basic Comprehension

**9** Constructive Reading

**10** Content Area Reading

**11** Children with Special Needs

**12** Literacy Assessment

**13** The Classroom & School Literacy Program

*She read it as if she were there;*
*We heard it as if we were with her.*
Anonymous

# READING ALOUD TO STUDENTS

When preservice teachers were asked what turned them "on" or "off" to reading in their youth, the greatest number said that "teachers reading to a class at any level was the thing they remembered and enjoyed most" (Artley, 1975, p. 27). This sentiment was also reflected in the commission report known as *Becoming a Nation of Readers* (Anderson et al., 1985). This highly regarded report mentions three times that reading aloud is the *best* literacy development activity for the classroom and the home (pp. iii, 23, and 51). Despite these strong endorsements, there are legitimate questions as to just what oral reading is supposed to improve. The endorsement also does not answer the question as to whether children should be encouraged to read aloud. That is not to say that there are not authoritative testimonials for both. Ruth Yopp and Hallie Yopp (1991), for example, list "reading to children" and "oral reading by children" as two of their *Ten Best Ideas for Reading Teachers* (in Fry, 1991). Nonetheless, most classroom teachers tend not to be aware of the solid reasons for teaching oral reading, so it often is not part of the reading–language arts curriculum (Ross, 1986). To help overcome the paucity of knowledge about why as well as how teachers and students should read aloud, these topics are taken up separately, beginning with oral reading by teachers and parents.

## WHY DO IT?

There are several good reasons for teachers and parents to regularly read aloud to children. McCormick (1977) and Simic (1991) have contributed greatly to this traditional list of benefits of this practice:

- It provides a model of proficient reading.
- Material is heard that is more appropriate to the intellectual level of children than what they can read.
- It increases attention span and listening capacity—the mode of learning every child will rely on the most throughout school.
- It tends to foster emotional ties with the reader and positive attitudes toward reading.
- It reinforces lifelong reading.
- It enlarges vocabulary.
- It allows for shared experiences.
- It demonstrates the connection between oral and written language.
- It arouses imagination.
- It increases knowledge of a variety of books and authors.

Trelease (1982), a career advocate of oral reading, further notes that teachers at all levels have discovered it to be a very humanistic management device when youngsters appear at loose ends. In such circumstances, he urges that the teacher have a small part of a book ready to share with the class. Lundsteen (1976) supports oral reading from a liberal arts perspective. She says simply that "the author's artistry—intonations, structures, and uses of language—come through best with oral reading" (1976, p. 189).

Captivating young audiences by bringing print to life

## GUIDELINES FOR READING ALOUD TO STUDENTS

The teacher needs to give a certain amount of special attention to preparation for oral reading. Suggestions range from selecting what to read to your place in the classroom when you do. These have been assembled from several sources (Durkin, 1989; Manzo & Manzo, 1993; Tompkins, 1992; Trelease, 1989; Vacca, Vacca, & Gove, 1991).

- **Build Attention** by selecting things to read that are interesting and colorful, and both fictional and nonfictional. Don't rely on book awards alone. Not all books given awards for good writing have read-aloud qualities.

- **Teach Effective Listening Habits** by stating what you consider to be acceptable and unacceptable behavior while you are reading to the class (books out? posture? doodling allowed? heads down?)

- **Sustain Attention** by not reading continuously for long periods without pausing to ask the class if you should continue a bit longer. It's OK, too, to skip over long descriptive passages.

- **Promote Active Listening** by providing opportunities for youngsters to express their thoughts and sentiments about the selection. When a difference of opinion occurs, tell the class to listen carefully to the next section for clues that will resolve the difference.

- **Ensure Fluency and Voice Control** by reading the material silently before reading it aloud. Check pronunciations of words as needed, and identify passages that could be skipped or shortened. If time and circumstances do not permit you to prepare for oral reading, it can be all right to read extemporaneously, but tell the children that you are doing so. It can be good for children to see the teacher stumble and then recover with reasonable grace. It tends to relieve some of their apprehensions about when they might stumble and err in oral reading.

- **Permit All Children to Follow** by speaking clearly and distinctly. This is best done by paying attention to pronunciation and elocution.

- **Permit Listeners to Gather in Meanings and Images** by reading slowly (never more than 90–130 words per minute). It also is a good practice to repeat phrases or sentences that are complex or may have been interrupted by some unexpected distractions.

- **Re-alert Drifting Minds** by raising and lowering the volume and pitch of your voice; also remember to pause and to emphasize those words that impart special meaning or connotations.

- **Help Youngsters to Focus on Key Elements** of the selection by giving them a specific purpose for listening before you begin to read aloud. This can be done simply by stating a purpose (precede *The Cat in the Hat* with, "Listen to find out whether the children got in trouble while their mother was away"), or by developing a brief discussion of students' related information or experiences, or by having students write a sentence or two that will tie to the story (e.g., write or discuss: "Do your friends sometimes talk you into doing things that may get you in trouble?").

- **Allow for the Time and Mood** by either sitting in one place and reading quietly or by moving about the room and surrounding youngsters with sound; maximize auditory effectiveness by experimenting with your voice in various parts of the room. If you have heaters, air conditioners, or other devices that emit a constant humming noise, position yourself near them so the youngsters closest to them will also be closest to you.

- **Build a Culture of Literacy** by doing some research on the authors of children's books, when feasible, and showing children how to do so as well. For help with this, see Lee Bennett Hopkins' paperback of interviews with authors, *Books Are by People,* and *More Books by More People,* and consult *Something About the Author,* a resource book that can be found in most libraries. You might also suggest writing to the author in care of the publisher. Authors love to receive mail because much of what they write is done in isolation from human response.

- **Connect a Reading Period to a "Third Dimension,"** as Trelease (1982) calls it. Trelease recommends things such as having blueberries to be eaten after reading McCloskey's *Blueberries for Sal,* or having a harmonica and lemon to pass around before reading McCloskey's *Lentil.* Tompkins (1992) also recommends using props to introduce books, giving examples such as a small vial of "magic" water for *Tuck Everlasting* (Babbitt, 1975) or a mouse puppet for *Abel's Island* (Steig, 1976). In this same vein, you could pass around pictures of owls, from books or the encyclopedia, before or during the time you read Morvat's *Owls in the Family.* Pictures and reading will almost always naturally stimulate interest and response.

## STRATEGIES FOR READING ALOUD TO STUDENTS

Reading aloud to students can achieve a host of literacy objectives. Examples follow. Note how the value or impact of each example are determined in some measure by the objective that the teacher chooses to pursue. Think through your objectives in planning periods so that you can have a set of priorities established. Ironically, the more you have "preplanned" a lesson or ongoing activity, the more flexible, spontaneous, and effective it often can be when the class happens. Here are a variety of holistic literacy objectives and specific suggestions as to how they can be advanced through reading aloud to students.

### For Reading Comprehension Empowerment

When youngsters need to read material, particularly nonfiction or class content material that may be a bit more difficult than they typically can handle, try the Oral Reading Strategy (Manzo, 1980). In the Oral Reading Strategy, the teacher reads the first few paragraphs, or pages of a selection, pausing to discuss with students what they understand it to be saying and what may be confusing. This simple strategy causes the teacher to impart a sense of the purpose and direction of a piece, its chief vocabulary, the author's style of writing, and the pace with which it should be read to achieve effective comprehension. This instructional conversation with students also tends to eliminate conceptual confusions, to bridge prior knowledge to present task, and to call up much of the relevant experiential background necessary to read the remainder of the selection. In brief, student empowerment occurs naturally as part of the conversation with the teacher, a more knowledgeable and interested party.

The Oral Reading Strategy can also be used to draw students' attention to inflection and punctuation and its effect on meaning. For example, explore with students how saying "He is leaving, now" can be said so as to denote a fact, or connote a like or dislike, or even a sense that the action is being taken or soon is to be taken. Consider the next suggestions for more on the speaking and listening aspects of oral reading.

### For Focused Listening and Comprehension

To improve students' ability to listen in a focused manner and to recall, try the TQLR (Tune in, Question, Listen, and Review) strategy. There is not much point in teaching youngsters to read aloud unless they also are taught how to be an attentive audience. TQLR has been in the repertoire of skillful teachers for at least forty years, but its origins are uncertain.

## STEPS IN TQLR

Step 1     *Tune in.* Get *ready* to listen, and to give the speaker your full attention. If you are still getting settled and miss the *beginning* of a lesson, a story being read, or an assignment being given, it's hard to understand what you are hearing. Failure to "tune in" early will leave you feeling as though you came in on a TV program five minutes late: confused and mildly annoyed. When this does happen, you have to listen even more carefully for clues that might put you on target. In the classroom, such clues could include a reference to something on the board or to a page in the textbook. Most teachers won't mind if you raise your hand and simply say, "Sorry, I wasn't 'tuned in' when you started; could you please repeat what you just said?"

Step 2    *Question.* Ask yourself questions while you are listening. Your job as a listener is to identify the main ideas. Here are some good questions to ask yourself when you listen:

- What is the *purpose* of what I'm listening to (to give me directions? to give me information? to give me an example of something? to get information *from* me? to amuse me?)
- What's *new* in what I'm hearing? How important is it? Do I need to try to remember it?

(For an interesting variation on this, try "Enabling Questions" in Box 4.1 below.)

---

**BOX 4.1    Enabling Questions**

Enabling Questions are questions students are taught to ask when they are listening to a speaker during a presentation, in order to maximize learning. The speaker may be the teacher, a guest, or another student making a report. The teacher will need to work with children to arrive at appropriate phrasing by age-grade level. Questions for three purposes are stated below. It is "ok" to introduce them all together, but learning will be more focused and manageable if you assign one set of questions to each of three groups to use and refine.

For an interesting collaborative learning experience between the teacher and the class, distribute the questions to three groups to use for a week or two. Then invite students to revise and edit the phrasing based on their experiences in using the questions in real situations.

*Questions for Organization and Clarity*

1. What is the main question or questions answered by your presentation?
2. What would you say are the key words and ideas?
3. What are we most likely to misunderstand (or confuse)?

*Questions to Slow Down the Speaker*

1. Could you say that again in different words? I didn't quite get it.
2. Would you please spell that word, or write it on the board for us?
3. What are the main points so far in what you have said?

*Questions to Increase Critical Listening and to Hear from the Class*

1. How does what you have said compare with what others might say?
2. Is there evidence for that point?
3. What do you think is the weakest or most questionable thing you have told us?
4. Could we pause for a moment to see what others think about this?

*Modified for elementary use, from Manzo & Manzo (1990a,b).*

**Step 3**     *Listen.* Now listen *to get answers* to your questions. Try to guess what is coming next. Were you right? Listen for clue words or phrases that help you predict what is coming:

There are three reasons why . . .      (here they come)
First . . . second . . . third . . .      (there they are)
And most important . . .      (here comes a main idea)
Also . . .      (here comes something similar)
Remember that . . .      (this is probably important)

**Step 4**     *Review.* The two important keys to remembering almost anything are: (1) to *want* to remember it, and (2) to *review* it. When you hear something important, repeat it to yourself *immediately*. Say it in your own words. Write it down in short form to review again later the same day. To make your review even stronger, say it out loud. To make it better yet, say it out loud *to* someone.

To give students practice in TQLR, ask them to listen in order to try to recall *all* that is read or spoken to them. Then help them to pick out the main and supporting ideas.

### For Following Oral Directions

Reading real or "doctored" directions aloud for a set of actions can be fun and good practice in improving focused attention through distractions. Students generally can be induced to listen more carefully when the purpose is lighthearted; try activities such as the following.

***Example:*** Listen carefully to follow the directions that I will give you. You will hear them twice. The first time I read them you must just *listen;* the second time you can begin to take the actions or make notes and complete the action within 5 minutes after I have stopped reading. Here are the directions:

1. Look through the books you have with you, select *one* that has at least 50 pages, and place it on your desk.
2. Take out a pencil and a single sheet of unused paper, placing these on your desk.
3. Remove everything else from the top of your desk, placing it neatly on the floor beside you.
4. Study the cover of your book, while counting silently to 50.
5. Turn your book face down and try to reproduce as much of the cover as you can, including the print and any designs or pictures you remember.
6. I will tell you when to stop.

Have students check each other's reproductions. Discuss and show the best ones. Discuss how students feel about the subject, the book, the cover, the typeface, etc.

*Example:* Instruct students to listen to and follow a series of directions for doing an ordinary task, but in an unusual and unexpected way. Give each direction only once. For example:

1. Take out a sheet of notebook paper and a pencil. Be sure the holes in the paper are to your right.
2. Write your name in the bottom right corner of the paper. Write your last name last, and your first name first.
3. Write the date above your name. Write the year, and then the day, and then the month.
4. Number your paper from ten down to one. (etc.)

### For Recreational Reading

Help students develop their interests by reading aloud from books of various types and on various topics. One practical way to do this is to read the first chapter or so of a book, and then ask who would like to be first to read the rest of the book on their own. By reading from a few books in this way each week, children will have been introduced to quite a large number and variety of books.

Poet Beatrice Schenk de Regniers says to teachers: "Keep a poem in your pocket" ready for an appropriate time (Larrick, 1987). Your "pocket" could just as easily contain a proverb, joke, or anecdote. Where poems are concerned, Larrick (1987) offers these further suggestions:

- Select a poem for the day, sometimes about the weather, sometimes about a school situation, sometimes funny, sometimes sad. Post the poem in the class-room afterward where the children can reread it during unstructured time.
- Invite children to bring you poems and to request poems that they may wish to hear again.
- Following your initial reading, have students do an impromptu choral reading of a poem to bask in the melody and the mood of it—such "spontaneity" usually requires writing it on the chalkboard or putting it on an opaque projector.
- Devote a week to a favorite poet (Shel Silverstein, Myra Cohn Livingston, and Jack Prelutsky are popular favorites) or to a unifying theme (adventure, hard times, fun times). Tell children what the theme is on some weeks; on others, ask them to try to figure out what it could be by inferring it from the poems through-out the week.
- Encourage spontaneity on these occasions by welcoming children to improvise appropriate rhythms or hum appropriate or ironic (in the sense of off-beat) back-ground music.

### For Building Community Involvement

There is a maxim in education that "much more is caught than is directly taught" in school. Where literacy is concerned, this is especially so, since visual media offers

> **BOX 4.2**
>
> ## Oral Reading Practice
>
> Practice reading these sentences yourself. Have students and volunteers discuss how they would read these contrasting sentences aloud:
>
> 1. The roaring wind banged the door shut.
>    A gentle breeze drifted softly by.
> 2. The giant pounded his fist on the table.
>    A wee fairy flitted to the rosebud.
> 3. The bass drum boomed like thunder.
>    The silver bells tinkled softly.
> 4. The Indian slipped silently through the trees.
>    The speeding car crashed into the bridge.
> 5. The great clock boomed out the hours.
>    The tiny watch ticked gently and steadily.
> 6. The girls tiptoed past the sickroom door.
>    The shouting boys dived with a great splash.
> 7. The sneaky cat crept up on the birds.
>    The elephant crashed through the brush.
>
> *Originally from Dawson & Newman (1969).*

such strong competition for how we spend our leisure. To highlight and encourage reading, invite parents, grandparents, and community people to be guest readers on selected days. Offer to help them to select an appropriate book and provide them with a one-page handout on how to prepare for and conduct a read-aloud. You may also want to consider holding a brief workshop for read-aloud volunteers. In one recent study of father–son reading, 35 percent of fathers surveyed said that they would be interested in such a workshop (Gray, 1992). See Box 4.2 for some practice lines to use in a workshop for guest readers, peer readers, or for yourself. See Box 4.5, at the end of this chapter, for further suggestions of books that are particularly suitable to be read aloud.

### For Building Silent Reading Comprehension

Tompkins (1992) offers this simple aid to "scaffold" silent reading: Pair the book that you read orally with an easier one for kids to read silently. For example, as part of a unit on the California gold rush, the teacher could read Fleishman's (1963) *By the Great Horn Spoon!,* a book too challenging for most fourth-graders. Afterwards, most students could silently read McNeer's (1950) *The California Gold Rush,* which is about on a fourth-grade reading level, while weaker readers might more easily tackle a simpler book on the same subject, such as Coerr's (1983) *Chang's Paper Pony* or Chambers' (1984) *California Gold Rush: Search for Treasure.* Consult your school librarian for help in finding books at varying difficulty levels on a subject.

### For Building Higher-Order Literacy (A Better Way to Read to Kids!)

The child is not only an emergent reader but an emergent thinker. Whitehurst, an early childhood psychologist, and associates (1988a) did a study supporting a better way to read to kids. Two groups of parents were urged to read to their young children. However, one group was trained to ask the children evocative questions while reading rather than "yes/no" questions like "Is that Eeyore?"; rather, "What is Eeyore doing?" and "How do you feel about that?" Within one month the children being asked such questions scored *six months* higher on tests of vocabulary (measuring conceptual growth) and expressiveness (measuring language growth) than students in a traditional method "control group" who were merely read to for an equal period of time.

In a follow-up study, Whitehurst et al. (1988b) discovered that the children in the higher-order questioning group also seemed to enjoy participating more and could be seen nine months later to be pacing their parents into more penetrating analysis. This finding offers further credibility to our assertion in the previous chapter that when children are properly empowered they can be a powerful catalyst to enrich their home and community life, rather than merely being shaped by their environment.

## HAVING STUDENTS READ ALOUD

### BENEFITS OF STUDENTS' ORAL READING

Some of the best arguments you will hear for *children* reading aloud have been made by Taylor and Connor. Ironically, these specialists support greater emphasis on *silent* reading with only incidental attention to oral reading, yet they argue that reading aloud may serve a developmental purpose in early years. That is, "young readers may need to go through an interiorization process in reading similar to that described for speech by Vygotsky" (Taylor & Connor, 1982, p. 442). Taylor and Connor further suggest two personal–social dimensions of children's early oral reading. One is what they refer to as the "see me" aspect of oral reading: reading aloud serves the young child's need to demonstrate personal and social competence. The second is that before and outside of school, when children encounter reading, it is usually in social situations that require reading out loud and/or discussing information from signs, labels, directions, nametags, etc.

Several commercial basal-reader manuals put a great deal of emphasis on inflection and performance in student oral reading—probably too much from the point of view of its impact on effective silent reading. For some youngsters this overemphasis may also be needlessly humbling; aspects of personality, quality of speech, and even brain organization influence the ability to read orally. (See the anecdote on our own son's reading in the previous chapter.) Nonetheless, there are reasons to pay *some* attention to elocution and to help children to do it better.

The soundest reasons for paying attention to it include the facts that: (1) it prepares students for the inevitability of having to read aloud periodically in impromptu, real-life situations (from birthday cards to position papers); (2) it gives youngsters who are naturally good at it a showcase for their strengths; (3) it gives

I can read it—all by myself

expression and poignancy to literature; and (4) because it is relatively difficult for some, it may deserve some special attention and practice.

Despite the advantage of having students read aloud, it can be stressful. Gentile and McMillan have identified five practices that should be avoided in order to minimize negativity and discomfort. These include:

1.  *Avoid* requiring children to read aloud and to others and then correcting them frequently

2.  *Avoid* requiring poorer readers to read aloud material that is very obviously for young children

3.  *Avoid* requiring reading materials that are too difficult and/or for which students have had no assisted preparation

4.  *Avoid* requiring students to read aloud and permitting mimicry or ill-stated comments on their reading

5.  *Avoid* requiring students to stop reading prematurely when they have made too many errors (1987, p. 4)

Two sets of oral reading teaching methods are developed next. One could be called "tactics," since they are brief methods requiring little preparation. The other set is better referred to as strategies, since they tend to be more elaborate or may require more planning and preparation.

## TACTICS FOR ENHANCING STUDENTS' ORAL READING

There are four solid brief ways to improve students' oral reading delivery.

- **Help First Tactic**  Be sure that anything a student is to read orally has first been read silently, and that there is an opportunity to ask for help with word pronunciation, meaning, and interpretation.

- **Practice Tactic**  Permit students to practice where this is possible with activities such as "buddy reading"—where one student reads to another, or choral reading—where several students read aloud together.

- **Audience Awareness Tactic** Prepare the audience and the reader to be attuned to one another. One popular way to do this is with Radio Reading (Greene, 1979). With this method, the reader simply pretends that he or she is doing a radio broadcast while those listening pretend to be the audience. Role play can put children into a more attentive and competent suit of clothing than the ones they typically wear. Just for fun, encourage children to make up radio salutations and sign-offs: "Good morning, this is Robbie Burns broadcasting from Prairie School in Toledo, Ohio. . . . Once again, this is Robbie Burns bidding you a major farewell."

- **Modeling Tactic** Be sure students are given an opportunity to hear and experience well-delivered oral readings. However, avoid professional records and tapes. While these may *seem* to serve as good models, it is better to have youngsters listen to the more realistic performances of the teacher and other students. Professional recordings tend to include electronic voice enhancements, sound effects, and musical accompaniment. These may make for enjoyable listening, but they also tend to make anything the student might try to do seem flat by comparison. When students do read aloud, remember to coach them by giving them adequate feedback on mispronounced and miscalled words that may warp meaning (Kozliski, 1989). Otherwise, don't "correct" *every* misspoken word or slight glitch. The former will help them to stay in touch with the meaning and sense of what they are reading, whereas the latter is distracting and can be felt as punitive.

## STRATEGIES FOR ENHANCING STUDENTS' ORAL READING

Engaging students in oral reading activities can meet a variety of holistic literacy objectives. See how the strategies discussed next are able to advance oral reading as well as public and conversational speaking and one or more other literacy objectives. Strategies that can legitimately serve more than one objective simultaneously are sometimes referred to as "concurrent" (Manzo & Manzo, 1990a) or "collateral" (Rubin, 1984) methods.

### For Entertainment and Sharing

Oral reading can be used to take advantage of the uplifting effects of performance. Encourage youngsters to collect and periodically read something to the class which is entertaining, such as a joke, a riddle, a tongue-twister, a humorous or touching portion of a trade book, or a poem.

In a related vein, there is another form of classroom entertainment, similar to Radio Reading, that is called Readers Theatre. (The British form of the word is written without an apostrophe and uses the British spelling of *theater*. Use either the British or the American spelling, but explain the British spelling if you use it with students.). In Readers Theatre, children select a story—one they have read, listened to, or even seen on television—and translate it into a script that can be read aloud in parts. Sloyer (1982) offered essentially seven steps for doing this, which we have slightly modified as shown below:

1. Capitalize on *children's interest* in a story or movie to select the material for creating a Readers Theatre production.

2. Guide a *discussion about theatre,* as compared to narrative, and what it would take to change a book into a movie.

3. Give students a *sample of a simple story* and the same story translated into scripted form (see Box 4.3). Discuss the changes that were needed to modify a story into a play (especially the role of the narrator).

4. *Review the key elements* of the story the students have chosen to translate into Readers Theatre: setting, characters' attributes, plot line, and theme.

5. Use large *poster paper,* the *chalkboard,* or an *overhead projector to write the script.* Begin with the title, then write the names of the characters, including the narrator, in the margin. As the script begins to develop, encourage children to make it interesting and realistic. When the script is complete, reproduce it for the class.

6. *Prepare for the reading as if it were a recording session.* You might use the occasion to discuss stage production by introducing students to basic elements of stagecraft, such as areas of the stage, props, and possible expressive body movement. However, it is more important to provide time for students to discuss and experiment with their lines and, finally, to rehearse with the full cast. Note: memorization of lines is *not* pursued in Readers Theatre, nor is the play typically acted out, but for voice intonations and possible facial and smaller gestural movements. It is best to keep the emphasis on fluent reading at this tender stage of development.

7. After the performance, lead a general discussion of the "production," including elements such as voice, projection, character portrayals, and pacing. This type of discussion leads to more careful analysis of the piece, its meaning, intent, and significance, while paying reasonable attention to those aspects of elocution and oral persuasion that once were taught separately and in some cases came to dominate elementary reading/language arts instruction.

There is a wide variety of resources for those who would like further guidance and examples for implementing Readers Theatre in their classrooms (see Busching, 1981; Coger & White, 1982; Maclay, 1971; Post, 1974; Sloyer, 1982; and Wertheimer, 1974). Some of these become more involved with the theatre and acting aspects of production. This tends to be more suitable for the upper elementary and middle grades. We have seen one of our favorite sixth-grade teachers, Joel Dempsey (Shawnee Mission, KS), use play productions not merely to excite enthusiasm for reading and theatre, but to teach vital study strategies such as memorization. Each year he proves to a new group of youngsters, who thought they would do well to remember their locker combinations, that they can remember and deliver heartfelt lines from the world's great plays.

Mr. Dempsey provides one other incidental benefit to his students that Guzzetti (1990) refers to as modeling the role of "raconteur." A raconteur is a narrator who operates in a casual and witty fashion. The manner of the raconteur should be impromptu, but steady and relevant to the topic. This is a vital skill in the

> **BOX 4.3**
>
> ## Readers Theatre Translation
>
> ### Sample Story
>
> #### The Shepherd's Boy and the Wolf
>
> A Shepherd's Boy was tending his flock near a village, and thought it would be great fun to hoax the villagers by pretending that a Wolf was attacking the sheep: so he shouted out, "Wolf! Wolf!" and when the people came running up he laughed at them for their pains. He did this more than once, and every time the villagers found they had been hoaxed, for there was no Wolf at all. At last a Wolf really did come, and the Boy cried, "Wolf! Wolf!" as loud as he could. But the people were so used to hearing him call that they took no notice of his cries for help. And so the Wolf had it all his own way, and killed off sheep after sheep at his leisure.
>
> Moral: You cannot believe a liar even when he tells the truth.
>
> *V. S. Verson Jones, Aesop's Fables. New York: Avenel Books (1912), p. 41.*
>
> ### Readers Theatre Script
>
> #### The Shepherd's Boy and the Wolf
>
> | | |
> |---|---|
> | Narrator I: | A shepherd's boy was tending his flock near a village, and thought it would be great fun to hoax the villagers by pretending that a wolf was attacking the sheep: so he shouted |
> | Boy: | Wolf! |
> | Narrator II: | And when the villagers came running up . . . |
> | Villagers: | Wolf? Where?! |
> | Narrator II: | he laughed at them for their pains: |
> | Boy: | Ha ha . . . I had you fooled! |
> | Narrator I: | He did this more than once, and every time the villagers found they had been hoaxed, for there was no wolf at all. |
> | Boy: | Ha ha . . . |
> | Villagers: | (grumbling) That boy! He's fooled us again. Look at him laugh. |
> | Narrator II: | At last a wolf really did come . . . |
> | Wolf: | Yum yum! Look at those tasty lamb chops! |
> | Narrator II: | and the boy cried . . . |
> | Boy: | Wolf! Wolf! |
> | Narrator II: | as loud as he could. |
> | Narrator I: | But the people were so used to hearing him call that they took no notice of his cries for help. |
> | Villagers: | Ignore him. He only wants to laugh at us. He's a liar. |
> | Narrator II: | Meanwhile, the wolf had it his own way, and killed off sheep after sheep at his leisure. |
> | All: | But no one ever came to help, for you cannot believe a liar even when he tells the truth. |
>
> *From: Tierney, Readence, & Dishner (1990), pp. 192–193.*

classroom, the boardroom, and in virtually *every* type of meeting. It is never too early to begin to try to master this art. Guzzetti's research showed that when teachers modeled the retelling of a previously read story in this way, attitudes toward English and reading *improved significantly.*

### For Fluency and Oral Language Development

Fluency, or the automatic recognition and smooth flow of "decoded" words while reading, is a key element of comprehension. Material is most easily understood when it is read, orally or silently, in a way that resembles smooth, well-articulated speech. Laberge and Samuels (1974) aptly refer to this fluency in word recognition as "automaticity." Three methods for developing greater automaticity are described below. These methods tend to involve: modeling, guided oral summarizing, word study, efforts to conceptualize the process, parent participation, and students evaluating their repeated oral readings in a variety of ways.

### Hoffman's (1985) Model Oral Recitation Lesson

1. The teacher demonstrates fluency by reading to the class in a model way.
2. The teacher discusses the selection with students, urging them to retell the selection in summary form. Story frames, the boxed-off lines and sentences previously discussed, can be used to help with summarization. The story frames should guide analysis of such critical features as: story setting, characters, goals, problems, plans, and resolution. Remember, too, to come back to "obvious" points. By this time, most youngsters have forgotten the name of the piece, and few if any remember the author's name.
3. Discuss and test key vocabulary. Have students add new vocabulary words to their "word ring"—each new word is written on a small card with a hole punched in the upper left-hand corner, and stored on a ring for independent review.
4. Discuss oral reading with students: what makes it good? difficult?
5. Students practice oral reading, first in choral fashion, and then in pairs.
6. Students evaluate their own oral reading and that of their partner and discuss their evaluations. (See sample Evaluation Form.)
7. Urge parents to have their children practice their stories at home until they become expert readers.

### Sample Evaluation Form

This kind of collaborative work among students, and of students with parents and teachers, has great potential for teaching students how to critique and be critiqued (Manzo & Manzo, 1990b; Topping, 1989) or, in the words of Hansen (1992), to learn the "language of challenge." This is a key element, you will recall, in progress toward reading, writing, thinking, and social–emotional maturity. In this same vein, consider now two related reading strategies by Lauritzen (1982) and Ross (1986) discussed next.

## Sample Evaluation Form

Your Name _____   Teacher _____

Your Buddy's Name _____   Date _____

*Circle your name if you are evaluating your <u>own</u> oral reading; circle your buddy's name if you are evaluating <u>his</u> or <u>her</u> oral reading.*

|  | very weak | weak | OK | good | very good |
|---|---|---|---|---|---|
| Smoothness | 5 | 4 | 3 | 2 | 1 |
| Words known | 5 | 4 | 3 | 2 | 1 |
| Expression | 5 | 4 | 3 | 2 | 1 |
| Understanding | 5 | 4 | 3 | 2 | 1 |

*When you are evaluating and coaching students' oral reading, you may wish to include these other indices of progress:*

|  | very weak | weak | OK | good | very good |
|---|---|---|---|---|---|
| Voice pitch | 5 | 4 | 3 | 2 | 1 |
| Interpretation | 5 | 4 | 3 | 2 | 1 |
| Contact with audience | 5 | 4 | 3 | 2 | 1 |
| Interest and enthusiasm | 5 | 4 | 3 | 2 | 1 |

**Lauritzen's Choral Reading Lesson**  Lauritzen (1982) offers a simple means of conducting an oral reading lesson with some of the characteristics of choral reading. It goes like this:

1. The teacher first reads the selection in its entirety while the class follows the printed words.
2. The children then "echo-read" portions of the selection with the teacher—that is, the teacher's voice leads that of students by just a moment.
3. Teacher and students then read the selection aloud together in choral fashion, with the teacher's voice now falling a bit behind the chorus, but ready to rise up to meet them like a vocal safety net.

Predictable books are especially fun to read in this manner. Lauritzen found that when she used this type of choral reading with second-grade children, the children would "arrive at school early, wait after class, and even return the following year [saying], 'Let me sing it again'" (p. 458). Joyce and Daniel McCauley (1992) cite Lauritzen's findings to support their use of choral reading as a means of promoting oral language learning and oral reading for ESL students.

**Ross's Oral Reading Homework Program**    Ross (1986) reports another approach to oral reading that she observed as part of an action research study by two veteran Tennessee teachers, Janice Neal and Brenda Vickers (1985). Ross reports that they achieved excellent results by soliciting parent support and by using tape recorders in the following ways:

1.  Parents were informed that children's oral reading would be evaluated each Friday and that these evaluations would be part of the child's total reading grade.

2.  Children took their books home during the week, and parents were asked to listen to their children read the assigned pages each night. Parents were told which skills they might emphasize (see Box 4.4 for the note that was sent to parents).

3.  Each child was assigned one page each week for the Friday evaluation. The assigned reading material was at each child's independent (easy) reading level, so that word recognition problems would not interfere with oral reading fluency. Children were given class time to practice reading their assigned pages in their reading groups and were shown how to practice their oral reading at home.

4.  Each Friday, each child was taken aside to read his or her assigned page into the tape recorder. The teacher used a checklist to record oral reading skills that needed improvement, and children could listen to the tapes to hear the kinds of mistakes they were making.

5.  As children gained oral reading proficiency, they were allowed to read stories to the kindergarten classes. This practice has a proven motivational value, causing readers to strive for fluency and proficiency.

---

**BOX 4.4**

## Oral Reading Program: Note to Parents

*Something for You to Do at Home!*

Beginning today, your child is bringing home a reader with a particular page assigned for the purpose of *practicing oral reading.* You may have him/her read any other story or all of the stories if you wish, but on Friday the assigned page must be read for an oral reading grade.

The book which is being brought home is one level below your child's reading group level; therefore, it should be easy to read. Listed below are the areas which will be considered:

1. Reads with proper expression (shows excitement, questioning, etc.).

2. Pauses for commas and dashes.

3. Stops at periods and question marks.

4. Reads in phrases and not by individual words.

5. Does not omit or change words.

6. Does not go back and repeat a word or begin again at the start of a sentence.

7. Pronounces the endings of words such as book*s* and go*ing.*

Enjoy reading with your child!

### For Externalizing Thinking Following Silent Reading

Most every discussion following silent reading offers an opportunity to practice oral reading and to reveal and reinforce logical thinking. This is done by linking postreading discussion to the expectation that each student may be called on to read the words or sentences aloud that verify a position taken in discussion or an answer given to a comprehension question. In this context, oral reading is practiced in a way that is natural and incidental. The driving force is the reader's wish to prove a point, support a deduction, interpret a character's emotion, or to bolster some other inference that occurred during silent reading.

This incidental approach to oral reading tends to be favored most by educators because it stresses reading as a meaning acquisition process, more so than a skilled performance task. However, the verification task itself is not easily learned, since it requires thorough comprehension, willingness to respond to text, and knowledge and experience in actually doing so. The next method was designed to foster these objectives in the sometimes intimidating social context of the classroom.

### For Discussion and Participation: The Note Cue Strategy

The Note Cue Strategy (Manzo & Manzo, 1987, 1990b) was designed to teach students how to participate in oral discussion about text. It provides a structured activity that *gets* language and discussion going, *keeps* it going, and keeps it *on target*. It tends to increase student participation in class discussion about textual material by building the behavioral and social learnings that come from actually doing something. It is a staged form of instructional conversation, similar in some ways to Readers Theatre. It builds oral reading and language experience in *asking* questions and, more importantly, in *commenting* on the text, as well as in the more familiar way of merely *answering* questions. Initially, it does this by relieving students of the complex burden of having to think about what to say and how to say it, leaving them only to think about *when* to say it.

Note Cue, as its name suggests, provides *cues* to students in the form of written *notes* that guide them through participation in a "model" discussion—"model" because it is prescripted by the teacher. Initially, almost the entire discussion is prescripted. Enactment of these *early* Note Cue discussions is a form of "strategic parroting" in which students are expected to participate with relatively little thinking. The potential value of strategic parroting was discovered separately by two sets of researchers working with reluctant learners (Manzo & Legenza, 1975a; Palincsar & Brown, 1984). You will be pleasantly surprised to see how this opportunity for class participation through simple parroting can provide a form of "instructional scaffolding" that can gradually be removed as students begin to internalize the many complex aspects of effective classroom discussion. As you read about Note Cue, notice its suitability for use with ESL students and others who may have underexposure to typical social and language conventions.

**Steps in Note Cue: Before the Lesson**   Prepare a set of "cue cards" for a prereading discussion of the material and/or a postreading discussion. The cue cards should be prepared as follows:

*For prereading questions:*

a. Write several **Questions** that will elicit students' background of knowledge about the reading selection or that urge predictions that could be made from a quick preview of the selection.

b. Write complete but brief **Answers** to each **Question.** When writing **Answer** cards, use complete sentences that include enough context to make it clear what **Question** it answers. The teacher's manuals for many texts and basals include prereading questions that can be used for Note Cue cards.

c. Write several **Comments**—relevant thoughts that might be sparked by previewing the reading selection.

d. Write each **Question, Answer, *and* Comment** on a *separate* 3″×5″ note card. Label each card at the top as appropriate: Question, Answer, or Comment.

Sample *prereading* Note Cue cards:

**FIGURE 4.1**

| Question | Answer | Comment |
|---|---|---|
| Where does it look like this story might take place? | From the cowboy-type pictures, the story probably takes place in the West or Southwest. | I wonder why kids in the West often are called by initials, like "T.J." |

*For postreading questions:*

Prepare **Question, Answer,** and **Comment** cards as you did for the prereading discussion, but based on information from the reading selection itself. Teacher's manuals that accompany instructional materials almost always include questions that can be used for postreading Note Cue cards.

Sample *postreading* Note Cue cards:

**FIGURE 4.2**

| Question | Answer | Comment |
|---|---|---|
| How long did it take the boys to build the raft? | T.J. and Bill worked on the raft for almost three weeks. | I wonder how a flood could start like that— almost before it rained. |

Teachers may prepare cards that contain messages that are personal or humorous:

"Who in this class do you think is most like Curious George?"

"With so many people now interested in animal rights, I bet some would be cheering for the wolf in *Little Red Riding Hood* or in *The Gunnywolf.*"

## PREREADING

Step 1   Students are helped to survey reading material and to make predictions about what it will be about. They may be told that a brief written test will follow reading and discussion of the selection.

Step 2   While students are surveying, the teacher places one or more of the prepared *prereading* cards on each student's desk. *A few students are given blank cards.*

Step 3   Students are instructed to read their card(s) silently and think about *when they should read it (them); students with blank cards are instructed to try to think of their own **Question** or **Comment** related to the material they are surveying, and write it on the blank card.

Step 4   The teacher begins the prereading discussion by asking who has a **Question** or **Comment** card to read that seems to provide a good idea of what the selection will be about. If a **Question** is read, the teacher asks who has an **Answer** that seems to fit it. This process continues until the teacher feels that students have a sense of what the passage will be about. This "Note Cued" prereading discussion should take *no more than 10 minutes.* The brisk pace and aura of evolving a purpose for reading will convey to students that Note Cue is driven by meaning, and *not* all cards *must* be read orally to establish a reasonable focus for reading.

Step 5   The teacher instructs students to read the selection silently to test their predictions. If reading is to be followed by a postreading Note Cue discussion, the teacher also reminds students to read their postreading Note Cue cards, which are placed on their desks while they are reading. (The teacher notes that he or she will come to the desks of any students who raise a hand for assistance in reading or understanding their card.)

## POSTREADING DISCUSSION

Step 6   The teacher opens the postreading activity simply by asking, "Who has a good **Question** to check comprehension of this selection?"; then "Who has a good **Answer** to that Question?"; then "Who has a printed **Comment** that seems right to say here?"; and finally, "Who has a personal reaction(s) or comment?" The last question is intended to encourage personal–evaluative thinking and responding apart from the statements on the cards, but somehow modeled after them in terms of relevance to the topic.

## FOLLOW-UP

Step 7    Within the same class period, or later if preferred, give a test of 5 to 10 questions that require brief written responses. Questions should be taken directly from the Note Cue cards and relevant comments made during the discussion. This builds appreciation of the value of reading one's card so that all might hear and learn, and respect for independent commenting.

**Gradual Removal of Note Cue's Instructional Scaffolding: From Strategic Parroting to Self-Initiated Participation:** As a group of students becomes familiar with the Note Cue procedure (as they quickly do), subsequent lessons should include *fewer teacher-prepared cards* and *more blank cards* for students to generate their own Questions, Answers, and Comments. In this way responsibility is gradually turned over to students as they become more equal to the expectation.

The second author piloted Note Cue in an inner city middle school with low-achieving minority youngsters who had an established pattern of low participation, poor oral reading, and ineffective participation in pre- and postreading discussions. Although these early trials of the strategy were not objectively measured, when these students' participation was prompted with Note Cue lessons, their behavior seemed to be more "on task" for longer periods of time, and their written responses on short tests showed higher levels of comprehension than they typically demonstrated. In a set of field-based studies that *did* include objective measures, three of four teachers obtained similar results (Fazzino, 1988; Roberts, 1988).

There are other incidental benefits in using Note Cue. The cards youngsters write offer insight into their thinking. Collections of student cards, and their placement in students' individual portfolios, can offer an overview of student progress in writing and oral communication. The next method also offers opportunities for eliciting diagnostic information and providing corrective feedback to the student.

### For Diagnostic Information and Corrective Feedback

Green (1986) has noted that the benefits of student oral reading are enhanced by an empathetic listener who gives subtle but potentially valuable feedback. These guidelines are offered for empathetic listening and teaching:

1. Behave more like a fellow reader than a judgmental listener by giving help and feedback to the struggling reader.
2. Reactions and help should be governed by the extent to which a miscue, word error, or omission distorts meaning.
3. Give total attention to the child reading.

Green suggests the use of professional and community volunteers to maximize the number of opportunities for children to read to an empathetic listener and coach. This is a common practice in England, where parents are trained to work as volunteers in listening to children read aloud.

In a comprehensive review of the literature on corrective feedback, McCoy and Pany (1986) found that "word supply" and "corrective cues" hierarchies were equal to or slightly better than approaches that stressed the phonetic aspects of decoding a word. However, in two of those studies, "word drill" proved very superior to "word supply" and three other corrective feedback systems (Jenkins & Larson, 1979; Jenkins, Larson, & Fleisher, 1982). Based on this review of the literature, McCoy and Pany developed a hierarchy of "corrective cues." These cues, in order from least to greatest assistance, are as follows:

1. "Try another way."
2. "Finish the sentence and guess at the word."
3. "Break the word into parts and pronounce each one."
4. Point to parts of the word and have the reader try each one.
5. Ask "What sound does (_____) make?" [Fill in the blank with letters for the troublesome sound, such as /le/ in *little; /ow/ in grow.*]
6. Finally, "The word is _____."

More research needs to be done to provide definitive guidelines for offering feedback and help with oral reading. Two things *are* clear from present research: (1) giving corrective feedback during students' oral reading *does* tend to enhance word learning and comprehension; and (2) this feedback is *most effective* when students perceive it as *nonpunitive* (Pany, McCoy, & Peters, 1981) and when it is coupled with "wait time" and with other clues such as sounding out the first letter (Allington, 1983b). It is difficult to say whether this contradicts the inclination of whole language proponents to overlook all misread words that do not affect comprehension. We suppose the reflective teacher will make the decision as to how much "corrective feedback" to give based on the objective of the lesson, whether it be to improve oral reading, reading for meaning, or to enhance word analysis and recognition skills.

A later chapter provides further information on explicit means of using oral reading in assessment. Oral reading can be used: (1) to estimate the student's listening capacity (or capacity to read and comprehend) when the student is read to; (2) to estimate word analysis needs and abilities when the student is permitted to read orally; and (3) to estimate their comprehension of what they have read from questions following oral reading.

### Peer Reading: For Weak Readers

Labbo and Teale (1990) have made the fascinating discovery that upper elementary grade youngsters, who were themselves weak in fluency, could be helped to read better when they were involved in a four-phase program that had them reading to kindergartners who also profited from the experience. The four phases included: preparation; preteaching/prereading; reading to kindergartners; and postcollaboration.

In the preparation stage, the teacher helps the older students to get ready by teaching them three things about oral reading that are similar to what could be said to any teacher or adult volunteer about to undertake such a task. The most important of these, as mentioned earlier, is that they personally should like the book, that the kindergartners should probably like it, that the illustrations be evocative and appropriate to the story, and that the words be manageable for the reader.

Older students then need to rehearse reading the selection. This can be done with the teacher or a same-age partner who is a better reader. It also can be done with a tape recorder at home or at school. The selection should be read through a minimum of three times before it is read to the kindergartners.

At the preteaching/prereading stage, the teacher should meet with the older students a few days prior to their reading to the kindergartners to help them make other teacher-like decisions, such as, how shall I introduce the book, where should I pause for discussion and questions, what else might I do to insure student involvement. At a final, or postcollaborative stage, the teacher and the cadet oral readers should meet again to see how things worked out and what might be done to improve their reading and teaching next time they meet with a kindergartner.

With this clever formula, the novice oral readers learn more than how to read better orally. They develop a sense of purpose, a sense of audience, and a sense of the job and thinking of the teacher. In turn, they give a good deal both to the kindergartners and to the teacher, who spends a considerable amount of time preparing them. Teachers' conversations with these youngsters inevitably cover topics such as the unusual ways different children relate and behave and, of course, the act of reading itself. All in all, this approach is a win-win-win situation: the novice readers learn to read better, the kindergartners get read to, and teachers learn from their conversations with the novice readers about the kinds of problems they encounter in reading and how they attempt to cope with them.

## ROUND ROBIN READING

No discussion of oral reading can be complete without reference to the practice of having youngsters read a portion of a selection while others follow along. This practice, sometimes known as Round Robin Reading, usually moves along from seat to seat in an orderly fashion with the teacher indicating when the next pupil should read by saying "next." To keep youngsters alert, the teacher might also skip around the room: "Kisha, please pick it up from there."

### WHY TEACHERS USE ROUND ROBIN READING

Round Robin practice, which has never received an endorsement from any teacher training institution, has been around since the nineteenth century, when most reading was done orally. Its persistence led Durkin (1989) to ask several elementary school teachers why they continue to use the practice. The reasons they cited most were as follows:

- It externalizes student reading and permits me to monitor their progress.
- Pupils' expressions tend to reveal whether they are comprehending.
- Kids seem to like it!
- Children should have a chance to read aloud, especially the younger ones.

*Durkin (1989), pp. 41–42.*

Exploring these points ourselves with several elementary school teachers, we have found some other reasons why elementary teachers gravitate toward this practice. They said that:

- It is one of the few things that can be done and shared by the entire class.
- It is orderly.
- It has a familiar feel, since they were taught that way.
- Following along at least appears to help poorer readers learn words and to develop a sense of fluency.
- It fills time in a quasiproductive way on those occasions when the teacher is feeling too tired or out of sorts to conduct a more intensive or complicated form of instruction.

These reasons tell us that Round Robin Reading serves some practical needs that cause it to persist. Therefore, let's consider why it is frowned upon and then look at some variations that might make it more beneficial for all students.

## PROBLEMS WITH ROUND ROBIN READING

Round Robin Reading is frowned upon essentially for these reasons:

- Poor readers are made to feel exposed and embarrassed.
- Pupils trying to follow along may be incidentally trained into greater subvocalization and to a silent reading rate that matches the slower oral reading rate.
- The child reading usually is too nervous to understand what he or she is saying, and those listening can be distracted from comprehending by the varying quality of the readers—points demonstrated by Luther Gilbert (1940) over fifty years ago.
- Instead of following along with the reader, some students may be looking ahead to find and practice their parts.
- Once readers have had their turn to read, they tend to lapse into inattention.
- Poor oral reading performance may not be connected to silent reading and may actually conceal a greater rather than a lesser degree of competence (Goodman, 1970). (See the anecdote on Anthony in Chapter 2.)

Consider now some variations on Round Robin Reading that tend to make it more acceptable. Each tries to preserve something of the low demand requirement on the teacher—a requirement that we support in principle, since realistically everyone who teaches cannot be expected to be at the top of his or her game each moment of each day.

## LOW DEMAND/HIGH IMPACT ORAL READING PRACTICES

1. The teacher introduces the selection by reading the first few paragraphs. Students then read orally in round robin fashion for the remainder of a selection.
2. Starting with the previous point, add two variations: a few students are selected to read orally, and after part of the selection has been read aloud, the remainder of the selection is read silently by all students.

3. Following 1 or 2, the teacher asks students to find and read aloud a short section that: (a) they found to be very descriptive; (b) or really got to the point about something; or (c) answered a specific question.

4. Most of the material in a longer selection is summarized by the teacher, using many of the vocabulary words in the selection. Students then read a few sections orally, and finally, the remainder is read silently.

5. Oral reading teams of about five students each are formed. Periodically, a selection is partitioned up among the groups, with some latter section held out for the teacher to read aloud. Students are given time to look over the group's portion of the material to be read aloud and to consult with one another about who among them will read orally on that day. The number of students who actually read, and how much they read, is determined by the group. Students can be encouraged to be playfully theatric. (One group we observed decided to have certain *words* always spoken by a designated group member: some words were spoken by a child with a deep voice and others by a youngster with a shrill voice.)

6. A different play is given to each group, with instructions to prepare to present a dramatic reading at any time after a given date. At any time after that date, the group may be called upon to give their dramatic reading. In this way, the teacher always has several oral reading activities ready to fall back on in a pinch.

7. Other acceptable combinations of oral and silent reading include the following strategies described elsewhere in the text: Read-Along Tapes, Paired Oral Reading, the Neurological Impress Method (NIM), the Listening–Reading Transfer Lesson, the Listen–Read–Discuss heuristic, and the Guided Listening Procedure.

Box 4.5 provides recommendations for books to read aloud that have some special feature worthy of note. The list is compiled from many sources, but especially from several elementary school teachers with whom we regularly consulted during this project.

---

**BOX 4.5** | **Books to Read Aloud**

***Baby Books*** come in a variety of formats for handling by toddlers, from durable cardboard covers to cloth books to plastic bathtub books, and emphasize simple labeling of familiar objects.

*The Blanket,* John Burningham (Crowell, 1976)

*I Can,* Helen Oxenbury (Random House, 1986)

*I Hear. I See. I Touch. (set),* Rachael Isadora (Viking, 1984)

***Beginning Stories*** are books with simple story lines for young listeners.

*The Baby's Story Book,* Kay Chorao (Dutton, 1985)

*Chicken Little,* Steven Kellogg (Morrow, 1985)

*Have You Seen My Duckling?* Nancy Tafuri (Penguin, 1986)

*Max's Bath. Max's Bedtime. Max's Birthday. Max's Breakfast. (set),* Rosemary Wells (Dial, 1979)

BOX
**4.5**
cont'd

## Books to Read Aloud

***Participation Books*** engage children in the story reading process through sensory elements such as flaps to lift, soft or scratchy surfaces to touch, scented pages to sniff, and built-in sounds to discover.

*Hand Rhymes,* Marc Brown (Dutton, 1985)

*My Very First Book of Shapes,* Eric Carle (Crowell, 1974)

*Peek-a-Boo!* Janet Ahlbert & Allan Ahlberg (Viking, 1981)

*Where's Spot?* Eric Hill (Putnam's, 1980)

***Concept Books*** develop a single idea by providing many examples in a nonfictional or fictional presentation.

*Circles, Triangles and Squares,* Tana Hoban (Macmillan, 1974)

*Colors to Know,* Karen Gundersheimer (Harper & Row, 1986)

*Is It Larger? Is It Smaller?* Tana Hoban (Greenwillow, 1985)

*The Supermarket,* Anne Rockwell & Harlow Rockwell (Macmillan, 1979)

*Truck,* Donald Crews (Greenwillow, 1980)

***Wordless Books*** tell stories from pictures, building the preschool child's sense of story and love of books.

*The Adventures of Paddy Pork,* John Goodall (Harcourt, 1968)

*Ah-Choo!* Mercer Mayer (Dial, 1976)

*Amanda and the Mysterious Carpet,* Fernando Krahn (Houghton Mifflin, 1985)

*The Angel and the Soldier Boy,* Peter Collington (Knopf, 1987)

*The Bear and the Fly,* Paula Winter (Crown, 1976)

*Bobo's Dream,* Martha Alexander (Dial, 1970)

*A Boy, A Dog, and a Frog,* Mercer Mayer (Dial, 1967)

*Breakfast Time, Ernest and Celestine,* Gabrielle Vincent (Greenwillow, 1982)

*Creepy Castle,* John Goodall (Atheneum, 1975)

*Deep in the Forest,* Brinton Turkle (Dutton, 1976)

*Do You Want to Be My Friend?* Eric Carle (Crowell, 1971)

*Dreams,* Peter Spier (Doubleday, 1986)

*Ernest and Celestine's Patchwork Quilt,* Gabrielle Vincent (Greenwillow, 1982)

*Frog Goes to Dinner,* Mercer Mayer (Dial, 1973)

*Frog on His Own,* Mercer Mayer (Dial, 1969)

*Frog, Where Are You?* Mercer Mayer (Dial, 1969)

*The Gift,* John Prater (Viking, 1985)

*The Great Escape,* Philippe Dupasquier (Houghton Mifflin, 1988)

*Little Red Riding Hood,* John Goodall (Atheneum, 1988)

*The Mystery of the Giant Footprints,* Fernando Krahn (Dutton, 1977)

*The Other Bone,* Ed Young (HarperCollins, 1984)

*Paddy Goes Traveling,* John Goodall (Atheneum, 1982)

*Paddy's Evening Out,* John Goodall (Atheneum, 1973)

*Paddy to the Rescue,* John Goodall (Atheneum, 1985)

*Pancakes for Breakfast,* Tomie dePaola (Harcourt, 1978)

*Peter Spier's Christmas,* Peter Spier (Doubleday, 1982)

**BOX 4.5 cont'd**

*Peter Spier's Rain,* Peter Spier (Doubleday, 1982)

*Rosie's Walk,* Pat Hutchins (Macmillan, 1968)

*Sleep Tight, Alex Pumpernickel,* Fernando Krahn (Little, 1982)

*The Snowman,* Raymond Briggs (Random, 1978)

*A Story to Tell,* Dick Bruna (Price, Stern, 1968)

*Up a Tree,* Ed Young (HarperCollins, 1983)

*Up and Up,* Shirley Hughes (Lothrop, 1986)

*Where's My Monkey?* Dieter Schubert (Dial, 1987)

**Alphabet Books** feature interesting formats, engaging pictures, and/or other special elements built around the letters of the alphabet. In *On Market Street,* for example, we follow a young boy who goes shopping on Market Street, and see what he buys from A to Z (Cullinan, 1989).

*ABC, an Alphabet Book,* Thomas Matthiesen (Putnam's, 1981)

*A, B, See!* Tana Hoban (Greenwillow, 1982)

*A City Seen from A to Z,* Rachel Isadora (Greenwillow, 1983)

*A Farmer's Alphabet,* Mary Azarian (Godine, 1981)

*A My Name Is Alice,* Jane Bayer (Dial, 1984)

*Animal Alphabet,* Bert Kitchen (Dial, 1984)

*Anno's Alphabet: An Adventure in Imagination,* Mitsumaso Anno (Crowell, 1975)

*Applebet: An ABC,* Clyde Watson. Illustrated by Wendy Watson (Farrar, Straus & Giroux, 1982)

*Ashanti to Zulu,* Margaret Musgrove. Illustrated by Leo and Diane Dillon (Dial, 1976)

*The Guinea Pig ABC,* Kate Duke (Dutton, 1983)

*Grandpa's Great City Tour: An Alphabet Book,* James Stevenson (Greenwillow, 1983)

*Jambo Means Hello,* Tom & Muriel Feelings (Dial, 1974)

*John Burningham's ABC,* John Burningham (Crown, 1986)

*The Most Amazing Hide and Seek Alphabet Book,* Robert Crowther (Viking, 1978)

*What's Inside: The Alphabet Book,* Satoshi Kitamura (Farrar, Straus & Giroux, 1985)

**Counting Books,** like alphabet books, feature interesting formats, engaging pictures and/or other special elements built around numbers and counting. *The Right Number of Elephants,* for example, explains that the "right" number of elephants depends on what you plan to *do* with them. Counting backwards from ten, the book ends with the idea that "when you need a very special friend for a very special moment, then the right number of elephants is one" (Camp, 1991).

*1, 2, 3,* Tana Hoban (Greenwillow, 1985)

*1, 2, 3, Play with Me,* Karen Gundersheimer (HarperCollins, 1984)

*Animal Numbers,* Bert Kitchen (Dial, 1987)

*Anno's Counting Book,* Mitsumasa Anno (Crowell, 1977)

*Count and See,* Tana Hoban (Greenwillow, 1985)

*Demi's Count the Animals 1-2-3,* Demi Hite (Grosset & Dunlap, 1990)

*Fish Eyes: A Book You Can Count On,* Lois Ehlert (Harcourt Brace Jovanovich, 1990)

*John Burningham's 1, 2, 3,* John Burningham (Crown, 1986)

*Mojo Means One,* Muriel Feelings. Illustrated by Tom Feelings (Dial, 1974)

## BOX 4.5 cont'd

# Books to Read Aloud

*Numbears: A Counting Book,* Kathleen Hague. Illustrated by Michael Hague (Holt, 1986)

*One Duck, Another Duck,* Charlotte Pomerantz. Illustrated by Jose Aruego & Ariene Dewey (Greenwillow, 1984)

*One Hungry Monster: A Counting Book in Rhyme,* Susan Heyboer O'Keefe. Illustrated by Lynn Munsinger (Little, Brown, 1990)

*Over in the Meadow: A Counting-Out Rhyme,* Olive A. Wadsworth. Illustrated by Mary M. Rae (Viking, 1985)

*Up to Ten and Down Again,* Lisa C. Ernst (Lothrop, Lee & Shepard, 1986)

*The Right Number of Elephants,* Jeff Sheppard. Illustrated by Felicia Bond (Harper & Row, 1990)

*Ten Little Mice,* Joyce Dunbar. Illustrated by Maria Majewska (Harcourt Brace Jovanovich, 1990)

*The Very Hungry Caterpillar,* Eric Carle (Philomel, 1969)

**Rhymes for the Young** build the preschool child's sense of language sounds and patterns,

*Finger Rhymes,* Marc Brown (Dutton, 1980)

*Hand Rhymes,* Marc Brown (Dutton, 1985)

*Listen, Children, Listen,* Myra Cohn Livingston (Harcourt Brace Jovanovich, 1974)

*Mother Goose, A Treasury of Best Loved Rhymes,* Walter Piper. Illustrated by Tim and Greg Hildebrandt (Platt, 1972)

*Oh, How Silly!,* William Cole. Illustrated by Tomi Ungerer (Viking, 1970)

*One at a Time,* David McCord. Illustrated by Henry B. Kane (Little, Brown, 1986)

*Read-Aloud Rhymes for the Very Young,* collected by Jack Prelutsky. Illustrated by Marc Brown (Knopf, 1986)

*Sally Go Round the Sun: 300 Children's Songs, Rhymes, and Games,* Edith Fowke (Ed.). Illustrated by Judith Gwyn Brown (Prentice-Hall, 1977)

*Side by Side: Poems to Read Together,* collected by Lee Bennett Hopkins. Illustrated by Hilary Knight (Simon and Schuster, 1988)

*Whiskers and Rhymes,* Arnold Lobel (Greenwillow, 1985)

**Predictable Books to Build Fluency** use text in which the next word, phrase, or event is easily anticipated and heightens the beginning reader's sense of confidence in independently getting meaning from print.

*Are You My Mother?* P. D. Eastman (Random House, 1960)

*Ask Mr. Bear,* Marjorie Flack (Macmillan, 1986)

*Brown Bear, Brown Bear, What Do You See?* Bill Martin, Jr. (Holt, 1983)

*The Cake That Mack Ate,* Rose Robart (Atlantic, 1986)

*Chicken Soup with Rice,* Maurice Sendak (Harper & Row, 1962)

*Do You Want to Be My Friend?* Eric Carle (Putnam, 1971)

*The Elephant and the Bad Boy,* Elfrida Vipont (Putnam, 1986)

*Fat Mouse,* Harry Stevens (Viking, 1987)

*Goodnight Moon,* Margaret Wise Brown (Harper & Row, 1988)

*Hattie and the Fox,* Mem Fox (Bradbury, 1987)

*Henny Penny,* Paul Galdone (Clarion, 1968)

*If You Give a Mouse a Cookie,* Laura Numeroff. Illustrated by Felicia Bond (Scholastic, 1988)

BOX
4.5
cont'd

*The House That Jack Built,* Rodney Peppe (Delacorte, 1985)

*The Little Old Lady Who Was Not Afraid of Anything,* Linda Williams (Crowell, 1986)

*Old Mother Hubbard,* Colin and Jacqui Hawkins (Putnam, 1985)

*Over in the Meadow,* Olive Wadsworth (Viking, 1985)

*The Teeny Tiny Woman,* Barbara Seuling (Puffin, 1978)

*The Three Little Pigs,* Paul Galdone (Clarion, 1970)

*Tikki Tikki Tembo,* Arlene Mosel (Holt, 1968)

*The Wheels on the Bus,* Maryann Kovalski (Little, Brown, 1987)

*Where's Spot?* Eric Hill (Putnam, 1980)

**Informational Books.** Nonfiction print satisfies and builds curiosity and reinforces the information value of books.

*Airplanes,* Byron Barton (Crowell, 1986)

*Animals in the Country,* Kenneth Lilly (Simon & Schuster, 1982)

*Do Animals Dream?* Joyce Pope (Viking Children's Books, 1986)

*Here a Chick, There a Chick,* Bruce McMillan (Lothrop, Lee & Shepard, 1983)

*How Much Is a Million?* David M. Schwartz. Illustrated by Steven Kellogg (Lothrop, Lee & Shepard, 1985)

*The Kids' Question and Answer Book,* by the editors of *Owl* magazine (Putnam, 1988)

*Life Through the Ages,* Giovanni Caselli (Doreing Kindevsley, 1992)

*The Milk Makers,* Gail Gibbons (Macmillan, 1985)

*The Post Office Book: Mail and How It Moves,* Gail Gibbons (Crowell, 1982)

*Trucks,* Byron Barton (Crowell, 1986)

**Picture Books** with particularly engaging pictures that enhance the theme, mood, and story line encourage children to identify with characters and events and heighten interest in the print.

*Alexander and the Terrible, Horrible, No Good, Very Bad Day,* Judith Viorst. Illustrated by Ray Cruz (K and up, 34 pp.) (Macmillan, 1972)

*Amelia Bedelia,* Peggy Paris. Illustrated by Fritz Seibel (K–4, 64 pp.) (Harper, 1992)

*The Carp in the Bathtub,* Barbara Cohen. Illustrated by Joan Halpern (K–4, 48 pp.) (Lothrop, 1972)

*A Chair for My Mother,* Vera B. Williams (K–3, 30 pp.) (Morrow, 1988)

*Curious George,* H. A. Rey (PP–1, 48 pp.) (HM, 1973)

*The Cut-ups Cut Loose,* James Marshall (K–2, 32 pp.) (Viking, 1987)

*The Day Jimmy Boa Ate the Wash,* Trinka Hakes Noble (PP–2, 32 pp.) (Dial, 1984)

*An Evening at Alfie's,* Shirley Hughes (PP–2, 32 pp.) (Lothrop, 1985)

*Frog and Toad are Friends,* Arnold Lobel (PP–2, 64 pp.) (HarperCollins, 1985)

*The Giving Tree,* Shel Silverstein (K–4, 52 pp.) (HarperCollins, 1964)

*Goodnight Moon,* Margaret Wise Brown (PP–K, 36 pp.) (HarperCollins, 1947)

*Ira Sleeps Over,* Bernard Waber (K–6, 48 pp.) (HM, 1973)

*Madeline,* Ludwig Bemelmans (P–2, 54 pp.) (Viking, 1958)

*Mike Mulligan and His Steam Shovel,* Virginia Lee Burton (K–4, 42 pp.) (HM, 1939)

*The Napping House,* Audrey Wood, illustrated by Don Wood (PP–K, 32 pp.) (Harcourt Brace Jovanovich, 1984)

**BOX 4.5 cont'd**

## Books to Read Aloud

*Tintin in Tibet,* Herge' (2–4, 62 pp.) (Little, 1975)

*Where the Wild Things Are,* Maurice Sendak (K–3, 28 pp.) (HarperCollins, 1985)

***Joke and Riddle Books for Fun and Imagination*** add a light note to school and help build a sense of humor.

*Bennett Cerf's Book of Animal Riddles,* Bennett Cerf. Illustrated by Roy McKie (Beginner, 1964)

*Bennett Cerf's Book of Laughs* (Beginner, 1959)

*Bennett Cerf's Book of Riddles* (Beginner, 1960)

*Buggy Riddles,* Katy Hall & Lisa Eisenberg (Dial, 1986)

*Spooky Riddles,* Marc Brown (Beginner, 1983)

*Ten Copycats in a Boat and Other Riddles,* Alvin Schwartz (HarperCollins, 1980)

*The Carsick Zebra and Other Animal Riddles,* David Adler (Holiday, 1983)

*The Purple Turkey and Other Thanksgiving Riddles,* David Adler (Holiday, 1986)

*The Twisted Witch and Other Spooky Riddles,* David Adler (Holiday, 1985)

*The Best Joke Book for Kids,* Joan Eckstein & Joyce Gleit (Avon, 1977)

*The Best Joke Book for Kids #2,* Joan Eckstein & Joyce Gleit (Avon, 1987)

*Haunted House Jokes,* Louis Phillips (Viking, 1987)

*How Do You Get a Horse Out of the Bathtub?,* Louis Phillips (Viking, 1983)

***Poetry*** collections expose children, early on, to the artistic potential in each of us.

*Sing a Song of Popcorn: Every Child's Book of Poems,* selected by Beatrice Schenk deRegniers, Eva Moore, Mary M. White, & Jan Carr. Illustrated by Maurice Sendak, Trina Schart Hyman, Arnold Lobel, et al. (Scholastic, 1988)

*Where the Sidewalk Ends,* Shel Silverstein (HarperCollins, 1974)

*A Light in the Attic,* Shel Silverstein (HarperCollins, 1974)

*You Read to Me, I'll Read to You,* John Ciardi. Illustrated by Edward Gorey (Lippincott, 1961; Harper & Row, 1987)

*The Random House Book of Poetry for Children,* selected by Jack Prelutsky. Illustrated by Arnold Lobel (Random House, 1983)

*Tomie dePaola's Book of Poems,* Tomie dePaola (Putnam, 1988)

***For Older Students.*** These largely nonfiction books help to build students' depth of knowledge in various topical areas.

*Paul Harvey's "The Rest of the Story,"* Paul Aurandt (Bantam, 1984)

*More of Paul Harvey's "The Rest of the Story,"* Paul Aurandt (Bantam, 1984)

***Scary Stories.*** Children are surrounded with frightening possibilities; scary stories seem to help them to acclimate and rehearse for the really fearful.

*More Scary Stories to Tell in the Dark,* collected by Alvin Schwartz (HarperCollins, 1986)

*Nightmares,* Jack Prelutsky (Greenwillow, 1976)

*Scary Stories to Tell in the Dark,* collected by Alvin Schwartz. Illustrated by Stephen Gammell (Lippincott, 1981; HarperCollins, 1983)

*Uninvited Ghosts and Other Stories,* Penelope Lively. Illustrated by John Lawrence (Dutton, 1985)

***Short Novels*** introduce readers to longer pieces of literature, in preparation for reading standard novels.

**BOX
4.5**
cont'd

*The Bear's House,* Marilyn Sachs (4–6, 80 pp.) (Dutton, 1987)

*The Best Christmas Pageant Ever,* Barbara Robinson (2–6, 96 pp.) (HarperCollins, 1972, 1988)

*Call it Courage,* Armstrong Sperry (2–6, 96 pp.) (Macmillan, 1968, 1973, 1990)

*Fantastic Mr. Fox,* Roald Dahl. Illustrated by Tony Ross (K–4, 62 pp.) (Puffin, 1988)

*The Friendship,* Mildred Taylor (4+, 53 pp.) (Dial, 1987)

*The Littles,* John Peterson (1–4, 80 pp.) (Scholastic, 1986)

*The Stories Julian Tells,* Ann Cameron (K–3, 72 pp.) (Knopf, 1989)

*The Story of Holly and Ivy,* Rumer Godden (K–5, 31 pp.) (Puffin, 1987)

*Twenty and Ten,* Claire H. Bishop (3–6, 76 pp.) (Puffin, 1991)

*The Velveteen Rabbit,* Margery Williams. Illustrated by David Jorgensen (2–7, 48 pp.) (Doubleday, 1991)

**Book Length Fiction.** These are books of intermediate length that contain enough space to develop characters and more elaborate plot lines.

*Bridge to Terabithia,* Katherine Paterson (4–7, 128 pp.) (HarperCollins, 1987)

*Caddie Woodlawn,* Carol Ryrie Brink (4–6, 288 pp.) (Macmillan, 1990)

*The Call of the Wild,* Jack London (6+, 126 pp.) (Puffin, 1983)

*The Cay,* Theodore Taylor (2–6, 144 pp.) (Avon, 1976, 1977)

*Charlotte's Web,* E. B. White. Illustrated by Garth Williams (K–4, 184 pp.) (HarperCollins, 1952, 1974)

*Dear Mr. Henshaw,* Beverly Cleary (3–6, 144 pp.) (Morrow, 1983)

*Homer Price,* Robert McCloskey (2–5, 160 pp.) (Puffin, 1976)

*The Indian in the Cupboard,* Lynne Reid Banks (2–6, 182 pp.) (Avon, 1982)

*J. T.,* Jane Wagner. Photographs by Gordon Parks (3–5, 128 pp.) (Dell, 1972)

*Jump Ship to Freedom,* James L. Collier & Christopher Collier (5–9, 192 pp.) (Delacorte, 1981)

*The Lion, the Witch and the Wardrobe,* C. S. Lewis (3–6, 186 pp.) (Macmillan, 1986)

*The Me Inside of Me,* T. Ernesto Bethan Court (5+, 156pp. ) (Lerner, 1985)

*Mrs. Frisby and the Rats of NIMH,* Robert C. O'Brien (4–6, 240 pp.) (Macmillan, 1971)

*My Side of the Mountain,* Jean George (3–8, 176 pp.) (Dutton, 1988)

*North to Freedom,* Anne Holm (4–8, 190 pp.) (Peter Smith, 1984)

*Ramona the Pest,* Beverly Cleary (K–6, 175 pp.) (BDD, 1990)

*Roll of Thunder Hear My Cry,* Mildred Taylor (5–9, 276 pp.) (Bantam, 1984)

*The Secret Garden,* Frances Hodgson Burnett. Illustrated by Shirley Hughes (2–5, 240 pp.) (Knopf, 1988)

*Sideways Stories from Wayside School,* Louis Sachar (2–5, 144 pp.) (Avon, 1985)

*Sing Down the Moon,* Scott O'Dell (3–6, 138 pp.) (Dell, 1976)

*Skinnybones,* Barbara Park (3–5, 112 pp.) (Knopf, 1989)

*Tales of a Fourth-Grade Nothing,* Judy Blume (3–5, 120 pp. (Dell, 1976)

*Understood Betsy,* Dorothy Canfield Fisher (2–6, 211 pp.) (Dell, 1986)

*Weird Henry Berg,* Sara Sargent (4–6, 114 pp.) (Dell, 1981)

*Where the Red Fern Grows,* Wilson Rawls (3–7, 212 pp.) (Bantam, 1974)

*Words by Heart,* Ouida Sebestyen (5–9, 144 pp.) (Bantam, 1983)

**W**here You've Been

### Reading Aloud, Listening and Speaking

**Reading Aloud to Students**
Why Do It?
Guidelines for Reading Aloud to Students
Strategies for Reading Aloud to Students

**Having Students Read Aloud**
Benefits of Students' Oral Reading
Tactics for Enhancing Students' Oral Reading
Strategies for Enhancing Students' Oral Reading

**Round Robin Reading**
Why Teachers Use Round Robin Reading
Problems with Round Robin Reading
Low Demand/High Impact'
  Oral Reading Practices

**W**here You're Going

While oral reading adds life to the printed word, it is largely through silent reading that we learn how to make meaning and correlate life to reading and reading to life. The next chapter highlights the current emphasis on encouraging children, from their earliest literacy experiences, to think about and respond to text. We shall refer to it as *emergent higher-order literacy.*

### *Reflective Inquiries and Activities*

1. Do you remember being read to in school? Tell what you remember the teacher did that made it pleasant, or otherwise.
2. Make Lesson Cards on oral reading methods that you think you will be able to personally experiment with soon.
3. Develop a pack of Note Cue cards on a selection and do a trial run with children or a simulation of the strategy with your college class. Videotape the lesson and critique it as if you were youngsters aiming to have a high quality discussion. To add an action-research dimension, assess comprehension on an

appropriate test and with comparable selections under a Note Cue and an alternative condition.

4. What's "wrong" with Round Robin Reading? Are there any variations that you might use? Why?

5. Plan a campaign and a workshop to involve more males in oral reading to children. Field-test the entire package with college students or volunteer community people before taking it public. (You will clearly strengthen your competitiveness for a good job if you can report that you have such a plan in hand.)

### CHAPTER 5

# READING AND RESPONDING: EMERGENT HIGHER-ORDER LITERACY

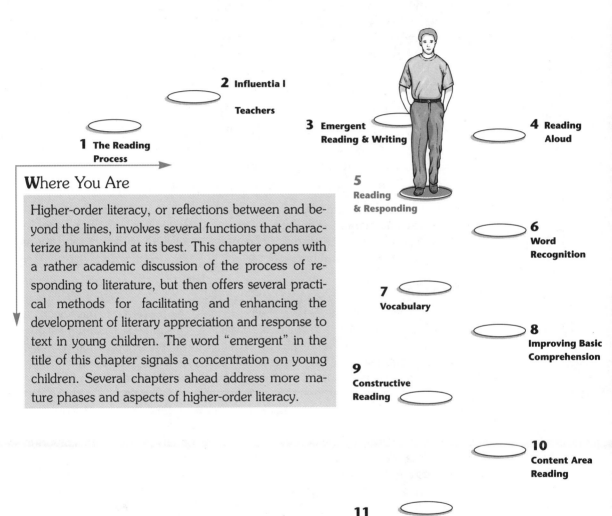

**2** Influentia l

Teachers

**1** The Reading
Process

**3** Emergent
Reading & Writing

**4** Reading
Aloud

**5**
Reading
& Responding

**6**
Word
Recognition

**7** Vocabulary

**8**
Improving Basic
Comprehension

**9**
Constructive
Reading

**10**
Content Area
Reading

**11**
Children with
Special Needs

**12**
Literacy
Assessment

**13** The Classroom
& School Literacy Program

## **W**here You Are

Higher-order literacy, or reflections between and be-yond the lines, involves several functions that charac-terize humankind at its best. This chapter opens with a rather academic discussion of the process of re-sponding to literature, but then offers several practi-cal methods for facilitating and enhancing the development of literary appreciation and response to text in young children. The word "emergent" in the title of this chapter signals a concentration on young children. Several chapters ahead address more ma-ture phases and aspects of higher-order literacy.

*Some books are to be tasted,
others to be swallowed,
and some few are  to be chewed and
digested.*

Francis Bacon

# STORY LITERATURE AND READER RESPONSE

Even before they learn to read, most children realize that story "meanings" usually go beyond the simple plot lines. The child may not be able to explain these deeper meanings, such as the sense of hope that is inspired by the story of the "Ugly Duckling." Nonetheless, it is with these early impressions that higher-order literacy begins to emerge. Recognizing the deeper meanings in stories is a satisfying feeling. When children begin to sense these meanings, they continue to reach for them thereafter as naturally as they reach for things that are sweet to the palate. From this point on, it can be argued that the chief functions of teaching become:

1. Pointing out where the good literature, or sweet stuff, is
2. Removing obstacles that come between children and the search for meaning
3. Encouraging children to respond to text with all that they feel and think
4. Understanding and appreciating children's different tastes
5. Helping children to use literature to acquire empathy for others

This chapter is about using story literature to promote the search for meaning. Several subsequent chapters elaborate on this topic, with special attention to those with different tastes, such as children who prefer nonfiction to fiction, and those with mechanical aptitudes and orientations.

## TEACHERS REDISCOVER CHILDREN'S LITERATURE

One very real outcome of the whole-language movement has been a groundswell of active interest in children's literature. This interest has been accompanied by increased attention to children's literature in professional journals and textbooks and publication of numerous listings and annotated bibliographies of various types of books and stories. A relatively new related phenomenon is the growing number of teachers across the country who are forming "Teachers Are Readers"[1] groups to gather after school and talk about children's literature. These discussions may center on the literary qualities of a book, its historical context, and/or teachers' personal responses. One teacher remarked that participation in these literature group discussions had "put a love back in my heart for reading. It's nice to be able to talk about books without having to relate them to students." This "rediscovery" of children's literature is generating increased interest in a more academic aspect of reader response, or "response to literature," as it sometimes is known. The next section summarizes one current view of how perspectives on response to literature have evolved over the years from a textbased perspective in which the reader was seen as relatively unimportant, to the current perspective in which the reader's role in interacting with and interpreting the text is essential to the literary experience.

---

[1] For information write or call the Association of American Publishers, Reading Initiative; 220 E. 23rd Street; New York, NY 10010; 212-689-8920.

## PERSPECTIVES ON RESPONSE TO LITERATURE

Perspectives on response to literature, or how, when, and why people read and react to narrative text, are closely tied to the values and context of the times. Eberdt-Armstrong (1990) has identified three historical perspectives on response to literature and has suggested a fourth that seems to be emerging from our current life and times. Each of these perspectives is described briefly here to provide a basis for understanding what has happened and is happening in the teaching of literature in general, and children's literature in particular. Following this discussion, you will find a diagram summarizing characteristics of these four perspectives (see Table 5.1, p. 140). As you read about these perspectives, compare them with your own attitudes about literature and its value to you personally, as well as your attitudes about teaching literature to children and its value to their educational, social, and emotional development.

The earliest views on how one should approach and respond to literature were from a *text-based perspective.* This perspective reached a peak in popularity in the years between 1912 and 1939. Literature, from the text-based perspective, is an objective entity with intrinsic qualities that can be evaluated completely apart from context, reader, or author. Knowledge of "good literature" was an accoutrement to be acquired for the same reasons one seeks to acquire other status symbols. The text-based perspective emphasizes the following propositions:

- Literature has specific product value—it is something to be learned.
- A beautiful poem is beautiful in all contexts, and a poor one can never be redeemed by its context—or who reads it and why.
- Not only poetry and literature, but all values, are fixed and context-free—good is good and bad is bad.
- Students and teachers need to learn the "proper" way to feel and understand literature.
- Literature is meant to act upon us, not to emerge from within us (Armstrong, 1991).

    *Example:* "Cinderella" is a classic tale that all children should know. It teaches us to persevere, even in the face of adversity, and that proper behavior will be rewarded.

This mechanistic view of literature was followed, in the period between 1935 and 1969, by a *social–political perspective.* In this view, literature is an essential means by which society hands down common allusions and values and maintains continuity. Literature is not seen as an objective entity, but as something whose value derives from the context in which it was created and into which it is placed. The social–political perspective is characterized by these propositions:

- Literature is a mechanism for recording and promoting cultural ideologies.
- The reader absorbs values and attitudes from textual accounts and spreads these into society.

- Values are not context-free, but emerge almost solely from whatever people are writing, saying, and doing (Armstrong, 1991).
- Literature is a form of safe experimentation for social change.

  *Example:* "Cinderella" teaches outmoded values. It teaches girls that they can expect to be rescued from adversity by a "prince"; therefore, they need not strive to improve their lot. Children should not be encouraged to read this book. It should be replaced by others that more fairly represent current values and roles.

In the early 1970s, with the emergence of the *transactive perspective,* the popularity of this social–political perspective began to fade. The transactive perspective, often attributed to Louise Rosenblatt (1938; 1978), focuses on the reader's role in the literary experience. The literary experience is not seen as a simple action of reading/absorbing the text, but as a *trans*action in which reader and text are mutually influenced. Although the text is a static entity, each reader brings something different to his or her reading of it; thus, the text "is" something different to each reader and influences each reader differently in turn. The transactive perspective can be characterized by the following propositions:

- Literature is a transaction between the reader and the text, as opposed to a transmission from text to reader.
- The literary experience is characterized by a fluid movement among the reader, the context, and the text.
- The value of literature is to be found in the literary process itself—especially effective writing in response to a literary experience.
- The literary experience is an important dimension of individual ethical and moral development.
- There is *no* "correct" way to respond to literature.
- Readers' personal responses to text are essential and may be unique to each reader.

  *Example:* "Cinderella" has different meanings for every reader. Children should be encouraged to express their responses to the behavior of the different characters and to tell how these are like or different from their own feelings and the behavior of people they know. They should be encouraged to distinguish between what parts of the story could really happen and what parts are pure fantasy. They might be asked to imagine what Cinderella might have done if there had been no "fairy godmother."

The fourth direction, and the one that response to text now seems to be taking, is being referred to as an *actualization perspective*[2] (Armstrong, 1991; Straw & Bogdan, 1990). It is characterized by the following propositions:

[2] This notion has been likened to the theory of holonomy proposed by a theoretical physicist (Bohm, 1978, 1986). The theory proposes that any piece of a hologram (such as the three-dimensional-looking logos on some credit cards) can be used to reconstruct the entire view of the original image (Armstrong, 1992).

- The reader is driven by a need to fulfill or actualize his or her *own* purposes.
- The external world of the text *and* the internal world of the reader are seeking to create meaning.
- It does not refute Rosenblatt's model, but refocuses emphasis on the text as a meaningful whole from which the reader can gain self-actualizing insights.
- Response to text is not so much a matter of bringing parts, such as reader and text, together in a dynamic state to make a whole; rather, eventual comprehension of the whole requires some level of taking it apart, or focusing upon one aspect or the other, until the whole can be regenerated.

*Example:* "Cinderella" does reflect outmoded values, but these are part of our shared experience, and it is a tale that children continue to enjoy. Children should be encouraged to respond to the characters, the story, and the values reflected—as parts and as a whole. Children should be made aware of the fact that "Cinderella" is a universal tale that emerged in various forms in different countries all over the world. Children enjoy comparing these different versions of the story and making up modern-day Cinderella stories that reflect different character traits and values.

This fourth perspective on response to text, like the New Eclecticism, does not exclude anything that has been previously held. Rather, it is a larger circle within which preceding perceptions are nested (Armstrong, 1991). Thus, the actualization perspective suggests that teachers should be encouraged to teach literature, initially, according to their personal perspectives, as long as instruction is carried out well and in a nondoctrinaire way. Whatever perspective the teacher starts with, it is likely to evolve toward a more "whole" or comprehensive perspective. This evolution is theorized to occur for the following reasons:

- There is a natural developmental process from the relatively primitive text-based perspective to the more sophisticated actualization perspective. As perspectives on response to literature become more advanced, they become more holistic.
- Education and experience tend to move thinking people away from narrow views and toward more holistic, encompassing ones.
- Regardless of what perspective we *teach* from, children *themselves* tend to lead us toward more holistic response modes, simply by reflecting the many and complex ways people can be, feel, and respond.
- In any given school, teachers are likely to represent a variety of perspectives. Typical social interaction is likely to bring about greater accommodation and a general movement toward a more encompassing perspective.

Table 5.1 provides a graphic summary of the developmental nature of these views along two continua: the effect of the *literature* on the *reader,* and the contribution of the *reader* to the *literary experience.* From a *text-based perspective,* for example, the reader contributes little to the literary experience, and literature has little personal effect on the reader. The *social–political perspective* emphasizes the effect of literature on the reader, while the *transactive perspective* stresses the reader's contribution to the literary experience. The more recent *actualization*

**Table 5.1**

### Four Perspectives on Story Literature

| | Social–Political Perspective / Actualization Perspective | | |
|---|---|---|---|

*(Diagram: vertical axis labeled "Effect of the literature on the reader" ranging from **low** to **high**; horizontal axis labeled "Contribution of the reader to the aesthetic experience" ranging from **low** to **high**.)*

**Social–Political Perspective (1935–1969)**
Literature is the means by which society hands down values and maintains continuity. The value of literature is entirely dependent upon the context in which it is created and/or encountered.

**Actualization Perspective (emerging view)**
The literary experience is part of a larger process of reader self-actualization. This larger "whole" occurs naturally, but can be enhanced by taking it apart, now and then, to focus on and develop the parts.

**Text-Based Perspective (1912–1939)**
Literature is a fixed "commodity," with fixed value irrespective of context. Knowledge of "good" literature is desirable as a kind of status symbol.

**Transactive Perspective (1970s to present)**
The literary experience is one in which the reader and the text interact with one another. The text may be different for each reader, depending upon what each brings to the reading experience.

*Contribution of the reader to the aesthetic experience*

*perspective* merges the social–political emphasis on the effect of the text on the reader with the transactive emphasis on the reader's own contribution. More importantly, the actualization perspective acknowledges that the holistic literary experience can be enhanced by periodically focusing on one or more of the other perspectives.

Be reminded that these perspectives on the literary experience address the fictional, or narrative, side of literature. These essentially are models for better understanding and promoting *aesthetic* reading—or seeing and appreciating the artistic-expressionistic aspects of literature. The chapters ahead describe additional models and methods for developing critical–creative responses to nonfiction, or facts and concepts, more so than stories, language, and forms. One such emerging model, called the "transformational theory," is being developed explicitly to address reading in a school context. It deals with the role of text as a way to guide and direct growth, or transform the reader, as well as to inform and entertain (Manzo, Garber, & Kahn, work in progress). For now, let's continue to explore the rather natural ways in which emergent higher-order literacy can be developed by eliciting children's responses to story-type literature.

## THE ROLE OF LITERATURE IN THE TEACHING OF READING

Alongside the movement to integrate the study of reading and literature, there is a growing sense that literature should be studied as art and not overly intertwined with reading. Maryanne Eeds put it rather directly when she says,

> We cannot confuse literature study with learning to read . . . Learning to read comes with writing and reading practice. Literature study is studying

about literature and how it came about, how the author did it. All children can take part in whatever literature study they want to. The choice should be theirs (Eeds, in an interview by Yvonne Siu-Runyan, 1991, p. 11).

There is merit in Eeds' view that the process of learning to read should be understood as a separate and different process from literature study. Still, there are several good reasons, with which Eeds probably would agree, for an emphasis on literature as part of the earliest literacy education of children. These reasons are addressed below, under the headings of "Why Teach Literature?" and "Why Teach Story Literature?".

### Why Teach Literature?

The most important reason for teaching literature is that it contributes, early on, to the development of evaluative thinking, an aspect of critical thinking, or higher-order literacy. It does this, ironically, precisely because it *is* art. Because evaluation of art is subjective, each child is free to like or dislike each piece, irrespective of an objective "right answer." In practical terms, this means that literature study provides the ideal context for asking the simple questions: "How do you feel about this piece?" (a higher-order evaluative question) and "Why do you feel this way?" (an equally challenging, higher-order explanatory question).

These two questions are inherent in any discussion of literature and are the chief vehicles for developing higher-order thinking in children and adults. More importantly, raising these and similar questions raises a classroom interaction between teacher and students from simple recitation to an instructional conversation. As Higgins (as cited by Eeds, 1991) puts it, every teacher sets out to orchestrate such a "grand conversation," only to have it turn, too often, into something more like an inquisition. Evaluative thinking about literature focuses discussion; it challenges thinking; and it is the most appropriate way to seek a reasonable middle ground between excessive recitation and formless conversation. In short, it is *teaching,* not telling. It is not simply conversation, it is "instructional conversation" (Tharp & Gallimore, 1989a).

Parts of the next question and answer are redundant with the above, but there are some special considerations as to why schools find it necessary to teach story literature. The reflective teacher will want to be familiar with both the pro's and con's.

### Why Teach Story Literature?

If you love literature, this question may seem odd. However, not all children love to read literature for pleasure. Some view reading as largely utilitarian, and there are those who simply do not like to read much of anything; they are not necessarily uncouth or insensitive.

Since we must teach all children, it seems reasonable to try to understand the perspectives of children as much as the perspectives on literature. One way to begin to understand others is first to understand ourselves. Let's see why teachers have tended to be strong advocates of story literature.

Cullinan (1987b) offers two main reasons for a literary emphasis in the primary grades: "to teach students how to read; and to make them want to read" (p. 2).

Cullinan asked *other* educators the question, "why teach literature?" and received equally simple and strong responses. Dorsey Hammond, for example, a professor and popular inservice teacher trainer replied, "Well, you can't teach reading comprehension if you don't have a good story to work with" (as quoted in Cullinan, 1987, p. 2).

Good literature is compelling and can be part of a collective social experience. Cullinan supports this point with an anecdote that will strike a note of truth in anyone who loves to read. She tells of how she was anxious to read Judy Blume's book *Blubber* the year it was published. When she asked a student in a school she was visiting for the book, the student answered that, "Nancy has it now but she promised to give it to Beth when she's done, and after that, Zoe gets it, then Lisa, then Nicole, and then ME! Maybe next time you come you can have it!" (1987b, p. 4). Blume's book paints a spellbindingly true picture of the behavior of fourth-graders. In so doing, it invites reflection on characters' motives and behavior and sparks insight and understanding of real-life acquaintances and situations—all of which are fundamental objectives of education at every level.

Another powerful, though more demonstrable, influence of story literature is upon language. We have noticed, for example, that children who are taught to read in a traditional basal-reader program begin to speak and write in the unnatural way basal sentences sometimes are constructed. Similarly, when children are exposed to good literature, their language becomes elevated, more imaginative, colorful, and conversational.

This response is not surprising since researchers have shown that children tend to assume the language and the attitudes inherent in the language to which they are most frequently exposed (Cazden, 1972; Chomsky, 1972; Whitehurst et al., 1988a,b). Considering, then, the power of language to influence how we interpret and organize our experiences, it seems only natural to expose children to the most poignant and insightful language available, and that is almost a definition of story literature.

Another reason to support story literature is its function in helping one to build empathy with and understanding of others. The writer C. S. Lewis put it simply when he said, "through literature I become a thousand [people] and yet remain myself" (as cited by Arthea Reed, 1988).

Literature can do more to naturally promote a multicultural and humane outlook than many an explicit lesson. In being a "thousand people," the child gets to walk in the life of protagonists who are culturally different, racially different, and of different ages and socioeconomic backgrounds. *Vicarious experience is experience* and can be a powerful means of learning to a profound level.

Additionally, literature feeds *fantasy* and *wonder*. Fantasy may be little more than diversion or embroidery for some people's tastes, but *wonder* is the basis of human motivation to learn. Another important reason to develop literary appreciation and thoughtful response to text in children is its match with the developmental patterns of early childhood. Let us explain. Young children do not have the informational and conceptual background for understanding much of what is taking place around them. They have only the vaguest idea of what a President is, or a Congress, or even where money comes from (we're all vague about where it goes!). However, what they do have, and use well, are life experiences, and in real life these unfold in a way that resembles story formats. Young children also have not yet come to be overly restricted in their thinking about what can and cannot be, so they remain more open and even joyful in their enthusiasm for fantasy and magical tales. Hence, story literature offers a potentially engaging and logical place for them to begin to engage life and its complexities and to acquire a sense of how to read and respond to text while incidentally building basic reading–writing skills, a fund of information and conceptual knowledge, and a pretty acute sense of how to think critically and creatively.

In summary, the values attached to story literature in the schools could be listed as follows:

- Literature study enhances reading fluency and builds further interest in reading.
- Literature is a model of what authors do; as such, it provides a means of improving oral and written expression.
- Literature is a major source of content information and vocabulary/concept acquisition.
- Literature is a transaction with text that permits personal meaning-making and social–emotional growth and adjustment (Ediger, 1991); it helps children "to relive and shape their own life experiences, to prelive or anticipate events, and to vicariously experience the lives of others" (Furner, 1991, p. 14).

It strikes us that the evolution of the theoretical perspectives on literature discussed earlier parallel and are becoming fused with the evolution of our understandings of the complex and multifaceted agenda of school, of society, and of individual growth and development. Teaching quality literature is one practical way to meet many of these complex needs with a minimum of additional demands on teachers and schools.

## QUALITY LITERATURE

It is said that there are some practical complications in teaching literary appreciation and response to text. One is the assumption that there is something that can be identified as "quality literature." Since literature is art, and art is a matter of personal taste, it will always be arguable whether some pieces should be singled out to be called "great" or important. In school programs, however, some pieces must be selected to be taught, for some very practical reasons:

1. A few common pieces make classroom instruction and discussion more focused and fruitful.
2. Some means of determining what constitutes quality literature needs to be undertaken by adults, since it is through these initial exposures that acquired tastes are developed.
3. A core literature offers a shared experience and common allusions to a society that demands that its cultural heritage and continuity be preserved in some way.
4. The identification of newer "important pieces" is now seen as equally necessary for expanding and reflecting the cultural and ethnic diversity within American schooling and the increase of contact with the larger global community.

5. Core literature is only one small part of the larger self-selected and teacher-guided exposure to quality literature—while it is inescapable that the pieces chosen are going to be deemed "important," it is a false inference that those that are not chosen are not great or important.

It simply is not necessary for a literature program that contains a "core" component to have this become the mechanism through which cultural diversity and outlook is pinched, or made exclusive. It can, in fact, be one of the best places for representing multicultural outlooks, as these compare and contrast with the world pictured in traditional literature. But this still leaves the irksome question of just what is a "good" or quality piece of literature. While there clearly is no easy answer to this question, it is the obligation of those who would be reflective teachers to pause and ponder the issue.

### What Is Quality Literature?

Jalongo (1988) points out that since quality literature essentially is art, it must be judged by the same criteria by which sculpture or music is evaluated. These criteria are a bit elusive and even may change with times and contexts. For example, *My Friend Leslie* (Rosenberg, 1983) is a picture book with characters who are physically disabled. It has sprung into popularity with our raised consciousness toward all children. Similarly, *Little Black Sambo* (Bannerman, 1923), has lost popularity because it perpetuates offensive stereotypes and offends good judgment.

So the term "good" book can rest on a "fragile raft of opinion" (Stewig, 1980, p. 10). Nonetheless, there are some terms and standards to guide teachers and parents. Among "good" books, it also is useful to distinguish between "classic" books and "important" books. As a rule, classics of children's literature: (a) cut across several stages of childhood; (b) contain writing that can be characterized as having fine style, originality of concept, and universal appeal; and (c) withstand the test of time (Oppenheim, Brenner, & Boegehold, 1986). But there are other pieces, as noted above, that can be called "important," and may become classics because they introduce fresh perspectives and broaden cultural outlook.

There are several ways to determine the likely quality of children's literature. One is to read reviews, discuss the books with others who have read them, and of course to read them oneself. Another is to buy or borrow books and magazines on books and to consult a librarian who specializes in children's literature—about 54 percent of public libraries have at least one designated specialist in children's literature (U.S. Bureau of Statistics Newsletter, March 1992). A growing number of bookstores stock only children's books. Their owners and buyers are very knowledgeable about what is available and what children like. They also tend to be particularly friendly toward teachers. Some even are willing to lend books to teachers to share with a class. See Table 5.2 for sources of reviews of children's books and Table 5.3 for books of reviews.

### Children's Responses to Quality Literature

Another means of determining whether a book is quality literature is to do some "kid watching." Children tend to exhibit certain behaviors when they are enjoying a

## Table 5.2

### General Sources for Reviews of Children's Books

| Journals and Magazines | | These journals and magazines regularly review picture books, publish articles about children's literature, and/or publish books about children's literature for teachers and parents. |
|---|---|---|
| American Library Association | School Library Journal and Booklist | |
| Association for Childhood Education International | Childhood Education | |
| Council on Interracial Books for Children | Interracial Books for Children Bulletin | |
| Horn Book, Incorporated | The Horn Book Magazine | |
| Human Sciences Press | Day Care and Early Education | |
| International Reading Association | The Reading Teacher | |
| National Association for the Education of Young Children | Young Children | |
| National Council of Teachers of English | Language Arts and Bulletin of the Children's Literature Assembly | |
| Allen Raymond, Incorporated | Early Years | |
| University of Chicago | Bulletin of the Center for Children's Books | |
| **Newspapers** | | This supplement publishes an annual review of children's books. |
| New York Times | New York Times Literary Supplement | |
| **Annotated Bibliographies** | | |
| R. R. Bowker Company | Best Books for Children and other annotated bibliographies | |
| National Council of Teachers | Adventuring with Books; Reading Ladders for Human Relations | |
| **Indexes of Reviews** | | These indexes synthesize the major children's book reviews that are published in a variety of sources. |
| Gale Research Publishing | Book Review Index and Children's Literature Reviews | |
| **Publishing Companies** | | These publishers produce catalogs, bound in large volumes, that advertise that company's award-winning books |
| Publishing companies such as Dial, Harper & Row, and Putnam | Trade Publishers Annual | |

Jalongo (1988), p. 23.

## Table 5.3

### Selected Books of Reviews and Recommendations for Children's Books

1. Children's Choices (1983). Nancy Roser & Margaret Frith (Eds.); International Reading Association; 800 Barksdale Road; Newark, DE 19711

2. Children's Literature in the Classroom (1987). Bernice E. Cullinan (Ed.); International Reading Association; 800 Barksdale Road; Newark, DE 19711

3. Comics to Classics (A Parent's Guide to Books for Teens and Preteens) (1988). Arthea J. S. Reed; International Reading Association; 800 Barksdale Road; Newark, DE 19711. This book also contains thoughtful recommendations for using television as part of the literary experience, a point discussed elsewhere in the chapter.

book. Specialists in children's literature (Cullinan, 1987b; Jalongo, 1988; Monson & Sebesta, 1991) say to look for these signs:

**Physical**   When children are enjoying having a book read to them, they act as they do when enjoying a television program or most anything else. They pull up close to it. They want to see the illustrations. They will even hug a book and ask to borrow it.

**Attentional**   They will lean forward, often with transfixed facial expressions, to blot out other possible distractions. They will protest if pages are skipped or turned too rapidly. Expect facial expressions and body movements that are connected to the prose, and an almost involuntary chiming in at an appropriate moment—especially in predictable or repetitive books.

**Verbal**   Children will say things that indicate that they are engaged and comprehending. They might question, as Jalongo notes, why everyone in the family recognizes their own dog in *Harry the Dirty Dog* (Zion, 1956). Children also will reflect appreciation and impact by incorporating some of the storybook language and vocabulary into their own, much as older children and adults do with movies that become part of their literary and popular culture experience, as in: "I'm going to make him an offer he can't refuse."

**Expressional**   Look for children to reflect aspects of their favorite stories in their artwork, dramatizations, and writing. See some samples of these in the pages ahead.

Jalongo (1988) further points out that there are even some ways to predict when children will respond favorably to a book. One is to try to select books that have great sensory appeal. *Pumpkin Pumpkin* (Tetherington, 1986) is an example of a book that offers great visual and tactile stimulation. A second way is to select books that are intellectually stimulating in the sense of fulfilling the natural inquisitiveness of children. Manzo and Legenza (1975b) developed a formula that was extensively validated (Legenza & Knafle, 1978; 1979; Legenza, 1980; Samson & Wescott,

| FIGURE 5.1 | **Children Write in Response to Reading** |

Diana
Grade 4

Dec. 11, 91
Creative Writing

Dear Mimi Brosky,
   I love the book you wrote, <u>The House at R</u>
<u>Rose Street</u>. I enjoyed it very much! I'm going to
try and get the continuation of it out of the library.
I think you made the characters seem alive. You made
me understand that even though people have different religions and
races, we all have feelings.

Sincerely,
Diana Seitelman

| FIGURE 5.2 | **Children Create in Response to Reading** |

1983) for estimating the degree to which children were likely to respond verbally to a given picture. They found that pictures containing children and showing action were the most stimulating of question raising and comments about the people and events depicted. (See Appendix A for the formula.) A third way to anticipate when a book will likely be engaging and memorable is if it contains affective appeal. The affective appeal can be to feelings of sympathy, humor, craftiness, or even anxiety. In recommending *Timothy Goes to School* (Wells, 1981), for example, Jalongo (1988) reminds teachers that starting school is not all instant fun and friendship, but also contains a certain amount of apprehension and having to contend with new and sometimes irksome personalities.

A fourth way to anticipate the likely appeal of a book is to select ones that involve a developmental issue facing children of that age. This is so powerful a factor that most of modern mass media marketing is based on matching television shows and products to the age and developmental demographics of the audience they may wish to reach. Doing this effectively requires the teacher to have some empathy and to engage in a little retrospection. Jalongo (1988) offers the example of selecting a picture book for a very small child by asking what the child faces. Two answers that she arrives at are the confusing and doubting moments waiting for a parent to return and facing a reprimand for making a mess. Omerod's (1985) *Dad's Back* and *Messy Baby* match this developmental woe and will catch even a baby's interest.

Finally, one of the most reliable guides to selecting a book that will suit a given child or small group is children's past preferences and their responses to interest inventories (Monson & Sebesta, 1991). There is a natural tendency to be drawn to things that are like our last pleasant experience. That is the simple reason why even adult readers will read most anything by a certain author or in a certain genre that is associated with an earlier pleasant experience. Of course, interests and tastes change, but they tend to evolve, more so than to change abruptly, so they generally are good bets to follow until evidence for a new direction emerges.

## DEVELOPING CHILDREN'S APPRECIATION FOR STORY LITERATURE

### Helping Children to Like Books

Classrooms that help children like books are not just happy accidents. They are the result of the carefully woven thoughts and actions of a reflective teacher, who sees classroom space as a conducive environment in which to cultivate literacy. Hickman (1983) has pulled together some very basic pointers to the teacher wishing to build such an environment. Some of these pointers are deceptively simple and have been alluded to earlier in the chapter on oral reading. Each needs to be reflected upon and converted into actions that come together like a musical composition to form an enveloping literary environment.

**Children Mirror the Teacher's Enthusiasm**   The teacher needs to provide signs of personal interest in books and reading. This may be done by sharing autographed copies of books from one's personal collection or by displaying a poster or stuffed toy character from a favorite book.

**Children Mirror the Teacher's Perspective**   The teacher who finds reason to say things like, "Now here is something that I didn't like at first but have learned to really enjoy!" is instructing children in a most powerful way to be open to new possibilities and to expect to be transformed by what they read and discuss. Such comments also encourage children to make similar observations that can be quite self-reflective and enlightening. One of the writers heard a fifth-grader making this surprisingly mature observation: "After I've tried to read something and still don't like it, I'm really interested to hear why other kids do. Then I may even try it again."

**The Classroom Itself Should Be Filled with "Well-Selected" Books**   The best and simplest meaning for "well-selected" is books that children at a particular age and grade level are likely to find interesting. Fourth-graders, for example, are likely to find immediate appeal in these recommendations: *Tales of a Fourth Grade Nothing,* by Blume; *How to Eat Fried Worms,* by Rockwell; and *The Mouse and the Motorcycle,* by Cleary (Hickman, 1983). Titles also should meet other meanings for "well-selected," such as stories of depth that would bear rereading and reflection. Using fourth-graders again as the example, Hickman (1983) recommends: Babbitt's *Tuck Everlasting;* Cooper's *The Dark Is Rising;* Steig's *Abel's Island;* and Konigsburg's *From the Mixed-Up Files of Mrs. Basil E. Frankweiler.* Another means suggested by Hickman for raising the attractiveness of books to the "well-selected" category is to group or connect them in some meaningful way. For example, books can be collected and made available by one author, or the same illustrator, or by some theme such as spooky, nature, or survival stories. The next point is highly related, and sometimes overlooked.

**Children Need Easy Access**   Books, Hickman says, need to be so accessible as to almost be unavoidable. This typically means having them at eye level and wherever children congregate. There are three ideal places for displaying books: on window sills, on the chalkboard rail, and on low bookcases. Some schools have installed narrow, upright shelves along a classroom wall that permit books to be displayed in an open position—either to an attractive inner page or with the back and front cover spread and exposed. In any case, books sitting neatly on shelves with only their spines showing rarely excite interest. Having books very accessible also pays off when children are asked to talk about what they have read. Children always seem to have much more to say about a book in informal interviews when they can handle it while they are talking (Hickman, 1983). We find that students and teachers often will pass a book back and forth between them, stirring reminiscences of what they read or felt. The presence of the book also helps to structure the conversation roughly into the sequence that has a clearer beginning, middle, and logical ending point. Attractive and accessible books are of little value without the next simple point.

**Time Must Be Made for Browsing and Choosing**   The easiest way to achieve this is to designate a specific time every day for free reading. Many different kinds of reading experiences can occur at this time. Some students may be selecting a book, others reading one previously selected, and some even quietly passing around one that they have read and sharing their experiences with it. The latter

Make time and space for browsing and choosing

may seem a bit distracting, but as Hickman reminds us, it tends to "amplify a book's natural appeal to add the attraction of a pleasant social contact" (1983, p. 4). If possible, the reading period should be followed by some other activity that could be used flexibly. This permits youngsters who are "hooked" on a book to complete it, or those in a particularly engaging conversation to see it through. Of course the teacher should never fear to call "time" and urge youngsters to move on.

**Provide Personal Introductions to Books**   Even the best and most accessible displays of books can leave a gap between the child and the book. Few things can close this gap as well as a personal introduction. Treat new books like "guests at a party," suggests Hickman. Introduce them around to youngsters who you think might wish to engage them and adopt them as friends. Influential teachers will do this with incidental comments in group settings, as well as privately to individual students when they are browsing to select a book, or even on informal occasions on the playground or while walking back to class from recess. The results of such efforts are greatly amplified by actually placing the book in the child's hands.

**Read Aloud and Be Seen Reading**   The old saying that "more is caught than can be taught" certainly applies here. The *teacher should be seen reading* and should read aloud to a class at least once a day. Remember especially to read aloud poems and more difficult pieces, since children may experience difficulty in accessing these by themselves. A poem or story read aloud can be used as an informal way to introduce youngsters to an author or style that is represented in a basal or trade book found in the classroom. (See the previous chapter for hints on reading aloud to a class, urging parents to do so, and providing opportunities for youngsters to do so as well.)

**Use Books to Stimulate Responding**   One of the basic purposes of reading is to enrich thought. It is essential that activities and opportunities be planned for youngsters to discuss a book formally. Many teaching procedures are recommended in the text for prompting and guiding serious analysis and discussion. Basically, however, these are all built on the simple proposition that students must react or respond to text. The teacher who fails to ask regularly for responses will lull children into a nonresponsive, nonconstructive mode of reading and thinking. The

**Reading Prompts Writing**

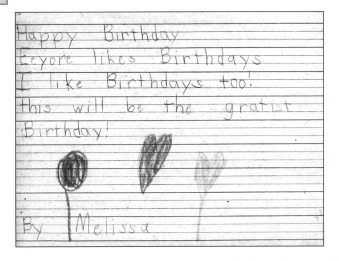

foundation of all efforts to build higher-order literacy skills very simply is to create a willingness and an opportunity for readers to respond. Be sure every contact with books and text is bathed in open-ended questions such as, "What did you think of _____?"; "Did you like this character/book/story?"; "Did you come away with any new ideas after reading this book?" It has been our observation that this is a distinctively American approach to reading that is founded on our high regard for individualism and innovation. In other parts of the world, approaches to evaluative reading and thinking seem to be more strongly based on heritage and/or consensus.

**Provide Opportunities to Represent Literature**    Once children realize that it is right and proper for them to have feelings or reactions to text, it becomes increasingly logical for them to wish to reflect these sentiments in a variety of ways. This is an excellent opportunity to encourage youngsters to work in alternate representational modes other than typical verbal responses. Children can be asked to make a drawing, collage, mural, clay sculpture, or other representation of their feelings or impressions of a story or some of its characters. Drawing can serve as a fine rehearsal for writing (Wells, 1992). Have youngsters explain what their artistic expression means to them. The process of trying to represent and articulate feelings is quite challenging at any level. Reinforce these early attempts at interpretation with verbal assertions and by displaying the actual representations in the classroom and about the school. Much of the success of such artistic efforts rests on having adequate space and resources available: paper, paints, felt tip pens, clay, etc.

**Build Appreciation from Cumulative Experiences**    Appreciation of some pieces of literature is an acquired taste that doesn't always happen easily or quickly. Take the time to build appreciation. To achieve this it may be necessary to teach

**FIGURE 5.4**   **Reading Stimulates Imaginative Responding**

children to delay immediate gratification and to welcome new possibilities. Hickman (1983) offers some vivid examples of how this occurred. In one case, a first-grade teacher shared *Say It!,* by Zolotow (1983). The children were less than enthusiastic. She then tied the seasonal content of the book to the time of the year (autumn) and to the study of trees and leaves and related writing. She read the story two more times aloud and encouraged discussion again. By this time the children were noting and responding favorably to words like "splendiferous" and "zigzagged." They even began to incorporate these words into their own stories. They also developed a new appreciation for the illustrator's techniques by talking about the effects created— such as how the lines up and down the trunk of a tree made it look very, very rough. In short, they came not only to appreciate a previously unappreciated work, but they expanded their capacities and will to appreciate some things that were a "stretch" for them. This is a step beyond greater literary appreciation to greater social and emotional maturity, and the basis for the kind of wonder and inquiry that leads to a desire to further converse and read.

### Developing Eclectic and Acquired Tastes

What about books that children don't seem to like? Should we not bother with these? In general, the golden rule of teaching literature is to meet the tastes of children so that they may be engaged and induced to read and grow. However, as mentioned previously there also are compelling reasons to expose children to books that are not initially received enthusiastically. Consider just two reasons for the moment. First, books that are not enthusiastically received tend to represent an undeveloped side of a child; as such they can be used as a staging area for developing broader tastes and empathy for people who are drawn to such books. Secondly, unenthusiastically received books often tend to reveal topics and styles of writing that are outside the child's present knowledge, interest, or taste. Hence, the information can be informally used to identify objectives for future lessons aimed at helping children to cultivate eclectic tastes and values (Knafle, Wescott, & Pascarella, 1988) and a knowledge base that is characteristic of students who are more mature and literate. Motivation to read, and more, to read broadly, begins early. See now how to help children like books and to use books to broaden tastes and encourage transactions with text.

### Obstacles to Reading Story Literature

Fiction tells about human experience in story form. If a child does not generally wish to engage in storybook reading, there are these reasons to consider:

1. The "messages" in the stories do not match their cultural outlook, experience, and/or ability to empathize.
2. The story itself is not engaging or well told.
3. The writing style is inconsiderate or assumes too much for its intended audience.
4. The student is not experientially, factually, or intellectually up to age-grade expectations.
5. The reader lacks the semantic and linguistic sophistication to handle the material.
6. The child has a nonfiction orientation or even a personal dis-orientation to story forms.

Having considered these sources of inhibition to enjoyment of reading, following are seven ways to enhance literary appreciation.

1. Provide special spaces and materials in early childhood classrooms (e.g., book displays, quiet reading areas, learning centers of various types).
2. Provide manipulative materials and opportunities for children to interact both with peers and adults (labeled cardboard "mailboxes," envelopes and notepaper, number- and shape-based puzzles and games, puppets, etc.).
3. Present concepts and topical material from an interdisciplinary perspective (develop activity units on topics that invite the use of information from many subject areas—listening, singing, counting, observing, etc.)
4. Plan classroom experiences that emulate functional life experiences (such as developing an activity unit that culminates in setting up a flea-market type sale).
5. Use and encourage attention to environmental print and labeling (label room sections and learning center areas; use additional labels within centers and around the room; collect reproductions of common signs such as stop signs, restroom labels, and frequently seen consumer logos to use in a separate learning center and in other activities).

6. Provide multiple opportunities for children to write or dictate for different purposes and to different audiences—the teacher, a parent, a peer, a volunteer (Morrow, 1988).

7. Have children keep a "character journal"—a written diary kept by the reader as he or she assumes the role of the main character. This is an especially good way to help youngsters build empathy and maturity, since they write in the first person, from the character's point of view, and interact with the teacher and buddies in that same voice (Hancock, 1993).

These and other recommendations are discussed in greater detail below. Specific suggestions are given for allocating space and materials and for teaching story-type literature in ways designed to promote emergent higher-order literacy.

## DETAILS OF SPACE AND MATERIALS ALLOCATION AND TEACHING FOR EMERGENT HIGHER-ORDER LITERACY

### CLASSROOM SPACE AND MATERIALS ALLOCATIONS

As the chief architect of learning, the teacher needs to give attention to the allocation of space and materials in the classroom. Three types of space and materials allocations deserve particular attention in the emergent literacy classroom. They are: the Library Corner, the Expressions Area, and the Learning Center.

Here are some tips for assembling each of these. Notice how these areas can provide most of the physical requirements necessary to meet many of the concerns previously noted.

The materials and space allocations suggested for the Library Corner and for what the writers call the Expressions Area are based largely on recommendations assembled from several sources, but especially Lesley Mandel Morrow (1988).

### The Library Corner

The Library Corner needs to be clearly defined and should afford privacy and some protection from most distractions. It should accommodate four to six children comfortably at one time. This can usually be accomplished by setting two bookcases at right angles to one another near a corner of the room. Most conventionally, it is necessary to have a table or some desks with headsets for listening to recorded stories. Some teachers also like to furnish the Library Corner with a rug, pillows, a rocking chair, and a cozy spot created from something like an old bathtub with some pillows in it or an oversized carton with door and window cutouts. This can be opened on one side and has an additional large hole cut in the top for extra light. The children can help in constructing it, painting it, or covering it with contact paper. It is best to have a rule that only one child at a time may use the "cozy corner."

The Library Corner may also include viewmasters with story wheels, puppets, felt stories, big books, and materials that children can use to play school. Children often will play school without coaching where seating and big books are conducive to one child reading to others or to turn-taking.

Create inviting places to read

Assemble a classroom library corner

The remainder of the library area should be dressed with posters that advertise books and reading [for posters, contact the American Library Association; 50 East Huron Street; Chicago IL 60611] and with various stuffed toys and representations from children's literature. Try to provide five to eight books per child at several reading levels. Replace about thirty books about every ten school days. Ask children to place a colored "sticky-note" tag with their name on it standing up out of any book they are currently reading so you won't remove it from the room before they have finished. Again, books should represent a wide variety of types and genre: poetry, pictures, joke books, information, fables, and even magazines and comics. Try to stock multiple copies of popular items.

Books and other print literature can be borrowed from the public or school libraries. They can be purchased at flea markets. Or, they can be acquired from donations and gifts from individuals, parents, and cooperating businesses. Many schools solicit a local store or industry at the beginning of each year that pledges to be a "business partner." Both the employer and employees of a business partner often will help with financial, material, and volunteer assistance.

### The Expressions Area

The most frequent forms of expression are writing, drawing, and paper constructions. However, some schools—particularly communications magnet schools such as the second author is affiliated with—now are encouraging students to make "TV commercials," videotaped plays, and content-based documentaries as well (Valmont, 1992). For more on how to do this, see "storyboarding" later in this chapter. In general, the Expressions Area requires little more than a table and chairs, felt-tipped markers, large and small crayons, regular and colored pencils and sharpener, chalk, chalkboard, and paper of a variety of types and colors. We have seen some youngsters who have otherwise been difficult to motivate participate for long hours in writing and practicing to make a videotaped commercial, whether it actually is videotaped or not. The Expressions Area should have a primer typewriter, a computer and printer, a tape recorder (for when a teacher is not available to take a child's dictation story), and a videocamera and VCR player. The latter should be

Involve children in productive expression

used only under supervision because of the potential dangers of breakage and bodily harm (from equipment falling on children or electrical shocks).

Another simple addition to the Expressions Area is a "mailbox," accompanied by stationery, envelopes, and some stamps. These can be used for writing to parents, pen pals, or children in other classes. A Notice Board can be used for within-class notes from one child to another or to and from the teacher.

Promote communication through a classroom mailbox area

The Expressions Area, like the library, should contain posters, puppets, drawings, and paper mache representations from children's literature, but these should be limited to samples of the children's own work, rather than commercial products or adult-made fare. The Expressions Area also is the ideal place to display some of the dictated and written stories of the children.

The teacher occasionally should find time to visit the Expressions Area as the lead member of the community of literate people and write or create something (appropriate to children) representing his or her own line of interest. The children will be bemused but also observant of how the teacher works: drafting, trying something, and then improving it, and finally, cleaning up afterwards.

### The Learning Center

There are several possible meanings and definitions of Learning Centers. In this context, they are meant to refer to some hands-on activities that connect literacy to content knowledge objectives and concepts. Morrow (1988) gives the example of a teacher who kept a setting hen whose eggs were about to hatch. The class discussed the care of the hen and kept an experience chart on which they recorded the hen's behavior each day and the eventual hatching of the eggs. Students also kept personal diaries of their feelings and thoughts about the hen and the arrival of the chicks. They were further encouraged to make index cards recording new "Very Own Words" that they acquired as a result of their experiences and discussions. See Box 5.1 for examples from our experiences with this idea.

Consider again now, in much more practical terms, the issue of balancing the direct and incidental teaching of reading. Lamme (1987) calls children's literature "the natural way to learn to read." She further points out that this "whole-language approach stems from research (Newman, 1985; Smith, 1981) on successful learners, especially early readers who learned how to read at home without school instruction" (p. 42). From this point on, we shall begin increasingly to present methods for assisting youngsters to learn to read and to become readers who have not shown, or are not showing, inclination to learn to read and to become readers.

These methods clearly are more direct and intentional. However, we think that you will not find them to be unnatural, but rather sound and appropriate parts of a professional teacher's total repertoire. They also will serve a host of purposes for those who do learn to read easily but still have much to learn about reading as a life-long process.

## LITERATURE-BASED READING INSTRUCTION

Lipka and Gaskill (1992) point out that, contrary to common belief, "Reading instruction in the western world has been literature-based until recently in history" (p. 20). By "recently," they mean until the introduction and growth in popularity of basal readers and, even more recently, when "phonics made its way into reading instruction" (p. 20).

In any case, it is clear that basal and whole-language approaches are moving closer together with each passing year and that some of the issue of literature base being very different is becoming largely a moot point. Let's see now how one might teach with literature, beginning with books that tell stories largely through pictures.

**BOX 5.1**    **Sample Experience Chart and Related Activities**

### EXPERIENCE CHART

|  | Week 1 | Week 2 | Week 3 | Week 4 |
|---|---|---|---|---|
| **Monday** | The hen pecks at anyone who comes near her eggs. | | | |
| **Tuesday** | The hen stands and fluffs her feathers some-times. | | | |
| **Wednesday** | The hen is getting dirty from her own droppings. | | | |
| **Thursday** | | | | |
| **Friday** | | | | |

### My Diary

Monday—My dog didn't fuss when we picked up her pups.

Tuesday—My dog brought some of her food to her pups.

rooster

dropping

Very Own Words    vitamin

inoculation

chicken wire

## Teaching with Picture Books

Picture books tell a story through a combination of *pictures and print.* Many of the things that can be taught with conventional print books can be taught with picture books as well, even at secondary levels (Neal & Moore, 1991). To achieve this requires little more than inducing and then guiding children to engage and make relevant responses to the pictures. There are essentially three ways to do this. These could be called basic paradigms, or models, for teaching with pictures and picture books. The first one epitomizes the whole language approach. The methods that follow move increasingly toward direct teaching, or more along the lines of a pointed intentional "instructional conversation."

**Show and Wait**   This paradigm takes an incidental, nondirective approach. It simply involves showing or introducing a picture book to children in a way that permits them to touch and inspect it in whatever ways they choose, and to simply *wait* until they express something about it. When they do, the teacher is expected to respond, in a caring and natural way, by entering into an authentic conversation about the book.

This incidental approach was used masterfully by the "professor" in Willa Cather's popular book, *Jack-O-Boy.* In the book the professor offers a picture book to Jack-O-Boy, a child who had recently moved into his building. However, the child had to promise to sit quietly and not disturb the professor. It was only a few moments, though, before Jack-O-Boy interrupted the professor's reading with his first irrepressible response: "These pictures are different from the ones in my books. What are these pictures about?" From that humble beginning, both Jack-O-Boy and the professor were drawn into a lively and on-going discussion of that and other picture books and pictures in print books in the professor's home library.

**Show and Comment**   If you are uncomfortable with the timelessness of "show and wait" in school, increase your level of involvement with "show and comment." In this paradigm the teacher shows the picture book and adds an initiating comment or question. "This is an alphabet book that shows an imaginary creature for every letter of the alphabet."

If this does not seem sufficient to stir imagination, then go to the next paradigm, which adds an element of inspection and analysis to generate discussion.

**Reciprocal Show and Tell**   This approach might also be called "show and interact reciprocally." Say to the child, "Take a look at this picture book. Ask me some questions about things in it that you would really like to know, or that you think that a teacher might ask about. I'll answer these, and then ask you some questions that I think of." An interaction such as the following is likely to occur in a typical classroom:

*Student:* What is the name of this book?

*Teacher: The Fairy Alphabet*

*Student:* What are fairies, anyway?

*Teacher:* They're imaginary—not real—people who, in stories, have magical powers.

[*Once the children have asked a few questions, the teacher raises a few that point students toward understandings and concerns that are part of the grade's curriculum.*]

*Teacher:* Does this book look as if it had been written recently or a long time ago?

*Student:* It looks new, but the pictures look old.

*Teacher:* Look inside with me for the "date of publication." Here it is. My, my, it was *first* written in 1877—over a hundred years ago! *This* book, though, is a copy that was made in 1991. How do you suppose we can find out who wrote it?

*Student:* It says it here on this part.

*Teacher:* Yes. It says it right here on the cover, "by Fanny Y. Cory," and if you turn to the first page of print, you will see it again. Look inside now at the imaginary creatures for each letter. See if you can find the one that matches the first letter of your first name. If you like, I'll read aloud the little verse on each page for the first letter of each of your first names.

There are several variations on this paradigm; one that is particularly relevant to school attempts to build recall and attention to detail. It could be called "Reciprocal Recall." It is accomplished by inviting children to study a picture carefully and then to turn their books (or an individual picture) face down. The teacher then asks questions that cause the children to try to recall aspects of the picture. Students then are invited to invert the process by asking the teacher questions in the same way about the same picture, or another one. Students can be paired off, or put in small groups, to engage in this same type of instrumental conversation.

The questions the teacher asks the first time are likely to be the ones that students will learn to ask as well. As importantly, as students learn how to articulate questions, their questions are likely to better reflect their particular interests and perceptions. The teacher should listen carefully for these, since this can be a powerful means of learning what kids care about, and also what they may not understand and need to be taught more about. In other words, this type of interaction also is the basis for diagnostic teaching, or the diagnostic conversation.

This type of reciprocal dialoguing allows the teacher to model good questioning and effective and coherent oral language. This permits students to emulate these, while offering an incidental opportunity for them to signal their special needs and interests. The practice of permitting children to challenge the teacher with questions also provides children with an incidental and thorough way to learn how to conduct a thoughtful, but courteous, line of inquiry. This "language of challenge," as Hansen (1992) aptly called it, is basic to learning how to critique and be critiqued, the essence of critical–evaluative thinking, personal social–emotional development, and school and community effectiveness.

Look now at the details on how to create Language Charts (Roser, Hoffman, Labbo & Farest, 1992) that can be used to elicit responses to text.

### Print Book Responding

It can be quite dreary to have to postpone delight in reading and the spontaneous origination of critical–creative thoughts until decoding strategies are mastered. Reflecting on the needs and nature of children, rather than merely that of reading acquisition, has given new life to the concept of teaching children from their earliest days to experience, read, and respond naturally and constructively to whatever they may be exposed.

Roser, Hoffman, Labbo, and Farest (1992) offer an excellent means to engage young children in an aesthetic response to literature that is personal and with literature that is more challenging than most basal reading fare. Roser and associates refer to their strategy as Language Charts. These are used in a read-aloud program that they call "Language to Literacy." Language Charts are a place to save ideas and responses to stories. They are gathered systematically at the close of "story time talk" (p. 44).

The Language Chart is intended to *follow,* not *replace,* "natural book talk" that grows out of reading. The chart is constructed with drawn boxes that pose questions to match a theme. The example shown in Table 5.4 is built around the theme "Being Different Is Being Special."

The primary purpose of this approach is to teach children how books can be connected thematically, or how they lean on one another. It is a legitimate early form of literary appreciation and criticism. As children build confidence with this process, they begin to talk across books, without prompts, "discovering for themselves how tales are bound" (p. 51). Box 5.2 illustrates how children self-bind, or connect books to personal feelings, experiences, and other books.

Of course the Language Chart approach also can be reversed. That is, students can be encouraged to respond freely, have their responses noted and recorded, and then prompted to organize them into charts that pose questions for which they already would have answers. This could be called learning what you know.

Language Charts can be constructed with empty space for children to add their personal written responses and small group responses. Space can also be provided for artistic works of favorite characters or scenes.

## Table 5.4

### Story Chart for the Unit: "Being Different Is Being Special"

| Title | Author | Who Was Different? | How Were They Different? | What Made the Character Special? |
|---|---|---|---|---|
| *Oliver Button Is a Sissy* | Tomie dePaola | Oliver | Some kids thought Oliver liked the same things as girls | Oliver had talent! |
| *Horton Hatches the Egg* | Dr. Seuss | Horton | Horton was an elephant but he sat on a nest! | Horton was a faithful friend to sit until the elephant-bird hatched. |
| *William's Doll* | etc. | | | |

## A Class Language Chart

*Our Observations*

1. Ezra Jack Keats is the author *and* the illustrator of his books. (Jimmy, Joy)
2. His characters look alike. They are lighter and darker brown. (Salvador)
3. So far, the cover has a picture and in the inside is the same picture. (Christopher)
4. All the stories make me happy. (Tara) What makes us happy is that all their wishes come true. (Christina, Joy, Salvador)
5. The colors that Ezra Jack Keats draws with are dark colors. His colors are different from the kind Tomie dePaola uses because they are light. (Jessica)
6. I am sad at the very beginning and at the end I feel happy. (Jennifer, Mike)
7. The characters of Ezra Jack Keats feel the same way as we do, first they're sad and then they're happy. Their names are mostly Peter and Louie. (Joy)

*From Roser, Hoffman, Labbo, & Farest (1992), p. 8.*

Language Charts provide tangible and historical accounts of children's experience with literature in the classroom. They also can serve to connect fiction and nonfiction material in basals, trade books, and content area study. Let's come back now to an earlier suggestion for the Expressions Area of the classroom.

### Storyboarding to Make Videos

Valmont (1992) urged teachers not to be afraid to make videos. More recently he has suggested the use of storyboards (Thomas, 1988) as a means of confidently tying video-making into all of the language arts (Valmont, 1992), particularly reading. The reading tie-in occurs when the video is used either to dramatize a book or simply to record a critical discussion of a book. See Box 5.3 (p. 164) for specific instructions for using storyboards to encourage a critical–creative response to text.

At the center of all literature-based reading is a collection of practices first formalized by Jeannette Veatch (1959). A brief description of Veatch's Individualized Reading program also serves to reconnect the previously described explicit teaching methods with her somewhat more incidental practices and with those considerably more incidental practices now considered part of the whole-language philosophy. Individualized Reading has four main parts:

**Selecting**   The child freely selects something to read from the student-made stories and books, school or community library, or other available sources of print.

**Reading**   The child reads at his or her own pace, but is encouraged to seek help from the teacher or a buddy with any word, sentence, or idea that may be confusing.

**Conferencing**  At the child's request, the teacher confers with him or her on what they have read, noting through questions and informal conversation how well the child may be understanding what has been read.

**Reacting and Extending**  The child is encouraged to share what has been read with others. Where common needs are realized among several children following individual conferencing, the teacher may conduct some small-group, teacher-directed instruction as part of this step.

This last step, focusing as it does on small-group, teacher-directed instruction, comes full circle back to the explicit teaching option that is part of most school-based literacy programs that would be comfortable under the umbrella of the "New Eclecticism." Notice that the decision to provide explicit instruction arose out of a child-centered need, and that the teacher's move to a directed teaching mode can only be called a reflective and responsive decision. Admittedly, there apparently is some distance between teachers who view individualized reading as part of direct instruction and those who view direct instruction as including some individualized reading. There should be ample room under most schoolhouse roofs for both perspectives to compatibly co-exist, and even positively interact.

For the last topic of the chapter, we shall elaborate on issues involving *book selection,* since this is central to explicit teaching and individualized reading. This section should help you to more clearly see and think about the kinds of children's literature that are available and appropriate for school use.

## SELECTING LITERATURE FOR CHILDREN

### Types of Children's Literature for the Emerging Reader–Writer

The perspective on "response to text" at the beginning of the chapter gave pretty convincing evidence that most of the style characteristics and dimensions of adult literature also can be found in children's books. It may not have been evident, however, that there are other literary elements and formats that are unique to children's books. These characteristics, such as eloquent illustrations and predictable structure and language patterns, are tools that provide support to young readers as they learn to read books on their own for entertainment and enlightenment. You should notice, in the supportive elements and formats described ahead, that some have been mentioned in previous chapters. This more comprehensive listing can be used as a grid, or schema-base, for adding to your ongoing knowledge of literary tools for emerging readers and writers.

**Wordless Books**  tell a story through illustrations alone. These nonprint books are intended to stir imagination, oral language, and to connect children to the notion of books as sources of wonder and enjoyment. Young readers enjoy "reading" wordless books on their own, particularly those that have previously been "read aloud" to them by an adult. For several examples, refer to the listing in Chapter 4. Again, see also Appendix A for a formula for estimating the power of pictures to elicit language from children (Manzo & Legenza, 1975b).

**BOX 5.3**
## Creating a Storyboard

A complete storyboard is made up of a series of cards which are created as the students think their way through the entire video production. In order to decide what to put in the "show" and on the cards, students need to brainstorm their topic, do research if they recognize that there are things they do not know about the subject, think about what the audience will need to see and hear, and plan to reveal the topic in a way that viewers will understand. Storyboarding involves students in all of the language arts: it calls for research and thinking skills, and it calls on both verbal and visual capabilities as well. Shown below is an example of a storyboard card and the types of information students need to consider.

On the **VIDEO** side of the card students can draw or describe what they want the audience to see. Simple stick figures may be used, and arrows can show movements. Rather than refined artwork, students simply need to "hint" at the visual aspects of the scene, since laborious artwork at this point can bog down the creative process. On the **AUDIO** side a sentence or two describing the content of what the audience will hear can be recorded. The full script will be developed after the storyboard is complete, so only key words or simple statements need to be put on the storyboard cards. In the **NOTES** section students can record the techniques they will use to make their video visually interesting. **Transitions** are the techniques students will use to string their smaller scenes and shots together into a flowing program. Angles of shots need to be considered both for visual effect and for dramatic effect, and shots need to be **predetermined** both for visual interest and to ensure that the audience sees exactly what the students want them to see. **Long shots, medium shots, closeups** are all used with intention, revealing just what the director wants the audience to see. Movement of the camcorder from side to side (**pan shots**), up and down (**tilts**), toward or alongside (**dolly** or **truck shots**), or around (**arcs**) the subject in the shot must also be planned before the videotaping takes place, ensuring visual interest.

Once individual cards have been created for each scene and/or shot, they can be tacked to a bulletin board, taped to the chalkboard, or placed flat on a large surface so students involved in the production can come to a consensus that the video is well planned and will communicate to the audience that which they want to communicate.

**Beginning Reader Books** support emerging readers' efforts to read alone by using a carefully controlled vocabulary and simple language to tell stories with interesting themes, plot lines, and characters. Cullinan (1989) recommends these examples:

Bonsall, C. (1974). *And I Mean It, Stanley.* New York: Harper & Row.

Gage, W. (1977). *Down in the Boondocks.* New York: Greenwillow.

Hoban, L. *Arthur's Pen Pal* (1976). *Arthur's Prize Reader* (1978). New York: Harper & Row.

Lobel, A. *Frog and Toad Are Friends* (1970). *Frog and Toad Together* (1972). *Frog and Toad All Year* (1976). *Days with Frog and Toad* (1979). New York: Harper & Row.

____. (1975). *Owl at Home.* New York: Harper & Row.

**BOX
5.3**
cont'd

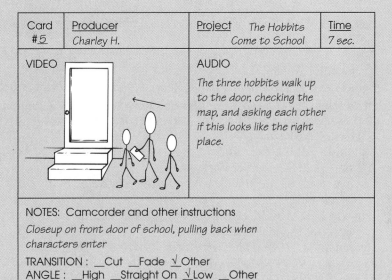

| Card #5 | Producer Charley H. | Project *The Hobbits Come to School* | Time 7 sec. |
|---|---|---|---|

VIDEO

AUDIO

*The three hobbits walk up to the door, checking the map, and asking each other if this looks like the right place.*

NOTES: Camcorder and other instructions

*Closeup on front door of school, pulling back when characters enter*

TRANSITION : __Cut __Fade √ Other
ANGLE : __High __Straight On √ Low __Other
SHOT : LS <u>MS</u> CU ECU PAN TILT DOLLY TRUCK ARC OTHER

Once the final order is determined, the cards can be numbered, and times can be determined. Students can estimate how long the audience should **see** the action and can estimate how long it will take a narrator to speak over each shot or scene. Again, planning for the time factor requires students to make critical judgments about their final production.

*Valmont (1992), p. 122.*

____. (1977). *Mouse Soup.* New York: Harper & Row.

____. (1986). *Grasshopper on the Road.* New York: Harper & Row.

Minarik, E. *Little Bear* (1957). *Father Bear Comes Home* (1959). *Little Bear's Friend* (1960). *Little Bear's Visit* (1961). *A Kiss for Little Bear* (1968). New York: Harper & Row.

Porte, B. *Harry's Dog* (1984). *Harry's Visit.* Illustrated by Y. Abolafia (1983). *Harry's Mom.* Illustrated by Y. Abolafia (1985). New York: Greenwillow.

Sendak, M. (1962). *Pierre.* New York: Harper & Row.

Sharmat, M. W. (1976). *Mooch the Messy.* Illustrated by B. Schecter. New York: Harper & Row.

Van Leeuwen, J. Illustrated by A. Schweninger. *Tales of Oliver Pig* (1979). *Tales of Amanda Pig* (1983). *More Tales of Amanda Pig* (1985). New York: Dial.

**Picture Books** are stories in which the theme and mood presented through words are accompanied by engaging illustrations that support the young reader's efforts to decipher print. Some popular picture books include:

Alexander, M. (1981). *When the New Baby Comes, I'm Moving Out.* New York: Dial.

Allard, H. (1974). *The Stupids Step Out.* Illustrated by J. Marshall. Boston: Houghton Mifflin.

Bemelmans, L. (1939). *Madeline.* Reprint. New York: Viking, 1962.

Brown, M. (1950). *Dick Whittington and His Cat.* New York: Scribner's.

Burton, V. L. (1939). *Mike Mulligan and His Steam Shovel.* Boston: Houghton Mifflin.

Clifton, L. (1976). *Everett Anderson's Friend.* Illustrated by A. Grifalconi. New York: Holt, Rinehart & Winston.

Dragonwagon, C. (1984). *Always, Always.* Illustrated by A. Zeldich. New York: Macmillan.

Emberley, B. (1967). *Drummer Hoff.* Illustrated by E. Emberley. Englewood Cliffs, NJ: Prentice-Hall.

Hauscherr, R. (1985). *My First Kitten.* New York: Four Winds.

Jaspersohn, W. (1980). *Bat, Ball, Glove.* Boston: Little, Brown.

Keeler, S. (1987). *Passport to China.* Philadelphia: Franklin Watts.

Kellogg, S. (1974). *The Mystery of the Missing Red Mitten.* New York:    Dial.

Locker, T. (1984). *Where the River Begins.* New York: Dial.

Ness, E. (1966). *Sam, Bangs and Moonshine.* New York: Holt, Rinehart & Winston.

Piper, W. (1976). *The Little Engine That Could.* Illustrated by R. Sanderson. New York: Platt.

Potter, B. (1984). *Yours Affectionately, Peter Rabbit.* New York: Warne.

Sendak, M. (1982). *Outside Over There.* New York: Harper & Row.

Spender, S. (1966). *The Magic Flute.* New York: Putnam's.

Stevenson, J. (1984). *Worse Than Willie!* New York: Greenwillow.

Tompert, A. (1976). *Little Fox Goes to the End of the World.* New York: Crown.

Weiss, L. (1982). *Chuckie.* New York: Greenwillow.

Wells, R. (1973). *Noisy Nora.* New York: Dial.

____. (1984). *My Teacher Sleeps in School.* Illustrated by E. Weiss. New York: Warne.

Wilhelm, H. (1985). *I'll Always Love You.* New York: Crown.

Williams, M. (1922). *The Velveteen Rabbit.* Illustrated by W. Nicholson. Reprint. New York: Doubleday.

Wood, A. (1984). *The Napping House.* Illustrated by D. Wood. San Diego: Harcourt Brace Jovanovich.

Zolotow, C. (1980). *If You Listen.* Illustrated by M. Simont. New York: Harper & Row.

**Story Structure Books** also referred to as "predictable books," are structured in a way that helps the young reader to anticipate words and actions. Despite this simplicity, pattern books also can contribute to higher-order processes. By imparting the concept of simple story structures, they teach formats for remembering, retelling, and writing stories. Several books of this type are listed in the read-aloud recommendations in Chapter 4. Neal and Moore (1991) offer these additional examples, noting the structure of each:

Cooney, B. (1985). *Miss Rumpus.* New York: Puffin Books. [flashback]

dePaola, T. (1978). *The Clown of God.* New York: Harcourt Brace Jovanovich. [linear]

Friedman, I. (1984). *How My Parents Learned to Eat.* Illustrated by A. Say. Boston: Houghton Mifflin. [flashback]

Jonas, A. (1983). *Round Trip.* New York: Greenwillow. [retraceable]

Noble, T. H. (1987). *Meanwhile Back at the Ranch.* Illustrated by T. Ross. New York: Dial. [parallel]

Numeroff, L. (1985). *If You Give a Mouse a Cookie.* Illustrated by R. Bond. New York: Harper & Row. [circular]

Pryor, B. (1987). *The House on Maple Street.* Illustrated by B. Peck. New York: Morrow. [flashback]

Turner, A. (1985). *Dakota Dugout.* Illustrated by R. Himler. New York: Macmillan. [flashback]

In addition to these examples, one of the most popular types of structure is the *circle story,* in which the character or characters go through a series of adventures, ending up in the same situation or place where they started. Crum (1991) recommends the following circle story books:

Brown, M. W. (1972). *Runaway Bunny.* New York: Harper Collins.

Carle, E. (1969). *The Grouchy Ladybug.* New York: Thomas C. Crowell.

Carle, E. (1989). *The Very Busy Spider.* New York: Putnam.

Hutchins, P. (1971). *Rosie's Walk.* New York: Macmillan.

Maccaulay, D. (1987). *Why the Chicken Crossed the Road.* Boston: Houghton Mifflin.

Numeroff, L. J. (1985). *If You Give a Mouse a Cookie.* New York: Harper & Row.

Sendak, M. (1985). *Where the Wild Things Are.* New York: Harper Collins.

Viorst, J. (1987). *Alexander and the Terrible, Horrible, No Good, Very Bad Day.* New York: Macmillan.

Ward, C. (1992). *Cookie's Week.* New York: Putnam.

Circle stories are simple and fun to diagram, as an aid to discussion of plot sequence and cause-and-effect relationships. Circle diagram forms can be used to help children write their own circle stories. See Figure 5.5 for Crum's (1991) diagram of *Rosie's Walk.*

**Genre Picture Books**[3] are especially suitable for introducing youngsters to the diverse types of fiction and nonfiction. Here are several examples of literary genre

---

[3] Genre (zhahn'-ruh)—a particular type or category of literature; may also be used to reference different categories of art or music.

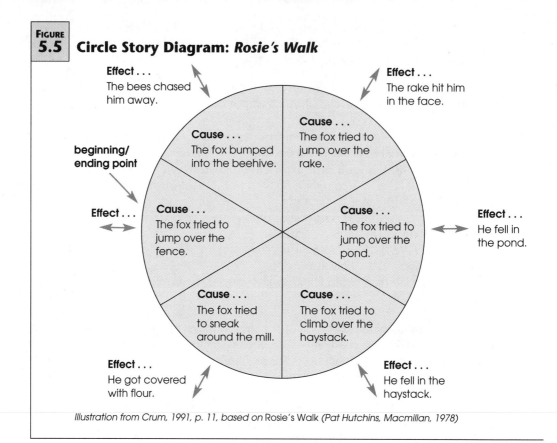

**FIGURE 5.5** **Circle Story Diagram: *Rosie's Walk***

**Effect . . .**
The bees chased him away.

**Effect . . .**
The rake hit him in the face.

**Cause . . .**
The fox bumped into the beehive.

**Cause . . .**
The fox tried to jump over the rake.

**beginning/ ending point**

**Effect . . .**

**Cause . . .**
The fox tried to jump over the fence.

**Cause . . .**
The fox tried to jump over the pond.

**Effect . . .**
He fell in the pond.

**Cause . . .**
The fox tried to sneak around the mill.

**Cause . . .**
The fox tried to climb over the haystack.

**Effect . . .**
He got covered with flour.

**Effect . . .**
He fell in the haystack.

*Illustration from Crum, 1991, p. 11, based on* Rosie's Walk *(Pat Hutchins, Macmillan, 1978)*

from Neal and Moore (1991), ranging from tall tales to allegory.[4] The genre represented is noted in brackets following each book listed below.

Barrett, J. (1978). *Cloudy with a Chance of Meatballs.* Illustrated by R. Barrett. New York: Aladdin. [tall tale]

Brown, R. (1983). *A Dark, Dark Tale.* New York: Scholastic. [mystery]

Bunting, E. (1990). *The Wall.* Illustrated by R. Himler. New York: Clarion. [realistic fiction]

dePaola, T. (1983). *The Legend of the Bluebonnet.* New York: Putnam. [legend]

French, F. (1986). *Snow White in New York.* Oxford: Oxford University Press. [parody]

Hodges, M. (1984). *Saint George and the Dragon.* Illustrated by T. S. Hyman. Boston: Little, Brown. [folktale]

Innocenti, R. (1985). *Rose Blanche.* Mankato, MN: Creative Education. [historical fiction]

---

[4] A story in which characters and events represent things not explicitly stated; an extended metaphor.

Lobel, A. (1982). *Ming Lo Moves the Mountain*. New York: Greenwillow. [allegory]

Maruki. (1980). *Hiroshima No Pika*. New York: Lothrop, Lee, & Shepard. [historical fiction]

Noyes, A. (1983). *The Highwayman*. Illustrated by C. Keeping. Oxford, England: Oxford University Press. [ballad]

Seuss, D. (1984). *The Butter Battle Book*. New York: Random House. [allegory]

Shulevitz, U. (1978). *The Treasure*. New York: Farrar, Strauss & Giroux. [fable]

Steptoe, J. (1981). *Mufaro's Beautiful Daughters: An African Tale*. New York: Scholastic. [folktale]

Turner, A. (1987). *Nettie's Trip South*. Illustrated by R. Himler. New York: Macmillan. [historical fiction]

Wilson, S. (1985). *Beware the Dragons*. New York: Harper & Row. [fantasy]

**Vocabulary Fun Books**   entice interest in vocabulary in any of a variety of ways. The accent is on fun and incidental learning more than on didactic vocabulary lessons. Lapp and Flood (1992) offer some examples that we also endorse.

Butterworth, N. (1987). *Nice or Nasty: A Book of Opposites*. Boston: Little, Brown.

Heller, R. (1989). *Many Luscious Lollipops*. New York: Grosset & Dunlap. Ages 8–12.

Keller, C. (1989). *Tongue Twisters*. New York: Simon & Schuster. All ages.

Kightley, R. (1987). *Opposites*. Boston: Little, Brown.

Limburg, P. (1989). *Weird! The Complete Book of Halloween Words*. Illustrated by B. Lewin. New York: Bradbury Press. Ages 10–14.

McMillan, B. (1989). *Spy on Vacation*. New York: Aladdin.

Roffey, M. (1989). *Mealtime and Bathtime*. New York: Four Winds Press.

Sperling, S. (1985). *Murfles and Wink-A-Peeps: Funny Old Words for Kids*. New York: Crown.

Terban, M. (1989). *Superdupers!: Really Funny Real Words*. New York: Clarion Books. Ages 9–12.

**Concept Books**   are books of literary quality that, through fiction or nonfiction, develop an idea that is derived or inferred form specific instances in some memorable way. Spicola, Griffin, and Stephens (1990) offer these excellent examples:

Ehlert, L. (1989). *Color Zoo*. New York: Lippincott. Uses bright colors and geometric figures to draw readers into an integration of content about zoo animals with concepts of shape and color.

Gans, R. (1984). *Rock Collecting*. New York: Harper & Row. Explains the fun and concept of rock collecting.

Goldin, A. (1989). *Ducks Don't Get Wet*. New York: Crowell. Explains clearly why ducks don't get wet, and, along the way, tells children much about how to set up science experiments.

Rockwell, A. (1989). *My Spring Robin*. New York: Macmillan. Describes the first day of spring in an insightful and easy to read manner.

Alphabet books and counting books are two types of concept books that young readers often enjoy reading on their own. Several popular books of these types are listed in the read-aloud references in Chapter 4.

**Big Books** also mentioned in an earlier chapter, are conventional children's books that are made larger so they can be seen by a class or used by a small group of students. Big Books can be purchased or made in the classroom. The traditional format for using Big Books also illustrates their value: the teacher reads the Big Book while youngsters follow along; students then read it together with the teacher; finally, students read it chorally, or alone. Big Books now include wonderful nonfiction literature as shown in the illustration. As suggested in a previous chapter, teachers can and should use these as models to help children make their own Big Books.

**Play-Acting Books** are books that lend themselves well to Readers Theatre, or are simply plays with roles marked off or which contain vivid scenes that youngsters can enact extemporaneously. Lapp and Flood (1992) and Cullinan (1989) recommend the following books as illustrative of this literary tool for teachers:

Bauer, C. F. (1987). *Presenting Reader's Theater: Plays and Poems to Read Aloud.* New York: Wilson.

Bemelmans, L. (1939). *Madeline.* Reprint. New York: Viking, 1962.

Crocker, B. (1988). *Words that Huddle Together.* Adelaide, Australia: Australian Reading Association.

Dr. Seuss (1939). *The King's Stilts.* New York: Random House.

Kamerman, S. E. (1987). *Plays of Black Americans: Episodes from the Black Experience in America,* dramatized for young people. Boston: Plays.

Kraus, R. (1980). *Mert the Blurt.* Illustrated by J. Aruego and A. Dewey. New York: Windmill Books/Simon & Schuster.

McMaster, B. (1986). *The Haunted Castle: Robena's Rose-Coloured Glasses: Two Children's Plays.* Toronto: Simon and Pierre.

Swortzell, L. (1985). *Six Plays for Young People from the Federal Theatre Project (1936–39).* Westport, CT: Greenwood Press.

**Humorous Books and Poems** set out to bring levity into reading and classroom life. Several educators have written strong endorsements for humor, not merely as a means of introducing mirth into one of those odd, joyless days that can sometimes occur, but also because it can contribute to critical analysis of language and text: "Can anyone explain how the author made us smile with his words?" (Gentile & McMillen, 1978; Whitmer, 1986). Most importantly, however, humor motivates and provides a relatively risk-free environment for playing with ideas. Face it, children love to laugh. Lach (1993) and Whitmer (1986) recommend the following humorous books and poems:

Blume, J. (1972). *Tales of a Fourth Grade Nothing.* New York: Dutton.

Ciardi, J. (1961). *Man Who Sang the Sillies.* New York: Harper & Row.

Doty, R. (1975). *Q's Are Weird O's.* Garden City, New York: Doubleday.

Dunbar, J., & Dunbar, J. (1991). *I Want a Blue Banana.* Boston: Houghton Mifflin.

Fitzgerald, J. D. (1967). *The Great Brain*. New York: Viking.

Green, A. (1957). *Pullett Surprises*. Glenview, IL: Scott Foresman.

Gwynne, F. (1976). *A Chocolate Moose for Dinner*. New York: Windmill Books.

Kohn, B. (1974). *What a Funny Thing to Say*. New York: Dial Press.

Meddaugh, A. (1992). *Martha Speaks*. Boston: Houghton Mifflin.

Prelutsky, J. (1984). *The New Kid on the Block*. New York: Greenwillow.

Rockwell, T. (1973). *How to Eat Fried Worms*. New York: Franklin Watts.

Shannon, G. (1992). *Laughing All the Way*. Boston: Houghton Mifflin.

Silverstein, S. (1981). *A Light in the Attic*. New York: Harper & Row.

Silverstein, S. (1974). *Where the Sidewalk Ends*. New York: Harper & Row.

Tremain, R. (1976). *Fooling Around With Words*. New York: Morrow.

Yee, W. H. (1992). *EEK! There's a Mouse in the House*. Boston: Houghton Mifflin.

**Coming of Age Books**   are books that are quality literature but also valuable for the way they can help youngsters to travel safely and securely through the passages to adulthood. Perhaps the most famous of these is *The Catcher in the Rye*, J. D. Salinger's now classic tale of a prep school boy who goes to New York City for three days while he tries to sort out his life. However, there are equally valuable, though perhaps less well-known stories for children across the age ranges. Reed (1988) and Maggart & Zintz (1992) offer these recommendations:

Blume, J. (1981). *Tiger Eyes*. New York: Bradbury, Dell.

Branscum, R. (1986). *The Girl*. New York: Harper & Row.

Cather, W. (1918). *My Antonia*. New York: Houghton Mifflin.

Cleaver, V., & Cleaver, B. (1969). *Where the Lilies Bloom*. New York: Lippincott, New American Library.

Clement, B. (1980). *Anywhere Else but Here*. New York: Farrar, Straus & Giroux, Dell.

Hall, L. (1981). *The Horse Trader*. New York: Scribner.

Hunter, M. (1985). *Cat Herself*. New York: Harper & Row.

Janeczko, P. (1986). *Bridges to Cross*. New York: Macmillan.

Paterson, K. (1977). *Bridge to Terabithia*. New York: Avon.

Peck, R. N. (1972). *A Day No Pigs Would Die*. New York: Knopf, Dell.

Powell, P. (1984). *Edisto*. New York: Holt, Rinehart & Winston.

Zindel, P. (1984). *Harry & Hortense at Hormone High*. New York: Harper & Row.

**Ethnically Diverse Stories**   are featured in books that represent the experience of minority ethnic groups in America: some still struggling to make their way into the mainstream of American life, or, having been assimilated, wondering whether it was the best thing to do. The books recommended below tell some of the stories of African-Americans, Polish Jews, and Czechs, among others.

Arrick, F. (1981). *Chernowitz*. New York: New American Library.

Baldwin, J. (1974). *If Beale Street Could Talk*. New York: New American Library.

Borland, H. (1963). *When the Legends Die.* New York: Lippincott.

Bosse, C. (1981). *Ganesh.* New York: Crowell.

Childress, A. (1973). *A Hero Ain't Nothin' but a Sandwich.* New York: Coward, McCann, & Geoghegan.

Childress, A. (1981). *Rainbow Jordan.* New York: Coward, McCann, & Geoghegan.

Ellison, R. (1951). *Invisible Man.* New York: Modern Library.

Fast, H. (1970). *Freedom Road.* New York: Bantam.

Gaines, E. (1983). *A Gathering of Old Men.* New York: Knopf.

Guy, R. (1973). *The Friends.* New York: Holt, Rinehart & Winston.

Hamilton, V. (1974). *M.C. Higgins, the Great.* New York: Macmillan.

Highwater, J. (1985). *Eyes of Darkness.* New York: Lothrop, Lee & Shepard.

Potok, C. (1967). *The Chosen.* New York: Simon & Schuster.

Quigley, M. (1981). *The Original Colored House of David.* New York: Houghton Mifflin.

Taylor, M. (1976). *Roll of Thunder Hear My Cry.* New York: Dial.

Yep, L. (1977). *Child of the Owl.* New York: Harper & Row.

### Selecting from New Books

With hundreds of children's books now being published each year, it would be very difficult even to review them, let alone to recommend them to students, parents, or for school purchase. However, the International Reading Association (IRA) operates a very helpful service that you may come to participate in. It is called the Teachers' Choice Project. The project is operated by seven regional teams that essentially circulate and collect reviews from teachers and librarians on 200 to 500 newly published books each year. Criteria for selection include: high literary quality; books students might not discover without guidance; and books with potential to meet various school curriculum objectives.

Ratings result in a national list, grouped into primary (K–2), intermediate (3–5), and advanced (6–8) levels. *The Reading Teacher,* an IRA journal, publishes the Teachers' Choice list along with a helpful annotation, suggested Curriculum Use (CU), an ISBN or library edition number, and other information, such as whether it is or will soon be available in paperback. See below for sample recommendations at each level.

## TEACHERS' CHOICE BOOKS

### Primary (Grades K–2)

**Dream Wolf**

Paul Goble, reteller. Ill. by the author.
A kindly wolf comes to the aid of two lost children, Tiblio and Tankis, when they wander away while gathering berries. Goble retells and illustrates the Plains Indian legend in glowing detail. **CU:** This excellent book enriched a social studies unit on the Plains Indians and a language arts focus on legends. A good read-aloud book. NF
Bradbury. 32 pp. ISBN 0-02-736585-9. US$14.95.

*Cover illustration from* **Dream Wolf.** *Copyright Paul Goble, 1990.*

## Intermediate (Grades 3–5)

### The Big Book for Peace

Ann Durrell and Marilyn Sachs, Eds.

An illustrious array of 34 authors and illustrators consider issues of peace and conflict from different viewpoints in short stories, poems, and songs. **CU:** Readers gained new insights into conflict and its resolution. The collection stimulated discussion on concern for peace, acknowledging diversity, taking a stand, and the genesis of conflict in both personal and global encounters. **CSR**

Dutton. 120 pp. ISBN 0-525-44605-2. US$15.95.

*Illustration from "There Is an Island" in **The Big Book for Peace**. Text copyright 1990 by Jean Fritz. Illustrations copyright 1990 by Teri Sloat. Reprinted by permission of Dutton Children's Books, a division of Penguin USA, Inc.*

## Advanced (Grades 6–8)

*Independence Avenue*

Eileen B. Sherman.

This book examines the life of a Russian Jewish immigrant to the U.S. in 1907. Elias Cherovnosky must learn to adapt his Old World traditions to a new environment in Galveston, Texas. Working in American society was a real shock to a man who had to change everything, including his name. **CU:** This book was part of a study of immigrants and adaptation to a new environment. Students learned about American life at the turn of the century and the difficulties faced by Russian immigrants who came to escape oppression and poverty. **ST**

Jewish Publication Society. 160 pp. ISBN 0-8276-0367-3. US. US$13.95. Paper ed., Jewish Publication Society, F.

*Cover illustration from **Independence Avenue**.*

*Copyright 1990 by M. Kathryn Smith.*

*Source: Teachers' Choices for 1991, The Reading Teacher. 45 pp. 213–220. (p. 214 Primary; pp. 216 & 217 Intermediate; p. 219. Advanced).*

## **W**here You've Been

**Reading and Responding: Emergent Higher-Order Literacy**

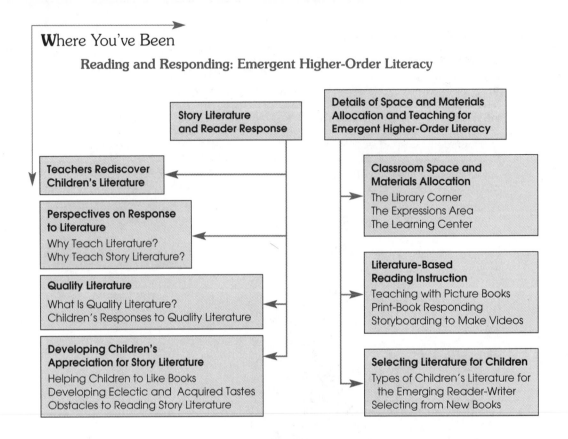

**Where You're Going**

In the previous five chapters we have largely addressed the most joyous aspects of promoting literacy. The next chapter opens a section that addresses the technical know-how for more direct teaching. The chapters ahead contain a distillation of the teaching practices acquired and largely tested in the past century—a century that could well be remembered as the one in which the franchise and benefits of literacy were actively brought to large numbers of people, rather than remaining the domain of a privileged few. The pages ahead may bulge with more than you can digest, but remember that as a teacher you are a lifelong learner, and one who, at some point, could well need all that is contained ahead, and more, to meet the challenges of a career that may well reach into the twenty-first century.

### *Reflective Inquiries and Activities*

1. Which of the reader-response to literature perspectives struck you as most valid? Explain.

2. Using the sections of the chapter on "Why Teach Literature" and "Why Teach Story Literature" as your base, describe a lesson or activity that you might do

with children at a designated grade level to make these points in terms that would be more relevant and engaging to them.

3. Which of the ideas presented for teaching literary appreciation seemed most appropriate to you for primary or for intermediate children? What might you do or add from your own experience and imagination?

4. Tell how you would allocate space in your classroom (primary or intermediate level) and what materials you would purchase if you had a reasonable budget. Explain your decisions.

5. Give a specific example of how you might connect children's knowledge of and interests in videos into a specific reading and writing activity. Explain especially how your project would accommodate different ability levels.

6. The examples in the chapter of literature representing America's ethnic diversity could not cover all possibilities. How would you go about finding suitable material for Germans and Italian-Americans, two of the most sizable ethnic groups by the 1990 census figures, and for Vietnamese and Pakistanis, two of the least sizable groups? Test your plan and see what you come up with, both in terms of recommended readings and by way of a strategy for doing such searching and updating.

# PART III

# LEARNING TO READ AND WRITE

### CHAPTER 6

# WORD RECOGNITION AND ANALYSIS

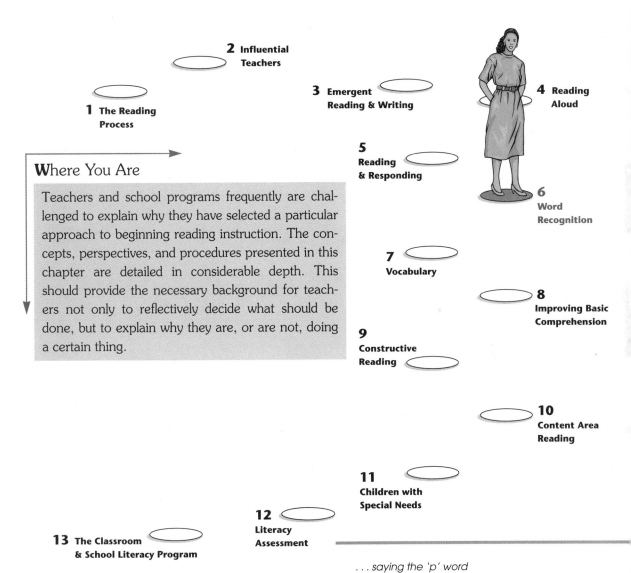

**2 Influential Teachers**

**1 The Reading Process**

**3 Emergent Reading & Writing**

**4 Reading Aloud**

**5 Reading & Responding**

**6 Word Recognition**

**W**here You Are

Teachers and school programs frequently are challenged to explain why they have selected a particular approach to beginning reading instruction. The concepts, perspectives, and procedures presented in this chapter are detailed in considerable depth. This should provide the necessary background for teachers not only to reflectively decide what should be done, but to explain why they are, or are not, doing a certain thing.

**7 Vocabulary**

**8 Improving Basic Comprehension**

**9 Constructive Reading**

**10 Content Area Reading**

**11 Children with Special Needs**

**12 Literacy Assessment**

**13 The Classroom & School Literacy Program**

*. . . saying the 'p' word*
Stephen A. Stahl

# WORD RECOGNITION MEANS . . .

The term "word recognition" often is used to refer both to the phonetic analysis and rapid recognition of words in print. For purposes of clarity, "word recognition" will be used here to refer primarily to rapid word identification, and the term "word analysis" to word attack strategies, or phonetic decoding.

## SOUND SOLUTIONS

Initiating a discussion of phonics, or ". . . saying the 'p' word," as Stephen Stahl (1992) puts it, tends to really turn up the heat of confusion and contention. No matter how often or how convincingly it is argued that learning to read begins with emergent literacy—with reading to children and establishing "concepts of print," with encouraging children to read wordless books—somewhere deep inside many of us there lingers the sense that "real" reading is the phonetic decoding of symbols back into words. This mis-impression probably stems from the fact that both children and adults have long viewed the mastery of this decoding process as a significant developmental step toward self-sufficiency, one right up there with toilet training and learning to talk. The mis-impression that phonics is "real" reading leaves many teachers in conflict about how to proceed. One first-grade teacher wrote about this conflict in a dialogue journal with her course instructors:

> I dreamed that all the first grade teachers had to come into a big gym. . . . In the middle of the gym was a volleyball net marked 'phonics' and we had to get on one side or another. I watched a few people march confidently to their chosen places, but I was part of the group that just stood at the door, feeling confused. I woke up in a cold sweat! (in Blachowicz, Bridgman, and Watson-Cohn, 1993, p. 15).

Many teachers feel that they face this kind of "either-or" dilemma with respect to phonics instruction. This being the case, we sense that the pages ahead will have your attention as keenly as you will have the attention of most children when it is clear that you are about to teach them to "read." Just as children tend to have high anticipation and a bit of apprehension when they are being taught to read, we suspect that you have some of the same feelings about teaching reading and would prefer that we jumped right in with a minimum of preparatory information. Unlike children, however, you are preparing to be professionals. In order to meet school, parent, and student expectations, you will need to develop the ability to be a reflective, strategic teacher of reading.

Accordingly, while the bulk of this chapter details the "how to's" of beginning reading instruction, it begins with a brief presentation of some of the basic concepts of word recognition and analysis. For example, Blachowicz et al. (1993), cited above, use the first-grade teacher's nightmarish dream to point out that the current controversy over phonics vs. "whole-language" has led them, and many others, to take a more holistic approach. Holistic, in this context, tends to mean that instruction in word recognition and analysis should have these characteristics:

- it should be both developmentally and philosophically appropriate;
- it should be consistent with a view of literacy development that centers on young readers;
- it should use children's language in meaningful ways;
- it should develop strategies rather than mere "skills"; and
- it should go beyond mere phonics to a more richly conceived view of word study (Blachowicz, Bridgman, & Watson-Cohn, 1993).

In sympathy with this more eclectic view, the "how-to" portion of the chapter details means and methods for advancing independent decoding and rapid recognition of words in isolation and in real reading situations. As in earlier chapters, the intent is to provide you with a fairly extensive and objective look at the various alternatives you are likely to encounter. This broad look should give you an opportunity to begin to identify and refine some personally preferred approaches, and to have a reference source for other approaches you might need to call upon to meet individual student needs and job role demands. In this way, too, you should be prepared to be a reflective, strategic teacher who is properly equipped and disposed to cultivate equally reflective and strategic reading in your students.

## WORD DECODING IS COMPLEX PROBLEM SOLVING

Strategy is important in word decoding, since it essentially is a form of recurring problem solving. The problem of determining just what a word in print might be is made all the more complex by "free-floating unknowns." English, unlike most other languages, does not have high phoneme (sound) to grapheme (symbol) correspondence. Rather, it seems more like what Goodman (1967) aptly called a "psycholinguistic guessing game." It must be more than a little unnerving to learn a word such as "beard" and then to learn that "heard" is pronounced quite differently. This challenges one of the basic strategies of human problem solving; namely, to look for an analogy, or a "known" that approximates what you wish to know or figure out, and then to proceed to make some logical manipulation—in this case, by substituting another known beginning consonant sound to come up with a workable solution. However, for some words the analogy, or "look-alikes," can be misleading. Consider the following words:

| sew | | few |
| horse | | worse |
| word | | cord |
| low | | cow |
| shoe | | foe |
| hose | dose | lose |
| doll | | roll |
| could | | mould |
| done | gone | lone |

George Bernard Shaw once suggested that we try recoding the very familiar (when spoken) word "ghoti." You would have to really dig into your phonological storehouse to come up with the pronunciation: "fish" (*gh* for the /f/ sound, as in "enou*gh*"; *o* for the short /i/ sound as in "w*o*men"; and *ti* for the /sh/ sound as in "defini*ti*on").

The difficulty inherent in recoding words like this have led some, such as Goodman, to conclude that the psycholinguistic guessing game can *only* be won by simultaneously drawing upon hints from three processes: the graphophonic (or symbol-to-sound), syntactic (or sentence structure), and semantic (or meaning aspects of words). Ehri (1978), on the other hand, puts much greater emphasis on phonological (or sound-matched-to-symbol) and far less on syntactic and semantic features. Consider now what proficient young readers actually do when faced with word decoding problems.

## THE DECODING STRATEGIES OF PROFICIENT READERS

The strategies used to determine how to decode or recode a word vary with the situation and task demand. For example, words presented in isolation from text need to be approached quite differently than do words found in context. Clay's (1991) interpretation of research yielded this range of choices available to the competent reader.

- They ask someone who might know the word.
- They make an estimate supported by the text and often get it right.
- They make estimates which are errors, detect them, and correct them—a self-correcting tutorial.
- They select rapid or slow processing to facilitate the pick-up of necessary information.
- They direct full or divided attention to selected features.
- They choose either precise search of detail or partial sampling of enough cues to solve the problem.
- They derive unknown words by *analogy* from known words. (Yes, this really works, despite the many exceptions.)
- They partially sound the words and complete the solving by using meaning.
- They sound the word in parts and link to known words.
- They sound the word and are unable to link it to any prior knowledge. (Clay, 1991, p. 340)

Notice that Clay's observations led her to believe that proficient readers approach new words in flexible ways and select from a range of problem-solving strategies which include checks and letter sound relationships. The principle behind trying to discover what proficient readers do is to get some clues as to what we should teach less proficient readers to do.

Let's now tackle "the 'p' word" by looking at some of the more traditional issues and general approaches to phonics instruction. Next we will detail several explicit means of teaching this aspect of *word analysis*. Following this detailed look at phonics instruction, we shall describe complementary systems for directly teaching *rapid word recognition,* and for stimulating word learning in general through contextual and literature-based reading approaches.

## BASIC ISSUES IN TEACHING PHONICS

Four basic issues, not to say controversies, surround phonics instruction. One viewpoint is that phonics should never be taught in isolation from real reading, if at all. According to this perspective, which is most popular among whole-language supporters, the rules governing phonetic decoding are undependable, and children learn to recognize and say words largely through immersion in a literate environment, through use of contexts, and through repeated exposures to words in meaningful reading. They argue, for example, that only textual *context* can tell you whether to say *reed* or *red* when you see the printed word "read." They would further argue that the words used most often in print are phonetically irregular, and hence "unpronounceable" by sounding them out. The latter position is based on an extensive study that showed that of the 80,000 core words that occur in the English language, the ones that occur the most *frequently* also are the most phonetically irregular (Hanna, Hodges, Hanna, & Rudolph, 1966). Word counts of books read by children further reveal that 50 percent of the print in such books is accounted for by only 109 different words and 90 percent by only 5,000 different words (Carroll, Davies, & Richman, 1971). Goodman (1973a), one of the chief opponents of explicit phonics instruction, goes one step further and says that words are not really even being decoded or recoded, since print is not really oral language written down. By this he means that the correspondence between graphemes and phonemes is too weak for the language even to be called alphabetic in the same sense that this term applies to languages such as Spanish and Italian. For example, in the English language, the letter *a* has four or five sounds (depending on how you count); in Spanish and Italian *a* has the same sound wherever it occurs. Goodman further adds that oral language patterns are quite different from formal writing, and that pronunciations vary so much from person to person and place to place that the same letters could not possibly represent the different sounds that individuals make. In other words, "recoding" is an illusion more than a fact. However, like the bumblebee, who by aerodynamic study cannot fly, phonics of a sort does seem to be part of word analysis and recognition, and some explicit instruction does seem to be profitable in the judgment of many other authorities in the field (e.g., Adams, 1990; Chall, 1983a; Cunningham, 1990).

## TWO BASIC APPROACHES

Among those who support explicit instruction in decoding, the issue has become more one of just how it might best be done. There are essentially two positions here. One is called *analytical,* or *gradual* phonics, and the other *synthetic,* or *intensive* phonics. It is no simple matter to clearly distinguish these from one another since various programs have used the same terms to mean different things. As a rule, however, the points found below will most often distinguish these for you.

**Analytical Phonics**   instruction usually has the following characteristics:

- It begins, in general, by teaching words that then are deductively analyzed into letter sounds.
- It presents children only with words that are in the child's oral language vocabulary, so that the child can know when he or she has correctly sounded it out through a deductive approach.
- It involves the initial teaching of approximately 250 irregular words by a "look–say," or whole-word method.
- It next teaches consonants (except low-utility consonants such as q, x, y, & z).
- It teaches vowel sounds later and gradually.
- It reinforces consonants and vowel sounds with context clues from sentences constructed to reinforce those sounds with no exceptions.
- It relies a great deal on structural analysis of words—the identification of prefixes, suffixes, roots, and smaller words within words.
- It encourages children to attend to the distinctive features of words (whatever experience and the mind's eye interprets these to be)[1]:

  perhaps  child-ren  minimum

- It teaches only high-utility phonics rules.
- It encourages students to see and use analogous parts of words to unlock words that are only slightly different (b and; s and; g rand).
- It encourages supported independent reading in materials carefully matched to the child's familiarity with words (where a minimum of 97% plus accuracy is assured).

**Synthetic, or Intensive Phonics**   instruction tends to be characterized by these differences:

- It begins, in general, by teaching letters and sounds and blending these into words.
- It typically begins first with alphabet letter names and then letter sounds.
- It teaches children to sound out each word, left to right, one letter sound at a time, much as does a computer that is programmed to synthesize language: r-a-t; b-a-t; d-o-g.
- It teaches vowel sounds and their variants early on.
- It teaches consonants next.
- It stresses syllabication and syllabication rules.
- It stresses the sounding or aural-auditory aspects of language, much more so than the visual.

---

[1] Analytic phonics proponents once emphasized teaching children to attend to the simple *configuration*, or outline shape, of words. The research of Marchbanks and Levin (1965) provided strong evidence that while simple configuration cues alone are unrelated to acquisition of decoding ability, attending to the *distinctive features of words* is an important part of effective word recognition.

- It teaches words in isolation from context and even creates and uses *nonwords* to sharpen effective left-to-right sounding: *ma-ger; do-ack; bo-jar.*
- It teaches many phonics (sound to print) and phonetic (language sound) rules, including those with relatively low utility.
- Phonics elements taught are practiced with a variety of exercises that have relatively little context.

Summarizing, there are three generic approaches to phonics instruction: (1) the analytical, or examine-in-many-ways-until-the-word-is-recognized approach; (2) the synthetic or code-emphasis, voice-synthesizer approach; and (3) the previously mentioned contextual and largely incidental approaches. The question of which is better is frequently investigated and debated, sometimes to a point that resembles the silliness of the argument in Gulliver's travels as to which end of the egg should be cracked first, the narrow or the broad one. Here now is a brief tour of the history of recent efforts to answer this question.

## PHONICS: THE "LITTLE" DEBATE

Once called "The Great Debate" (Chall, 1967), there really is little question any longer about whether a reader needs phonics. The important question, as suggested above, has become one of how phonetic analysis strategies can be most easily imparted to novice readers. Venezky (1967) made this point clearly over thirty years ago when he wrote, "Most literates form spelling-to-sound generalizations regardless of the method which they encounter in initial reading instruction. What these generalizations are, how they develop, and how they differ from one literate person to another is at present unknown" (p. 102). While somewhat more is known today, progress has been slow, and the question of "how it all happens" still is shrouded in mystery. Let's see why this is the case.

### Problems with Phonics Research

It would seem to be a relatively simple matter to determine which of the three most basic approaches to phonics is the best. However, there are factors that continue to cloud the research and hence the conclusions that can be drawn. These are especially worth your consideration since they will help you to read and digest the literature in the field by spotting some of the subtleties that can change or cloud findings.

1.  First and foremost, relatively few studies have been done on instructional practices. Most have been addressed to theoretical aspects of "the reading process" (Cunningham, 1991).
2.  When instructional methods *are* studied, it isn't always clear what the method in question actually involves. For example, when one of the methods being tested is called a "phonics" method, the tendency is to assume that it is the *only* method used, to the exclusion of other aspects of literacy development such as context-based exposures to words and emphasis on oral language and writing. Often, however, a closer look at the method proves otherwise. For

example, the Gillingham–Stillman phonics method is reputed to be one of the most intensive synthetic phonics programs. Yet a close examination of the training manual for this method reveals a good deal of attention to context-based applications, oral language development, and writing.

3. It is difficult to know how individual teachers in various experimental groups actually used a particular method. For example, in one heavily funded group of studies, previously referred to as "The First-Grade Studies" (Bond & Dykstra, 1967), it was informally discovered that teachers were using a variety of supplementary materials and methods to round out what they saw as weaknesses or inadequacies in whatever experimental treatment they had been assigned to use. As a result the large-scale study showed relatively few clear differences among individual methods being compared but quite significant differences among the teachers, no matter which method they ostensibly were using.

4. Often, important information regarding the precise amount of time spent on each treatment is not noted, or is obscured. Since "time-on-task" is known to be a powerful factor in learning outcomes, failure to note this clearly can seriously cloud findings and result in misleading conclusions.

5. Results tend to be reported for groups with little attention given to individual learning outcomes. In other words, individual differences are masked; there could be some youngsters who did not learn well at all with the method that seemed best, or others who did exceptionally well with the method that proved less favorable.

6. A good deal of what is found and concluded from a study is tied to the nature of the instruments selected for assessing progress. If, for example, the measure used for first-grade reading success depends on a youngster's ability to decode "nonsense" or nonwords and/or correct spelling, then intensive phonics programs generally will tend to look stronger than analytical or incidental approaches. Conversely, if samples are taken of children's writing and examined for naturalness, sentence length, and content, the incidental, or whole language methods tend to look better. Ideally, a study tries to use a variety of measures. However, time constraints often make this quite difficult.

These and other such subtleties of research design and reporting aside, there have been some noteworthy attempts to summarize findings from many studies by eliminating those studies that fail to meet some stringent requirements. Here now is a brief review of some of the most frequently cited studies (mostly studies of studies) and their findings. You should find this to be a handy resource that can be easily reviewed, added to, and probably modified in the future.

### Findings from Research

The reviews of the early stages of learning to read reported here are drawn in large measure from mega-analyses reported by Adams (1990), Chall (1967; 1983), Cunningham (1991), Ehri and Robbins (1992), Juel (1991), Stahl (1992), and Yopp (1992). These findings should provide a firm footing for you to evaluate the relative merit and appropriateness of the next section of the chapter, which offers a full range of methods for teaching independent word analysis and recognition, as well as a source for future reference and study.

### Phonics Instruction: Necessary but Not Sufficient to Learning to Read

- As noted in a previous chapter, the relationship between phonemic awareness and learning to read is marked by this paradox: (a) phonemic awareness improves as a consequence of learning to read, yet, (b) an optimal level of phonemic awareness is a prerequisite to learning to read (Yopp, 1992).

- Acquisition of word analysis and recognition strategies is neither "easy" (Gibson & Levin, 1975, p. 265) nor "natural" (Gough & Hillinger, 1980, p. 180). For some children it can be so demanding as to actually impair or stifle interest in learning to read. Nonetheless, they must be taught and learned, for early success in these skills is a solid predictor of eventual growth in decoding (Lundberg, 1984), comprehension (Lesgold & Resnick, 1982), and opportunity for subsequent exposure to words: good decoders encounter roughly twice as many words as poor ones in the earliest stages of reading (Juel, 1988).

- Analysis of the First-Grade Studies (Bond & Dykstra, 1967) suggested that early reading programs that included *most any* systematic phonics instruction consistently exceeded the nonphonics emphasis programs in word recognition achievement scores. More importantly, the approaches that combined systematic phonics with an emphasis on meaning-seeking and reading connected prose surpassed the basals (of that time) alone on virtually *all* outcome measures (Adams, 1990).

- Both inductive and deductive approaches should be incorporated into teaching decoding generalizations (Harris & Sipay, 1990).

- A little bit of phonics can go a long way. It takes a fairly minimal amount of explicit phonics instruction to induce the learning and use of even untaught spelling-sound relationships when the text children are exposed to contains a number of regular decodable words (Juel & Roper-Schneider, 1985).

- The least time should be spent teaching specific phonic rules per se, and the most time actually reading (Cunningham, 1991; Juel, 1991).

### Developing a "Phonetic Sense" May Be More Important Than Learning Phonics Rules

- Reading depends first and foremost on visual letter recognition. Curiously, while we do not seem to need to depend on the phonological (or sound) aspects of a word to read it, skillful readers seem to be relying upon them in some way (Elly, 1989). Such phonological verifying seems to add a critical quality of redundancy to the system (Adams, 1990) that supports and reinforces reading and spelling.

- It appears that it is the learned associations among individual letters, or how letters cluster and "excite" one another to form familiar clusters, that ultimately is responsible for the easy, holistic manner in which we come to respond to words in print (Adams, 1990; Cunningham, 1991; Glass, 1973)

### Readers Use a Variety of Cue Systems in Addition to Phonics

- Several studies and theories have led to the belief that there are essentially three stages to developing decoding skill:

    1.  *The pre-decoding stage:* At this stage, the child tends to rely upon three categories of cues in roughly this order:

        a.  Random cues—most any visual clue which is present is used to remember what a word might mean, even an accidental thumbprint (as reported by Gough, in Juel, 1991)
        b.  Environmental cues—such as where the word is located on the page
        c.  Distinctive letters (the *y* in "pony," or the double letters in "balloon")

    2.  *The spelling-sound stage:* At this stage, the child tends to recognize some words by a combination of visual recall of its spelling and a beginning sense of sounds of some of the letters. The pinnacle of this stage is sounding out and plausibly decoding most words.

    3.  *The automatic response stage:* At this stage, a fair-sized vocabulary of frequently occurring words is recognized automatically. Juel (1991, p. 783) notes that "we do not know exactly what it is about word recognition that becomes automatic"—recognition of whole words, due to frequent exposure to a small number of words, or letter-sound relations, due to exposure to letter-sound patterns in many different words.

- There is little evidence to suggest that good readers use context as a clue to word recognition more than poor readers. On the contrary, good readers decode words using word analysis techniques that then strengthen their understanding of the context. Readers can only predict about one out of four words from context (Gough, Alford, & Holly-Wilcox, 1981); hence, context cannot take the place of orthographic (or symbol to sound) information (Adams, 1990).

- Skillful readers' ability to read long words seems to depend to a large extent on their ability to break words into syllables, although this ability generally is not firmly developed until during the fourth grade (Friedrich, Schodler, & Juola, 1979).

- Reading words by analogy (that is, by recognizing previously learned words or word parts in an unfamiliar word, such as the nonsense word "yave," and trying to pronounce the unknown word based on knowledge of analogous word parts in familiar words such as "have" or "gave") is imperfect at first, but develops earlier than reading words by sequential decoding (Goswami, 1990).

- Several simple practices noted in previous chapters help to build strategic cue use:

    1.  Labeling objects with printed cards
    2.  Language experience activities based on children's dictated sentences or stories

3. Using Big Books for read-alouds, enabling children to see the words the teacher is reading (Holdaway, 1979)

4. Using patterned, predictable chart stories (Bridge, 1986; Bridge, Winograd, & Haley, 1983)

5. Using songs and games to strengthen phonemic awareness (Yopp, 1992)

## Readers Have Varying Personal Learning Strategies

- Most poor readers have a "strategy imbalance." They tend to rely excessively on one tactic to the exclusion of others (e.g., context but not sounding, or glued-to-print, laborious sounding to the exclusion of visual imprinting and context; Sulzby, 1985).

- In a longitudinal study, early readers who had a strong preference for whole-word decoding strategies showed progressive deterioration on most measures, a problem *not* noted among early readers with a strong preference for alphabet phonics strategies (Byrne, Freebody, & Gates, 1992).

## Frequent Exposure to Words Is a Key Factor

- Reading errors tend to be made in inverse proportion to the number of times a word has been previously exposed in print (Gough, Juel, & Roper-Schneider, 1983)—or the greater the number of times a word is encountered in print, the more likely it is to be mastered.

- It has been difficult to establish just how many exposures it takes to a new word before it is learned. It depends, of course, on several factors, such as the length of the exposure, the nature of the word, the way the practice and reinforcement sessions are "distributed": e.g., five exposures over one day (?), 3 days (?), 5 days (?). The number of needed exposures also depends on precisely what the child is asked to do or say during those exposures. Nonetheless, it is possible to say with confidence that the greater the period and frequency of exposure to a word, the greater will be each student's opportunity to process and store it in some way that is characteristic to them (Bloomer, Norlander, & Richard, 1991; Cunning-ham, 1991; Fernald, 1943; Glass, 1973; Manzo & Manzo, 1993).

## Writing and Spelling Complement Reading

- Writing and spelling greatly aid in developing alphabetic phonetic sense (Frith, 1985).

- Arguments to include spelling instruction in a reading program are strongly supported. The best differentiation of good and poor readers at a young age is found to be their knowledge of spelling patterns and proficiency with spelling-sound translations (Adams, 1990). Hence, learning about spelling clearly reinforces knowledge of letter sequences. More specifically, the process of copying new words, while thought to be an old-fashioned practice, has been shown to strengthen memory for them in a rather enduring way (Whittlesea, 1987). Nonetheless, there are many extremely bright, and eventually good readers, who remain terrible spellers for much of their lives; e.g., Robert Louis Stevenson, Mark Twain, Thomas Edison (Fernald, 1943, p. 174).

- Students permitted to use "invented" spellings learn to spell *better,* perhaps because they write more and are permitted to move through more stages in less time, hence instructing themselves sooner and better (Adams, 1990).

### The Key Question

- When a child asks the question "What's this word?" this gives the strongest evidence that he or she is thinking about reading and print decoding, and hence is on the way to becoming a generative, or self-directed and self-teaching learner (Clark, 1976; Durkin, 1966; Manzo, 1987).

As we continue now to tell the story of the ways that educators have come to teach or impart those aspects of phonics that seem to be essential, we realize that you may never have been taught about phonics, per se, yourself, or that you may have forgotten what you were taught. More likely you have simply internalized the rules and are no longer aware of what you know. For these reasons, we have assembled a "Teacher's Primer on Phonics" from works by Cordts (1965) and Hull (1976) (see Appendix B). You should find this information useful even if you ascribe to the incidental teaching of phonics—in fact you may especially need the primer in that case, since incidental teaching requires the teacher to have such information almost instantly available whenever an appropriate situation arises. In sum, these studies seem to support two seemingly opposing positions, both of which are reflected in most modern basals—namely, a need for:

- Increased attention to phonetic training with decreased time on workbooks
- Increased time in reading selections of literary quality with *less* stringent concern for a grade-level controlled vocabulary

Furthermore, while the preponderance of evidence suggests that one can be taught to read and spell without being taught rules, it can be profitable to teach phonics rules if the rules are used to enhance concepts about language, and, to put it frankly, if the teacher does not become obsessive and rule-bound in his or her approach. Consider the argument made in another context by Leopold Stowkowski, the famous music conductor. He said in a "Today Show" interview (6/22/89) that even to learn a "weak rule," such as that the letter "e" at the end of a word generally signals that the preceding vowel takes a long sound, instantly converts words like those shown below into a lawful body of decodable and potentially new words:

*tap + e = tape*
*hop + e = hope*
*tub + e = tube*
*pet + e = Pete*

More than that, he added, it imparts to the learner a sense of the need and value of seeking order in apparent chaos. The Maestro's comments were in the context of whether it was necessary to learn to read music in order to be a great musician.

# MODELS AND METHODS OF TEACHING WORD ANALYSIS

The perspective of this section is how to impart independent word analysis *in reading and spelling,* not to teach phonics rules, as such. Hence, the methods offered tend to frankly stress reflex training more than concept learning. Our impression is that frequent exposures to words is necessary to permit each child to reach a personally effective strategy for rapid word recognition with a minimum of reference to "rules." Notice, however, that the methods offered attempt to represent different possible learning needs and different learning and teaching styles, including almost purely conceptual approaches. Our assumption is that every teacher will work to develop a rich range of methods to meet the varied needs that any class of children tends to represent and need, rather than doing only that which fits his or her own experiences or personal learning styles. Reliance on personal intuition is fundamental to effective teaching. However, over-reliance on personal intuition is unacceptable in professional life, where there is a knowledge base to draw upon that exceeds any individual's personal experiences, or even some group's shared but limited perspective.

## EXPLICIT METHODS

The first method presented for explicit teaching of word recognition and analysis is a generic form of word coaching (Gaskins, 1988). It can be used any time a word is encountered in context or in isolation. It is a method that is particularly compatible with the whole language philosophy.

### Word Coaching

In general, when encouraging a student to decode a word in context, first ask if the student can think of a word that seems to fit in that position. Then draw the student's attention to the first letter and sound (often a strong clue). Next draw attention to any easily recognizable larger parts (a small word or familiar cluster, such as *ing*). Next, direct attention to distinctive consonants, then medial sounds, and finally to blending.

This sequence is not necessarily the way words are finally stored, but it is a good way to bring about recognition of a known word and to show how natural language is represented in print. This is essential because of the differences that exist between the way a word is used in print, the way it is spelled when natural language is represented, and the way it is actually spoken—which may be different yet. For example, the word "grandfather" appears much more frequently in print than in real life. But even when the more familiar word "grandpa" is used, it still does not represent the way it most often is said in natural language, which is "grampa."

The next method for teaching word analysis is so basic that it could be considered a paradigm, or foundational model. It is an analytical phonics approach that has been the method of choice in basal readers for nearly half a century, and in several essential ways matches the intent of several modern programs such as Reading Recovery (detailed in a later chapter on special needs students) and those suggested for raising "phonemic awareness" (Stanovich, 1988; Yopp, 1992).

### Gray's Paradigm for Teaching Phonic Elements

Gray's paradigm (1948) for teaching phonic elements probably was assembled from the work of many researchers and practitioners. It represents the earliest and most complete articulation of the analytic phonics approach to early reading instruction. It is widely used and adapted in most basal programs. The method does little to teach phonic rules, but goes far in focusing visual and aural attention to key letters and letter clusters, a well as in teaching blending and use of context clues. The paradigm is explained and illustrated below using the **squ** blend.

## STEPS IN GRAY'S PARADIGM

Step 1    *Visual and Aural "Fixing"*

a. *Recognizing visual similarities:* Words are written on the board. The student circles the part(s) that all the words have in common:

*squirrel      squeeze      squeak      square      squaw*

b. *Recognizing aural similarities:* Using the same list as above, the teacher reads each word from the board, giving only slight emphasis to the **squ** sound. The students try to identify the sound that each word has in common. The auditory step may precede the visual step if the student tends to have an auditory orientation.

Step 2    *Visual and Aural Discrimination*

a. *Visual discrimination:* Presenting words in groups of three, the student first underlines **squ** in each word in which he or she finds it. Next the student attempts to say only those words containing the **squ** sound:

| | | | |
|---|---|---|---|
| *queen* | *retire* | *squirrel* | *shrimp* |
| *squat* | *squirt* | *squirm* | *spring* |
| *whom* | *whenever* | *sprint* | *squeaky* |

b. *Auditory discrimination:* The teacher says three words. Without seeing the words, the student identifies the word(s) containing the **squ** sound:

| | | | |
|---|---|---|---|
| *squeal* | *squash* | *shield* | *squelch* |
| *spur* | *squid* | *square* | *squeak* |
| *dig* | *send* | *squash* | *squat* |

Step 3    *Blending (substitution)*
The teacher shows the student how to blend and substitute sounds to form new words.

*Example: Substitute the **squ** sound for the existing sound at the beginning of each word:*

| | |
|---|---|
| *ball − b = all + squ = squall* | *wire − w = ire + squ = squire* |
| *what − w = at + squ = squat* | *tint − t = int + squ = squint* |

**Step 4**   *Contextual Application*
The student underlines words containing the **squ** sound, which are embedded in sentences, and learns to identify the sound when encountered in narrative reading.

> *1.   He led a **squad** of men into battle.*
> *2.   He leads a **squadron** in the army.*
> *3.   Try not to **squash** it, please.*

*Blending and Contextual Reinforcement* need not be a dreary affair. For example, activities like the poem "Rhyme Time Fun" in Table 6.1 can be used to reinforce the concept of substitution.

There are several ways to select which letters and sounds to teach using Gray's paradigm or the "teaching songs" in Table 6.1. The most popular of these are based on:

- A "scope and sequence" chart as can be found in most basal-reader programs
- Informal systematic observation of children's oral reading errors and miscues
- Frequency counts of *predictable* phonics rules and elements (See Table 6.2, p. 196, for assistance in developing your own "sequence.")
- The most frequently occurring letter clusters identified by Gerald Glass, which is used most frequently with the teaching procedure called Glass-Analysis (described ahead)

# Table 6.1

## Rhyme Time Fun!

Think of words that rhyme with *cat.*
(bat—fat—hat—mat)
Did you forget to think of *that?*
*(Wait for a choral ''yes'' or ''no!'' response)*

Think of words that rhyme with *red.*
(bed—fed—led—wed)
Did you happen to think of *Ned?*

Think of words that rhyme with *pig.*
(big—dig—jig—wig)
Did you forget to think of *twig?*

Think of words that rhyme with *hop.*
(flop—mop—pop—top)
Did you happen to think of *stop?*

Think of words that rhyme with *bug.*
(dug—hug—mug—tug)
Did you forget to think of *snug?*

Think of words that rhyme with *cake.*
(bake—lake—make—rake)
Did you happen to think of *snake?*

Think of words that rhyme with *feet.*
(beet—meet—sheet—sweet)
Did you forget to think of *street?*

Think of words that rhyme with *kite*
(bite—quite—white—write)
Did you happen to think of *polite?*

Think of words that rhyme with *nose.*
(chose—close—hose—rose)
Did you forget to think of *those?*

Think of words that rhyme with *cube.*
(                              )
All I can think of is a toothpaste *tube.*

*Author unknown.*

The next method sets out to teach phonics by teaching some phonics rules. While it relies on inductive and deductive thinking, it stresses a highly conceptual, inductive approach. As such, it can be a good match for children with a scientific bent, as well as a solid means of incidentally teaching inductive reasoning to those who are more literary or artistic.

### Botel's Discovery Technique

The Discovery Technique is a conceptual approach refined by Botel (1964). It is designed to help students to discover for themselves some of the phonetic and structural patterns that make many words decodable. The teacher helps students to "discover" these patterns through inductive questioning, hence developing their powers of observation, sensitivity to language, and capacity to form concepts about word recoding.

## STEPS IN BOTEL'S DISCOVERY TECHNIQUE

Step 1    The teacher provides accurate sensory experiences.

        Example: When teaching that some words drop the *e* before endings are added, the teacher might:

    a.   Put the following known words on the board:

        *make—making*        *hope—hoping*  *ride—riding*

    b.   Ask students to enunciate the words accurately.

    c.   Ask students to note how the base words are alike, and what change to the base word took place each time we added the *ing*. If response comes quickly and accurately, move to Step 2. If not, do not move on to Step 2 for a while. Even when students are ready for Step 2, the teacher always reviews Step 1, at least briefly.

Step 2    Students examine the structural pattern with teacher guidance, but the teacher does not state the rule.

        Example: In adding *ing* to words that end in a silent *e*, the teacher questions students until they arrive at the following findings:

    a.   The base words have a silent *e* preceded by a long vowel sound.

    b.   The base words drop the *e* when *ing* is added.

Step 3    Students collect words that fit the pattern.

    Students practice finding other words in their word lists and in general reading that fit the pattern, such as:

        *chase—chasing*     *close—closing*     *skate—skating*

Step 4    Students generalize the pattern.

    A written or oral statement of the rule is formulated. For example, the rule on dropping the *e* before adding *ing* could be stated: *"If a base*

> *word contains a long vowel sound and ends in a silent e, you drop the e before adding* ing."

Botel adds that it is important to the Discovery Technique also to teach students that rules can have many *exceptions*. As students begin to apply rules, he points out, they will find words that do not "behave" according to principles. Therefore, teach rules by pointing out that:

> *"A rule tells us what sound to try first. If the word makes sense in the sentence, it is probably right. If not, try another sound. The final test is always the meaning of the word in context" (Botel, 1964, p. 49).*

For example,

She is my *niece.*     Mother baked *bread* for us.

Assume that the italicized words in each of these sentences are unfamiliar at sight to the student. If the child has learned the rule that when two vowels appear together the first is generally long and the second silent, the first attempts to decode the word will be to use a long /i/ sound in *niece* and the long /e/ sound in *bread*. In each case, however, if reading is meaning-driven, the student will reject these choices and keep trying to find a context-appropriate alternative.

The next method offers a strong contrast in terms of its lack of reference to phonics rules. However, neither of these methods need to be used to the exclusion of the other.

### Glass-Analysis: A "No Rules" Phonics Method

Glass (1973) developed a method for teaching what he calls the "decoding aspects of reading." The method, called Glass-Analysis, is a form of analytic phonics that is compatible with his research on how *successful* decoders acquired word decoding strategies (Glass & Burton, 1973). This research is supported by the conclusions being reached by many others as to how this ultimately is achieved (Cunningham, 1991; Manzo & Manzo, 1993; Stahl, 1992). Glass-Analysis resembles an old-fashioned approach that taught high-utility letter-sound combinations (such as /bl/, /og/, and /th/) as single sounds. However, it is a distinct improvement in several ways. Most particularly, it teaches students to segment sound combinations and distinctive features of words.

In Glass-Analysis, the act of *decoding* is *temporarily decontextualized* from comprehension in order to maximize the student's focused attention on target words and word elements. Students are trained in conventional and personal word-analysis strategies that center on studying and learning how certain letters "excite one another" (Adams, 1990)—meaning that because the reader has seen and sounded a particular letter cluster in whole words many times in many words, when the letters appear as a cluster in an unfamiliar word, the reader automatically identifies them and test-pronounces them as they are pronounced in the known words. Two simple verbal "scripts" are used in the Glass-Analysis method to help

## Table 6.2

### Letter Clusters (by Difficulty Level)
### Recommended for Use with Glass-Analysis

| STARTERS | MEDIUM 1 | MEDIUM 2 | HARDER 1 | HARDER 2 |
|---|---|---|---|---|
| 1. at | 1. ed | 1. all | 1. fowl | 1. er |
| 2. ing | 2. ig | 2. aw | 2. us | 2. air |
| 3. et | 3. ip | 3. el(l) | 3. ll(l) | 3. al |
| 4. it | 4. ud | 4. eck | 4. ite | 4. ied |
| 5. ot | 5. id | 5. ice | 5. es(s) | 5. ew |
| 6. im | 6. en | 6. ick | 6. om | 6. ire |
| 7. op | 7. ug | 7. if(f) | 7. oke | 7. ear |
| 8. an | 8. ut | 8. ink | 8. ore | 8. eal |
| 9. ay | 9. ar | 9. ob | 9. tow | 9. tea |
| 10. ed | 10. em | 10. od | 10. a̅s̅t̅ | 10. e̅e̅ |
| 11. am | 11. up | 11. og | 11. ane | 11. care |
| 12. un | 12. ate | 12. ub | 12. eat | 12. d̅e̅a̅f̅ |
| 13. in | 13. ent | 13. uf(f) | 13. as(s) | 13. o̅a̅t̅ |
| 14. ap | 14. est | 14. ush | 14. ev | 14. ue |
| 15. and | 15. ake | 15. able | 15. ind | 15. oo |
| 16. act | 16. ide | 16. ight | 16. oss | 16. ou |
| 17. um | 17. ock | 17. is(s) | 17. oem | 17. ound |
| 18. ab | 18. ade | 18. on | 18. ost | 18. ure |
| 19. ag | 19. ame | 19. or | 19. rol(l) | 19. ture |
| 20. old | 20. ape | 20. l(l) | 20. one | 20. ur |
| 21. ash | 21. ace | 21. ac | 21. ate | 21. ir |
| 22. ish | 22. any | 22. af(f) | 22. ave | 22. ai |
|  | 23. enk | 23. ook | 23. ove | 23. au |
|  | 24. ong | 24. tion | 24. folly | 24. oi |
|  |  |  | 25. a̅g̅e̅ |  |

the child sound-test possibilities in a given word. One script asks what *sound* a given letter or letter cluster "makes"; the other script asks what *letter* or *letter cluster* represents a given sound. This is a functional definition of phonics instruction, which Stahl conceptually defined as "forcing students to focus attention on the internal structure, or patterns, in words" (1992, pp. 623–624).

Glass' research has identified 119 letter clusters by their frequency of occurrence in early basal reading material. These counts have been used to rank-order the difficulty level of learning each cluster. While there is nothing sacrosanct about one list versus another, the idea of having a frequency-generated word list to guide instruction has been shown to have a reasonably good basis in the research literature (Juel, 1991). See Table 6.2 for letter clusters that can be used to identify and select words for use with the Glass-Analysis strategy. A "shoe box" of word cards, arranged by letter cluster difficulty, is available to facilitate the use of the Glass-Analy-sis decoding approach.[2] These relatively inexpensive, nonconsumable materials can include a quick program for teaching the names of the letters of the alphabet.

[2] Easier-to-Learn, Inc.; P.O. Box 701; Garden City, NY 11530; 516-475-3803.

The Glass-Analysis method emphasizes the following basic ideas:

- Students should look at the target word throughout the lesson.
- Students should avoid undue attention to word meaning during the initial emphasis on sound decoding and word recognition.
- Lessons should keep a brisk pace.
- The teacher should avoid an emphasis on word meaning (while engaged in the Glass-Analysis interaction). If a student asks the meaning of a word, the teacher simply gives the meaning and proceeds with the lesson.
- The teacher should avoid discussion of phonic rules (again, while engaged in this specialized interaction) such as reminding the student to drop the final "e" before adding a suffix.
- The teacher should avoid breaking up units that logically belong together (e.g., *th, wr, ing, st*).
- The teacher should reinforce correct responses and not punish incorrect ones. If a student cannot answer a question about a cluster, a brief answer should be given, and the cluster should be returned to again before leaving that word.

## STEPS IN GLASS-ANALYSIS

**Step 1** Check to make sure students know the alphabet and most of the letter sounds.

**Step 2** Pick a set of word cards that teach a particular letter cluster.

> *Example:* the letter cluster "eck"

**Step 3** Seat the child or group of children before you and show the first word card. Ask if they can pronounce the word; if not, pronounce it and have students repeat the word as a group, or by calling on two or three for individual responses.

> *Example:* What is the word? (*pecking*)

**Step 4** Starting with the letter cluster of the packet, focus on as many letters and letter clusters as is reasonable, asking what *letters* make a given sound.

> *Example:* What letters make the *eck* sound?
>
> What letters make the *ing* sound?
>
> What letters make the *p* sound?

For words that contain only the teaching cluster plus an initial letter (e.g., *cat*), treat the initial letter as you would a cluster so that the student has been exposed to all the letter sounds in the word.

Step 5    Focus on sounds next, asking what *sound* is made by a given letter cluster or letter.

> *Example:* In the word "pecking," what sound does the letter *p* make?
>
> What sound do the letters *p-e-c-k* make?
>
> What sound do the letters *e-c-k* make?
>
> What sound do the letters *i-n-g* make?
>
> What is the whole word?

The ease and rapid pace of Glass-Analysis seem to offer several special advantages for promoting word analysis training at any level, including for upper grade remedial, learning disabled, and even adult students. The first is that paraprofessionals and volunteer tutors and parents can be easily trained to use the method with children or adults. The second is that a classroom teacher can set up a "decoding station" (just two desks facing one another in a quiet place) where students with word analysis and recognition problems can be called over for 5- to 15-minute training sessions several times a day until they become proficient decoders (Manzo & Manzo, 1990). The third advantage offered by the Glass-Analysis is that the two language scripts, once they become familiar to students, can be contextualized in the sense that they can be used by the teacher, or *as a personal decoding strategy by the student,* when challenging words are encountered in literature or in content area texts. This also can be done with key words before and/or after they are encountered in print, instead of interrupting the flow of meaning.

For further practice and fun, youngsters can be sent on a "sound search" through designated pages: "See if you can find the *air* sound, as in the word 'bear,' in any of the words on pages 210–214." In searching, students will find both examples (*tear, fair,* and *stare*) and nonexamples (*clear*), but in either case they will become better "programmed" and more "wordly wise" to the wily ways of the English language.

### Synthetic, or Intensive Phonics

Some educators take a "scorched earth" attitude toward intensive phonics. They feel that they must totally discredit and destroy it before it destroys or comes to dominate and destroy them. This sentiment stems at least in part from the fact that advocates for intensive phonics have included some highly commercialized interests (see Box 6.1 for a review of one called "Hooked on Phonics") and several active and vocal community-based groups.

This oddity aside, most of the synthetic, or intensive phonics, programs that are available today are supplementary or remedial offerings. They are distinguishable from most main line programs only in their tendency to rely more heavily on one or more of the following elements:

- A visual–auditory–kinesthetic feature which typically involves seeing, saying, and handtracing of letters and words

> **BOX 6.1**
>
> ## Hooked on Phonics: "Buyer Be Wary"
>
> Several members of the International Reading Association organization recently were charged with looking into the hotly advertised program called "Hooked on Phonics." Here is a summary of some of their comments:
>
> - "Hooked on Phonics" concentrates only on decoding.
> - No instruction is provided in blending letter sounds.
> - The materials fail completely to engage learners.
> - It is difficult even to deduce what they mean by reading in this program.
> - How does the program propose to move children or adults through ten years of reading instruction, practice, and experience with a mere two hours of listening to tapes?
> - Clearly, the program will not hurt a child, but there is little evidence that it will help. The evidence cited in ads has been requested several times but none has been forthcoming.
>
> *In:* California Reader, 25(2) Winter 1992, p. 17.

- A highly aural-auditory, or speaking and listening component
- A highly structured, often whole-class kind of lock-step training
- Highly linguistically controlled reading passages that repeat certain letter clusters, such as: Dan has a fan. The fan is tan. Dan's fan is tan (Lapp & Flood, 1992, p. 438). Oddly, these highly contrived passages are not too different from the familiar nursery rhyme, "Jack Spratt would eat no fat," which, in turn, is not too far removed from a familiar muscial form that is known today as rap.

As with the previously cited Gillingham–Stillman phonics approach, the presence of one or more of the above elements often belies some of the other main line features and special values that these programs do have to offer. A full review and description of some of these, such as the popular DISTAR mastery learning program and of the research available on these is presented in the chapter on special needs students. For the moment, we shall stay with more main line approaches such as syllabication. Even this topic, however, is not without some surrounding controversy. Glass (1973), for example, thinks it is a waste of time and effort.

### Syllabication: Phonics Back-Up

Syllabication is part of structural analysis, which often is considered to be part of phonics. Actually, structural analysis is a way of examining the way a word is built and hence, what it may mean; it is only incidentally related to pronunciation. The meaning aspects of structural analysis are taken up in a separate chapter on vocabulary. Structural analysis typically includes five aspects of words:

1. Prefixes, suffixes, and roots (morphemes)
2. Inflectional endings
3. Contractions

4.  Compound words
5.  Syllabication

It is the syllabication aspect of structural analysis that is most often taught as an aid to decoding. As noted in the previous research findings section, syllabication is a form of phonic or phonemic awareness; hence, those who do it well naturally also tend to learn to read and spell more easily. For example, the ability to read long words clearly is linked to the ability to break words into syllables (Friedrich, Schodler, & Juola, 1979). What is arguable, however, is whether the direct *teaching* of syllabication results in significant improvement in word recognition and word analysis skills.

Goodman (1973b) once called syllabication instruction "an easy way to make learning to read difficult." In fact, there is one criticism in particular of teaching syllabication that should be noted. It is the fact that "dialectic differences in readers make for differences in syllable pronunciation" (Tierney, Readence, & Dishner, 1990, p. 413). Dialect is a difficult obstacle to overcome in a linguistically diverse society. Nevertheless, there is evidence that practice in syllabication can significantly improve youngsters' ability to decode print into oral language (Cunningham, 1975–76; 1978).

Since several phonics rules are tied to syllabication, those pupils who find syllabication easy and natural to learn also find syllable-based phonics rules to be useful in decoding and reinforcing of rapid word recognition. Such students really enjoy listening for sound dividers and may cause the teacher to overvalue this strategy. It is good to be reminded that other children do not find syllabication easy or natural, and that there is no convincing evidence to suggest that great attention to syllabication will cause them to be able to easily recall and apply such rules to pronunciation or spelling. Nonetheless, this may not argue convincingly against teaching syllabication. One of the primary means of teaching word decoding skills, you will recall, is to keep a word in front of a student long enough and frequently enough for him or her to identify its distinguishing features and to internalize it in some personal way. Syllabication instruction does seem to accomplish this basic objective: the stimulus word is present, it is divided into logically pronounceable parts, and both analysis time and frequent repetitions are provided.

What then should guide instruction in syllabication? First, and foremost, it should not be obsessive or excessive. Beyond that, the general idea is to teach students to recognize letter clusters in an automatic, almost a conditioned response manner, rather than have them memorize complex rules. There are a few rules, however, that might be taught—if it is done deftly and with recognition that this instruction could benefit some children more than others, depending on their learning styles. For example, some children, even among those who are not natural syllabicators, are "sequential processors"—that is, they learn and do best with rule-based processes and step-by-step, or linear operations. They will tend to approach tasks by carefully studying and assembling the parts to construct a meaningful whole. These children can and do profit from instruction in syllabication and phonics rules. Other children, sometimes referred to as "simultaneous processors," do *not* benefit much from learning syllabication and phonics rules. These children operate on a more intuitive level, with a low level of tolerance for sequential processing. If they also are not natural syllabicators, they will need the kind of time that Thomas Edison, Robert Louis Stevenson, and others previously mentioned seemed to need to find some personal way to decode and recognize words. For such children, their initial approach to a rule-based task generally is to attempt to rapidly infer the whole and then to fill in the important parts as needed. In this way these children often reach impressive and inventive solutions. For such children, the whole-language philosophy is much more appropriate and charitable.

Another simple way to determine how profitable it is to teach syllabication is to introduce it as an appealing option, and then take a class vote to see how much and how they feel they could/should be taught about syllabication. Let the children negotiate with one another on the amount of time and the ways to be spent doing this, perhaps compromising on other tasks and instructional options that you may offer at other times.

This is a good time, too, to remember Burnett's (1991) suggestion to teach periodically as if we were salespeople who had to please our customers. Done on a limited basis, from reasonable choices, it can make teachers and students more astute about what is needed to get a job done, and no doubt will raise children's sense of participation in and control over class work.

Should you decide that it is appropriate to teach aspects of syllabication, you may wish to review the most useful rules for guiding syllabication and pronunciation that are provided in the Primer on Phonics (Appendix B). Here are some explicit ways to consider teaching syllabication:

1. Teach syllabication through *known* words, and preferably in context (teach *apple,* not *grap-ple*).

2. Use a deductive approach. Cite one appropriate rule and have students apply it to several words until they see how it applies (having discussed the rule of dividing a word between repeated consonants, using the example of *ap-ple;* how would you syllabicate *little* and *rattle?*).

3. Alternate this with an inductive approach. Show students several words that have the same syllabication rule in common and ask them to try to state the rule (*little, battle, carried*—division between repeated consonants).

4. Teach students to use this sequence when trying to syllabicate a word:

   a. Look for prefixes, then suffixes, and then familiar root words (these are all syllables).

   b. Try applying the rules we have studied (these can be recorded on a cue card for easy reference).

   c. Check the dictionary—it is the final arbiter, and every word listed in it is syllabicated.

Regarding the last point, any time a student, a list of words, and a dictionary can be brought together, there is an incidental means available for practicing syllabication in a self-pacing and self-correcting way. Encourage students to use the dictionary to look up definitions of words they don't know and even of words that they do "know." This activity keeps the emphasis on the semantic or meaning side of

FIGURE
6.1 **Sample Interlocking Word Analysis and Recognition Program (K–3)**

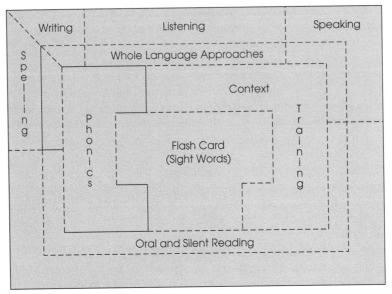

Notice that the lines between portions of most activities are permeable, permitting actual integration and fusion to occur, but that the modular, or componential approach is the more dominant factor in the realistic school model.

words and reading while building greater incidental familiarity with syllabication and other aspects of structural analysis.

### Fluency, or Word Recognition Training

Lewkowicz boldly states that "decoding *is* comprehension" (1987, p. 42). This statement is not just verbal play: effective comprehension and thinking are most achievable when one can move past the distraction of trying to decode words and on to a more natural sense of conversation, or transaction with text. In fact most readers reach a point where comprehension and thinking are facilitated *better* by reading than by listening or even discussion. This is because the fluent reader has a high degree of control over the reading process. Reading rate can be increased or decreased, and the reader is free to pause to reflect on personally relevant ideas and even to seek information to clarify words, phrases, allusions, or concepts.

Figure 6.1 illustrates one of the more popular ways of teaching and promoting effective word analysis and recognition. Notice that it is less than fully integrated but more than separate skills-based. We have found it convenient to refer to it as an "interlocking" model: each of the relevant language arts is involved in some contiguous or touching manner, and ideally in ways that interact with one another (as indicated with dotted lines in the diagram). In this realistic model, most of the language arts are presented as interrelated lessons, rather than as a single authentic and integrated instructional unit. The size of each component in the illustration below and the degree to which the components invite integration (as indicated by the dotted lines) tends to vary with school policy, teacher know-how, nature of available materials, and so on. See Cunningham's Piece Plan toward the end of the chapter for another example of an interlocking plan, though more from the perspective of a basal-based total reading–language program.

In the next section on contextual approaches to decoding, we look at some implicit ways to build word-decoding fluency, or rapid word recognition. Most authorities agree that fluency training is needed to connect phonics instruction with whole word, flash card training, which is covered a bit further ahead in the chapter.

## CONTEXTUAL APPROACHES TO DECODING

Contextual approaches center on reading for meaning, with the assumption that children will acquire the needed phonetic and word recognition skills in incidental ways. Contextual approaches are the methods of choice in whole-language teaching. In these approaches, word recognition is advanced through reading, with an emphasis on stories created by the children themselves. Children's own stories contain more natural language, topics, and concerns clearly of interest to children. Further, stories told by children are said to contain more colorful and "difficult" words that are in the children's speaking vocabularies, and thus are more likely, in the view of whole-language advocates, to transfer into children's reading vocabularies. Contextual approaches also encourage children to use pictures and context as clues to help in decoding unfamiliar words. Word deletion exercises are encouraged (Y. Goodman, 1975), as is the use of familiar children's stories, rhymes, and songs that contain repetitions and other predictable elements that support children's early efforts to associate meaning with printed words (see Box 6.2).

Most importantly, reading *to* children is seen as an essential means of sparking and extending children's interest in reading and building familiarity with redundant patterns in language. Words tend to be taught as "wholes," with phonic elements taught incidentally or not at all. In basal programs this approach is most often combined with analytical phonics (described earlier) and is an integral part of the interlocking word recognition and analysis package of most early reading programs. The

**BOX 6.2**

### Word Deletion Exercise

I dropped my dolly in the __1__.
I __2__ my dolly if it hurt.
The only thing my __3__ said was
Wah, wah, wah!

next method is one of the oldest and most respected traditions in integrated reading and language arts.

## Dictated Story

This approach is not teacher-directed, nor does it attempt to be "teacher-proof," as do some word recognition training methods. Rather, it relies on teacher sensitivity and agility in making the most of children's language experiences to teach word learning and writing. The method has been known and used for generations as one of several Language Experience Activities (Hall, 1981; Stauffer, 1980). LEAs now are more familiarly referred to as part of *the* "whole-language" approach. In fact, what the whole-language movement seems to have done is to provide LEAs with a fuller rationale and context (Y. Goodman, 1989).

The basic assumption of all contextual approaches to word learning is that word recognition and analysis can be learned, for the most part, incidentally through the process of being read to, writing down spoken language, and reading that which was written. Of the several variations on Language Experience Activities, the one called the Dictated Story, or Language Experience Story, is the most often recommended for use with novice and remedial level readers. The Dictated Story is described here as it might be employed with a small group, or for one-on-one remedial, or peer tutoring use. The method has been around for many generations and cannot be attributed to anyone in particular.

## STEPS IN THE DICTATED STORY APPROACH

**Step 1**   A discussion is generated around a question, event, storybook, or some concrete object.

**Step 2**   Youngsters are asked to compose a story or set of thoughts and reactions in response to the question, event, story, or object (see Box 6.3).

**Step 3**   The teacher records the story as told by the students, saying back what is being printed (50 to 250 words).

**Step 4**   The teacher reads the story back to the group, asking if there is anything that they would like to change or correct.

**Step 5**   Corrections and changes are made.

**Step 6**   The story is reread and individual words are stressed in a variety of optional ways:

   a.   Students attempt to read the story while the teacher or student partner underlines *every* word they *know* (rather than marking those they do not know). The teacher/partner may tell students the words they miss, but they should *first* encourage the student to try to use context clues (including pictures), letter sounds, and syntactic (word order) clues to decipher the words not immediately recognized.

   b.   Students reread the story, again underlining words they know. In this way words read correctly both times will be marked with a

| BOX 6.3 | **Students' Dictated Story** |

*Stimulus:*

The teacher has read the story of Winnie-the-Pooh aloud to the class.

*Students' Story:*

We got to do the book of Winnie the Pooh. It was a good story. Eeyore was so sad that he had a tear. Roo wanted to have a party for Eeyore, so he went to find Pooh and Tigger and Piglet for the party. He went to get Pooh, but Pooh was eating honey. He was eating so much honey that he would not eat at the party. Tigger did not want to come to a party. But then everyone came and they had lots of fun. They played games and had some cake and ice cream. Christopher Robin was taking a walk and he came to the party. Roo was singing "happy birthday to you," and they had lots of things to do.

    double line; words they figured out the second time will be marked with a single line.

c.   Students make a list of the words underlined once or not at all and convert these to flash cards for further analysis or practice as described later in the chapter.

d.   Students attempt to read some sentences composed by the teacher that contain essentially the same words as their story and, ideally, are along the same story line.

    A word of caution related to using the Dictated Story Approach has been offered by McCormick (1990), based on her research with nonreaders at the Ohio State Reading Clinic. McCormick notes that the stories dictated by severely disabled readers reflect these *older* students' more developed oral language; their stories tend to have too *many* words and too few *repetitions* of words for these nonreaders to learn and remember (1990). Thus attempts to use these students' Dictated Stories as instructional materials can result in lessons that are more frustrating than they are empowering. McCormick has developed an alternate strategy for nonreaders that introduces new words gradually and provides intensive practice with these words in a variety of contexts. McCormick's method and two related strategies for building fluency and rapid word recognition in struggling readers are presented in the chapter on special needs children.

## Little Books

    Clay (1991) has a slightly different perspective on the problems, previously noted, in using children's dictated stories for instruction: too many words, too few repetitions, and too many difficult words. She sees these as possible "transition texts" that can be used to help students make a smooth transfer from text with oral language characteristics to more formal writing. To produce text which helps with this transition, she suggests having the teacher work with youngsters to produce Little Books—or collections of their stories that have been edited and enhanced to more closely resemble formal writing.

**FIGURE 6.2**

| Our Trip to the Zoo | Nekita's Zoo Story | Ian's Zoo Story |
|---|---|---|

**Our Trip to the Zoo**

**Nekita's Zoo Story**

The zoo wants to change its name. They asked us for new names. The zoo-keeper said that he liked the name "Reserve" better.

**Ian's Zoo Story**

The ape was trying to pull a tire down off the ceiling. He is supposed to swing on the tire. We thought that he was mad about something.

cover                    page 1                    page 2

### Martin's "Sensible Phonics"

Just before whole language became the chief movement in reading education, there was a strong movement to return to phonics instruction. In an effort to deal with that movement, people like Bill Martin, Jr., who advocated for a Humanistic Language Reading Program, offered some wonderfully inventive ways to teach phonics incidentally as part of oral language. In fact, the poems and songs in Table 6.3 and those by Yopp in an earlier chapter were largely inspired by Bill Martin's work. Martin himself would involve children in a lot of what he called "sensible phonics" through such rhymes and poems.

Few of us can claim his special talent, but we can use his books and creative lessons. For example, when Martin decided that children needed to learn the "x" sound, he did not lay out a lesson in the step-by-step manner called for in Gray's Paradigm for teaching phonic elements. Rather, he collapsed the essence of the paradigm into an activity that could be used to teach a phonic element incidentally. Martin's Sensible Phonics goes something like this:

- A story is written or rewritten to give aural and visual distinction to a choice phonic element.
- The story is read aloud to students.
- Each sentence in the story is rewritten with scrambled word sounds. These are read aloud, pausing at the end of each sentence for the children to unscramble it orally (see Table 6.3).

An approach such as this has the obvious advantage of being playful. However, it has possible disadvantages:

- It can be demanding to a fault on one's ability to be creative all of the time.
- It is nonsystematic, and hence hit and miss.
- It may not be easy or appeal to youngsters who do not have the verbal dexterity that such verbal play requires, although this is overcome somewhat by choral responding.

**Table 6.3**

## Sensible Phonics: Sample Lesson

First the teacher reads "A Maker of Boxes" aloud to the class. Then the scrambled sentences are read, one at a time, pausing at the end of each sentence for children to say the unscrambled sentence.

| *The first part of a story for teaching the sound of "x"* | *sample scrambled sentences* |
|---|---|
| ### A Maker of Boxes | |
| Hello! My name is Albert | Lelho! Ny mame is Albert. |
| I'm a maker of boxes. | I'm a baker of moxes. |
| I make paper boxes, | I bake maper poxes, |
|    and cardboard boxes, | and bardboard coxes, |
| and wooden boxes . . . | and booden woxes, |
|     and square boxes, | and bare squoxes |
|   and round boxes, | and bound roxes, |
| and long boxes, | and bong loxes |
|   and short boxes, | and bort shoxes, |
|    and little boxes, | and bittle loxes, |
|   and big boxes, | and big boxes |
| . . . and all of them are empty. | . . . and all of em are thempty. |

*From Bill Martin, Jr., Workshop*
*Kansas City Public Schools, 1975.*

These disadvantages notwithstanding, it is a good example of exciting and creative teaching of phonics, an otherwise unexciting topic. As such, it provides reflective teachers with another alternative to the basic paradigm and invites all of us to be a bit more creative.

The next group of methods, known as Repeated Readings methods, addresses the circular problem that those very youngsters who are having difficulty in learning to read *also* are the ones who tend to avoid reading, and to read *least*. Lack of practice further limits their ability to become fluent, to acquire new information, and may even result in poor habits of reading, such as reading haltingly or with emotionally disruptive levels of apprehension. Repeated Readings methods counteract this problem by structuring regular, ongoing opportunities for youngsters to read who otherwise would not.

### Repeated Readings Methods

Repeated Readings refers to a cluster of methods that has a student do one or any combination of the following:

1.   Read the same material more than once.
2.   Listen to it before reading.
3.   Read it with immediate support from another on first or subsequent readings.

These methods also provide for review and further exposure to new words, practice in reading out loud with a natural rate and fluency, and opportunity to experience the four major benefits of reading: pleasure, knowledge growth, vocabulary enrichment, and better understanding of one's self and surroundings. Research evidence tends to suggest that poor readers with decoding problems benefit the most from Repeated Readings Methods (Carver & Hoffman, 1981; Dowhower, 1987; McEvoy & Homan, 1991).

There are several versions of Repeated Readings. We have fashioned the version described here (Manzo & Manzo, 1993) from pioneering works by Allington (1983a), Clay (1985), Dowhower (1989), Samuels (1979), Ballard (1978), Topping (1987), and Koskinen and Blum (1986).

## REPEATED READINGS: STEPS AND POINTERS

**Step 1**    Help a child select an interesting portion of a selection (100 to 200 words) at the student's "instructional" or medium difficulty level and set a goal for an appropriate oral reading rate, in words-per-minute (usually 60–110).

**Step 2**    Time the student's initial, unrehearsed oral reading of the passage (See Box 6.4 for time charting).

**Step 3**    Instruct the student to practice in pairs and at home.

**Step 4**    Time and graph reading rate again for the student to see, following the previous practice step.

**Step 5**    Continue oral rereadings, timing, and graphing of times, at intervals of several days.

**Step 6**    When the preset goal is reached, begin a new passage or continue reading the remainder of the passage.

## SOME OPTIONS TO STEPS 1–6

**Step 7**    The teacher, buddy, or parent can serve as a "talking dictionary," providing any word that the student calls for with the phrase "word please." (Ballard, 1978; Topping, 1987).

**Step 8**    The teacher, buddy, or parent can give the reader feedback and have the reader self-evaluate progress (see Figure 6.3 for guidelines from Koskinen & Blum, 1986). The latter is best done from audio recordings, which also are inexpensive enough to be kept for a child's individual portfolio.

**Step 9**    Do choral repeated reading with a large group using poems, song lyrics, folk tales, or some other such compelling sequence or predictable pattern (Lauritzen, 1982).

Research, as well as reports from teachers and parents, indicates that this simple method is highly motivating and results in increased word recognition and fluency (Herman, 1985). This approach also improves rate, comprehension, and confidence in reading new passages, and not merely those used in repeated practice (O'Shea,

**FIGURE 6.3**

## Self-Evaluation of Reading 1, Reading 2, and Reading 3

### Reading 1 (Self-Evaluation)

How well did you read? (Circle one)

| terrible | not so good | fair | good | fantastic |

### Reading 2 (Peer Evaluation)

How did your partner's reading get better? (Check *all* that apply.)

____ He or she read more smoothly
____ He or she knew more words
____ He or she read with more expression

  ** Tell your partner one thing that was
     better about his or her reading.

### Reading 3 (Peer Evaluation)

How did your partner's reading get better? (Check *all* that apply.)

____ He or she read more smoothly
____ He or she knew more words
____ He or she read with more expression

  ** Tell your partner one thing that was
     better about his or her reading.

*Inventory from Koskinen & Blum (1986).*

*Drawings provided from experimental IRTI © Anthony & Ula Manzo.*

Sindelar, O'Shea, 1985; Topping, 1987). There now, too, is evidence that learning disabled students derive some special benefits from repeated readings (Roshotte & Torgensen, 1985).

To further heighten the positive effects of repeated readings, the teacher can orally read portions of a selection, pausing to discuss the first few paragraphs with students. This approach, previously described as the Oral Reading Strategy (Manzo, 1980), also is an easy way to get youngsters started on *silent* repeated readings by modeling an appropriate reading rate, giving help with unknown words, and providing an introduction to new concepts that will be encountered. This combination of the Oral Reading Strategy and Rereadings of an initial paragraph is an especially useful prereading strategy for introducing challenging, content-rich material.

Aulls and Graves provide a handy chart (see Box 6.4) and excellent commercial materials (from Scholastic, Inc.) for practicing and visualizing progress from Repeated Readings.

To avoid getting all wrapped up in the procedural aspects of repeated readings, try to remember a simple suggestion of Rasinski (1988). It is to use natural classroom events to encourage repeated readings. These should include activities such as putting on plays and having older students read short books to younger ones (Rasinski, 1989).

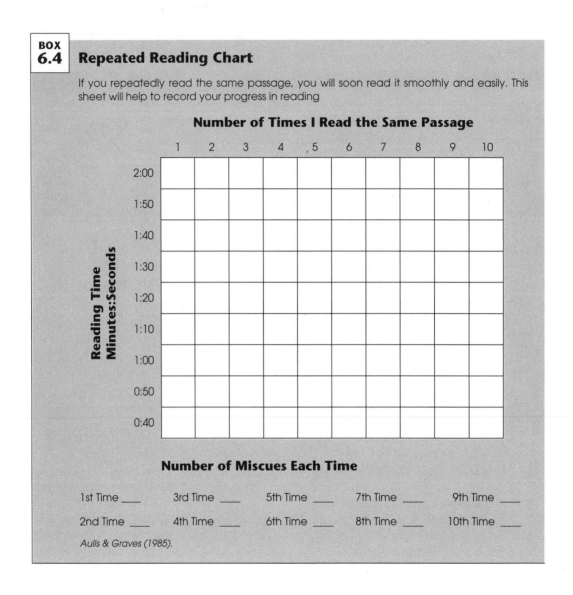

**BOX 6.4**

## Repeated Reading Chart

If you repeatedly read the same passage, you will soon read it smoothly and easily. This sheet will help to record your progress in reading

**Number of Times I Read the Same Passage**

|  | 1 | 2 | 3 | 4 | 5 | 6 | 7 | 8 | 9 | 10 |
|---|---|---|---|---|---|---|---|---|---|---|

Reading Time Minutes:Seconds

2:00
1:50
1:40
1:30
1:20
1:10
1:00
0:50
0:40

**Number of Miscues Each Time**

1st Time ____     3rd Time ____     5th Time ____     7th Time ____     9th Time ____

2nd Time ____     4th Time ____     6th Time ____     8th Time ____     10th Time ____

*Aulls & Graves (1985).*

Now let's look at some often maligned methods of teaching sight words. See if you don't find some sense in having these techniques in your professional repertoire.

## MODELS AND METHODS OF TEACHING SIGHT WORDS

### RATIONALE FOR TEACHING SIGHT WORDS

As previously noted, it cannot be firmly established just how many repetitions it takes to learn to easily recognize and say a word. This is due to a number of possible confounding variables, such as whether the word looks like a child's name (e.g., "mark") or like nothing familiar (e.g., "gargoyle") or familiar to the point of interfering with similar-looking words (e.g., "these"). Nonetheless, seeking some kind of average, Gates is said to have estimated that it takes between 20 and 44 exposures. Whatever the actual number of times may be, it surely is more than most teachers tend to provide. Therefore it is necessary to have a solid grasp of the rationale, means, and methods by which to conduct and sustain whole-word instruction. The rationale for doing so has three bases. One is in the nature of the language; another is in the nature of the task or purpose for reading; and the third is in the nature of a developmental strength in most children in the primary grades. Each of these requires a bit of elaboration.

Although approximately 85 percent of the words in the English language are phonetically regular, that still leaves about 15–20 percent that are *not* phonetically regular, and these, as previously noted, are the words that appear most frequently in print—about 80 percent of the time. Hence, when samples of words from typical school books were fed to a computer programmed to apply phonics rules, the computer could correctly interpret only 49 percent of them (Hanna, Hodges, Hanna, & Rudolph, 1966). This happens neither by conspiracy nor by accident. It is in the nature of language: the more a word is used, the more its sounds tend to become relaxed, clipped, or otherwise suitable to oral use, while its print, or graphemic, characteristics remain fairly constant. This is especially the case with *function words*. These are words that do not convey much meaning in themselves, but aid in sentence building, or syntactical construction: "they," "you," "other," "who," "could." These words traditionally are taught as *sight words*. You learn to say the word when you see it, without paying much attention to the sounds of the letters or application of phonetic rules. In order to do this, the reader needs to be taught to practice selective inattention. This seldom-referenced but essential skill makes it possible to easily learn to *say* "nite" for "night" rather than a guttural pronunciation of the 'gh'—or an /f/ sound pronunciation of the 'gh,' as in "rough," which would convert "night" to "nift"!

Teaching children to recognize words on sight also is justified on the grounds that eventually all words need to become sight words. That is, words must be quickly and automatically recognized with 100 percent accuracy in order for meaningful and fluent reading to occur. As previously noted, LaBerge and Samuels (1974) have referred to this process of instant and accurate recognition as *automaticity*.

The basic principles of sight word instruction are fairly simple:

- Get students to *see* words, to recognize their distinguishing features.
- Have students *say* the words aloud in flash presentation.
- Have students look for and silently *practice* saying these words wherever they are encountered, until they are learned to 100 percent accuracy.

Some of the ability to acquire rapid sight word recognition rests upon an innate human capacity called *eidetic imagery*. This is the ability to first see something as a whole and then to continue to picture it before you in great detail a few moments after it has been removed. Eidetic imagery is one of those "use it or lose it" things. This ability peaks in most children between the ages of six and nine, and then begins to recede or atrophy since it apparently is not called upon to any great degree in contemporary life. Knowing about this developmental phenomenon is useful in seeking out a strength that can be fairly safely relied upon in initial reading instruction (Manzo & Manzo, 1993). Unfortunately the ability is not present in all children to an equal degree, nor at precisely the same time, and there are some youngsters for whom it is in such short supply and hence are somewhat learning disabled. Boder (1972) has identified some youngsters whose skill in whole-word memory of this type is so poor that she uses the term *dyseidetic dyslexia* to describe their condition. Fortunately this dysfunction does yield to effective teaching, and the teaching actually helps to improve overall (very) short-term memory, which is highly similar, though not identical to eidetic imagery.

## GENERAL TIPS ON SIGHT WORD TEACHING

The role of the theory of early learning, discussed in a previous chapter, applies in great measure to sight word instruction. While the use of sight word instruction implies repetition, it should be noted that as the reader's achievement level increases, the need for repetitions decreases (Hargis, Terhaar-Yonkers, William, & Reed, 1988). For example, once a child has learned to recognize that his name is spelled M/a/r/k, learning the word m/a/r/k/e/t is much easier; once the word "these" is recognized with high accuracy at sight, words like "there" and "those" are more easily learned.

Of further note in teaching sight words is the extent to which they are functional words or words that conjure images. Words that conjure images, like "horse," require far fewer repetitions than abstract words like "if" (Hargis et al., 1988).

One other key point to remember in *initial* teaching of sight words is to avoid words that look alike, as in what/when; their/then. Just as with initial teaching of the alphabet, it is best to select words that have clear featural differences. Where similar words are concerned, first teach one of the confusing words until it is learned well, saving comparing and contrasting of like words for a later phase in learning (Wiesendanger & Bader, 1987).

Following is a collection of ways to enhance eidetic imaging and short-term memory, as well as to improve long-term memory for sight words.

## FLASH CARD APPROACHES TO SIGHT WORDS AND EIDETIC IMAGERY

There are many variations on the flash card approach. The one described here is a synthesis of several methods, based largely on those described by Cunningham (1980), Ekwall and Shanker (1988), and the authors (Manzo & Manzo, 1993). The method uses voice intonations and pivotal questions about each word to provide the necessary repetitions, attention to its distinguishing features, and to strengthen short-term memory. Since it incorporates several traditional and modern techniques, we have come to call it the *New Eclectic Sight Word Strategy.*

### New Eclectic Sight Word Strategy

This strategy can be done with a whole class or a small group in a tutoring situation. The teacher first selects appropriate words. These may be taken from children's charts of dictated stories. These are printed on flash cards or written on the chalkboard. The words then are brought to the children's attention and taught to rapid and automatic response in the manner illustrated below. Be advised that some educators find approaches such as this offensive, referring to such recitation as teaching children to "bark at words" (Stahl, 1992). We respect their sensibilities, but see conditioned response training as a viable teaching tool with a proven track record.

**Sample Script for the New Eclectic Sight Word Strategy**    The word "and" is used because it has a high frequency of occurrence and is an important connective. Most children are hard pressed even to say what it means (also, furthermore).

*Teacher:*    See this word? The word is **and**. Everyone look at this word and say it together.

*Students:*    And

*Teacher:*    That's correct. Now say it five times while looking at it.

*S's:*    And, and, and, and, and

*T:*    Good. Now say it louder.

*S's:*    **And!**

*T:*    Come on, you can say it louder than that!

*S's:*    **AND!**

*T:*    OK, I have three other cards here ("again," "answer," "arrange"). When I show a card that is *not* "and," say "No!" in a loud voice. But when you see "and," say it in a whisper.

*S's:*    No!

*S's:*    No!

Make time for directed word study

| | |
|---|---|
| **S's:** | (whisper) "and" |
| **T:** | Great. Look at it carefully, and when I remove it, close your eyes and try to picture the word under your eyelids. Do you see it? Good. Now say it in a whisper again. |
| **S's:** | "and" |
| **T:** | Good. Now—all together—spell it. |
| **S's:** | A . . . N . . . D |
| **T:** | Now pretend to write it in the air in front of you with your finger while saying each letter. |
| **S's:** | A . . . N . . . D |
| **T:** | Good. Now describe the word the way you would describe a new kid to a friend who hasn't met him or her yet. |
| **S1:** | It's small |
| **S2:** | It has a witch's hat in the beginning |
| **S3:** | It has a belly at the end |
| **T:** | What's its name again? |
| **S's:** | AND! |
| **T:** | Let's search for "and's" throughout the day and especially after you get home tonight. We'll ask you later if you found any in school, and again tomorrow morning if you found any at home. |

In the morning, have on the board, "Did you find any *and*'s last night?" Over the next few lessons, ask if the student has seen an "and."

Up to three words a day usually can be taught in this general way. Again, for initial learning trials, try to select target words that do not *look* alike. To reiterate from above, even words that are shown in context with the target word and that look like it should be treated lightly. At this tender stage in the process, the student is facing the grittiest part of early learning—the establishment of those first semblances of accuracy in word recognition. In very short order, students should be ready to begin to rapidly learn similar looking and sounding words, largely from context and incidental exposure. This initially guarded, almost contrived way of teaching rapid word recognition is supported by a large body of research in theories of learning called *proactive and retroactive learning* dilemmas. Basically, what it says is that if not done properly (as described above), things taught immediately before or after one another can interfere with each other, causing them both to be confused and forgotten.

## Word Lists

One of the earliest sources of high frequency sight words was compiled by Dolch (1951). Two more recent sight word lists, by Fry (1980) and Eeds (1985), are found in Table 6.4 (pp. 216–218) and Table 6.5 (pp. 220–221). Fry's list is based on the frequency of occurrence of words in more recent school texts and trade books. Eeds' list is shorter, containing 227 words, also in order of frequency of occurrence, but derived from 400 storybooks for beginning readers, making it more suitable for a literature-based or individualized reading program. The Fry and Eeds lists have the further advantage of being easily used for diagnostic assessment of a child's approximate level of progress in learning higher and lower frequency words. Quite reliable tests of progress can be made by selecting a total of about twenty words from the three lists.

### Other Flash Card Activities

To further reinforce targeted sight words, try these traditional methods, collected for use in preventing and treating eidetic imaging and whole-word learning disorders (Manzo & Manzo, 1993).

1. Put the words on oak tag and place them around the room. If you add other clues, such as pictures, remember to remove them after a short time.

2. Have the child put the words on a ring that can be carried about for self-review.
3. Create a buddy system that has students checking and helping one another to learn the words. Have frequent and spaced practice sessions.
4. Distribute prepared word cards to students and have them sort them into known and unknown words. Have them say all the words they (think) they know. Next begin to use the unknown words to teach self-reliant decoding. Ask students to first try to figure out what each word says, so that word analysis becomes an embedded consideration. Informally note the letters and sounds that may be giving trouble and include those elements as priorities in teaching letter clusters, phonetic analysis, and syllabication.
5. Have students try to construct sentences from their flash cards. Tell them that you will help them to add any words they wish, but that the words added then become part of their personal word card file, and they must add them to their word ring for frequent practice.

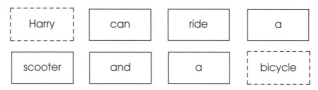

6. Use media-assisted reinforcement devices. There is an excellent (older) device called a Language Master (product of Bell & Howell Corporation) that was designed for training in sight word recognition. It is a card with a piece of magnetic tape across the bottom of both sides. The student pushes it through a tape recorder while saying what he thinks the word is. The card then is

## Table 6.4

### Fry's "The New Instant Word List"

**FIRST HUNDRED**

| First 25<br>Group 1a | Second 25<br>Group 1b | Third 25<br>Group 1c | Fourth 25<br>Group 1d |
|---|---|---|---|
| the | or | will | number |
| of | one | up | no |
| and | had | other | way |
| a | by | about | could |
| to | word | out | people |
| in | but | many | my |
| is | not | then | than |
| you | what | them | first |
| that | all | these | water |
| it | were | so | been |
| he | we | some | call |
| was | when | her | who |
| for | your | would | oil |
| on | can | make | now |
| are | said | like | find |
| as | there | him | long |
| with | use | into | down |
| his | an | time | day |
| they | each | has | did |
| I | which | look | get |
| at | she | two | come |
| be | do | more | made |
| this | how | write | may |
| have | their | go | part |
| from | if | see | over |

reversed and put through with a prerecorded voice saying the word correctly. There also are computer programs that now do essentially the same thing. Cutler and Truss (1989) have designed one that pronounces and gives meanings for targeted words in popular teenage novels.

7.  Connect sight words to meaningful contexts by having youngsters group new words into categories, such as words associated with activities and tools used in the classroom (chalkboard, eraser, desk, etc.) or words that might describe books (big, colorful, hard, soft, etc.). This categorizing activity adds a further and proven dimension of meaning and concept enhancement to word manipulations.

8.  Connect sight words to authentic experiences with "Postcard" and other Language Experience Activities. Have students write brief postcard letters to friends and family. Mention the weather, what they are doing, how they are feeling, and some special salutations and closings, such as *Dear cousin;* and *Your grandson.* These are excellent writing/reading/learning opportunities.

## SECOND HUNDRED

| First 25<br>Group 2a | Second 25<br>Group 2b | Third 25<br>Group 2c | Fourth 25<br>Group 2d |
| --- | --- | --- | --- |
| new | great | put | kind |
| sound | where | end | hand |
| take | help | does | picture |
| only | through | another | again |
| little | much | well | change |
| work | before | large | off |
| know | line | must | play |
| place | right | big | spell |
| year | too | even | air |
| live | mean | such | away |
| me | old | because | animal |
| back | any | turn | house |
| give | same | here | pint |
| most | tell | why | page |
| very | boy | ask | letter |
| after | follow | went | mother |
| thing | came | men | answer |
| our | want | read | found |
| just | show | need | study |
| name | also | land | still |
| good | around | different | learn |
| sentence | form | home | should |
| man | three | us | America |
| think | small | move | world |
| say | set | try | high |

9. Use word games—commercial and teacher-made (word bingo, consonant lotto, word dominoes, crossword puzzles, word wheels). See the chapter on basals and practice materials for specific suggestions. "Hangman," one of the oldest word games, can be used with little preparation and can be used as a large-group, small-group, or paired activity. Also play "Wheel of Fortune," which Merv Griffin said he made up as a simple variation on Hangman.

10. Have students try to act out with their hands and/or body what they think a certain word "looks" like. Select one of the pantomimes or gestures offered by the students and have everyone do it while saying the word. For example, for "church," the pantomime might be hands in steeple shape. This step adds an encoding, or personal transformation step to word recognition learning as well as a certain degree of motor involvement. This method was suggested to us by a veteran primary school teacher who modeled it after Motor Imaging (Casale, 1983), a meaning vocabulary strategy detailed in the vocabulary chapter ahead.

## Table 6.4—cont'd

**THIRD HUNDRED**

| First 25 Group 2a | Second 25 Group 2b | Third 25 Group 2c | Fourth 25 Group 2d |
|---|---|---|---|
| every | left | until | idea |
| near | don't | children | enough |
| add | few | side | eat |
| food | while | feet | face |
| between | along | car | watch |
| own | might | mile | far |
| below | close | night | Indian |
| country | something | walk | real |
| plant | seem | white | almost |
| last | next | sea | let |
| school | hard | began | above |
| father | open | grow | girl |
| keep | example | took | sometimes |
| tree | begin | river | mountain |
| never | life | four | cut |
| start | always | carry | young |
| city | those | state | talk |
| earth | both | once | soon |
| eye | paper | book | list |
| light | together | hear | song |
| thought | got | stop | leave |
| head | group | without | family |
| under | often | second | body |
| story | run | late | music |
| saw | important | miss | color |

*Fry (1980), pp. 286–287.*

After reading about the many controversies and different tacks for teaching word analysis and recognition, you probably are ready for a proposal as to how to reconcile the controversies and put these pieces together into a sensible and balanced program for your classroom. Fortunately, such a plan has recently been offered by Cunningham (1991). She presented her plan at a meeting of the National Reading Conference as part of a larger report on the state of phonics instruction. She said she had no name for it yet, so we took the liberty of calling it a Piece Plan. The small pun on peace aside, the plan has some of the ingredients of the New Eclecticism: it values proven teaching traditions and reflectively draws upon newer findings and considerations.

### Cunningham's Piece Plan

This plan is based on Cunningham's work with primary school teachers and on recent research-based understandings of how children develop quick, accurate word identification systems and effective habits of reading and writing. Its structure is similar to that used in the successful Reading Recovery Program—the New Zealand plan for early intervention that is more fully described in a later chapter on special needs children.

Before describing the Piece Plan, it seems necessary to comment on the question of whether a plan based on "pieces" satisfies the longstanding interest in achieving reading–language arts integration, as opposed to reading–language arts component parts. Very simply, we believe that the Piece Plan does this for some explicit and metaphoric reasons. Before things can be brought together, they need to be permitted to gather momentum, as a gentle brook flows into a stream, then the stream flows more rapidly into larger bodies of water whose gathered momentum is increasingly rapid and strong. The fusion of brooks into streams, and streams into rivers is most likely to occur when they are in close proximity to one another. An increasing number of educators are realizing that to dam up a brook, or temporarily isolate it, is to permit it to amass the critical level of depth it may need to make its way more forcefully to the stream. To dam up the stream is to permit it to build the energy it needs to continue its flow and integration into the main flow of literacy.

Three examples of this kind of "damming-up" to build strength come to mind: Glass's temporary decontextualization of word decoding training discussed earlier in the chapter; Eeds' argument for treating literature as art more so than reading lessons in order to stimulate more "grand conversations" than inquisitions with children; and the implicit argument in the previous chapter that children be taught, rather explicitly, through "instructional conversations" to say what they feel about what they read, why they feel that way, and whether they really understand what they have read. Let's look more closely now at Cunningham's Piece Plan and see whether the parts are close enough together to merge in some natural and integrated way.

The Piece Plan model teaches reading and writing in a multilevel, multimethod approach. It unfolds in a two-hour-long language arts block. The key feature of the program, according to Cunningham, is the lack of any fixed ability groups and the division of 120 minutes of instructional time into four roughly equal blocks, or interlocking components of structured activities. The four blocks are:

- **Basal Block**   This involves teacher-guided reading and discussion of selections from basal readers and tradebooks, with children reading and working with partners.

- **Writing Block**   This involves employing the Writing Process format (detailed in another chapter). Teachers conduct a compressed writing process lesson that has children writing on topics of their choosing, using invented spellings as these may be needed. They then share their work in an "author's chair" format, and finally publish their Little Books with help in revising and editing.

- **Self-Selected Block**   This involves having children read trade books, literature, and other materials, essentially of their own choosing. While Cunningham did not say so explicitly, we presume that this block also includes conferences with students about what they are reading and incidental teaching such as it is called for in Individualized Reading (Veatch, 1978) and whole-language classrooms.

**Table 6.5**

### High Frequency Words from Children's Literature

**FINAL CORE 227-WORD LIST BASED ON 400 STORYBOOKS FOR BEGINNING READERS**

| | | | | | | | |
|---|---|---|---|---|---|---|---|
| the | 1314 | her | 156 | could | 90 | friend | 65 |
| and | 985 | what | 152 | good | 90 | cry | 64 |
| a | 831 | we | 151 | this | 90 | oh | 64 |
| I | 757 | him | 144 | don't | 89 | Mr. | 63 |
| to | 746 | no | 143 | little | 89 | bed | 63 |
| said | 688 | so | 141 | if | 87 | an | 62 |
| you | 638 | out | 140 | just | 87 | very | 62 |
| he | 488 | up | 137 | baby | 86 | where | 60 |
| it | 345 | are | 133 | way | 85 | play | 59 |
| in | 311 | will | 127 | there | 83 | let | 59 |
| was | 294 | look | 126 | every | 83 | long | 58 |
| she | 250 | some | 123 | went | 82 | here | 58 |
| for | 235 | day | 123 | father | 80 | how | 57 |
| that | 232 | at | 122 | had | 79 | make | 57 |
| is | 230 | have | 121 | see | 79 | big | 56 |
| his | 226 | your | 121 | dog | 78 | from | 55 |
| but | 224 | mother | 119 | home | 77 | put | 55 |
| they | 218 | come | 118 | down | 76 | read | 55 |
| my | 214 | not | 115 | got | 73 | them | 55 |
| of | 204 | like | 112 | would | 73 | as | 54 |
| on | 192 | then | 108 | time | 71 | Miss | 53 |
| me | 187 | get | 103 | love | 70 | any | 52 |
| all | 179 | when | 101 | walk | 70 | right | 52 |
| be | 176 | thing | 100 | came | 69 | nice | 50 |
| go | 171 | do | 99 | were | 68 | other | 50 |
| can | 162 | too | 91 | ask | 67 | well | 48 |
| with | 158 | want | 91 | back | 67 | old | 48 |
| one | 157 | did | 91 | now | 66 | night | 48 |

*Eeds (1985), p. 420.*

- **Working with Words Block** This involves a variety of activities designed to "help children develop automatic reading and spelling of the highest frequency words and a daily Making Words[3] activity designed to help them learn that words are made up of letters which form predictable spelling patterns" (Cunningham, 1991, p. 14). This component of the Piece Plan program includes the types of sight word and phonics training presented immediately above in this chapter, and, where necessary, the more intensive approaches described ahead in the chapter on special needs students.

Cunningham and associates have collected data on the first two years of instruction under the multilevel, multimethod Piece Plan. Their research indicates that

---

[3] See Chapter 11 for a description of the Making Words activity (Cunningham & Cunningham, 1992).

| | | | | | | | |
|---|---|---|---|---|---|---|---|
| may | 48 | mom | 35 | fast | 28 | ball | 24 |
| about | 47 | kid | 35 | next | 28 | sat | 24 |
| think | 47 | give | 35 | only | 28 | stay | 24 |
| new | 46 | around | 34 | am | 27 | each | 23 |
| know | 46 | by | 34 | began | 27 | ever | 23 |
| help | 46 | Mrs. | 34 | head | 27 | until | 23 |
| grand | 46 | off | 33 | keep | 27 | shout | 23 |
| boy | 46 | sister | 33 | teacher | 27 | mama | 22 |
| take | 45 | find | 32 | sure | 27 | use | 22 |
| cat | 44 | fun | 32 | says | 27 | turn | 22 |
| body | 43 | more | 32 | ride | 27 | thought | 22 |
| school | 43 | while | 32 | pet | 27 | papa | 22 |
| house | 42 | tell | 32 | hurry | 26 | lot | 21 |
| morning | 42 | sleep | 32 | hand | 26 | blue | 21 |
| yes | 41 | made | 31 | hard | 26 | bath | 21 |
| after | 41 | first | 31 | push | 26 | mean | 21 |
| never | 41 | say | 31 | our | 26 | sit | 21 |
| or | 40 | took | 31 | their | 26 | together | 21 |
| self | 40 | dad | 30 | watch | 26 | best | 20 |
| try | 40 | found | 30 | because | 25 | brother | 20 |
| has | 38 | lady | 30 | door | 25 | feel | 20 |
| always | 38 | soon | 30 | us | 25 | floor | 20 |
| over | 38 | ran | 30 | should | 25 | wait | 20 |
| again | 37 | dear | 29 | room | 25 | tomorrow | 20 |
| side | 37 | man | 29 | pull | 25 | surprise | 20 |
| thank | 37 | better | 29 | great | 24 | shop | 20 |
| why | 37 | through | 29 | gave | 24 | run | 20 |
| who | 36 | stop | 29 | does | 24 | own | 20 |
| saw | 36 | still | 29 | car | 24 | | |

both more able and less able children are making better than expected progress in decoding and fluency (Cunningham, Hall, & Defer, 1991; Hall & Cunningham, 1991). Cunningham's larger conclusion from this research is that children and teachers are best served by a *balance* and *variety* of activities, some more teacher-centered and others more student-centered. Together such balance and variety increase the probability of meeting the needs of children at different reading levels and with different learning styles in the same classroom. This aspect of the Piece Plan is more in the tradition of the "old" eclecticism since a general potpourri of methods is assembled to meet a range of probable needs. To bring this aspect of the plan into alignment with the New Eclecticism, the teacher would need to collect some additional information on the more specific needs of the pupils, and then adjust the amount of time and possibly the intensity of some of the four aspects of the plan to those needs. Cunningham's plan implicitly allows for this, since the teacher can begin with the equal-parts plan and then modify as need suggests.

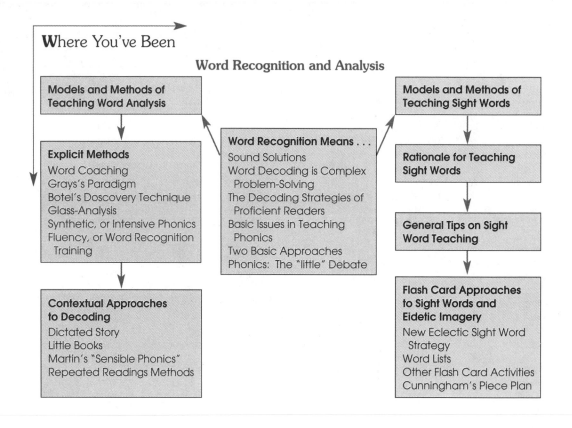

**W**here You've Been

## Word Recognition and Analysis

**Models and Methods of Teaching Word Analysis**

**Explicit Methods**
Word Coaching
Grays's Paradigm
Botel's Doscovery Technique
Glass-Analysis
Synthetic, or Intensive Phonics
Fluency, or Word Recognition Training

**Contextual Approaches to Decoding**
Dictated Story
Little Books
Martin's "Sensible Phonics"
Repeated Readings Methods

**Word Recognition Means . . .**
Sound Solutions
Word Decoding is Complex Problem-Solving
The Decoding Strategies of Proficient Readers
Basic Issues in Teaching Phonics
Two Basic Approaches
Phonics: The "little" Debate

**Models and Methods of Teaching Sight Words**

**Rationale for Teaching Sight Words**

**General Tips on Sight Word Teaching**

**Flash Card Approaches to Sight Words and Eidetic Imagery**
New Eclectic Sight Word Strategy
Word Lists
Other Flash Card Activities
Cunningham's Piece Plan

**W**here You're Going

The next chapter continues the emphasis on words, but this time from the arguably more important dimension of word meanings. The chapter discusses vocabulary acquisition and enrichment in reading, listening, writing, and in terms of its implications for effective thinking.

### *Reflective Inquiries and Activities*

1. Beginning reading instruction tends to be based on generalizations about proficient readers. Do you think that reading educators are on the right track when we try to teach less proficient readers to do more of what proficient readers do? Can you find relevant information in your experience or in the chapter that sheds some light on this practice? Can you think of reasonable *alternatives* to this assumption?

2. Characterize yourself in terms of how you think that you might best have been taught to decode and recognize words. Ask this same question to someone close to you, but whom you suspect of having a different general orientation. Share your findings in class. What implications do you draw from the class summary about how to best teach to a heterogeneous class?

3. Which research findings related to teaching and learning word analysis and recognition struck you as most significant(?) most surprising(?) most necessary for you to remember as a teacher(?) most what you wished you could have told your teacher(s) about when you were a student?

4. Which specific word analysis methodologies do you think that you will try to master first? Why?

5. Check a basal teacher's guide and compare and contrast its recommendation for teaching phonics with those recommended in this chapter.

6. Do you think you will teach syllabication? Why/why not? If so, how? If not, with what would you replace it?

7. Select two incidental, or whole-language, based methods for teaching word recognition and analysis that appeal to you. Why do they appeal to you?

8. Would you use "recitation" training to teach whole words? Why/Why not?

9. Which word list would you work from to teach sight words? Why?

10. Tell specifically what you would do under each component of Cunningham's Piece Plan.

11. Compare the "interlocking" reading/language arts approach (Figure 6.1) with the analogy of the dammed-up brook that was used to justify Cunningham's Piece Plan. How do these highly similar ideas compare in theoretical and practical terms with whole-language and integrated reading/language arts?

12. Write a paragraph for your resume telling what you now know about word recognition and analysis and how you think this may qualify you to handle a position that you seek.

13. Class Project: Make up a set of three questions per class member from the Primer on Phonics (Appendix B), to be submitted to the class instructor. Take a week or so to prepare, and then hold a group competition to see who has learned the most about this tricky business. For fun, give your groups names, elect a leader for each group, have a group cheer, but mostly, come up with a nifty study plan and some study and recall techniques (see the chapter on study strategies for some suggestions).

### CHAPTER 7

# VOCABULARY FOR READING, LISTENING, THINKING, AND WRITING

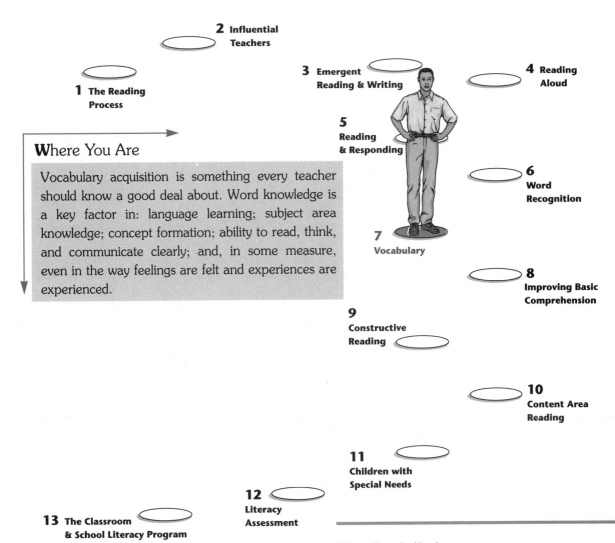

**2** Influential Teachers

**1** The Reading Process

**3** Emergent Reading & Writing

**4** Reading Aloud

**5** Reading & Responding

**6** Word Recognition

**7** Vocabulary

**8** Improving Basic Comprehension

**9** Constructive Reading

**10** Content Area Reading

**11** Children with Special Needs

**12** Literacy Assessment

**13** The Classroom & School Literacy Program

**W**here You Are

Vocabulary acquisition is something *every* teacher should know a good deal about. Word knowledge is a key factor in: language learning; subject area knowledge; concept formation; ability to read, think, and communicate clearly; and, in some measure, even in the way feelings are felt and experiences are experienced.

*When the mind is at sea,*
*a new word provides a raft.*
Goethe

## THE FUNCTIONS OF LANGUAGE

"Teacher," asked Mark, "if the emperor of Russia was called the Czar, what were his children called?"

The teacher frowned, thinking, and then shrugged.

"Well, I know," said Mark, "they were called czardines."

Jokes like this illustrate our natural fascination with words and language. Jokes based on word play can be used to signal the latent George Carlins and Eddy Murphys in most any class that his or her contribution to word learning is welcomed in this context. In this way children will realize that while vocabulary building is serious business it need not always be conducted in a serious way.

There is a bit of vocabulary "fun" built into this chapter. Throughout the next sections, you will find several words printed in bold and marked with subscript numbers. These are low-frequency words that may be unfamiliar. As you encounter these terms, particularly those unfamiliar to you, take a moment to reflect on what you typically would do when seeing a "new" word in print. At the end of the chapter you will be asked to tell what strategies you used with these low-frequency terms.

We turn now to why vocabulary building is serious business, so that you may fully grasp the significance it deserves, though seldom is given, in schooling.

In previous chapters reading and writing have been presented as extensions of language development itself. The role of vocabulary enrichment, on the other hand, is to promote language development. It is a well-documented fact that vocabulary level has the highest correlation with all other measures of achievement and aptitude. The words we know are a reflection of the concepts we have formed based on the experiences we have had and the extent to which we have struggled to make sense of them. More importantly, acquisition of new words seems to stretch intellectual capacity. The words we know enable us to understand the world around us, just as words we don't know can blur and distort our perceptions.

A friend who is a kindergarten teacher gave us an example of how unfamiliar vocabulary can distort the child's understanding of the simplest experience. Calvin, one of her kindergarten students, had arrived at school one morning with the news that his mother had remarried, and that his last name now would be Thompson instead of Green. A short time later, during the reading lesson, the teacher reminded the students to write their names on their worksheets before turning them in. Calvin quickly raised his hand. "Teacher," he said, "I don't know how to *spell* Thompson." Slightly distracted, the teacher replied, "Oh Calvin, your first name will be sufficient." After a short pause Calvin slowly raised his hand again. "Teacher . . . but I don't know how to spell *Sufficient*."

Almost every child enters school with a basic vocabulary, a developing sense of grammar and sentence structure, and a natural inclination to learn words as a means of communicating needs and coping with the world. Fostering the development of these language functions should be a central and explicit objective of the classroom and school literacy program.

## HALLIDAY'S OVERLAPPING FUNCTIONS OF LANGUAGE

Halliday (1975) delineated several separate but overlapping functions of language. These functions are useful in understanding the role of words in thinking, feeling, social interactions, and learning. A checklist of these functions also can be used for informal assessment of children's language development:

1. **Instrumental Function**    Language used for satisfaction of material needs ("I'm hungry.")

2. **Regulatory Function**    Language used to control behavior of others ("Do what I'm telling you.")

3. **Interactional Function**    Language used to get along with others, or simply to socialize ("Hi, how are you doing?")

4. **Personal Function**    Language used to build self-identity ("My name is Judith Ann, and I'm in the sixth grade.")

5. **Heuristic Function**    Language used for exploration, examination, and learning ("I wonder why she said that; what's so annoying about a tapping pencil?")

6. **Imaginative Function**    Language used to wonder, pretend, help visualize and express perspective ("So bacteria are tiny bugs. I think that I can picture them without even looking in a microscope.")

7. **Representational Function**    Language used to represent concepts, content, and ideas; that is, to help one to mediate or think about various things through a symbol system ("Revolution and evolution are interesting words. One is a fast, uncertain change, and the other is a slower and more secure change.")

To realize that the functions of language tend to overlap, or participate in one another, is to understand the most significant point of this chapter; namely, that language is not merely a means of receiving and sending communications, but—as suggested in functions 5 and 7—it is also a means of understanding and thinking about the world around us. In other words, language **mediates$_1$,** or gives voice to thinking.

The expression that words are *mediators* means that symbols (words, gestures, or signs) can be held in mind and used to make distinctions and generalizations, even when these are not readily apparent to the senses. For example, with the proper words, one can teach a child to treat as equivalent a stack of four quarters and a dollar bill (see Figure 7.1). Words can, in effect, permit the mind to manipulate and transfer familiar objects and concepts to unfamiliar ones.

Language influences thought at intellectual and at emotional levels. Teaching a child word meanings and language patterns is analogous to installing a computer's machine language that determines how it must be spoken to thereafter. The child's experiential associations with words and phrases influence future emotional responses to those language forms. The words and phrases a child knows greatly

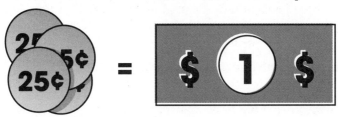

| FIGURE 7.1 | **Words Can Be Used to Mediate Concrete Concepts** |

"Four quarters, worth twenty-five cents each, add up to the same amount of money as a dollar."

influence what the child will say to him- or herself. It is with appreciation of the enormous power inherent in language learning that the Jesuits have said "Give us a child at five, and that child will be ours thereafter." It was this appreciation for the power of language that led Vygotsky (1978) to suggest that there really are only two functions of language: communication and self-direction. The developmental sequence of these, he further noted, is from the interpersonal, or between people, to the intrapersonal, or self-guiding inner speech variety. It is the latter which gives children the adaptive ability that they need to take charge of their frustration when faced with a difficult learning task. A similar picture of the relationship of words to language to deeds is told by anthropologists Sapir and Whorf (Sapir, 1921).

## THE SAPIR-WHORF HYPOTHESIS

According to this **hypothesis$_2$,** the words one is taught greatly influence what one "sees," thinks, comprehends, feels, and to some extent even what one does with one's life. It does this by instilling a values-based filtration system for everything we experience, read, hear, and express. The more refined the filtration system (the more words we know), the more information we receive, and the richer are our experiences. This hypothesis derives its name from the two anthropologists who documented the high correlation between a tribe's cultural concerns and the number of words they have for things and ideas related to those concerns. As English-speaking Americans, we have some definite preoccupations as well as other areas of little or no concern. For example we have only a few words to describe cold weather precipitation (sleet, snow, hail), while there are at least fourteen words for these same conditions in most Eskimo dialects.

It seems evident that the goals of vocabulary instruction are multiple:

- To aid in concept formation
- To permit effective oral and written conversation
- To mediate, or see and converse with oneself about, experiences in symbolic form

- To help one think and see beyond the limitations of our **domestic$_3$,** or home-based language

Furthermore, since most people associate a rich vocabulary with intelligence, it can be argued that vocabulary acquisition has some fairly strong social values as well. A rich vocabulary can make one more articulate and influential.

Let's look now at some facts and **precepts$_4$** that can be used to interpret and guide vocabulary instruction. We will begin with a look at how vocabulary is typically acquired and then combine this with related research to come up with a general formula—a five-point plan for promoting vocabulary growth.

## CONSIDERATIONS FOR TEACHING VOCABULARY

Several comprehensive reviews of the literature on vocabulary acquisition have made it possible to summarize research-supported findings for promoting vocabulary instruction (Baumann & Kameenui, 1991; Manzo & Sherk, 1971; Petty, 1967). A number of consistent considerations have emerged. The primary consideration that runs through all the others is that vocabulary instruction needs to be tied to the functions of language learning.

### ALIGNING VOCABULARY INSTRUCTION WITH LANGUAGE LEARNING

Vocabulary is learned and internalized in four basic contexts:

- Incidentally, through direct experience in social contexts and vicarious experience in reading and viewing
- Through direct instruction, as when a teacher or instructional material presents lessons intentionally designed to build vocabulary power

From *The Study Reader: Fifth Year,* by Alberta Walker and Mary R. Parkman, New York: Merrill, 1924, p. 85.

- Through self-instruction, as when words are looked up in a dictionary or their meanings are sought from others in a conscious manner
- Through manipulation of words while thinking, speaking, and writing

In each of these contexts, effective word learning occurs when all or some of these conditions are present:

- The learner is engaged in an active, meaning-seeking process (***disposition*$_5$**)
- The learner narrows attention to a specific word or words *(focus)*
- The learner understands the new word to be a *label* for some concrete object or abstract aspect of personal experience or feelings *(integration)*
- The learner has frequent exposure to the word(s) in similar and differing contexts *(repetition)*
- The learner has the opportunity to participate in social situations that are conducive, thereby making new words a dynamic part of thinking, listening, reading, writing, and speaking *(interaction)*

Any of these conditions alone should result in some degree of vocabulary growth. For example, almost *any* kind of instructional emphasis on word meanings will evoke the simple conditions of *repetition* and result in measurable growth. When instruction is designed to present new words in the ways that integrate new learning with prior experience, attitudes, and feelings, vocabulary tends to be learned more quickly and lastingly. But the most dramatic gains in vocabulary can be achieved when the instruction is designed to evoke most or all of the conditions listed above.

Word learning, as shown in Figure 7.2, may also be accelerated or hindered by the social climate and particular community of language that one lives within (Manzo & Manzo, 1990a; Vygotsky, 1962). Many authorities feel that vocabulary is best acquired through a dynamic process that involves incidental learning, direct instruction, self instruction, and frequent use—within a social climate and community of language that impel word learning, as pictured below (Baumann & Kameenui, 1991; Manzo & Manzo, 1993). The social climate and community of language are like a stick driving a hoop. When they are withdrawn, the hoop has only its forward momentum to impel it, and that unfortunately is not enough. Words in the process of being learned are lost, and even words that are known begin to shrivel and fade. This forward momentum is essential because words generally are acquired in stages. These stages also define the level, or depth of one's knowledge of a word. Beck, McKeown, and Omason (1987) characterize these levels of knowledge of word meanings as follows:

- No knowledge
- General informational level
- Narrow recognition (usually context-bound)
- Need to hesitate to remember a meaning
- Easy recognition and full knowledge

Vocabulary study, essentially, is a process of moving words through each of these stages. It especially involves taking steps to keep a healthy number of words

**Figure 7.2** **Vocabulary Acquisition**

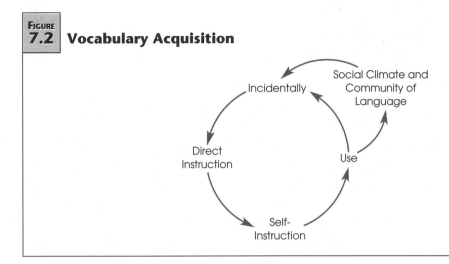

flowing into the general informational or awareness level and then to keep them moving along into the *easy recognition and full knowledge*, or permanence stage. Relatedly, it is important to note that there are five acceptable ways, according to Rapaport (1950), to define and teach about words:

- Giving a synonym (*childish,* for **puerile₆**)
- Classifying it (*humans* are "rational animals")
- Enumerating words to which it relates (*spices* are cinnamon, cloves, paprika, etc.)
- Providing an example (pointing to the object and saying "goat")
- Operationally defining it—telling what to do to experience or recognize it (your *heart* is that thing you feel thumping in your chest)

It also is notable that, depending upon what you count, there are four, maybe five types of vocabulary: speaking, reading, writing, listening, and "visual." During childhood, listening and speaking vocabularies appear to be dominant. With further schooling, all aspects of vocabulary grow, but reading vocabulary tends to grow the most since written language contains the greatest reservoir of factual, technical, and literary information.

Some educators believe that there is a fifth, or "visual vocabulary," as it has been called by Debes (1962). Visual vocabulary is composed of representations of reality that are usually *photovisual surrogates* for words. These surrogates, or stand-ins for conventional words, are mental pictures of things we know about but do not yet have words for. In a sense these vague mental pictures may be necessary early stages of new word learning. Subsequent experiences and word learning gradually bring these images into clearer focus, until at some point they are sharpened into concepts that can be clearly articulated. For example, consider how one's personal meaning for the word "grandeur" (meaning great and wonderful) comes increasingly into focus as one sees and hears about things like the Niagara Falls, Mount

Everest, and the Grand Canyon. Soon its metaphoric value also becomes apparent in the many things and events that are called by the short form, "grand," as in a "grand opening," a "grand finale," and even "grandparents."

## IMPARTING A POSITIVE DISPOSITION TOWARD WORDS

Since disposition and self-instruction are essential qualities of effective word learning, teachers need to do at least four things in teaching vocabulary. First, view *every* instructional episode as an opportunity to model a genuine interest in new words. Second, aim to impart strategies that can be used for learning the meanings that are associated with words. Third, strive for lessons that are varied and engaging. Vocabulary instruction needs to be more dynamic and relevant than just "look-ups" and worksheet exercises. Ideally it should draw on all domains of langauge learning—cognitive, affective, and sensorimotor. Fourth, ensure that student involvement is active and generative. For example, ask *students* to select some words and even methods that they find interesting and profitable. Note, however, that it is not a good idea to surrender the right and responsibility to use less preferred teaching methods. Occasionally a less popular method may have benefits that children do not fully grasp or that require more commitment than some are willing to make. Before going on now to specific teaching methods, it is necessary to address a **paradox,** that has often perplexed teachers and researchers.

**FIGURE 7.3**

" MY INSTRUCTOR SAID MY VOCABULARY WAS EXECRABLE. I WONDER WHAT HE MEANT BY THAT? "

## RESOLVING THE INCIDENTAL VERSUS DIRECT TEACHING PARADOX

A paradox reported in the research literature on vocabulary needs to be anticipated in order to be properly resolved. Put simply, the paradox is as follows: Direct instructional approaches tend to be more effective than incidental means of promoting word learning (Nagy & Herman, 1984; Nelson-Herber, 1986). However, most of our knowledge of word meanings is acquired through incidental means, such as through wide reading (Harris & Sipay, 1990, p. 533), television viewing (Neuman & Koskinen, 1992), and normal conversation. The reason for this is that the enormous number of words that can and must be learned cannot all possibly be taught, even by the most ambitious vocabulary program. Furthermore, as Nagy speculates (1988), the "sheer volume" of new words encountered in reading and listening must have a significant effect on learning. It seems that wide reading and other such incidental influences may *appear* to be "weak forces," but in the way that gravity appears to be a weak force when compared with strong forces such as wind and waves. However, when a weak force is pervasive, it can be very powerful, as is the gravitational force that holds the solar system in place. Based on these observations, a solid vocabulary development program should include indirect (gravitational) methods. It is also evident that direct instruction is just as important when it is desirable to make more rapid progress. Before we consider some specific methodologies that embody these considerations, let's say a few words about the dictionary. The dictionary is a vital piece in the total literacy picture. It really is not so much an approach to vocabulary instruction as it is an important component of various approaches.

## DICTIONARY STUDY

The dictionary, according to Henry David Thoreau, is a "concentrated and trustworthy natural history of the [American] people" (as cited in the *American Heritage Dictionary,* 3rd edition). As such, it is a convenient, incidental means of meeting the obligation to teach American heritage while teaching precision in thinking and speaking.

Studies comparing the effectiveness of different vocabulary strategies tend to show that direct teaching methods are better than dictionary methods that amount to "looking up words" (Casale & Manzo, 1983; Eeds & Cockrum, 1985; Gipe, 1978–79). However, such results must be interpreted with caution, since they rarely involve explicit and extensive teaching of the use of the dictionary and often do not account for the long-term effects of becoming an habitual user. The dictionary is another seemingly "weak force," though it is more like light than like gravity. Inquisitive minds slowly turn to it, as plants turn to a nearby window.

A review of the parts and functions of the dictionary reveals its intrinsic worth. It is a key that opens the treasure chests of language and literacy **artifacts**[8] (see Figure 7.4).

Much of what is described ahead on how to promote dictionary study is derived from two classical sources: Gray's text, *On Their Own in Reading* (1948, 1960), and Roberts' *Teacher's Guide to Word Attack* (1956). These exercises can be done independently or in cooperative learning pairs. Activities such as these are part of most every comprehensive basal-reader package.

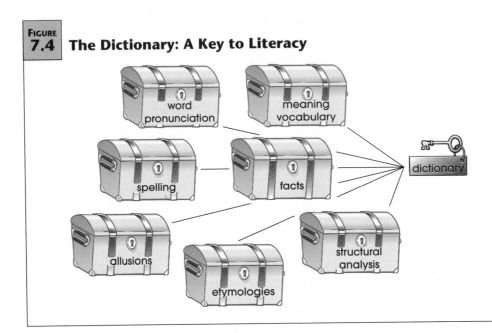

**FIGURE
7.4** **The Dictionary: A Key to Literacy**

1. A good place to begin dictionary study is to show that it can be a fun book to browse through. One way to do this is to use it to learn what certain unusual things are or what some very usual things are called, or are *also* called. Gray (1960) recommends uncommon animals for the first category, e.g., rhea, marten, pelican. The second category would be covered by words such as: hinge (as on a door) and **mucilage₉**.

2. Show how words in the dictionary are arranged in alphabetical order, and how this can be used to help spell words correctly as well as to look up their meanings. Illustrate how to look up the spelling of a word by considering several possible ways it might be spelled other than the way it immediately sounds (e.g., the word "mucilage" sounds like *mu-sill-age,* but is spelled *mucilage*). Take this point a bit further and show how the dictionary can be used to discover, more or less, how to pronounce words encountered in print, e.g., rhea = rē′·ə. Give students practice in doing this with known words then less known and finally unknown words. Have them study and associate pictorial representations of key sounds (see p. 235). In this way a student could conceivably learn how to pronounce most any word in the language. Attention to word parts, you will recall, also is an effective means of improving basic word recognition skills.

3. Write adjectives such as "agile," "smug," and "arrogant" with dictionary page numbers after each and ask students to decide whether they would like to have these words used to describe them.

4. The dictionary contains a wealth of information on the origins of words, or etymologies. Looking for this can be a helpful way to remember meanings and spellings. When it's combined with Vocabulary Classmates (described ahead in

## **Vowel Sounds**

  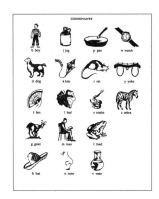

Roberts (1956)

this chapter), it can be as interesting as learning the background of a new acquaintance. Teach students to look at the information between the brackets—[  ]—where these are used. It is here that the dictionary tells what is known of the origins and special features of a word; for example, "*bonfire* [literally, bone fire, fire for burning corpses] now, a fire built out-of-doors."

5. Familiarize students with any additional informational values the particular dictionary available may have; e.g., geographical and biographical information. Older dictionaries, which can be acquired quite inexpensively at garage sales, often include fascinating color illustrations and historical notes. The word "bonfire," for example, is said to have been coined during the Spanish Inquisition to describe the way the Spaniards dealt with human remains.

Dictionary and word study are most engaging when combined with authentic experiences in reading, writing, and conceptual undertakings. Have youngsters write letters to a grandparent or other relative suggesting that they might consider giving them a dictionary, even an old one, for a birthday or holiday present. If a new one is desired, you might recommend *The American Heritage Dictionary,* 3rd ed. (Houghton Mifflin, 1992). It has many pictures and illustrations and interesting current usage notes.

# **VOCABULARY PROCEDURES FOR THE ELEMENTARY CLASSROOM**

In general, students should be expected to learn about 3,000 words per year from kindergarten through grade 12. The average high school senior should know about 40,000 words (Nagy & Herman, 1984). It takes a variety of approaches to meet this standard and a great deal of professional knowledge to help youngsters to exceed it. The vocabulary acquisition methods presented here are grouped under four general types that represent a framework for planning vocabulary instruction and assembling an overall vocabulary program for your classroom or school. The categories are as follows:

- Pre- and Post-Reading Word Study
- General Word Study and Concept Development
- Incidental Instruction
- Reinforcement and Practice Formats and Games

## PRE- AND POST-READING WORD STUDY

Most basic reading lessons, such as the Directed Reading Activity described in the next chapter, call for previewing the reading selection to identify and teach difficult *meaning* vocabulary (as well as unfamiliar "sight words") before students read. Word study also is a recommended part of the skills extension, or follow-up portion of such lessons. At primary grade levels, attention to word meaning is a minor concern. Reading materials generally do not include words with unfamiliar meanings, since the objective at the primary level is to teach children to recognize or quickly decode words they already know and use. It is never too early, however, to support and encourage children's natural inclination to learn new words. Several of the methods ahead, as you will see, can easily be adapted to begin to instill effective word-learning strategies in even the youngest children. Early effort is important because by about the middle of second grade, textbooks begin to contain an increasing proportion of words with unfamiliar meanings—a potential obstacle to fluent decoding and reflective reading. Each of the teaching strategies described in this first section on vocabulary acquisition is designed to introduce students to a set of preselected target words that they will encounter in a particular reading selection. Each strategy also evokes most of the key conditions of effective word learning. The very first strategy, in fact, is based on a natural strategy that is used by most anyone who reads.

### Contextual Redefinition Strategy

Typically, new words are encountered in the following sequence: context, isolation, context (Putnam, Bader & Bean, 1988). What this means is that when readers encounter a word in context that they don't know, they try to figure out its meaning from the context, and then, if unsuccessful, seek meaning from another source, such as a dictionary or another person. Finally, they return to the original context to make better sense of the word and its context. The Contextual Redefinition Strategy (Cunningham, Cunningham & Arthur, 1981) applies this natural process to a simple format for classroom instruction (Tierney, Readence, & Dishner, 1990).

The most important feature of this method is that while it teaches youngsters that context can provide clues to word meaning (Gipe, 1978–79), it also teaches them not to *over-rely* on this sometimes false prophet. Word *mislearning* often is due to misinterpreting a word's meaning in some initial context. It is remarkable how longlasting such misimpressions can be. They often remain with us for years, warping the contexts and meanings of many messages we read and hear thereafter (Manzo & Manzo, 1993). Each of us can tell a story of at least one word we were entirely wrong about well into adult life. Learning from context alone will do that. Contextual Redefinition is a method that teaches the use of context, as well as the dangers of over-reliance on it.

## STEPS IN CONTEXTUAL REDEFINITION

Step 1    Select target words from the reading selection.

Step 2    Write at least a sentence for each on the chalkboard. The sentence(s) may come from the selection itself, if it provides reasonable clues.

Step 3    Write the new word in isolation and ask for a pronunciation. If an incorrect one is forthcoming, give the correct pronunciation and ask for additional insights into meanings as may be derived from the word itself—that is, from a structural analysis of its prefixes, suffixes, and of possible root words that look or sound similar.

Step 4    Return to the context and try again to derive a definition from these two analyses.

Step 5    A dictionary is consulted to test the accuracy of the contextual and structural analyses. This step can stir a very productive instructional conversation, since dictionary definitions can sometimes be too abstract for easy interpretation or the word could have been used in some unusual or ironic way.

The next method is one of the most popular and well studied to come along in recent years.

### The Keyword Vocabulary Method

The Keyword Vocabulary Method is based on an ancient memory improvement technique that dates back to the time when unschooled messengers had to recall long and explicit details. It links relatively unfamiliar things to familiar things that are similar in some way, and then combines the two in some thematic way into an odd and therefore memorable mental image. For example, to recall the meaning of the word **plateau$_{10}$,** it could be linked with the image of a huge upside-down "dinner plate" forming a grassy flatland; the meaning of the word "collage" could be linked to an image of word spelled with the letters overlapping; or, to recall the meaning for "amicable," it could be pictured as *AMI* walking hand-in-hand with *CABLE*.

The Keyword Vocabulary method can be especially demanding for youngsters under eleven years old. They tend to require several explicit examples (Pressley, Levin, & Miller, 1981). This has led some critics to maintain that it is cumbersome and artificial (Moore, 1987). Nonetheless, the method has been reported to be effective in learning content material (Konopak & Williams, 1988; Levin et al., 1986) and in working with learning disabled students (Condus, Marshall, & Miller, 1986; Guthrie, 1984). Those who have studied Keyword the most extensively maintain that it helps students to learn how to form connections and to develop elaborations on concepts (Pressley, Johnson, & Symons, 1987; Pressley, Levin, & McDaniel, 1987; Pressley, Levin, & Miller, 1981).

Keyword does create an interesting instructional conversation in which the teacher and students come to the word workbench together in an authentic attempt to capture and represent word meanings in some memorable ways. It also inculcates a potentially useful memory training device (see Chapter 11 for additional memory devices, including one with a name similar to this one: The Key Word Study Strategy). Keyword Vocabulary also tends to incidentally reveal students' thought processes, thus making it a useful diagnostic teaching tool.

The next method resembles the old standby of using a new word in a sentence. It has, however, some subtle but important differences. Try to spot the differences.

### Possible Sentences

Possible Sentences is a method that teaches vocabulary, comprehension, and writing. Stahl and Kapinus (1991) recently visited and tested the value of this method, first developed by David and Sharon Moore (1986). Stahl and Kapinus showed the method to be a valuable and easy-to-use approach to vocabulary development in a content class or a remedial setting. When used as described below, Possible Sentences significantly improved vocabulary acquisition and textual recall (Stahl & Kapinus, 1991). Stahl and associates emphasize that it appears to be the *discussion*—or pointed instructional conversation—that seems to make Possible Sentences really work (Stahl, 1986; Stahl & Vancil, 1986; Stahl & Kapinus, 1991).

## STEPS IN POSSIBLE SENTENCES

Step 1    The teacher lists several key concept words from a selection, pronounces them, and elicits and/or gives meanings for them.

Step 2    Students are encouraged to predict sentences that could possibly appear in the textual material containing these words.

Step 3    Students read the textual material to check the relative accuracy of their sentences, in the sense that their sentences seem to be compatible with, though not identical to, those in the text.

Step 4    The students' sentences are then analyzed, evaluated, and corrected as needed.

Step 5    New sentences are invited that reflect the sum of learnings from the prediction, reading, and sentence analysis steps.

Try this method soon, to get a better grasp of the solid ideas for effective teaching that are built into it. The next method helps in the learning of words that can seem rather **ethereal**[11] to young readers.

### Subjective Approach to Vocabulary (SAV)

The Subjective Approach to Vocabulary (Manzo, 1983) is a focusing method that builds on students' personal views and associations with a word. It uses these "knowns" to anchor fleeting word meanings, keeping them from drifting off and being forgotten. The method imparts a self-instructional strategy that teaches students how to use their own prior knowledge and experiences to build word knowledge.

The teacher, using a "talk-through" technique, simply helps students to tie their lives and experiences to new words. Thus, the biographies of individual lives become part of the on-going biography of a word (see "Classmates" ahead for a related method). When used in a group situation, SAV offers diagnostic opportunities for discovering how individual youngsters think and what they might be saying to themselves that is facilitative or disruptive of learning and personal–social adjustment. The conversations that ensue also give students a chance to hear the perspectives of others. In this way multicultural learnings and insights can occur in a very natural incidental manner.

## STEPS IN THE SUBJECTIVE APPROACH TO VOCABULARY

Step 1    The teacher identifies two to four words to be taught, or "pretaught" if SAV is used as a prereading activity. If a word list is used, be sure to include as many words as possible that impart concepts and feelings that you would wish students to learn.

Step 2    The teacher tells the student the full meaning of a word, much as it might be found in a dictionary. It is recorded in a Word Study Journal as the "objective," or dictionary meaning.

Step 3    The teacher asks students, "What does this word remind you of?" or "What do you picture or think of when you hear this word?" (Explain that discussion of a personal association with a word can be very helpful in remembering and clarifying its meaning).

Step 4    The teacher talks the student through this personal search for meaning by asking further clarifying questions, and in group situations by pointing up those images suggested that seem most vivid. The teacher may add his or her own images, especially where student images appear vague or the word itself is vague or abstract. Students are then directed to write some "subjective," or personal associations for the new word under the previously written dictionary definition in their Journals. Drawings can also be added (see Box 7.1 and Figure 7.5).

Step 5    Silent reading follows next when SAV is used for prereading vocabulary development. When it is being used for general vocabulary development, students are given 5–10 minutes to study and rehearse the new and previously recorded words.

Step 6    The teacher has students close their Word Study Journals and asks them the meanings of the words studied that day and a few others from previous days. This step can be tied to seat exercises in conventional workbooks such as crossword puzzles, category games, etc. This manipulation and reinforcement step can be made easier by selecting the words to be taught from the exercise material.

## Subjective Approach to Vocabulary

*The Target Word Is "Magnetic"*

*Teacher:*    Do you know what a *magnet* is?

*Student:*    Yeah, you have one on your desk with paperclips stuck to it.

*Teacher:*    Well, the word *magnetic* comes from *magnet,* and, according to the dictionary, it means two things: 1. having the properties of a magnet—that is, doing what magnets do; and, 2. being attractive and charming, and therefore drawing people to you, such as having a "magnetic personality." Let's write these meanings down in your Word Study Journal. (Pause to record meanings.)

*Teacher:*    What do you think of when you hear the word *magnetic*? (Explain).

*Student:*    My brother Billy. Mr. Ablomp, our neighbor, is a grump, but he gave Billy some of his old golf clubs. Everyone likes Billy, and they give him things.

*Teacher:*    I guess you'd say that he had a "magnetic personality"?

*Student:*    He has a *lot* of "magnetic personality."

*Teacher:*    Another way to say that is, "He has a great deal of *personal magnetism.*"

*Student:*    He's got it, whatever you call it.

*Teacher:*    Do you think that you'll mention Billy's "magnetic" personality to anyone at home? It's good to use new words quickly, after you learn them.

*Student:*    Yeah, I guess I'll tell my dad, because he's always saying that being *pleasant* is important in selling stuff.

*Teacher:*    You mean, as in being *magnetic*?

*Student:*    Right.

*Teacher:*    Let's write out your ideas about "magnetic" on the board to help us to remember them. See if you can illustrate the word with a drawing.

*Student:*    OK.

*Teacher:*    Who else wants to tell us about what they picture when they hear "magnetic"?

The reader's subjective associations with words play an important role in meaningful reading. Rosenblatt has emphasized this role by reminding us that "The reader brings to the text a reservoir of past experiences with language and the world. . . . All readers must draw on past experiences to make the new meanings produced in the **transaction**$_{12}$ with the text. This experience then flows into the reservoir brought to the next reading event" (1991). In reading, as in all language-based events, individual words tend to have both "public" dictionary meanings and "private" meanings based on associations with the feelings, ideas, and attitudes that accompanied them in previous life experiences (Bates, 1979). The Subjective Approach to Vocabulary can be a pleasant means of helping students to acquire the habit of linking private with public meanings of words. Figure 7.5 illustrates a useful worksheet format for recording SAV experiences.

**Variations on SAV**    Eeds and Cockrum (1985) developed a similar format for students to record their subjective associations with words, adding the identification

FIGURE
7.5 **SAV Worksheet**

Divide a full-size sheet of paper into four quarters. Have students label each of the four squares, and complete each square using public and private meanings of the target word.

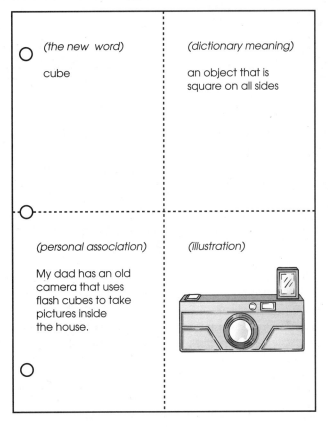

of *non*examples of the target word's meanings. They suggest that the worksheet be structured to include: the target word in square 1; the student's subjective association in square 2; a *non*example of the word meaning in square 3 (e.g., for the target word "soothing," students might identify *non*examples such as "the sound of a lawnmower," "scary movies," "fingernails on the chalkboard," etc.); and a definition of the word in square 4. Eeds and Cockrum report the results of an experimental study that compared students taught in this way with two other groups—one in which words were taught by a dictionary approach and the other in which the target words were presented incidentally in an interesting context. The results were dramatic. Students taught through the subjective approach "actually either out-performed or equalled the performance of students identified as high ability and randomly assigned to the other treatment groups" (Eeds & Cockrum, 1985, p. 496).

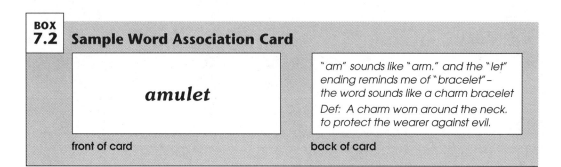

Students can be encouraged to use a variation on SAV as an independent study strategy. Have them keep a few blank index cards handy while reading. Show students how to use these as Word Association Cards in the following way. When an unfamiliar word is encountered, write the word on the front of the card, and on the back write a personal association (see Box 7.2). Then write the precise, dictionary meaning under the personal association. Finally, try to connect the initial personal association with the dictionary meaning. Encourage students to spend some time on this part: their associations probably have something to do with the way they have heard a word used, even though they didn't know exactly what it meant. Remind students to review the cards in short, but frequent sittings: look at the word on the front of the card, recite the meaning (aloud if possible), and use the back of the card as a self-check.

The next strategy is based on *creating* experiences that can be linked with new words. You could start work on it and continue to build and improve on it for years to come.

### Vocabulary Skits

Duffelmeyer (1980) developed a way to create actual contextual experiences in the classroom that can form the basis for effective word learning. The teacher writes a short skit that revolves around the meaning of a *single* target word, and a group of students acts out the skit for the rest of the class. Duffelmeyer provides this straightforward rationale for development and use of vocabulary skits:

> Children never forget the meanings of many of the words they learn during their preschool years. This is partly because these are frequently repeated, common words. Another reason is that these words are learned through experience, a method that makes for real understanding. (1980, p. 35)

Vocabulary Skits are, admittedly, somewhat labor-intensive on the teacher's part. However, they also have an intense impact on student learning. Not only do students have experiences that intensify their learning of a few important vocabulary terms, but they also are made more aware of the power of their everyday experience as a means of acquiring vocabulary independently.

## STEPS IN THE VOCABULARY SKIT STRATEGY

**Step 1**    Prepare short skits, each designed to convey the meaning of a single target word. Skits should take no longer than about one minute each to enact.

**Step 2**    Skit scripts are distributed to small groups of students, who then select roles and read through the scripts.

**Step 3**    The teacher writes the first target word on the chalkboard and directs students to pay close attention to the way in which it will be used.

**Step 4**    The group that has the skit for the target word enacts the skit (see Box 7.3 below).

**Step 5**    The teacher asks several questions relevant to the target word just enacted.

**Step 6**    Students are asked to volunteer a personal experience that would convey the meaning of the word.

Teachers hearing of this method are quick to suggest that students be encouraged to write their own skits, thereby providing more exercises than the teacher would have time to generate. It is also a good idea to ask parents and volunteers to try writing these little one-act plays.

The next strategy makes further and deeper use of personal associations. It taps into a seldom-used domain of learning.

---

**BOX 7.3**    **Sample Vocabulary Skit**

**Target word: Celerity**[13]

Setting:    *Booth at a carnival. A small crowd is gathered around a carnival*

Worker:    *Step right up! Step right up! Is there any among you who would dare risk a small amount to prove that the hand is* not *quicker than the eye? You sir, you look like a man of action. For the mere sum of 25 cents—just one quarter of a dollar—I will demonstrate such quickness as you have never seen.*

Man:    *(Shrugs) Why not? (Takes a quarter from his pocket and throws it on the counter.)*

Worker:    *(Gesturing to three small cups and a tiny object no larger than a pearl. Holds it up so all can see.) Under the middle of the three it goes, and where it stops, nobody knows. (Maneuvers cups, then stops.) Now, sir, would you care to point to the cup under which the tiny object lies?*

Man:    *(Points to one of the cups.) This one. (Worker lifts the cup.)*

Woman:    *(Turns to a friend.) Did you see the* **celerity** *with which he moved his hands? So swiftly. It was amazing!*

Worker:    *(Having overheard.) Did I hear the word "celerity?" Celerity is* all *in this trade. If I'm not quick, I'm out of business. (Crowd begins to move away.) Step right up! Step right up!*

### Motor Imaging

Motor Imaging (Casale-Manzo, 1985) involves the sensorimotor, as well as affective and cognitive domains. There has been little recognition even of the existence of this learning domain. It was not even acknowledged by Bloom (1956) nor by Krathwohl and associates (1964), the chief architects of the handbooks of the cognitive, affective, and attitudinal domains. Motor Imaging relies on a form of learning that incorporates muscle movements to supplement conventional means of word learning. It sometimes is known as **_proprioceptive_**[14] learning, or sensorimotor learning that comes to reside within the nervous system.

The basic idea is very old, though generally overlooked in the design of instruction for all but seriously disabled readers with basic word recognition problems. Developmental psychologists such as Jean Piaget have observed that young children first respond to a stimulus with gross motor movements. Over time these motor responses are "abbreviated" into more subtle motor responses, and eventually are "interiorized" (Piaget, 1963). Closer to home, Betts (1936), writing on reading, said the following about motor learnings: "It is well established that the young learner gets a feel and reinforcement for language through the speech and writing _muscles_" (p. 8). He goes on to say that, "it is mandatory for the teacher in some cases to design a definite program of motor augmentation to promote learning" (p. 8).

## STEPS IN MOTOR IMAGING

Step 1    The teacher writes the first target word on the chalkboard, pronounces it, and tells what it means.

Step 2    The teacher asks students to imagine a simple pantomime for the word meaning ("How could you 'show' someone what this word means with just your hands or a gesture?").

Step 3    When the teacher gives a signal (such as pointing, or saying "now"), students do their individual gesture pantomimes simultaneously.

Step 4    The teacher watches these, and selects the most common pantomime observed. The teacher then demonstrates it to all the students and directs students to say the _word_ while doing the pantomime (this may require several repetitions for all students to do the pantomime while saying the word).

Step 5    After all target words have been presented and pantomimed, the teacher repeats each new word, this time directing the class to do the pantomime while saying a brief _meaning or simple synonym_.

Step 6    The students' next encounter with these words is in the assigned reading material.

Step 7    The teacher should try to casually use the pantomime whenever a target word is used for a short time thereafter.

Box 7.4 presents some examples from a Motor Imaging lesson.

| BOX 7.4 | **Motor Imaging Examples** | | |
| --- | --- | --- | --- |
| *New Word* | *Language Meaning* | | *Motor Meaning* |
| appropriate | right or fit for a certain purpose | | both palms together, matching perfectly |
| convey | take or carry from one place to another | | both hands together, palms upward, moving from one side to the other |
| woe | | | great sadness or trouble— one or both hands over the eyes, head slanted foward |
| dazzle | shine or reflect brightly | | palms close together, facing outward, fingers spread |
| utmost | the very highest or most | | one or both hands reaching up as far as possible |
| abode | place where you live | | hands meeting above the head in a triangular "roof" shape |

The effects of the Motor Imaging strategy were tested by comparing it to two other approaches to vocabulary instruction. The study compared dictionary study— a cognitive approach, the Subjective Approach to Vocabulary (SAV)—an affective approach, and Motor Imaging—a proprioceptive approach. Fifth- and sixth-grade students were rotated through each of these three instructional treatments in different orders. The study showed that Motor Imaging and SAV were superior to the dictionary method, and that Motor Imaging was superior to both of the other approaches on four of the five measures used. This was true across ability levels (Casale & Manzo, 1983).

It appears that even the highest forms of vocabulary and concept learning have psychomotor foundations, or equivalents. Hence, motor movements associated with certain stimuli can become interiorized as a "symbolic meaning" (Piaget, 1963). This presents certain advantages in classroom teaching and learning that are worth reviewing:

- Since sensorimotor learnings can be interiorized, they also can be self-stimulating, and therefore are easier to rehearse and recall with even the slightest mental reminder, as well as from external stimulation.
- Sensorimotor activity is so basic to human learning that it is common to all learners, fast and slow, and hence, ideal for heterogeneously grouped classes.
- The act of identifying and acting out a word becomes a life experience in itself with that word—a value that Duffelmeyer (1980) demonstrated with his "experiential" Vocabulary Skits.

Some teachers have told us that they have successfully used this same basic approach in teaching youngsters letter sounds, as well as word meanings. A hand gesture or expression is selected for a troublesome sound; the same gesture then is used each time the sound occurs, no matter what grapheme is present (e.g., a finger pointing to the eye, for the long sound of "i," whether in *sigh, lie,* or *by;* a hand compressing any vowel forming a schwa—the neutral vowel sound of most unstressed syllables in English (as of "*a*" in *ago* or in *cobra*).

The next method uses elements of Vocabulary Skits and Motor Imaging in a more ongoing way.

### Vocabulary Classmates

This child-centered approach to vocabulary puts a child in a classroom, imaginary or real, made up of "classmates" named after new words taken from literature selections, content area materials, or from a standard grade level vocabulary list (Manzo & Manzo, 1993), as illustrated in Figure 7.6.

The teacher helps children to get to know their new vocabulary classmates by asking questions and by leading activities that build personal associations as well as cognitive acquaintance with their new-found word friends. The idea of Vocabulary Classmates is to have fun with the words in a way that is also instructive. It helps children learn about words in some of the same ways they learn about other unfamiliar things—including new people. Sample questions and activities include the following:

• How do you say this Vocabulary Classmate's name (pointing to the word)?

  *wonder—"wun - der"*

• Check the dictionary to find out more about this Vocabulary Classmate:

  – What does this Classmate's name mean? (A good lead-up to this is to illustrate that many popular names, first and last, have meanings. The library will have a book of these.)

    *wonder: curiosity, surprise, marvel; also: doubt about something*

  – Where is this Classmate from? (Check the derivation of the word.)

    *from: old Norse - Scandinavia*

  – Check the dictionary to learn about this Classmate's family heritage. (Check the dictionary for the word's "parentage"—meaningful affixes and morphemes brought together to form the word.)

    *None noted in the dictionary.*

  – Who is this Classmate related to? (synonyms)

    *astonishment*

  – From whom is this Classmate most different? (antonyms)

    *None noted, but ordinary, and expected come to mind.*

  – What is this Classmate's job in a sentence? (part of speech)

    *Wonder is a noun (it names a feeling).*

**FIGURE 7.6**

**Illustrations from Vocabulary Classmates as Assembled with "Mandy" (age 10)**

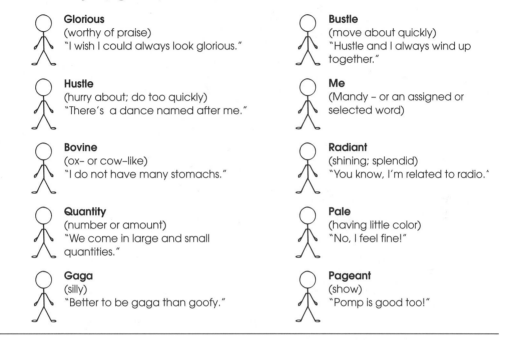

**Glorious**
(worthy of praise)
"I wish I could always look glorious."

**Hustle**
(hurry about; do too quickly)
"There's a dance named after me."

**Bovine**
(ox- or cow–like)
"I do not have many stomachs."

**Quantity**
(number or amount)
"We come in large and small quantities."

**Gaga**
(silly)
"Better to be gaga than goofy."

**Bustle**
(move about quickly)
"Hustle and I always wind up together."

**Me**
(Mandy – or an assigned or selected word)

**Radiant**
(shining; splendid)
"You know, I'm related to radio."

**Pale**
(having little color)
"No, I feel fine!"

**Pageant**
(show)
"Pomp is good too!"

- Tell a story about this Classmate on the playground: what is he or she doing(?) saying(?) feeling(?)

  *Wonder is surprising everybody by speaking different languages. There are two of them, and they are twins. Marvel Wonder is the boy. I think the girl is called Astonishment. They look and sound a lot alike.*

- Would you like to have this Classmate sit near you? Why or why not?

  *Yes. They're always doing something surprising and fun.*

- Which Word Classmates do you think would be friends with this Classmate? Why?

  *I think Drudgery would, because he really needs a friend. Merriment would like Astonishment because they look and even sound alike.*

- Draw or describe the clothing each would wear and what they might look like physically (see Figure 7.6).

  *The Wonder twins are wearing matching jeans and bright red shirts. They look radiant and glorious. (See also Figure 7.7)*

- Have each Classmate say something they might have on their minds. The teacher can provide some statements that may stimulate deeper understandings, associations, and further word study (see Figures 7.6 and 7.7).

**FIGURE 7.7** **Vocabulary Classmates—Associations with Words**

Wonder
(surprise, marvel, doubt)

My dad would like the Wonder twins.
They're on his favorite record:
"Oh I wonder, wonder, wonder,
wonder, who — who wrote the book
of love."

(dictated by Jennifer)

Here are some additional activities and considerations related to Vocabulary Classmates:

- Start with an imaginary classroom or lunchroom. Have youngsters fill about a third of the seats in the room with words they have selected themselves. Have them fill other rooms at upper and lower grade levels with words they think to be easier and more difficult. Transfer words to other schools once they have been learned well. As a reminder of meaning, have an occasional note jotted on the chalkboard from the old friend.

> *Dear Miss McGee's Fourth-Grade Class:*
> *Miss you all, but I like my new school in Springfield. I'm always busy, busy, busy.*
> *Your friend,*
> *Bustle*

- When using an actual classroom, avoid assigning real children names that may have derisive meanings or connotations (such as "gaga"). Have students select their own middle and last names and even nicknames from words they have encountered. Have them say something about the names they have selected.

> *My name is Wonder Q. Mandolin. The "Q" stands for Quantity. I got my last name from a picture in the dictionary of this instrument that is the same as one my grandmother was playing in a picture we have of her.*

- Have youngsters create "autobiographical notes" for their Vocabulary Classmates, complete with illustrations. Encourage them to add places they subsequently find the word in context. (See Figure 7.8.)

## GENERAL WORD STUDY AND CONCEPT DEVELOPMENT APPROACH

The methods discussed above for teaching target words from reading selections will cover a lot of ground in vocabulary instruction. However, a well-rounded vocabulary

**FIGURE 7.8** **Autobiography of Pale Hustle**

Pale Hustle

Gaga Hustle

Bovine Hustle

Radiant Hustle

My name is Pale Hustle. This is my little brother Gaga Hustle. Dad is called Bovine, 'cause he's as strong as an ox. Mother is Radiant, because she has happy eyes.

I heard a man on TV say that he made a movie with my name in it, called He Rode a Pale Horse. I think that he meant the horse was light gray and ghostlike.

program should also include a general word study component, in which vocabulary is taught as an extension of concept development. This concept-based approach to vocabulary helps students to convert words into richer concepts, and concepts into more precise words. Several writers have offered guidelines for teaching concepts (Rentel, 1971; Taba, 1967) and words as concepts (Frayer, Fredrick, & Klausmeier, 1969; Graves and Prenn, 1986). Frayer's model is the most widely known.

### Frayer's Concept-Based Approach

Frayer's Concept-Based Approach to teaching meaning vocabulary has much in common with Gray's **paradigm**₁₅ for teaching phonics, or sight word vocabulary. It is a paradigm in that it covers all the necessary elements of teaching children to form a concept. It can be used to teach most anything from "what is electricity," to the concept of a "sphere."

## STEPS IN FRAYER'S CONCEPT-BASED APPROACH

**Step 1** Identify the *relevant and irrelevant features* of the concept you wish to teach. For example, a relevant attribute or feature of the concept of "sphere" is that it is three-dimensional, and round in all directions. It is not a circle, as in a two-dimensional picture, and it is not simply a three-dimensional circle, like a car tire. Note these features on a semantic map on the chalkboard or overhead (see Figure 7.9).

**Step 2** Provide *examples* of the concept. For example, show a classroom globe—pointing out that the globe is a more perfect sphere than the actual Earth.

**Step 3** Provide *examples of irrelevant but loosely related concepts* with which it might be compared, such as drawing of a two-dimensional circle and a three-dimensional tire.

**Step 4** Relate the concept by some possible smaller, or subordinating concepts, such as a ball, an egg, or the moon.

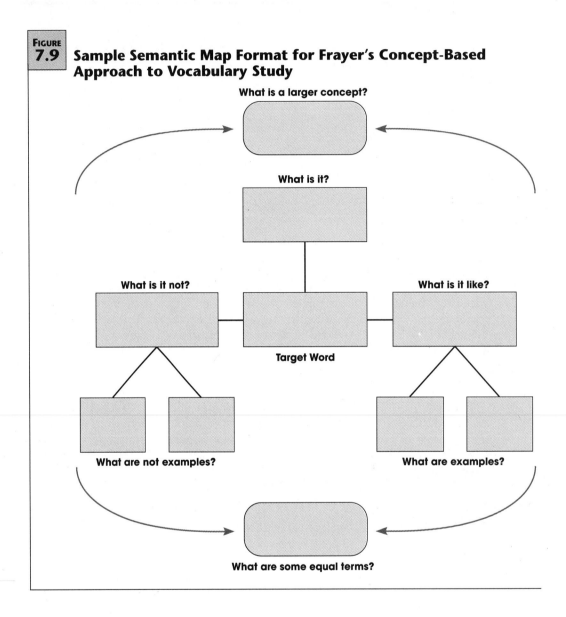

**FIGURE 7.9** **Sample Semantic Map Format for Frayer's Concept-Based Approach to Vocabulary Study**

**What is a larger concept?**

**What is it?**

**What is it not?**

**What is it like?**

**Target Word**

**What are not examples?**

**What are examples?**

**What are some equal terms?**

**Step 5** Relate or categorize the concept by some possible larger, or **superordinating**[16] *concepts,* such as "spherical objects" and stars (which are not really star-shaped but only appear that way due to the effect of viewing them through an atmosphere that causes them to appear to twinkle).

**Step 6** Relate or categorize the concept alongside equal, or *coordinating terms,* such as other planets.

As suggested before, Frayer's model leaves little to chance. It covers most possible areas in which a youngster's grasp of a word's meaning might go astray. This also means that it tends to be a bit **arduous**[17] for the teacher. Nevertheless, it is an effective way to teach concepts that are likely to contribute "early learning" for most of the class (such as "sphere"). It also is particularly appropriate for youngsters with serious reading or language disabilities and those who are developmentally disabled or mildly retarded.

The next method for general word study also is an effective means of promoting concept development. It helps youngsters to understand subtle differences within a single category.

### Themed Vocabulary Study

One of the most traditional means of vocabulary enrichment is based on grouping words by themes. Themed Vocabulary Study has also been called Semantic Clusters by Marzano and Marzano (1988). It permits students to take well known, partially known, and barely recognized words and link them together into a semantic web that will catch and hold new word meanings as well as **nuances**[18] of meaning for familiar words. It helps children understand that words do not always have precise, distinct, and unchanging meanings (Anderson & Nagy, 1989). Most importantly, themed vocabulary study imparts an effective strategy for lifelong word learning.

## STEPS IN THEMED VOCABULARY STUDY

**Step 1**   Identify a theme (see "talk" as it would be treated by second-graders in Figure 7.10, and how the same word would be elaborated by sixth-graders in Figure 7.11 and by college students in Figure 7.12).

**Step 2**   Ask students to state words they think are related to the theme.

**Step 3**   If necessary, use dictionaries to check word meanings and to find additional synonyms, antonyms, and subtly different meanings.

**Step 4**   Link the relevant words to one another (with brief definitions) in the form of a semantic map, as shown.

**Step 5**   Reinforce and evaluate by testing students' recall of word meanings and by having them write sentences or descriptive pieces designed to elicit the new words in the theme.

The traditional practice of having students write a sentence or two containing a new word still makes sense, despite the criticism it tends to receive. It can reveal whether the students' knowledge of the word includes the often context-specific way in which it was encountered in print. Anderson and Nagy (1989) give the example of the word "correlate." The dictionary definition says "to be related one to the other." This led a student to write: "Me and my parents *correlate,* because without them I wouldn't be here" (p. 719). In a teaching situation this would immediately reveal that the term and possibly the concept, "correlate," is not yet within the student's grasp.

**Selecting Themes for Themed Vocabulary Study**   Themes can be selected based on the guiding concept of instructional units in reading or other subject areas:

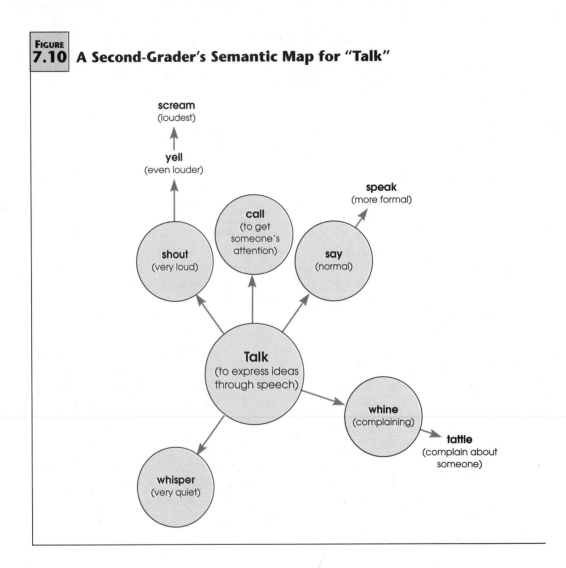

**FIGURE 7.10** A Second-Grader's Semantic Map for "Talk"

the possibilities are as broad as one's imagination. Here are some themes to consider in word study:

- Noncomplimentary but nonvulgar terms (pesky, brusque, prissy, scattered, antsy, bawdy, addlebrained)
- Behavior-related terms (manners, antsy, comportment, deportment, inappropriate, maladaptive, poised, irascible)
- Character traits (endurance, restraint, perseverance, reflection, tolerance)
- Thinking terms (abstract, concrete, rational, irrational, creative, critical, cognitive, diffusive, constructive, coherent)
- Temperament labels (sanguine, industrious, hyper, choleric, mercurial, pensive)
- Attitudes (positive, negative, hostile, aggressive, assertive, constructive)

(See Marzano & Marzano, 1988, for other recommendations.)

**FIGURE 7.11** **A Sixth-Grader's Semantic Map for "Talk"**

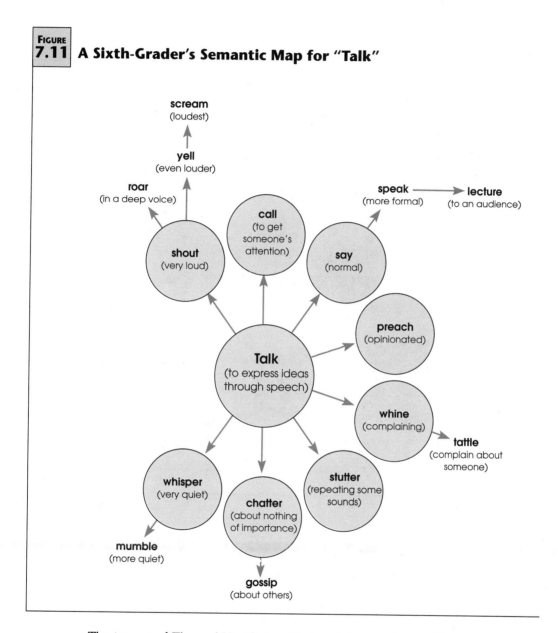

The impact of Themed Vocabulary Study can be greatly amplified by combining it with other vocabulary strategies previously described. A more specific subset of Themed Vocabulary is described next.

### Sensory Experience Word Study

Earlier it was noted that sensorimotor learning is basic to all human efforts to understand. Motor Imaging was offered as a method that heightens and takes advantage of the motor aspects of sensorimotor learning. Now let's address the sensory side more fully. One of the more interesting ways of developing vocabulary

**FIGURE 7.12** A College Students' Semantic Map for "Talk"

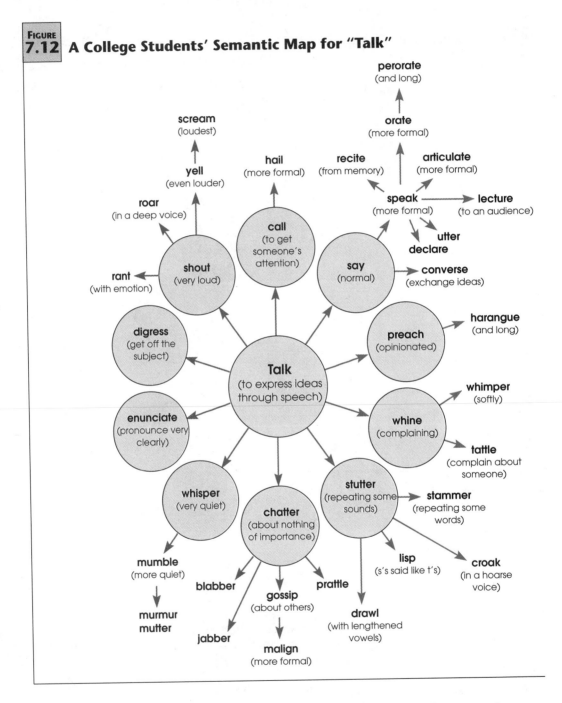

is to heighten youngsters' abilities to sort out and label the steady stream of sensory experiences that bombard us each day. A rich vocabulary of the senses is fundamental to reading, writing, and—this may be a surprise—scientific orientation. Both

| BOX 7.5 | **Sample Frazier's Vocabulary of Senses** | | | |
|---|---|---|---|---|
| *Hearing* | *Seeing* | *Touching* | *Tasting* | *Smelling* |
| babble | admire | alive | acid | aroma |
| bang | appear | blush | appetizing | bouquet |
| bark | array | blushing | biting | deodorant |
| bawl | attractive | bristly | bitter | fragrant |
| • | • | • | • | • |
| • | • | • | • | • |
| yell | watchful | vibrating | unripe | spicy |
| yelp | well-groomed | warm | unseasoned | stench |
| yip | white | warmth | untainted | strong-smelling |
| yowl | yellow | wooly | yummy | whiff |

*Frazier, (1970).*

the physical and biological sciences rely on one's powers of sensory observation and expression. As with Themed Vocabulary, the study of sensory experience vocabulary words is on-going and self-reinforcing: The themes serve as categories for *sorting* and *storing* new words.

The most challenging aspect of teaching a vocabulary of the senses is assembling an appropriate word bank. Happily, Frazier (1970), in what must have been a life-long work, assembled, categorized, and alphabetized many of the terms a teacher would ever need to heighten sensory awareness and expression. A few examples are provided in Box 7.5. The full list can be found in Appendix C.

Donlan (1975) has provided a basic teaching design for enhancing students' sensory vocabularies.

### Donlan's Strategy for Teaching a Vocabulary of the Senses

1. Students' senses are stimulated through an experience—such as that of sounds made by tapping several different objects, playing a tape recording, or showing objects or pictures of objects of different textures or colors, or things that evoke the sense of taste.
2. Students describe and discuss the sensory experience.
3. New words related to the experience are introduced.
4. These same words are applied to other situations.
5. Words are applied in personal writing.

**Using the Vocabulary of the Senses for Themed Vocabulary Study**    Sensory vocabulary provides a wealth of ideas for themed vocabulary study. Simply select a sensory theme and follow the steps for Themed Word Study to develop a semantic map, as shown in Box 7.6. Additional suggestions are provided below.

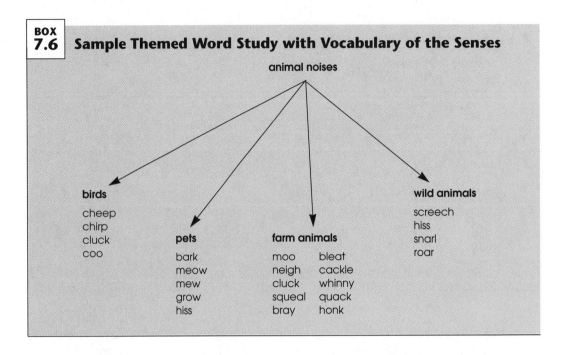

**BOX 7.6  Sample Themed Word Study with Vocabulary of the Senses**

animal noises

**birds**
cheep
chirp
cluck
coo

**pets**
bark
meow
mew
grow
hiss

**farm animals**
moo       bleat
neigh     cackle
cluck     whinny
squeal    quack
bray      honk

**wild animals**
screech
hiss
snarl
roar

**How Many Ways?**   "How Many Ways?" is a sensory-based variation on themed vocabulary study. The idea is to explore different ways that something can be described. This approach builds new concepts, new vocabulary, and new awareness. It does so by having students describe comparable and contrasting ways of talking about experiences. It can be used in conjunction with Donlan's strategy and requires much less preparation. Examples are from Platts' book, *Anchors* (1970):

*How many ways can a castle look?* (quaint, luxurious, elegant, charming, magical, haunted, bewitched, spooky, unoccupied, run-down, seedy, cold, frightening, enchanted, deserted, vacant, etc.)

*How many ways can sandpaper feel?* (gritty, grainy, granular, scratchy, hard, stiff, abrasive, raspy, rough, etc.)

*How many ways can a dancer move?* (spin, flit, leap, jump, dip, frisk, frolic, prance, hop, bound, vault, gambol, rotate, whirl, turn, sway, cavort, etc.)

*How many ways can a person speak?* (scream, shout, whisper, bellow, stutter, stammer, screech, orate, murmur, boom, babble, yell, sputter, drone, etc.)

*How many ways can a scream sound?* (shrill, loud, piercing, frantic, powerful, deafening, blatant, lusty, thunderous, noisy, etc.)

Consider now some additional language arts activities for building sensory vocabulary.

**Other Lesson Activities for Vocabulary of the Senses**

1.  **Connotations**[19]  On the chalkboard, list sensory words preselected from a story students are about to read. Have students simply try to define these

words from their current perspectives (to be sure they know the basic **denotations**[20] of the terms), then read the story and study the words in context to identify and extend their connotative possibilities.

2. **Conceptual Sorting**  Provide students with five to fifteen words, depending on the age and grade level of the children or the difficulty level of the words. Have students categorize the words under the five senses (see the sample worksheet format in Figure 7.13). This activity improves important aspects of basic thinking as well as reinforcing vocabulary. It is best done in three stages: first with each child working independently, then in designated groups, and finally in a whole-class discussion. Again, see Appendix C for lists of words categorized by the five senses.

3. **Phonemic Representation**  To teach the concept of **onomatopoeia**[21], give students a list of such words and discuss how the letters in each word help to convey a familiar sound. Point out that while onomatopoetic words are close approximations of the sounds they represent, they are not accurate *reproductions* of the sounds. This point is easily made by showing how one word, such as "bark" applies to many different barking sounds. Sample onomatopoetic words from a fourth-grade basal story are listed below:

*bark*     the sound a dog makes when somebody approaches whom he does not know

*bang*     the loud noise like the shot of a gun or the sound made by dropping an object

*blare*    the loud blast of a trumpet or horn

*bray*     the cry of a donkey or burro

*cackle*   the cry of a hen when she lays an egg

*purr*     the sound a cat makes when she is comfortable or happy

*neigh*    the noise a horse makes when he is afraid of something, like fire

*chirp*    the sound a bird makes when it is happy

*giggle*   a noise that sounds a little like laughing that you make when you are tickled, when you are nervous, or when you find something a little funny

*peep*     the sound made by a baby bird when it wants to eat

The next method also involves a form of sorting. However, it invites the student to consider overlapping as well as exclusive categories.

### Semantic Feature Analysis

Semantic Feature Analysis is a method designed to teach students how to think systematically about words in terms of their relevant and irrelevant **semantic**[22] features (Johnson & Pearson, 1984). It resembles the paradigm, previously described, by which concepts are learned. The method has been shown by Anders and Bos (1986) to be especially effective in improving reading vocabulary and comprehension. The version described and illustrated below was refined by Stieglitz and

**FIGURE 7.13** **Worksheet for Categorizing Words by Senses**

Name _____

# A Collage of Senses

Find and cut out words or pictures in the newspaper that you can:

| smell | taste | hear | touch | see |
|-------|-------|------|-------|-----|

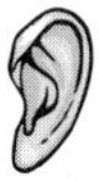

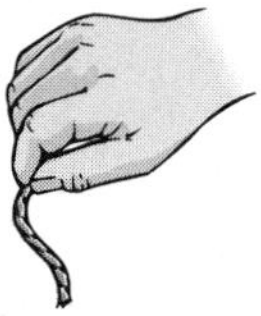

Make a collage of your "five senses" pictures and words. On a separate sheet of paper, write a story about some of the pictures and words you found.

Stieglitz (1981) for use with content material. They call it SAVOR, for Subject Area Vocabulary Reinforcement.

## STEPS IN SAVOR

**Step 1**    The teacher identifies a category of words highly familiar to students. For a fun example, try "monsters," a category within the interest range of many students (see Table 7.1). The teacher first **elicits**[23] words from the pupils that fit in this category (King Kong, Hulk, Dracula, Cookie Monster, Godzilla) and has the students list these examples in a column on their own paper.

**Step 2**    The students list some features of these monsters (hairy, huge, strong, mean, form-changing) across the top of the page. Following this, they fill in the blank chart by using plus (+) or minus (−) signs to indicate whether a monster has or does not have each feature.

**Step 3**    After the **matrix**[24] is filled in, the teacher leads a discussion based on the patterns of pluses and minuses. The object of the discussion is to state how each word (or in this case, creature) is similar to and different from the others and to discover the possible uniqueness of each.

Johnson and Pearson (1984) state that as pupils gain more experience with Semantic Feature Analysis, the teacher may wish to switch from a plus/minus system to a graduated numerical system (0 = none, 1 = some, 2 = much, 3 = all). The method is particularly suitable for helping young children to clarify frequently confused terms, such as: *square, rectangle, octagon.*

The next method is a game format. It enhances vocabulary development by heightening attention to the written and spoken words in the child's daily environment.

### Cultural Academic Trivia (Treasures)

The CAT game (Manzo, 1970; 1985) is designed to build *prior knowledge,* or power to read and understand, by making students more attentive to words and allusions in their environment. It does this by inviting students to make a note on a $3 \times 5$ card of anything that they hear or read but don't quite know. Cards are given

## Table 7.1

### Sample SAVOR Worksheet

**"MONSTERS"**

|  | Hairy | Huge | Strong | Mean | Transforming |
|---|---|---|---|---|---|
| King Kong | + | + | + | + | − |
| Hulk | − | + | + | − | + |
| Dracula | − | − | − | + | + |
| Cookie Monster | + | − | − | − | − |
| Godzilla | − | + | + | + | − |

out periodically to serve as a reminder to be alert for unknown words, facts, and ideas in and outside of the school situation.

Students bring their CAT cards to class, where the teacher and a resource team of three to five youngsters try to determine quickly what they know about each item, checking references as needed. The information is written on the back of the card and returned to the student who submitted it. The student then resubmits it if he or she chooses, and it is placed in a pack to be used to play the "trivia" game. The trivia game is played by dividing the class into two groups. The groups are challenged, in turn, to state the meaning and significance of words or phrases randomly chosen by the teacher from the card pack.

The game can be played competitively by keeping score, or noncompetitively, simply by having students keep count of their number correct out of ten cards each time they play the game. It also can be tied to a random factor to make it more game-like. For example, each time a correct answer is given, the student gets to roll a die; the number shown is recorded and added until a winner is declared (25 points or more to a game).

CAT is an especially good means of helping youngsters to begin to acquire some of the many allusions or referents that are used by others in speaking and writing. To that extent, it could be called a Heritage Game; that is, one that helps students to become familiar with common cultural allusions, such as Mesopotamia, Marie Curie, and Buddha. When the teacher and resource team find related information of interest, they note it in parentheses and share it incidentally and in a way that matches age/grade interests: e.g.:

> Mesopotamia: Ancient country in southwestern Asia between the Tigris and Euphrates Rivers (sometimes known as the "Cradle of Civilization"; today it is roughly the same as the country of Iraq).
>
> Marie Curie (1867–1934): Chemist (and physicist) who discovered two new chemicals (radium and polonium). She was the wife of a famous French chemist and physicist, Pierre Curie. She was Polish, and her maiden name was Sklodowska.
>
> Buddha: Name given to a great sixth-century religious leader. The name really means "enlightened one," and was given to others. "The" Buddha was named Gautama Siddharta. Buddhism teaches right living, right thinking, and denial as the way to overcome release from worldly woes.

A variation on CAT, called a "Friday Quiz Bowl Competition," is a major component in one of the most successful programs for helping black minority youngsters to be academically competitive for medical school (Whimbey & Lochhead, 1980). The best part of this game is that it gently turns students toward the light of words and conversation about important subject area concepts. The next method is based on a slightly larger definition of vocabulary building. It addresses some of the challenges inherent in the English phonemic system.

## Multiple Meanings

The idea of this activity is to help students overcome their puzzlement about the fact that the English language has many words that are identical in spelling but with different meanings—sometimes several different meanings. Because the idea of the same word having different meanings doesn't make a lot of sense to most youngsters, they often will try to spell such words differently in different situations. This tactic is reinforced by the fact that many English words with identical pronunciations but different meanings are spelled differently, such as two, too, and to.

Platts (1970) provides a word list and accompanying set of words and practices that we have modified slightly for teaching about multiple meanings.

### Sample Words with Multiple Meanings

| | | | |
|---|---|---|---|
| strike | fast | scale | cast |
| stern | train | quarter | pitch |
| cabinet | stand | run | post |

### Protocol for Teaching Words with Multiple Meanings

**Teacher**  Will you use the first word, "strike," in a sentence, Alan?

**Student**  Yes. When the batter missed the ball, the umpire yelled, "Strike one!"

**Teacher**  What does the word "strike" mean in this sentence, Alice?

**Student**  To miss.

**Teacher**  Can you give a sentence in which "strike" has an entirely different meaning, Dick?

**Student**  Yes. The workers voted to strike.

**Teacher**  What does the word "strike" mean in this sentence, Ann?

**Student**  Not go to work.

**Teacher**  Yes, it means to cease or stop working.

Continue in this fashion until additional meanings for the word "strike" have been mentioned and discussed. Then turn to the dictionary to search for some others. You may need to set limits on how many more—there are about 32 meanings for "strike" in an unabridged dictionary. As a followup, write several other words on the board. Have students write two sentences showing two *different* meanings for each word on the board. When children have completed their work, encourage class discussion of the multiple meanings of each of the words listed.

*Platts (1970, pp. 106–107).*

Let's turn now to some "gravitational," or "weak force," approaches to the improvement of vocabulary acquisition. The impact of these approaches tends to be linked to the student's interest in and attention to words as a means of labeling and thinking about experience.

## INCIDENTAL INSTRUCTION APPROACH

As previously discussed, the highest level of mental processing occurs when a person self-monitors, self-corrects, and self-guides his or her own learning.

Collectively these functions are known as *metacognition*—or awareness of one's own cognitive processes. Where vocabulary is concerned, learning can never be great unless these self-guidance systems are activated. There simply are too many words in the English language that occur too infrequently to teach all that must be learned. Rather, it is necessary to teach students strategies for independent word learning. This *also* means disposing children toward *seeing and hearing* the words, in their reading and *everyday* experiences, that are out there waiting to be learned, and imparting to them a sense that words are something about which they should be both curious and excited.

The next four vocabulary methods address this important matter of student *disposition* toward words. They resemble the CAT game, described above. Each is **cognate**[25] to the idea of "organic words." "Organic words" was the name used by Sylvia Ashton-Warner (1959) to describe her chief method of encouraging the **indigenous**[26] Maori children of New Zealand to become literate. They would tell her what words they wanted to be able to read and write, and she would show them how to spell their words. The children then would "own" the words, with the stipulation that they were expected to read their words any time she asked them to do so. If a child missed a word three times, he or she would lose it. The methods presented next extend this organic, or *words-as-an-extension-of-self-and-environment,* approach from the word recognition to word meaning level.

## Wide Reading

As suggested earlier in the chapter, wide reading is a valuable means of developing vocabulary, and to *compare it with* direct instructional approaches is to miss the point. Instead, it should be thought of as a complement to direct instruction. Through wide reading, children: (1) have the **vicarious**[27] contextual experiences necessary to conceptually grasp new words; (2) have increased exposure to the words and referents they need to learn (e.g., "sputnik"—as used to refer to the beginning of the space age or to the height of Soviet power and influence); (3) build familiarity with various forms of known words (e.g., bicycle, bicycling, bicyclist); and, (4) learn multiple meanings of known words.

Wide reading alone is not enough to build vocabulary significantly. To amplify its impact, the teacher can do a variety of things. Three *previously* mentioned suggestions are especially valuable:

- Encourage students to truly "see" the words that they typically read past by encouraging self-collection of unfamiliar words and allusions.
- Teach students how to use context to interpret meanings of unfamiliar words, as in the Contextual Redefinition method, but also to be aware of the sometimes misleading effects of overreliance on context.
- Teach, reinforce, and model dictionary usage.

The environmental/organic method described next seems especially useful for amplifying the effects of Wide Reading on vocabulary acquisition. It ties vocabulary learning to real-world contexts and learning.

### Community of Language Approach

This approach, which recently has been called "Cross-Curriculum Word for the Day" (Switzer, 1991), is simple and fun (Manzo & Manzo, 1990a). It begins with the identification of a **corpus**$_{28}$ of words that children should learn. Then all teachers, the principal, and even the support staff of a school simply are asked to *use the words* as often as they can in the natural situations and conditions throughout the school day. In this way words as **esoteric**$_{29}$ as "bucolic" are learned through immersion and multiple exposure as naturally as we learn more frequently used synonyms like *rural, rustic, countryside,* and *pastoral.*

Teachers and staff members are asked to tape the word list to their desk or outside a frequently used notebook as a constant reminder to use the words whenever possible. Children begin to hear these words used in many contexts by different people. They also begin to *notice* that the word list is being used in different places by different people in the school. The fact that the adults in the building are making this cooperative effort sends a clear message to children: words are important, and we are committed to helping you learn them.

Repeated exposures to words in many contexts not only teaches surface meanings of words; it teaches the layers of meaning that are needed to see, image, and conceptualize new things and ideas. The new words become part of the "toolkit" the child uses to explore the world. One sixth-grade child, for example, observed that the classroom window blinds must contain some form of *pulley* system, prompting the teacher to have his class take down and examine the blinds.

Now consider some exercise and game formats for reinforcing vocabulary learning. These formats are widely used in workbook-type practice materials.

## REINFORCEMENT AND PRACTICE FORMATS AND GAMES

Of all the things that can be said about word learning, none is simpler and more certain than the need for repetition and use: "Use a word three times," the old saying goes, "and it will be yours forever." Words worth teaching are worth practicing until they are learned. When word meanings are "forgotten," more often than not, they simply have not been adequately learned.

There are several ways to ensure that the benefits of repetition are achieved without boredom to students or teacher. The most convenient way, as suggested above, is simply through classroom conversation. Once words have been identified and taught, the teacher must follow up by encouraging students to use the words in typical classroom talking. This simultaneously puts the new word into a familiar context, deepens learning by using it in varied settings, and provides incidental repetition. In a related vein, the teacher should not overlook a plain, old-fashioned oral recitation-review. The snappy, five-minute-a-day, oral review of unfamiliar, low-frequency words can be an effective means of keeping word learning in high gear throughout the term.

Other popular means of providing practice and reinforcement in exercise formats are described next. As noted earlier, some educators condemn exercises of this type on the basis that they fragment "whole language." Edelsky (1992), for example, warns that no matter how cute or interesting the exercises are, they are not the way that language is learned naturally. Study the exercises and see if you agree, or if you believe, as others do, that school need not always be "natural" any more than must vitamins, medicines, air conditioning, or other aids to health and comfort.

**Vocabulary Practice Formats and Exercises**

**Categorization**    To teach word meanings and concept formation.

Directions: Choose the one word in each group that does not relate to the others and should be excluded. Write this word in the blank labeled "Exclude." In the blank labeled "General Concept," write the concept that describes the remaining words. The examples shown are from a science unit on the "Mechanics of the Human Body."

digestive            Exclude _____ *organism* _____

circulatory          General Concept *moving parts inside us*

organism             _____

muscular

veins                Exclude _____ *blood* _____

arteries             General Concept *vessels (tubes) that*

capillaries          *carry blood to and from the heart*

blood

**Analogies**    To teach categorization and abstract thinking. Following are examples from *Worksheet Magazine* (1989, p. 11).

Directions: Read the analogies below in the following manner: ____ is to ____ as ____ is to ____. Think how the first word pair is related. Look at the third word. Then fill in the blank with a word from the word bank that has that same relationship.

*Word Bank:*    birds      person    hand
                children   grass     down
                people     bird      train
                feet       black     duck

1. Ducklings are to ducks as babies are to _____.
2. Chirp goes with bird the way quack goes with _____.
3. A house is to a person as a nest is to a _____.
4. Toe goes with foot the way finger goes with _____.
5. A wing is to a bird as an arm is to _____.

As students become familiar with the basic form of analogies, teach them to look for specific types of relationships among the word pairs, including:

size or proportion
*large : enormous :: small : tiny*

antonyms
*black : white :: good : bad*

part/whole
*toe : foot :: finger : hand*

language forms
*come : came :: run : ran*

action/object
*sail : boat :: drive :car*

singular/plural
*man : men :: dog : dogs*

cause/effect
*wound : blood :: accident : damage*

number relationships
*1 : 3 :: 3 : 9*

synonyms
*cool : chilly :: copy : imitate*

object/function
*cup : water :: frame : picture*

object/composition
*pencil : wood :: cup : glass*

**Word Lines**   To teach subtleties of word meanings. This is basic to concept formation (see below).

*Sample Word Line*

Directions: Place the following words on the word line. Arrange them in order from hottest to coldest. Be ready to defend your arrangement.

| | |
|---|---|
| temperate | chilly |
| cool | hot |
| torrid | moderate |
| warm | sweltering |
| frigid | cold |

*hot*                                                      *cold*

**Antonyms Matching**   To reinforce word meanings by considering and labeling opposite meanings. This, too, is basic to concept formation as well as word learning.

Directions: Circle the letter of the word that is most nearly the *opposite* of the first word.

1. prevalent
   a. uncommon   b. unwilling   c. unknown   d. unexciting   e. unfounded

2. precise
   a. impossible   b. incorrect   c. excited   d. clinging   e. receptive

3. adequate
   a. aware of    b. short of    c. jealous of   d. demand of   e. expect of

**Translating Idioms**   To teach figurative language forms. This exercise tends to build appreciation of the wonder and poetry of language as well as of word meanings.

The concept of idioms is interesting since it is a handy way of using a simple expression to say something that could sound quite stuffy if said in the most correct terminology. For example: "This book is over my head" obviously does not mean that "this book is suspended above my head," but rather that "this book is too difficult for me," and might mean, more precisely, that "this book uses so many hard words that I can't make much sense of it." Here are seven other sample sentences containing idiomatic phrases that students can translate into simpler language first, and then into more precise statements:

He's up to his neck in work.          I could eat a horse.
I think I'll hit the hay.              He shot off his mouth.
It's raining cats and dogs.           That's not my cup of tea.
He's just letting off steam.

### Word Games

Word games can help to build motivation for vocabulary study. Bowman (1991) suggests that two classes of games based on word pairs, "Wordy Gurdy Puzzles" and "Oxymorons," are especially useful because they are based on cues within words and word relationships. By providing focused practice in attending to these types of cues, these games may even reinforce reading comprehension.

**Wordy Gurdy Puzzles**   Develop a list of definitions that could be associated with two rhyming words—each of the rhyming words having the same number of syllables. Give the definitions to students, indicating the number of syllables in each word of the "answer":

principal plumbing outlet [1]    (main drain)
Henry's practical jokes [1]      (Hank's pranks)
comical rabbit [2]               (funny bunny)

Once students have provided the answers to several Wordy Gurdy Puzzles, challenge them to make up their own "definitions" and trade puzzles. Compile these in a bulletin board display.

**Oxymorons**   An oxymoron is a word pair in which the two words contradict each other, as in *permanent press, cruel kindness,* and *eternal moment.* Introduce several such oxymorons to students, pointing out their seemingly contradictory nature. Have students compose definitions for a list of oxymorons. Then furnish definitions and compare. Also, have students add to a list throughout the term; e.g. "hot ice."

**Vocabulary Hot Potato**   Use small metal rings and paper tags. Put a vocabulary word on each of the paper tags and hang the tags on the ring. Hang the ring of

**FIGURE 7.14** **Pundles**

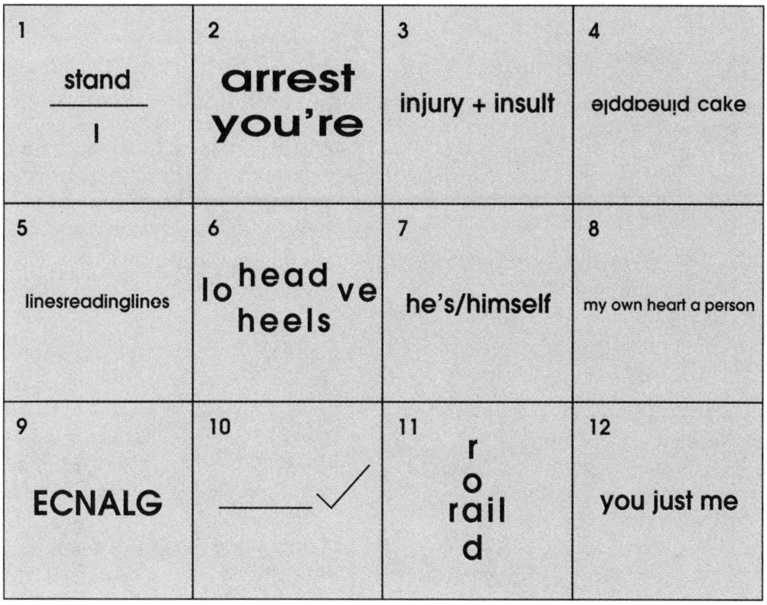

| 1<br><br>stand<br>─────<br>I | 2<br><br>**arrest<br>you're** | 3<br><br>injury + insult | 4<br><br>pineapple cake |
|---|---|---|---|
| 5<br><br>linesreadinglines | 6<br><br>lo<sup>head</sup>ve<br>**heels** | 7<br><br>he's/himself | 8<br><br>my own heart a person |
| 9<br><br>**ECNALG** | 10<br><br>───── ✓ | 11<br><br>r<br>o<br>rail<br>d | 12<br><br>you just me |

*Translations:*

1-I understand 2-you're under arrest 3-adding insult to injury 4-pineapple upside down cake 5-reading between the lines 6-head over heels in love 7-he's beside himself 8-a person after my own heart 9-a backward glance 10-blank check 11-railroad crossing 12-just between you and me

*Adapted from Vail, 1981, pp. 166-167.*

words near your desk as a reminder to integrate them into conversation. To play "hot potato," toss the ring to a student, who then has ten seconds to use the top word in a sentence before turning the top word over and tossing the ring to a classmate.

**Pundles** These visual plays on words enhance interest in words and understanding of figurative language. Number 1, in Figure 7.14, for example, is a visual representation of "I understand." See how you do with the others before checking the translations that are printed upside down below the illustration. Children enjoy translating a few pundles and then creating their own.

To **reiterate**[30], there is no method of teaching vocabulary study that can generate greater and more continuous and contagious growth in vocabulary than a teacher who enjoys words and talks about them. Think of *every* method presented in this chapter as a way to remind teachers and students to be interested in conversing about words and language usage. Watch for comments like this from one of two boys who were looking at the classroom's new *American Heritage Dictionary*

(1992): "Teacher! Charlie found where the word *moped* came from! It comes from the *mo* in *motor* and the *ped* in *pedal*."

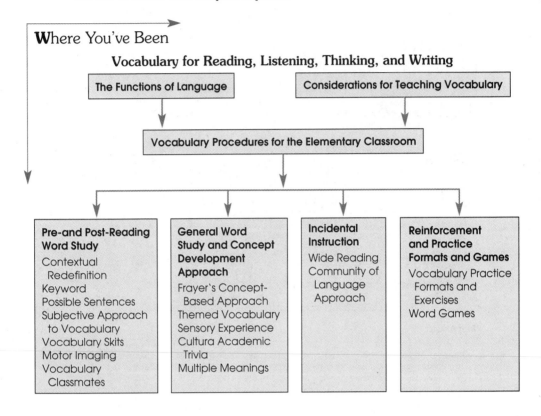

## **W**here You've Been

### Vocabulary for Reading, Listening, Thinking, and Writing

| The Functions of Language | | Considerations for Teaching Vocabulary |

**Vocabulary Procedures for the Elementary Classroom**

| **Pre-and Post-Reading Word Study** | **General Word Study and Concept Development Approach** | **Incidental Instruction** | **Reinforcement and Practice Formats and Games** |
|---|---|---|---|
| Contextual Redefinition | Frayer's Concept-Based Approach | Wide Reading Community of Language Approach | Vocabulary Practice Formats and Exercises |
| Keyword | Themed Vocabulary | | Word Games |
| Possible Sentences | Sensory Experience | | |
| Subjective Approach to Vocabulary | Cultura Academic Trivia | | |
| Vocabulary Skits | Multiple Meanings | | |
| Motor Imaging | | | |
| Vocabulary Classmates | | | |

## **W**here You're Going

Words, or semantics, are the building blocks of comprehension. When those words are strung together, however, they can create some special problems to understanding. The next chapter is devoted to the recent explosion of theories, means, and methods for teaching basic comprehension strategies, or how to impart to children the means to help themselves to generate meaning from their interactions with the printed page.

### *Reflective Inquiries and Activities*

1. Identify three facts about vocabulary acquisition that you found to be most interesting for a teacher to know.

2. Tell a story of a word whose meaning you mistook for sometime due to learning it from context alone. Do you remember how you finally learned its correct meaning?

**Table 7.2**

### Personal Ratings of Vocabulary Methods

| Name of Method | resembles the way language is learned naturally | can be used as a strategy for independent word learning | can be used to introduce words from a given selection or unit | has been tested and shown to be effective | would tend to heighten students' interest in words and language | I plan to use this method regularly |
|---|---|---|---|---|---|---|
| example: Motor Imaging | 5 | 4 | 5 | 5 | 3 | 4 |
| | | | | | | |
| | | | | | | |
| | | | | | | |

3. Review each method and rate it in Semantic Feature Analysis style on a 5-point scale, from 1 low to 5 high, on factors such as those shown in the sample Semantic Feature Analysis chart in Table 7.2. Table 7.2 also provides sample ratings of one method.

4. Identify the three methods you are most and least likely to use, and tell why.

5. Try designing a means of measuring student progress that you could use to evaluate your word study program. For guidance refer to the different ways the words can be defined.

6. Try designing a means of measuring student progress that you could use to evaluate your word study program. For guidance refer to the different ways words can be defined.

7. How many low-frequency words used in this chapter do you know? Check your knowledge of these words by completing the vocabulary exercise below. Check your choices against the answer key at the end of the test.

VOCABULARY EXERCISE

    1. mediate
        a. treat        b. intervene        c. renounce        d. ponder
    2. hypothesis
        a. testable        b. axiom        c. theory        d. tentative
           observation                              explanation
    3 domestic
        a. intolerant        b. unemployed        c. native        d. natural
                                                         resource

4. precept
   a. principle    b. general idea    c. condition    d. glimpse

5. disposition
   a. general climate    b. shifting    c. orientation    d. upkeep

6. puerile
   a. noxious    b. childish    c. mature    d. peripheral

7. paradox
   a. analogy    b. pattern or model    c. simple lesson    d. seeming contradiction

8. artifact
   a. deception    b. ancient    c. man-made    d. natural

9. mucilage
   a. glue    b. air-tight tank    c. brackish fluid    d. detergent

10. plateau
    a. wide basin    b. flat highland    c. crest    d. grassy slope

11. ethereal
    a. gaseous substance    b. obvious    c. moral    d. intangible

12. transaction
    a. forward motion    b. agreement    c. communication    d. rising above

13. celerity
    a. swiftness    b. relating to the heavens    c. renown    d. sluggishness

14. proprioceptive
    a. learnable    b. sensorimotor    c. suited to a purpose    d. audible

15. paradigm
    a. celestial body    b. contradiction    c. pattern or model    d. misquote

16. superordinate
    a. outside the laws of nature    b. numerical    c. above-ground    d. more abstract form

17. arduous
    a. definite    b. strenuous    c. passionate    d. steep

18. nuance
    a. subtle distinction    b. bother    c. close approximation    d. essence

19. connotation
    a. suggested meaning    b. indirect relationship    c. exact alignment    d. unwritten agreement

20. denotation
    a. acknowledg-    b. specific    c. public    d. resolution
       ment         meaning     renunciation

21. onomatopoeia
    a. using a part to    b. unrhymed    c. nonsense    d. using words to
       symbolize the     verse       words       imitate sounds
       whole

22. semantic
    a. elements of    b. related to    c. simple    d. irrelevant
       grammar      meaning     logic       argument

23. elicit
    a. draw out    b. unlawful    c. deliver    d. precise

24. matrix
    a. point of    b. a system of    c. a chart with    d. a female
       convergence    measurement   rows and columns  supervisor

25. cognate
    a. international    b. related in nature c. subset of a    d. ponder
       organization     or function     larger concept

26. indigenous
    a. native    b. unschooled    c. melded    d. mixed

27. vicarious
    a. direct    b. real-life    c. changeable    d. substitute

28. corpus
    a. excessive    b. material    c. largest part of    d. group or
       fat       evidence     a collection     unit

29. esoteric
    a. complex    b. known by a    c. highly    d. superficial
             few       abstract

30. reiterate
    a. repeat    b. return    c. justify    d. claim

### Exercise Key:

1. b  2. d  3. c  4. a  5. c  6. b  7. d  8. c  9. a  10. b  11. d  12. c  13. a
14. b  15. c  16. d  17. b  18. a  19. a  20. b  21. d  22. b 23. a  24. c
25. b  26. a  27. d  28. d  29. c  30. a

### Score Interpretation:

28 or more = *excellent;*   23–27 = *good;*
18–22 = *on target;*   below 17 = *needs improvement*

# 8 IMPROVING BASIC COMPREHENSION

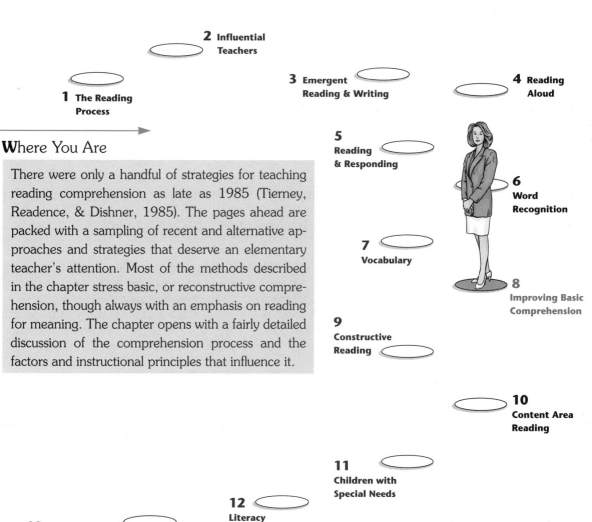

**2** Influential
Teachers

**1** The Reading
Process

**3** Emergent
Reading & Writing

**4** Reading
Aloud

## Where You Are

There were only a handful of strategies for teaching reading comprehension as late as 1985 (Tierney, Readence, & Dishner, 1985). The pages ahead are packed with a sampling of recent and alternative approaches and strategies that deserve an elementary teacher's attention. Most of the methods described in the chapter stress basic, or reconstructive comprehension, though always with an emphasis on reading for meaning. The chapter opens with a fairly detailed discussion of the comprehension process and the factors and instructional principles that influence it.

**5** Reading
& Responding

**6**
Word
Recognition

**7** Vocabulary

**8**
Improving Basic
Comprehension

**9**
Constructive
Reading

**10**
Content Area
Reading

**11**
Children with
Special Needs

**12**
Literacy
Assessment

**13** The Classroom
& School Literacy Program

*Time, which diminishes all things,
increases understanding.*
Plutarch,
*The Education of Children*

# COMPREHENSION PROCESS

The act of silently reading and comprehending a single page of print is one of the most highly integrated and recently evolved functions of humankind. It was not so very long ago, in fact, that most educators and psychologists believed that comprehension could not be taught—one simply comprehended or failed to comprehend according to one's inborn talents. Thorndike's 1917 article entitled "Reading as Reasoning" presented a different scenario. As you can see in the excerpt below, Thorndike described comprehension as a *process* rather than a *product:*

> The mind is assailed, as it were, by every word in a paragraph. It must select, repress, soften, emphasize, correlate, and organize, all under the right mental set or purpose or demand.

Years of subsequent study have provided varying views of the nature of reading comprehension. One thing, however, has become clear: Reading comprehension is a process that can be taught. More importantly, the more a teacher understands about the comprehension process, the better able he or she is to anticipate and prevent many problems their students are likely to encounter and to help them to overcome other problems that inevitably will arise.

## INTERACTIVE MODES

The particular interactive view of reading that most authorities support is one in which the reader assembles a personal understanding of print through a selective process of applying two opposing modes. At times the reader applies a part-to-whole, or "bottom-up" mode, and at other times a hypothesis-driven, "top-down" mode. The effective reader switches rapidly back and forth between these modes until a sense of the author's meaning is achieved and is translated into some personalized form. Most current views of the comprehension process differ only in the degree of emphasis that is placed on one or the other of these interactive modes.

Pearson and Fielding (1991) argue that reading is essentially a *reconstructive,* or a "get-the-author's-meaning," process, since each moment of actual reading begins with some bottom-up level of decoding of at least some words. Initially it is necessary to establish just what the author intended to say, rather than what one might imagine or like it to be. In other words, initial reading comprehension by definition is an act of trying to acquire the ideas being conveyed or *transmitted* by the writer.

Other authorities, such as most whole-language advocates, tend to emphasize the *constructive* side of the process, arguing that the reader uses the author's words as a stimulus to construct meaning. In this view the definition of reading is broadened to include the thoughts, knowledge, and experiences that must be called up and applied to the construction of meaning from print. Even on initial reading, individual words and word parts call up our innate search for meaning. Wilson and Gambrell (1988) put it simply when they said that reading comprehension is "the process of using one's own experiences and text clues to infer the author's intended meaning" (p. 12). In this constructive definition, reading is seen as a *transaction* that inspires the reader's imagination.

## TRANSMISSION, TRANSACTION, TRANSFORMATION

The reconstructive/constructive (R/C) view of interactive reading that is advocated here places equal emphasis on *transmission* and *transaction,* but adds an emphasis on *transformation.* Transformation is the process of being changed by what one reads. The implication is that effective reading requires a willingness to be influenced and possibly changed by what one reads, assuming that it is logical and compelling.

With respect to the transmission, or reconstructive aspect of reading, the R/C view stresses the importance of teaching youngsters to do a very effective job of literal level reading as a necessary facet of being able to assemble a sturdy point of reference for reading and thinking between and beyond the lines. The rationale for accurate reconstructive reading in the R/C Interactive model is best exemplified by an analogy.

## HITTING THE "BULL'S EYE"

Think of the reading act as an arrow aimed at a target that is three feet in diameter, six feet away, with a bull's eye that is six inches in diameter. If the rate of error for the arrow in flight is one inch per foot, the aim could be off by three inches above, below, or to either side, and the arrow will still hit the bull's eye. If the target is moved back even one foot, and precisely the same shot is repeated, even the slightest error in aim will be multiplied. Within just a few additional feet the arrow will miss the bull's eye, and by the time it is thirty feet away the arrow will miss the target entirely. So it is with reading between and beyond the lines. Unless the reader starts with a pretty accurate shot, thinking beyond the lines can easily deteriorate into misguided shots all over the textual landscape. Thus instructional emphasis on reconstructive reading is an essential element of on-target constructive reading. This emphasis also supports the institutions and values, such as democracy, that rely on schools to teach the voting public to read and consider complex issues with a minimum of the distorting effects of bias and prejudice. The higher the target, the more important the initial aim. In other words, facts are important, and reader ability and willingness to check and correct aim (interestingly called "attitude" in aerodynamics) greatly affects one's ability to be on target. It also permits one to have the confidence to raise and then hit targets that others initially might be too distracted to even see. This is the essential nature of the highest act of the constructive process, that of creative reading–thinking.

To clarify, we are *not* saying that teachers should concentrate on reconstructive, or "just the facts, ma'am" reading, and then after some interminable delay go on to teach or excite critical and creative reading and thinking. On the contrary, this book has already offered, and will offer, many examples of how youngsters can be drawn into, or be engaged in the process of active, reconstructive reading by appealing *first* to higher levels of thinking. Whitehurst and associates' (1988a, b) research (first cited in Chapter 3) showed how this can be done easily, even with very young children, when the person reading to them merely remembers to ask some open-ended questions. Nonetheless, schools must pay close attention to building a correct "attitude" in youngsters to try hard to hit the comprehension bull's eye whenever any piece of text is put before them.

## HUMAN EMOTIONS MAKE ATTITUDE IMPORTANT

An attitude of high regard for literal level reading needs to be stressed and taught simply because there is a great deal of natural emotionality and apprehension built into most everything humans see, do, and encounter. Our perception of "facts" is colored by our feelings, attitudes, and expectations. It is for this reason, for example, that there usually are marked differences in the recollections of any three witnesses to the same incident. Feelings, attitudes, and expectations can also enhance or distort basic reading comprehension (Goetz et al., 1992). Comprehension, like remembering, is an act of reconstruction, not reproduction. This means that even our best efforts to read the author's message will result in subtle differences in our perceptions of word associations and allusions. Mental images will differ, causing details, and even main ideas, to be perceived differently from person to person, between each person and the author, and even in the same person at different times or under different circumstances.

In considering this point, keep in mind that there are some "proficient" readers who need to be taught how to awaken their passions and capacity for associations and constructive thoughts. In fact, the "neutering" of comprehension also could be considered a form of emotionality. It is based, technically speaking, on repression—an involuntary denial that can be quite warping, as opposed to suppression—a voluntary rejection of biases that tends to be clarifying. So, while this chapter focuses largely on reconstructively reading the lines and between the lines, the next two chapters pay equally focused attention to constructive reading, thinking, and writing beyond the lines. As you read ahead, note that many of the reconstructive reading practices advocated in this chapter excite and invite the kind of constructive reading–thinking–writing that is developed more fully in the next chapters on higher–order literacy.

## EVIDENCE THAT COMPREHENSION CAN BE TAUGHT

It was noted above that until recently, many educators did not believe that reading comprehension could be taught (Pearson et al., 1992). The belief was that one could be taught word attack and recognition and then be encouraged to read until the upper limits of one's intelligence and the outer limits of one's experiences came together to act as a governor on one's ultimate ability to comprehend. Reading comprehension occurs between the ears and can not be seen. Thus it was assumed that it could not be explored or tutored except in some marginal ways through postreading recitation, discussion, and lots of practice reading.

In 1969, two teaching methods were published that quietly incorporated some radical newer ideas. These methods were based on the assumption that reading comprehension *could* be *taught,* and each came to be widely used. Together, the ReQuest Procedure (Manzo, 1969b) and the Directed Reading–Thinking Activity (Stauffer, 1969) offered convincing evidence that comprehension could be improved through direct instruction when teaching was characterized by these then-pioneering ideas:

- Thinking can be externalized through mental *modeling.*
- *Reciprocity,* or the use of an intimate and analytical "give and take" between a

teacher and students, amplifies the effects of modeling by permitting teacher and students to subtly poke at and influence one another.

- Teaching students to think and acquire learning strategies, such as *self-purpose setting* and *hypothesis testing,* is more effective than merely helping them to comprehend the page before them.

Some authorities, such as Carver (1981), continued to hold to the proposition that reading comprehension is learned largely, if not exclusively, from reading—a proposition he has more recently retested and found wanting (Carver, work in progress). In general, however, the greatest number of authorities believe that with the better identification of the factors, functions, and strategies involved in reading comprehension, we now have much of the knowledge base needed to more directly *teach* comprehension effectively.

Let's look now at a listing of these elements to see what would most likely need to be addressed in some way to develop a successful reading comprehension program for the majority of children. This listing is drawn from several sources, including meta-analyses of the research literature done by: Manzo and Manzo (1993); Mason, Herman, & Au (1991), Pearson, Roehler, Dole, & Duffy (1992); and Robinson, Faraone, Hittleman, & Unruh (1990). In many cases the sources cited for each factor are only representative of those that could be included. Several other relevant sources are cited ahead in the chapter where specific methodologies are presented.

## FACTORS, FUNCTIONS, AND STRATEGIES INVOLVED IN READING COMPREHENSION

1.  Orientation and motivation to read (Mason, Herman, & Au, 1991)
2.  Willingness and ability to engage in inner conversations and conversations with others about what has been read (Helfeldt & Lalik, 1979; Tharp & Gallimore, 1989a, b)
3.  Accurate and resourceful word recognition and analysis (Chall, 1983a; Holmes & Singer, 1961; LaBerge & Samuels, 1974; Lewkowicz, 1987)
4.  Knowledge of word meanings and ability to further infer meanings from context (Graves, 1986; Hafner & Palmer, 1980)
5.  Adequate schema, or appropriate prior knowledge and experience, especially where processing involves learning and memorizing, as opposed to simpler story or expository reading (Anderson & Pearson, 1984; Bartlett, 1932; Carver, 1992; Gray, 1948; Langer, 1981; Meeks, 1991; Rumelhart, 1980; Yopp & Singer, 1985)
6.  Adequate mental aptitude and basic thinking skills such as identifying a main idea, seeing details, and being able to make logical inferences (Marzano, 1991)
7.  Fundamental curiosity and the ability to ask purpose-setting questions (Baker, 1979a, b; Maw & Maw, 1967; Manzo, 1969a)
8.  Familiarity with the language patterns in prose, and hence with the syntactic and semantic cues used to anticipate meaning (Mason, Herman, & Au, 1991; Reed, 1968)

9. Adequate social-psychological maturity to respond empathetically and objectively to information and story narratives (Mason, Herman, & Au, 1991; Rumelhart, 1980)

10. Continuously developing "metacognitive" skills that permit one to self-monitor and self-fix comprehension problems as they arise (Flavell, 1981; Paris, 1986), including the ability to self-activate appropriate prior knowledge when reading (Bransford & Johnson, 1972; Dooling & Lachman, 1971), and to put aside mis-information that can interfere with understanding (Hynd & Alvermann, 1986; Swafford, 1991)

11. Ability and willingness to see and find *larger* structures and organizational patterns in print (Greenewald & Rossing, 1986; Meyer, 1975)

12. On-going development of higher mental processes, such as the ability to reason analytically and to think metaphorically, evaluatively, and constructively (Gaskins & Elliot, 1991; Hayes & Tierney, 1982; Manzo & Manzo, 1990a; Readence, Baldwin, & Head, 1987)

13. Ability and skill in taking notes and summarizing (Bean & Steenwyck, 1984; Bromley & McKeveny, 1986; Rinehart, Stahl, & Erickson, 1986)

14. Ability and skill to critique, or write reflectively in response to what one has read and thought (Anderson & Hidi, 1988–89; Graves, 1983; Eanet & Manzo, 1976)

15. Inclination to continue the evolution of a "world view" (Chall, 1983b), including time-tested values (Hoffman, 1977; Schell, 1980), interests, and understandings of how things are and ought best to be (Shannon, 1990)

Researchers and practitioners have sifted through these factors and translated them into some general and more manageable principles to guide the selection of methods and techniques for teaching comprehension under both "in-flight" and more reflective conditions. With time and experience, you undoubtedly will wish to add your own guiding principles to this list.

## PRINCIPLES GUIDING SUCCESSFUL COMPREHENSION INSTRUCTION

The principles stated here are essentially comprehension-specific *elaborations* from the guidelines for Influential Teachers noted in Chapter 2 and from suggestions found in other textbooks and reviews of the literature on reading comprehension instruction (Duffy et al., 1987; Gaskins, 1981; Levin & Pressley, 1981; Manzo & Manzo, 1990a, 1993; Maria, 1990; Pearson & Fielding, 1991; Pearson & Gallagher, 1983; Santa & Hayes, 1981; Tierney & Cunningham, 1984). Six principles for guiding comprehension instruction are described below.

1. **Use *Front-Loading Techniques*** *Front-loading* refers to attempts to empower pupils before they read. Front-loading techniques are used to reduce potential vocabulary obstacles to comprehension, activate relevant prior knowledge, and provide specific information on text structure and actual facts cov-

ered in the text. This enables students to engage a reading selection with what amounts to an elevated reading quotient. Use of front-loading techniques obviously is more important with content-rich material than narrative and is important with young, remedial, or culturally or linguistically different youngsters.

2. **Use Strategies That Cause Students to Make *Transformations*** Readers are made more alert, active, and engaged by a requirement to manipulate and transform the text from the author's words into those of the reader. Try to include this "active ingredient" in *every* teaching episode and with any teaching method you may be using. Reconstructive transformations include tasks such as:

   a.  Translating, or retelling what one has read, with the text available
   b.  Recalling and retelling, without looking back at the text
   c.  Rewriting, or summarizing, with the text available
   d.  Summarizing without consulting the text
   e.  Outlining with and without available text
   f.  Representing the text in a student-constructed graphic overview or illustration, with the text available for reference

   Additional types of transformations that are conducive to more constructive thinking are discussed in the chapters on content reading and higher-order literacy. These include compressing and categorizing information for long-term memory (study strategies) and various other means of writing, reflecting, connecting, and creating.

3. **Base Instruction on *Authentic Text and Tasks*** There are many possible ways to achieve some level of authenticity in school. None, however, can be ideal, since schools are designed to teach about and simulate life conditions in ways that control for erratic and potentially negative effects. Nonetheless, teaching methods and materials need to be selected that come closer to the ways that real interests are built and language is used and learned. This is best done largely through the careful construction of a conducive environment that can excite interest and has a life-like or problem-based orientation. The next point offers a small but highly effective way of building authenticity.

4. **Create *Instructional Conversations*** As previously noted, the instructional conversation is known by several other names, such as "responsive teaching," "reciprocity," and "cognitive apprenticeship." By any name, the idea is to create an authentic interaction between people who just happen to be teacher and students, or students with one another. Such interactions tend to rouse minds to life (Manzo & Manzo, 1983; Tharp & Gallimore, 1989a) and provide opportunities for effective thinking to be modeled, or made public (Ehlinger, 1988), and for ineffective thinking to be detected and fixed in an "on-line" way while you are teaching.

5. **Teach *Strategies,* not Skills** Each lesson should be crafted so as to impart possible strategies for students to use in reading and learning situations.

Accordingly, it is important to focus on teaching students to use strategies such as self-monitoring and self-fixing, and hence to encourage them to assume increasing responsibility for their own reading and learning needs. "Skills instruction" is not a way of teaching. It is an objective that is achieved when teacher and student commitment and practice result in students acquiring a variety of personal learning strategies for making sense out of print.

6. **Use *Question Types* That Match Instructional Objectives** Question types typically are categorized according to some perceived organization of the cognitive domain. Box 8.1 describes the most popular categories. However, questions also can be categorized in a variety of other ways that reflect the

---

**BOX 8.1  Cognitive Domain Question Types**

Several popular taxonomies were drawn upon to describe the nine cognitive domain type questions illustrated below:

1. *Recognition questions* require identifying answers from available choices. (Mary had a little: a. goat; b. ham; c. dog; d. lamb)

2. *Recall questions* require remembering answers with very little prompting. (In what state was the battle of Bull Run fought?—Answer: At Bull Run Creek in Virginia)

3. *Translation questions* entail transferring something from one symbolic form to another. (Can you describe this picture?; Can you tell in your own words what the author said in this paragraph?; Can you say what you just heard in your own words?)

4. *Inference questions—Level 1* have the reader combine available textual information to reach an answer that is relatively simple, logical, and implicit in the passage, though not explicitly stated. (What is the relationship between Jack and Joseph in this story?)

5. *Inference questions—Level 2*, better known as *conjecture* questions, require the reader to read between and a little beyond the lines to make an inferential "leap" or prediction, beyond what can be strictly inferred from stated facts alone. (As we read ahead, do you suppose that Brent and Nancy will be friends again?)

6. *Explanation questions* require thoughtful arrangement of information, typically to verify a point. These involve reference to the text but also may call upon other sources, such as familiarity with similar stories, a sense of how and why things happen in the world, and so on. (Why do you think Brent and Nancy will become friends again?)

7. *Application questions* require the abstraction of an idea presented and its transfer to a situation in which the new idea can improve understanding or be used to solve a problem. (Based on what we have learned about hamsters, where is the best place in the room to put Joey's cage?)

8. *Evaluation questions* are a specialized type of application question that require critical analysis, aesthetic sense, and personal judgment. (How do you feel about the story? The characters? The style of writing? The moral or ethical issues raised?)

9. *Synthesis questions* also are a form of application question, but require the bringing together of parts—some far afield—toward the creation of what may be a new solution or hybrid. Such questions tend to require some divergent as well as convergent thinking. (How is this story like another we have read? Who would you like to have read this story, and why? Does this story remind you of anything that is happening in the world today?)

multitude of purposes and subtle lessons that teachers may wish children to learn. See Box 8.2 for some other hints on effective questioning. It is important to remember that questioning is only one way that the teacher plays an important role in determining what will be learned from text (Yopp & Singer, 1985). The teacher also chooses the textual material, helps students develop reader resources, sets reader goals, and guides thinking by the tests, and activities that are selected to accompany reading.

---

**BOX 8.2 | Hints on Effective Questioning**

1. A hierarchy of question types does *not* imply that questions need to be asked in order from lowest to highest levels; most question types should be covered, however, in most lessons.

2. Use retelling formats as well as specific questions to get a better understanding of what readers are thinking when reading silently (Schell, 1988; Gauthier, 1990). Retellings tend to provide purposeful practice in orderly thinking, oral delivery, and preparation for responsive writing. Invite youngsters to assist one another in retellings.

3. Train yourself to ask *translation* questions. Translation questions, again, simply require that something be expressed in a different way or in another symbolic form: "What did Jack just say?" "What, in your own words, did this paragraph say?" "Could you draw a picture to show what the story is saying?" Translation questions are important because: (a) they act as bridges in most question taxonomies (Bloom, 1956; Aschner et al., 1962) from literal level to higher-order thinking; and (b) they demand active reading and thinking. Nonetheless, teachers tend to ask questions of this type less than *one percent* of the time (Guszak, 1967; Manzo, 1969a, b).

4. Remember especially to ask evaluative questions. The evaluative question requires active reading. It requires one to pull together all that one knows, feels, and values in order to render a defensible judgment. Thus evaluative questions build values and wisdom as well as knowledge.

5. Use questioning strategies that establish a reciprocal relationship, or give-and-take between teacher and students and among students. These heuristic strategies (such as the ReQuest, InQuest, and IntraAct Procedures, described ahead) can cause teachers and children to self-discover the art of effective questioning, in much the same way that a block of wood informs the sculptor to go carefully over its knots and to follow its grain.

6. Every day, in some way, ask some questions that encourage synthesis. Students need to make connections, transfer information, test their concept formation, and to try to read and think creatively. Many seemingly proficient, but literal level readers need this as much as do weaker readers. Use questions such as: "How would you solve the problem presented here?"; and "Where else might the solution offered here also work?"

7. Periodically students need to be asked how they feel they are being changed or "transformed," as well as informed and entertained, by what they read, learn, and experience: "Would anyone like to say how they felt/thought, before reading, about something in this story/selection, and how they are feeling/thinking about it now?" This question, while rarely asked, is the implicit basis of education. It gets at the issue of whether children are maturing in what they understand and the way they understand it, as opposed to simply what they "know."

The remainder of the chapter is a compendium of strategies for teaching reading comprehension. The term "strategies," as used here, refers primarily to methods that are selected, upon reflection, to meet students' characteristic and situational reading–learning needs. The overall objective of all these methods is for the student to become reflective and selective in choosing the personal strategies he or she will use in becoming an independent reader. Most of the methods presented are basal-compatible, but, more importantly, they are adaptable to books of any type and to most any print material that is within a student's reasonable age-grade range. These methods are the teacher's "stock in trade." Among the many that are presented here, you should find some that are particularly suitable to your current teaching style and many others that will serve as a handy source of options for reference as you evolve professionally and encounter students with a variety of needs. With them, you should be able to teach anyone to read and comprehend better wherever printed material is available. Many of these methods also could be used in any other language in which the child is proficient. This is useful to know in the event that you have foreign-speaking students and access to tutors who speak their language. More pointers for teaching the linguistically different are offered in Chapter 11.

## COMPENDIUM OF STRATEGIES FOR TEACHING READING COMPREHENSION

Instruction in reading can be provided in equal measure or with greater or lesser weight at each of three points in a lesson. These are referred to as the:

- Prereading, or readiness phase
- Silent reading, or "during" reading phase
- Postreading, or discussion and follow-up phase

A method that provides extensive assistance at *each* of these three phases is not necessarily better than one that stresses one phase. The relative value of one strategy over another is best determined by reflectively taking several factors into consideration. Among the more important of these are some that are redundant with points previously made regarding good comprehension and influential teaching. These include the following:

- Is there research and clinical/experiential support for the method?
- Is it flexible and easy to use? Does the method require a certain kind of material, considerable preparation time, or extensive training and orientation of students or of teachers?
- Does it match the needs of the particular students with whom it would be used?
- Is it *efficient* in the sense of being fast-paced, or in the sense of accomplishing more than one objective at a time, and how long does it take to conduct it?
- Does it impart a sense of *strategy* for independent reading comprehension, or does it merely help youngsters to read a given *selection* with greater comprehension?

Remember, too, that it is not wise to judge any new method after only one use. It may take a few trials to get past your own unfamiliarity, or the possibility of a bad day on the part of the class. The first method presented probably is the most comprehensive and widely used approach in education. Many consider it to be a paradigm for all reading comprehension instruction.

## DIRECTED READING ACTIVITY

### Background

The Directed Reading Activity (DRA) was pulled together by Betts (1946) from the manuals of basal readers of that time. There are many variations on it. The one presented here includes elements of the Directed Reading Lesson (Maggart & Zintz, 1992), and of the more thinking-oriented version that Stauffer (1969) referred to as the Directed Reading–Thinking Activity (DR–TA). This combined form can be used with narrative or expository materials of most any reasonable length (Gill & Bear, 1988); however, it is especially suitable for group instruction with traditional basal-reader material.

The DRA is one of those methods that addresses all three instructional phases: prereading, active silent reading, and postreading. It tends to incorporate attention to vocabulary and word recognition as well as comprehension and may include special attention to certain aspects of thinking, writing, and study skills. Despite strong research evidence for its overall efficacy (see ahead), the DRA is sometimes criticized as having too many steps and taking too long to implement. The reflective teacher undoubtedly will need to be selective and adaptive in its use, but also to be sure to deliver a full DRA on those occasions when the material and opportunity seem appropriate.

## STEPS IN THE DIRECTED READING (THINKING) ACTIVITY

**Step 1**  *Prereading: Relate, Motivate, Anticipate*

   a. Discuss students' background experience and knowledge related to the selection with them.

   b. Preview the material by discussing the pictures and other graphics that accompany it.

   c. Reduce obstacles to comprehension by preteaching difficult words and concepts (Many basal versions of the DRA list this as a separate step. Stauffer advised *against* preteaching vocabulary *if* the material is at the student's *instructional or independent reading level*. It is better, he believed, to have children try to figure out such words for themselves, much as any effective reader needs to do while reading.)

   d. Conclude the prereading discussion by encouraging students to make reasonable predictions of what the remainder of the selection is likely to be about.

**Step 2**  *Silent Reading: or Active "Predict–Read–Prove" Reading (most typical of the DR–TA)*

a. Provide silent reading guidance by reminding students to read to check their predictions.

b. Have students read silently—either the entire selection (in a DRA) or in short sections, pausing at the end of each to discuss the accuracy of their predictions and to make new predictions (Stauffer's strongest suggestion).

c. Where student predictions are correct, ask for verification from the material; where predictions are incorrect, ask why.

**Step 3**    *Postreading: Check, Refine, Relate, Re-anticipate*

a. Check comprehension by discussing answers to general purpose-setting questions and by additional recognition, recall, inferential, explanatory, and evaluative questions.

b. Refine understanding by seeking verifications for comprehension questions that require silent and oral rereading and citing of the material.

c. Read orally some conversational parts, or just favorite parts, of the material for practice and interpretation.

d. Relate the story or information covered to other materials read or to common experience or mass media events.

e. Engage in some follow-up activity that extends selected strategy areas. These may include any of the following:

- Write a personal reaction or a different ending.
- Study key meaning or sight vocabulary from the selection.
- Retell the story in sequence.
- Outline or summarize the story.
- Use words in the story to practice phonic or structural analysis strategies.
- Build or create some artistic expression, dramatization, or unusual perspective on the story or expository (Galda, 1982; Pellegrini & Galda, 1982; Walker, 1985). For example, have children retell the story from the perspective of an inanimate object or a minor character. Youngsters are usually shy or perplexed by this at first, but later they can't wait to show their creativity.

f. Build fresh anticipation of something to be read at a later time by connecting it to some relevant aspect of the postreading discussion: For example, regarding the previous point on inventive perspectives, the teacher could hold up a copy of Shel Silverstein's poem "It's Dark in Here," written from the perspective of a person inside a lion, and a copy of *All About Bones* by Joselyn Stevenson, and say, "Tomorrow we're going to read these unusual views of the world from inside living things. Would anyone like to take either of these home tonight and tell a little about it tomorrow before I read it out loud?"

When properly orchestrated, Directed Reading Activities can have an attractive symmetry that begins and ends with anticipation, hence creating an impelling reason to read immediately, and again on the same or a related topic at a later time. The DR–TA format also is a comforting structure that can hold a lesson together through the sometimes dizzying array of classroom distractions that can arise.

### Support for the Directed Reading Activity

The overall DRA format has been shown to be quite effective for improving reading comprehension and the quality of classroom interactions (Bear & Invernizzi, 1984; Davidson, 1970; Grobler, 1971; Petre, 1970). The DR–TA, in particular, offers a practical and effective means of improving critical thinking (Haggard-Ruddell, 1988) and content area learning (Shepherd, 1978). Under modified conditions the DR–TA also can build remarkable levels of independence. Schmitt (1988) showed this rather dramatically with third-grade students who were trained to: activate their own prior knowledge; set their own purposes for reading; raise and answer their own questions; verify or reject their own predictions; and monitor their own success. This was accomplished merely by this teacher-researcher gradually releasing greater responsibility to pupils for each of these key strategic reading functions. This focus resulted in students in an experimental group scoring higher than the traditional DR–TA control group on all post-test measures. Students effectively learned how to conduct their own Self-Directed Reading Activity (Schmitt & Baumann, 1986), thus enhancing the value of the DR–TA as a means of acquiring strategy control and independence. Several other means and methods of achieving self-directed silent reading are discussed ahead. First, however, consider some recent innovations on the traditional Directed Reading Lesson.

## RECONCILED READING LESSON

The Reconciled Reading Lesson (RRL), developed by Reutzel (1985; 1991), inverts the traditional steps in the sequence of the basal-type DRA. In so doing, it takes advantage of the well-established value of "frontloading" to empower young readers with more of the relevant "prior knowledge" and concepts necessary to read effectively and also to learn from what is read.

### Three RRL Inversions

Reutzel's simple means for doing the first of the three inversions is to have the teacher check the basal manual's suggestions for language enrichment and follow-up activities that accompany a reading selection, and then, more or less, to do these *before* reading the selection. He gives the example of a lesson built on a basal story called "Stone Soup" (M. Brown, 1947). Inverting the suggestion of the manual of a basal, Reutzel says that the teacher should stimulate children actually to make some stone soup and write a recipe from their experience prior to reading the story, rather than after (Reutzel & Cooter, 1992).

The second inversion he proposes is to teach the skill extension step *prior to* the reading selection rather than after, and, more importantly, to select a skill that complements and is reinforced *by* the story to be read. Unfortunately, in many basal programs the skills activities that follow a reading selection are completely unrelated to the selection. Reutzel gives two examples of typical nonaligning lessons. In one, there was a vocabulary activity that did not contain any of the words from the story. In another, the word analysis lesson did not use any of the words that appeared in the story. Both of these skills activities missed golden opportunities to have students apply what they were taught in an immediate and contextual way.

The third RRL inversion relates to the postreading comprehension and discussion questions. Again Reutzel's suggestion is simple. Instead of saving all of the postreading questions for the end, use some of them as questions to build anticipation *before* having students read a selection.

### Support for the Reconciled Reading Lesson

Reports by Prince and Mancus (1987) and Thomas and Readence (1988) testify that using the RRL significantly increases students' comprehension and recall over the traditional sequence of the basal-based DRA (in Reutzel & Cooter, 1992). A word of caution, however: We have observed several classrooms where the prereading step was extended for too long. Discussions were permitted to wander far off the subject, and extensive time was spent in marginally relevant activities like coloring, cutting, and pasting. This can seriously cut down on the time for reading. It was precisely the extensiveness of this condition that inspired the creation of the ReQuest Procedure, a method that tends to move youngsters along at a faster pace and with more of an orientation toward discussion. The discussion of this method which follows is more elaborate than that of most others because it embodies several ideas that have come to influence contemporary theories of teaching and learning.

## THE RECIPROCAL QUESTIONING (REQUEST) PROCEDURE

### Background

The ReQuest Procedure was developed to teach students to independently set their *own* purpose(s) for reading (Manzo, 1969a, b; 1985). ReQuest builds student independence largely through three mechanisms: "instructional conversation" (Tharp & Gallimore, 1989a, b), "mental modeling" (Duffy, Roehler, & Hermann, 1988; Manzo, 1969a, b), and teacher-student "reciprocity" or structured interacting (Manzo, 1969; Palinscar & Brown, 1984). ReQuest is a form of apprenticeship training that brings students and teacher together much as apprentices and craftsperson are brought together at a workbench.

Prior to ReQuest, "modeling" was used almost exclusively in trade crafts (such as bricklaying, plumbing, pottery making, etc.) and for teaching external social and language behaviors (for example, to teach a child to say "thank you," a teacher might say a slightly exaggerated "thank you" each time a child complied with a request). However, the modeling process, as structured by the ReQuest procedure, proved to be an effective means of externalizing and teaching internal mental processes, as well as the related attitudes and social behaviors that are involved in reading. Ehlinger (1992) found that strategies learned through modeling resulted in students reporting 70 percent transfer effects, a remarkably high proportion. Modeling and emulating have a way of becoming part of one's cognitive, affective, and sensorimotor experience. Importantly, behaviors learned in this way can be self-initiated thereafter (Bandura & Walters, 1963).

In the ReQuest procedure, the teacher engages students in an instructional conversation marked by reciprocal interactions that permit the sharing of "cognitive secrets" (Pearson & Fielding, 1991) about how to read and think. ReQuest interactions tend to sharpen students' attention to the "functional value" of the teacher as a model of effective thinking and related conduct (Ehlinger, 1992, p. 2). The teacher also gains a great deal of diagnostic information about the student's thinking and level of development as the student externalizes questions as well as answers.

ReQuest also can be used to concurrently, or "collaterally" (Rubin, 1984) attend to several other reading, language, thinking, and personal–social adjustment needs. It is instructive to note how this is achieved. While most modern-day teaching strategies have their theoretical basis in cognitive psychology, ReQuest's can also be found in the influence of the social context on learning. This is a domain recently made popular in education by the rediscovery of the work of the Russian psychologist, Lev Vygotsky, who died in 1963, but whose works were being published as late as 1978. A related American branch of this research, known as *social and imitation learning theory,* was pioneered by Miller and Dollard (1941) and by Bandura (1987). The social learning theories of Vygotsky, Miller and Dollard, and Bandura provide the basic rationale for the structure of ReQuest interactions. The social-imitation learning connection is important to know about because much of children's inability to make progress in reading and other schoolwork often can be traced to dealing with a variety of social and emotional inhibitions, such as fear of failure, feeling conspicuous in class, and other social concerns.

From a broader theoretical perspective, the union of cognitive and social-imitation learning theory re-casts the teacher as a facilitator of learning and as more of a partner with students in a community of literate individuals. This impression led Pearson and Fielding (1991) to conclude that methods employing such cognitive apprenticeships and responsive teaching modes "may be the bridge that spans the chasm" (p. 850) that exists between largely teacher-directed forms of instruction, and more student-centered approaches, such as those associated with whole language. See below for how these ideas are incorporated into this relatively simple teaching method.

## STEPS IN THE REQUEST PROCEDURE

**Step 1**   Both teacher and students read the *title and first sentence* only of the first paragraph of a selection and look at any pictures or graphics that are part of the introduction.

**Step 2**   The teacher invites students to ask as many questions as they wish about the title, first sentence, and/or pictures or graphics. The teacher turns his or her copy of the selection face down, but students may continue to look at their copies. Students are told that they should ask the kinds of questions that they think a teacher might ask. (This permits students to ask "ego-protective" questions since they need not reveal whether *they* know the answers to the questions they ask.)

**Step 3**    When all student questions have been fully and politely answered, the teacher turns his or her book face *up* while students are instructed to turn theirs face *down*. The teacher than asks as many additional questions (about the title, first sentence, and illustrations) as seem appropriate to bring about a sense of focus and purpose for reading the selection. The last question of each episode of questioning should be, simply, "What do you suppose the remainder of this selection will be about?"

**Step 4**    The next sentences are handled in the same way, with the student again leading off the questioning, followed by teacher questioning, and again concluding with the question, "What do you suppose the remainder of this selection will be about?" The number of sentences covered is based on the teacher's judgment: the ReQuest activity should conclude as soon as a *plausible* (as opposed to correct) purpose for reading has been evolved but should not last *more* than about fifteen minutes.

**Step 5**    At the conclusion of the ReQuest activity, the student is encouraged to continue reading the selection silently for the purpose(s) developed.

**Step 6**    Following silent reading, the teacher should *first ask the evaluative question:* "Did we read for the right (or best) purpose?"

This final question is asked even before the purpose-setting question itself for three reasons. First, it helps to overcome what has been called "confirmation bias" (Garrison & Hoskisson, 1989), or the tendency to conclude only what has been predicted. Second, it helps to keep the focus of instruction on the development of effective strategies for independent reading and learning, more so than merely on comprehending a given selection. Third, it further develops the important metacognitive habit of monitoring and appraising one's own comprehension and strategy use while reading.

The ReQuest procedure can be used across subject areas and grade levels. Use of ReQuest over time and in a variety of settings helps the student to proceed in self-governed stages from explicit questioning to a greater awareness of the implicit questions in the world around them.

ReQuest-induced instructional conversations are a solid way to enhance teaching as well as learning. Several anecdotal accounts in Boxes 8.3–8.7 illustrate discoveries teachers have made by using it in a variety of situations: The Impact of Modeling (Box 8.3); ReQuest in Teaching Decoding (Box 8.4); ReQuest in Peer Modeling (Box 8.5); the ReQuest Pictures (and Objects) Procedure (Box 8.6); and ReQuest Picture Procedure: Strategic Parroting (Box 8.7). Look these over as examples of how teachers can learn from teaching. The vehicle here is the ReQuest procedure, but the point is to develop comfort and mastery of any of the other methods described in the book and then to use them as probes with which to learn as well as to teach.

### Support for the ReQuest Procedure

ReQuest has a strong body of research and field trials to support it. It has been shown to be successful in both individual and group settings in the improvement of

BOX
8.3

## BOX 8.3  The Impact of Modeling

One of the earliest lessons learned by using ReQuest was how to get the students to select and home-in on the teacher as an effective model of questioning behavior. Very early in the development of ReQuest, Thomas Estes (now professor at the University of Virginia) raised an intentionally tricky question to a fourteen-year-old boy who had no questions of his own to ask. The boy sat as if defying Estes to ask anything about that first short sentence that he could not easily answer. Thinking fast, Estes asked, "What was the fifth word in the sentence?" Startled, the boy fumbled around. Tom then told him that he could turn his book over to check for the fifth word. When it was the boy's turn again, he quickly asked Tom a similar question about the next, much longer sentence. Instead of cringing, Tom remained composed and said, "Gee, I thought you might ask me a question like that, but I knew that if I tried to remember all those words in order, I'd probably miss the whole point of the sentence. So I guess I don't know." The student was stunned by this response. He said, in so many words, that *he* had felt foolish for not being able to answer such a question, but Tom sounded *smart* when he couldn't answer the same kind of question.

What happened next was a textbook case illustration of social and imitation learning theory in operation: Having observed Tom's demonstrated mastery over this environment, the boy began to emulate Tom's thinking and language style. The same reciprocal interaction that caused the young man to see Tom Estes as a model of *questioning behavior* soon was causing him to take note of Tom as a model of *question answering behavior*, and much more. Tom's clever question couldn't have worked better in communicating to this frightened and socially failing student (he had been expelled from school for being "incorrigible") that here was a competent and caring person worth watching and emulating.

Please note that following this "clever" question that caused the student to home-in on Tom as a model of language and social competence, Tom then asked several conventional questions to settle the student down and turn him more to the task of analyzing the text: "What was the name mentioned in this sentence?", "What happened to this person?", "What do you suppose happens next?", and finally, "What do you suppose the remainder of this story will be about?" A failure to return to a more expected pattern of questioning here could have resulted in the slippage of the lesson into an unproductive game of who could ask the quirkiest, rather than the most meaningful, questions.

comprehension and questioning skills of students (Larking, 1984; Manzo, 1969a), and incidentally in improving the questioning of teachers (Manzo, 1969a; Helfeldt & Lalik, 1979). It has been used effectively with juvenile delinquents (Kay, Young, and Mottley, 1986); with learning disabled youngsters who have been "mainstreamed" (Alley and Deshler, 1980; Hori, 1977); with second-language students (McKenzie, Ericson, & Hunter, 1988); and in content area reading sittings (Gaskins, 1981), as well as in teaching purpose-setting to elementary school students (Dreher & Gambrell, 1985; Spiegel, 1980b). Additionally, ReQuest provided the basis for a more encompassing and also well-validated strategy called Reciprocal Teaching (Palincsar and Brown, 1984), a method based on peer teaching. The only drawback to Reciprocal Teaching is that it requires a great deal of training of teachers and students just to use it properly. However, you should put it on your list of things to learn about in the future.

<table>
<tr><td>**BOX<br>8.4**</td><td>## ReQuest in Teaching Decoding</td></tr>
</table>

Once the teacher and student have established an apprenticeship relationship, the teacher can easily shift from modeling comprehension processes to "think alouds" (Davey, 1983) that even model decoding processes.

One way to step into this more basic function is to ask questions that use either of the two "scripts" of the Glass-Analysis system covered in a prior chapter. For example, after showing and pronouncing the word 'lakefront,' one script would go: "Which letters make the /ache/ sound in *lakefront?*; Which letters the /fr/ sound?; Which make the /ont/ sound?" The second script reverses the process: "What sound do the letters 'a-k-e' make?; What sound do the letters 'l-a-k-e' make?; What about 'f-r'?; 'o-n-t'?"

In using this approach, the teacher typically externalizes a great deal of inner speech (e.g., "Let's see now where should this word first be divided? What are the regular sounds? Which are irregular?). It is OK in this situation *not* to be so smooth that one never considers asking about a cluster of letters that don't go together very well (e.g., "Should I ask what sound the letters 'e-f' make in this word? No, the 'e' clearly belongs to the 'l-a-k' part of the word."). Oddly, even these misses, or rejected questions, can turn out to be informative and more than a bit comforting to youngsters who are faced with the humbling nature of "early learning."

## Cautions in Using ReQuest

While mature conversation between teacher and students is a frequent incidental benefit of ReQuest interactions, there are two factors that may turn a teacher away from its use. One is that when students reflect back the questions of their teacher, they sometimes do so in some emotionally convoluted way. This can be disconcerting, since some of our less thoughtful questions can really come back to haunt us when we put ourselves up as models. The best way to deal with this problem is to listen carefully to the twisted or potentially hostile questions that students may ask, and then begin by assuming that there is something that we are doing or saying

<table>
<tr><td>**BOX<br>8.5**</td><td>## ReQuest in Peer Modeling</td></tr>
</table>

A sixth-grader named Clarence taught us how to achieve effective peer modeling during a ReQuest group interaction. The second author had been leading a demonstration lesson on a passage from a sixth-grade social studies text.

Students first were given some background information about the three "Estates" that comprised the Estates General of Paris. Once the reciprocal questioning portion of the lesson began, Clarence proceeded to ask five or six unusual questions about each sentence. The other students noticed the unique nature of Clarence's questions and tended to follow with similar ones. So, when he asked "What does 'watched' mean here?," someone else would say, "What does 'turns to' mean here?" And when he asked, "Did the king think that he was a hero?," others asked, "Did the clergy think they were heroes?"

From this simple heuristic experience we learned that whenever a student asks an interesting or potentially generative question, the teacher can shift the class' attention toward an appropriate peer model simply by saying, "Can anyone ask another question like that one?"

## BOX 8.6 The ReQuest Pictures (and Objects) Procedure

Several experiences with younger children have shown how the inquiry and comprehension aspects of emergent literacy, or nontext based literacy, can be taught with pictures and objects as well as with text. During development of the ReQuest *Picture* Procedure (Manzo & Legenza, 1975), Alice Legenza asked kindergartners to study a picture and then to ask her some "good" questions about it. She told the children that after they asked questions, she would ask *them* some questions back to see how carefully they had studied the picture.

In this context it was possible to impart a sense of story analysis to youngsters who were not yet even reading:

- "What is the main thing shown in this picture?" (main idea question)
- "What do you suppose came just before?" (inference question)
- "What do you think will happen next?" (conjecture question)
- "If these people/objects could speak, what do you suppose they would say?" (language and personal connection question)
- "How do you feel about what is pictured?" (evaluative and transfer question)

A student, viewing a picture of a little girl teetering on a stepstool to reach a cookie jar, said sheepishly that he never realized how dangerous this was until he really looked at this picture (see the Picture Potency Formula in Appendix A for a reprint of this picture). This struck us as a wonderful display of reading "beyond the lines."

that is evoking those questions; then try to ask better questions. It is important, too, to realize that it may not be *your* questioning that is at fault. It may be that the *child* is carrying some heavy emotional baggage quite apart from your efforts. If you are tolerant of the sometimes taunting questions that children may ask, they soon come around and behave more thoughtfully and respectfully.

The other problem that sometimes inhibits use of ReQuest is that teachers can be overwhelmed by the flood of diagnostic information that they receive through

## BOX 8.7 ReQuest Picture Procedure: Strategic Parroting

In another situation with kindergartners, Legenza found one student who seemed to be totally devoid of all curiosity (Manzo & Legenza, 1975). The child was very attractive, and used to being the center of attention; however, in school activities, she seemed content to stand by and watch. In desperation, Alice said to the child, "Here is a question that you could ask, repeat it after me. . . . Now ask me that question." The child repeated Alice's question, and Alice then answered the question fully and thoughtfully, as if the child had thought of it herself. After just a few such parroted questions, the child began to initiate her own twists on these strategic questions, and thereafter to ask many of her own.

Palincsar, Brown, and Martin (1987) report equally remarkable success with a related procedure. They couldn't seem to impart the idea of a student leading a discussion until they had one student "mimic" the teacher's discussion-leading statements. Thereafter the discussion began to flow rather naturally.

The Note Cue Procedure (Manzo & Manzo, 1990b) for promoting classroom participation was based on this discovery. (See the chapter on oral reading for a description of Note Cue.)

such interactions. Some teachers become immobilized when they realize how much some students don't know. They wonder how they can begin to fill these needs without frustrating the rest of the group. Experience has shown that when the teacher stays with the procedure and tries to help those who do not understand even the simplest of things, the other students often are patient and touched by the teacher's caring. Children seem to sense that they might need the same thoughtful assistance at some time in the future.

The next three methods presented are especially effective for improving the reconstructive, or "get-the-facts," level of comprehension. The first two rely heavily on listening, and the third can be *converted* into a listening comprehension activity.

## LISTENING–READING TRANSFER LESSON

### Background

Cunningham (1975) designed this essentially "front-loading" method to teach students to find the main idea by listening to a passage, and then to transfer the same task to a different passage that is read. In our experience, pupils tend to sense and appreciate the extra level of assistance the teacher provides when using this method. It tends to communicate affection and concern, as well as aid with comprehension. Look for more positive body language and voice tone, especially when the method has been preceded by conventional postreading question methods.

## STEPS IN THE LISTENING–READING TRANSFER LESSON

Step 1    Prepare three sentences related to a passage that the student will listen to, with one of the three being the best representation of the main idea.

Step 2    Tell students that the main idea of the selection that they will listen to is stated in one of three sentences that you will present to them (either as a handout, on the board, or on an overhead).

Step 3    Following listening, have youngsters indicate which sentence best captures the chief ideas.

Step 4    Repeat the same process with a passage that is read.

For a variation on this, see the Listen–Read–Discuss heuristic (Manzo & Casale, 1985) in the content reading chapter. With younger children and with remedial level readers, try "talking books" (Carbo, 1978; Gawby, 1983) for the listening portion of the lesson. These are books and basal selections that have been taped by the teacher, parents, volunteers, or older students and made available for youngsters to listen to and then read, or follow along in their own books while listening. Many public libraries now have these prepared and in plentiful supply.

### Support for the Listening–Reading Transfer Lesson

Several teachers and researchers have offered support for the basic idea underlying the Listening–Reading Transfer and the Listen–Read–Discuss lesson approaches. Key among these are Moore and Readence (1980), Sticht et al. (1974), Seaton and Weilan (1979), and Watkins, McKenna, Manzo & Manzo (in progress, 1994). The study by Seaton and Weilan is especially notable since it demonstrated that higher-order comprehension, such as interpretation and appreciation, were the most significantly improved by listening before reading. In a critique of this study, Flippo (1981) adds a point that keeps recurring in recent research: "Children enjoy being read to and it is possible that this enjoyment factor . . . positively affect(s) their comprehension of the intricacies of the story" (1981, p. 108).

A variety of other strategies rely on students' listening ability to compensate for, or otherwise enhance comprehension. Several are based on reading lesson formats, such as Choate and Rakes' (1987) variation on the Directed Reading–Thinking Activity and Kelly and Holmes' (1979) variation on the Guided Reading Procedure, described next.

## THE GUIDED READING PROCEDURE

### Background

The Guided Reading Procedure (GRP) was developed to *demonstrate* to under-achieving students that they can greatly increase their reading comprehension through a metacognitive act of self-determination (Manzo, 1975a), or strategy control. The GRP does this by having students engage in a learning activity that urges them to re-tell what they have read in a great deal of detail. This requires students to self-monitor their level of attention, concentration, and commitment. Strong reinforcement for doing this follows from their seeing and experiencing the rewards of their improved recollection and comprehension. This outcome is achieved through built-in redundancy features of a GRP lesson: Facts and ideas in the selection are stated, repeated, and reviewed in various forms. In this way even students who were not willing or able to read a selection initially acquire a firm grounding in the story or information when it is presented in these overlapping ways.

In examining the steps of the GRP, notice that it guides students toward greater independence by stressing one of the most pervasive but least acknowledged secrets of real schooling; namely that, whatever else is said, teachers tend to value factual reading, notetaking, organizing, and test performance. Notice, too, how steps 4 and 8 especially reinforce metacognitive development and strategy control.

## STEPS IN THE GUIDED READING PROCEDURE

**Step 1** *Teacher Preparation*

Identify a selection, to be read or listened to, of moderate to high difficulty. This generally means not exceeding 50–250 words for a primary grade class, 600 words for an intermediate class, or 900 words for a middle school class. Prepare a 10–20-item test on the material to be given at the end of the class period. Recognition type questions, such as multiple choice, tend to ensure early success.

**Step 2** *Student Preparation*

First ask students what they know about the topic, then explain that they are to "Read to remember *all that you can,* because after you have read, I will record what you remember on the chalkboard just as you tell it to me." When literature is being read, this question can include a phrase asking that students try to remember events in the story, as well as "all that you felt and thought while reading." Record these comments in parentheses alongside the related plot elements. It is OK to say "feelings?" and "thoughts?" periodically to remind students that they can express these.

Step 3   *Reading and Recalling*
Following silent reading, begin asking for free recalls. Record all information on the chalkboard until students have retold all that they can remember. Difficulties in remembering and differences in what students do remember stir excitement and implicit questions for the next steps.

Step 4   *Self-Monitoring/Self-Correcting*
Instruct students to review the material read and self-correct inconsistencies and information overlooked in their initial attempts to retell. Note changes and additions on the chalkboard. (See Box 8.8 for an illustration of steps 2, 3, and 4).

Step 5   *Restructuring*
Encourage students to organize their retellings into outline form. Having students record the outline in their notebooks lends a sense of authenticity and purpose to this effort. The outline can be as simple or elaborate as student ability level permits. Ask guiding questions at this time, such as: "What was discussed first?"; "What details followed?"; "What was brought up next?"; and "What seems to be the main idea?" Keep students focused on the outlining task by avoiding questions that are too specific.

Step 6   *Teacher Monitoring and Correction*
If it appears that students have overlooked any important ideas, raise focusing questions about these points, such as: "What do you suppose is the most important of the five points made by the author?"; "How do you suppose this information relates to what we talked about last week in the selection, 'Man and the Moon'?"

---

**BOX 8.8**

## Detail of Children's GRP Recalls of Story, Feelings, and Thoughts

Teacher:   Tell me about this story.

Student A:   The story is about Little Red Riding Hood, and how she met a wolf on her way to Grandmother's house; Oh yes, in the woods.

Teacher:   What feelings or thoughts did you have about the story?

Student A:   I wondered why wolves always are the bad guys in stories in books, but they're the good guys in those stories about real animals that you see on TV.

Student B:   Not me; I'm still afraid of them. This story is a lot scarier than the Gunnywolf.

Teacher:   What else was important in the story?

Student A:   The wolf pretended to be good and helpful at first.

Student B:   That's what makes wolves scary—they can pretend to be good.

Step 7    *Evaluation*

Give the test prepared in step 1. A score of 70 percent to 80 percent should be required for a "pass." Students will surprise you by seeing this as a fair "pass" level due to the extraordinary level of help and empowerment they have received. They also tend to look forward to the test as an opportunity to show what they have learned.

Step 8    *Introspection*

Discuss any insights students may have reached about their own learning processes as a result of the GRP experience. The insight you most want students to reach is that accuracy in comprehension and recall can be improved simply by an internal "act of will" to do so.

Step 9    *Optional but Important Study Step*

Several days later give a second test on the same material. Questions should be the same as those on the original test. Allow students about 15 minutes prior to the test to review material from their notes. This step also can serve as a "teachable moment" for coaching study skills and memory techniques of the type presented in the chapter ahead on higher-order thinking and study skills.

### Support for the Guided Reading Procedure

The GRP has been supported by several experimental and field studies testing its use from fourth grade through high school levels. Culver (1975) found it to be as effective as a full DR–TA; other comparison studies have found it to be significantly more effective (Ankney & McClurg, 1981; Bean & Pardi, 1979; Colwell, Mangano, Childs, & Case, 1986). There also are several field accounts of the value of the GRP in the professional literature, including its use at elementary levels (Gaskins, 1981) and at secondary levels (Maring & Furman, 1985; Tierney, Readence, & Dishner, 1990). Importantly, the basic paradigm has struck a sound note with many educators who have used it to develop a variety of related teaching methods such as in writing (Eanet, 1983; Hayes, 1988), science (Spiegel, 1980b), and listening (Cunningham, Cunningham, & Arthur 1981; Kelly & Holmes 1979). Some of these variations on the GRP are presented in other chapters.

The next method described has been evolving for decades due to the work and experiences of many teachers and researchers. The format discussed below is used to concurrently teach familiarity with the subtle language patterns needed to anticipate the next word in print, as well as to heighten inferential thinking and comprehension.

## CLOZE PROCEDURE TRAINING

### Background

Cloze procedure, or the fixed deletion of every fifth to ninth word, is a way to measure a student's familiarity with the language and phrasing forms that are commonly used in text. These are known as the "language redundancy patterns" of prose (Weaver & Kingston, 1963). Bowman (1991) notes that "Redundancy helps readers predict, thereby increasing their odds in favor of suitable comprehension" (p. 66). However, its value as a method for *teaching* reading has been called into question at times (e.g., Culver et al., 1972; Shanahan & Kamil, 1983). These doubts have been raised primarily because cloze passage performance has a low level of correlation to known comprehension factors such as background knowledge, ability to follow connections between sentences, and rate of reading. In addition, several early studies of cloze training failed to show significant gains in comprehension, vocabulary, or rate of reading (cf. E. Jongsma, 1980).

After considerable trial and error, reading researchers and practitioners have discovered some rather inventive ways to use cloze passage training exercises in ways that take advantage of its connection to language patterns, while overcoming its more limited connection with overall comprehension (Cunningham & Tierney, 1977; Y. Goodman, 1975; Guice, 1969; Guthrie, Barnham, Caplan, & Seifert, 1974; Jongsma, 1980; Schell, 1972).

The Inferential (Cloze) Training Technique, developed by Dewitz, Carr, and Patsberg (1987), drew from these earlier works. This technique has been shown to improve general inference, overall reading comprehension, self-monitoring, and familiarity with language redundancy patterns. The "active ingredient" in the Inferential (Cloze) Training Technique seems to be the instructional conversation it generates, more so than any inherent value in Cloze exercises.

Note how inference training occurs on two levels in the Inferential (Cloze) Training Technique described below. On one level word replacements are inferred from the remaining context of the sentence. On the next level inference questions are raised on the content of the overall passage. Strictly speaking, there is a third dimension of inference training that occurs when the teacher models how she or he thinks aloud and tries to replace deletions, and then asks students to follow and infer from his or her thinking to their own efforts with similar sentences.

## STEPS IN THE INFERENTIAL (CLOZE) TRAINING TECHNIQUE

**Step 1**  Begin with a cloze passage of 5 to 25 words deleted following every fifth to ninth word—on a fixed basis depending on the age/grade level of the children.

**Step 2**  Preteach students essential vocabulary from the passage (an important meaning–building step).

**Step 3**  Beginning first with one sentence and increasing progressively to paragraphs, demonstrate to students, by sample talk-throughs, how to infer a correct word replacement by using semantic (context) clues, syntactic (grammatical structure) clues, and background knowledge. This can be done with the teacher and then the students alternately "talking-through" their thoughts on word replacement for a single deletion or for sentence units containing more than one deletion.

**Step 4**  During the talk-through, try to use these self-monitoring guidelines from Cambourne (1977):

a. Does the replacement make sense?

b. Does the replacement cause the sentence to make sense?

c. Does the replacement combine prior knowledge with clues in the passage?

d. Is there a forward clue in the same sentence, paragraph, or passage?

e. Is there a backward clue in the same sentence, paragraph, or passage?

f. Did the clue cause you to change your replacement?

Step 5  The teacher expresses him- or herself by explaining why a certain replacement seems correct (see Box 8.9) and then helps the student to do the same thing by asking the student questions that aid in inferring why certain replacements are more correct than others. (Occasionally students will generate a better choice of word than the author may have used. Acknowledge these where they occur. It shows respect for children's thinking and their own growing sensitivity to language.)

Step 6  The teacher asks students to read a second intact sentence, paragraph, or passage (ideally continuing from the one read, again to build meaning).

Step 7  The teacher checks overall comprehension of the deleted and intact portions of text with typical main idea, detail, and especially inferential questions.

This same cloze task can be made even more accessible in teaching and testing situations by having the space represent the number of letters in the deletion and/or by offering choices for the words which are deleted. For example:

Jack could have been in (class) / (school) on time. He was in the building. Nonetheless,

he arrived late for (class). / (running).

---

**BOX 8.9**

## Inferential Cloze Training: Teacher Modeling

### Cloze Passage:
Once upon a time, there were ___1___ bears. There was a Momma Bear, ___2___ Daddy Bear, and a Baby Bear.

### Teacher Talk-Through:
Let's see, the word I need here in the first blank could describe the bears. It could be big, dark, or something like that. I think I'll read ahead for more clues. 'There was a Momma Bear (blank), Daddy Bear, and a Baby Bear. The second blank must be 'a,' because it probably is the same as in 'a Momma Bear' and in 'a Baby Bear.' Oops, that's it, the first space must be the number of bears—which is three! Who would like to try to figure out the word that fills in the next space?

This "Maze" format (Guthrie et al., 1974) is used in several major comprehension tests, such as the Gates–MacGinitie tests (MacGinitie & MacGinitie, 1989), and has been shown to much more closely resemble conventional reading comprehension measures. The absence of choices in the Standard Cloze Test tends to put the emphasis on language pattern clues and training, while the presence of choices in the Maze Test tends to shift the task to comprehension, or meaning seeking. Select the emphasis that best meets the students' language and comprehension needs.

As an uplifting variation, Gauthier (1990a) has devised Inverse Cloze: Delete *all but* every fifth word of a passage and ask students to try to write in a connected story of their own making. Have students share their creations. Students tend to really enjoy this unlikely-looking task. This can also be done with dictated stories. It is interesting, and occasionally amusing, to see how youngsters construct remarkably different tales from essentially the same stimulus.

## LOOKBACK TECHNIQUES

Because it is as basic as sliced bread is to a sandwich, teaching "Lookbacks" can sometimes be overlooked for its important strategic value to readers at all levels and ages. The idea of "lookbacks" very simply is to get students to *reread* material that is not fully comprehended, in an effort to independently self-fix misapprehensions or to figure out word meanings from context. Waern (1977a), a Scandinavian researcher, found that many student comprehension problems could be overcome by reading the material just one more time. Successful "lookback" procedures have been described by several authorities (August, Flavell, & Clift, 1984; Garner, Hare, Alexander, Haynes, & Winograd, 1984). Good readers tend to do it, and poor readers do not (Garner & Kraus, 1981–82; Garner & Reis, 1981). Poor readers seem not to realize that whenever there is the slightest bit of confusion, one must reread for clarification. Clarifications might be needed for a variety of reasons, such as mis-reading a tense, missing the significance of a punctuation mark, or simply because one's mind has drifted.

Sanacore (1984) has suggested interspersing questions during reading, either orally or in written form, as a way to systematically urge students to look back. The questions that he recommends also tend to reveal text structure, thereby building a sense of what is clear and what yet needs to be clarified. He recommends questions such as: "Who is the leading character? What is the leading character trying to accomplish in the story? What stands in the way?" (see Figure 8.1).

The next method also urges lookbacks.

## PARAPHRASING

Several authorities in the field believe strongly in the value of paraphrasing orally as one reads, starting at the sentence level and building up to paragraphs and even passages (Haynes & Fillmer, 1984; Kalmbach, 1986; Shugarman & Hurst, 1986). Paraphrasing also is known as translating, transforming, and encoding or recoding in a more personal form. This technique can be used comfortably in the ReQuest procedure as a question type ("Can you tell me in your own words what this sentence says?") and in the verification step of the DR–TA ("Tell in your own words what part of the story supports what you are predicting/answering/saying").

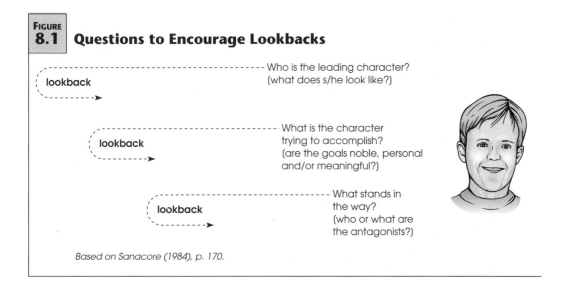

**FIGURE 8.1** **Questions to Encourage Lookbacks**

lookback — — — — — — — — — — — — — — — — — — — — — — Who is the leading character?
(what does s/he look like?)

lookback — — — — — — — — — — — — — — — — — — — What is the character
trying to accomplish?
(are the goals noble, personal
and/or meaningful?)

lookback — — — — — — — — — — — — — — — — — — What stands in
the way?
(who or what are
the antagonists?)

*Based on Sanacore (1984), p. 170.*

Since this simple technique tends to expose misapprehensions in reading, it is a most natural way to encourage "lookbacks." It is a basic routine for building comprehension of main idea, identification of supporting details, and an inclination to self-monitor and self-fix these while reading.

## SUMMARIZING

When the practice of paraphrasing is extended, without the text to refer to, it is known as "retelling," or free recall. When the text may be referred to, it generally is known as summary or precis writing. The latter has been studied and recommended by several authorities for its positive influence on active comprehension (Yopp & Singer, 1985), knowledge building (Pearson & Fielding, 1991), and expository writing (Bromley, 1985; Cunningham, 1982; Davey, 1987; Eanet & Manzo, 1976; Hayes, 1988; Simpson & Nist, 1990).

Summary writing is part of a rich tradition in England and most of Western Europe. Only in America is it not taught routinely from the earliest grades. The absence of such an emphasis would seem, in itself, to explain much of the difficulty experienced by students in reconstructive reading and specifically in unaided recall and expository writing. Summarizing is a form of encoding that requires the student to do something with what is read; hence it has been growing in popularity in recent years. Pearson & Fielding (1991) note that studies done prior to 1980 concluded that summarizing did not significantly improve comprehension; studies done after 1980 give it high marks. The differences between the two groups of studies can be important to the reflective teacher. The earlier ones tended to use standardized reading test measures and not consider the benefits to writing. The latter studies used selection-specific comprehension questions and assessed changes in writing. Hence, at least on the short term, teaching summarizing may not be the most immediate way to improve comprehension as measured by standardized tests; however, when the gains in selection-level comprehension are added and extrapolated with gains in writing and active reading, there is definite progress in raising and teaching children to be literate.

Please note, too, that there is something of a self-fulfilling prophecy working against teaching summarizing. The fact that many youngsters cannot do it tends to discourage teachers from requiring it, hence decreasing the likelihood that they ever will. To make summary writing more approachable, try "slicing" the task into more manageable parts and offering students some guidelines, or "Rules for Summarizing." Teach these rules one at a time:

1. Delete unimportant information.
2. Delete repeated information.
3. Provide a category label for listings of specifics (e.g., "flowers" for roses, petunias, daisies).
4. Find and restate any main idea that is stated in the selection (usually in the first or last sentence).
5. Try to create a main idea statement if the author has not provided one (Brown & Day, 1983; Simpson & Nist, 1990).

The deletion rules usually can be taught incidentally from kindergarten through third grade, and more explicitly in the fourth and fifth grades. Rules 3, 4, and 5 take longest to acquire. Provide the rules on "cue cards" or on a wall display for ease of reference (McNeil & Donant, 1982). See Figure 8.2 for an example of a summary of a book section that a fifth-grade teacher used to teach application of the Rules of Summarizing.

Beyond rule-guided approaches to summarizing, Cunningham (1982) experimented with a self-discovery approach that urges students to simply get the "GIST"—*Generating Interactions between Schemata and Text*—by writing lots of 15-word summaries. A comparison of McNeil's and Donant's rule-governed approach with Cunningham's more incidental-intuitive approach, found them to be equally effective (Bean & Steenwyck, 1984). Of course nothing prevents the reflective teacher from doing both alternately, or in a near-simultaneous way.

Other studies on summarizing provide these additional pointers for promoting effective summarizing:

1. Focus on main idea searching (Baumann, 1984).
2. Teach summarizing initially from pieces organized in familiar patterns such as chronological order (Hill, 1991).
3. Provide frequent and extensive feedback about the general effectiveness of strategy use, especially to weaker readers (Schunk & Rice, 1987).
4. Combine and integrate summarizing with questioning, clarifying, and predicting (Palincsar, Brown, & Martin, 1987).
5. Provide a lead-in sentence (Cassidy, as cited in Gaskins, 1981) or key words for constructing one: "Ralph's great adventure began when . . . ."
6. Provide a simple word grammar to follow, such as: First this happened . . . Then . . . Then . . . and Finally . . . (Pincus, Geller, & Stover, 1986).
7. Give students an outline of a story that has been read, or elicit one from them, and then have them reconnect it into a summary (Eanet, 1983; Hayes, 1988).

---

**FIGURE**
**8.2**    **Application of Summary Rules**

*Summary Rules Applied to a Summary of "The McKennas Learn About Snakes":*

~~All along their route,~~ the McKennas -- ~~Angie, Michael, and son David,~~ noticed that the ~~viper and rattle~~ snakes were most active ~~and likely to bite~~ during the day, ~~but not as likely to do so at night~~.

~~As their wagon train moved on,~~ they talked about this ~~at evening meals~~ with their friends the ~~McCoys, the Grummers, and the Prices. Finally,~~ they ~~began to~~ realize ~~that~~ it was because the desert ~~that they were traveling through~~ grew cold at night that the snakes came out in the daytime ~~when the sun was out and the ground was warm~~.

*New Summary:*

The McKennas noticed that the snakes were most active during the day. They talked about this with their friends. Finally, they realized that it was because the desert grew cold at night that the snakes came out in the daytime.

---

8. Use Al-Hilawani's (1991) Keyword Strategy (detailed in another chapter) to teach youngsters how to identify pivotal words, phrases, and concepts upon which summaries and retellings can be mapped and then connected.

9. Teach aspects of text structuring and outlining as suggested next in the chapter.

See the chapter on higher-order literacy for other methods that use this reconstructive level of encoding to promote transformations beyond summarizing. If children cannot be led beyond summarizing, they would have made only minimal progress toward becoming literate: They would be overly practiced in reconstructing messages, but unaccustomed to constructing new ones.

## TEXT STRUCTURE: OUTLINES, STORY GRAMMARS, AND STORY MAPS

The ability to see and follow the larger and lesser organizational patterns with a selection is one of the most durable operations isolated in research on "good readers" (Davis, 1944; McGee, 1982, Meyer, 1975). While no single method has yet proven to be the "most" beneficial in teaching text organization and accurate comprehension, several have proven useful in heightening awareness of text organization, and to that extent can be said to contribute to reading comprehension proficiency. However, where reconstructive comprehension is concerned, the value of text structuring has yet to be fully validated. This may explain why reading specialists, responding on the basis of experience and intuition, have ranked text structure instruction 14th out of 23 possible teaching practices for comprehension improvement (Gee & Raskow, 1987). Nonetheless, attention to organizational patterns can be especially useful when it is made a part of a more inclusive operation that puts a greater emphasis on students' transforming text more than on the teacher doing it for them. There are several popular practices for drawing attention to text structure. These include outlining, paragraph pattern analysis, and various uses of story grammars and reading guides. Most of these strategies are best used with nonfiction material, and hence are covered in the chapter on reading and writing across the curriculum. However, story grammars and maps are nicely suited to following a story line and are detailed here.

### Teaching Story Grammar Through Story Maps and Frames

Comprehension of stories depends largely on following the basic story line. The use of graphic methods for teaching this basic element of comprehension appears to have begun with the pioneering research of Barron (1969) on Structured Overviews and Hanf (1971) on mapping. An examination of basal reader teacher manuals by Beck and associates (1979) led them to conclude that the questions typically offered for checking and teaching comprehension did not follow any discernible pattern. In a similar study quite recently, Taylor (1992) found that basal questions do not follow a logical line of reasoning and do not reflect the major elements of the story. In a follow-up of their earlier study, Beck, Omanson, and McKeown (1982) had *teachers* revise the DRA's of a basal manual to prereading, during reading, and postreading questions that mapped into the organization of the story (see Table 8.1). The teachers then used their DRA's with their second-grade students. These second-grade students had significantly higher scores on comprehension measures than students who received instruction based on the basal teacher's manual.

Two other mapping studies are worth noting here. In one study learning disabled and low-achieving readers in a heterogeneously grouped class were shown to be able to better participate in and follow materials up to a year or more above their level when story grammar information was provided to guide reading and discussion (Idol, 1987). In a second study, it was shown that story grammar instruction of very low-achieving fourth-graders resulted in their producing much more complex and fully formed language experience stories than did a control group (Spiegel & Fitzgerald, 1986). These findings are consistent with many anecdotal reports of the value of various means and methods of structuring, mapping, and charting. Again, the simple thesis is that: (1) students will be better able to follow a story, or line of exposition, if they have a set of logical categories to help them properly anticipate and recognize information or story parts when they see them; and (2) guides are more effective when students are actively engaged in identifying at least some of the

**Table 8.1**

## Story Map and Related Questions for *Madge's Magic Show*, by Mike Thaler (second grade)

| STORY MAP | QUESTIONS |
|---|---|
| *The Setting* | |
| Characters: Madge, Jimmy | Who are the main characters in the story? |
| Place: Madge's house | |
| *The Problem* | |
| Jimmy isn't impressed with Madge's magic tricks | What problem does Madge have with Jimmy? |
| *The Goal* | |
| For Jimmy to think Madge is a good magician. | What does Madge hope will happen? |
| *The Events* | |
| Event 1 | |
| Madge pulls a chicken instead of a rabbit out of a hat. | What are three things that happen when Madge tries to pull a rabbit out of a hat? |
| Event 2 | |
| Madge pulls a fox instead of a rabbit out of a hat. | |
| Event 3 | |
| Madge pulls a cow instead of a rabbit out of a hat. | |
| Event 4 | |
| Madge pulls a rabbit out of a hat. | |
| *The Solution* | |
| Jimmy finally thinks Madge is a good magician. | How does Jimmy react when Madge pulls a rabbit out of a hat? |

*Beck, Omanson, & McKeown (1982).*

information that goes into the categories (see Figure 8.3 for an example of a student's story map.

A simple technique for introducing students to story structure prior to teaching Story Mapping is to explain and demonstrate how a story can be reduced to a series of "frames" detailing factors such as setting, characters, time, place, problem, action, and resolution or outcome. Students then are led through several stories as the teacher gradually fades support and urges students to complete more and more frames for themselves. The next step usually is to have students begin to make maps that others might use to follow a story. See Figure 8.4 for a Story Frame example.

Once children have become familiar with story structure through Story Frames and Maps, mapping techniques can also be effectively used with subject area reading materials. Heimlich and Pittelman (1986) compiled an entire monograph that detailed classroom applications of Mapping (see Figure 8.5).

The next method returns to the concept of frontloading, but with greater emphasis on calling up relevant prior knowledge, and includes steps that move through the other stages of guided reading. This method is being widely adopted with many basals and supplementary materials.

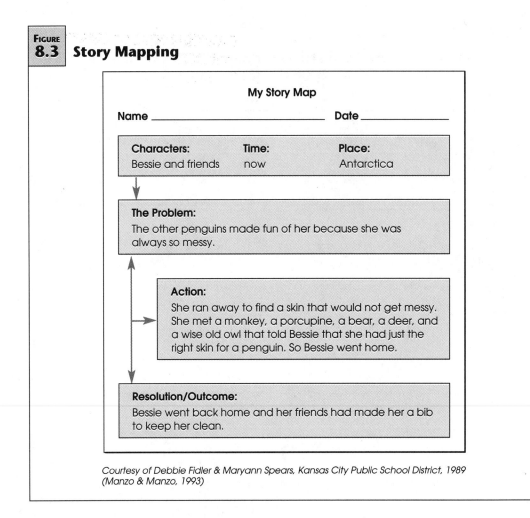

**FIGURE 8.3 Story Mapping**

My Story Map

Name _____ Date _____

| Characters: | Time: | Place: |
|---|---|---|
| Bessie and friends | now | Antarctica |

**The Problem:**
The other penguins made fun of her because she was always so messy.

**Action:**
She ran away to find a skin that would not get messy. She met a monkey, a porcupine, a bear, a deer, and a wise old owl that told Bessie that she had just the right skin for a penguin. So Bessie went home.

**Resolution/Outcome:**
Bessie went back home and her friends had made her a bib to keep her clean.

*Courtesy of Debbie Fidler & Maryann Spears, Kansas City Public School District, 1989 (Manzo & Manzo, 1993)*

## KNOWLEDGE ACTIVATION AND INTEGRATION TECHNIQUES

The general rule to activate relevant prior knowledge and experiences has been part of reading instruction from the earliest days. As you will recall, Betts (1946) included social forms of frontloading as the first phase of the Directed Reading Activity. The method that follows describes a recent effort to activate relevant prior knowledge and experience and to see it through to postreading.

### K–W–L Plus

K–W–L Plus, developed by Carr and Ogle (1987), can be used as a total lesson plan since it has prereading, guided silent reading, and postreading components. Its most significant contribution, however, is in the activation step and in the postreading follow-up step. The idea of the method is to stir students to want to say what

**FIGURE 8.4** **Story Framing**

Title _The Sad Mule_

GOVERNORS STATE UNIVERSITY
UNIVERSITY PARK
IL 60466

The problem in this story was _a mule that was too old to work._

This was a problem because _the farmer was going to sell the mule._

The problem was finally solved when _the farmer's children had fun riding the mule._

In the end, _the farmer kept the mule as a pet for the children._

**FIGURE 8.5** **Classroom Map for *Stores***

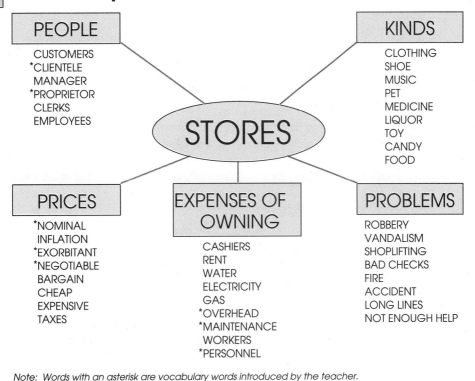

Note: Words with an asterisk are vocabulary words introduced by the teacher.

they **Know (K),** express what it is they **Want (W) to Know** from the textual material, and then tell what they have **Learned (L)** following reading. The **Plus** refers
to an important follow-up step. It involves having students generate maps or summaries, either cooperatively or individually. This step seemed to provide the active
ingredient that an earlier K–W–L version of this method seemed to need to bring
about more predictable benefits to comprehension (Ogle, 1986). See Table 8.2 for
a sample K–W–L Worksheet.

## STEPS IN K–W–L PLUS

*Before Reading*

**Step 1**    Students "brainstorm" and note on individual worksheets what they think
they know about a topic. Ogle (1989) recently suggested that the best way
to direct this step is to ask, "How is/should this content be structured?"

**Step 2**    Students categorize information they have generated and anticipate categories of information that they may find in the selection.

**Step 3**    The teacher models categorizing by "thinking aloud" while combining and
classifying information.

**Step 4**    Students generate a list of questions they want answered as they read.

*Silent Reading*

**Step 5**    During reading, students pause to answer the questions raised in the
"want to know" list. (New questions can be added as they read.)

**Step 6**    Students list things they have learned while reading.

*Postreading*

**Step 7**    Discussion of what was learned takes place, and questions raised before
reading are reviewed to determine whether they were resolved.

*Follow-Up*

**Step 8**    Students are encouraged to map and/or summarize the information from
their "learned" list.

For an interesting variation on K–W–L Plus, see Heller's (1986) metacognitive
method in the chapter on higher-order literacy. The next method also is a front-
loading activity and a good way to get kids talking—constructively.

## PreP

The PreP, or Pre-reading Plan, was developed by Langer (1981) to simultaneously provide opportunity for assessing the adequacy of students' prior knowledge
while raising and focusing topic awareness. It is primarily a small-group method.
This three-phase process has the teacher first identify key terms, then the teacher:

## Table 8.2

### K–W–L Worksheet for "Killer Whales"

| K (Know) | W (Want to Know) | L (Learned*) |
|---|---|---|
| They live in oceans. | Why do they attack? | D They are the biggest members of the dolphin family. |
| They are vicious. | How fast can they swim? | |
| They eat each other. | What kind of fish do they eat? | D They weigh 10,000 pounds. |
| They are mammals. | What is their description? | F They eat squid, seals, and other dolphins. |
| | How long do they live? | |
| | How do they breathe? | A They have good vision underwater. |
| | | F They are carnivorous (meat eaters). |
| | | A They are the second smartest animal on earth. |
| | | D They breathe through blow holes. |
| | | A They do not attack unless they are hungry. |
| | | D They are warm-blooded. |
| | | A They have echo-location (sonar). |
| | | L They are found in the oceans. |

*A = Abilities; D = Description; F = Food; L = Location
Carr & Ogle (1987).

1. Asks students for their associations with the terms
2. Builds a discussion around the question, "What made you think of that association?"
3. Prompts further discussion and focus by asking, "Now that we have discussed this, have you any new ideas before we read?"

PreP tends to get students talking very freely. However, it does not seem to convert easily into "instructional conversation," since it often calls up too much irrelevant information that is difficult to channel back into analysis of the textual material. Studies of PreP indicate that the quality and quantity of the information it calls up are predictive of reading comprehension but not necessarily related to the *improvement* of comprehension (Langer & Nicholich, 1981). PreP probably should be thought of as a component of a more inclusive method, such as the first step of a Directed Reading Activity.

### Inferencing (Non-Cloze)

Inferencing, a technique developed by Hansen (1981), improves on some of the limitations of the PreP model. With Hansen's approach, there are three front-loading steps. The first step has the teacher explain *why* the group will try to relate new information to old. The second leads students into a prereading discussion based on having them express *what they think* the story characters might do based on their own experiences. The third and continuing phase has the teacher ask a steady stream of *inferential questions* that require the integration of student experiences with events in the story. Hansen suggests limiting questions to no more than three preselected concepts.

Maria (1990) gives the example of a teacher leading children to discuss the central concept of "boredom" in preparation for reading Krasilvosky's story, *Cow Who Fell in the Canal*. The teacher then asks the text-related question: "Henduka, the cow in the story we are going to read, is bored. When do you think she will do so that she won't be bored anymore?" (p. 106) [She wanders off, falls in a canal, and floats into many adventures.]

This strategy has been found to have relatively *little* impact on good readers. However, it helped poor readers to perform about as well as good readers who received traditional basal instruction on the same stories (Hansen, 1981; Hansen & Pearson, 1983). This makes Inferencing a useful strategy for initiating reading in a heterogeneous group.

For two other front-loading techniques that rely on writing, you may wish to consult Blanchard's (1988) Plausible Stories technique and Wood's (1984) Probable Passages. Consider now a popular method to keep reading going.

### Sustained Silent Reading

The essence of reading power is to read silently and to sustain it for some reasonable period of time. From this perspective, Hunt (1970) and McCracken (1971) independently created the notion of Sustained Silent Reading (SSR). Recent name variations on SSR include Sustained Quiet Reading Time (SQUIRT), and DEAR (Drop Everything and Read) (Lipson & Wixson, 1991).

By any name, the purposes are pretty much the same: To provide opportunity, during the school day, for students to read connected text, to provide adult reading models, and to increase the duration of reading from a few minutes up to an hour or more. Mork (1972), also a pioneer of SSR, reminds us to begin with a period of time that is so brief that it is no serious challenge to youngsters. McCracken & McCracken (1978) further advise that the rules be made clear, and that the teacher and anyone else in view also obey the basic rules of being *silent and reading.* Other helpful features of SSR include "book floods," in which reading areas are equipped with paperback book libraries (Elley & Mangubhai, 1983; Ingham, 1982) and where the reading area is regularly spruced-up to be attractive (Morrow & Weinstein, 1986).

SSR can be a valuable means of starting or ending a school day. In our experience, the ritual of silent and focused reading the first thing in the morning proved comforting to inner city students in schools that were otherwise disruptive and appeared unmanageable. Importantly, the entire staff of the schools were required to participate, including clerical, cafeteria, and janitorial workers, and even security guards in one volatile middle school (Manzo, 1973).

The success of SSR can be further ensured by giving considerable attention to explaining to students what they are doing and why, and by helping them to select appropriate material. SSR now tends to be linked to a second period of time for guided "recreational reading" (Morrow, 1989), direct instruction, "buddy type" reading (Koskinen & Blum, 1986), or expressions, such as writing and "make and takes."

The evidence supporting SSR is mixed. Several studies have shown outcomes related to better attitudes toward school (Cline & Kretke, 1980) and faster movement through basals (Collins, 1980), but only two studies seem to offer a link to achievement, and each of these studies contained an additional ingredient. Pearson and Fielding (1991) note that one of these studies was accompanied by peer and teacher interaction about books (Manning & Manning, 1984), and the other had poor readers spending a good deal of time writing as well as reading (Holt & O'Tuel, 1989).

Since no one seems to doubt that sustained silent reading ought to be a serious goal and practice in most every reading program, it is our inclination to think of it as the "inert substance" in a pill; that is, as a significant bonding agent but generally in need of an active agent to promote more careful encoding, or restating. This can be achieved with plain conversation, which can result in at least a minimum level of active manipulation and transformation of text (Manzo & Manzo, 1993). Here now are three systems for initiating a more active level of reading.

## CUEING SYSTEMS

There are few methods that rely heavily on a *behavioral training* model to help inculcate certain desirable reading, language, and even thinking behaviors. When used judiciously, this general approach can be a powerful pump-primer in developing the physical and emotional experience base that sometimes is necessary to get a certain type of thought process and action flowing naturally. To this extent, cueing is similar to the "strategic parroting" technique described earlier with the ReQuest Picture Procedure and to Note Cue (Manzo & Manzo, 1990b). The first is something of a reading-study method based on providing direct, explicit instruction in *how, when,* and *why* to employ specific reading strategies. The second attempts to alter the text to focus attention on idea units.

## Monitoring Cards

Babbs (1983) developed a method that actually teaches students about the reading process over several sessions. The discussion, she says, should center around five questions related to a reader's strategic planning and decision making:

1. What is reading?
2. What is my goal?
3. How difficult is the text?
4. How can I accomplish my goal?
5. How can I check on whether I have achieved my goal?

Once students become reasonably proficient in handling these questions, they are trained in the use of nine prompt cards that can be employed in silent reading in class or at home. The cards are used in the following manner:

After silently reading the first sentence, students refer to the *first two* of these nine cards to remind themselves to monitor their own reading comprehension:

1. *clink*—"I understand"
2. *clunk*—"I don't understand"

If their reading has resulted in a *clunk,* the student attempts to classify it as a *word* problem or a *sentence* problem. Then the student reviews the next strategy cards, *in order,* until the problem is resolved. The strategies recommended are in this order:

3. Read on (to see if further information brings greater clarity).
4. Reread the sentence.
5. Go back and reread the paragraph.
6. Look in the glossary (or dictionary).
7. Ask someone (such as a fellow student, a volunteer, or a teacher).
8. What did the paragraph say?
9. What do I remember at the end of the page?

Using this method, Babbs found that fourth-graders in an experimental group spent more time on the reading task and had more than twice as many recalls of important ideas (Babbs, 1983). However, strategy use did not transfer as well as she hoped when the cards were withdrawn from these fourth-graders.

## Chunking Cues

"Chunking," also sometimes known as *phrase* training, attempts to focus students' attention on meaningful units of language by breaking sentences up into phrases, or ideational chunks. For example, the sentence below would be "chunked" as indicated by the slash marks:

*Careful, / Catherine, / the cabinet door is open above you, / and your crayons are on the floor / in front of you.*

Training in reading prechunked material, and in chunking material with slashes (/) can draw attention to phrasing, ideas, and sequencing, but it also needs to be accompanied by a good deal of discussion about meaning, which really is the chief dictate of phrasing. Asking students to indicate where they would place phrase markers evokes discussion about meaning in a close-knit, analytical way that draws them into thinking like writers.

Stevens (1981) found such chunking procedures to be of considerable value with high school students. Brozo and associates concluded that such training helps poor readers in high school and college but has little positive effect on *competent* readers at these levels (Brozo, Schmlzer, & Spires, 1983). This suggests that phrase training and related activities may not be needed for more mature and competent readers; however, it clearly is a problem for remedial level readers, and it is likely to be a problem for most younger readers. Try it and see whether it promotes the kind of activity and instructional conversation that seem to sharpen comprehension with elementary school children.

At an anecdotal level, several specialists have noted that phrase training can be effectively used to teach the use and connection between punctuation and communication. They have done this by stressing the role of clause markers such as "but," "and," "if," etc. Phrase training predates the mid-1960s, but lapsed into disuse for no apparent reason. Currently it is growing in popularity due to the renewed interest in having children learn to be writers as well as readers.

Consider now some techniques that make use of the mind's eye to image and follow analogies. Imaging, or picturing from print, is not quite the same as imagining. Imaging is something that proficient readers apparently do quite naturally, but poor readers do not.

## IMAGING

It has been shown that the act of attempting to construct mental images can help young readers to better integrate (Pressley, 1977) and detect inconsistencies (Gambrell & Bales, 1986) in textual material. Sadoski (1983; 1985) found that those students who were able to *image* the climax of the story from the information available also comprehended it best. This is not conclusive proof that imaging improves comprehension, but imaging does require a personalized transformation of textual material, and therefore is a good way to call up relevant knowledge and to promote active comprehension.

The following model for guided imagery instruction has been synthesized from several sources: a volume called *200 Ways of Using Imagery in the Classroom* (Bagley & Hess, 1982); from our own experiences with children; and from recommendations (steps 1 and 6) found in works by Aulls (1978) and Maria (1990).

## STEPS IN GUIDED IMAGERY

Step 1    Demonstrate (model) for them what you mean by imaging by selecting a common place or thing and expressing how you "see" it in your mind's eye: "When I close my eyes and picture a kitchen, I see a warm room that has a refrigerator, a stove, a sink, and a small table."

**Step 2**   Have children relax, breathe a bit more deeply than usual, and attempt to focus themselves on your voice as you tell them what to imagine.

**Step 3**   Have them try to form an image of a place or object that will be featured in the story they will read: "We are going to read a story about a fire engine. Picture a fire engine in your mind. Picture it from the side, from the front, from the back. Picture its color, its size, the equipment on it . . ."

**Step 4**   Have them attempt to broaden their image to include a larger setting and to add details.

**Step 5**   Ask students to imagine what they see, smell, hear, and feel in their picture.

**Step 6**   (optional) Have students write or draw a simple picture of what they pictured before they tell about it aloud (this is done in order to permit them to first find their own images before being unduly influenced, and perhaps distracted, by the images offered by others).

A recent study by Gambrell and Jawitz (1993) suggests that reading comprehension can be enhanced when students are taught to form vivid mental images and to attend to illustrations. Gambrell and Jawitz found this type of instruction to be particularly effective in promoting the ability to answer higher-order or text-implicit questions. However, they note that these results need to be further validated since they are based on a single story, with illustrations that were judged to be highly text-relevant, and that had a high language stimulation rating on the Manzo–Legenza picture potency formula (1975b).

On a related note, Maria (1990) notes that visual images can be so powerful in young children as to be potentially emotionally disquieting for them. We concur, but also feel that experienced teachers are professionals who can be trusted to use certain potent techniques judiciously: Most things that are powerful also are potentially dangerous when used inappropriately or in excess. We have found that inviting children to talk about some of their scarier images, such as from *The Wizard of Oz,* can give them strength and courage. Discussions about fears also can help the teacher to gain insights into where children are and how they deal with their fears. Understanding the seemingly "senseless" fears of children can be an intriguing and beneficial topic for a Parent Focus Group meeting, as described in Chapter 2.

## DRAMATIZATION

*Dramatics* are activities in which children translate ideas from text into action. Several ways have been mentioned for doing this, such as dramatizing literature with puppets and teaching vocabulary through skits. The type of dramatization referred to here is more of a simulation variety. One of the simplest and most imaginative of these is called Investigative Questioning, or InQuest, developed by Shoop (1986). The strategy involves the reader or listener with narrative text through student questioning and spontaneous drama techniques. InQuest is a natural for video-taping and use in an integrated language arts program or a communications magnet theme school.

As a precondition to InQuest, students are led through a discussion and practice of the techniques involved in journalistic interviewing. The following points are made to students in the discussion:

- Questions that get longer responses are more desirable.
- Yes/no questions should be followed by a "why?"
- Interview questions should try to elicit reflections and evaluations as well as simple information.
- It is best to use a variety of question types.

## STEPS IN THE INQUEST DRAMATIZATION PROCEDURE

**Step 1**  The teacher selects an interesting story that is read by the teacher or students up to a critical point or incident.

**Step 2**  The teacher suggests to students that they try to think of questions that they would like to ask one of the characters as the narrative unfolds.

**Step 3**  Students role-play a news conference in which someone plays the character and everyone else assumes the roles of investigative reporters. (The teacher may model role-play either of these parts initially.)

**Step 4**  Students are directed to read on to a next point and repeat the interview process with a different or the same character.

**Step 5**  Have students evaluate which questions proved most interesting, in the sense of bringing characters to life.

The benefits of InQuest to inquiry training can be magnified by using it in combination with the ReQuest and Question-Only Procedures. The next topic, Following Directions, once was considered sedentary, if not boring. However, it too can be taught through simulation, dramatization, and high-activity approaches. In fact, in the hands of some children and teachers, it can be clever and fun.

## FOLLOWING DIRECTIONS

The ability to follow written directions is an important key to independent learning and functioning. It has been aptly said that "At various points in almost every schoolday, students are expected to follow some form of written directions, and that life outside school is full of basic life demands that require [all of us] to follow written instructions" (Henk & King, 1984, p. 62).

Some of the earliest "specific skills series" materials included practice in "Following Directions." These were *not* well received by students, largely because they were tedious and nonengaging. However, when teachers and students get involved in making such materials, they naturally become more engaging as a result of raised levels of physical activity and the inclination of children to be playful (Calder & Zalatimo, 1970).

Maring and Ritson (1980) offer this example of an activity that can be done in physical education class, at recess, or to break up routines that are becoming stale.

### Read and Do Sheets

Prepare Read and Do instruction sheets so that students will learn required content and at the same time improve their ability to follow written directions.

Example: Motor Development Exercise

*Single-heel click:* Jump into the air, click your heels together once, and land with your feet apart (any distance).

This can be turned into an *even* more amusing and exacting exercise in which students try to write totally unambiguous directions for their peers to follow. It's a real test of thinking and writing craft to write so clearly that what is directed is actually what can occur.

Other related Read and Do direction activities for school include:

1.  Having students write out explicit directions for others to follow on how to get from one very specific place in the school to another.
2.  Having students read and follow directions for drawing a certain graphic or folding a sheet of paper.
3.  Having students working in groups to write up directions for a scene from a play that another group must enact.
4.  Having students work to assemble something from the manufacturer's directions, such as a model car, plane, or a dollhouse.

If the "real-life" directions pose too great a challenge for young or poor readers, consider Henk and King's suggestions (1984) for rewriting them:

1.  Use one sentence per direction.
2.  Substitute simple synonyms for difficult words.
3.  Avoid taking background information for granted.
4.  Ensure that essential intermediate steps have not been omitted or just implied.
5.  Avoid using lengthy or complex sentence structures.
6.  Avoid ambiguous statements.
7.  Omit irrelevant information.
8.  Use numbers to mark the steps to follow (1984, p. 63).

Conversely, to add a further bit of challenge to the task of following directions, have students try to anticipate (and perhaps record) where they think other students will have trouble understanding or following a set of directions. This takes careful reading, imaging, and thinking.

## **W**here You've Been

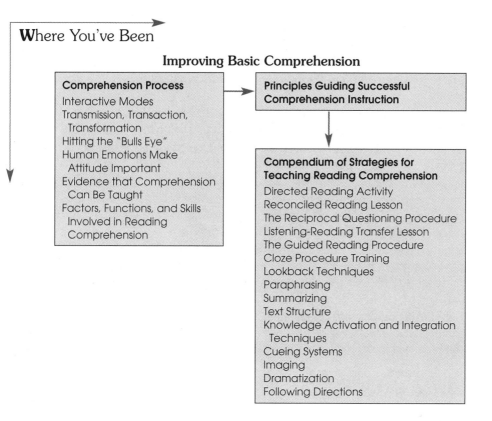

**Improving Basic Comprehension**

**Comprehension Process**

Interactive Modes
Transmission, Transaction,
  Transformation
Hitting the "Bulls Eye"
Human Emotions Make
  Attitude Important
Evidence that Comprehension
  Can Be Taught
Factors, Functions, and Skills
  Involved in Reading
  Comprehension

**Principles Guiding Successful
Comprehension Instruction**

**Compendium of Strategies for
Teaching Reading Comprehension**

Directed Reading Activity
Reconciled Reading Lesson
The Reciprocal Questioning Procedure
Listening-Reading Transfer Lesson
The Guided Reading Procedure
Cloze Procedure Training
Lookback Techniques
Paraphrasing
Summarizing
Text Structure
Knowledge Activation and Integration
  Techniques
Cueing Systems
Imaging
Dramatization
Following Directions

## **W**here You're Going

Now that you have a firm foundation in how to improve reconstructive comprehension, you will want to be equally knowledgeable about how to build constructive (critical–creative) reading. The next chapter is devoted entirely to this eternally new area of literacy. You should notice at least two things as you read ahead: (a) *Many* of the methodologies studied in this chapter on reconstructive reading also contribute to higher-order comprehension; and (b) *Every* method that teaches higher-order thinking also promotes basic comprehension.

### *Reflective Inquiries and Activities*

1. Explain this statement in your own words: Reading essentially is a reconstructive act, but it also is a personally driven one that must be active to be truly beneficial.

2. The meaning of "reading comprehension" can be summarized in three words: transmission, transaction, and transformation. Can you explain what is meant by each of these terms?

3. Why might it be necessary, in a program designed to nurture literate children, to be so concerned about accurate, reconstructive reading?

4. Why did (and do) some educators believe that it was almost impossible to directly teach toward comprehension improvement? What occurred to change many minds?

5. Go to the list of Factors, Functions, and Skills Involved in Reading Comprehension (p. 277) and select a half-dozen that you currently value most highly. Tell why.

6. Select two principles for Guiding Successful Comprehension Instruction that you feel are the most important and argue for full implementation by your school.

7. Without looking back, what are two types of questions that are especially important in comprehension work? Why? (This can be tackled in small groups.) Now *look back*. Did you forget anything important? What are you going to do so you remember these points when you are teaching?

8. Why would Stauffer, author of the Directed Reading-Thinking Procedure, prefer that youngsters try to figure out words for themselves when reading instructional material? Go back to the chapter on word recognition and analysis and see if you can find research to support the rationale for this practice.

9. Select two comprehension teaching methods that in your view best meet each of the objectives stated below. A method can be chosen for more than one category (be prepared to defend your choices).

   a. Improves accurate recall.
   b. Goes well with basals.
   c. Goes well with content material.
   d. Is likely to stimulate a quality instructional conversation.
   e. Has significant diagnostic value.
   f. Has significant concurrent, or collateral values beyond mere comprehension.
   g. Builds metacognitive traits.
   h. Really sharpens reconstructive, read and recall, reading.
   i. Are very well documented by empirical and field trials.
   j. Can improve familiarity with oral and/or written language patterns.
   k. Couldn't be simpler.
   l. Fosters translation thinking and skills.
   m. Offers guidance during silent reading.
   n. Looks like it could be fun.
   o. Promotes curiosity and inquiry skills.
   p. Needs to be done, one way or another, no matter what.
   q. Frankly, doesn't look that good to me.

10. Try to create a comprehension improvement strategy, activity, or technique that you think would be especially useful with children who are not proficient with the English language. (See the chapter on special literacy needs to see how well you anticipated and may have met such needs.)

11. Working in small groups, have each group member select one of the comprehension strategies to demonstrate to the group. Each group member will have the chance to prepare and demonstrate a selected strategy and to participate in demonstration lessons prepared and presented by other group members.

# PART IV

# HIGHER-ORDER LITERACY

# 9 CRITICAL AND CREATIVE READING, WRITING, AND THINKING

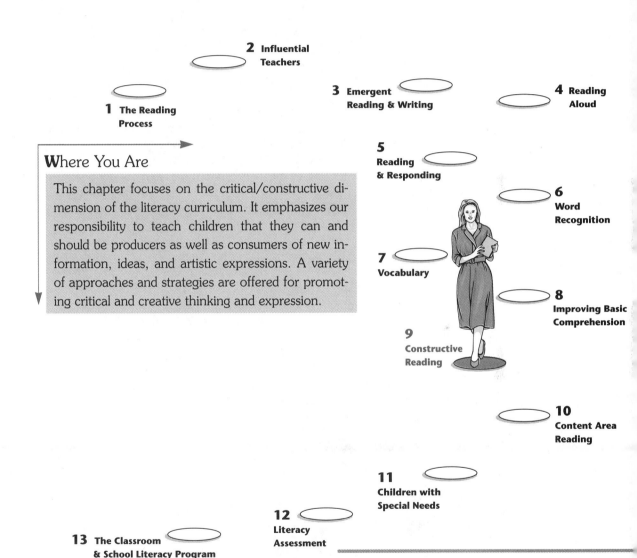

**2** Influential
Teachers

**1** The Reading
Process

**3** Emergent
Reading & Writing

**4** Reading
Aloud

**5**
Reading
& Responding

**6**
Word
Recognition

**7** Vocabulary

**8**
Improving Basic
Comprehension

**9**
Constructive
Reading

**W**here You Are

This chapter focuses on the critical/constructive dimension of the literacy curriculum. It emphasizes our responsibility to teach children that they can and should be producers as well as consumers of new information, ideas, and artistic expressions. A variety of approaches and strategies are offered for promoting critical and creative thinking and expression.

**10**
Content Area
Reading

**11**
Children with
Special Needs

**12**
Literacy
Assessment

**13** The Classroom
& School Literacy Program

*Where some see problems, others
see possibilities*

Anonymous

## WHOLE-CHILD DIMENSION

This chapter expands the whole-child theme of this book to the often-overlooked critical and creative thinking potential within each child, and to those children who may have unrecognized special talents in this area. The reading–language arts curriculum has been considered one of the most suitable places to address effective thinking since Thorndike (1917) showed reasoning to be a close relative of effective reading over seventy-five years ago. Yet American education has been slow to respond with anything more than lip service to higher-order literacy functions. This reluctance is reflected in the children we teach. For example, although the 1990 National Assessment of Educational Progress (NAEP) report showed that over the previous seven years the nation's students had made significant improvement in reading performance, there was no group of students who had made *any* improvement in related reasoning abilities. Collins-Block (1993) reports a longitudinal study showing that 84 percent of kindergartners ranked high in creative aptitude, but that only 10 percent were able to sustain this level after three years of schooling (p. 347). These findings suggest that we may be facing a national crisis in thinking, and a clear call for schools to implement a substantial shift in emphasis from recall to reasoning and creative problem solving.

Elementary school teachers of the twenty-first century will need to heed this call. To prepare you to do so, this chapter provides an introduction to the critical/creative thinking process and a variety of practical means of promoting and applying it through instruction in reading, writing, listening, and speaking. In this "creative process" approach, the reading and language arts curriculum is the vehicle through which students are taught to question, to explore, and to try things that might ini-

### *This Wonder-Filled World*

I Wonder Why? *Elizabeth Gordon, M. T. Illustrations by M. T. (Penny) Ross. Chicago: Rand McNally & Co., 1916.*

tially appear to be beyond their reach. In this way, "they learn to define problems and to test solutions. . . . They learn, in other words, to deal with the inevitable challenge of their constantly changing lives—and our constantly changing society" (Haas, 1988, p. 4). As children learn to be more capable observers and problem identifiers, they learn how to organize events, experiences, and information into well-stated problems and possible solutions. This emphasis better prepares them not only to adapt to change and to meet crises, but to form an image of an anticipated future that they can work toward. It is an effort to give students the power to shape, not merely react to the forces that will shape their futures.

Many new terms have been coined to describe this new emphasis, but a very old term probably still captures it best: it is "Wonder!" The simple idea of teaching children to wonder still is the "wind beneath the wings" of all critical thinking, discovery, invention, and creation. Hence, while it may seem a bit new, emphasis on critical and creative thinking is part of an old tradition of helping children to see that it's a "wonder-filled" world.

Read ahead now and see how elementary teachers are becoming part of this rediscovery. Let's begin to address this newer aspect of the reading–language arts curriculum by further refining what we mean by "critical and creative thinking."

## CRITICAL AND CREATIVE THINKING: DEFINITIONS AND ATTRIBUTES

Critical and creative thinking are the essence of higher-order literacy. As discussed in previous chapters, higher-order literacy is based on reading the lines, reading between the lines, and reading and thinking beyond the lines. Higher-order literacy involves critical analysis of the author's message, creative response, and the willingness to be transformed as well as informed by relevant information from credible sources. As essayist John Locke expressed it in 1706, "Reading furnishes the mind only with materials of knowledge; it is thinking that makes what we read ours."

Writing and reading permit us to store, recover, and share what we have discovered. However, creativity, ingenuity, and wonder are humankind's most powerful tools for envisioning adaptive possibilities where there are constricting problems. Remarkably, this potential seems to be a built-in part of the human psyche. Why else, for example, would we work extra hard to make a twisted, rather than a straight pretzel? Surely not just to celebrate the odd discovery made by a monk over 400 years ago. And why do we need so many varieties of pasta? Whatever the answers to these whimsical questions, here are our philosophical and practical reasons for having a high regard for ingenuity and the creative process in education:

1. It is satisfying and intrinsically motivating.
2. It doesn't stop when school lets out: the mind that is beset with creative possibilities stays active beyond the classroom walls.
3. It clearly is the highest act of the mind. As such, it is the means by which we continue to define ourselves.
4. It is playful and uplifting.

5. It can cause children to be subtly influential by bringing them together with parents and teachers.

6. It is a respectable way to venture outside some of the petty rules and regulations that constrain us in modern life.

7. It raises hope by offering possibilities where there were problems.

8. It provides the mental tools for building a better life.

9. It is procreative and enduring: "All it takes is one person with a new idea and our lives are all made different" (Discovery Channel, June 1992).

10. It offers anyone who can do it an opportunity to leave something behind that is bigger and more durable than our finite stay here, whether it be a twisted pretzel or a children's book with the enduring quality of *Green Eggs and Ham* (thank you, Dr. Seuss, who died in 1992).

Attributes of higher-order thinking have been identified by several researchers (Gentile & McMillan, 1991; Manzo & Manzo, 1990a; Marzano, 1991; Resnick, 1987). Five attributes are particularly relevant here:

- It is *dispositional,* or driven by orientation and will as much as ability.
- It is the *mediational* system, or method of inner speech by which we are able to impose meaning and find structure in apparent disorder.
- It involves aspects of *self-examination* and "strategic reading" that have come to be known as study strategies and metacognitive functioning (two topics that are covered more fully in Chapter 11).
- It implies effective *memory* and the acquisition of a rich fund of information (also in Chapter 11).
- It suggests command of the *related language arts* (especially writing, which, as previously noted, is a chief means by which to "mediate," or reflect on, experience as well as communicate it).

Interestingly, higher-order literacy does not appear to be simply an upward extension of basic reading comprehension, as intuition might lead one to believe. Certain types of higher-level thinking disorders are almost as likely to be found among proficient readers as among remedial readers, and certain higher-order thinking strengths are almost as likely to be found among average and even some below average readers as among proficient readers (Casale, 1982; Manzo & Manzo, 1990a; Ratanakarn, 1992). In Chapter 12 on assessment, you will read about a new reading test that is designed to assess strengths and weaknesses in critical and creative reading as well as basic comprehension.

Creative thinking often is the result of a simple rearrangement of existing knowledge—a rearrangement that is, of itself, an addition to knowledge (Kneller, 1965). Thus, most people have the reconstructive thinking ability, the background knowledge, and the human experience that are the necessary elements in creativity. Yet few people actually create. More often than not, in fact, we fail to acknowledge or appreciate creativity when we see it. This irony requires further examination if we are to be successful in promoting the critical/creative process.

# HOW MUCH DO WE REALLY VALUE CRITICAL/CREATIVE THINKING?

Most people value, in retrospect, the insightful criticisms and creative solutions that have led to current life conditions. Yet, when similar innovations are encountered in everyday life, they often are met with skepticism if not outright hostility. The primary reason for skeptical reactions to critical and creative thinking seems to be that it interrupts the patterns and assumptions from which we tend to draw a sense of security and comfort. Since creativity fits no familiar pattern, it must be analyzed and evaluated each time it occurs. It often can mean wandering off the beaten path, or coloring outside the lines. It raises doubt and uncertainty—two feelings human beings try to avoid. In order to keep these feelings of doubt and uncertainty in check, we tend to do what we have done, see what we expect to see, and hear what we have been taught to listen for.

To get an idea of just how pattern-bound we are by nature, give a few people this simple "test." Ask someone to spell "STOP." Then say, "What do you do when you come to a green light?" Most people will say, "stop"—or pause in confusion. Similarly, ask someone to read this message:

CA  RETA  KER

It's easily decipherable, once you realize that a familiar spacing pattern has been broken.

Our tendency to maintain patterns influences how we tackle life's problems. For example, when something isn't working, there are four possible types of response: (1) ignore the problem; (2) say that the problem is unsolvable, and accept it; (3) work harder at doing the same things; and (4) consider more inventive possibilities. The first three responses are by far the most common, probably because they permit us to maintain a pattern that has come to be familiar. Only the fourth, least typical, response represents an attempt to alter the existing pattern. Chester Finn, former Assistant Secretary for Education, once used this analogy to remind us of the need to break out of our typical patterns of response: "When you're navigating by the wrong stars, pulling harder on the oars won't get you to your destination" (in Gentile & McMillan, 1991, p. 74).

As teachers, it is useful to first note that creative thinking often *does* break patterns and make us uneasy. However, when it is encouraged as part of a fuller program that teaches and explains traditional values and conventions, those ideas and values that are correct and supportable will survive, and even be strengthened by the review. Let's see now what can be done to teach ourselves and this generation of children to think more inventively.

# CAN CRITICAL/CREATIVE THINKING BE TAUGHT?

Some educators, such as Smith (1990), wonder whether higher-order thinking can even be taught. Smith argues that it is temperamental and dispositional more so than cognitive. Nonetheless, evidence continues to mount that it *can* be taught easily and profitably. Recently, for example, Collins (1991) showed that simply by infusing explicit thinking training into the reading–language arts curriculum, experimental groups of average middle school students outperformed comparable youngsters who received a traditional curriculum. This improved performance was evident in a variety of areas, including measures of reading comprehension, vocabulary, and self-esteem. In addition, and most importantly, they transferred their training to writing samples. This illustrated that their feelings and thoughts were more deeply touched than by the traditional reading–language arts program.

Cooter and Flynt (1986) provided an interesting and telling test of what they called the Cognitive Caboose Theory with third- and fourth-graders. According to this theory, if students were asked only inferential and higher-order questions, these would serve as the locomotive that pulled along a caboose of literal facts and skills. Two groups of average ability children were compared: an experimental group that was asked only higher-order questions, and a control group that was asked a conventional blend of questions that generally began at a literal level. The experimental group performed significantly better on inferential comprehension questions and slightly better on literal and detail questions. While this study lends considerable credibility to the caboose theory, it does not prove it unequivocally, since many of the questions used tended to be more of a "between the lines," or inferential type than of a "beyond the lines," or applied, evaluative, or conjectural type. In other words, the questioners asked more literal-level questions than they realized. Nonetheless, when these findings are added to the research of others, such as is described next, the caboose theory gains considerable credibility.

Writing on the history of thinking, Dillarosa (1988) reports of several studies of this higher-order literacy approach with disadvantaged youngsters. This research led him to identify essentially the same points called for in the "New Eclectic" approach:

- Build on what students know and do (e.g., instead of teaching spelling, have youngsters write their city council regarding matters of concern to them and their families; rather than assigning math drill, have kids calculate how many cold lunches are ordered each day in their school cafeterias).
- Teachers should ask more open-ended, rather than concrete recall questions.
- Teachers should provide "scaffolding" for difficult tasks by furnishing whatever support information and assistance is necessary to engage the critical part of the learning task.
- Teachers should make dialogue the central medium for teaching and learning.

Haggard-Ruddell (1976) discovered strong evidence for the value of higher-order cognitive training even with remedial readers. In this study, remedial readers, aged 7 to 17, were assigned to either an experimental or a control group. The experimental group received about 15 minutes of "warm-up" creative thinking exercises prior to reading instruction. In the control group, regular reading instruction was preceded by about 15 minutes of reading games such as Hangman, "consonant lotto," and the like. Posttest results showed that the creative thinking (experimental) group performed significantly better on all reading measures. Examples of these Creative Thinking-Reading Activities (CT–RA's), as Haggard-Ruddell (1979) came to call them, are provided ahead in the chapter. They contain three elements shared by most of the creative thinking approaches described ahead: a challenge to think creatively, opportunity for group interaction, and guidance in transferring creative thinking to new situations and challenges.

## TEACHING CRITICAL AND CREATIVE THINKING

Ironically, there is not much mystery in what it takes to promote thinking. Recent research (Comstock, 1992; Khatena, 1989; Hayes, 1989; Ripple, 1989) is suggesting that seven elements are essential. A conceptual overview of these will help you to follow as each of these is developed more fully throughout the chapter.

### SEVEN INSTRUCTIONAL ELEMENTS THAT FOSTER CREATIVE READING, WRITING, AND THINKING

1. Remember to *ask for it;* that is, for discovery, invention, and artistic/literary creation (see the anecdotes in Boxes 9.1, 9.2, and 9.3).
2. Greet curiosity and new ideas with enthusiasm "ideas are themselves intrinsically pedagogic . . . they have heuristic power (McEwan & Bull, 1991, p. 332).
3. Expose learners to new twists on old patterns. (The very titles of Jon Scieszka's "twisted" versions of popular tales excite the imagination: *The Frog Prince* [1991], *Knights of the Kitchen Table* [1991], *The Not-So-Jolly Roger* [1991], *The Stinky Cheese Man and Other Fairly Stupid Stories* [1992], and *The True Story of the Three Little Pigs* by A. Wolf [1989], also available on audiotape]).
4. *Constructively* critique new ideas, since they almost always require fine tuning.
5. Believe more fervently in our collective and individual ability to be constructively critical.
6. Reset our expectations to the fact that there will be many more "misses" than "hits" when reaching for workable new ideas (doing more of 1 through 4 accomplishes this best).
7. Learn to invite *contrary,* or opposing, positions; new possibilities often are discovered in this way.

Despite their generally weaker capacities for "formal reasoning," children may actually have an advantage in being creative: They have not yet learned all of the patterns of living and interacting that tend to inhibit its expression. Furthermore, teachers have the opportunity to etch into children's "basic programs" the sense that one of the patterns that life offers is the ongoing invitation to be creative and positively influential.

As stated above, the term *creative,* in a literacy context, means "reading beyond the lines" and being willing to write to learn. It suggests adopting a mind set that is

## BOX 9.1 Just Ask for It

The first author was having a discussion about creativity over lunch with three graduate students. Two said, modestly, that they tended to be uninventive in their thinking. The third said the same thing, but with the conviction of those who speak only when necessary.

Violating the unspoken agreement teachers tend to have with shy students, not to challenge them, I said, "No, you are not uninventive, you are unwilling to act assertively—to determine where there are problems and to intervene with plausible solutions."

"No," she replied insistently, "I am totally uncreative."

I persisted, "What are you doing right now, and how is it a problem for the shy?" The other two students tried to help but, ironically, could not because they were not self-conscious about the problem I had in mind. Finally, I asked, "Do you like your hot and sour soup?"

"Yes," she replied.

"Why aren't you finishing it?" I asked.

"I did," she murmured.

"No you didn't, you left some in the bottom."

"Well, I couldn't finish all of it to the bottom!" she snapped back, somewhat annoyed.

"So then, you have acknowledged a problem! Can you solve it?" I asked.

"You mean how to get the soup out of the bowl without lifting it to your mouth or even tipping the bowl to spoon it out?" she asked.

"Yes," I replied.

Overwhelmed with all this attention, she responded in moments. "Well, I suppose the bowl could have been made with an indentation in the shape of a spoon at the bottom. No wait," she quickly added, "how about just forming the inside of the bowl at an angle so the soup drains to one side?

There it was. Despite the fact that pottery has been made in the same way for thousands of years, this shy 'totally uncreative,' but prolific reader became a creator with two plausible solutions with no more training than a sharp prompt to do so!

*Manzo & Manzo (1990), p. 263*

## BOX 9.2 The Teacher Who Asked for It

A primary school teacher told this story on herself. She had gotten into the habit of keeping an account on the board of the number of times during the day that the "boys" or the "girls" misbehaved. The best behaved group received various privileges and prizes, such as being the ones to choose the story that would be read to the class. The girls rarely misbehaved, so they almost always received the rewards.

One little girl, Kristin, kept trying to tell the teacher that this was not a good idea. She said that because the boys never "won," they were being spiteful and mean to the girls. Finally one day, when Kristin brought it up again, the teacher replied rather curtly, "All right, Kristin, just what would you have me do about this?"

Kristin thought just for a moment, and said, "Why can't you just make groups that have both boys *and* girls in them?"

The teacher's question, even when raised in exasperation, proved to be the interruption necessary to create new possibilities where a pattern had gotten to be a rut.

**BOX
9.3** | **The Dolphin Researchers Who Asked for It**

Louis Herman, founder and director of the Kewalo Basin Marine Mammal Laboratory, has taught dolphins to respond to directions communicated through hand gestures. When told, through gestures, to perform in tandem, and to do "something creative," two dolphins submerged, swam in tandem, and then "leap(ed) into the air and simultaneously spit out jets of water before plunging back into the pool." On another occasion, given the same command, they performed a "synchronized backward swim culminating in a simultaneous wave of the tails."

*Time, March 22, 1993, p. 54*

intent on moving the reader (or writer) *through* literal and inferential thinking and *on* to a sense of wonder and commitment to seeing possibilities and connections beyond those explicitly presented or even implied. Doing this typically involves little more than extending current practices that tend to stop just short of this mark.

In practical terms, it generally means leading the reader to slowly but securely internalize a set of "paradigmatic," or model, questions that can guide reading and thinking down paths not typically taken and to questions not typically raised. Most everyone does this in their reading and thinking sometimes, and to some degree. It is the extent to which it is valued, taught, and done that can make a difference. Consider now how the teacher can ease his or her way into promoting critical and creative thinking by only slightly modifying one of our basic teaching tools— *questions*.

## PARADIGMATIC QUESTIONS THAT INVITE CRITICAL AND CREATIVE READING, WRITING, LISTENING, SPEAKING, AND THINKING

If each teacher were merely to add certain questions to his or her lesson activities, we probably could unleash a good deal of critical and creative thinking, reading, listening, and expression. See if you agree as you consider these question formats:

- *How is this study like another you/we have read?* This question encourages students to make connections and see analogies.

- *Does this story/information make you aware of any problems that need attention?* This amounts to asking youngsters to see themselves as active participants in problem identification as well as problem solving.

- *What does this mean to you, and how might it affect* others? This pair of questions gives students the right to feel and express their own best interests, but also to empathetically consider and understand the views of, and possible consequences to, others.

- *Is there anything wrong with this solution, and how else might this problem be solved?* These questions are the heart of successful critical analysis. A classic study with engineers showed that when two groups were given a third group's solutions to some difficult problems, they responded quite differently based on the verbal directions they were given. One group was directed to "critically" review the solutions, while the other group was directed to "constructively" review them. The latter group produced many more constructive solutions; while the former almost none (as reported in Baker & Schutz, 1972).

- *What more needs to be known, or done, to understand or do this better?* This is the pointed request for creative problem solving that invites thinking beyond what is known and written. It is a question that is rarely asked at any level of education, though it should be at *every* level of education.
- *Who thinks they can say this, or picture this differently than it is said or pictured here?* This is the same question as the previous one, but posed from a more artistic or aesthetic point of view. This question invites personal imaginings and expressions.
- *What is the author trying to get you to believe, understand, or know, and why?* Regularly asking this two-fold question in some form helps students to understand the fallibility, and possible biases, of even the best-intentioned authors. As such, it is a cornerstone of critical thinking (McKeown, Beck, & Worthy, 1993).
- *What is a contrary way of seeing this?* This question is basic to teaching dialogical thinking, a form of critical thinking described ahead in the chapter.

Needless to say, these questions need not *always* be asked, and they should be posed in authentic and conducive situations. Such questions do need to be asked with enough regularity so that the request for creative thinking becomes an expected means of social reward and personal validation. This is the classical means of building internal motivation. The remainder of the chapter details several practical ways that this can be done in the reading–language arts curriculum. Three overlapping categories are considered:

- Critical and Creative Reading
- Writing: Its Role in Improving Reading, Thinking, and Social–Emotional Development
- Higher-Order Thinking: Head-On Approaches

## CRITICAL AND CREATIVE READING PRACTICES

Good sense suggests that one of the first things to do in the teaching of anything new is to establish that students understand what they are being asked to learn. The first method is designed to impart a key concept about reading and thinking beyond the lines.

### QUESTION–ANSWER–RELATIONSHIPS (QARs)

Developed by Raphael (1982, 1986), Question–Answer–Relationships (QARs) are the three most common ways to look for answers in text. These are based on

FIGURE
9.1 **Question–Answer Relationships**

Type 1                                                    Right There

The answer is in the story, easy to find.   The
words used to make the question and the words
that make the answer are Right There, in the
same sentence.

Type 2                                                    Think and Search

The answer is in the story, but a little harder
to find.  You would never find the words in
the question and words in the answer in the
same sentence, but would have to Think and
Search for the answer.

Type 3                                                    On My Own

The answer won't be told by words in the story.
You must find the answer in your head.  Think:
"I have to answer this question On My Own, the
story won't be much help."

*Raphael (1982), p. 188.*

the relationship that exists among text, questions about the text, and the reader's existing knowledge (Pearson & Johnson, 1978). Students can be taught to use QARs as an effective strategy for answering comprehension questions. These QARs are described in Figure 9.1.

The steps below for teaching children to use QARs typically need to take place over several stages. Raphael recommends that these steps, or "phases" as she calls them, be adapted as needed, according to the children's age and grade.

## PHASES IN TEACHING QARs

Phase 1    Introduce students to the three Question-Answer-Relationships. This can be done using an overhead transparency of the illustration above. Then have the students work in small groups to practice recognizing these QARs, using the following format:

*Why did Ralph find himself sitting on the floor?*
*Right There* _____
*Think and Search* _____
*On My Own* <u>He rocked too hard</u>_____

This practice may need to be provided in several phases: In the first phase, have students read a short selection and provide them with a set of questions with answers and QARs identified. Discuss each QAR and how the answer was obtained. In the second phase, after students have read a passage, provide questions with the format above and have them simply circle the QAR they would need to use to answer the question. In the final phase, have them write their answer to each question next to the QAR they select as the appropriate information source.

**Phase 2**   Provide students with additional short passages (approximately 75 to 150 words) and QAR question worksheets. Students may work in small groups on an initial passage, but then should work individually on others, checking their answers with a small group. As a class, discuss students' responses, including selection of a QAR strategy as well as the answer for each question.

**Phase 3**   Divide a longer passage, about the length of a basal reading story, into four questions, with QAR question worksheets for each section. QAR worksheets should contain six questions: two of each type of QAR. When all students have completed the first section, discuss students' selection of QAR strategies and their answers to the questions. Students should then complete the remainder of the sections independently.

**Phase 4**   Provide a six-question QAR worksheet for a longer passage (600 to 800 words).

Raphael further notes that:

- A student can identify a Question-Answer-Relationship incorrectly but still offer an acceptable response. In such cases, the teacher should move discussion toward recognition of the best *possible* answer to the question. This will lead to careful analysis of the question and, in turn, recognition of the most appropriate QAR.
- QAR is a transition teaching strategy that should be phased out, but for occasional reminders, once students get the idea and practice down.

Raphael and Pearson (1982) have found that fourth-graders taught to use QARs were significantly better able to answer questions about reading selections than students who did not receive this instruction. Further, Raphael and Wonnacott (1981) found that teachers require very little training in QAR in order to successfully implement the strategy. This suggests that it has the heuristic quality of promoting self-discovery in teachers and students. Gentile and McMillan (1991) offer the example shown in Box 9.4 of QARs in action.

## PREDICTION TASKS

Prediction is use of knowledge about language and context to anticipate what is coming next in oral or written discourse. Teaching procedures that encourage prediction greatly facilitate learning (Anderson, 1976). Prediction arouses pupil interest

**BOX 9.4**

## Sample QARs

*Excerpt from:* **Laughing Boy**

The next time they met, he contemplated the man, and guessed at the dimensions of his soul. Taking an opportunity when they both were taking horses to water, he rode up beside him, sitting sideways on his barebacked pony, one hand on the mane, one hand on the rump—a casual post for a careless chat. Red Man greeted him noncommittally. Laughing Boy responded, "Grandfather, let us not run around things, let us not pretend," he said. "You have not said anything, but you have said too much. Do not pretend not to know what I mean. If you like what you are doing so much that you are willing to fight about it, go on. If not, stop it. I say, not just do less of it, or do it differently, but stop it entirely. That is what I mean. I have spoken."

*O. La Farge (1929), New York: Houghton Mifflin.*

### QARs:

### Right There

Where were both men taking their horses?
How was the man seated on his pony?
How did the man strike a casual pose?
What does Laughing Boy mean when he responds, "Let us not run around things"?

### Think and Search

Where does this casual chat take place?
What does "guessed at the dimensions of his soul" mean?
What does "You have not said anything but you have said too much" mean?
What is the main point of this conversation?
What group of people is represented in this passage?

### On My Own

What led to this "chat"?
How does Red Man respond to Laughing Boy?
Has anyone ever had a "chat" like this with me or have I ever heard one like this between two other people?
What happened?
What comparisons were there in these situations with the one between Laughing Boy and Red Man? How were they the same? How were they different?
What happens next? What do they say and what do they do?

*Gentile & McMillan (1991), pp. 77–78.*

(Nichols, 1983) and helps students focus on details (Ferguson & Kennedy, 1985). As such, it has long been held to be a basic means of helping students to set reconstructive purposes for reading (Cramer, 1978). However, Spears and Gambrell (1991) have theorized and proven that such tasks also influence constructive, or creative, reading and thinking.

Basically, the Spears and Gambrell (1991) study showed that prediction training of fourth-graders helped these students improve significantly more on both prediction tasks and composing tasks. They wrote stories that contained more story structure elements than students who were trained in a reread procedure. This was accomplished at no cost to reconstructive reading; the prediction group's free and aided recall was comparable to that of a "reread" method. The prediction strategy used in this study was Nichols' (1973) Prediction Guides.

## STEPS IN PREDICTION GUIDES

**Step 1**   The teacher prepares statements that relate to the story or passage to be read, but only some of which are actually contained in the story.

*Example:*

_____ *When Little Red Riding Hood was walking through the woods, she met a wolf.*

_____ *When Little Red Riding Hood was walking through the woods, she met a man on a horse.*

_____ *Little Red Riding Hood decided to go to town to buy a gift for her grandmother.*

_____ *The wolf seemed nice at first.*

**Step 2**   Students read the statements and check the ones they think will be answered by the text (prediction).

**Step 3**   After silent reading, students indicate and discuss which predictions were upheld by the text.

The next method builds creative reading by moving students smartly along from concrete to abstract levels of thinking. Abstraction permits information to be converted to ideas with which the brain is much more comfortable in arranging and rearranging.

## PROVERBS STUDY

A proverb is like a small book. It is the condensed wisdom of the ages. Efforts made to grasp and understand proverbs provide several far-reaching benefits. Skill in interpreting proverbs has been found to be significantly related to a number of language, thinking, and comprehension factors (Manzo & Casale, 1981). Because proverbs tend to be value-laden, they are an excellent medium for incidentally teaching evaluative thinking, for learning about children's concerns and values, and for helping them to understand the values and concerns of others. Proverbs study is useful with a broad range of students. It is appropriate for building higher-order thinking in youngsters who may fail to see the deeper meanings in literature and in everyday human experience. Here now is an adaptation of the original elementary classroom version of the Proverbs Mastery Paradigm (Manzo, 1981b; Manzo & Manzo, 1987b) for use in building abstract thinking through reading. Notice how it links class sessions one to another, as well as offering a "carry-out" and "carry-home" capability. Notice too how the same basic method can be used from kindergarten to adult levels.

## STEPS IN PROVERBS STUDY

Step 1    Present a proverb at the students' reading level and commensurate with age and grade development (see Box 9.5 for a starter list).

Step 2    Show and discuss with students how proverbs can have a literal meaning and a deeper, abstract meaning. Take, for example, "Look before you leap," and consider which translation is literal and which is abstract:

> *Watch before you step down.*
> *Do not act in haste.*

Step 3    Present a second proverb, and discuss its literal meaning; help students to *translate* it into their own words.

Step 4    Ask students to suggest a possible deeper, or more abstract meaning.

Step 5    Ask the students whether the proverb seems to relate to anything in their own experience, reading, or viewing (including movies and television).

Step 6    Discuss and help students to clarify any misconceptions or misunderstandings.

Step 7    Provide "carry-out": Post a proverb on the chalkboard or a bulletin board, or have students copy it on an index card to carry with them through the week. Tell students to watch for examples of the proverb's meaning at school, at home, and in their reading. You will be pleasantly surprised at how this weekly proverb serves as a magnet to draw insights out of everyday experience and reading.

For another interesting "carry-out" and "back-in" activity, consider this related suggestion from Renner and Carter (1991). Have students collect "*family* sayings" in the tradition of *Poor Richard's Almanac.* These need not be famous sayings. Then have them match a collection of *famous* and *family* sayings for similarities. The discussions about matches induce the kind of analysis and transformations that spur growth in abstract thinking, critical thinking, and schema.

Renner and Carter cast their advocacy of proverbs study in the larger multicultural context of folklore. "Folklore," they point out, "is concerned with recurring traditional beliefs such as art, customs, stories, songs, sayings, charms, speech, jokes, proverbs, and riddles" (1991, p. 602). Otte, Knafle, and Cramer (1990) note that *riddles* provide an especially good and cheerful medium for teaching inferential/abstract thinking: How do you say "hello" to a farmer? Answer: You say, "Hay you!"

There are many other variations and options on this basic read, translate, delve into, and discuss model for teaching proverbs. Most will arise naturally as teachers and students engage in comprehension-oriented instructional conversations (Goldenberg, 1992) that reference other proverbs and maxims that are similar and opposing.

The value of proverbs study reaches beyond reconstructive comprehension to constructive problem solving, or "social comprehension." This type of comprehension helps one to begin to build a rational "worldview," and a rich schema for

---

**BOX 9.5** **Sample Proverbs, Adages, and Quotations**

---

### CODING KEY

**Language Difficulty**
1. primary
2. intermediate
3. secondary
4. archaic or otherwise
   unusual language form

**Age Level Difficulty**
A. 5 to 7 years old
B. 8 to 12 years old
C. 13 to 16 years old
D. 17 to 21 years old
E. adult life

---

| Proverb (difficulty code): Meaning | Comparison Proverb (difficulty code) |
|---|---|
| HE WHO MAKES NO MISTAKES MAKES NOTHING. (1 D): The person who is afraid of making mistakes never does anything of value. | Same: A BURNED CHILD DREADS THE FIRE. (2C) |
| A MISS IS AS GOOD AS A MILE. (2 C): Failure by however little is still failure. | Opposite: OMELETS ARE NOT MADE WITHOUT BREAKING EGGS. (3 C) |
| MONEY BEGETS MONEY. (4 E): Money that's put to use generates more money | Opposite: A PENNY SAVED IS A PENNY EARNED. (2 B) |
| THE LOVE OF MONEY IS THE ROOT OF ALL EVIL. (2 D): People's drive to acquire money and things causes them to do evil things. | Same: POVERTY IS THE ROOT OF ALL EVIL. (2 E)  Same: MONEY IS A GOOD SERVANT BUT A BAD MASTER. (3 C) |
| REVENGE IS SWEET. (2 D): It feels good to get back at someone who has wronged you. | Opposite: TWO WRONGS DON'T MAKE A RIGHT (2 B) |
| THERE IS NO ROSE WITHOUT A THORN. (2 C): There is nothing good that doesn't have negative aspects as well. | Opposite: EVERY CLOUD HAS A SILVER LINING. (2 C) |

---

understanding the "universal truths" and wisdom found in longer books. The Proverbs Mastery Paradigm also can be adapted to assess reading comprehension, as you will see ahead in Chapter 12 on assessment.

## DIALOGICAL THINKING

Another important way to spur both critical and creative thinking is to teach a special kind of critical thinking. This form of thinking, which can be traced back to Socrates and ancient Greece, is enjoying a much-needed rediscovery. Contemporary writers are referring to it by both its ancient name, *dialectical thinking* (Manzo, Garber, & Warm, 1992), and a modern one called *dialogical thinking* (Commeyras, 1993; Paul, 1987). In this form of thinking, first a popular position is considered, then an opposing position is stated and considered, even if one must be made up. The class then works toward an alternative or inventive new position,

**BOX
9.5
cont'd**

| Proverb (difficulty code): Meaning | Comparison Proverb (difficulty code) |
| --- | --- |
| WHAT IS SAUCE FOR THE GOOSE IS SAUCE FOR THE GANDER. (4 A): What applies to one person applies equally to another. | Opposite: CIRCUMSTANCES ALTER CASES. (3D) |
| SILENCE GIVES CONSENT. (2 E): Have the courage of your convictions, or live with the consequences. | Opposite: THERE IS TIME TO SPEAK AND TIME TO BE SILENT. (2 D)<br>Opposite: SPEECH IS SILVER BUT SILENCE IS GOLDEN. (2 D)<br>Opposite: DISCRETION IS THE BETTER PART OF VALOR. (4 D) |
| SPARE THE ROD AND SPOIL THE CHILD. (1 A): Love means being critical, at times, of the ones you love. | Contrast: BOYS WILL BE BOYS. (1 A) |
| THREATENED FOLK LIVE LONG. (2 E): People who must struggle learn how to survive. | Same: A CREATIVE GATE HANGS LONG ON ITS HINGES. (2 E) |
| NEVER TROUBLE TROUBLE TILL TROUBLE TROUBLES YOU. (3 C): Don't spend your time imagining difficulties which may never come about. | Same: DO NOT CROSS THE BRIDGE TILL YOU COME TO IT. (2 C)<br>Opposite: PREVENTION IS BETTER THAN CURE. (2 C)<br>Opposite: FOREWARNED IS FOREARMED. (3 D) |
| IT IS BETTER TO WEAR OUT THAN TO RUST OUT. (1 C): It is better to act than to live in fear. | Opposite: A LIVING DOG IS BETTER THAN A DEAD LION. (1 C)<br>Opposite: IT'S BETTER TO BE SAFE THAN SORRY. (1 C) |
| WHERE THERE'S A WILL THERE'S A WAY. (2 C): If you are determined to do something, you will find a way to do it no matter how difficult this might be. | Same: NECESSITY IS THE MOTHER OF INVENTION. (2 C)<br>Opposite: WHAT CAN'T BE CURED MUST BE ENDURED. (3 D) |

usually somewhere between the two, but possibly one at an "extreme," if it makes the most sense.

This may seem to be difficult for children to do, but it can be introduced playfully through children's stories like "Little Red Riding Hood." The popular interpretation of this story is that Little Red Riding Hood is an innocent child, and that a sly and evil wolf tries to devour her. A contrary position might be that the wolf is innocent and never meant to harm her. To help get youngsters to engage in contrary thinking, remind children of Oscar, the contrarian grouch on "Sesame Street." Most children will remember his antics and have a better idea of how to start to be "critical." Be sure then to move them along to more *constructive* criticism by urging thoughtful new solutions. For example, one inventive interpretation of "Little Red Riding Hood" would be that the wolf is not *evil,* even though Little Red Riding Hood is innocent, but that he is hungry and might devour her because wolves do eat meat. Of course, there can be more than one *popular* position, *contrary* position, and *new* position suggested—and these can serve to make discussions even more lively and interesting. It is also important to clear up any *wrong* impressions children may have. For example, *National Geographic* and the Discover Channel on cable television remind us often that while wolves do eat meat, they do not seem to eat humans. In fact, they point out, there is not a single documented case of a person being eaten by wolves in North America.

Commeyras has designed a relatively simple procedure for teaching dialogical thinking through conventional reading/language arts lessons. She views Dialogical-Thinking Reading Lessons (D-TRL), described below, as a complement to other cognitively based approaches to reading instruction that teach readers to use reasoning and critical thinking to reconstruct and to construct meanings from text (Commeyras, 1993).

From a theoretical perspective, she sees D-TRLs as being consistent with the belief that effective language and thought patterns are internalized from conducive social interactions. Hence, she designed a lesson format that invites participation from all members of a class, including those identified as learning disabled.

**Dialogical-Thinking Reading Lessons**    There are two phases of D-TRLs, a *reading* phase and a *discussion* phase. The discussion phase consumes the most time, since it is the most important.

**Reading Phase**
1.  Select a story that is intriguing and lends itself to discussion from more than one perspective (see Box 9.6 for Commeyras' recommendations).
2.  Conduct a reading lesson that ensures that students understand the selection well enough to participate in the discussion phase. (To aid LD students, Commeyras had them silently read one page at a time, pausing to informally share understandings of the reconstructive portions of the story. She provided additional information on details and events that they missed.)

**Discussion Phase**
1.  Identify a central question that has two possible perspectives. Write the question on the chalkboard.
2.  Divide the board under the central question to reflect each side, or perspective (see Figure 9.2).
3.  To raise personal involvement, invite students to take one position or the other.
4.  Invite students to undertake an in-depth exploration of the story in search of reasons that can be classified on the board under the words "TRUTH" as true (T), false (F), or depends (D), and under the word "SUPPORTS" as relevant (Y) or not relevant (N).
5.  Accept all reasons given so that they can be evaluated for truth and relevancy; however, since students often will engage in "exploratory talk" (Barnes, 1976) before they are ready to say something meaningful, it is ok to ask some general questions like "Can you rephrase that?" without putting words in their mouths.

**Commeyras' Story Recommendations for Teaching D-TRLs**

| *Reading phase* | *Discussion phase* |
|---|---|
| 1) Nolan, M. S. (1978). *My daddy don't go to work.* Minneapolis, MN: Carolrhoda. | What should the daddy do?<br>(A) He should leave his family to go find work.<br>(B) He should stay with his family. |
| 2) Asimov, I. (1980). A boy's best friend. In *A hundred circling camps* (pp. 178–185). Oklahoma City, OK: Economy. | Did Jimmy make the right decision?<br>(A) Yes, he should keep Robutt.<br>(B) No, he should trade Robutt for a real Earth dog. |
| 3) Blos, J. W. (1987). *Old Henry.* New York: Morrow. | What should the mayor do about Henry?<br>(A) The mayor should ask Henry to return.<br>(B) The mayor should tell Henry to stay away. |
| 4) Olson, H. (1986). The sack of diamonds. In *Mystery sneakers* (pp. 138–144). Lexington, MA: Ginn. | Was the old woman foolish or wise?<br>(A) The old woman was foolish.<br>(B) The old woman was wise. |
| 5) Wilhelm, H. (1985). *I'll always love you.* NY: Scholastic. | Do you think the boy should have taken the neighbor's puppy?<br>(A) Yes<br>(B) No |
| 6) Litchfield, A. B. (1991). Making room for Uncle Joe. In *Crossroads* (pp. 23–33). Chicago: Harcourt Brace Jovanovich. | What should Uncle Joe do?<br>(A) Uncle Joe should stay with the family.<br>(B) Uncle Joe should move to the apartment. |
| 7) Lexau, J. M. (1971). *Me Day.* New York: Dial. | Did Rafer have a good birthday?<br>(A) Yes<br>(B) No |
| 8) Ludwig, L. (1991). The shoemaker's gift. In *Fanfares* (pp. 6–13). Chicago: Harcourt Brace Jovanovich. | Did the shoemaker do the right thing?<br>(A) Yes<br>(B) No |
| 9) Holmes, E. T. (1988). Amy's goose. In *On the horizon* (pp. 242–251). Needham, MA: Silver Burdett & Ginn | Do you think Amy made the right choice?<br>(A) Yes<br>(B) No |
| 10) Giff, P. R. (1991). Ronald Morgan goes to bat. In *Come one, come all.* Boston: Houghton Mifflin. | Would you have let Ronald play ball?<br>A) Yes, I would let Ronald play on my team.<br>B) No, I would not let Ronald play on my team. |

*From Commeyras, (1993), p. 494.*

6. Allow students the opportunity to say what they have come to believe as a result of the dialogical examination (*see* Figure 9.2 for a sample lesson with steps 1–6).

**FIGURE 9.2  Dialogical-Thinking Reading Lesson**

This lesson is based on Sheila Greenwald's (1972) *The Hot Day*, a story about some mischievous children who used Mr. Peretz's fan and their mother's talcum powder to keep cool on a very hot day. The children used the fan when Mr. Peretz, a boarder in their home, was supposed to be out for the day. Returning unexpectedly, he opened the door, looked, screamed, ran away, and never came back.

**Central Question**
**Why did Mr. Peretz run away and never come back?**

| Support (Y) (N) | Truth TFD | Side A | Side B | Truth TFD | Support (Y) (N) |
|---|---|---|---|---|---|
| | | He was scared. | He was angry. | | |
| Y | 1. He thought they were ghosts. | | | 1. Because children broke into his room and made it cold. | N |
| Y | 2. He thought a bomb went off. | | | 2. Because the children came into his room without permission. | Y |
| N | 3. The children yelled at him. | | | 3. Because the children wasted talcum powder. | N |

*Adapted from Commeyras, (1993).*

## Options and Alternatives

- *Writing:* As an alternative to talking through step 6, first have students write out their conclusions, and then share them.

- *Simplifying:* In early lessons, especially with primary school children, concentrate only on identifying reasons to support two hypothesized positions that you offer.

- *Release of Responsibility:* To eventually disengage the teacher as the sole discussion leader, divide the class into two groups, first to evaluate two positions that are *given,* then to generate hypotheses (possibly more than two), and finally to identify a possible central question on the selection they have read.

- *Diagnosing:* By taking note of students' initial positions, these can be compared to their conclusions following discussion. This will give you a sense of a student's willingness to change positions or withhold judgment in the face of compelling contrary evidence. Situations such as these, in our judgment, provide important anecdotal insights into students' willingness to be potentially *transformed* as well as *informed* by what they read and learn.

# WRITING TO PROMOTE READING, THINKING, AND SOCIAL–EMOTIONAL DEVELOPMENT

All writing is something of a plunge into the unknown; hence, it requires a certain degree of willingness to venture within. But this is only one of several other factors that tend to inhibit effective instruction in writing and thinking in American schools. The first is that it doesn't happen much, although there are many efforts under way to change this. Second is the problem of getting youngsters over the fear that they have "nothing to say." Third is the simple prerequisite of getting language and ideas flowing so that words and thoughts can begin to stimulate and excite one another. The fourth factor is the difficulty of getting young writers to critically review and edit their personal patterns of writing and thinking.

Getting youngsters to edit and review their own thinking is the aspect that tends to be least acknowledged and most poorly handled. This shortfall would be acceptable if the purpose of school was fully defined by the narrow meaning of the terms "reading" or "language arts," but it isn't. It is neither effective language nor art that constitute the schools' primary mission; rather, it is teaching and promoting clarity and purposeful thought. The craft of writing, while it can and should reach for some level of art, is secondary to the education of the mind. For this reason, this section is organized to promote effective *writing* and *thinking,* or what some have called languaging (Manzo & Manzo, 1990a; Postman & Weingartner, 1969), more so than just language. Languaging is the use of language to talk to oneself as well as to others; that is, to better mediate, clarify, and excite effective thinking. This can be fun, it can be cute, it can be colorful, but it also will always be difficult, simply because it requires a great deal of self-examination. There is a growing sense of the importance of this ingredient even among formerly strong advocates of writing for writing's sake. Hansen (1992), for example, writes of the need for "classrooms characterized by the *language of challenge*" (p. 100); that is, of the importance of imparting to children the inclination and ability to critique and to be critiqued (Manzo & Manzo, 1990a). However, she goes on to add, and we agree, that this element should increase in vitality and emphasis at the upper elementary levels. The primary grades clearly should be retained largely as the time for children to be enveloped in wonder and to be encouraged simply to feel, express, and become enamored of language and thought.

The remainder of this section is divided largely into the overlapping functions of using writing to improve reading, thinking, and social–emotional adjustment.

## WRITING TO STIMULATE READING

The demand for a writing component to any reading program now is an established part of the literature of the field. Writing also is a key facet of the whole language movement (Lamme, 1989). A summary of the reading–writing connection is paraphrased below, from Fitzgerald (1989).

### The Two-Way Relationship Between Reading and Writing

| Reading to Writing | Writing to Reading |
|---|---|
| • Reading increases the knowledge individuals have to write about. | • Writing clarifies understanding of subjects, making subsequent reading easier. |
| • Reading instills knowledge of linguistic patterns and forms. | • Writing helps one to read like a writer; hence, sparking insights into writer mechanisms, and enhancing comprehension. |
| • Reading builds vocabulary and familiarity with writercraft. | • Revision in writing, or making changes at the various points in the process, involves many of the same higher-order thinking strategies involved in critical reading. |

While a good deal of empirical evidence and logic supports the connection between reading and writing (Loban, 1963, 1964; Shanahan & Lomax, 1986), there is recognition that reading and writing also represent *some* "quite different patterns of cognitive behaviors" (Langer, 1986). Put another way, while one undoubtedly benefits from progress in the other, this is not the only or the greatest justification for teaching both. Rather, the justification for teaching writing along with reading is that together they contribute to the wholeness of an individual, or to total literacy. A *synergistic* outcome can be expected; that is, an educational outcome that is greater than the sum of the parts. It is rather like combining aerobic exercise with good diet. It doesn't merely produce one who is stronger and lighter, but stronger, lighter, and physically and potentially mentally healthier.

A study by Tierney and associates (1989) examined the nature of the thinking that students engaged in under a variety of treatments, such as reading with no writing; draft writing but no reading; and drafting, reading, and rewriting. Their findings provide solid support for the growing emphasis on writing across the curriculum. They found that students who wrote prior to reading tended to read more critically, and that whenever reading and writing were combined in any way, students generally were more thoughtful in their treatment of ideas than they were if they had only read or only written. This was especially evident in the changes students made in their drafts, such as additions, deletions, and fresh points of view (Tierney, Soter, O'Flahavan, & McGinley, 1989).

It is of further significance to note that prior research has demonstrated that different types of writing affect thinking in different ways (Applebee, 1986; Applebee et al., 1987; Copeland, 1987; Hayes, 1987). This finding is especially relevant to the improvement of higher-order thinking, as will be illustrated ahead.

To review, writing can be expected to advance reading and full literacy in the following ways:

- Writing activates the reader's background knowledge before reading (Langer & Applebee, 1986).
- Writing builds anticipation of story events (Short, 1986).

- Writing raises the reader's level of intellectual arousal and activity (Newell, 1984).
- Writing encourages meaningful comparisons of the reader's perspective with that of the writer (Penrose, 1988).
- Writing helps the student to begin to better appreciate the writer's craft, and therefore to think like a writer (Smith, 1984).
- Writing helps the reader to better formulate a "world view," or a personally examined perspective on key issues (Gentile & McMillan, 1990; Hayes, 1987).
- Writing builds critical reading, for the thought processes involved in revision in writing and critical reading are highly related (Colvin-Murphy, 1986; Ericson et al., 1987; Fitzgerald, 1989; Flower & Hayes, 1981).
- Writing builds metacognitive as well as cognitive abilities because writing forces deeper levels of introspection, analysis, and synthesis than any other mediational process (Duffy, Roehler, & Hermann, 1988; Flood & Lapp, 1987; Gentile & McMillan, 1991).
- Writing contributes to creativity, since every phase of it requires creative effort—from initial impressions, to attempts at expression, to the discoveries and changes that occur within each student, no matter what age, as she or he writes, revises, and edits.

### Guidelines for Teaching Writing

Hittleman (1984), in reviewing the literature on writing research, found support for guidelines which say that writing should be:

- Daily rather than infrequent
- Done for real audiences and purposes
- More student- than teacher-initiated
- Allotted sufficient time for stages of thought and editing to occur
- Set in a writing community environment
- Peer-guided, reviewed, and supported
- Done with an initial emphasis on "reacting and responding" to the intended message rather than on "proofreading and editing"

To these general points, four more can be added from the more recent literature and experience:

- Children must be carefully taught to accept and to give constructive criticism, especially during the revision process (Hansen, 1992; Hayes, 1989; Manzo & Manzo, 1990a; 1993).
- Students' writing improves most when responders (teachers or peers) end their comments with encouraging remarks: "Good work, I'm looking forward to your next draft" (Neubert & McNelis, 1990).
- Someone must read what children write. Reading and responding to children's writing helps them to grow in the sense of the uniqueness of their identities and the specialness of their work: "When you write something, it will be different from anyone else's anywhere in the world. Let me see what you have written."

- Children will write if they think they have something to say. Teach them to see the lessons in their own lives, artifacts, and relationships. Rice (1975) notes that children from poor families are not at a disadvantage because their environments lack objects with which to associate language, or because their experiences are droll—rather, they lack the kind of encouragement that imparts a sense that their experiences are worthy of account.

Good writing can transform pathos into tragedy, tragedy into humor, and a life of despair into one of dignity and challenge. Teaching children to tell their stories, and those of their families and friends, builds bridges from the less fortunate to the more fortunate. Most great stories were once small stories: from *Little House on the Prairie,* to *The Grapes of Wrath,* to *The Last Picture Show.* Most of the stories children love are simple and small. The traditional story "The Teeny Weeny Woman" (Modern Curriculum Press, 1987), for example, is about little more than an elderly woman who finds a bone, and her resistance to a tiny voice that keeps telling her to "Give me back my bone," until she shouts "Oh, take it!"—and that was the end of that.

The general guidelines for writing instruction can be applied in many ways. Several of these are described ahead. We shall begin with a basic design for writing instruction, called the Writing Process.

## THE WRITING PROCESS

The Writing Process essentially is a description of the stages that good writers tend to go through in producing a written piece—much as the Directed Reading Activity roughy parallels what a good reader does, moving from schema activation, to reading, to schema enhancement. The Writing Process is a straightforward master plan for teaching writing. As noted above, it also is an exercise in creative production.

### Prewriting: "Getting It Out"

In this phase the teacher helps students get ready to write by:

1. Raising motivation and interest
2. Encouraging students to select and/or explore a topic
3. Calling up relevant prior knowledge and experiences
4. Laying out the basic expectations for the final product
5. Assisting students in identifying an audience they can keep in mind to guide the form and character of the composition

### Drafting: "Getting It Down"

In this phase the student attempts to channel the simultaneous din of ideas, purposes, facts, personal feelings, and biases into the linearity of words and structure. This includes finding out what you really think and then whether you can, or dare, say it. Typically the teacher's role in this phase is to:

1. Help students express initial thoughts and ideas on paper.
2. Urge students to use prewriting notes and experiences.
3. Encourage the free flow of ideas, even where they seem to contradict one another.
4. Build personal conviction that learning and clear thinking are desirable and attainable goals.

### Revising: "Getting It Organized"

This is an evaluative phase that requires a good deal of introspection and willingness to critique oneself, to be critiqued, and to think like an editor when critiquing the work of others. In this phase the teacher's role is to:

1. Set up peer editing teams: students read and evaluate their partner's paper, using a revision checklist.
2. Encourage students to reorder, rewrite, and revise for fluency and coherence as suggested by their peer editor.
3. Guide discussions that clarify and thereby point to specific areas of composition that require rewriting.
4. Encourage redrafting as needed with an eye toward initial purpose and audience.
5. Help students to learn how well others have understood and interpreted their writing.

### Editing: "Getting It Right"

In this phase the composition is reviewed for correct mechanics such as spelling, grammatical usage, and punctuation. The teacher assists by:

1. Encouraging students to fine-tune their work
2. Noting common mechanical problems and providing class instruction in these areas
3. Providing an editing checklist for peer editing teams
4. Helping children to learn to write for different audiences

### Publishing: "Going Public"

In this phase children's writing is read by others as reinforcement for future writing. The teacher facilitates by:

1. Using methods that ensure that there will be readers for students' efforts
2. Offering opportunities for the work to serve as a foundation for reading, discussion, expression, or study
3. Offering evaluative feedback based on the guidelines for the assignment
4. Offering reactions from different perspectives that teach how to write for different audiences

While the Writing Process, like the DR–TA, provides an excellent master plan, it leaves a lot of "how-to" questions unanswered. The next topic answers these questions with some representative methods that were selected for their compatibility with the overall objective of the book: Teaching children to be well read, well spoken, clear headed, and socially and emotionally secure and responsible; i.e., *literate*.

## WRITING METHODS

### Dialogue Journals

When students record their thoughts in brief notes and teachers pause to write back their responses, a dialogue journal is created. Dialogue journals map into some of literacy's most prized objectives. They are "written conversations between two persons on a functional, continued basis, about topics of individual (and even mutual) interest" (Staton, 1980, p. 312).

Good readers tend to read as if they were wide-eyed and attentively listening; good writers also tend to write as listeners (Witty, 1985). Dialogue journals offer an on-going means for teachers and students to learn to write as naturally as youngsters learn to talk (Gambrell, 1985). Students also learn to think more clearly about what they are saying: Written language invites reconsideration, or editing and critical review (Reid, 1990). The presence of a written record of a student's thoughts, along with the opportunity given the teacher to be informed by as well as to further inform those thoughts, could serve equally well as a definition of both whole-language learning and diagnostic teaching, two ways of saying *simultaneous teaching and assessing*. Here are some accounts of how dialogue journals have been used to promote higher-order literacy.

- Wollman-Bonilla (1989), a teacher turned researcher, writes that her greatest awakening came when she realized that conventional writing assignments failed to tap the potential of writing to stimulate thinking. Abandoning structured assignments dealing with analysis of plot, author's technique, and the like, she simply invited students to use their journals to write whatever thoughts were triggered by what they read. Curiously, their written responses revealed greater depth than had been evident in previous assigned writings and oral responses to conventional questions.

- Isakson (1991) reports that students invited to exchange personal letters with her (a form of dialogue) found a way to express their interests and objections to certain stories and books. In this way they were motivated to read a great deal more.

- Gauthier (1991) showed that reciprocity can be naturally built into aspects of journal dialoging. He had teachers offer students opportunities to comment on their schoolwork. Invariably, they found statements from the students that directly influenced what they taught and how they taught it. Students, on the other hand, became increasingly aware of their own learning needs and ability to seek help.

- Bode (1989), an elementary and middle school principal, encouraged an entire staff of teachers to engage students in journal dialogues. The teachers learned simple and useful things from students. One teacher had a student point out that his class had been "doing" [studying] India for about a month and that now they were coming to hate it!

Dialogue journals have several of the most natural, interactive features of the most carefully thought through prescribed teaching strategies. They can be intimate, personal, empowering, and corrective. As previously noted, they can reveal the diagnostic needs of children, but they also can alert us to miscalculations that may creep into our teaching, such as the teacher (above) who didn't realize that he was taking theme study a bit too far. In such cases, it is important to "stay with the program" and permit our own sometimes delicate egos to learn from being "talked back" to.

To get journal writing started, it may be necessary to demonstrate it with some simple formats that may begin conversationally and then become part of written journal dialoging thereafter. H. Jackson Brown wrote a popular volume called *Life's Little Instruction Book* (1992). The book is based on the story starter "*What I've Learned . . .*" Brown says, for example, that he has learned that if you're in a motel, the side of the bed closest to the phone will be the lumpiest, so sleep at the farther side. We have enhanced his scheme by encouraging teachers to first use Brown's story starter to stimulate student writing (*I have learned that . . .* ), and then to write *back* questions to students like:

- How did you come to learn this?
- What do you wish others would learn?

There's no telling where these questions will go, but they will generate dialogue, and it often will be amusing, informative, and generative. See Boxes 9.7 and 9.8 for some examples.

### Imitative or Pattern Writing

It could be argued that the overlearning, or over-reliance on patterns is the single most stifling factor to creativity. Patterns invite clichés and predictable stories, with predictable outcomes. Nonetheless, patterns can further self-development when they are introduced in a timely way, offer encouragement to use and experiment with a medium, and are properly faded and replaced with less confining options. It is this way with reading, and so it is with writing.

Just as predictable books encourage reading by building a secure sense of linguistic and story redundant patterns, the same is possible in writing. Bohning (1991b), summarizing the work of other authors (Cramer, 1978; Townsend, 1989), put it this way: "Book instruction is using the writing pattern presented by an author and fitting one's ideas and responses into that pattern" (p. 17). Look ahead now for some nifty patterns that can lead to creativity more than to mere reproduction.

***ABC Book Imitations*** Developing readers and writers enjoy selecting and following a pattern to write simple ABC books as a whole class or in small groups. More advanced forms of ABC books can be used as a novel format to stimulate research and expository writing by older students. Start by collecting a variety of ABC books of appropriate types and sharing these with students. Bohning (1991a) describes four types of ABC books to look for:

> **BOX 9.7** **Dialogue Journal Exchange Between Jackie (5th grade) and Mr. Wilson**
>
> Mr. Wilson,
> i learned that stores always run out of whatever I seem to like.
> Jackie
>
> Jackie,
> I've noticed the same thing. What do you wish others would learn from this?
> Mr. Wilson
>
> Mr. Wilson,
> I wish store managers would learn that an empty space in the cereal section means they should order more of that kind of cereal.
> Jackie
>
> Jackie,
> Wouldn't it be fun to make up little notes saying that? I know a lot of places I'd like to put them.
> Mr. Wilson

- In a *Collection* ABC book, each letter is represented by a member of a category of animals, objects, or people. On each page an alphabet letter is printed in upper and lower case, along with a word representing the letter and an illustration (drawn or cut from a magazine). Bohning recommends: *An Alphabet of Animals,* (Wormell, 1990) and *Brian Wildsmith's ABC* (Wildsmith, 1963).

- A *Central Subject* ABC book is based on a topic, and tends to include more information than the simple collection format. This format can be used by older students to report information gained in a research project. Some examples include *Ashanti to Zulu: African Traditions* (Musgrove, 1976), *The Farm Alphabet Book* (Miller, 1981), *A Caribou Alphabet* (Owens, 1988).

- *Word Fun* ABC books are based on rhymes, alliteration, and other language-based patterns. Some sample books to stimulate student interest in this format include: *A My Name is Alice* (Bayer, 1984), *An ABC Bestiary* (Blackwell, 1989), and *The Guinea Pig ABC* (Duke, 1983).

- *Specials* is a final category of ABC books that have unusual formats such as lift-up pages or other extraordinary artwork, as in *The Most Amazing Hide-and-Seek Alphabet Book* (Crowther, 1977), *I Unpacked My Grandmother's Trunk* (Ramsey, 1983), *The Glorious ABC* (Eden, 1990), and *Anno's Alphabet* (Anno, 1975).

The teacher can assist the class, small groups, or individual students to produce an ABC by following these steps:

- Select a favorite ABC book as a model.
- Decide on the basic format for each page.

---

**BOX 9.8**

## Dialogue Journal Exchange Between Kristin (2nd grade) and Mrs. Price

Mrs. Price,
i learned that flees are badder than I thought.

Kristin
(June 1, 1993)

Kristin,
How did you learn that fleas are worse than you thought? You can tell me at recess, or write back.

Mrs. Price
(June 4, 1993)

Mrs. Price,
I learned it from letting our dog in the house and get on my dad's favorite chair.

Kristin
(June 5, 1993)

Kristin,
What do you wish your dad would learn from what happened?

Mrs. Price
(June 9, 1993)

Mrs. Price,
To not make Randy stay outside where the fleas are.

Kristin
(June 10, 1993)

Kristin,
Did you learn anything from this?

Mrs. Price
(June 14, 1993)

---

- Brainstorm words to use for each letter.
- Produce and edit a draft version.
- Create or assemble illustrations.

Employing this same basic format, teachers can show children more advanced patterns to induce creativity. Two of our favorites are "circle stories" and "By Definition."

***Circle Stories***   Circle stories, you will recall, capitalize on visual diagrams to guide students' comprehension, discussion, and the writing of their own stories (Jett-Simpson, 1981). This strategy follows a predictable pattern that students can learn to identify and duplicate. The main character starts at one location and, after a series of adventures, returns to the starting point. Stories like Sawyer's *Journey Cake Ho,* Gag's *Millions of Cats,* and Brown's *The Runaway Bunny* are examples of this circular pattern.

FIGURE
**9.3** **Circle Story Diagram**

In *The Runaway Bunny*, the baby rabbit playfully tests the limits of his mother's love by threatening to run away to all kinds of adventures, while his mother resourcefully assures him of how she would always be there to protect him. When he says he will run away and become a flower in a field, she says she will become a farmer, to water and care for him; when he would become a sailboat, she would become the wind to blow him safely home; when he would be an acrobat swinging through the air, she would be a tight-rope walker to catch him if he falls; and when he would be a little boy and run into the house, she would be the mother, there to welcome him home.

Based on Brown's The Runaway Bunny *(1942, rev. 1972) Harper & Row. Figure based on a design from the Wisconsin Department of Public Instruction, 1986*

To teach this strategy, draw a large circle on the board or butcher paper and divide it into as many pie-shaped parts as there are adventures in the chosen story. At the top of the circle a house is drawn to represent the beginning and ending of the character's journey, whether that place is "home," the cabin of the journey cake, or Mother Rabbit's lap.

Read the story aloud and have the class recall the story to decide what events should be pictured in the circle diagram. For example, Figure 9.3 below shows the sequence of imaginary adventures in *The Runaway Bunny.*

The circle story strategy can be extended for small-group work. Each group is given a story to diagram on large paper. Each student in every group is given a portion to illustrate in order to complete the whole diagram. Using large paper for this process allows students in each group to draw pictures simultaneously, an activity that motivates a great deal of oral language. Some students will want to label pictures while others may write descriptive sentences or even include written quotations for their character as the activity progresses. Sharing the finished products increases opportunities for language, reinforces the story pattern, and above all adds to the fun of reading and discussing.

Teachers will recognize the success of this strategy when students are offered the opportunity to use this pattern independently or in small groups to write their own original stories. Equally satisfying is the spontaneous recognition of the circle story pattern weeks later when a new book or a story is read.

**Writing from Less-Defined Patterns**  The next logical step in teaching children to be writers is to further reduce the structure of the pattern. To do this successfully, it is necessary to turn them over to a less explicit structure, such as the implicit routines and stories that are the structures in their own lives.

One of the ways that we have used this is by offering youngsters a theme that reaches into their experiences such as one we call, "Annoying Kid." This calls for youngsters to tell of incidents or behaviors that really seem to annoy and irritate others or just generally aggravate any already tense situation. When it is presented in a humorous vein, such as by allusion to the "Annoying Man" character from *Saturday Night Live,* youngsters follow in a similar pattern.

This theme has evoked wonderfully interesting, sometimes joyous, and always enlightening stories—everything from the sad to the perversely funny. There was one story of a child who, when he was "little," made his grandmother cry by calling her "cracked face," because she had age lines in her face. Another told of the annoying habit of one girl's brother, who always said that the kitchen "stinks," no matter what his mother was cooking.

In a similar vein, children then can be encouraged to talk and write about how they can help to correct such annoyances. This also proves to be a way to show children how they can become a constructive force in their homes immediately, and perhaps even later in teenage and adult life. Responses such as the following have been elicited from children when asked to solve annoyances:

- Kids shouldn't play with their trucks and cars in the kitchen while their mom is cooking.
- It's not nice to call your unmarried father's new girlfriend a "space queen."
- You should tell your little brother not to pick his nose and wipe it on the wallpaper.
- You should try not to whine about every little thing.

Of course, it's a long way from thought to action. Hence, talking and writing about "Annoying Kids" will not in itself correct such behaviors, but it is a solid way to have children think, say, and write about what they are doing and experiencing while considering consequences. As a further bonus, it can lay the foundation for addressing similar annoyances that occur in the classroom. It could appear too self-serving, even to children, for the teacher to go for this benefit right off, however. You may wish to note that "Annoying Kid," and a variation such as "Annoying Mom/Dad/Brother/Sister" or even, if you dare, "Annoying Teacher," seem to be particularly engaging themes for drawing reluctant students into the writing process.

The next few methods involve a good deal of higher-order thinking, but are focused a bit more on the craft aspects of creative writing. Toward the end of the chapter we will return to the creative reading–thinking–writing theme with activities that are explicitly addressed to the improvement of creative, inventive, and imaginative production.

### Teaching Creative Writing

The *most* important element in teaching craft is in providing a reason to be doing it that is authentic and engaging. The next method does this in a generally compelling manner.

**Language Shaping Paradigm (LSP)**    The Language Shaping Paradigm (Manzo, 1981) offers a framework for taking youngsters' writings public, treating them respectfully as something to be carefully read and comprehended, and then analyzed in terms of the language and writing craft techniques used. The LSP is similar to two other methods: Santeusanio's (1967) Read-And-Meet-the Author and Lamme's (1989) "Author's Chair."

### STEPS IN THE LANGUAGE SHAPING PARADIGM

Step 1    The teacher begins with a *stimulating topic for discussion* that can engage children's interest and eventually provide an authentic purpose for writing ("dreams" and "misdeeds," for example, are always discussion-provoking topics.)

Step 2    *Students write stories or themes* in the conventional way, or the teacher can write a student's dictated story. (See Charlie C's story of a "misdeed" in Figure 9.4.

Step 3    The teacher *selects a student story* or essay and revises and edits it jointly with the student-author, informing the student that his or her work was selected for the class to read and analyze. This teacher-assisted revision can be guided by simple *who, what, where, when, why* and *how* questions.

Step 4    The teacher, with the student's approval, prepares *comprehension questions* and language analysis and improvement exercises for the material.

Step 5    The teacher duplicates the story and exercises for the *group to read and discuss.* The student-author is urged to do a lot more listening than speaking during the initial discussion.

Step 6    The teacher then *invites the student-author to participate* more openly as the discussion moves from the comprehension check to the language

---

**FIGURE 9.4**    **Ralphie Eight the Dogs by Charles C.**

Ralphie is my friend from next door. He is my brother's grade and they play together alot to. Ralphies mother gave us a bag of gumy dogs. Before we could get them Ralphie eight them all. We were playing in a big box and didn't see him doing it.

While the class divided into groups to share their stories, the teacher selected Charles' for a quick one-to-one editing session. The quick edit eliminated most of the obvious spelling and grammatical errors. While Charles wrote his story on the front board, the teacher wrote these questions on the back board:

1. Who is the main character in Charles' story?
2. What was his misdeed?
3. Where were the other children when this happened?
4. Why didn't the writer's mother help?
5. Whose brother did the misdeed?
6. What would you have done if this had happened to you? (Following discussion, the teacher could ask Charlie what he did.)

For language improvement exercises, the teacher asked students to study the sequence of the story and say what they thought could be improved. They soon volunteered that telling about the boys playing in the box needed to be the first or second thing said, in order to get the setting for the story straight.

*Fourth grade, Nelson School, Kansas City, KS (1991).*

---

analysis and improvement exercises. This is the student-author's greatest learning opportunity in terms of writing, speaking, and learning to properly receive and benefit from constructive criticism.

Note that the Language Shaping Paradigm follows all the steps of the Writing Process, with particular emphasis on the "publishing" stage. The "publication" of a student's piece offers its own justification for some pretty straightforward editing and revision. It is a good time to correct the more glaring grammatical and logical inconsistencies that occur in most unedited works at any level.

The language-shaping exercises developed by the teacher in Step 5 can take many forms. Some examples are given below:

- Word choice. Select certain key words in the selection, and ask students to determine whether the word used, or another word, best communicates the intended meaning and effect.
- Improving style and mood. Select key phrases, and ask students to decide whether the phrase used, or another one, best communicates the intended style and mood.

- Rewriting. Select a short section of the selection, and ask students to rewrite it in a way that has greater impact on the reader.
- Reorganizing. Ask students to consider the selection as a whole and create a different organization by listing reordered events in abbreviated form.

Four additional thought-shaping exercise formats are described in more detail ahead.

- Sentence-Combining exercises
- Reducing/Expanding Sentences exercises
- Rewriting for Different Audiences
- Writing in Response to Reading

**Sentence Combining**   Sentence combining is an easy way to give students practice with the basic patterns of language. It does this by simply having them combine two or more simple sentences into one or more complex ones. Sentence combining improves both writing fluency (Combs, 1975; Green, 1972; Mellon, 1969; O'Hare, 1973; Perron, 1974) and reading comprehension (Machie, 1982; Obenchain, 1971; Stotsky, 1975; Straw & Schreiner, 1982). It can be used with students from primary grades through college to improve familiarity with written language patterns at increasing levels of linguistic complexity. Simple levels of sentence combining include insertion of modifiers, connecting subjects or predicates, or connecting two or more sentences in sequence:

**Insertion of Modifiers**
- She sat behind a table.
- The table was long.
- The table was wooden.
  
  [*She sat behind a long, wooden table.*]

**Connecting Subjects**
- Football is one of my two favorite sports.
- Baseball is one of my two favorite sports.
  
  [*Football and baseball are my two favorite sports.*]

**Connecting Predicates**
- Marvin topped the pizza dough with sauce and cheese.
- Marvin popped the pizza in the oven.
- Marvin waited hungrily for his dinner.
  
  [*Marvin topped the pizza dough with sauce and cheese, popped it into the oven, and waited for his dinner.*]

**Connecting Sentences in Sequence**
- I had lost my gloves.
- I did not worry about losing my gloves.
  
  [*I had lost my gloves, but I did not worry about it.*]

More complex sentence-combining exercises, for upper elementary and middle school, include inserting modifying clauses and phrases and combining a list of short sentences into a fluent paragraph.

**Insertion of Modifying Clauses and Phrases**

- My mother always worries about our being clean.
- My mother wants me to wash my hands three times a day!

  [*My mother, always worried about our being clean, wants me to wash my hands three times a day!*]

**Combination of a List of Short Sentences**

To create this type of exercise, "de-compose" a selection from a content textbook or an encyclopedia entry. The uncluttered sentence-by-sentence layout makes it possible to use much more challenging material than you otherwise might. The sentences below were used with a middle school class.

- Thomas Carlyle wrote about what makes a "great man."
- Thomas Carlyle had strong views on the divinity of heroes.
- It is hard to relate Thomas Carlyle's views to current thought.
- There is a basic difference between Thomas Carlyle's time and ours.
- Thomas Carlyle's ideas fit the mood of the Victorian era.
- In the Victorian era, men agreed on certain values.
- In the Victorian era, heroes could be measured by those principles.
- Today, things are different.
- Today, values are more a matter of individual choice.
- Today, heroes are more a matter of individual choice.
- Today, we each have our own heroes.

  [*Thomas Carlyle's strong views on the divinity of heroes are hard to relate to current thought. There is a basic difference between his time and ours. Carlyle's ideas fit the mood of the Victorian era, when men agreed on certain values and heroes could be measured by those principles. Today, things are different. Values and heroes are more a matter of individual choice. Today, we each have our own heroes.*]

Sentence-combining activity lends itself well to whole-class, small-group, or individual instruction. It is introduced by showing two sample sentences and demonstrating how they might be combined. After students have tried their hand at combining sentences, instruction should focus on how well and why different combinations work. As students discuss the exercises, they should be encouraged to use any grammatical labels they might know. The teacher can use this instructional conversation to introduce grammatical terms and conventions of language usage. In the first example above, the teacher might say, "This combination works well because the words 'long' and 'wooden' are both adjectives that tell us about the noun 'table.'" However, sentence combining can also be used to provide intensive instruction in language patterns and usage *without* the need to use the cumbersome terminology of traditional grammar. You will need to decide for yourself which is best for your situation.

**Reducing/Expanding Sentences**    Bill Martin, Jr., children's author and enthusiastic supporter of children's writing, suggests two variations on sentence combining for improving writing: Reducing Sentences and Expanding Sentences.

Reducing/Expanding Sentences is especially useful when done as a whole-class activity using samples from students' own writing. It concentrates attention on the main ideas of sentences and the subtle changes of meaning evoked by slight changes of words and punctuation. It also encourages *constructive* criticism.

At a more language-based level, the process of "reducing" and "expanding" sentences helps students figure out how sentences work. To *reduce* a sentence, the student underlines all words, phrases, and clauses that are unnecessary to the essential meaning of the sentence. The danger in reducing a sentence is that one is apt to alter or destroy subtleties of sentence meaning or the author's style of writing. Let's reduce a few sentences and analyze the results.

> Underline any words that can be removed and still keep the basic sense of the sentence.
>
> - A bird <u>also</u> has another way to <u>help</u> keep <u>himself</u> warm in winter.
> - By seeing to it that the birds <u>near your home</u> have plenty to eat, you can "keep <u>their furnaces roaring" and</u> their bodies warm in winter.
> - The bird's outer feathers <u>are staggered like shingles on a roof to</u> keep out the rain and snow.
>
> From "How Birds Keep Warm in Winter," *Sounds of Mystery.*

> Discussion: In the first sentence, the reducing sharpened the sentence. The eliminated (underlined) words are truly unnecessary. In the second sentence, the meaning is preserved but the charm seems to suffer. In the third sentence, the basic sentence is unchanged, but an important detail is left out.
>
> Source: Bill Martin, Jr., lecture, Kansas City, Missouri (July 1985).

Expanding Sentences is done by providing students with kernel sentences, such as the examples below.

- *The children heard a noise.*
- *They ran to the window.*
- *They could hardly believe their eyes.*

Students are encouraged to add elaborative words and phrases to each sentence, and/or to connect these into a continuous narrative. This activity also lends itself well to whole-class, cooperative learning groups, or individual work.

**Mood and Audience**    One of the most sophisticated ideas in creative writing is in how to establish and sustain a mood appropriate to the piece. Initially, students will expect the teacher to always opt for the more formal way of saying things in print. The best way to teach the relationship between phrasing and mood is to select a piece that is written in a humorous vein. Then select a paragraph to edit as a group. Students' initial decisions will be to go for "correct" phrasing, but they soon will realize that this often can dull a snappy line or alter a humorous piece. For example, when reviewing "Version A," below, students might initially suggest changes of the type shown in "Version B," which is more "correct" but less authentic:

> Version A: "Mom," Sally yelled, "what's my weird brother doing in the tub with all his clothes on?"

> Version B: "Mother," cried Sally, "why is Jonathan in the bath with his clothing on?"

A good guidance is to see whether the more "correct" language alters the credibility of the characters. Listen for statements from children like, 'A bunch of kids wouldn't talk that way."

An equally important and corresponding idea is that of *audience*—or whom you're writing to. To teach both mood and audience simultaneously, have students write pieces as if they are going to be read by different types of individuals (a friend, a teacher, a neighbor) or for different purposes (a grocery list, a thank-you note, a letter of complaint). Note differences in wording, punctuation, sentence length, etc. Start with a situation such as: "You have observed an accident between two cars. Describe what happened."

| In a police report: | "The car coming south on Montrose Avenue struck and collided with the car headed east on Troost Street." |
|---|---|
| A child telling parents: | "I saw two cars crash on Montrose Avenue today." |
| A child telling children: | "You won't believe what I saw today. Mrs. Ratter smashed into some old guy in a van on Montrose!" |

**Guided Reading and Summarizing Procedure (GRASP)**   For teaching formal composition, Eanet (1983) and Hayes (1989) have independently designed methodologies that expand the Guided Reading Procedure (GRP) into a method for teaching writing from reading.

Eanet's idea, called DeComposition, uses GRP to teach students how textual material is composed. The steps of the GRP then are inverted to "de-compose," or break the material into component parts (see the example in Box 9.9 p. 356). Then students are asked to use their notes to "recompose" the text in their own words. Hayes' Guided Reading And Summarizing Procedure (GRASP) also begins with the textual analysis of the recall material recorded and organized into an outline on the board, as required in the Guided Reading Procedure. Students then use their outline as the basis for composing their *summaries* of the material. The strategy described below is a combination of Eanet's and Hayes' methods. Note that Step 5, while optional, raises the activity to a higher level of critical/creative reading and writing.

---

**BOX 9.9**    **De-Composing and Summarizing**

*Original Text:*

Evidence continues to grow that some mountainous areas, such as the region where Noah's Ark is said to have settled, were under the sea at one time. The remains of ocean fish and plant life can be found in the rock layers far above sea level. The thing that remains unclear is whether the waters rose from heavy rains, or from melting polar ice caps. It is even said that the rock forming these mountains may have been pushed up from the ocean floor.

*De-Composing:*
- Some mountains were once under the sea.
- The area where Noah's Ark is said to have settled is one of these mountainous areas.
- Remains of ocean fish and plants can be found in the rocks.
- Heavy rain and melting ice caps from the poles may have covered these areas.
- The rock now forming mountains may have been pushed up from the ocean.

*Re-Composing:*

Some mountains were once covered by water. Sea life found in the rock of these mountains proves this. The water may have come from rain or from melting polar ice caps. Another explanation is that the rock that forms these mountains was pushed up from the ocean floor.

*Reaction:*

I don't think the mountains rose up from the sea. How is that possible? I'm going to ask our science teacher.

---

## STEPS IN MODIFIED GRASP

Step 1    *GRP lesson.* The teacher conducts a conventional Guided Reading Procedure lesson up through the outlining step.

Step 2    *Decomposing.* The teacher asks students, "Can you describe how the author put this information together?"

Step 3    *Recomposing.* The teacher asks the class, "Can you think of other ways that this could have been written or organized?"

Step 4    *Summarizing.* The teacher has students write their own summaries, following these guidelines:

   a. Include only important information (leave out unimportant details).
   b. Where possible, compress information by combining it.
   c. Add any information, questions, or comments as needed to avoid "loose ends" and to achieve coherence. Hayes suggests that the teacher demonstrate how the first cluster of information can be written into a single sentence, explaining why certain information is omitted and why other information can be combined. Then students are directed to write the next sentence while the teacher does the same on

an overhead transparency (not displayed at this time). Students then compare their sentences with each others' and with the teacher's (now shown on the overhead). The teacher should be prepared to revise his or her sentence, writing changes above or below the original sentence to leave a visible record of the revision process. Students then work individually (or in pairs) to compose additional sentences to complete the summary.

Step 5 (Optional) the teacher encourages students to write a brief reaction to the material read, recalled, outlined, decomposed, and then summarized.

The next method further helps students to reap critical and creative ideas in response to text. The method can be extended to become a system that reaches far beyond the classroom to building a literate environment that can be most conducive to critical and creative reading, writing, and thinking.

### REAP: A Reading and Responding Strategy

Read–Encode–Annotate–Ponder, or REAP (Eanet & Manzo, 1976), uses writing as a means of promoting deeper thinking and reading. REAP is a way to teach children a variety of possible ways to write in response to reading. As such, it offers them both options and individual control over how they might respond to text. The basic REAP procedure is summarized by its title:

| | |
|---|---|
| **R**ead | to get the writer's basic message |
| **E**ncode | to translate the message into your own words |
| **A**nnotate | the message by writing a response in one of several possible forms |
| **P**onder | what you have read and written, by yourself and then by sharing and discussing it with others |

Students are introduced to several different annotations, or ways to write in reponse to text. Eleven response forms are described in Box 9.10. A sample passage is annotated in these ways in Box 9.11.

**How to Teach REAP** Each response form can be taught using the basic paradigm below. To begin, collect several short, interesting selections at the independent reading level of most students in the class. These same selections can be used, over a period of time, to teach the other response forms. The example below illustrates teaching of the *critical* response. Like tying a bow, these may seem quite difficult when described in step-by-step fashion. However, the parts are logically linked, and so will feel more natural in the doing than in the describing.

### STEPS IN TEACHING REAP

Step 1 *Feeling.* Students read or listen to a selection. They are encouraged to express their initial, "gut level" responses to the piece. If the teacher wishes, this can be structured by having students record their responses on a scale such as shown below:

| BOX 9.10 | **REAP Annotation Types** |
| --- | --- |

*Reconstructive Responses*

1. *Summary response.* States the basic message of the selection in brief form. In fiction, it is the basic story line; in nonfiction, it is a simple statement of the main ideas.

2. *Telegram response.* Briefly states the author's basic idea or theme, with all unnecessary words removed. The result is a crisp, telegram-like message.

3. *Poking response.* Restates a snappy portion of the selection that makes the reader want to respond. It is best to use the author's own words.

4. *Question response.* Turns the main point of the story or information into a question that the selection answers.

*Constructive Responses*

5. *Personal view response.* Answers the question "How do your views and feelings compare with what the author said?"

6. *Critical response.* Supports, rejects, or questions the main idea, and tells why. The first sentence of this type of response should restate the author's position. The next sentence should state the responder's position. Additional sentences should explain how the two differ.

7. *Contrary response.* Attempts to state a contrary position, even if it is not one that the student necessarily thinks or feels. As with the previous form, this one lays the foundation for improving dialogical/dialectical thinking, which in turn improves creative reading and writing.

8. *Intention response.* States and briefly explains what the responder thinks is the author's intention, plan, and purpose in writing the selection. This is a special version of the critical response that causes the reader/responder to try to think like the author.

9. *Motivation response.* States what may have caused the author to create or write the story or selection. This is another special version of critical responding. It causes the reader/responder to do even more than think like the author, and attempt to feel what the author may have felt or experienced.

10. *Discovery response.* States one or more practical questions that need to be answered before the story or facts can be judged. This type of response to text is the mode of thinking that leads to lifelong reading and learning.

11. *Creative annotation.* Suggests different and perhaps better solutions or views. (Children usually need a question or two to get their "creative juices" flowing to produce this type of response.)

| *Directions:* | *Circle the number closest to your feelings about what you have just read (heard):* | | | | | |
| --- | --- | --- | --- | --- | --- | --- |
| *A. Boring* | | | | | | *Interesting* |
| *1* | *2* | *3* | *4* | *5* | *6* | *7* |
| *B. Cold* | | | | | | *Hot* |
| *1* | *2* | *3* | *4* | *5* | *6* | *7* |
| *C. Stale* | | | | | | *Fresh* |
| *1* | *2* | *3* | *4* | *5* | *6* | *7* |

**Step 2** *Expressing.* Students attempt to explain their feelings about the piece in twenty-five words or less.

**BOX 9.11**

## Sample REAP Responses-to-Text

*Selection:*

"Travelers and the Plane-Tree"

Two travelers were walking along a bare and dusty road in the heat of a mid-summer's day. Coming upon a large shade tree, they happily stopped to shelter themselves from the burning sun in the shade of its spreading branches. While they rested, looking up into the tree, one of them said to his companion, "What a useless tree this is! It makes no flowers and bears no fruit. Of what use is it to anyone?" The tree itself replied indignantly, "You ungrateful people! You take shelter under me from the scorching sun, and then, in the very act of enjoying the cool shade of my leaves, you abuse me and call me good for nothing!"

*Adapted from* Aesop's Fables *(1912). New York: Avenel Books.*

### Reconstructive annotations:

1. *Summary response*
   Travelers take shelter from the sun under a large tree. They criticize the tree for not making flowers or fruit. The tree speaks, and tells them that they are ungrateful people for taking shelter under her leaves and then criticizing her.

3. *Telegram response*
   Travelers stop for rest and shade under big tree. Travelers say tree is useless. Tree tells them off.

2. *Poking response*
   In this story, a tree talks back to people. The tree says, "You ungrateful people! You come and take shelter under me . . . and then . . . abuse me and call me nothing!"

4. *Question response*
   What if the things we use could talk back?

### Constructive Annotations

5. *Personal view response*
   a. We use resources like coal without thinking. Then we criticize the resource for damaging our lungs and dirtying our air.
   b. I guess kids sometimes use their parents the way the travelers used the tree, and then criticize them without thinking about their feelings.

6. *Critical response*
   Not every word spoken in criticism is meant that way. The travelers were just grumpy from the trip. The tree is too sensitive.

7. *Contrary response*
   The travelers could be right, a better tree could produce something and also give shade.

8. *Intention response*
   The author wants us to be more sensitive to the people and things we depend on—especially those we see and use often.

9. *Motivation response*
   It sounds like the author may have felt used, after having a bad experience with friends or family.

**BOX 9.11 cont'd** **Sample REAP Responses-to-Text**

10. *Discovery response*

I wonder how many of us know when we are being "users." We could take an anonymous poll to see how many class members secretly feel that they have been used and how many see themselves as users.

11. *Creative response*

a. This fable reminds me of how Dobie Gillis uses and then abuses that nice, but plain girl who always hangs around him.

b. This fable made me think that teachers are sometimes used unfairly. They give us so much, and then we put them down if they make little mistakes. They're only human.

c. We should put this fable on the bulletin board where it will remind us not to be ungrateful "users."

d. How would you re-title this fable if you were writing it? I'd call it "Travelers in the *Dark*," to show that we go through life without knowing how many small "gifts" come to us along our way.

**Step 3** *Sighting the Objective.* The teacher provides students with a well-written example of a critical response (see example ahead) and asks them how it is like, or about, what they have read.

**Step 4** *Selecting.* Students read a second selection. This time the teacher shows three or four critical responses to the selection: One of the sample responses should be a good critical response, and the others should each be faulty in some way—too emotional, too narrow, not directly related to the idea(s) in the selection, and/or lacking sufficient support. Students discuss the sample responses and choose the best one. They are asked to defend their choice and explain why the others are unsatisfactory.

**Step 5** *Modeling Response Writing.* Students read a third selection. This time, the teacher "thinks aloud" to show students how to write a critical response to text. This involves showing students how to draft initial thoughts, and then reorganize and rewrite these as necessary to compose an honestly felt but balanced statement.

**Step 6** *Practicing.* Students read a fourth selection and individually try writing their own critical response. A few of the students' productions are duplicated or put on the chalkboard and then discussed and evaluated by the teacher and class.

**Step 7** *Sequencing.* Once students have tried their hand at writing a few critical responses, the teacher introduces another form of response to text.

**Step 8** *Reinforcing Dialogue.* The teacher has students exchange their brief responses and try to write in response to one another's work. At this point the teacher should introduce the idea of letters to the editor from newspapers and magazines as examples of dialogue centered on issues and text, and as print models of effective writing from which students can learn incidentally each time they read a newspaper or magazine.

The response types listed and described in Box 9.10 are roughly in order of difficulty: lower numbers tend to indicate more reconstructive and literal level thinking, and higher numbers more constructive and sophisticated patterns of responding. It is not necessary, however, for a student to master the "lower-level" response types before attempting "higher-level" ones.

A good index of a student's general level of literacy development can be inferred by noting the kind of response he or she tends to prefer and to construct. Students can be asked to select and save their best written responses for review at a later time. This is an excellent way to show progress in writing and thinking (see the chapter on assessment for details on organizing and evaluating student Assessment Portfolios).

REAP is based on four simple propositions: (1) students need a conceptual grasp of what it *means* to think more deeply, constructively, and creatively before they can do it; (2) students need a classroom environment that is "safe" enough to risk deep thinking; (3) students learn from each other when they share their responses to text; and (4) students need to be *challenged* to exert the extra mental energy necessary to engage in a higher-order task before they are likely to commit to ratcheting-up the few notches necessary to do so. Hayes (1987) demonstrated the soundness of the latter point by asking students to engage in a variety of writing tasks from literal to higher-order levels—paraphrasing, formulating questions, and developing compare-and-contrast statements. As he had hypothesized, students asked to do higher-order tasks, such as writing questions and compare-and-contrast statements, had better recall of what they had read. More importantly, these students recalled more of the abstract and structuring information from what they read. Hayes concluded that the greater level of challenge resulted in greater and more profound levels of integration of text information with learner knowledge. In other words, the demand of the writing task itself can result in higher levels of *constructive* thinking and reading, or—ask for it, and you just might get it!

See the last chapter on classroom and schoolwide literacy programs for an interesting way to convert individual student text responding into an exchange reading program. Read now about how to promote imaginative writing, largely by asking for it.

### Reading and Writing Poetry—For the Imagination

Poems are beautiful ways of saying "come use your imagination." The reflective teacher will collect poems for different occasions and different developmental stages of learning. You might recall from Chapter 3, for example, that primary grade children prefer poems that are rich in rhythm, rhyme, humor, and straightforward language and that do *not* contain visual imagery or figurative language. Three collections recommended by Galda and West (1993) are especially suitable for moving children to the higher grounds of imaginative thinking and writing. One is *Always Wondering* (1991), a collection of the favorite poems of Aileen Fisher, a former winner of an excellence in poetry award from the National Council of Teachers of English (1978). Another, by Esbensen (1992), is called *Who Shrank*

*My Grandmother's House? Poems of Discovery.* This collection takes a childlike perspective of ordinary phenomena such as doors, clouds, and pencils, to show primary and intermediate grade children that there are discoveries to be made every day and all around us. For upper grade readers, the teacher can turn to Cohn Livingston's (1992) *I Never Told and Other Poems.* This collection presents her unusual perspective on common events such as a flock of geese flying overhead and nighttime rainfall. Like Esbensen's book, *I Never Told* inspires readers to look and look again at the world around them (Galda & West, 1993).

Poetry reading leads naturally to poetry writing, a topic on which Comstock's pioneering research gives valuable insight. Comstock (1992) undertook a study of children's poetic creativity by first studying the literature and then carefully observing and interacting with children writing poetry to see what she could learn. Remarking on the creative impulse to write poetry, she noted these things that her research made clear:

- "Almost all poets credit the legacy of other poets who preceded them and the support of an existing poetic community of which they are a part" (p. 261).

- Accomplished poets often felt that their "beliefs in themselves as poets seemed to spring from, or at least coincide with, the invitation to write" (p. 264).

- Once children begin to compose, it is easy to take up the technical elements of poetry, such as fluidity, alliteration, juxtaposition of images, and so on.

It should be noted that Comstock worked largely with a volunteer group that no boys elected to join. Nonetheless, this was a place to start. Of course, the classroom teacher has the obligation to involve all youngsters in the process. For that reason, you will be interested in the following strategy. Its structure parallels Comstock's findings but also attempts to fold in some inducements for fuller participation from all students.

**Communal Poetry**    Communal Poetry (Manzo & Martin, 1974) enables students to better understand and relate to poetry as an option for expression. It serves as a useful means of gaining access to youngsters' feelings, thoughts, and experiences, and a valuable heuristic for helping children to self-discover the inner workings of the constructive/creative processes involved in poetic expression. It also is a collaborative task that can build memorable bonds among a group.

### STEPS IN COMMUNAL POETRY

**Step 1**    Select a topic that students know well, or for which preparation is given (see Notes on Readiness ahead).

**Step 2**    Read and discuss other poems on the topic (save some of these to read and discuss following the creative effort as well).

**Step 3**    Ask the class questions designed to evoke fresh language, personal experiences, and sensory responses to the topic. Record students' responses on the chalkboard. Clichés and hackneyed phrases may be edited as they occur, or accepted in unedited form to keep the language flowing. (Follow your instincts here.)

Step 4 Once the board is filled with "raw material," ask students to carefully select a beginning line for the poem from the material on the board.

Step 5 Copy the first line, and help students to select other phrases to follow. In doing so, guide the group through decisions about establishing rhythm, rhyme, continuity of meaning, etc.

Step 6 Read the drafted poem aloud, and ask students to consider whether there is additional raw material left out that they want to add, or whether other changes need to be made. Make changes as students indicate.

Step 7 Prepare a final version, with the names of student participants, and distribute copies to the class.

Step 8 (Optional) Read additional published poems on the topic and have students compare these with their own poem. This can be a valuable step. It improves comprehension of poetry, and heightens students' awareness of their own thought processes, of their increasing control of language, and of their ability to express themselves artfully.

**Notes on Readiness**    Once a topic has been selected, the teacher decides how much preparation students will need. There ar two types of readiness to consider.

**Conceptual Readiness**    If the topic lends itself to unit study, the teacher may wish to spend several days exploring related literature and poems with the class. This conceptual readiness helps students to discover that their own experiences and thoughts often resemble those expressed in the poems and stories published in books. It also enriches their general fund of information and cultural literacy. One third-grade class explored the topic of "school humor." In preparation, the teacher read a variety of poems that were rather irreverent, such as David Etter's "As You Travel, Ask Us." In response, the third-graders, who had been harboring some "special" feelings for Miss Moore, their lunchroom supervisor, produced "Ronald":

*Ronald*
Ronald took his fork,
and went wump
to Miss Moore
right in the rear end.
The fork got bent.
Three cheers for Ronald!
(Hurrah!!!)

**Perceptual Readiness**    Help students to discover and create the fresh language and captivating images that are the raw material of poetry by challenging them to look at the topic from some intentionally divergent points of view. Here are four types of questions for enhancing students' perceptual readiness:

- Questions that have students look at the topic from another perspective, such as:

*Pretend you are a puppy, and describe what autumn means to you.*

*Pretend you are a grandmother, and tell what autumn means to you.*

- Questions that personalize in an inanimate topic, such as:

*What kind of costume does autumn wear?*

*If autumn came in the door, what would it look like?*

*If autumn were a person, how would it walk? What would it say?*

- Questions that connect to ordinary events, such as:

*What games and events are popular in autumn?*

*What might you be doing during this time of the year? Your brother/sister? Your mother/father?*

- Questions that evoke sensory responses, such as:

*Pretend you have a metal bucket over your head and are walking outdoors in autumn.*

*What do you hear? smell? touch?*

*Pick one object that represents autumn. What does it look like? smell like? feel like?*

For a simpler format, try a "sense poem" (Jones, 1985). These can be done individually as well as communally. Here is a pattern for a sense poem:

| | |
|---|---|
| Line 1 | Tell the color of the subject. |
| Line 2 | Tell what it sounds like. |
| Line 3 | Tell what it tastes like. |
| Line 4 | Tell what it smells like. |
| Line 5 | Tell what it looks like. |
| Line 6 | Tell how it makes you feel. |

Here is a communal poem written by sixth-graders:

*Basketball*

Basketball is neon green.

It sounds like thunder.

It tastes like sweat.

It smells like new sneakers.

It looks like popcorn popping.

It makes you feel like

jumping,

shouting,

hollering,

hyperventilating,

*exploding!*

To maximize the effects of this activity on comprehension, appreciation, and the writing of poetry, invite a local writer to lead the communal poem. While our experience shows that even the most unpoetic of us can lead a group, when we have used real poets, it always resulted in better poetry—even when they weren't as patient or nurturing as a teacher might be.

See further ahead for how to use writing in a more direct way to build other aspects of creative thinking. First, we will look at the possibilities inherent in teaching creative thinking in a rather explicit manner.

# HEAD-ON APPROACHES TO TEACHING THINKING

In addition to the methods that have been described for teaching critical and creative thinking *through* reading and writing, there is a good deal of support for the idea that teaching thinking strategies *directly* has beneficial effects on both reading and writing. Haggard's study (1976), described in the beginning of this chapter, found that remedial readers made significantly more improvement in *reading* when their instructional sessions were begun with a 15-minute creative thinking activity. Following are several examples of these Creative Thinking-Reading Activities (CT–RAs), as she came to call them, followed by Haggard-Ruddell's lesson design for using CT-RA's in reading and language arts lessons.

## CREATIVE THINKING–READING ACTIVITIES (CT–RAs)

### Sample Creative Thinking–Reading Activities

**Word Creation**   Language is constantly changing. To help students be participants in our living language, provide exercises such as the following, provided by one of our favorite teachers, Maria Manzo Wiesner:

- Define the word "squallizmotex"—explain how your definition fits the word.
- If dried grapes are called raisins, and dried beef is called beef jerky, what would you call these items if they were dried: lemons, pineapple, watermelon, chicken.

**Unusual Uses**   Have students try to think of as many unusual uses as they can for common objects. Objects may vary from "a red brick" to "used toys." Ask students to identify objects that challenge inventive thinking. Here are a few that kids have brought to class:

- old tennis balls, handballs, racquetballs
- soda bottles
- old 8-track cassette tapes

As you can see, this activity can easily be tied to a unit on recycling. Weekly magazines often carry stories of how something is being recycled in a clever way. One recent article told the fascinating story of how the rubber from old tires is being used to make the very asphalt road beds that ate them up in the first place.

**Circumstances and Consequences**   What would happen if . . .

- school was on weekends and not during the week?
- water stuck like glue?

- all babies looked alike at birth?
- there were no colors?

This type of CR–TA can be made quite sophisticated by upping the caliber of the "ifs" to things like:

- we all had identical genetic makeup
- everyone would vote on every issue that now is decided by representatives to Congress

**Rational Problem Solving**   These are questions and problems to which young-sters ought to be able to deduce answers using their current levels of knowledge and experience. The activity can also be conducted so as to encourage further study by permitting students to ask three informational questions of the teacher, or to search in reference books. Examples of problems or questions that can be solved by ratio-nal thinking would be as follows:

- Is it possible for someone to fly the way Superman does?
- Can there really be mermaids?
- Why do scientists say that it probably isn't possible to go faster than the speed of light?

**Product Improvements**   These *questions* require as much or more imagination than do the answers. They are best used to set the stage for the last two activities that basically ask, "What is broken?" Here are some sample product questions:

- How could school desks be improved?
- How could living room furniture be improved to provide better storage and even exercise while we watch television?
- How might tables be designed so children would be less likely to spill and drop things?
- How can we better equip book-carrying bags to handle lunches and other needs that you can think of?

**Problem Identification**   What's the problem? What doesn't work? What's needed? These questions lead to creative thinking. When asked these challenging questions, fifth-graders identified problems that included the following:

- Some way to keep water pressure up when I turn on a faucet when Dad is in the shower
- A place to put toys and stuff in your house
- A way to always know what our homework is
- A quick way to find out how to check your spelling when you are writing

**Systems and Social Improvements**   The major breakthroughs in world order, peace and sanity are the result of the creative vision of a few individuals who have pictured social and systems changes such as democratic government, the post office, better teaching methods, and medical procedures. However, there is little incentive provided for this type of thinking. To encourage such thinking, pose prob-lems and reward plausible solutions to questions such as:

- How can we get ourselves to be as courteous to people who aren't attractive as we are to people we think of as pretty?
- List some ways you can think of to tell someone that they have bad-smelling breath, other than saying "your breath smells."
- How can we help people who are not very bright, or are less able due to aging, to meet the complex obligations of modern life? (give some examples by category, such as owning a car: renewing a driver's license, getting car insurance, getting license plates and safety inspections for a car).
- How can schools be made more fun without hurting learning?
- List some "pet peeves" and use these to think about other social, or people, problems that need to be solved.

### Making the Thinking–Reading Connection

The most popular sequence for using CT–RAs has been these four steps suggested by Haggard (1976):

1. *Pose a stimulating question* (such as those listed above).
2. *Brainstorm.* Initial responses should be generated in small groups, following standard brainstorming ground rules: *all* responses are permitted, without criticism; as many ideas as possible are to be listed; unusual, even "wild" ideas are encouraged; and new ideas can be formed by combining ideas already mentioned.
3. *Compare Ideas.* After brainstorming, each small group should share their ideas with the class for review and evaluation. Students may wish to choose the "funniest" or the "wildest" response generated by each small group. At this point also, ideas are assessed for "reasonableness," or practicality. It is important to point out that all creative solutions are at best just "possibles" until tried and proven.
4. *Transfer to Reading.* The whole point of reading and thinking is to transfer new knowledge and power to solving life problems. This is most likely to occur when real problems are allowed to surface and drive reading and thinking. However, this same mindset can be used to drive reading so that it connects to the creative thinking activities:

"Maggie Magpie was determined to never read or write in cursive. We know that she eventually came to like it, but what might the teacher have done to help her sooner?"

"Before we find out how Huck saved Jim, think of all the possible ways for him to do so" (Haggard, 1980, p. 2).

"Remember our CT-RA on new inventions? What new invention (or system) could you come up with that would change the end of this story?" (Haggard, 1979, p. 2)

After reading *Liang and the Magic Paintbrush:* "What would you paint if you had a magic paintbrush and whatever you painted would then come to life?" (Gross, 1990)

Collins (1991) offers several other transfer activities similar to those above. One of these methods is especially relevant here. Students were taught to ask certain clarifying questions of material presented to them in oral or textual form. Seven questions were stressed:

1. Could you give me an example?
2. What do you mean by _____?
3. What is *not* an example, but similar to the idea that you are describing?
4. Is this what you mean: _____?
5. Would you say more about _____?
6. Why do you believe (feel or think) that _____?
7. What is the main point?

Collins provided a context for these questions by asking students to first report times in their lives when they benefited from asking clarifying questions. (We have found it just as useful to ask students to tell when they got into problems for *failing* to ask a clarifying question.) Then they were urged to select books with vivid characters, and to write up incidents in the books where characters asked questions for clarification, and how it affected the plot. Finally, students practiced using the clarifying questions with one another in group discussions.

Consider now how writing activities can also be used to promote creative thinking.

## CREATIVE THINKING-WRITING ACTIVITIES

Writing can be as powerful a tool as reading and discussion for building constructive/creative thinking. Here are some examples of Creative Thinking-Writing Activities that were selected from a ditto master program by Drake (1982):

**Writing About Everyday Life:**   Write a good or funny excuse for the following:

- Why are you so late in getting home from school?
- Why is there spaghetti on your math paper?

**Writing About What *Might* Happen:**   What happens next?

- When the spaceship landed . . .
- As the door slowly opened . . .

**Writing About Problem Situations:**   If this happened to you, how would you solve the problem?

- Your dog does not come when you call. You have not seen him since this morning. It is getting dark now.
- You are riding your bicycle home from a friend's house. The chain breaks and you are losing speed.

Of course, the objective of such exercises is to have children use their imaginations freely, *without* prompts such as these. To further this objective, ask children

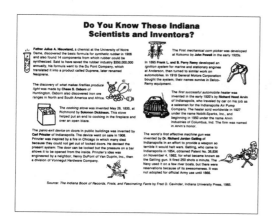

**Sample Project on Scientists and Inventors**

to come up with their own "starters" in each of the categories above. As an incentive to do so, have a revolving group of children designated to give out certificates each week for Great Writing Ideas (similar to the Great Idea award illustrated in photo above). The next idea also has built-in incentives.

## BOOKS AND PROJECTS ON CREATIVITY AND INVENTION

In planning to heighten creative output, don't overlook one traditional means of doing anything new in school; namely, to study about it. There are wonderful books and even some computer software that can be used to study about topics like invention. Here are some especially interesting ones:

### Books

Konigsburg, E. L. *Samuel Todd's Book of Great Inventions*. Atheneum, 1991, Grades K–2.

Lasson, K. *Mousetraps and Muffling Cups: One Hundred Brilliant and Bizarre United States Patents*. Arbor, 1966. Grades 3–12.

Olsen, F. H. *Inventors Who Left Their Brands on America*. Bantam Books, 1991, Grades 5–9.

Provensen, A., & Provensen, M. *Leonardo da Vinci: The Artist, Inventor, Scientist in Three-Dimensional Movable Pictures*. Viking, 1984, Grades K–6.

### Software

*LogoWriter, LCSI*. (Apple II, Macintosh, IBM). Grade Levels K–12.

*Kid Pix*. Borderbound. (Macintosh, IBM). All ages/grades.

For a more project-oriented approach, consider having youngsters check libraries and write to various state agencies to try to discover who in their own areas or states have invented things of note. The illustration above was constructed in conjunction with a science unit on accomplishments by citizens of Indiana.

Creative thinking and writing activities of the types described are valuable and useful to any educators who are willing to test them for themselves. As noted earlier, it seems that the tendency of the mind to follow mind-numbing patterns can be interrupted and reset on more imaginative paths rather easily. Experience suggests that even the most convergent thinkers can be much more creative and imaginative

**FIGURE 9.5** Great Idea Awards

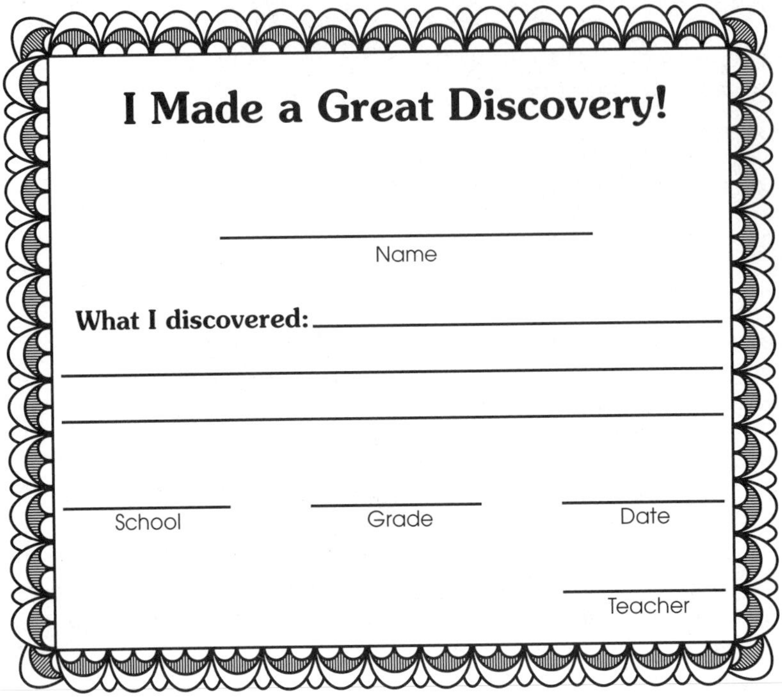

# I Made a Great Discovery!

_____
Name

**What I discovered:** _____

_____

_____

_____        _____        _____
School                        Grade                        Date

_____
Teacher

if we just remember to "ask for it!" (Cecil, 1990; Manzo & Manzo, 1990a). However, we still need more heuristic teaching methods with built-in reminders to us, as teachers, to ask for inventive thinking. A key characteristic of heuristic methods is that they get us to do what we know we should but somehow don't. Thus far, no natural means has been developed for raising pattern-interrupting questions, but now that we are asking for it, perhaps one of you will think of a better way. In the meantime, one popular way to remind ourselves to make creative thinking a priority is by designating a day of the week for a concentrated dose, as in "Thinking Thursdays." Another is to give awards for great ideas (see Figure 9.5).

## TEACHERS AS CREATORS

Should it not be apparent, this chapter was dedicated not only to teaching creativity, but to teaching _creatively_. In the introduction to his book _Expecting the Unexpected_, Donald Murray (1988) offers this valuable hint for keeping teaching fresh and creative: "The unexpected, not only the expected, teaches us and allows us through our writing to teach" (p. xi).

"Spur-of-the-moment curriculum development," writes teacher Sheila Siegfried (1992), "should be occurring regularly in our classrooms" (p. 285). Accordingly, she tells of how her 5-, 6-, and 7-year-old students were totally preoccupied with the "Teenage Mutant Ninja Turtles." She learned that their names were Leonardo, Donatello, Raphael, and Michaelangelo. She also learned that the children had no idea that other, somewhat more durable souls, had once borne these names as well. From this, she created a curriculum that divided the class into four groups. Each group was to investigate one of these names. When the groups finished their research, they shared their findings at a celebration pizza party (pizza is the Ninja Turtles' favorite food).

Before they were finished with this invented curriculum, the class had made maps of Italy, listened to Renaissance music, and become immersed in the culture of that time. This kind of spontaneity can occur with some regularity when the teacher is willing to follow Graves' (1983) simple dictum to "know the children" (p. 22).

Actually, what he said was "*Just* know the children." We don't mean to quibble, but we take this to mean that you should *also* know the children. School programs based *only* on spontaneous curricula could turn into a quirky and diminished rather than an enhanced curriculum.

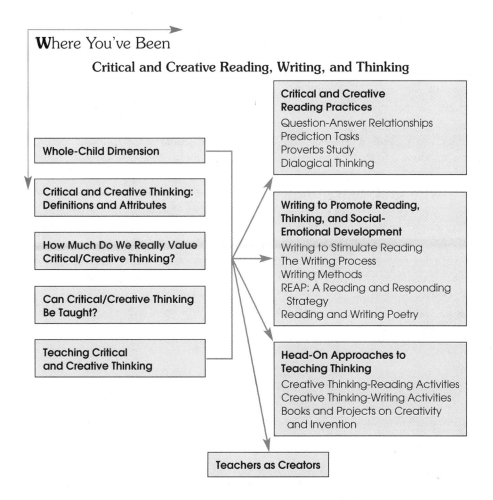

**W**here You've Been

**Critical and Creative Reading, Writing, and Thinking**

Whole-Child Dimension

Critical and Creative Thinking: Definitions and Attributes

How Much Do We Really Value Critical/Creative Thinking?

Can Critical/Creative Thinking Be Taught?

Teaching Critical and Creative Thinking

**Critical and Creative Reading Practices**

Question-Answer Relationships
Prediction Tasks
Proverbs Study
Dialogical Thinking

**Writing to Promote Reading, Thinking, and Social-Emotional Development**

Writing to Stimulate Reading
The Writing Process
Writing Methods
REAP: A Reading and Responding Strategy
Reading and Writing Poetry

**Head-On Approaches to Teaching Thinking**

Creative Thinking-Reading Activities
Creative Thinking-Writing Activities
Books and Projects on Creativity and Invention

**Teachers as Creators**

**W**here You're Going

The next chapter attempts to further and strengthen the critical and creative reading–writing–thinking themes developed in this and previous chapters. It does so by explaining and illustrating how these themes can be applied to teaching reading in subject areas like social studies, science, and mathematics.

## *Reflective Inquiries and Activities*

1. Start a dialogue journal with either your course instructor, a peer, or a school-age child.

2. Can you see a connection between the examples of our propensity to follow patterns and Glass' approach to teaching decoding? Read the section on Glass-Analysis again for clues. Explain.

3. Evaluate and discuss QAR as a method for improving comprehension.

4. Write out what you remember most about the value and means of using proverbs study. Explain how it can be used to reconnect children to the oral language traditions and wisdom of the past. How does any of this result in improved reading comprehension and better thinking?

5. Explain how dialogical thinking can promote creative as well as critical thinking.

6. Conduct a communal poetry session on the same theme with: your class; a younger/older class of children; and/or some special interest or minority group. Consider these as possible topics: money; school days; police; good eats. Compare and discuss your experiences.

7. Describe how one or more of the methods or ideas described in this chapter can be connected to a basal- or literature-based classroom reading program.

8. Add further examples to each of the CR–TAs and CR–WAs described in the chapter. Can you think of other categories of such activities?

9. Research the topic of teaching creativity. See what others are saying about this growing movement in education. Here are some starter names: Fisher; Feuerstein; de Bono; Lipman.

10. Look for *examples* of inventive thinking and problem solving in children's literature that can be used to connect thinking activities to reading and writing.

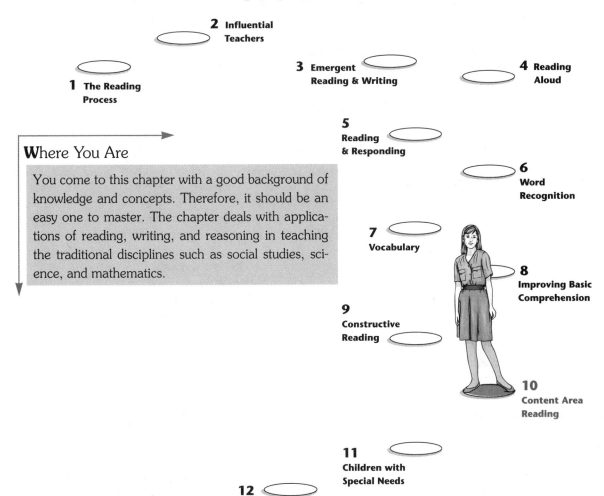

CHAPTER

# 10 CONTENT AREA READING, WRITING, REASONING, AND STUDY

**2** Influential Teachers

**1** The Reading Process

**3** Emergent Reading & Writing

**4** Reading Aloud

**5** Reading & Responding

**6** Word Recognition

**W**here You Are

You come to this chapter with a good background of knowledge and concepts. Therefore, it should be an easy one to master. The chapter deals with applications of reading, writing, and reasoning in teaching the traditional disciplines such as social studies, science, and mathematics.

**7** Vocabulary

**8** Improving Basic Comprehension

**9** Constructive Reading

**10** Content Area Reading

**11** Children with Special Needs

**12** Literacy Assessment

**13** The Classroom & School Literacy Program

*Facts and ideas themselves enlarge our vision and capacity to learn.*
Richard S. Prawat (1993)

# THE STORY OF CONTENT AREA READING

The term "content area reading" (CAR), as used here, refers to reading, writing, reasoning, and study in the subject disciplines, which include social studies, mathematics, science, and so on. In the last thirty years, content area reading has grown from a small subset of reading education into a large body of knowledge. There are entire courses, and in some institutions, more than one, dedicated to this subdiscipline. This chapter provides a fair sample of this newer "educational technology," from its inception to its current state. We refer to it as a technology because it has been developed in recent years in an atmosphere marked by more careful research than ever before. It could be called the first child of this more scientific period.

You already have a pretty good background in the concepts and practices covered here. However, should you wish to more fully activate this relevant "prior knowledge," turn to exercise #1 at the end of the chapter before going on.

## THE TORCH IS LIGHTED BY FRUSTRATION

About thirty years ago, junior and senior high school teachers began to voice their frustration with students that elementary teachers were "sending up" to them. They began to carp out loud about students' reading, writing, and spelling, and later about their uncritical thinking and poor study habits (Austin & Morrison, 1963). Elementary teachers responded to these accusations at first with surprise and then with an appropriate poke. They pointed out that upper grade teachers did more telling than teaching: they taught subjects by lecture and out of books that were not appropriate for students' developmental reading levels. The term "inconsiderate text" was coined for written materials that are dense with concepts and difficult vocabulary, and assume prior knowledge that many youngsters would not have. This public argument finally stimulated sustained attention to the problem.

About seventy years ago, a conference of elementary and secondary teachers came together and agreed that educators at all levels must work together to take youngsters who have been *taught to read* and teach them to *read to learn* (Gray, 1925). It was many years, however, before any real effort toward this goal was begun, and many more years until any real progress was made. Some efforts initiated in the 1950s led to incomplete or impractical answers and blind alleys. One such incomplete answer was the concept of simply helping poor readers to *compensate* for their weak reading. Various means were designed to circumvent textual material and, hence, the problem. By the mid 1960s, these compensations included:

- Purchasing multiple textbooks at varying difficulty levels for a single course
- Rewriting textbooks to lower their difficulty levels
- Developing lessons in ways that required poorer readers to read less
- Audiotaping texts and tests for poorer readers
- Giving poorer readers watered-down versions of a particular course of study

These general approaches made intuitive sense because the texts were largely "inconsiderate," and it seemed a monumental task to change the way they were written. However, there were flaws in this general approach that were revealed slowly, with experience and further research. These led to the following newer conclusions:

- Crutches alone do not help weak readers to become proficient. Compensatory methods tend to camouflage real problems, depriving weaker readers of opportunities to build independence.
- Help needs to be blended with challenge. Teaching can be thought of as a staircase: if each step is too high, little progress can be made, but if the staircase is leveled, no upward progress is made.
- Average, and even some proficient, readers need to be taught to *read to learn.*
- In some sense, every teacher needs to be a teacher of reading (Gray, 1951), just as every teacher needs to be a teacher of content and concepts (Manzo & Manzo, 1990a).

With these realizations, the focus of the CAR movement gradually shifted to teaching *all* youngsters to be strategic readers—or independent selectors and users of the strategy or strategies that make for effective, self-directed reading and learning. This shift led to the adoption of some basic premises that now guide the CAR movement.

## GUIDING PREMISES EMERGE

Several premises now guide the content area reading movement. Three, in particular, are relevant here:

1. Make specific provisions for transition and transfer. It is well documented that the transfer of previously acquired strategies does not tend to occur naturally. Youngsters need on-going assistance in making the transition from learning to read to reading to learn. In other words, learning how to effectively question, set purposes, and analyze the content of pictures and story literature does not lead most students to automatically do so when faced with social studies and science material. One means of helping children to make this transition is through the use of high interest content trade books. Very young children, for example, learn useful anatomy concepts from Stevenson's (1980) *The Amazing Mumford Presents: All About Bones,* featuring the Sesame Street Muppets. Older children learn basic concepts in physics from Cobb and Darling's (1980) *Bet You Can't,* featuring science impossibilities that fool and astonish (see below for one illustration from this resource).

2. Take advantage of "teachable moments." The previously stated "teachable moments" hypothesis is very pertinent here, for two reasons. The moment when a student is struggling to understand content material is the moment when that student will be most open and responsive to a teacher's guidance in how to effectively question, set purposes, and analyze textual material. Thematic instructional units are an excellent way to prompt and be prepared for teachable moments. In this kind of instructional planning, reading and writing are connected with relevant concepts and information from the subject disciplines. (Several anecdotal examples are provided later in this chapter.)

### High Interest Content Trade Books
### Aid in Transfer of Reading Strategies to Content Materials

Women and men have different centers of gravity. Because of this, a woman standing with both feet together, can easily pick up a stool placed close to a wall, but a man cannot. Try it!

Cobb & Darling (1980) *Bet You Can't*, p. 17.

3. Since learning to read is a life-long developmental process, it needs attention and consideration throughout school. Content area reading methods offer practical means of fostering reading, writing, speaking, and thinking in all subject disciplines, and for all students.

## CHALLENGE TO CAR

A recent challenge to content area reading instruction is based on teachers' observation that while children may learn easily enough to read to identify facts, they have difficulty when they are expected to read to acquire *concepts*. This observation has led some educators to propose that demonstration and hands-on experiences need to *replace* conventional reading and study.

Swafford's (1991) research has shown pretty convincingly that *both* reading and related experiences are necessary. Youngsters who observed a science demonstration and then read a related text made more accurate predictions about the outcome of subsequent demonstrations than did those who participated in the demonstration only. It should be noted that this was more true for girls than for boys: boys learned almost as well from demonstrations alone as from the combination with textual material, but girls benefited far more when reading preceded observation.

Swafford suggests that the value of combining reading with observation is that the textual material provides youngsters with more language to think about and describe what they had seen. We suspect that the textual material also provides youngsters with a greater capacity to see and conceptualize the demonstration. While Swafford's study used reading as a follow-up for an experiential activity, it probably is a good idea to have youngsters read relevant material both before and after such activities.

Get ready now for some other relatively quick and easy ways to help youngsters become proficient users of text. Print, after all, still is a more practical resource than demonstration for independently acquiring knowledge, studying it in depth, and reviewing it any time thereafter.

# FIVE "UNIVERSAL" STRATEGIES FOR GUIDING CONTENT AREA READING

Most strategies for teaching reading comprehension through basal-reader material and children's literature also are effective means of helping children to read and understand content material. The guiding concept of content area reading methods is to provide the types of guidance called for in the Directed Reading Activity for before, during, and after reading. Across all subject areas, and at *every grade level*, students need some degree of guidance with setting purposes for reading, handling difficult vocabulary, applying active study reading strategies, and reflecting upon and personalizing what they have read. Some of the strategies that have been developed to meet these objectives have been quite specialized. Others are more "universal," in that they can be used with almost any kind of content reading materials and at most grade levels (Manzo, 1980). The universal strategies that follow also have these characteristics:

- They are relatively easy to use.
- They require little preparation.
- They have "heuristic," or learn-by-doing and self-discovery, properties for both teachers and students (Manzo & Manzo, 1990a).

Look for each of these characteristics in the first universal strategy, the Listen–Read–Discuss Heuristic, described below. Notice especially how the teacher, *while* helping students to learn from text, also has an opportunity to observe and better understand the needs of young learners.

## LISTEN–READ–DISCUSS HEURISTIC (L–R–D)

A common school practice is to have students read a section of text, often for homework, then to listen to the teacher's explanation of the information, and then to participate in question–answer recitation and discussion. The problem with this read–listen–discuss approach is that students receive little, if any, help with silent reading. Consequently, they typically are ill-prepared to participate in the postreading recitation and discussion. The L–R–D (Manzo & Casale, 1985) offers a simple alternative to this approach. Simply by changing the *sequence* of conventional instruction, students are better prepared for reading. Notice, in the steps below, how this approach quickens the pace of instruction and provides for several repetitions of the information. You may recall from Chapter 1 that pace and repetition are two of the most powerful practices for learning enhancement.

## STEPS IN THE LISTEN–READ–DISCUSS HEURISTIC

**Step 1**    Select a portion of text to be read.

**Step 2**    Present the information from that portion of text in a well-organized lecture format for about 5 to 15 minutes.

**Step 3**    Have students read the book's version of the same material. Students now will be reading in an "empowered" way, since they have just listened to an overview of the information.

**Step 4**    Discuss the material students now have heard and then read. Three questions, adapted from Smith (1978), are useful in guiding this postreading discussion:

- What did you understand *most* from what you heard and read?
- What did you understand *least* from what you heard and read?
- What *questions or thoughts* did this lesson raise in your mind about the content and/or about effective reading and learning?

The L–R–D has "heuristic," or learn-by-doing, effects for both teachers and students. Following the empowering lecture presentation, teachers observe even the more reluctant readers approaching the text with more confidence. Teachers also find that following empowered reading, all students bring more information and enthusiasm to the postreading discussion. Students learn by doing that they are capable of reading with greater understanding than they may have imagined, and that, having read, they have more to contribute to class discussion.

Several variations on the L–R–D have been designed to teach other components of strategic teaching and strategic reading. These variations also serve to keep the learning process fresh and on-going for both teacher and students. The variations are listed in Box 10.1 in order of increasing difficulty. This "ladder" of variations can be thought of as a suggested sequence for further exploring and developing your knowledge and skill base as a reflective, strategic teacher of content area reading. Using the basic L–R–D and the ten variations could be a self-guided, year-long professional development project in itself. The L–R–D has been found to be a powerful means of improving reading comprehension and content learning in both weak and proficient readers (Watkins, McKenna, & Manzo, in progress, 1993).

## ORAL READING STRATEGY

The Oral Reading Strategy (Manzo, 1980), briefly described in an earlier chapter, is a simple way to model the complex "inside the head" processes that enable the reader to comprehend and think about text. The teacher reads content-rich material aloud to students, pausing at logical points to comment or pose simple translation questions. In effect, the teacher models the active reading process of an effective reader and urges the student readers to come along. In addition, the

| BOX 10.1 | **L-R-D Ladder of Variations** |
|---|---|

1. Have students reread the information covered in the L-R-D format rapidly to increase their speed of reading and thought processing. Reading speed tends to rise as a result of increases in prior knowledge, although it can also be easily improved simply by systematic attention and practice.

2. Inform the class that as you tell them about the content material, you will intentionally leave out a few important details that they will need to read their texts to discover. This gives practice in careful reading and in recognizing what is not yet known or experienced. This can be supplemented with an incomplete graphic, as shown ahead in the chapter.

3. Inform the class that your presentation will cover all the details of the material, but that they will need to read to discover what *questions* these details answer. This is one way to teach students to actively seek an understanding of the concept, or main idea around which an area of study is focused.

4. Inform the class that a quiz will follow the L-R-D sequence. Allow a short study period. This is recommended to activate a high level of focused attention, give practice in test-taking, and set the stage for questions and discussion about how to study effectively.

5. Invert the core process *occasionally* by having the class R-L-D: read (for about 15 minutes), then listen, then discuss. This variation tends to focus and improve independent reading as well as the ability to learn from subsequent listening—a frequent format in all further schooling. This can be even more effective when combined with the other listening activities and notetaking techniques covered in the study strategies section of this chapter.

6. Watch an informative videotape on a text topic before reading. This format is compatible with the habits of contemporary youngsters and can help them build new bridges to print.

7. Ask students which parts of the text seemed most difficult. Ask if it was poorly written, or poorly organized, or just poorly explained. This can help students learn when to ask for help with reading. It also helps the teacher become more alert to student learning needs. Analysis of the writing in texts is also a good way to informally teach some of the basics of effective writing.

8. Give students a clear purpose for reading and discussing that will require critical and/or creative expression or application. State that purpose clearly on the chalkboard for easy reference: "As you read this section on the steam engine, try to figure out why it was sure to be replaced by the gasoline engine."

9. Have a postreading discussion on teaching and learning strategies. Make the discussion positive by asking students what they or you may have done that helped them learn. Such discussion gives credit to student intuition and develops "metacognitive" processing, or thinking about thinking. It also builds rapport with and regard for the teacher as a source of personal help and comfort, as much as of challenge and fair criticism.

10. Create research teams and provide time for students to delve into a topic in greater depth. One group could simply see what other textbooks say on the topic. Another could check with other authoritative references—persons and books. Another could write their best estimate of which real-life problems the information learned might help solve or answer. Still another group, where appropriate, could try to identify and discuss theme-related stories, poetry, music, or art. Activities such as these provide links between text topics and nonprint resources and among school learning, artistic expression, and the real world.

strategy builds student familiarity with the cadence and patterns of language and thought that are characteristic of different subject areas, and introduces correct pronunciations of new words in a straightforward, informal manner.

## STEPS IN THE ORAL READING STRATEGY

**Step 1**   In preparation, the teacher should always preread the selection that will be used. This makes oral reading more fluent and poignant. At the most basic level, the teacher should be sure about how to pronounce all the words.

**Step 2**   The teacher reads the first few pages of a selection to the class while they follow along in their texts. The teacher pauses periodically and comments or asks a few simple translation questions of the text: "What do you suppose this word means here?" or "Tell in your own words what point was just made here." At first the teacher may have to answer his or her own questions, because students are unaccustomed to translating what they read and could have difficulty understanding what they are being asked to do. It also is helpful, especially the first few times the teacher uses this strategy, to jot down some comments or questions to use during this step.

| | |
|---|---|
| *Teacher reading from text:* | *The Jura (joo'-ruh) is a mountain range that lies between two rivers, the Rhine and the Rhone.* |
| *Teacher question to class:* | What do you picture when you hear that the Jura lies between two rivers? |
| *Teacher comment:* | This reminds me of a row of tall office buildings between two streets. |
| *Teacher reading from text:* | *The Jura forms part of a natural boundary between Switzerland and France. The Jura extends from the northeast to the southwest in parallel ridges.* |
| *Teacher question to class:* | What other kinds of "natural boundaries" do you know of? Can someone define "parallel ridges?" |

**Step 3**   The teacher reads the next page or so with fewer questions and comments. Students are told to listen for the main ideas presented, to pronunciation of unfamiliar words, and for questions they might want to ask before they are asked to continue reading silently.

**Step 4**   The teacher tells the class to read the next portion of the selection silently. It is important that time be provided for students to continue reading *immediately,* to apply the active reading strategies the teacher has been modeling.

The next universal strategy shifts the emphasis from *information* to the *questions* the information answers.

## C/T/Q Strategy

The C/T/Q strategy (Manzo, 1980) focuses both teaching and learning by teaching students to identify the key concepts, terms, and questions answered (C/T/Qs) in a section of text or other subject area reading material. When teaching students to identify these, the teacher comes to better understand, anticipate, and provide for the idea load students face when they read content material. When students hear the teacher identify C/T/Qs, they are led to observe and practice what expert readers and accomplished thinkers do to construct meaning; namely, combine textual information with prior knowledge and experience.

Instructional conversations based on identifying C/T/Qs are characterized by frequent repetition of the important facts and ideas in the text. This redundancy factor alone would justify the effort. However, C/T/Q interactions also help to impart the *process* of seeking conceptual meanings, teaching youngsters a strategy for independent learning as well.

## Steps in C/T/Q

**Step 1**  The teacher selects *three* brief selections of text for analysis.

**Step 2**  The teacher notes and "talks through" the key concepts, terms, and questions underlying the first selection, writing these on the chalkboard or overhead.

*Example*

*Concept:*  Rivers often are found at the bases of mountains.

*Terms:*  Jura mountains; parallel ridges

*Question:*  How did Switzerland's geography help Switzerland to form itself into a country separate from France, Germany, and Italy?

**Step 3**  The class reads that portion of the text. A brief discussion follows to check students' comprehension of the material. A good way to do this is to ask students to answer the C/T/Q "question."

**Step 4**  Students read the second short selection, and the teacher and class together develop a C/T/Q for it.

**Step 5**  Students read the third selection and develop C/T/Qs independently, without peer discussion or teacher assistance.

**Step 6**  The teacher shows his or her own C/T/Qs for the third passage on the chalkboard or overhead. Students compare their versions with the teacher's and discuss similarities and differences.

### C/T/Q Options

- Once students have been taught to write C/T/Qs, these can be used as a component of a Reading Guide (described ahead).

- The *teacher* can create a reading guide by writing and distributing C/T/Qs to assist students in reading difficult homework assignments.
- Student groups can be assigned to write C/T/Qs for various portions of a text, which then are reproduced and shared with the rest of the class.

## QUESTION-ONLY STRATEGY

The Question-Only strategy evolved from studies on why children slowly but surely cease to express curiosity and how this problem might be remedied (Legenza, 1978; Manzo & Legenza, 1975a). Research and field experience have shown that students of all ages can be taught to ask more and better questions—an important component of higher-order thinking and active comprehension. One version of the Question-Only strategy, adapted for kindergarten children, was discussed under "emergent higher-order literacy" as a variation on show-and-tell. The basic Question-Only strategy, described below, can be used in any subject area, at any grade level.

## STEPS IN QUESTION-ONLY

Step 1    The teacher announces a topic to the class and explains that they must learn about it solely through their questions, and that they will be tested on the topic. The test should cover all the information the teacher considers important, whether or not the students actually extract the information with their questions.

Step 2    The class questions, and the teacher answers. The teacher should answer fully, but avoid providing more information than is specifically called for in the question. The purpose is to challenge students to form relevant questions that elicit the important information. Of course, the teacher should also be ready to take advantage of "teachable moments" that may occur.

Step 3    The test is given.

Step 4    In a whole-group discussion, the teacher and students note which questions were raised and which *should* have been raised but were not.

Step 5    Students are directed to read their texts carefully or listen to a short lecture to discover what they failed to learn through their initial questions.

*Example*

*Teacher:*    The topic today is the Jura. You can find out about it by asking me any questions you wish to. When you are finished asking questions, there will be a short test, so try to ask good questions!

*Student:*    You said "*the* Jura." Does that mean Jura is a thing?

*Teacher:*    Yes.

*Student:*    This is geography, so is it a country?

*Teacher:*    No.

*Student:*    A river?

*Teacher:*    No.

*Student:*    Mountains?

*Teacher:*    Yes!

*Student:*    It sounds foreign. Is it in India?

*Teacher:*    No.

*Student:*    South America?

*Teacher:*    No.

*Student:*    Eastern Europe?

*Teacher:*    No, but close.

*Student:*    Western Europe?

*Teacher:*    Yes.

Ten minutes later, students will have deduced facts such as that the Jura is in Switzerland and France and its highest peak is 6,000 feet. The quiz that follows should teach the class more about the topic, but also more about how to inquire. *Quiz Questions*

1. What is the Jura?
2. What does it divide?
3. What happened to the valuable forests that once covered the mountainsides?
4. What do you think is the relationship between mountains and rivers?

### Question-Only Options

- The teacher can add a 5- to 10-minute period of "comments-only," encouraging students to say what they feel they learned about the topic and/or about how to learn in class. Record their comments in brief form on the chalkboard to emphasize their importance. Students can also be asked to write their comments before they speak them.

- A natural tie-in exists here to Shoop's (1986) InQuest strategy (see Chapter 9). To take advantage of this connection, the teacher can have students interview other students on a report they have written or book they have read that may relate to the content topic.

## The Discussion Web Graphic

While prior knowledge is a powerful ingredient of content area reading comprehension, when the knowledge called up is *incorrect*, it can have an equally powerful negative effect (Guzzetti, 1992a, b; Hynd & Alvermann, 1986; Lipson, 1984).

The Discussion Web Strategy is a special type of graphic aid developed by Alvermann (1991) as a way to help students confront misconceived ideas that may be hindering their comprehension. After reviewing twenty-three studies of strategies designed to counteract the negative effect of misconceptions, Guzzetti, Snyder and Glass (1992) recommend the Discussion Web as one of a very few strategies that were shown to be effective in eradicating these misconceptions.

## STEPS IN USING THE DISCUSSION WEB GRAPHIC

**Step 1**   Prepare students to read the selection by activating background knowledge, introducing new vocabulary, and setting purposes for reading.

**Step 2**   Identify, from the reading selection, a central concept or "yes/no" question that students may have misconceived ideas or unexamined opinions about. Distribute the graphic aid form to students (see example in Figure 10.1) along with the reading assignment. Students are directed to write the central concept or question in the center box, and then work with a partner to list, on one side of the graphic, evidence from the text in support of the concept statement, and on the other side evidence that refutes it (or evidence that supports a "yes" or "no" answer to the question). Suggest that partners work on the same sheet but take turns writing. Alvermann stresses that students should try to give an equal number of reasons on each side. This is the most fundamental way of teaching contrary thinking, discussed in Chapter 9 as a key ingredient in "dialectical" or critical thinking. During this step and the next, the teacher should circulate, asking leading questions, helping students find sections in the text to support their ideas, and helping them to summarize their thoughts. This provides an opportunity to informally model the active reading processes of questioning, verifying opinions, and translating information into one's own words.

**Step 3**   When a student pair has completed their graphic, they are directed to join another group of two, and defend their positions in working toward consensus on a group conclusion. It is acceptable for individual students to disagree with the group conclusion, and dissenting views should be heard during the final whole-class discussion.

**Step 4**   One person from each small group is selected to report to the class. The spokesperson also should report any dissenting viewpoints from their group. In the whole-class discussion, the teacher helps to further correct any misinformation. In particular, the teacher should watch for cases where students supported a misconception by taking incomplete information from the text.

**Step 5**   As a follow-up, students are directed to write their individual response to the central concept or question, including their own ideas and those expressed by others. These individual responses should be put up around the room to be read by others.

**FIGURE 10.1** **Discussion Web Graphic**

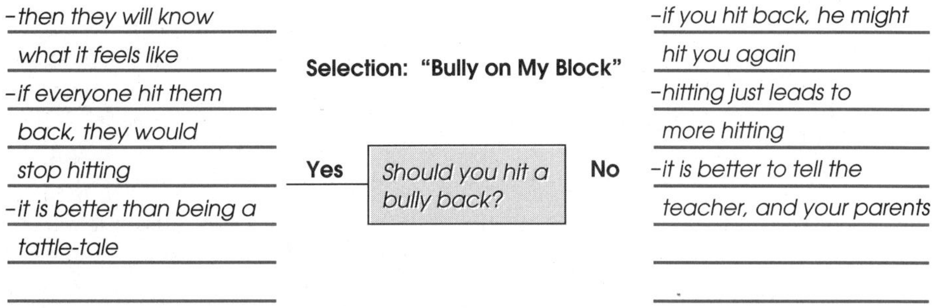

–then they will know
what it feels like
–if everyone hit them
back, they would
stop hitting
–it is better than being a
tattle-tale

Selection: "Bully on My Block"

**Yes**

Should you hit a bully back?

**No**

–if you hit back, he might
hit you again
–hitting just leads to
more hitting
–it is better to tell the
teacher, and your parents

*Alvermann notes that the right and left column labels can also be labeled: supports/refutes; relevant/irrelevant (as for a mathematics word problem), hypothesis 1 and hypothesis 2 (as for a science concept); or with names of historical figures, to be completed by stating the position of each on the central concept.*

To really test the value of "Just Asking for It" mentioned in the previous chapter, you might wish to add a sixth step to the Discussion Web Graphic, asking for further criticisms and constructive solutions from "your own head."

The Discussion Web method imparts an appreciation for the importance of careful reading *of* the lines, as the basis for reading between and beyond the lines. Alvermann notes that the Discussion Web has been successfully used with children as young as kindergarten, though at this level it should be done as a whole-class activity.

In addition to the five interactive Universal Strategies described above, content area reading can be guided and enhanced through thoughtfully developed reading guides that accompany the students on their journey through the printed page. These, too, can be called "universal," since they can be adapted to most any kind of textual material.

## READING GUIDES

Reading Guides are printed worksheets designed to guide the reader's thinking process (Durrell, 1956). They differ from conventional workbook exercises both in when and why they are used. Where workbook exercises are used almost exclusively *following* reading, Reading Guides are generally used before and during, as well as after reading (Manzo & Garber, 1995, in press). This is because Reading Guides are oriented more toward the "process" than the "product" of reading: They are intended to be with the student along the way, and to coach and support the process of thoughtful reading, more so than just testing the student's ability to get a "right" answer. There are several types of Reading Guides (Wood, Lapp, & Flood, 1992) described ahead. Those include Three-Level Guides, Process Guides, Reading Guide-O-Ramas, Text Connection Questions, Anticipation–Reaction

Guides, and Graphic Organizers. These can be combined or adapted according to the type of reading material and the needs of your students.

Guides tend to have some shortcomings. They are time-intensive to prepare and to use. Further, they have tended to be overly occupied with the reconstructive elements of reading. However, as you will see with the Three-Level Guide, this is not a structural flaw. Reading Guides simply reflect the concerns of their authors. To date, they often reflect our tendency to emphasize the acquisition of facts, with only a marginal concern for development of critical and creative thinking. In short, Guides can not only be made more inventively, but also can be made to require more invention. We simply must remember to ask for it! Just ahead, you will see how Vacca and Vacca suggest that a guide be constructed so that the "applied" level, which easily can be extended to a creative level, will not be overlooked.

## THREE-LEVEL GUIDES

The Three-Level Guide (Herber, 1978) leads students from literal levels of understanding what the author has *said,* to interpretive levels of understanding what the author may have *meant,* and to applied levels of understanding and generating meaningful *uses* of the information. To create this kind of Reading Guide for students, the teacher needs first to determine why the information is important and how it might be appropriately used. Accordingly, Vacca and Vacca (1986) suggest the following procedure for constructing a Three-Level Guide:

## STEPS IN CONSTRUCTING A THREE-LEVEL GUIDE

Step 1    Review the textual material and determine what *applications* students should be able to make after reading. Develop the last part of the Guide first: *Part 3: Applying the Information.* To do this, think of reasonable uses of the information and develop questions related to these. (To heighten the critical–creative value of this level, remember to ask questions that intentionally connect to other material and issues, and remember, too, to ask if any problems were sidestepped or alternatives overlooked by the author.)

Step 2    Next, determine what information is needed to make these applications, and whether it is explicitly stated in the text or must be inferred. Develop the second part of the Guide next: *Part 2: Inferring from Facts.* To develop this section, ask questions that cause students to make the inferences that will be necessary for them to go on to the applications you have identified.

Step 3    Finally, the necessary literal information is used to develop questions for *Part 1: Getting the Facts.* Typically, this part of the Guide is designed to be used by students while they are reading. The questions follow the sequence of the text, with page numbers noted to assist the student in locating the answers. *Part 2* and *Part 3* of the Guide typically are written to be answered after reading.

Step 4 Reassemble the sections of the guide: *Part 1: Getting the Facts; Part 2: Inferring from Facts;* and *Part 3: Applying the Information.*

## PROCESS GUIDES

Karlin (1984) emphasized the distinction between conventional fact-oriented worksheets and Reading Guides by referring to the former as "Content Guides," and the latter as "Process Guides." The variety of forms that the Process Guide may take is as wide as your imagination. Following are some general guidelines for creating this type of reading aid for your students.

## STEPS IN CONSTRUCTING A PROCESS GUIDE

Step 1 Pick an *important* section of text. Process Guides are time-consuming to construct, so you will want to spend your efforts on something of value.

Step 2 Read the selection carefully, putting yourself in your students' place: "If I didn't know much about this, what would I need to do?"

Step 3 Construct questions/directions that lead the reader to apply these strategies. Some examples are given below (adapted from Karlin, 1984).

- *Identification of key terms.* Select key vocabulary terms from the passage. List these, with page numbers for students to watch for and check off as they read.

  Example
  Directions: Check off the terms listed below as you come to them in reading. Review them after reading to see what you can remember about each.

  | Page | | | |
  |------|-----------|----------|------------------|
  | 166  | stealthily | regulars | Bunker Hill |
  | 173  | summit | redcoats | Breed's Hill |
  | 175  | ill-matched | tactics | continental army |
  | 178  | Tories | man-of-war | |

- *Categorization.* Construct category labels for the identified vocabulary terms. Have students categorize the terms in one or more ways as a means of further reflecting on the new word meanings.

  Example:
  Directions: Use the context in which you encounter the above terms in your text to place them in the categories listed under "A" below. Should you finish early, try recategorizing the terms in the categories listed under "B."

  A. Part of Speech
     1. Words for an action or state of being (verbs)

2. Words that describe people, places, things, or events (adjectives and adverbs)
3. Words that name persons, places, or things (nouns, pronouns)

B. Meaning
1. Words related to war
2. Words that describe people
3. Words that describe the English and their sympathizers

- *Using Text Structure.* Determine the basic structure of the passage and develop questions that guide students to effective use of this structure.

Example
Directions: Chapter 9 answers three basic questions. The first and third are listed below. What is the second question this chapter answers?

A. Why did the Thirteen Colonies decide to declare their independence?
B. _____
C. How did the Thirteen Colonies win their independence?

- *Identification of Important Details.* Identify the details that are essential to understanding the passage. Construct questions to focus attention on these details. List these in order, or label them with page numbers to aid students in watching for these details as they read.

Example:
Directions: *As you read,* mark each statement as true (T) or false (F). Where a statement seems false, cross out the incorrect information and replace it with the correct information.

T or F:
_____ A. The Battle of Bunker Hill actually was fought on Breed's Hill.
_____ B. Breed's Hill is in Pennsylvania.
_____ C. The "Continental Army" was made up largely of Europeans against England.

- *Use of Effective Reading Processes.* See the Reading Guide-O-Rama and Text Connection Questions, below, for examples of exercises of this type.

## READING GUIDE-O-RAMA

Developed by Cunningham & Shablak (1975), the Reading Guide-O-Rama is a set of prompts that helps the student to read and think about the selection. It does not necessarily require written responses. To construct a Reading Guide-O-Rama, consider how you, an expert reader, would approach the selection. Provide page number references, and point out unimportant as well as important information. Notice how the very first question in the example below seems to say, "Hey, don't just take this in—think about it!"

Example:

page 93, paragraphs 3–6:   Pay attention to this section. Why do you think Hunter acted in this manner? We will discuss your ideas in class.

page 94:   See if you can rewrite (convert) the boldface print at the top of this page into a question. You should pick up five ideas under this topic very quickly. Jot these down.

page 179, column 1:   The author has provided us with some interesting information here, but it isn't important to our course of study. Just skim it, unless, of course, it is of special interest to you.

*Example from Tierney, Readence, & Dishner (1990), pp. 240–241.*

## TEXT CONNECTION QUESTIONS

Muth (1987) developed this form of Reading Guide to improve reading comprehension by teaching students to use the structure of written material. The most common paragraph patterns used to structure text include:

1. Introductory
2. Definition
3. Transactional (shift attention from a previous pattern)
4. Illustrative
5. Summary
6. Main Idea and/or supporting details
7. Chronological order
8. Compare–contrast
9. Cause–effect
10. Problem–solution
11. Descriptive (attempting to evoke a mental picture)
12. Narrative (containing a sequence of story-like events)

Tonjes and Zintz (1987).

Each of these text structures is a way of connecting ideas. Muth's Text Connection Questions approach teaches students to use these text structures incidentally, through questions that cause them to use a particular text structure to make meaningful connections. This is done by first identifying a selection that follows one of the basic structures listed above. Then the teacher constructs questions that cause the student to use the text structure to make "internal connections" between and among the facts and ideas in the selection. Finally, the teacher constructs questions that cause the students to make "external connections" that go beyond the information provided. See Box 10.2 for sample compare–contrast and cause–effect selections, with "internal" and "external" connection questions that teach students to use those text structures.

**BOX 10.2** **Text Connection Questions**

*Compare-Contrast*

*People who want to buy a horse for pleasure riding usually choose between the Quarter horse and the Saddle horse. The Quarter horse has a thick mane and tail. It is strong and is able to carry heavy riders over rough trails for several miles. It is also very healthy and does not catch diseases easily. However, the Quarter horse is not comfortable to ride. It has a jerky walk, which bumps its rider up and down. Also, it is nervous and is hard to control when something unexpected happens.*

*The Saddle horse is usually brown with dark eyes. It has a steady walk, which is comfortable for riding. It is also easy to control; it responds instantly to commands and is always ready for unexpected things that might lie in its path. The Saddle horse is not very healthy though, and tends to catch diseases easily from other horses. Also, it is not strong enough to carry heavy loads.*

The teacher's questions should focus on helping students understand the author's purpose for using the compare-contrast structure and on the relationships among the ideas in the passages. Here are some questions (and possible student answers) which could help students build "internal connections" among the ideas in the passage:

1. What is the author comparing and contrasting? (the Saddle horse and the Quarter horse)
2. Why is the author comparing and contrasting these two types of horses? (so we can decide which horse is best for pleasure riding)
3. Why did the author use the compare-contrast structure in this particular passage? (to show us that each type of horse has advantages and disadvantages for pleasure riding)
4. What are the advantages of the Quarter horse for pleasure riding? (strong and healthy)
5. What are the advantages of the Saddle horse? (comfortable and easy to control)
6. What are the disadvantages of the Quarter horse for pleasure riding? (uncomfortable and hard to control)
7. What are the disadvantages of the Saddle horse? (not healthy or strong)
8. What other characteristic of the two horses does the author include in the passage? (physical appearance)
9. Is the appearance of the horses important in determining which horse is best for pleasure riding? (no)
10. According to the passage, which of the two types of horses is best for pleasure riding? (there is no clear-cut answer)
11. How would someone decide which of the horses to buy based on what he or she read in this passage? (they would have to decide which horse is best for their particular needs)

## ANTICIPATION–REACTION GUIDES

Anticipation–Reaction Guides emphasize the prereading processes of active prediction and application of prior knowledge. Students are asked to respond to several questions *before* they read, and then reconsider their answers to these questions *after* they read. This type of Reading Guide provides a simple and effective means of structuring small-group or whole-class discussions before and after

**BOX 10.2 cont'd**

Here are some questions which could help students build "external connections":

1. Which of the two horses would you pick, and why? (I'd pick the Saddle horse because I'm light and wouldn't be carrying heavy loads; also, I don't have any other horses, so it would be hard for my Saddle horse to catch a disease if there aren't any other horses around.)

2. Do you know anyone who might be concerned with the appearance of the horses? (My aunt would. She participates in horse shows, and appearance is very important for show horses.)

*Cause-Effect*

*Why do some things become rusty? Perhaps you found out if you left a shovel or rake out overnight. When you picked them up a few days later, you might have seen rough, brown spots of rust on them. Air is composed partly of oxygen. Oxygen combines with iron to make rust. Moisture or water helps to bring about the change. Tools like rakes and shovels are made of iron, and they rust quickly if they are left out in wet or damp air. If you left them out long enough, they would rust completely and crumble away.*

Again, teacher's questions should focus on helping students understand why the author used the cause-effect structure and how the ideas in the passage are related to each other. Here are some questions which could help students build "internal connections" among the ideas:

1. Why did the author use the cause-effect structure for this passage? (to describe a process; to give an example of one thing causing something else to happen)

2. What is the cause-effect process that the author is describing? (how things rust)

3. Describe the process of how some things rust. (oxygen and moisture in the air combine with the iron in the objects to cause rust)

4. What causes the process? (the oxygen and the moisture combining with the iron)

5. What is the effect of this combination? (rust)

6. What are the three necessary "ingredients" for rusting? (oxygen, moisture, iron)

These questions could help students build "external connections":

1. Why don't most things usually rust inside your house? (there's not enough moisture)

2. When do you think things might rust in your house? (when the humidity is very high)

3. Can you think of some things that might rust in your house? (the scale in the bathroom, the pipes in the basement)

4. Can you think of some things that you own that might rust if you left them outdoors long enough? (bicycle, wheelbarrow, car)

5. Can you think of some things that you own that won't rust if you leave them outdoors? (basketball, book, sweatshirt)

*Muth (1987).*

reading. When developing items for an Anticipation–Reaction Guide, look especially for points on which the text may differ from students' pre-existing ideas and attitudes. See Box 10.3 for two examples of Anticipation–Reaction Guides. Duffelmeyer, Baum, and Merkley (1987) developed what they called the Extended Anticipation–Reaction Guide. When students review the statements after reading, they are directed to rewrite any statements that do not correspond to the

---

**BOX
10.3** **Sample Anticipation-Reaction Guides**

**Anticipation-Reaction Guide based on the short story "Caged," by Lloyd E. Reeve**
Directions: Read each statement below. If you agree, put a check in the "Before Reading" blank. If you do not agree, do *not* put a check in the blank. Directions for the "Author's Ideas" column will be given later.

| *Before Reading* | | *After Reading* |
|---|---|---|
| _____ | The creatures in pet stores are happy and contented. | _____ |
| _____ | People sometimes commit cruel acts without realizing that they are cruel. | _____ |
| _____ | Freedom is more valuable than money. | _____ |
| _____ | Unusual behavior sometimes frightens people. | _____ |
| _____ | Two people can be a part of the same event yet have totally different understandings of it. | _____ |

**Anticipation-Reaction Guide based on a selection entitled "Ranchers and Cowboys"**
Directions: Read each item and decide if you agree with it or disagree. Put a "yes" on the line next to the item labeled "Before Reading" if you agree, a "no" if you disagree. Think about how you would defend your point of view.

| *Before Reading* | *After Reading* | |
|---|---|---|
| _____ | _____ | Cattle raising techniques were developed by American ranchers (p. 513). |
| _____ | _____ | You would enjoy life as a cowboy (p. 514). |
| _____ | _____ | You would not mind a cattle drive going through your land (pp. 515–516). |
| _____ | _____ | You would have a comfortable life as the wife of a cowboy (pp. 520–521). |
| _____ | _____ | Overstocking cattle and overgrazing resulted in the end of open range ranching (p. 523). |

*Ericson, Hubler, Bean, Smith, & McKenzie (1987), p. 434.*

---

information in the passage. This is a challenging "teach-up" activity, as Estes (1990) referred to those occasions when you ask students to stretch.

## GRAPHIC ORGANIZERS

Graphic Organizers display information to pictorial form. Any one of a number of Graphic Organizer formats can be used alone or in combination with the Reading Guide formats described above. They give concrete form to the otherwise abstract structural patterns of text and can be especially useful in teaching students the elements of outlining. See Figure 10.2 for a few sample Graphic Organizer formats.

To build student independence in using any of these graphic organizers, start by filling one in with the whole group, asking for student input, and modeling the reasoning processes involved. Then distribute the graphic with some parts already filled

**FIGURE 10.2** **Sample Graphic Organizer Formats**

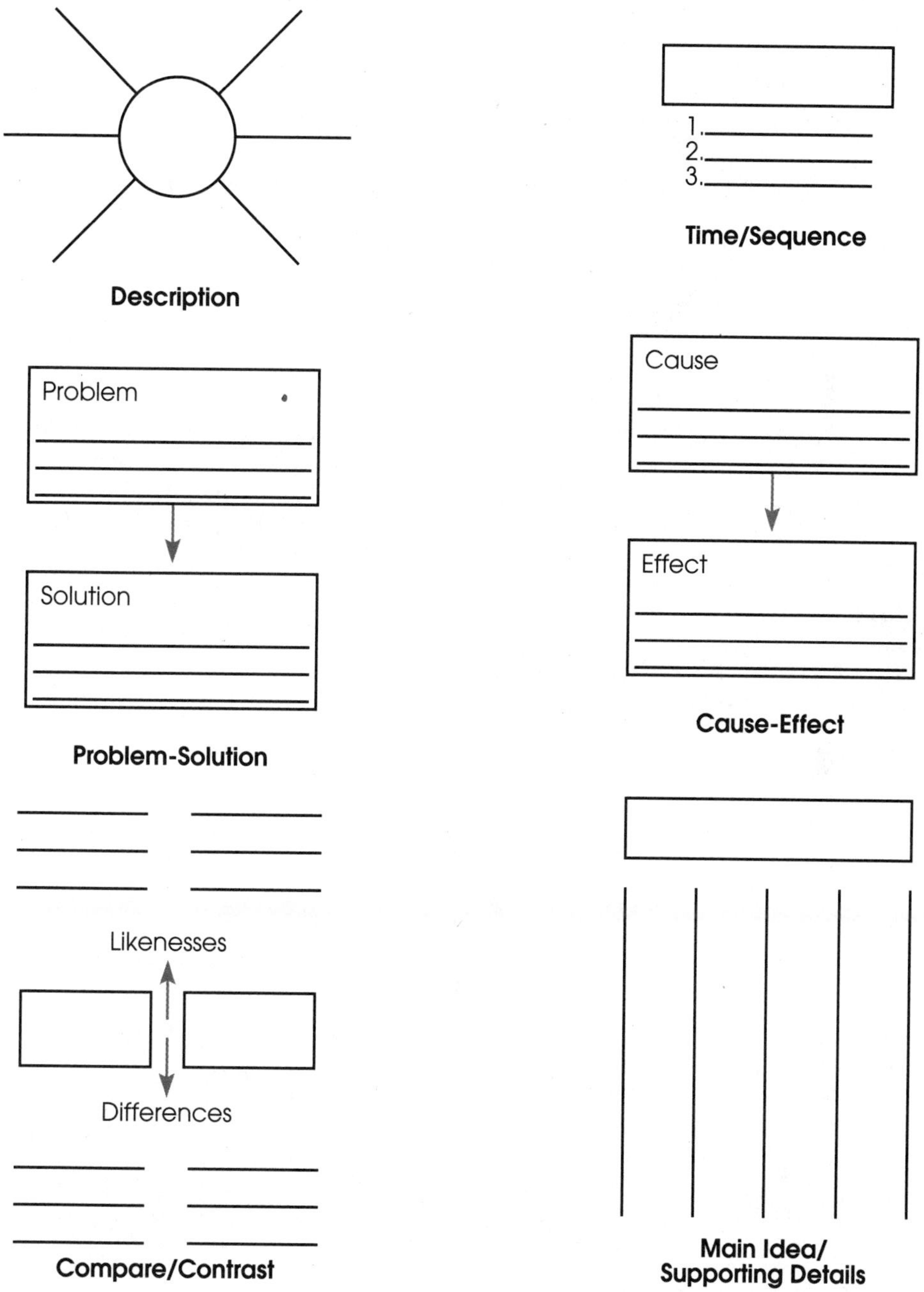
Description
1.
2.
3.
Time/Sequence
Problem
Solution
Problem-Solution
Cause
Effect
Cause-Effect
Likenesses
Differences
Compare/Contrast
Main Idea/
Supporting Details

### FIGURE 10.3   Partially Completed Graphic Organizer

Pets can be dangerous to your health.

1. There are many kinds of animal diseases.

2. _____

3. _____

4. Insect pests are attracted to animals.

5. _____

**Main Idea/Details**

in and have students fill in the remaining information on their own or working with a partner. Eventually, eliminate these supports and have students complete the entire graphic on their own. See Figure 10.3 for an example of a partly completed organizer.

A somewhat more complicated graphic is called the "pyramid" (Clewell & Haide-menos, 1983). As shown in Figure 10.4, the pyramid starts with a simple subject at

### FIGURE 10.4   Pyramid Graphic Organizer

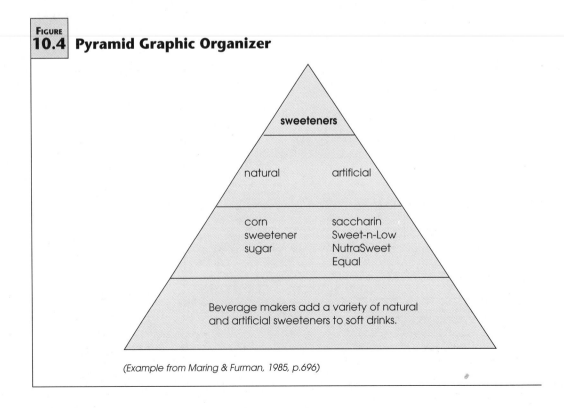

sweeteners

natural     artificial

corn
sweetener
sugar

saccharin
Sweet-n-Low
NutraSweet
Equal

Beverage makers add a variety of natural and artificial sweeteners to soft drinks.

*(Example from Maring & Furman, 1985, p.696)*

the top, adds details through the body of the graphic, and ends, at the base, with a good statement of the main idea or thesis of the reading selection. It should be noted that graphic organizers are more effective when students participate in their construction. One way to increase student participation is to have them work in groups to make structured overviews that they then will use in an oral presentation.

# WRITING TO LEARN

Despite a growing body of evidence that writing improves thinking and learning (Newell & Winograd, 1989), it is rarely used as a means of helping students explore content area information. Having already discussed the use of writing at emergent and higher-order levels, we shall limit ourselves here to two questions that are relevant to content area learning:

- What type(s) of writing are most appropriate in the content areas?
- How can the teacher encourage youngsters to use writing to learn?

## TYPES OF WRITING THAT ARE APPROPRIATE IN THE CONTENT AREAS

Several observational studies have determined that there are four types of writing that tend to be used in the content areas (Applebee, 1981; Marshall, 1987; Newell, 1984):

- Mechanical, or noncompositional writing—copying or recording
- Informational, or expository writing—responding to questions based on textual information
- Personal writing—focusing on students' interests, activities, and feelings in order to connect new learnings to these personal frameworks (e.g., journal writing, letter writing)
- Imaginative writing—writing stories, plays, and other literary forms

To complete the picture of writing options, we would add:

- Reflective essay writing—asking students to critically analyze information
- Constructive essay writing—inviting students to better *articulate* a position and/or offer possible constructive solutions to issues and problems

At present, essay writing occurs quite infrequently in our nation's classrooms: a mere 3 percent of the time, according to Applebee's (1981) findings. Even if we allow for a recent increase in attention to writing, the current figure, in our estimation, would not exceed 6–8 percent. More discouraging is the fact that critical and constructive writing does not occur often enough to even receive mention in observational studies. Research in progress is suggesting that the reason why teachers are not teaching critical and constructive writing is simply because they have never been taught to do so (Manzo, Mocker, & Manzo, report in preparation).

How then, can the teacher encourage youngsters to use writing to learn? Research has clearly established that different types of assignments result in different patterns of thinking (Langer, 1986; Tierney & Shanahan, 1991; Tierney, Soter, O'Flahavan, & McGinley, 1989). Generally, when writing tasks have been compared—such as writing answers to comprehension questions, taking notes, and essay writing—it is the latter that almost always results in greater gains in knowledge, more elaborative responses, and more abstract associations (Vacca & Linek, 1992).

The key ingredient in writing to learn seems to be the same one that facilitates effective reading comprehension. Both reading and writing require an "encoding" process that gets the student to engage, review, relate, restate, personalize, explain, and evaluate. These formations and transformations are the mental manipulations to look for in writing-to-learn activities and methods. You already know of several of these from the previous chapters. These include: the Writing Process; the Language Shaping Paradigm; writing REAP annotations such as simple summaries and critical–creative responses; and keeping Dialogue Journals. Let's look now at some specific suggestions for uses of writing in the content areas. These are drawn from three sources: Tchudi and Huerta (1983), Vacca and Linek (1992), and Manzo and Manzo (1990a).

- Initially, keep content at the center of the writing process. Focus on *what* the writing says, rather than *how* it says it.
- Design writing activities that help students structure and synthesize their knowledge, not merely restate it.
- Provide real or imaginary audiences for student writing so that students have a sense of writing for some real person or group.
- Look for writing activities that allow the student to play different roles: learner, researcher, inquiring reporter.
- Attend to the *process* of writing. Provide prewriting activities to help students acquire a solid grasp of the material; provide assistance and support as students write, helping them solve problems as they arise rather than waiting until an assignment has been turned in; and, offer help with final editing.
- Let students help one another with revisions and final editing. Provide support through revision and editing checklists and guidelines—also called *rubrics*. (See Box 10.4.)
- Don't confuse revising with editing. Approach revision first, having students clarify the content and substance of their work. Then focus on editing of spelling, grammar, punctuation, and usage.
- Make a conscious effort to provide pupils with an audience that enables them to write what they really think, an audience that will provide constructive (as opposed to generally negative) criticism.
- Display or otherwise publicize student writing through shows, demonstrations, book publishings, discussions, and oral readings. Don't be the only reader of your students' work.
- Provide a low-risk environment that values and encourages thinking—a supportive, we're-in-this-together, learning community.

- Provide well-thought-out themes, including some options to drive thinking and writing.
- Remember to ask for critical analysis and constructive thinking.

One way to teach students to evaluate their own and each other's writing is through the use of rubrics, or structured evaluation guides. The rubric shown in Box 10.4 can be used at any or each stage of the writing process. It can be used for self, peer, or teacher evaluation. Notice that 40 percent of the evaluation includes attention to critical and constructive thinking. Add elements to the rubric that serve your interests and situation. For example, you might wish to add spaces for "overall rating," for "too lengthy/too brief," or for "contribution to group effort." The rubric

---

**BOX 10.4** | **Rubric for Writing Evaluation**

Author's name _____      Writing Stage (circle one):
Evaluator's name _____      Draft/Revision 1/Revision 2/Edit/Final Copy

*Rate the author's piece on each item below: "1" is a low rating, "4" is high. Circle the number that shows your rating.*

1. The information provided seems to be accurate (for        1        2        3        4
   nonfiction) or believable (for fiction)

   *Explanation or examples:* _____

2. The piece is well organized, with a clear beginning,        1        2        3        4
   middle, and end.

   *Explanation or examples:* _____

3. The piece is original. It presents ideas or information        1        2        3        4
   in ways that are interesting.

   *Explanation or examples:* _____

4. Words and sentences are used in ways that help to        1        2        3        4
   emphasize the main idea or theme or mood of the piece.

   *Explanation or examples:* _____

5. The mechanics of writing (spelling, grammar, phrasing,        1        2        3        4
   punctuation) are accurate.

   *Explanation or examples:* _____

   _____

   _____

**FIGURE 10.5** Graphic Organizer: Clustering, Webbing, Semantic Mapping

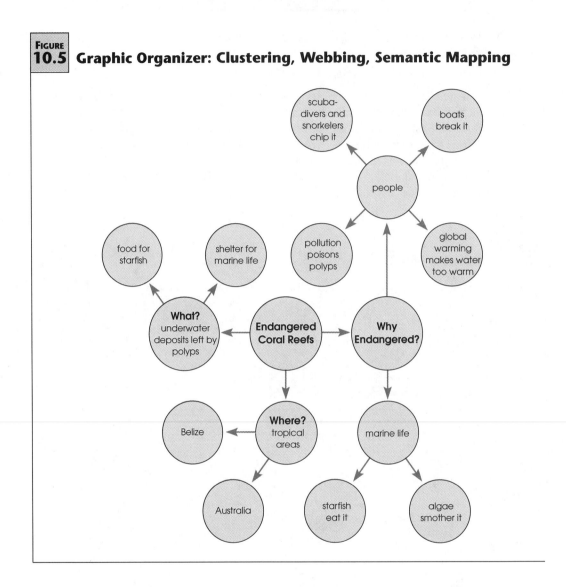

can also be an effective way to encourage greater precision in word choice and language usage.

Now that you have seen how easy it can be to fuse writing, reading, and thinking in constructive/creative ways, let's look at some appropriate ways to pay closer attention to promoting reconstructive/fact-based writing in the content areas.

## RECONSTRUCTIVE WRITING IN THE CONTENT AREAS

The methods described in this section teach students to use several additional graphic formats to guide thinking and writing about what they have read. Guided

FIGURE
10.6 **Graphic Organizer: Chart Format**

| Title | *How to Make a Kite* |
|---|---|
| Materials | *large sheet of sturdy paper, glue, lightweight strips of wood, strips of cloth, large roll of string* |
| Step 1 | *Draw kite shape on paper and cut out* |
| Step 2 | *Lay wood strips top-to-bottom and side-to-side on kite shape and cut to fit; cut notches close to ends of wood strips* |
| Step 3 | *Place string around edges of kite, wrapping around ends of wood strips* |
| Step 4 | *Fold paper edges down around string and glue securely* |
| Step 5 | *Attach string to bottom point of kite; starting about a foot from the bottom of the kite, wrap string around center of a 1"×8" strip of cloth and knot; add two more cloth strips, a foot apart* |
| Step 6 | *Decorate front of kite as desired, and you're ready for flight* |

practice in these methods enables students to add these basic thinking and study strategies to their personal array of options for strategic reading.

### Clustering, Webbing, and Semantic Mapping

Easily modeled on the chalkboard or overhead projector, the simple graphic organizer format called by these various names teaches students to organize their thoughts by making connections among key ideas. Simply place the topic or main idea in the center of the page and branch out to important subtopics. Illustrate the connections among items with lines or arrows. To welcome connections and elaboration, stand back, look at the board, and say (in some way): "Does anyone see any connections to any other things we are studying or that you have read?" You may need to offer an example or two to get the ball rolling. However, youngsters are usually quite responsive to such invitations. A fifth-grader offered this powerful connection to add to the example shown in Figure 10.5. "Energy! Lots of those things are forms of energy."

### Charts

When reading instructions, narrative information, and sometimes even fictional stories, charts can be a useful way to organize the information and ideas presented. Distribute blank chart forms to students. Direct students to use the chart form to fill in the steps (or events) as they read. The chart will eventually provide a summarized sequence of key points read (see Figure 10.6).

**FIGURE 10.7** **Graphic Organizer: Inverted Triangle Format**

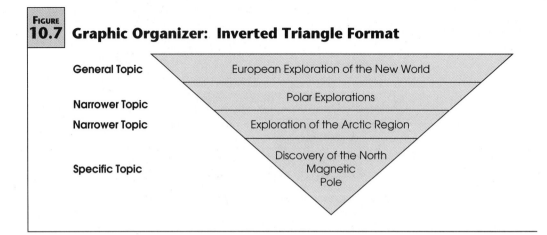

**General Topic** — European Exploration of the New World

**Narrower Topic** — Polar Explorations

**Narrower Topic** — Exploration of the Arctic Region

**Specific Topic** — Discovery of the North Magnetic Pole

### Inverted Triangles

This graphic form helps students to recognize large, general topics, as distinct from focused, specific ones. This is a useful format for guiding students' understanding of expository writing (see Figure 10.7).

### Time Lines

Constructing time lines helps students think about material that is based on chronological presentation. They provide a broad overview of a topic and solid touchstones for exploring how one piece of information relates to other events and people (see Figure 10.8).

As you can see, writing activities begin to blur the lines between subject and strategy instruction. This brings us to the next highest level of challenge for teachers, that of integrating reading and language arts lessons with subject area study.

**FIGURE 10.8** **Graphic Organizer: Time Line Format**

**Space Travel**

| 1961 | Russian cosmonaut orbits Earth. |
|------|----------------------------------|
| 1962 | John Glenn orbits Earth. |
| 1969 | Neil Armstrong and "Buzz" Aldrin land on the moon. |
| 1976 | NASA launches Mars space probes Viking 1 and 2. |
| 1981 | Two US astronauts orbit Earth 36 times in space shuttle Columbia, the first reusable spacecraft. |

# INTEGRATED LANGUAGE ARTS AND LITERATURE-BASED APPROACHES

Just as the content area reading movement has tried to demonstrate that reading, language, and thinking can be taught through the disciplines, so too has the whole language movement stirred deeper commitment to teaching content and concepts through literature. This same movement also has been largely responsible for giving new life to an emphasis on theme study. In theme study, a general topic is used as the basis for integrating language arts and subject area instruction to create cohesive units of reading, writing, thinking, and content study.

Theme study typically has the following characteristics:

- It teaches and reinforces content through literature.
- It is based on a conceptually unifying theme.
- It involves reading, writing, speaking, listening, and study.
- It flows from one part to the next, following some natural and relevant lines of inquiry.

Sounds good, you might think, but is it worth the effort to develop such units of study, and can teachers be so inventive all of the time? Having tested the first proposition very carefully, we can say that it definitely is worth the effort: an integrated approach improves learning to a significant degree. In a study comparing an integrated theme study program with a more traditional reading and language arts program, children in the integrated program did statistically significantly better on every measure employed—including the year-end standardized tests. The students, by the way, were all fourth-graders in an inner city school (Manzo, Manzo, & Smith, in preparation, 1993).

The second question—can teachers be so inventive all of the time?—is a bit more difficult to answer. In our study, teachers were carefully trained and were provided with materials that had been designed by curriculum specialists. However, the professional literature reports an increasing number of schools embracing the concept of theme study, and a wide array of teacher-developed theme units and curricula.

Pond and Hoch (1992) provide a convincing rationale for an integrated language arts curriculum:

> Pressure to include more topics and issues in the elementary school curriculum has reached a crisis point. It seems the only way to add something new to the curriculum is to take something away, so integrating the curriculum makes the most effective and efficient use of class time (p. 15).

This convincing rationale has gained recent support from a study by Guzzetti and associates (1992). This study provides empirical support for literature-based content units. Sixth-graders who studied China largely through literature scored significantly higher on a concept-based test than did those studying China in a traditional textbook (Guzzetti, Kowalinski, & McGowan, 1992).

In the sections that follow, you will find a broad sampling of integrated theme study units. These should help you grasp the concept of theme study in very concrete terms.

## LITERATURE-BASED SCIENCE UNITS

Pond and Hoch (1992, pp. 13–15) provide a number of examples to illustrate how literature can set the stage for activities that teach science concepts in meaningful ways. Three of these are detailed below:

| | |
|---|---|
| Literature Base: | *Charlotte's Web* (E. B. White, 1952) |
| Story Line: | A spider named Charlotte uses her web not to only catch insects for food, but also to save a pig's life. |
| Science Concepts: | How do spiders make their webs? How strong are spider webs? Why do spiders make webs? |
| Activity: | Have children catch a spider (a large black and yellow garden spider is ideal) and place it in a large terrarium or similar container. The children can then observe the spider spin its web. Live insects are then placed in the container to see how the insects are caught in the web. |
| Literature Base | *The Tough Winter* (Robert Lawson, 1979) |
| Story Line: | The story is about how animals work hard to survive a tough winter. |
| Science Concepts: | Why do we have seasons? What happens to plants during the winter? Where do animals spend the winter? What is hibernation? What foods can animals find during the winter? |

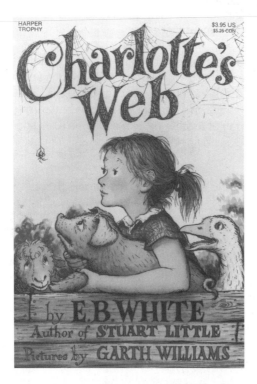

*E. B. White, New York: Harper & Row, (1952).*

| | |
|---|---|
| Activity: | Collect some cocoons from tall grass during February and March. Bring them into the classroom. Put them in a wide-mouth gallon jar. Cover with flyscreen. Observe. |
| Literature Base: | *Landslide* (Veronique Day, 1963) |
| Story Line: | Five children are trapped by a landslide while hiking. |
| Science Concepts: | What is erosion? What is the function of plants in maintaining a balance in nature? |
| Activity: | Construct a box that has two parts with a board separating those parts. Fill each side with dirt. Cover one side with grass seed. Let it grow. Then tilt the box and run water evenly down the two sides. Observe what happens to the dirt on the side without grass. |

Children's literature is rich with books that can make science concepts richer and more understandable. Maggart and Zintz (1992, pp. 400–402) offer these examples for developing units on animals and weather:

## Books for a Unit on Animals
- *Born in a Barn* (Gemming, 1974). Primary grades.
- *Panda* (Curtis, 1978). Primary grades.
- *Animal Superstars: Biggest, Strongest, Fastest, Smartest* (Freedman, 1984). Intermediate grades.
- *Here Come the Dolphins* (Goudey, 1961). Intermediate Grades.
- *Born Free* (Adamson, 1960). Upper grades.
- *Whale Watch* (Graham & Graham, 1978). Upper grades.

## Books for a Unit on Weather
- *Blizzard at the Zoo* (Bahr, 1982). Primary grades.
- *The Snowy Day* (Keats, 1962). Primary grades.
- *Listen to the Rain* (Martin & Archambault, 1988). Primary grades.
- *The Cloud Book* (dePaola, 1975). Intermediate grades.

## LITERATURE-BASED MATHEMATICS UNITS

For knowledge to be retained and transferred to other situations, it needs to be relevant and interesting to the student (Farris & Kaczmarski, 1988). Jamar and Morrow (1991) and Pauler and Bodevin (1990) have assembled integrated units for first- and second-graders. See the illustration below for a practical example of how "the natural language in good children's literature provides a vehicle that allows teachers to present interrelated activities in reading, writing, and mathematics" (Jamar & Morrow, 1991, p. 29).

| | |
|---|---|
| Literature Base: | *Cross-Country Cat* (Calhoun, 1979) |
| Story Line: | Henry, a sassy Siamese cat, takes matters into his own "paws" when his family accidentally leaves him behind at a ski lodge. Henry skis home, meeting a variety of animals along the way. |

| Mathematics Concepts: | Counting by twos; one-to-one correspondence; comparison; sequencing; map-making and map-reading. |
|---|---|
| Activity: | Use cut-out pairs of skis to practice counting by two's; use items of ski-clothing to reinforce the concept of one-to-one correspondence (2 shoes for 2 feet; 1 scarf for 1 neck; 2 mittens for 2 hands; 1 hat for 1 head, etc.); reinforce the concept of sequencing by having children list the animals that Henry met on his journey home; have children create maps of Henry's journey, illustrating where he met each of the other animals; have children use a cut-out ski to measure the length of Henry's trip, and to spark a discussion with questions such as, "How long do you think Henry's trip took? How long did it take Henry to get as far as he did before the family found him? How did you decide this? What clues did you find in the story or the pictures?" The map-making activity can be extended to creation of a neighborhood map, and estimation of distances. |

Jamar & Morrow (1991), pp. 29–33.

| Literature Base: | *Millions of Cats* (Wanda Gag, 1928) |
|---|---|
| Story Line: | Includes a refrain children can join in on when the story is read aloud, about hundreds, thousands, millions, billions, and trillions of cats! |
| Mathematics Concepts: | Place value, a mnemonic device for reading "big" numbers (a great motivator and confidence builder for young children). |
| Activity: | Note and list on the board the names of the number places: hundreds, thousands, millions, billions, and trillions. Explain how to read each hundreds and tens place ("three hundred seventy-eight *million* . . ."). Then show children how they can use the *Millions of Cats* refrain as a way to remember how to read numbers with as many as fifteen places. |

Pauler & Bodevin (1990) pp. 33–35.

Wood, Lapp, and Flood (1992) offer some additional examples of content area reading in mathematics that you might wish to examine. The methods they offer rely heavily on collaborative activities in reading, writing, and thinking aloud. One method, for example, uses a variation on "Big Books." Children produce enlarged versions of math word problems, then, using a pointer, show how they solved the problems (See Figure 10.9).

## OTHER LITERATURE-CONTENT TIES

Wooten (1992) gives several examples of how the Martin's books can be tied to subject area instruction. In one example, *Chicka Chicka Boom Boom* (Martin &

**FIGURE 10.9 Math Word Problems**

Archambault, 1989), a colorful illustrated alphabet book typically used with kindergartners was used with fourth-graders to release these "layers of learning" (see Figure 10.10).

Indrisano and Paratore (1992) offer this other literature-to-content connection. The book is a nonfiction piece by Barbara Bash (1989) called *Desert Giant—The World of the Saguaro Cactus.* Indrisano and Paratore's graphic organizer for *Desert Giant,* shown in Box 10.5, illustrates its potential for teaching science and ecology in an altogether engaging manner.

Children's literature is also full of natural connections with social studies. Select children's literature that illuminates the values of the people about whom the social studies text is written; books that teach something of the lives of the people, what daily living was like, what was fun, what games they played, what caused happiness and unhappiness, as well as fears and anxieties. Following are a few suggestions from Maggart and Zintz (1992, pp. 400–402):

- Biographies of historical figures, such as *Abe Lincoln Grows Up* (Cavanah, 1959).
- Fictional accounts of historical periods, such as the Laura Ingalls Wilder series (Harper & Row, 1951, 1953).
- Books representing varied cultural worlds, such as *Fifth Chinese Daughter* (Wong, 1963) that reveals the conflict between parents and the children growing up as first-generation immigrants in San Francisco; and *Owl in the Cedar Tree*

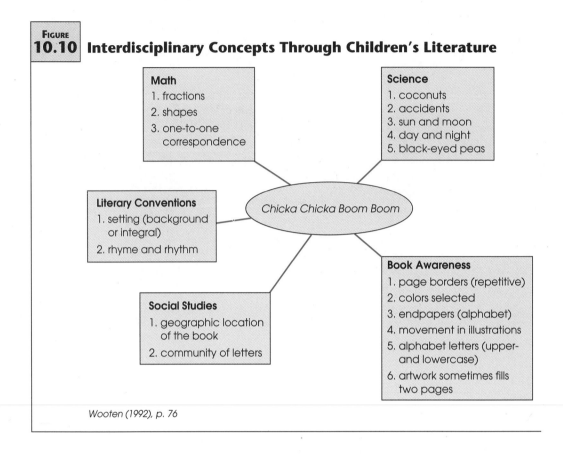

**FIGURE 10.10** **Interdisciplinary Concepts Through Children's Literature**

*Chicka Chicka Boom Boom*

**Math**
1. fractions
2. shapes
3. one-to-one correspondence

**Science**
1. coconuts
2. accidents
3. sun and moon
4. day and night
5. black-eyed peas

**Literary Conventions**
1. setting (background or integral)
2. rhyme and rhythm

**Social Studies**
1. geographic location of the book
2. community of letters

**Book Awareness**
1. page borders (repetitive)
2. colors selected
3. endpapers (alphabet)
4. movement in illustrations
5. alphabet letters (upper- and lowercase)
6. artwork sometimes fills two pages

*Wooten (1992), p. 76*

(Momaday, 1975) that presents a conflict between the culture of the Native American and the culture of the European settlers.

## LITERATURE-BASED INTERDISCIPLINARY UNITS

Once a teacher begins using literature as a springboard for content-based activities, the boundaries between subject areas begin to fade. A science lesson leads naturally to the introduction of a math concept, for example, and on to a social studies activity, and back to a writing activity. This is the height of excellence in teaching because it reflects the real world, where subjects do not exist as separate entities, but as threads in a richly woven fabric. See the lesson developed by Post (1992, pp. 29–35), below, for an illustration of how a single piece of literature can spark activities across the curriculum.

Literature Base:      "The Camel Caper" (Kristin Casler, *Grand Rapids Press;* see Post, 1992, for reprint)

Story Line:      In this humorous article Casler chronicles the escape of the camel, Roxanne, from the John Ball Zoo, her trav-

## Graphic Organizer for *Desert Giant—The World of the Saguaro Cactus*

### How It Looks

- can grow as tall as 50 feet
- can weigh several tons
- has sharp spines
- has accordion-like pleats that expand when it rains to store water

### How It Grows

- begins under the canopy of a larger tree or "nurse plant"
- after 50 years it produces its first flowers
- after 75 years, arms start to appear
- at 150 years, it towers over the desert
- can live for 200 years

### How It Is Used

- male woodpeckers make holes in the cactus for their mates' eggs
- elf owls and hawks live in them
- bats, doves, bees, and butterflies eat its flowers
- thrashers, lizards, and ants eat its fruit
- fruit used for jams, candy, and wine
- hardened parts of dead cactus can be used as food containers
- termites feed on dead cactus
- snakes, geckos, and spiders use the dead stalks as a home

Indrisano & Paratore (1992), p. 146.

els through the neighborhood, the reactions of stunned observers, and finally, her capture.

Language Arts Activities:

*Introduction.* Show a picture of a camel on an overhead and have students brainstorm what they know about camels. Distribute the article for students to read.

*Getting the Facts.* Distribute note cards and have students work in pairs to jot down the basic "who, what, when, where, why/how's" of the article.

*Application 1.* Distribute a map of the area in which the camel wandered and have students trace the camel's route from the zoo to where she was captured. Have students compare their maps with those of a partner. Where differences occur, reread for clarification. Show the map on an overhead and have one or more students or groups share their results with the whole class.

*Application 2.* Ask several students to volunteer to give an extemporaneous radio broadcast, using their "who, what, . . ." card as notes. Tape-record the speaking exercises. The teacher begins each "broadcast" by saying,

> "Good evening. This is station
> WGRX, Grand Rapids, Michigan,
> here to bring you the latest news."

Students speak into a real or pretend microphone. Replay each "broadcast," giving the speaker positive comments and constructive criticism. Later, transcribe these "broadcasts." Instead of writing them as a paragraph, list and number the sentences and use these as the basis for teaching aspects of grammar.

*Writing in Response to Reading*

A.    Have students use their "who, what, . . ." cards as the basis for writing a summary of the article.

B.    Brainstorm writing activities that are a stretch beyond summarizing, such as:

- "Write another chapter: 'Roxanne Escapes Again' or 'Roxanne is Banished from the Zoo.'"
- "Write poetry about Roxanne in the form of haiku, a limerick, an alliterative sentence, etc."
- "Write a different ending. Let's pretend she wasn't captured and tell what happened."
- "Rewrite the story from the camel's point of view. Use the first person, 'I,' for Roxanne."
- Present students' works in the "Author's Chair" format noted above.

**Mathematics Activities:**    Use elements from the article to make up story problems ("How much older is Bob Jester than Lisa Kolker?"); have students use story elements to make up their own story problems to trade with a partner and solve.

**Science Activities:**    Have students list things they know and do not know about camels, including living conditions, eating habits, and other characteristics. Assign research teams to discover the information they do not know.

**Social Studies Activities:**    Explore the role of the camel in certain societies and geographic regions, including map skills and locational skills.

**Grammar Activities:**    Find two colorful verbs in the article and explain what they mean; find two figures of speech in the article and explain what they mean.

As a follow-up to this discussion and illustration of theme study, it is necessary to consider the topic within a larger context. This is done by considering how *far* theme study should reasonably be taken.

## Can Subject and Literature Integration Be Taken Too Far?

Simply put, yes it can. The drawbacks to theme study can outweigh the advantages if subject area instruction loses all continuity and becomes entirely "hit-and-miss." Theme study can and should enhance instruction of the full scope and sequence of each subject. However, because it is so labor- and time-intensive, theme study can reach a point where it detracts from or actually replaces subject area study. Furthermore, some degree of formal subject area study probably is needed for students to reconstruct the facts and concepts on which each field of study is based. For example, story literature may give interesting historical accounts from ground level, but it is the explicit study of history that provides a look-out over the larger picture. Taken together, views from "the ground" and from "above the ground" can stimulate meaningful learning; when separated, they can be misleading. Hence, it could be said that theme study *alone* can be as fragmenting of subject area learning as trying to learn how to read from sequential instruction alone.

On a practical level, it also should be noted that textbook-based subject area instruction is efficient, manageable, and cost-saving. Bantam Doubleday Dell Books alone lists 150 titles for teaching history through literature. The process of selecting, buying, storing, replacing, and managing this collection alone can be quite expensive in dollars and human terms. Of course, given enough lead time, the school librarian usually can help to assemble a collection of books that correlate to unit themes. However, there remains the monumental task of correlating the concepts illustrated in these trade books to a reasonably thorough and sequenced presentation of social studies concepts in even one grade level. More to the point, consider the instructional planning that is needed to help children abstract social studies concepts from fictional accounts. Clearly, the organizing structure of textbook instruction is the most practical means of implementing theme study in a way that supports learning.

Let's look more carefully now at the important curriculum objective of teaching critical thinking. While a good deal can be taught about it in the abstract, critical thinking has little meaning or attraction without a context; hence its place in this chapter on content reading, language arts, and thinking.

# CRITICAL READING ACROSS THE DISCIPLINES

## Traditional Methods

There are several methods for promoting critical reading and thinking across the curriculum that are part of a long tradition in education (McKee & Durr, 1966). Learn these, and you will have a solid and tried set of practices that are largely adaptable to most any level of education, but clearly are most appropriate from fourth grade upward.

1.  Help youngsters to activate relevant prior knowledge and make predictions about material that you would have them read critically. Dole and Smith (1989) offer "Think Sheets" as a simple means for doing this:

**A Think Sheet for Social Studies**
Central Question: What is the government like in China?

| My questions | My ideas | Text ideas |
|---|---|---|
| How many rulers are there in China? | One | There is one ruler in China. There are three organizations, however—the communist, the socialist, and the military. |

2. Compare at least two biographies of the same person. Check the facts each source gives, then compare them with those presented in other sources. Which facts are historically true, and which seem legendary?

3. Compare ideas represented in books with present-day practices in areas such as family relationships, standards of living, ideas about discipline, nutrition, climate, geography, ethics, and so on. It's always fun to do this with movies by looking for things that are misplaced in time.

4. Read and compare reports of the same event in newspapers from different publishers and/or media sources and note the differences.

5. Find differing views on a subject. Discuss which are most valid and why.

6. List authorities in specific areas and discuss whether or not their writings should be accepted. Determine why or why not.

## Children's Magazine

*Science World, November 17, 1989, 46:6.*
*Scholastic Publishing Co.; 730 Broadway 10003*

## Children's Non-Fiction Trade Books

*EDC Publishing (8141 E. 44th St; Tulsa, OK 74143).*

7.  Explore several books or articles by the same author to trace the origins of or changes in his or her interests, viewpoints, and feelings.

8.  Examine articles from the editorial pages of various newspapers and discuss each in terms of personal opinion versus facts, biases, radical ideas, and attempts at sensationalism. The same procedures can be used with magazine articles, pamphlets, and books.

9.  Use *children's trade books and magazines* to build knowledge, interest, and wonder related to various topics and disciplines (see integrated language arts and literature-based approaches ahead in the chapter).

10. Develop criteria with the class such as author's background, position, experience with the subject, biases, writing style, and date of publication for use in determining the author's competence. (The teacher, as expert reader, should help students learn the following: Who is the author? What are his or her interests? Occupation? Experiences? What is the author's background in the subject? How did the author gather his or her information? Why did the author write this book or article? Is his or her reasoning sound? What evidence does the author provide to support his or her conclusions or generalizations? What appears to be the author's intent? Does the author attain this objective?)

11. Develop an idea and have pupils find information for subsequent evaluation. Classify each piece of information as valid, invalid, or questionable.

12. List facts and opinions offered in a selection and discuss how these may be distinguished.

13. Teach students to recognize "propaganda techniques"—see ahead for details.

## Propaganda and Advertising: Same Old–Same Old

Critical reading often involves recognizing an author's use of propaganda, or techniques designed to convince, persuade, or move the reader to action. In teaching this aspect of critical reading, it is useful to have a set of words and concepts for thinking about and discussing these techniques. The language is especially useful and transferable to teaching youngsters certain aspects of persuasive writing and oral presentation. Following are some of the most commonly used terms and ideas that provide useful reference points for critical analysis of argument or persuasion. Invite students to find examples of these and other "selling" techniques they encounter in their listening, viewing, and reading.

- *Bandwagon.* Everyone else is doing a certain thing, so jump on the bandwagon and go along with the crowd. ("More kids want _____ than any other toothpaste.")
- *Testimonial.* A well-known person, or person chosen to represent a class (such as the elderly) endorses a certain product or course of action even though he or she is not an authority on the subject. ("Take it from me, _____ is the greatest video game you can buy for the money.")
- *Plain Folks.* People who appear to be "just plain folks," or "just like you and me," suggest that we think or act in a certain way. ("My family has been in farming for 50 years; you know I won't forget you when I get to Washington.")
- *Snob appeal.* The opposite of plain folks. ("These beautiful designer jeans were created for the with-it girl.")
- *Name calling.* Applying a put-down to a person or movement, whether or not it really applies. ("That teacher is a geek—look at those ancient-looking clothes.")
- *Glittering Generalities.* Words or phrases with favorable connotations that lead us to favor a person or movement without examining the evidence (can also be used with unfavorable words). Such abstract words or phrases (e.g., "public spirit," "time for change," "patriotic duty," "fiscal responsibility") are used to make us support some person or idea with little further analysis. ("We need a leader who will guide us to greater fiscal responsibility, an improved standard of living, and a fairer system of taxation. It's time for a change!")
- *Transfer:* A commercial symbol that trades off our support for something to which it really is not connected. ("Buy Red Cross shoes"; "You can count on Veterans' Insurance Company.")
- *Scientific slant.* Use of scientific terms to persuade us to accept something as being more than what it really is. ("The titanium light bulb burns for 7,000 hours"; "Four out of five doctors surveyed . . .")

The ability to recognize the use of propaganda techniques in advertising is an important characteristic of knowledgeable and alert consumers. The ability to spot propaganda techniques in political events is perhaps even more important, since these same techniques are used in "selling" political options and candidates.

Let us now turn to a topic that can easily be overlooked in elementary school reading and language arts, but that is essential to content and concept acquisition: "study strategies."

# STUDY STRATEGIES

Study strategy instruction is a must for any literacy program that presumes to be child-centered. The reason for this is simple. Study strategies might be best thought of as the "practical" side of literacy. The term refers to all those things one can do to apply literacy to one's best advantage in a school setting. A typical study strategy curriculum, for example, includes topics like time management, note taking, study reading, memory techniques, test taking, report writing, and even reading rate. Such topics are essential in a program that is concerned not only with knowledge acquisition, but also with helping students to be efficient and effective in handling the demands of school.

Study strategies of every sort are strongly grounded in personal attitudes and habits. Acquiring a "new" study skill often means changing an "old" study habit. It means reflecting on what one typically does, and why, and then trying to do it better. The development of study strategies is an extension of metacognition. It is a personal, introspective process that can be quite difficult because study habits and attitudes—good ones or bad ones—are formed in the earliest years of school. The next sections describe approaches and strategies that help students form good study habits early and build on them as they grow.

## PRIMARY GRADES FOUNDATIONS FOR STUDY STRATEGIES

In the primary grades children begin to develop their personal response patterns to the requirements of school. The teacher has much of the responsibility for children's learning, but, even in these early years, children are expected to begin to assume increasing responsibilities. The primary school teacher can help to lay positive study strategies foundations in the following ways:

- Use strategies that reward questioning and critical and creative thinking.
- Impart the understanding that the purpose of writing is to express one's ideas and feelings.
- Teach reading lessons using strategies that permit the teacher to model effective behaviors for the three stages of the reading process: prereading, silent reading, and postreading.
- Teach vocabulary in ways that also teach children how they can learn words on their own.
- Teach children to organize their school materials so that they can find the proper supplies when they are needed.
- Teach children to record important information and assignments from the chalkboard.
- Use strategies that encourage effective listening.

## INTERMEDIATE GRADE STUDY STRATEGIES

### Involving Students in Study Strategies—PASS

The selection and use of effective study strategies essentially is a problem-solving process. It requires, as we have said, thoughtful analysis of one's habits, an honest evaluation of one's strengths and weaknesses, and an exploration of other possible ways of approaching reading and study tasks. The Problem-solving Approach to Study Skills (Manzo & Casale, 1980), abbreviated as *PASS,* is one way to help students to develop this personal problem-solving orientation while introducing them to a variety of study strategy options. It also is, by definition, a form of metacognitive control.

### STEPS IN PASS (MODIFIED FOR ELEMENTARY USE)

Step 1    *Count.* The teacher presents students with a list of common study skills problems and asks them to check those that apply to them (see Table 10.1).

Step 2    *Characterize.* The teacher guides students in defining selected study and learning problems in specific terms. With older students this can be done with inventories of learning style, temperament, skills, abilities, and attitudes.

Step 3    *Consider.* Students consider how they typically have dealt with their particular needs and problems and the possible advantages of these intuitive ways of dealing with school requirements.

Step 4    *Collect.* Students discuss and judge the value of standard techniques for dealing with reading/study problems. Where these seem to be inadequate, they are set aside for reconsideration in the next step.

Step 5    *Create.* Students seek inventive modifications and alternatives that match their personal strengths and needs. This step can be handled initially in

## Table 10.1

### Common Study Problems

*Directions: Check all that are problem areas.*

| | |
|---|---|
| _____ 1. Accurate and complete class notes | _____ 11. Attention while studying |
| _____ 2. Basic reading comprehension | _____ 12. Vocabulary knowledge and strategies |
| _____ 3. Identifying the main idea | _____ 13. Informational background |
| _____ 4. Noting important details | _____ 14. Homework |
| _____ 5. Drawing inferences from facts | _____ 15. Writing |
| _____ 6. Memory | _____ 16. Test-taking techniques |
| _____ 7. Test anxiety | _____ 17. Outlining/text notetaking |
| _____ 8. Concept formation | _____ 18. Library and reference strategies |
| _____ 9. Attention span in class | _____ 19. Classroom discussion |
| _____ 10. Attention span while reading | _____ 20. Critical/creative thinking |

individual and small-group settings, then in larger group discussions from which all may benefit.

Casale and Kelly (1980) found this technique of introducing study strategies to be an effective way to involve students in an examination of their own study habits and exploration of new possibilities.

### Study Reading—SQ3R and Strategy Families

It now is axiomatic that reading instruction should be planned and delivered in ways that give children opportunities to observe, select, and practice personal strategies for effective independent reading and learning. By intermediate grades, children are ready for a greater emphasis on metacognitive understandings—knowing what they know, and what they need to know—about reading. Robinson's (1946) "SQ3R" study technique is a simple means of introducing students to this metacognitive side of reading to learn. The acronym SQ3R is a way to remember to apply active reading strategies when reading independently.

## STEPS IN SQ3R

Step 1: **S** urvey—Look over the material before you begin to read:

    a.  Read the title and think about what it says or implies.

    b.  Read the headings and subheadings.

    c.  Read the summary if there is one.

    d.  Read the captions under pictures, charts, graphs, or other illustrations.

Step 2: **Q** uestion—Ask yourself questions about what you are going to read:

    a.  What does the title of the chapter mean?

    b.  What do I already know about the subject?

    c.  What did my instructor say about this chapter when it was assigned?

    d.  What questions do the headings and subheadings suggest?

Step 3: **R** ead—Read *actively:*

    a.  Read to answer the questions you raised when doing the survey/question routine.

    b.  Read all the added attractions in the chapter (maps, graphs, tables, and other illustrations).

    c.  Read all the underlined, italicized, or boldface words or phrases carefully.

Step 4: **R** ecite—Go over what you read by either orally summarizing it or by making notes of some type.

Step 5: **R** eview—Periodically survey what you read and learned:

    a.  Use your notes or markings to refresh your memory.

    b.  Review immediately after reading.

    c.  Review again before taking an exam on the subject.

Research on the effectiveness of SQ3R has shown that the "Recite" step of SQ3R is highly effective (McIntyre, 1991). Research on the general effectiveness of SQ3R as a whole, however, has not yielded clear support (Wark, 1964; Stahl & Henk, 1986; McIntyre, 1991). This is probably because, as Robinson himself observed, the strategy cannot be effective until it becomes "automatic" and "subordinate to the task of reading" (1946, p. 21). Intermediate grade students need a great deal of teacher guidance in the use of SQ3R. For many students, SQ3R requires substantial changes in habitual study reading behaviors. Elementary school teachers can help students develop effective study reading habits by providing guided practice in the use of SQ3R as a simple extension of any basic reading lesson.

Another way to help students to build metacognitive awareness of their reading and study behaviors was suggested by Dana (1989). Dana suggests introducing students to four major cueing strategies or "families" as she calls them. These cueing families are labeled with acronyms to help students remember effective strategies to apply before, during, and after reading:

| | |
|---|---|
| **Before Reading:** | **RAM** |
| as preparation for reading | Relax |
| | Activate your purpose |
| | Motivate yourself |
| **During Reading:** | **SIPS** |
| to focus on the content | Summarize natural sections |
| | Image—visualize the contents |
| | Predict what's coming |
| OR | |
| to make repairs | **RIPS** |
| | Read further/read again |
| | Paraphrase the troublesome section |
| | Speed up/slow down/seek help |
| **After Reading:** | **EEEZ** |
| to set your memory | Explain what it all means to you |
| | Explore other versions |
| | Expand with related material |

Once students have become familiar with these, you can encourage students to make up their own strategy families, as one group of boys did:

**BURP**

Breathe

Understand

Reread

Predict

One field-based study of the effectiveness of strategy families showed that remedial reading students (aged 7 to 15) who used these strategy families with fiction and nonfiction materials made significant gains on standardized reading tests (Dana, 1989). Children can make posters of strategy families for display. To amplify their value and use, leave space for testimonials: "When I began to use BURP, I realized that I was holding my breath whenever I had to do something I was afraid of. Just remembering to breathe normally really can help" (Jackie M., 5th grade).

### Listening

Listening is a skill that can be rather easily improved. Kelly and Holmes (1979) developed a variation on the Guided Reading Procedure, called the Guided *Lecture* Procedure to teach students to improve their ability to learn from listening during classroom presentations. A major part of school learning takes place through talking and listening. Teach children early on how to learn from this widely used mode of instruction.

## STEPS IN THE GUIDED LECTURE PROCEDURE

Step 1    Students are directed to *take no notes* as they listen carefully to the lecture. (The idea here is to have students focus, initially, on listening for concepts rather than details.)

Step 2    The teacher writes the objectives of the lecture on the chalkboard along with key technical terms.

Step 3    The teacher presents for about half the class period, then stops.

Step 4    Students attempt to write down everything they can recall from the presentation.

Step 5    Students form small cooperative learning groups to review and discuss their notes. This discussion component involves important manipulations of ideas and facts as well as involving the related language arts of speaking, writing, and listening.

This simple but effective activity provides a sound basis for teaching students to take better notes *while* listening—the next topic.

### Taking Notes in Class

By the intermediate grades, much content instruction is presented through a combination of lecture/discussion and related reading. Palmatier (1971) developed a notetaking method that integrates these two presentation forms and also provides a built-in study system. Palmatier's Unified Notetaking System (PUNS) is one of the few notetaking methods that has been validated through empirical research (Palmatier, 1971, 1973; Palmatier & Bennett, 1974).

## STEPS IN PUNS

Step 1    *Record.* Use only one side of regular-sized notebook paper, with a *3-inch margin* line drawn on the left side. (Many school supply stores now stock this type of paper for this purpose.) Record lecture-presentation notes to the right of the margin. Use a modified outline form to isolate main topics. Leave space where information seems to be missing. use the front side of the paper only, and number each page as you record the notes.

**Step 2**   *Organize.* As soon after the lecture as possible, add two sections to the notes. First, place *labels* in the left margin. These should briefly describe the information in the recorded notes. Second, insert *important text information* directly into the recorded notes. If you need more space, you can use the back of the notebook paper.

**Step 3**   *Study.* Remove the notes from the looseleaf binder and lay them out so that only the left margin of each page is visible (see Figure 10.11). Use the labels as memory cues to recite as much of the information on the right as you can recall. The labels can be turned into questions: "What do I need to know about ____[insert label]____?" Check your recall immediately by lifting the page to read the information recorded to the right of the label. As you learn the material on each page of notes, set that page aside in an "I already know" stack.

In a related method, called the Directed Notetaking Activity (DNA), Spires and Stone (1989) recommend adding a self-questioning component to the split-page notetaking approach. This addition offers a relatively easy and direct means of teaching metacognitive thinking. Students are taught to ask themselves these questions before, during, and after listening:

**Before Listening**
- How interested am I in this topic?
- If my interest is low, how do I plan to increase interest?
- Do I feel motivated to pay attention?
- What is my purpose for listening to this lecture?

**While Listening**
- Am I maintaining a satisfactory level of concentration?
- Am I taking advantage of the fact that thought is faster than speech?
- Am I separating main concepts from supporting details?
- What am I doing when comprehension fails?
- What strategies am I using to deal with comprehension failure?

**After Listening**
- Did I achieve my purpose?
- Was I able to maintain satisfactory levels of concentration and motivation?
- Did I deal with comprehension failures adequately?
- Overall, do I feel that I understand the information to a satisfactory level?

**10.11 Sample PUNS Study Layout**

Step 1: Record. Use the right-hand side of a specially divided page, leaving space to add text notes.

Step 2: Fill in labels. Write key word labels in the left-hand margin and text notes in the space provided for lecture notes. Use the back of the page if more space is needed.

Step 3: Study key words. Lay out pages so that only key words show, and try to recite the information from the notes. Remove each page as you master its contents.

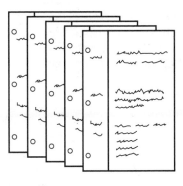

One of the best ways to teach notetaking is to begin by providing several pages of *partially completed* notes for students to follow and complete as they listen to short lecture presentations. Teaching notetaking does take some preparation on the teacher's part. However, the benefits to students will more than justify the effort. In a summary of the research on notetaking, Kiewra (1985) drew these conclusions:

- *Notetaking helps.* 35 out of 38 recent studies have demonstrated that taking notes increases attention and learning during lectures.
- *Review helps.* 24 out of 32 studies have found that students who review their notes learn and remember significantly more than those who do not.
- *Use the chalkboard.* Locke (1977) found that 88 percent of students recorded information from the chalkboard but only 52 percent recorded even the critical ideas when these were stated.
- *Pause briefly.* Providing occasional pauses during a lecture enriches lecture notes and increases recall (Aiken, Thomas, & Shennum, 1975).
- *Take breaks.* There is a 17 percent decrease in notetaking in the second 20 minutes of a 40-minute class period (Locke, 1977). (This finding is based on junior high students. The decrease very likely is much greater for younger children.)
- *Vary test formats.* Students who expect multiple choice examinations take notes of lower structural importance and recall more details recorded than students who expect an essay test. On the other hand, students who expect an essay exam take notes of higher structural importance and recall more concepts (Richards & Friedman, 1978).

When helping students to learn to take notes, be sure they know it's "OK"—even smart—to abbreviate! Intermediate grade students are usually intrigued by coded messages: They enjoy learning of and even creating their own abbreviations. See Box 10.6 for some examples of Speedwriting (or, more appropriately, "Spdwrtg").

Very few curricula even include attention to this easy way to help students to help themselves. The same is true of the next topic—memory. The absence of these topics from school programs is the strongest evidence that our schools are not yet "whole-child" centered. If they were, the needs of children for these easily acquired strategies would be a top priority.

## Memory Training

Much of the basic information we expect students to acquire in school requires simple rote memorization—at least until enough information and experience has been acquired to link the information into larger concept structures. Teaching students to use memory strategies can help them to tolerate times when school learning seems quite arbitrary and can give them a useful strategy for future school learning and success in business. Business and industry often pay huge sums of money to have these very methods taught to their employees. Harvard psychologist George Miller has determined that two-thirds of the population can only remember between five and nine unrelated pieces of information (the rule of $7 \pm 2$, cited in Pauk, 1974). Almost everyone, however, can easily increase this capacity by making items more meaningful or manageable in one or more of the ways discussed next.

For fun and painless practice, flexibly group students into teams and have them compete periodically to see who can best "learn and recall" the most on topics

> **BOX 10.6**    **"Spdwrtg" Abbreviations**
>
> ### Use symbols for words:
>
> | & | and |
> |---|---|
> | c | around, about, approximately |
> | @ | at |
> | # | number |
> | w/ | with |
> | w/o | without |
> | ? | questionable |
> | ! | surprising |
> | vs | versus, against, as compared with |
> | = | equals, is, the same as |
> | ≠ | does not equal, is different from |
> | < | is less than, less important than, etc. |
> | > | is greater than, more important than, etc. |
> | ∴ | therefore |
> | → | causes, results in, produces, yields |
> | e.g. or ex. | for example |
> | cf | compare, look this up |
> | i.e. | that is |
>
> ### Shorten words by eliminating final letters:
>
> | max | maximum |
> |---|---|
> | subj | subject |
> | info | information |
>
> ### Shorten words by omitting vowels, but keeping enough consonants to make the word recognizable:
>
> | rdg | reading |
> |---|---|
> | bkgd | background |
> | gvt | government |
> | clsrm | classroom |
> | lrng | learning |
>
> ### Shorten frequently used words and phrases by using first letters or acronyms:
>
> | GNP | gross national product |
> |---|---|
> | NDP | National Democratic Party |
> | S/L | standard of living |
> | CW | Civil War |
>
> *Manzo & Manzo (1990).*

from geography to parts of the body. As mentioned in an earlier chapter, such "quiz bowl" competitions even once a week, are of proven value for all students, but especially for slower learners, and especially when better students serve as incidental tutors by describing the memory techniques they use.

**Key Word Study Strategy**    The most frequent problem with "forgetting" occurs as a result of inadequate initial learning: The reason we don't remember names is most often because we didn't hear them to begin with. Accordingly, Al-Hilawani

(1991) recommends a variation on reciprocal teaching to get things learned deeply the first time. In the Key Word Study Strategy, students and teacher first discuss the topic of the lesson in general terms, to help retrieve prior learning of specific related ideas and vocabulary. They then try to identify key words in a paragraph as they read silently. Students and teacher then take turns asking what happens before and after each word without rereading the paragraph. Next, students write questions for each paragraph in the selection and take turns asking them. Finally, they summarize what they have learned. The teacher models this step before having youngsters try it.

Al-Hilawani credits Mann and Sabatino (1985) with the idea of writing down important words that can serve as memory tags for retrieving stored information. The further steps of questioning one another and summarizing the passage clearly add strong memory traces and rich associations. It also is consistent with basic research that shows that remembering incoming information depends, as suggested above, on the initial levels of processing of that information (Craik & Lockhart, 1972). (Note that the Key Word *Study* Strategy is different from the strategy with a similar name: the Keyword *Vocabulary* Method described in the chapter on vocabulary.)

**Imaging**    Teach children to take the time to form clear visual images of material studied. Have them close their eyes, while you describe the object or event in minute detail. In one study, Meier (1978) taught the elements of a brain neuron by telling students to imagine that they were floating around in the cytoplasm of a neuron. Students were told to picture the cell, to touch it and feel a mild electrical charge, and to carefully picture and even feel various parts of the neuron. They were told that they were inventing a vivid, memorable experience. These students' comprehension was compared with another group of students who were taught the same information via lecture accompanied by attractive props and illustrations. The group taught through imaging performed 12 percent better on a test of immediate recall and 26 percent better on a test on long-term retention.

**Loci Imaging**    This is a specific type of imaging that has been used since the time of the ancient Greeks. Have students pick a familiar location, such as the classroom, and to identify specific locations, or "loci points" within it. The items to be remembered are then mentally placed and pictured in the different loci points. When the items are to be recalled, students need only retrace their steps and retrieve the images from where they were placed.

**Spatial Arrangements**    Spatial Arrangement is similar to Loci Imaging, but simply uses a familiar shape, such as an $X$ or a $K$ or a $2$ to organize and picture the information to be recalled (see Figure 10.12).

**Clustering**    When there is much information of a certain type to be learned and remembered, help students to break it into parts, or "clusters." For example, in trying to learn the names and discoveries of early explorers of North and South America, it helps considerably to simply group them by threes, or better, by the continent or parts of continents they explored.

**Acronyms**    This is probably the most commonly known memory strategy. It involves the creation of "memory words" from the first letter of each word in a list

**FIGURE 10.12** **Spatial Arrangement Memory Technique**

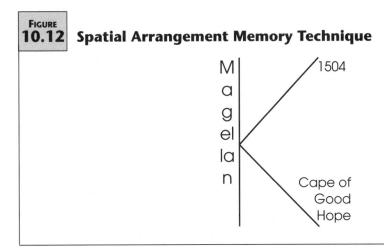

of words to be memorized. How many of us, for example, use the acronym ROY G. BIV to remember the colors of the spectrum (red, orange, yellow, green, blue, indigo, and violet)? Similarly, students of geography are always pleased to learn HOMES—an acronym for the names of the Great Lakes: *H*uron, *O*ntario, *M*ichigan, *E*rie, and *S*uperior (Uttero, 1988).

### Report Writing

While much of the current focus of writing instruction is on writing to learn and writing in response to reading, the traditional report continues to be an often-used means of assessing student learning. Report writing often requires effective use of the library and related resources materials, as well as application of notetaking, expository writing, and referencing. Box 10.7 provides a listing of the essential components of report writing as a guide for instruction. You will have to give some thought to just how to *teach* each of these points. For example, you could walk students through some of the broader and narrower topics. You will need to review and/or teach students the basic procedures for accessing information in the library prior to having them attempt to use these resources. Students may be organized in small groups to help one another formulate report topics and search for relevant information in the library. Later in the report-writing project, group members can review each other's draft material to make suggestions about organization, word choice, and mechanics such as spelling and punctuation.

### Test Taking

The object of test-taking instruction is to familiarize students with the testing formats they will encounter, so that they can use them easily and comfortably. When children are not able to do this, their test scores reflect what they know about tests, rather than what they know about the subject the test is presumed to be measuring. Here are some ideas to share with your students for taking typical standardized tests,

---

**BOX 10.7** | **Components of Report Writing: A Guide for Instruction**

Formulating a report topic (not too broad: not too narrow)
Collecting information

    Using the library card catalog (hard copy and electronic)
    Using guides to periodicals
    Conducting personal interviews
    Taking notes from reading
    Documenting reference source information
    Taking notes during interviews (or from taped interviews)

Organizing a report

    Developing an introduction, a sequenced presentation of information, and a conclusion
    Constructing paragraphs
    Using descriptive words

Targeting the audience

    Writing in a style that matches the intended audience
    Selecting and presenting information that matches the intended audience

Preparing the final copy

    Eliminating errors in grammar, punctuation, usage, etc.
    Following a style guide for appropriately referenced information sources
    Producing legible final copy

---

summarized largely from Pauk's (1974) recommendations to college students. These are best adapted and presented in combination with practice standardized tests that can be purchased (from the test publisher or from teacher supply sources) or made yourself.

1. Read the directions for the whole test and for each subsection.
   a. Note the number of items, and set a rough schedule for the amount of time you have to work. Leave time to check your work.
   b. Ask about guessing penalties—whether points will be subtracted for incorrect answers or items left blank. If not, you should guess when you don't know the answer.
2. Answer the easy items first.
   a. Spending time on difficult questions will make you tense and could cause you to forget information you knew when the test began.
   b. As you go through the test, you often will come across information that will help you remember answers to earlier items.
3. Read each question carefully.
   a. Cover the choices and read the question; try to state it in your own words. If the question is long and complex, underline the subject and the verb.

    b. With the choices still covered, make a guess at the answer. Predicting your own answer first puts you more in control. You are not as easily led astray by an incorrect answer, or as confused by two similar answers.

    c. Uncover the choices one at a time, noting each as "probable" or "not probable" before deciding. (Test makers often put a correct but not best choice at the top of the list.)

4. Try to think simply and clearly: try not to read too much into the question.

    a. If a question is in the negative form—for example, "One of the following is *not* a cause"—it is helpful to look for three "true" answers; then the remaining false answer will be the correct one.

    b. Make sure that the grammatical structure of your choice matches that of the question stem.

    c. General statements are more likely to be correct than very detailed statements, especially if you think of *even one* exception.

5. Keep a positive attitude.

    a. Don't assume that the test is loaded with trick questions. If you look for tricks, you will read too much into the questions and trick yourself.

    b. As an overall approach, read each question carefully but concentrate on the main point rather than the details.

6. Watch yourself for signs of worry.

    a. During the test, pause briefly two or three times to consider whether you are overly tense: Neck muscles tight? Palms clammy? Weak stomach? Holding your breath?

    b. Avoid stress-related behaviors that break concentration: glancing frequently at the clock or the teacher, examining fingernails, gazing at the wall or ceiling, excessive yawning or stretching.

7. Check your work.

    a. Make sure you answered all questions you had skipped to come back to later.

    b. Check your answer sheet against your question sheet to make sure the numbers match (check about every fifth question or so).

    c. Don't waste time reviewing answers if there are still questions unanswered.

    d. Change your answers if you have reason to. Research shows that contrary to common belief, three out of four times your *changes* will be correct. This may be because during a final check, the tension begins to lessen and thought processes are clearer.

    There are many other topics and techniques that can be covered under study strategies. Some of these, such as reference skills and report writing, are covered quite well in most basal-reader programs, or are taught incidentally in more whole-language and strategy-based methods such as those described throughout the text where meaning and inquiry drive research and writing. However, the crowning moment in all study is the opportunity to reach some level of being well informed in an area of personal concern. Consider this next idea for building this option into your reading–language–thinking content programs.

**FIGURE 10.13** **Be-an-Expert Kits**

"You can be an expert. You can know more about _____ than anyone else in this room, this school, this block, and maybe this town. Here's what you do. Unpack this kit. Listen to the tapes. Study the maps. Read the books. When you're ready, ask for the EXPERT QUIZ. You can do this by yourself or with a partner.

"My first Be-an-Expert Kit was on Mozart, celebrating the 200th anniversary of his death. I taped the best-known, most sprightly airs from my Mozart records. I also taped the brief but rather difficult text of Lisl Weil's _Wolferl: The First Six Years in the Life of Wolfgang Amadeus Mozart._ I added two fairly easy, well-focused biographies: _Mozart Tonight_ by Julie Downing and _Mozart: Scenes from Childhoods of the Great Composers_ by Catherine Brighton. As an option, I added _The Mozart Season_ by Virginia Euwer Wolff, a novel about a 12-year-old violinist getting ready to play a Mozart concerto in competition.

"Students can check out the kit for three weeks. When they finish, they request the EXPERT QUIZ, which I prepare and seal in an envelope. The quiz isn't picky, but it does require information that a person ought to have if she or he claims to be an expert on, say Mozart: _Which opera has a statue that moves? If you play a clavichord, do you sit down at it, blow into it, or tuck it under your chin?_

"Put the Be-an-Expert materials in uniform-size boxes bought at the hardware store. Start the year with six of them on a range of arts-related topics. Invite contributions. I'm waiting for a family to come back from Salzburg with more Mozart materials!"

_Sebesta (1992), p. 59._

Certificate
of
Proficiency

(name)

Mozart Expert

(signature)

(date)

## Certified Expert

It has long been held that concentrated study in almost any subject for 15 minutes a day for four years will make one an expert. More importantly, concentrated study in a field reveals the structure of knowledge in that field. The mind begins to make conceptual maps, especially if taught and encouraged to do so.

We have long recommended that libraries and teachers act as guides and certifiers of independent study by students in areas of their special interest (Manzo, 1973; Manzo & Manzo, 1990a). However, it took Sam Leaton Sebesta (1992) to suggest a neat package for making it work.

See Sebesta's account of the Be-an-Expert Kit (Figure 10.13) to see how this can be done. To give a further sense of importance and tangible achievement to such study, check your computer software supplier for some of the wonderfully official-looking certificates that you can make to certify a student's special expertise (see Figure 10.13). Work collaboratively with other teachers (especially those with interesting avocations) and other school personnel to assemble "Be-an-Expert" kits.

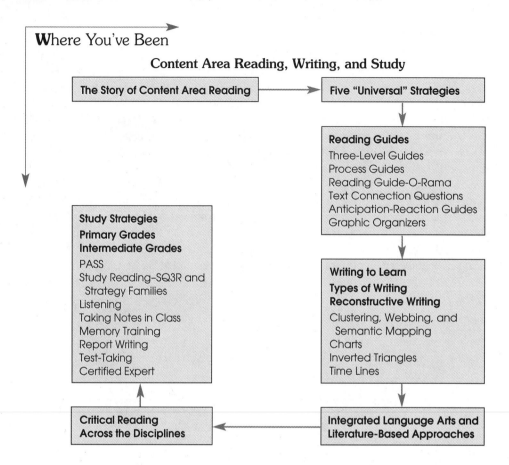

**W**here You've Been

**Content Area Reading, Writing, and Study**

The Story of Content Area Reading ➔ Five "Universal" Strategies

**Reading Guides**
Three-Level Guides
Process Guides
Reading Guide-O-Rama
Text Connection Questions
Anticipation-Reaction Guides
Graphic Organizers

**Study Strategies**
**Primary Grades**
**Intermediate Grades**
PASS
Study Reading–SQ3R and
　Strategy Families
Listening
Taking Notes in Class
Memory Training
Report Writing
Test-Taking
Certified Expert

**Writing to Learn**
**Types of Writing**
**Reconstructive Writing**
Clustering, Webbing, and
　Semantic Mapping
Charts
Inverted Triangles
Time Lines

**Critical Reading**
**Across the Disciplines**

**Integrated Language Arts and**
**Literature-Based Approaches**

**W**here You're Going

Chapters 1 through 10 have prepared you to teach and address the needs of most children of average ability and from conventional backgrounds. In the final section of the book you will learn about a range of literacy support provisions, ranging from special methods to assessment to organizing the classroom and school literacy program. The next chapter, which introduces this final section, will help you to better understand and help children with more specialized needs.

### *Reflective Inquiries and Activities*

1. Search your memory, and then the book (run your finger through the index), for some ideas and methods that seem particularly relevant to content area applications:

    *From My Memory*
    *(e.g., K–W–L Procedure)*

    *From the Book*
    *(e.g., Cultural Academic Trivia Game)*

2. List the forms of thinking that were addressed in the chapter and (very briefly) how each can be promoted.
3. Review the "Primary Grades Foundations for Study Strategies" on page 413. List two or three teaching strategies you have learned about in previous chapters that accomplish each point listed.
4. Go back to the chapter on reading comprehension and find a method or two that strongly foster initial learning as a means to achieve long-term memory. Explain your reasons for selecting these methods for this purpose.
5. Use a memory device described, or another of your choosing, to show how you can remember everyone's name in a class.
6. Assemble an Integrated Reading–Language Arts Content Lesson around one or more pieces of children's literature.
7. Why is attention to study strategies, such as memory training and speedwriting, a sign of concern for the whole child? Would you include typing in this list? Why?

# PART V

# LITERACY SUPPORT PROVISIONS

# LITERACY PROVISIONS FOR CHILDREN WITH SPECIAL NEEDS

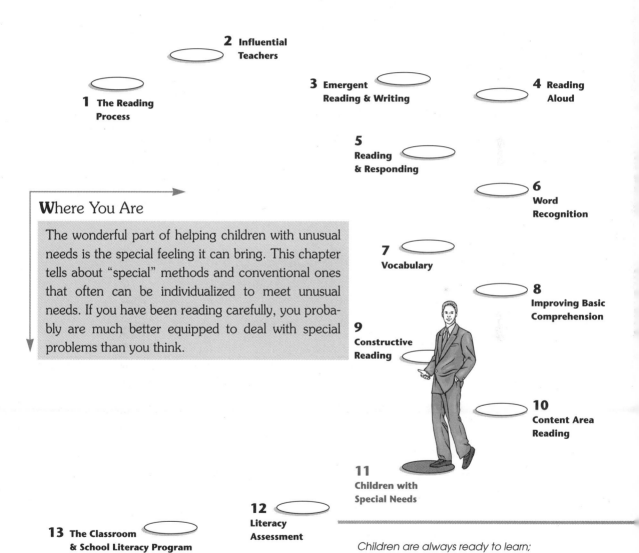

**2 Influential Teachers**

**1 The Reading Process**

**3 Emergent Reading & Writing**

**4 Reading Aloud**

**5 Reading & Responding**

**6 Word Recognition**

**W**here You Are

The wonderful part of helping children with unusual needs is the special feeling it can bring. This chapter tells about "special" methods and conventional ones that often can be individualized to meet unusual needs. If you have been reading carefully, you probably are much better equipped to deal with special problems than you think.

**7 Vocabulary**

**8 Improving Basic Comprehension**

**9 Constructive Reading**

**10 Content Area Reading**

**11 Children with Special Needs**

**12 Literacy Assessment**

**13 The Classroom & School Literacy Program**

*Children are always ready to learn; they're just not always ready to be taught.*

*Anonymous*

## "SPECIAL NEED" DEFINED

If the term "special need" were defined simply as unique and individual learning characteristics, it would apply to *all* children, since all children are unique. In this context, however, "special need," is more narrowly defined. The term refers here to particular types of problems that every teacher now is expected to address. These typically include children who have various types of reading and learning disabilities; those whose cultural or learning styles are under-represented; and those who come from linguistically different backgrounds. Students in each of these categories may be "at risk" of failure in school unless some special instructional provisions are made.

Several categories of at-risk students are *not* addressed in this chapter. Needs of the physically handicapped and the emotionally distressed, for example, are covered only incidentally, since these are covered thoroughly in other courses. This chapter is written to address the more traditional categories of the disabled reader, the poorly motivated, and students with limited English proficiency (LEP).

Let's begin now by talking about prevention. Most literacy specialists agree that efforts are better spent on *preventing* reading failure than on attempts to remediate problems once they have become evident and serious. The people of New Zealand have done something about this, and Americans are catching on.

## A POUND OF PREVENTION: "READING RECOVERY" AND "SUCCESS FOR ALL"

### READING RECOVERY

Developed in New Zealand, and pioneered by Marie Clay (1985), Reading Recovery is designed to help children having difficulty in reading and writing after the first full year in school. The primary purpose of Reading Recovery is to serve as a safety net by undercutting early reading failure and reducing the need for subsequent remediation in the later grades (Pinnell, 1989, 1992). As such, it has become known as a "preventative program," even though it begins after a full school year.

Characteristics of Reading Recovery for children include:

- It is designed for the lowest achieving readers in the first grade.
- Each child's program is individually constructed and focuses on strengths.
- The program involves intensive one-on-one tutoring by a trained adult.
- It is supplementary to the classroom: classroom and Reading Recovery teachers work as a team.
- Reading Recovery is temporary, lasting 12 to 20 weeks.
- The program is discontinued, and another child is entered, as soon as a qualitative assessment, supported by an outside consultant, provides evidence that the child can continue to learn in the typical class situation.
- The Reading Recovery teacher "teaches for strategies"—or the construction of "in-the-head" operations that are characteristic of good readers.

- It relies on story books and does not use highly controlled readers or workbook sheets.

Reading Recovery lessons consist of a framework of writing and several levels of reading. It is not a step-by-step plan, but one that unfolds more like an extended conversation between teacher and child. There typically are four phases to a Reading Recovery lesson. These are worth noting, since many teachers are adapting these phases for use in regular classroom instruction.

1. *Rereading.* The lesson begins with the child rereading several familiar, or previously read books. The textual material tends to contain language close to children's oral forms, but otherwise is not overly controlled for vocabulary and sentence length.

2. *Yesterday's New Book.* The most recently read new book, which was introduced the previous day, is read orally and independently while the teacher makes a record of the reading using those observations to guide her teaching decisions.

3. A short period of letter and word work with magnetic letters follows.

4. *Writing.* Every day the child writes and then reads a message which the child has previously written. This is not meant to take the place of the writing process which, Clay says, should continue to be taught in regular class. The messages typically are connected to the stories and tend to be personal responses to text. The child writes as much as he can alone, the teacher writes some words for the child, and she selects some words for them to work on together on the practice page. This is a shared activity. The sentences are composed in the child's unique way: "I wish I had a basket like Little Red Riding Hood had. I like her hood to." The teacher encourages the child to hear the sounds he needs to write and uses judgment as to when to correct grammar, punctuation, and spelling. If there is conversation, it can occur quite naturally as part of the chit-chat of writing and reviewing: "When you mean that you 'also' like her hood, it's spelled t/o/o; this way it isn't confused with 'to' as in 'to do something.'"

5. *New Book.* A new book is introduced every day. Ideally, it is one that offers a bit more challenge.

6. The book will then be read successfully with the teacher's support. (No two children need read the same books or follow the same sequence. Teachers do not read these books to the children. This time is considered reading and practice time for the child.)

To achieve projected results, Reading Recovery requires a year of in-service training. This takes the form of extensive conferencing on what a teacher is facing and doing with each child. It is a clinical training model that deals with whatever comes up in a collaborative problem-solving way, more so than training in a set of procedures. Hence it requires schoolwide, if not districtwide, financing, restructuring, and support. Teachers are trained to be decision makers about the needs of hard-to-teach children. When this type of training and support has been implemented, the Reading Recovery program has had impressive results, even when compared with other one-to-one tutorial programs (Pinnell, DeFord, Lyons, Bryk, & Seltzer, 1991).

The next program described has also been receiving high marks for prevention of reading failure. Like Reading Recovery, it is also based on one-to-one tutorials but adds enhancements of the regular reading program as well.

## SUCCESS FOR ALL

The objective of this program (based on the work of Slavin, 1987; Slavin, Madden, & Dolan, 1990; Slavin & Yampolsky, 1991) is to do "whatever it takes" to ensure reading success for every child. Madden and colleagues (1991) describe Success for All as a combination of approaches, containing the following elements:

**Reading Tutors**    Children who are not keeping up with their reading groups are placed with individual tutors for 20 minutes of an hour-long social studies period. Reading tutors are certified teachers who receive a two-day training in the program. In tutoring sessions they teach the regular reading curriculum but use different strategies than those used in the classroom program. Teachers and tutors meet regularly to coordinate their efforts. Student progress is evaluated every eight weeks using curriculum-based assessments, teacher judgment, and other formal measures.

**Reading Program**    Students are grouped in heterogeneous classes for most of the day. For the 90-minute reading period, however, students in grades 1–3 are regrouped in *cross-grade* groups according to reading level: a reading class working at second grade, first semester level, might include first-, second-, and third-grade children. This type of grouping, a version of what is known as the "Joplin Plan," has been found to increase elementary school reading achievement (Slavin, 1987). Teachers receive a two-day training when the progam is initiated. At every level, the 90-minute reading time begins with the teacher reading children's literature to children and leading a discussion of the story. Other instructional components include:

- At K–1, emphases on listening, retelling, and dramatizing stories, oral and written composing activities, and vocabulary development. Phonetically regular minibooks used for oral reading to partners, to the teacher, and for instruction in story structure, comprehension strategies, and writing in response to reading.
- Beginning with primer reading, use of cooperative learning activities based on story structure, prediction, summarizing, vocabulary building, decoding, and story-related writing.
- Direct instruction in comprehension strategies, followed by team practice activities.

**Eight-Week Reading Assessments**    Students in the regular program, as well as those in additional tutorials, are evaluated at eight-week intervals to identify candidates for tutoring, for a change in reading group, or for specialized assessment or other type of intervention.

A program facilitator and a family support team also are important parts of the Success for All program. The facilitator helps to plan, schedule, and monitor the program. The family support team encourages parent participation in school activities and in working with their children at home.

The seven schools in which Success for All has been implemented and evaluated are among the most disadvantaged and low-achieving schools in their districts; five of these schools are almost 100 percent African-American (Madden et al., 1991). In these schools, students' reading achievement has exceeded that of students in matched comparison schools. More importantly, achievement gains increase from year to year from first through third grade. The program's proponents suggest that results of Success for All indicate a need for *both* early intervention tutorials *and* improvement in classroom practice throughout the early grades.

Several of the ideas developed ahead can be used with Reading Recovery, Success for All, or with any in-class remedial program. Some have been part of "remedial reading" for several generations.

# DISABLED READERS IN THE REGULAR CLASSROOM

You should be pleased to know that if you have been reading carefully, you already are well prepared to deal with many of the issues discussed ahead. The "specialness" of approaches and methods used with special needs students lies largely in the fact that they are reflectively selected for application in some more intense or adapted way to correct or compensate for some specific area of apparent need. Therefore, much of what you have learned to this point is more than a prologue to assisting special needs children; it is immediately and directly applicable.

As a reflective teacher, you will realize that any method is potentially a special method when it is applied in response to an unattended need. Special does not need to mean exotic—though it can be; nor does it have to be specialized—which it also can be. However, it always must be thoughtful and provisional: If it doesn't work, change it, and if you find a match, light it!

Let us now consider some general tips for working with disabled readers in the regular classroom.

## GENERAL GUIDELINES

Nine general tips have been suggested by Ford and Ohlhausen (1988) for teachers to consider in working with disabled readers in regular classrooms. They are as follows:

1. *Organize instruction around* themes that *focus on real, meaningful learning.* In a theme approach, children can engage in a variety of individualized and small group activities to which readers of all levels can contribute.

2. *Capitalize on these children's* oral language *strengths to maximize their participation in class activities.* Whole-class activities such as brainstorming and semantic map techniques actively involve readers in content learning.

3. *Use whole-class activities that have built-in* individualization. Activities such as Sustained Silent Reading and Journal Writing are inherently individualized— each student reads or writes at levels that suit his or her abilities and interests.

4. *Develop open-ended class projects that allow students to contribute at various levels and in various modes.* Publishing a class newspaper or producing a dramatic presentation are examples of class projects that require many different kinds of contributions from students. When guiding projects such as these, find ways to incorporate the talents of all students.

5. *Plan writing activities that allow children to respond at their own levels.* Using patterned stories and poetry is a good way to ensure that all children have access to the writing activity. Even the most reluctant writers become involved when they realize that it's okay to "borrow" another author's pattern.

6. *Use group incentives and internal competition to motivate disabled readers.* Avoid subjecting these children to the inevitable failure that results from unequal competition by establishing group goals to which all members make a contribution. Students also can be encouraged to set individual goals and decide how to chart their progress—again avoiding unnecessary competition among classmates.

7. *Implement cross-age tutoring with a group of younger students.* In these settings, disabled readers have the opportunity to practice reading materials and writing forms that are appropriate for their reading level but may not be socially acceptable by their peers.

8. *Obtain the help of the school psychologist to implement relaxation techniques in the classroom.* Some disabled readers suffer from attention deficit disorder, as well as a good deal of stress, that can contribute to feelings of frustration, anxiety, and avoidance. Training in muscle relaxation, deep breathing, and visualization techniques teach children some coping strategies for dealing with such stresses. (See Manzo & Manzo, 1993, for a critique of various relaxation techniques.)

9. *Organize and participate in a support group with other teachers who work with disabled readers.* Sharing and receiving feedback on teaching techniques stimulates the reflective teaching approach that is difficult to maintain in isolation and with press of daily pressures and responsibilities.

## METHODS YOU KNOW

As suggested above, there are several methods that you have already read about that are especially appropriate for meeting the special needs of disabled readers within the regular classroom setting. Some of the more pertinent are summarized here with accompanying connections:

| Method | Connection |
| --- | --- |
| 1. *Phonemic Awareness Methods* | • To help students to better *hear* unfamiliar sounds |
| 2. *Gray's Paradigm for Teaching Phonic Elements* | • To systematically teach the auditory and visual discrimination and contextual use of new sounds |

3. *Glass-Analysis*

- To induce attention and play with English letter clusters and phonemes (sound combinations)

4. *ReQuest Procedure*

- To stir interactive conversations that are driven by analysis of text

5. *Note Cue*

- To build comfort with classroom participation in a low-risk way

6. *Know, Want-to-Know, Learned, and Question-Answer-Relationships*

- To build bridges from knowns to un-knowns in comprehension and metacognition; to help children build a deeper awarness of their own thought processes

7. *Vocabulary Self-Selection and Cultural Academic Trivia Game*

- To keep youngsters alert to the flood of new words and allusions that are all around them waiting to be learned

8. *Subjective Approach to Vocabulary and Motor Imaging*

- To help youngsters personalize and internalize meanings of new terms

9. *Writing Process and Related Activities*

- To create avenues for expressive and thoughtful speaking and writing

10. *Journal Writing*

- To offer opportunities to state unique concerns and thoughts in an interactive manner

11. *Cloze Passage Exercises*

- To offer close-up analysis and training in context usage, and to build familiarity with the "language redundancy patterns" in prose

12. *Language Shaping Activities*

- To provide contextualized exercises in language usage beyond Language Experience Stories

13. *Question-Only Strategy and InQuest*

- To improve abstract thinking and provide opportunities for spontaneous, thought-guided oral language experience

14. *Proverbs Study*

- To offer opportunities to connect American language and culture to the students' more familiar native language, cultural sayings and values

15. *Pattern Book Reading and Writing*

- To provide a well-structured avenue for building familiarity with language patterns and story elements in English, as well as opportunity to use these patterns to express aspects of one's native language and culture

16. *Universal Strategies* and *Study Strategies Techniques*

• To help youngsters read to learn—thus continuing to increase their fund of information despite reading and/or language lags

17. *"Teach-Up"*—Use higher-order reading, writing, and thinking activities

• To exercise and free minds that can become numbed by literal, repetitive tasks

The next topic is rarely treated as a topic in remedial programs. Hence, it is seldom given the attention it deserves. The methods mentioned above are vital here as well.

## REMEDIATING CONCEPT DEFICIENCIES

Concepts are gatherings of relevant associations. They are like nets that can catch and pull together otherwise loose bits and pieces of experience and information into meaningful units. Everyone forms concepts; it is one's purpose and orientation that determine what kinds of concepts are formed. Children with learning problems, for whatever reason, often are concept and schema deficient in things academic but not necessarily in other aspects of life. Of course, there also are some children who lack the orientation, strategies, and experiences for forming anything but the most basic concepts. You will need methods for reaching them as well.

You already have read about several ways to build relevant concepts in various parts of this text. Let's review some of these and elaborate on a few, to build your proficiency in dealing with this need.

### Vocabulary: Concept-Based Approaches

The first and perhaps easiest way to teach concept acquisition is to show how *words* are used to represent known concepts and are also used as tools for building new concepts. Semantic Feature Analysis (SFA) is especially useful for these purposes. SFA, you will recall, is a system for characterizing words by attributes and nonattributes. This categorization activity is an effective paradigm for concept building. You have also read about several alternative approaches to building word concepts. Motor Imaging, for example, helps a word concept to find a sensorimotor home and a symbolic gestural representation. The next approach to concept building is not limited to words. It is more appropriate for scanning and building concepts from larger textual meanings.

### Concepts by Interactions

Most any activity that involves a two-way interaction has potential for developing academic concepts and for teaching how to actively form academic concepts. The key ingredients of effective interactions are:

• Opportunity for students to talk back, and signal whether they are correctly seeing examples of the concept
• Teacher modeling of the thought processes involved in concept formation

FIGURE
11.1

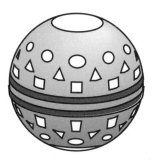

Several children are kicking a ball around during recess. It hits the teacher. She holds it behind her and says, smiling slightly, "I suppose you think this ball is yours."

"Yes," they respond sheepishly.

"How do I know you didn't just find it?" the teacher asks. Then, before they can answer, she says, "Prove it—what are its colors?"

Thinking a minute, the children shout out, "Blue and red." The teacher brings the ball into view, and the children say, "See, we're right!"

"Not really," the teacher says. "Look, the ball is *white*, with red and blue markings." Then she adds, "OK, maybe that was tricky. Look at the ball for a minute, and I'll bet you still can't answer questions about it." They do, and then return the ball to the teacher. "All right," she says, "tell me all the forms that are on the ball."

Having anticipated this, the children quickly respond, "squares and circles and things like—" (drawing shape in the air).

"Do you mean triangles?" the teacher asks.

"Right—yeah—that's it," they retort.

"Are you sure that is all?" the teacher prompts. The children look puzzled. Taunting them a little, she adds, "Want to look at it again?"

They study the ball again, and reply confidently, "That's it!"

"Wrong!" the teachers says challengingly. "Look at the blue and red rings around the ball, and the big circles filled in with color at the top and bottom. You see? There are rings and large circles as well."

While the children are dealing with this oversight, the recess bell rings. When they get back to the classroom, the teacher discusses geometric shapes and labels them. Together, they write an experience story about the event on the playground. Next, the teacher introduces them to "Question-Only," as the technique that they will use to learn about an ant colony she has brought to class, and about which they will be reading shortly.

- Opportunity for relevant peer interactions (and modeling)
- Opportunity to apply the concept independently and to get constructive feedback

There are strategies, such as ReQuest, InQuest, and Question-Only, that are particularly good matches to these requirements. However, the direct instruction provided by strategies such as these should be reinforced by incidental learning opportunities as well. A recent summary of over thirty years of research on concept learning stresses the importance of such "informal experiences" as well as "formal education[al]" ones (Klausmeier, 1992). See the anecdotal illustration in Figure 11.1 for an example of how to combine these two teaching/learning systems. As

**King Tut Revisited**

*Introduction*

- Show pictures from books that include inside and outside views of pyramids, pictures of the Sphinx and treasures from King Tutankhamen's tomb. (See Glubok's *Tut-ankh-Amen's Tomb*, Donnelly's *Tut's Mummy Lost . . . and Found*, and Reiff's *Secrets of Tut's Tomb and the Pyramids.*

- Have children generate a list of assumptions they may have about the Egyptian culture: What can you tell me about the people who made these things? When do you think these people lived? How do you think these people lived? How do you think these treasures were made, and of what materials?

- Develop a list of questions students would like answered about the ancient Egyptian culture. Write the questions on chart paper and hang them in the classroom. As answers are found, they are written on the chart. Sample questions: How were the pyramids made without modern equipment? How were the mummies preserved? Why were King Tut's treasures still intact when they were found? How do archaeologists go about finding such sites?

*Math and Science Connections*

- Use cement blocks to demonstrate the use of simple machines and the inclined plane.

- Have students calculate the number of blocks in a real pyramid, and their total weight—make the activity more concrete by having students construct a pyramid of wood blocks and determine its height, width, and weight. (See Maccaulay's *Pyramid*, Millard's *History Highlights: Pyramids*, and Weeks' *The Pyramids*.)

*Language Arts Connections*

- Write stories about what it would be like to live as a child in ancient Egypt, as a member of one of the social classes. Illustrate the stories and make a class library book. (See Grant's *How They Lived: The Egyptians* and Neurath's *They Lived Like This in Ancient Egypt.*)

- Make paper, or write on paper that is rolled on cardboard tubes to simulate papyrus rolls.

- Write stories using hieroglyphics, and pass them around for translation. (See Katan's *Hieroglyphs: The Writing of Ancient Egypt.*)

- Enhance vocabulary and word origin study with terms such as pyramid, Sphinx, pharaoh, scarab, hieroglyphics, and archaeology. Enhance study strategies by having children help each other devise techniques for remembering correct spellings.

you read the interaction in Figure 11.1 below, picture the teacher's manner as play-fully challenging these first-graders who were having trouble adjusting to school.

This anecdote also illustrates the basis for the next means of building concepts with all children, but most particularly those with reading–learning problems.

## Themes and Integrations

Few activities can be as powerful for building multiple concepts in students of all levels of ability as themed study (Shaw, 1993). This is due to the fact that themed study is based on finding and following relevant associations and connections, and that's pretty much a definition of the concept formation process. Several examples

**BOX 11.1** cont'd

- Include children's literature on the theme, such as Tomie dePaola's *Bill and Pete,* Shirley Cline's *The Egyptian Cinderella.*

**Music Connections**

- Read Leontyne Price's *Aida,* followed by listening to the operatic version on record or tape. Compare the book version with the operatic version.
- Have children compose their own songs about the war between Egypt and Ethiopia.

**Art Connections**

- Design a paper maze to find a mummy. (See Aliki's *Mummies Made in Egypt,* Lord's *Explorer Books: Mummies,* Milton's *Secrets of the Mummies,* and Perl's *Mummies, Tombs, and Treasures.*)
- Have children create drawings of their own Egyptian gods, give the god a name, and write a story describing the importance their new gods might have to ancient Egyptian culture. (See the November 1987 issue of *Ranger Rick* magazine for drawings of Egyptian gods that were part animal and part man.)
- Make a large paper mosaic that looks like those found on the walls in tombs and temples.

**Social Studies Connections**

- Discuss why so many objects were buried with the pharaohs. Have children bring in shoe boxes of objects or picture of objects they would take with them on a long journey. (See Bendick's *Egyptian Tombs.*)
- Build models of boats, towns, or pyramids. (For examples, see Unstead's *See Inside: An Egyptian Town* and Scott's *Egyptian Boats.*)

**Culminating Activity**

Incorporate social studies and art by having students make Egyptian artifacts from clay. Paint the objects, seal them in zip-lock bags, and bury them in a corner of the playground. Rope off the area and post signs declaring "No Trespassing—Archaeological Dig." Discuss what archaeologists do, and some techniques used to find treasures without damaging them. About a week later, begin the expedition to uncover the artifacts. Use small garden trowels for the dig. Each student must find an artifact that is not his or hers. Examine the pieces and determine what their uses might have been. Display the pieces in a "museum"—a hall table covered with black roll paper, with typed labels numbering and describing the objects. Send out invitations and make posters for the opening of the display. Invite the superintendent, the local newspaper and parents.

were offered in the previous chapter. Here is one more from Drum (1992) that webs into math, science, language arts, music, art, and social studies. It all springs from study of King Tut, a frequent allusion in literature, newsprint, and media (see Box 11.1). See the last chapter in this text for help in selecting themes that were identified for teaching important concepts, rather than leaving it all to chance.

## Pattern Books to Stimulate Reading, Writing, and Concept Development

Perhaps the greatest single advantage of writing is the amplifying and elevating effects it has on all previous experience, and related thoughts. When children attempt to write, their comprehension of the paradoxes and mysteries of experience become focused, and they teach *themselves* much about what is found in books and school subjects. In this way, concepts are clarified and *comprehension* of related textual material is enhanced.

Even reluctant or emergent writers, of any age, can be drawn into writing activities that are based on pattern books. The structure provided by writing to a pattern book model enables any child to produce a cohesive written piece. There are many types of patterns, and probably many yet to be developed. Roberts (1988) describes the following possibilities for pattern books:

- Interlocking structure. These are books in which each short story segment links to the next. In Bill Martin, Jr.'s *Silly Goose and the Holidays,* for example, the ending phrase or word of one sentence becomes the beginning phrase or word of the next. This pattern provides the remedial level reader with an enriched schema in the form of additional clues to decoding.
- Cultural sequence patterns. As in *The Very Hungry Caterpillar* by Eric Carle, where the reference source is the days of the week.
- Time sequence patterns. As in *The Grouchy Ladybug,* also by Eric Carle.
- Animal names and body parts patterns. As in Sandra Rokoff's *Here Is a Cat!*
- Cumulative pattern structure. As in "The Twelve Days of Christmas" song and Bill Martin Jr.'s *Old Devil Wind.*
- Rhyming scheme patterns. Here the child uses the rhyming expectation to sound out new words (even where the endings have different spelling patterns) as in Bill Martin Jr.'s *Whistle, Mary, Whistle* and *Fire! Fire! Said Mrs. McGuire.*

Lauritzen (1980) points out that an additional benefit of working with pattern books is that these predictable materials also help remedial and early readers to overcome oral reading problems such as jerky, hesitant, word-by-word reading.

To help remedial level and younger children to write at any early age and to explore their world, the first author developed a particular pattern book called *By Definition.* The pattern in this book is the development of multiple meanings for familiar words. In separate but coordinated studies, Roberts (1988) and Fazzino (1988) used the *By Definition* pattern to teach the concept of multiple meaning vocabulary to remedial level intermediate grade children. In both studies, the children made significant gains in vocabulary. More importantly, they wrote very credible stories, showing real gains in sensitivity to story structure and subtleties of language. See Figure 11.2 for an example of one of the renditions generated by these children.

*By Definition* pattern books are equally appropriate for use with limited English Proficiency students. Students' writing tends to reveal and teach words and idioms that often cause confusion. The pattern can also be used for getting a sense of what children with various other handicapping conditions are feeling and thinking; for example, "What's physically challenged?"

For more information on pattern or imitation books, see Cramer (1978) and Townsend (1989).

**FIGURE 11.2** **Pattern Book for Multiple Meaning and Complex Concept Words**

*What Is Run?*

What is *Run*?

Title

Authors:

Justin
Tequila
Jeremy
LaKeisha
Kasiya
Jason

Grade 4
February 29, 1988

Credits

Albert the bear likes to run.

What is run?

p. 1

Run is moving one's legs rapidly.

p. 2

**FIGURE 11.2 cont'd** **Pattern Book for Multiple Meaning and Complex Concept Words**

However, today Albert's nose runs.

But I thought run was moving one's legs rapidly.

p. 3

You're right.
Run is also a nose discharging matter.

p. 4

Look! Albert has a run in his socks.

Wait. I thought run was moving one's legs rapidly, or a nose discharging matter.

p. 5

Yes. But run is also a lengthwise ravel.

p. 6

**FIGURE 11.2 cont'd**

Albert made a run in baseball.

Great! But I thought run was moving one's legs rapidly, a nose discharging matter, or a lengthwise ravel.

p. 7

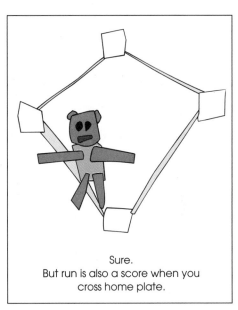

Sure.
But run is also a score when you cross home plate.

p. 8

Did you know Albert is going to run for president?

Really? I thought run was moving one's legs rapidly, or a nose discharging matter, or a lengthwise ravel, or a score when you cross home plate.

p. 9

It is.
But run is also to be a candidate.

p. 10

**FIGURE 11.2 cont'd** **Pattern Book for Multiple Meaning and Complex Concept Words**

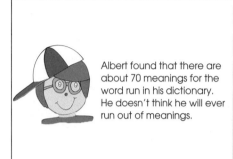

Albert found that there are about 70 meanings for the word run in his dictionary. He doesn't think he will ever run out of meanings.

Gosh! I thought run was to move one's legs rapidly, a nose discharging matter, a lengthwise ravel, a score when you cross home plate, or to be a candidate.

p. 11

That's correct. But run is also to come to end.

We've run out — for now!

p. 12

## HIGHER ORDER LITERACY APPROACHES TO REMEDIATION

"*Teach Up,*" Tom Estes (1991).

The previous chapters introduced and offered empirical support for the rather radical idea that at-risk and remedial students would not merely profit from attention to higher-order thinking, but might actually flourish under such approaches. To reiterate this position, let us review three compatible theories from previous chapters that underlie this fresh assumption:

- The "Caboose Theory" says that if higher-order thinking is used as the instructional locomotive, then basic literacy will be pulled along, like the caboose on a train.

- The Whole Language Theory says that when reading and learning are driven by meaning (good stories and themes) then the other language arts and subjects can be integrated and learned largely in incidental ways that avoid fragmented, decontextualized practices.

- The New Eclectic, or Whole-Child Theory says that higher-order thinking and attention to personal–social adjustment can and should be taught directly in contextual and noncontextual exercises (rather like aerobics), but also incidentally by infusion into content and reading–language arts instruction. The rationale for this selective eclecticism is that (1) it addresses more of the different ways in which people learn; (2) it has built-in repetitions when things are taught both explicitly and implicitly; (3) it doesn't unseat traditional methods, but merely adds another option; (4) it calls for constructive thinking that can be psychologically and cognitively uplifting; (5) it offers the opportunity for remedial and at-risk students to build on possible unrecognized strengths; and (6) it challenges students who may appear to be proficient readers on conventional measures, but who may have unrecognized deficiencies in higher-order thinking.

On these bases, two activities that stimulate constructive reading–thinking are described next that can be added to those recommended in the previous chapter. These activities are the Literary Report Card and the Advice Column. You're going to like these, and experience tells us, so do children who are at risk or already in need of remedial assistance.

## LITERARY REPORT CARD

Johnson and Louis (1987) suggest the Literary Report Card as an activity that teaches evaluative and inferential thinking and writing. It also provides an opportunity for students to engage in self-examination in a safe and incidental way. More importantly, it can be used quite effectively as part of conventional reading–language arts instruction.

To use this method, have students select a character from a story they have just read and create a "report card" based on the character's qualities and actions. Introduce the activity to the whole group by selecting a character together and asking students to think of some qualities of the character that could be judged. If a negative quality is suggested, try to rewrite it as an antonym, since it seems a little odd to give a person an "A" in *cowardice* rather than a "D" or "F" in *bravery*. The example in Box 11.2 is based on Evaline Ness's *Sam, Bangs and Moonshine*. If adjectives or adverbs are suggested, provide the appropriate noun without comment: if a child says, "Max wasn't very happy to begin with," say, "Then we can give him a grade for happiness." For each "subject" suggested, decide on a grade for the character in that subject, and relevant comments. After the whole group has graded the character on a few "subjects," have students work in cooperative learning groups to do a report card on one of the characters in the story. They may select the character that has been started by the whole group, or select a different character. Have groups share their report cards with the class, and display completed report cards in

**REPORT CARD**

School: *Harbour School*

Name: *Samantha*

Grade: *3*

Teacher: *Ms. Kirbstoan*

*A = Outstanding*
*B = Good*
*C = Satisfactory*
*D = Needs Improvement*
*F = Failure*

| Subject | Grade | Comments |
|---------|-------|----------|
| *Creativity* | *A* | *Samantha has a very powerful imagination.* |
| *Honesty* | *D* | *Sometimes she tells lies.* |
| *Courage* | | |
| *Happiness* | | |
| | | |
| | | |

*Johnson & Louis, 1987, p. 70.*

the room. Johnson and Louis report that children have little difficulty assigning grades and providing explanatory comments.

## ADVICE COLUMN

The Advice Column is a strategy for developing children's evaluative thinking and writing in response to reading. Have students select a character from a story they have read and write a letter from that character to an advice columnist (Dear Abby . . . , Dear Ann Landers . . . , etc.). The letter should state the character's problem, using the language the character might use. Then have students write a response to the character. Some variations include:

- Introduce the activity by writing the problem letter yourself and having children write responses. This provides an opportunity to teach, by example, how the problems may be inferred from the story, and how these might be stated.
- Have children trade papers after they have written their first letters and have *another* student write the response.

- Provide a list of proverbs and have children include a proverb in their response letter.
- Show some sample advice columns and point out how advice columnists often shorten the names of the writer in humorous ways. Have children try this technique in their letters.
- Have children make up a name for the columnist, such as "Dear Wise-One."

**Samples:**

Dear Wise-One,
   We have these neighbors, the Bears, who don't want to be friends with anyone. They have a kid about my age, but he can never come out to play with me. I went over to their house the other day, but nobody was home. I had a little snack, and (this is sort of embarrassing) I fell asleep. I don't know what they were so mad about, though.
   What can I do to get the Bears to like me?
   Yours truly,
   Goldilocks

Dear Locks,
   It sounds like your *neighbors* need some locks. You went in their house when no one was there? Where were you brought up, in a barn? After this little housebreaking stunt you pulled, I suggest you mind your manners, and not be so pushy. And next time, look before you leap—or sleep!
   Yours truly,
   Wise-One

Dear Wise-One,
   Two years ago I was transformed from an overworked step-sister into a Princess. My problem is that I kind of miss my family, even though they weren't the best. I'm also finding it a little bit boring trying to just "live happily ever after," but with nothing really to do. Please advise.
   Yours truly,
   Princess Cinderella

Another variation is to have children write letters to the fictional advice columnist about real-life issues, for other students to answer:

Dear Wise-One,
   Our city now has everyone separating their garbage and putting it in bins and all this stuff.
   Is it really a good idea for everyone to have to be handling garbage rather than just the few who were being paid to do it before?
   Why can't we make more jobs for garbage collectors and sorters, and have the rest of us return to normal living?
   Sincerely,
   A Reluctant Garbage Guy

The next topic area is one of the major concerns in helping remedial level readers. You will notice that the two previous activities could comfortably fit under this category.

# INTRINSIC MOTIVATION: REGULAR CLASSROOM-BASED APPROACHES

One of the more difficult aspects of working with children who are at risk in a regular classroom setting is that they are not internally motivated. They also do not respond easily or consistently to external rewards such as gold stars or nods of approval. There are some few approaches, however, that actually help to heighten internal motivation. These include, but are not limited to, the following:

- Biblio-Support and Journal Writing
- Homilies, Proverbs, and Fables
- "Leading from Behind"
- "When I Teach, I Learn"
- Media Connections
- Attitude Adjustments (to borrow a phrase from a country and western song)
- Personalization Techniques

There has been a flurry of activity among researchers to bridge the gap between the role of cognition and affect in explaining reader responses to literature (Goetz et al., 1992). Ahead is one way that teachers have been combining the two in a very practical way for many years.

## BIBLIO-SUPPORT

Biblio-support is a classroom form of "bibliotherapy." The basic ingredient is a teacher who loves to read, knows books, and cares about children. It is a means of emotionally and intellectually "empowering" students to deal with personal–social adjustment problems in a largely incidental way. The simple act of matching a student with a book or selection that deals with the situation he or she is facing can trigger three therapeutic psychological processes: empathy, catharsis, and insight. *Empathy* is the act of associating some real or fictional character in literature with oneself. *Catharsis* occurs when the reader identifies with a character and observes that character working through a problem to a successful solution, or "release of emotional tension." Through empathy and catharsis comes further *insight*. Insight is the sense of the enlightenment that comes with recognizing aspects of oneself and one's situation in a written tale. This can be uplifting and often lends a sense of dignity to one's woes. This shift in perspective on one's personal situation is referred to by literary critics as the distinction between a tragedy (the failing of great people) and pathos (the problems of the weak and pathetic).

When described in these terms, this process may sound too complex for children. However, it is quite a natural progression with which children generally are quite at ease. To activate the process, the teacher, librarian, or reading specialist who recommends a book to a student should invite the student to retell the story, highlighting incidents and feelings that are relevant to the situations portrayed. Changes in behavior, feelings, and relationships should be looked at closely to permit vivid identification and empathy with the characters. Most important, the reader should have an opportunity to form a conclusion about the consequences of certain behaviors or feelings to determine whether or not these behaviors or feelings improve human relationships and happiness (Heaton & Lewis, 1955).

Biblio-support may be used in either of two ways. First, it can be used to help a student to solve an *existing* emotional problem or anxiety by recommending a book that recounts an experience or situation similar to the student's own. By recognizing the problem and its solution in literature, students often can gain insights about their own problems and begin to take steps to solve them. Second, biblio-support may be used as a *preventative* measure. A student who has experienced a situation through literature can be said to have vicariously experienced it and should be better able to deal with similar situations encountered in real life. This technique can be compared to the process of inoculation against contagious diseases. Stories, in general, have been used in this way by the wise for thousands of years because they work. Whether they are called parables, fables, or tales, the effect is the same: the right story at the right time crosses the line from vicarious to actual experience. Such stories can remain with the child as a ready "teacher" for a very long time.

Biblio-support can be enhanced by the addition of a writing component. The easiest way to do this is to have students keep personal journals in which they write brief reactions—at least one sentence—to whatever they read. These can be accumulated and, with the student's prior approval, the teacher may read through them on occasion and write back personal notes and thoughts. Of course, notes and dialogue need not be limited to textual material; they can be extended to anything a student wishes to write about. The idea of *dialogue journals* (Staton, 1980), as previously noted, is as old as conversation between caring friends. Teachers who use this approach regularly report touching insights revealed and warm relationships formed with students who at first appeared apathetic, hostile, or just plain reluctant to learn (Kirby & Liner, 1981).

Together, biblio-support and dialogue journals offer students help in making progress toward reading, language, thinking, and personal–social adjustment by:

1. Teaching students to think positively
2. Encouraging students to talk freely to appropriate adults about their problems
3. Helping students analyze their attitudes and modes of behavior
4. Pointing out that there are alternative and constructive ways to solve most adjustment problems
5. Helping students compare their problems with those of others as a means of lessening internal tension and conflicts in a society that sometimes can appear uncaring (Rongione, 1972, as cited in Edwards & Simpson, 1986)
6. Preparing youngsters, with vicarious experiences, to anticipate and handle the inevitable difficulties of living and growing

Several sources list children's books by biblio-support type topics. See, for example:

- Bernstein, Joanne E. *Books to Help Children Cope with Separation and Loss.* New York: R. R. Bowker, 1983.
- Dryer, Sharon S. *The Bookfinder, A Guide to Children's Literature About the Needs and Problems of Youth Aged 2–15.* 2 volumes. Circle Pines, MN: American Guidance Service, 1985.
- Gillespie, John T., & Gilbert, Christine B. (Eds.) *Best Books for Children: Preschoool Through the Middle Grades.* 4th ed. New York: R. R. Bowker, 1990.
- White, Mary Lou, (Ed.) *Adventuring with Books: Booklist for Pre-K–Grade 6.* Urbana, IL: National Council of Teachers of English, 1981.

Box 11.3 (pp. 454–457) provides a "starter list" of books on topics that may be of concern to children. These were selected with the able assistance of Betsy Reese, at the University of Missouri–Kansas City's Instructional Materials Center.

In a slight but important extension of biblio-support, called "Teletherapy," O'Brube, Camplese, and Sanford (1987) suggest having children share the stories that have touched their lives. This, they say, can be done with creative dramatics, finger plays, a puppet show, or a movie or tape.

Puppets can also be used to engage children in conversation. With no attempt at ventriloquism, a teacher can get children to talk to a puppet with great candor. The teacher also can have the puppet answer with more candor than could ever be attempted in one's own persona. We once watched a foreign language teacher make very pointed criticism of children's pronunciations in Spanish without offending them in the least. He simply held a large scruffy puppet on his lap and had it say things that were almost outrageously frank. The children laughed, talked back, and tried again! You may have to try this to believe how effective it can be for broaching subjects that otherwise would be very difficult to handle. For example, the puppet turns to one child and says about another, who is characteristically loud and boisterous: "Does this kid need to chill-out, or what?" The entire class chimed in with some form of "Yeah!" and "No kidding!" This may not have permanently quieted the bouncing lad down, but it did mellow him for a while, and it gave the teacher a way to express some of his frustration without injury to anyone. The teacher said that "Frank" came to look forward to talking with the "Dummy" as he called him. "Dummies" can be more easily forgiven for being too direct, or tactless.

For further information on bibliotherapy, including possible problems with taking it too far, see Harris and Sipay (1990), and Manzo and Manzo (1993).

## HOMILIES, PROVERBS, AND FABLES

Homilies, proverbs, and fables can help reduce emotionally disruptive thought patterns and heighten common sense. They are brief forms of the universal truths often sought in great literature. They provide a powerful way to communicate basic values and life management skills, especially when spoken at a needed, and therefore "teachable moment." These compressed bits of wisdom can reset our "emotional clocks" when they become erratic from the effects of stress, conflict, or depressing times. They are to mental health what vitamin supplements are to diet: great when you need them and harmless otherwise.

To simultaneously teach and monitor progress in clear thinking, use the Proverbs Mastery Paradigm from the chapter on comprehension, or the format shown below. The form shown below can be used either in a class discussion format or as an independent worksheet activity.

**Sample Multiple Choice Proverbs Format** Proverb worksheets like the example below can be constructed to evaluate students' response patterns. Of the four choices offered, one should be a simple miscue, or misinterpretation of the literal meaning of the proverb (labeled "M" in the examples below); another choice should be an emotional level response (labeled "E"); another should be an accurate but concrete, or literal translation ("C"); and the best translation should be an abstract interpretation of the proverb's meaning ("A").

**Directions:** Choose the answer that is the best and most *general* way of saying what the proverb means. Be sure to read all choices before selecting one. Place an (X) in front of the letter of your choice.

**1. The grass is always greener on the other side of the fence.**

(C) ____    A. A neighbor's grass often looks better than yours, because you cannot see its flaws.

(E) ____    B. Your efforts will make your neighbor richer.

(M) ____    C. There are two sides to everything.

(A) ____    D. The things we see often look better than the things we have.

**2. He who laughs last laughs longest.**

(C) ____    A. If you are the last person to begin to laugh, you will be the last one to finish laughing.

(M) ____    B. If you want to laugh best, always laugh loud.

(A) ____    C. Be careful not to celebrate a victory until you are sure you have won.

(E) ____    D. Laughing is important; always have a sense of humor.

**3. You can catch more flies with honey than you can with vinegar.**

(C) ____    A. Flies are attracted to sweet things, not to bitter things.

(E) ____    B. To get what you want you sometimes have to be tricky.

(M) ____    C. People who are pleasant have more friends than those who are grouchy.

(A) ____    D. You can get further by being thoughtful than by being demanding.

**4. Out of the frying pan and into the fire.**

(C) ____    A. You no sooner solve one problem than another one comes up. That's life!

(M) ____    B. If something falls out of the pan it will drop into the fire.

(E) ____    C. Trying to hide your mistakes can be dangerous.

(A) ____    D. Some bad situations can never be improved.

Proverbs study is especially useful with remedial level readers, since each proverb is—as suggested in an earlier chapter—like a miniature book. For each proverb spoken, it is possible to construct a prologue, or situation which preceded it, an event or events that make it timely, and an epilogue telling what can be learned from it. For this reason, proverbs can easily be connected to discussion and writing in response to children's stories and books. By putting a few proverbs around the room, connections will form naturally as life and reading unfold.

---

**BOX 11.3    Books for Biblio-Support**

**Adoption**

grades 3–6     Girard, Linda Walvoord. *We Adopted You, Benjamin Koo.* Niles, IL: A. Whitman, 1989.

grades 4–8     Sobol, Harriet Langsam. *We Don't Look Like Our Mom and Dad.* New York: Coward-McCann, 1984.

**Aging**

grades K–3     dePaola, Tomie. *Now One Foot, Now the Other.* New York: Putnam, 1981.

grades 4–6     Rappaport, Doreen. *"But She's Still My Grandma!"* New York: Human Sciences, 1982.

**Child Abuse**

grades 7–12    Nathanson, Laura. *The Trouble with Wednesdays.* New York: Bantam, 1986.

grades K–3     Stanek, Muriel. *Don't Hurt Me, Mama.* Niles, IL: A. Whiteman, 1983.

**Death**

grades K–3     Brown, Margaret Wise. *The Dead Bird.* Reading, MS: Addison-Wesley, 1958.

grades 4–6     Buck, Pearl S. *The Big Wave.* New York: Day, 1948.

grades K–3     Carrick, Carol. *The Accident.* New York: Seabury, 1976.

grades K–3     Fassler, Joan. *My Grandpa Died Today.* New York: Human Science Press, 1971.

grades K–6     Greenberg, Judith E. *Sunny: The Death of a Pet.* New York: F. Watts, 1986.

grades 1–3     Hickman, Martha Whitmore. *Last Week My Brother Anthony Died.* Nashville: Abingdon Press, 1984.

grades K–6     Kubler-Ross, Elizabeth. *Remember the Secret.* Berkeley, CA: Celestial Arts, 1982.

grades 5–8     Paterson, Katherine. *Bridge to Terabithia.* New York: Crowell, 1977.

grades K–3     Simon, Norma. *The Saddest Time.* Niles, IL: A. Whiteman, 1986.

grades 4–6     Simon, Norma. *We Remember Philip.* Chicago: A Whitman, 1979.

grades 4–6     Smith, Doris B. *A Taste of Blackberries.* New York: Crowell, 1973.

grades K–3     Varley, Susan. *Badger's Parting Gifts.* New York: Lothrop, Lee & Shepherd, 1984.

**Divorce**

grades 7+      Blume, Judy. *It's Not the End of the World.* Scarsdale, NY: Bradbury Press, 1972.

grades K–3     Goff, Beth. *Where Is Daddy? The Story of Divorce.* Boston: Beacon Press, 1969.

**BOX 11.3** cont'd

### Divorce

grades 4–6     Mann, Peggy. *My Dad Lives in a Downtown Hotel.* NY: Doubleday, 1973.

grades 5–8     Ruby, Lois. *Pig-Out Inn.* Boston: Houghton Mifflin, 1987.

grades 4–6     Schuchman, Joan. *Two Places to Sleep.* Minneapolis: Carolrhoda Books, 1979.

### Drugs

grades 7+     *Go Ask Alice.* Englewood Cliffs, NJ: Prentice-Hall, 1971.

grades 7+     Wojciechowska, Maia. *Tuned Out.* New York: Harper & Row, 1968.

### Fear

grades 4–6     Sharmat, Marjorie Weinman. *Frizzy the Fearful.* New York: Holiday House, 1983.

grades K–3     Stolz, Mary. *Storm in the Night.* New York: Harper & Row, 1990.

### Foster Care

grades 5–8     Byars, Betsy Cromer. *The Pinballs.* New York: Harper & Row, 1977.

### Homelessness

grades 4–6     Chalofsky, Margery Schwartz. *Changing Places: A Kid's View of Shelter Living.* Mt. Rainier, MD: Gryphon House. 1992.

grades K–3     Guthrie, Donna. *A Rose for Abby.* Nashville: Abingdon Press, 1988.

grades 5–8     Hahn, Mary Downing. *December Stillness.* New York: Clarion, 1988.

grades 5–8     Jones, Adrienne. *Street Family: A Novel.* New York: Harper & Row, 1987.

### Illnesses

grades 4–6     Dacquino, V. T. *Kiss the Candy Days Good-bye.* New York: Delacorte Press, 1982.

grades 3–6     Jordan, MaryKate. *Losing Uncle Tim.* Niles, IL: A. Whitman, 1989.

grades 4–6     Roberts, Willo Davis. *Sugar Isn't Everything: A Support Book in Fiction Form for the Young Diabetic.* New York: Atheneum. 1987.

### Immigrants

grades K–3     Bunting, Eve. *How Many Days to America?: A Thanksgiving Story.* New York: Clarion, 1988.

grades 3–6     Cohen, Barbara. *Molly's Pilgrim.* New York: Lothrop, 1983.

grades 4–6     Surat, Michele Maria. *Angel Child, Dragon Child.* Milwaukee: Raintree, 1983.

grades 3–6     Tran, Khanh Tuyet. *The Little Weaver of Thai-Yen Village = Co Be Tho-Det Lang Thai-Yen.* San Francisco: Children's Book. 1987.

### Individuality

grades K–3     dePaola, Tomie. *Oliver Button Is a Sissy.* San Diego: Harcourt Brace Jovanovich, 1979.

grades K–3     DeVeaux, Alexis. *An Enchanted Hair Tale.* New York: Harper & Row, 1987.

grades K–3     Lester, Helen. *Tacky the Penguin.* Boston: Houghton Mifflin, 1988.

grades K–3     Munsch, Robert N. *The Paper Big Princess.* Toronto, Ont.: Annick Press, 1986.

grades K–3     Otey, Mimi. *Daddy Has a Pair of Striped Shorts.* New York: Farrar, 1990.

### Lying

grades 4–6     Levy, Elizabeth. *Lizzie Lies a Lot.* New York: Delacorte, 1976.

**BOX 11.3 cont'd** | **Books for Biblio-Support**

### Mental Retardation

grades 3–6    Bergman, Thomas. *We Laugh, We Cry: Children Living with Mental Retardation*. Milwaukee: Gareth Stevens, 1989.

grades 7+    Byars, Betsy. *The Summer of the Swans*. New York: Viking Press, 1970.

grades 4–6    Cleaver, Vera, & Bill Cleaver. *Me Too*. Philadelphia: Lippincott, 1973.

grades K–3    Litchfield, Ada Bassett. *Making Room for Uncle Joe*. Niles, IL: A Whitman, 1984.

grades 4–6    Shyer, Marlene Fanta. *Welcome Home, Jellybean*. New York: Scribner, 1978.

### Moving

grades K–3    Hughes, Shirley. *Moving Molly*. New York: Lothrop, 1988.

grades K–3    Komaiko, Leah. *Annie Bananie*. New York: Harper & Row, 1987.

grades 4–6    Sharmat, Marjorie Weinman. *Mitchell Is Moving*. London: Collier Macmillan, 1978.

grades K–3    Smith, Miriam. *Annie & Moon*. Milwaukee: Gareth Stevens, 1989.

### New Sibling

grades K–3    Alexander, Martha. *Nobody Asked Me If I Wanted a Baby Sister*. New York: Dial, 1971.

grades K–3    Keats, Ezra Jack. *Peter's Chair*. New York: Harper, 1967.

grades 4–6    Klein, Norma. *Confessions of an Only Child*. New York: Pantheon, 1974.

### Nontraditional Families

grades 7–10    Brooks, Bruce. *Midnight Hour Encores*. New York: Harper & Row, 1986.

grades 3–6    Jenness, Aylette. *Families: A Celebration of Diversity*. Boston: Houghton Mifflin, 1990.

grades 4–6    Jukes, Mavis, *Like Jake and Me*. New York: Knopf, 1984.

grades 4–6    Maury, Inez. *My Mother the Mail Carrier = Mi Mama La Cartera*. New York: Feminist Press, 1976.

grades 5–8    Roberts, Willo Davis. *Megan's Island*. New York: Atheneum, 1988.

grades 3–6    Walter, Mildred Pitts. *Justin and the Best Biscuits in the World*. New York: Lothrop, Lee & Shepard, 1986.

grades K–3    Williams, Vera B. *A Chair For My Mother*. New York: Greenwillow, 1982.

grades K–3    Williams, Vera B. *Music, Music for Everyone*. New York: Greenwillow, 1984.

grades K–3    Williams, Vera B. *Something Special for Me*. New York: Greenwillow, 1983.

### Physical Handicaps

grades 3–6    Bergman, Thomas. *Finding a Common Language: Children Living with Deafness*. Milwaukee: Gareth Stevens, 1989.

grades 3–6    Bergman, Thomas. *Going Places: Children Living With Cerebral Palsy*. Milwaukee: Gareth Stevens, 1991.

grades 3–6    Bergman, Thomas. *On Our Own Terms: Children Living With Physical Disabilities*. Milwaukee: Gareth Stevene, 1989.

grades 3–6    Bergman, Thomas. *Seeing in Special Ways: Children Living with Blindness*. Milwaukee: Gareth Stevens, 1989.

BOX
**11.3**
cont'd

### Physical Handicaps

grades K–3    Caseley, Judith. *Harry and Willy and Carrothead.* New York: Greenwillow, 1991.

grades K–3    Cohen, Miriam. *See You Tomorrow, Charles.* New York: Greenwillow, 1983.

grades K–3    Goldin, Barbara Diamond. *Cakes and Miracles: A Purim Tale.* New York: Viking, 1991.

grades K–6    Kuklin, Susan. *Thinking Big: The Story of A Young Dwarf.* New York: Lothrop, Lee & Shepard, 1986.

grades 7–12    Rosen, Lillian. *Just Like Everybody Else.* San Diego: Harcourt Brace Jovanovich, 1981.

grades 3–6    Rosenberg, Maxine B. *My Friend Leslie: The Story of a Handicapped Child.* New York: Lothrop, Lee & Shepard, 1983.

### Prejudice

grades 7+    Fox, Paula. *The Slave Dancer.* Scarsdale, NY: Bradbury, 1973.

### Responsibility

grades 7+    Cleaver, Vera, & Bill Cleaver. *Where the Lilies Bloom.* Philadelphia: Lippincott, 1969.

### School

grades K–3    Giff, Patricia Reilly. *Today Was a Terrible Day.* New York: Viking, 1980.

grades 5–8    Martin, Ann M. *Yours Truly, Shirley.* New York: Holiday House, 1988.

grades 7–10    Peck, Richard. *Princess Ashley.* New York: Dell, 1988.

grades K–3    Schertle, Alice. *Jeremy Bean's St. Patrick's Day.* New York: Lothrop, 1987.

grades K–3    Schwartz, Amy. *Annabelle Swift, Kindergartner.* New York: Orchard, 1988.

### Shyness

grades K–3    Hazen, Barbara Shook. *Very Shy.* New York: Human Sciences, 1982.

grades K–3    Yashima, Taro. *Crow Boy.* New York: Viking, 1955.

### Siblings

grades K–3    Hazen, Barbara Shook. *If It Weren't for Benjamin (I'd Always Get to Lick the Icing Spoon).* New York: Human Sciences, 1983.

grades K–3    Henkes, Kevin, *Julius, the Baby of the World.* New York: Greenwillow, 1990.

grades K–3    Titherington, Jeanne. *A Place for Ben.* New York: Greenwillow, 1987.

### Vandalism

grades 4–6    Addy, Sharon. *We Didn't Mean To.* Milwaukee, WS: Raintree, 1981.

## LEADING FROM BEHIND

As effective as direct instruction can be with disabled readers, it cannot generally be counted on to get youngsters interested in reading and learning. To really meet youngsters "where they are," you must learn to "lead from behind." This simply means negotiating certain parts of the curriculum with students and then improvisationally tying what they may want to know about or to do to whatever you and the conventional curriculum call for. Andrea Butler[1] made the following points about "leading from behind":

- *You probably don't need a science period and a math period where integration and options can co-exist.* (We're not sure we would go quite this far.)

- *Intrinsic motivation is best achieved when "instead of trying to make sure that every content area is covered or tied in, you pull in what is most relevant to your purpose"* (p. 7).

- *The basic approach is simple. Say the topic is hippos. Well, there are many aspects that can be explored, so just ask, "What do we already know about the hippo? What do you want to learn? . . . Then you divvy up the inquiry. Some kids investigate the hippo's habitat, others its food needs, and so on."* (p. 7)

- *"In other words, choice is not a free-for-all. The teacher stakes out the turf upon which the kids can crawl"* (comment by the interviewer, p. 8).

- *Theme in school is like theme in music—"it can tolerate a good deal of improvisation when the teacher permits kids to form small jazz quartets as well as large orchestras. That's leading from behind, as Gordon Wells refers to it"* (p. 8).

## "WHEN I TEACH, I LEARN"

Human experience, as well as several pieces of solid research, have shown that the act of teaching can aid the *teacher's* learning as well as the students'. What has been overlooked until fairly recently is that the act of teaching to learn applies to weaker readers and even learning disabled children as well as to children with average and above rates of learning (Coleman, 1990; Labbo & Teale, 1990). Hence, it seems wise to have programs that allow students who are at risk, for any reason, to teach as well as to be taught. Teaching is uplifting to morale and to commitment to learn to deeper and more fluent levels. The next chapter on programs and materials spells out the whys and hows of doing this in some detail. It also addresses ways to involve at-risk children in various forms of cooperative and collaborative learning experiences. But for now, suffice it to say that children can and should teach one another, and that even those who are below grade level can work with younger children. See the previous chapter on oral reading for more information about Labbo and Teale's (1990) cross-age tutoring system.

Beyond direct instruction, there is the need when working with children at risk to touch them with the worth of learning, as much as the fact of it. The next several ideas and methods are cast in this more affective and attitudinal direction.

---

[1] Co-author of *Towards a Reading–Writing Classroom* (Portsmouth, NH: Heinemann Books, 1984) in an interview with the editors of the *Virginia State Reading Association Journal* (vol. 16, 1991).

## MEDIA CONNECTIONS

Even weak readers are learning and experiencing all the time. Find their base of interest, and build on it. One sensible way to do this, as hinted in earlier chapters, is to use children's exposure to media as a backdrop for promoting reading and critical analysis. Where books once were made into movies, now movies are being made into books. Recommend these connections to parents of reluctant readers—they make great stocking-stuffers. Seeing the movie first should have the same effect on reading comprehension as the Listen–Read Lesson (Cunningham, 1975) and the Listen–Read–Discuss Heuristic (Manzo & Casale, 1985). Of course, some previewing activities, similar to the prereading steps of the DRA, can be expected to amplify learning from viewing.

Another means of building on media connections is to use captioned television. Originally developed for the hearing impaired, captioned TV has proved to be highly motivating to remedial level readers and to enhance vocabulary comprehension (Adler, 1985; Koskinen, Wilson, Gambrell, & Jensema, 1987). It also has been shown to improve word identification, word meaning, and content learning among bilingual students who viewed the same material with and without captions (Koskinen, Wilson, Gambrell, & Neuman, 1993; Neuman & Koskinen, 1992).

Currently, a special electronic TeleCaption decoder (costing in the neighborhood of $160) is required for older television sets to pick up the captions being sent out on almost all public broadcasts. However, televisions manufactured after June 1993 are required to have this feature built in. For additional information on TeleCaption decoders and their use, write or call: The National Captioning Institute; 5203 Leesburg Pike; Falls Church, VA 22041 (1-800-533-WORD).

## ATTITUDE ADJUSTMENT

Children who are failing or are at risk of doing so often labor under a compound negative state: low achievement, loss of hope, and a generally dreary view of life's possibilities. This is another way of saying that important internal guidance systems are not leading them toward learning; hence, little that is offered in a conventional lesson can take hold. One way to help such youngsters to see the brighter side was suggested first by Edward L. Kramer, a St. Louis native, back in 1948 (Lenehan, 1992).

Each evening, after dinner, Kramer would sit down with his children and ask them for an accounting of the good they had observed that day. Then postcards expressing their appreciation were mailed to those individuals. At first the children found this difficult to do. They really hadn't thought before in terms of the many acts of kindness and generosity that were expended each day by parents, friends, teachers, relatives, and various service people (e.g., postal, sanitation, and security personnel). After a time, their thoughtfulness was returned tenfold in warmth and thankfulness by the many people who felt appreciated. More interestingly, people who experienced kindness wished to share it.

It all grew so quickly that Mr. Kramer came to design a card patterned after the once-popular yellow telegram. He called it a Thank-U-Gram. He offered a two-week supply, free, to anyone who requested them. He received requests from

---

**BOX 11.4** **Good Things Are Happening!**

<table>
<tr>
<td>

### Thank-U-Gram

TO: Our Sanitation Workers
FROM: Katie Prine, 5th grade
c/o Miss Debra Eubanks,
Carter Elementary School,
15 Waits Ave., Texarkana, TX

I saw your crew picking up the mess left by the dogs that tore the garbage bags open. Thank you for the extra effort in keeping my neighborhood clean. Have a good day.

</td>
<td>

Sanitation Department
Texarkana, Tx

Dear Katie,
You helped settle an argument about whether we should clean up the messes dogs make, or leave them for the home owners.
Now that we know that someone cares, we will do our best to pick up the mess.
Thank you.

Bud, Willie, Don,
& Anthony

</td>
</tr>
</table>

---

President Eisenhower, Robert Frost, Leonard Bernstein, Bob Hope, Walt Disney, and thousands of others.

Many years have passed since that time, but the idea still is viable. Create Thank-U-Grams with your computer software, or have children make up their own to spread good will again. It will cause them to think about their lives more positively, to write and to read with purpose, and to give them an additional way in which to constructively influence the environments that so influence them. To add to the fun, be sure a return address is included, and leave these in obvious places to be picked up when it is not realistic to mail them. Keep a teacher-made book of some of the Thank-U-Grams and of responses that are received. Call it a "Good Things Are Happening!" (See Box 11.4.)

Another way to bring learning closer to home is to personalize otherwise abstract information. This idea has been around for many years, but it comes out differently each time it is used, so it always seems fresh.

## PERSONALIZATION TECHNIQUES

There are two basic forms of personalization techniques: one that uses *concrete parallels,* and one that uses *dramatizations.*

*Concrete parallels,* as suggested by Moore and Readence (1980), develop comprehension by beginning with pictures. Students are shown a picture and asked to state the main idea and supporting details. The teacher first models the task, then offers the student some supportive practice with similar pictures accompanied by multiple choice options for main idea and details. The teacher then does the same with textual material, having students read aloud with the teacher.

Elliott and Carroll (1980) report a similar procedure. In their version, students read a selection and then are asked to manipulate objects on a story board in ways that retell or otherwise reflect that they understood the story and what characters said or could have said to one another. The "could be saying" portion can provide some powerful insights into children's hopes, fears, and aspirations.

BOX
**11.5** **Parallel Form Strategy**

The class was asked to pretend they were sixth-graders attending a progressive elementary school that held an annual prom for its graduates. (There was such a school nearby.) An attractive new girl in class was said to have two boys vying for her attention. Their names were written on the proverbial love triangle: Alpha at the top, Donnie Ray and Osceola at either angle of the base. A situation was provided to stir the pot: Donnie Ray's father owned a florist shop, and Osceola's father was a candy maker.

The simulated scene was a schoolyard at recess some days before the prom. Donnie Ray's friends, the teacher said, were gathered about him demanding, "How will you win a date with Alpha?" To which he responded, "First I've got to let her know I exist." Suiting action to words, he proposed to dash past her several times to display his blazing speed.

Osceola was asked to suggest a countermove. He got on the athletic high bar and began to chin as his friends loudly counted, proclaiming his awesome strength to all within earshot.

Not very subtle, but it stirred Donnie Ray to suggest a persuasive countergesture: "In the morning, I will send Alpha a single rose" (by emissary).

Osceola immediately countered, "I will send candy" (in the same manner). "Tomorrow," Donnie Ray returned, "I will bring a bouquet."

But Osceola matched and surpassed his rival: "And I'll bring a box of candy and a cozy sack lunch for two."

The vying continued, to the cheers and jeers of the class, until Alpha was asked to choose her date. "Couldn't I wait another day or two?" she coyly asked.

"No way!" Donnie Ray snapped. "In fact, you're not deciding nothing!"

"Right," Osceola volunteered. "Me and this turkey are going to settle this thing right here and now!"

While the class was still laughing and jabbering at that macho proposal, the teacher began to slowly erase each name from the triangle and write in new ones. The class grew quiet and perplexed as they observed these changes on the chalkboard:

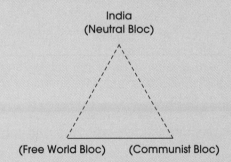

India
(Neutral Bloc)

(Free World Bloc)    (Communist Bloc)

"You won't believe this," they were told, "but if you read pages 29 to 36 in your modern history book, you will find a story very much like the one you 'sixth-graders' just made up." This was true enough. Between 1955 and 1961, the United States and the Soviet Union were wining and dining India and the neutral nations to get their support in the General Assembly of the United Nations. When the giveaway programs appeared to be faltering, both countries began to test bigger and bigger hydrogen bombs while seemingly chanting the macabre refrain "My bomb's bigger than your bomb." In fact, the kids had anticipated the next chapter, which told of the near catastrophe at the Berlin Wall, where the world learned a new word: brinkmanship.

*From Manzo & Manzo (1990a).*

*Dramatization* activities before reading, such as the Parallel Form Strategy (Manzo, 1977), provide a way for students to translate the main ideas of difficult textual material into more familar, personal terms. See Box 11.5 for an illustration of how a group of underachieving youngsters first acted out a situation that paralleled a fairly difficult piece of textual material. By doing so, they were able to achieve rich comprehension of material that otherwise would have been too remote for them to handle.

Analogous thinking not only serves the mind, but it is the aesthetic underpinning of metaphors and similes. The famous French author Marcel Proust once noted that "analogies link two unlike things in a magical way."

If you are thinking that it would be better if children came up with their own analogies, you will be interested to learn that Bean and associates (1987) showed that this approach was much more difficult and not very productive. Apparently providing an analogy is helpful; expecting one is too great a demand, especially for lower-achieving youngsters. Nonetheless, don't be afraid to ask for it. Sooner or later, someone will be able to offer one that works, and you will have one of those teaching experiences from which you will be drawing meaning for many years to come.

Now consider a fresh way of approaching spelling and word analysis that taps into intrinsic motivation by raising participation among students who may be lapsing into apathy. This method was designed for the regular classroom.

## EVERY-PUPIL-RESPONSE TO "MAKING WORDS"

Cunningham's and Cunningham's (1992) Making Words is a fast-paced, every-pupil-response system that also involves active manipulatives. The strategy combines elements from Reading Recovery (Clay, 1985), Glass-Analysis (Glass, 1973), and a modified form of anagrams—a game of forming new words from the letters in a given word (e.g., *satin* is an anagram for *stain*).

Making Words does require considerable preparation and following a set of fairly complex directions. For a quick conceptual fix on the process, think of yourself as giving students a set of scrambled letter cards that can be put together to form a long word. You then guide students into making smaller and then larger words from those letters. Two sets of steps follow: steps for planning Making Words and steps for teaching it.

## STEPS IN PLANNING A MAKING WORDS LESSON

Step 1     Decide what the long word will be (e.g., tricks). Consider the number of vowels, children's interest, curriculum tie-ins, and letter-sound patterns you can reinforce (short i, ir, sk).

Step 2     Make a list of shorter words you can make from the letters of the long word (is it kit sit sir stir sick Rick tick skit skirt stick trick **tricks**).

Step 3     From the words listed, pick 12–15 words that include: (a) words that fit the pattern you want to reinforce; (b) little words and big words; (c) words that can be made with the same letters in different places (skit, kits); (d) a proper name or two to reinforce capitalization; and (e) words that most students have in their listening vocabularies.

**Step 4**     Write all the words on index cards and sort them from shortest to longest.

**Step 5**     Order the words further to emphasize letter patterns and how changing position of letters or adding just one letter results in a different word.

**Step 6**     Store the cards in an envelope, labeled with the words in order, and the patterns you will sort for at the end.

**Step 7**     Prepare a reusable set of small letter cards, with a set of each letter stored in a resealable plastic bag. Both large and small letter cards should have the lower case on one side, and the upper case on the other side.

## STEPS IN TEACHING A MAKING WORDS LESSON

**Step 1**     Place the large letter cards in a pocket or chart or along the chalk ledge.

**Step 2**     Have designated children give matching small letter cards to each child, so that each child has letter cards that match the large ones. (Let the passer keep the reclosable bag containing that small letter and have the same child collect that letter when the lesson is over.)

**Step 3**     Hold up and name the letters on the large letter cards and have the children hold up their matching small letter cards.

**Step 4**     Write the numeral 2 (or 3 if there are no two-letter words in the lesson) on the board. Tell them to take two letters and make the first word. Use the word in a sentence after you say it.

**Step 5**     Have a child who has the first word made correctly make the same word with the large letter cards. Encourage anyone who did not make the word correctly at first to fix the word when they see it made correctly.

**Step 6**     Continue having them make words, erasing and changing the number on the board to indicate the number of letters needed. Use the words in simple sentences to make sure the children understand their meanings. Remember to cue them as to whether they are just changing one letter, changing letters around, or taking all their letters out to make a word from scratch. Cue them when the word you want them to make is a proper noun and send a child who has started that name with a capital letter to make the word with the big letters.

**Step 7**     Before telling them the last word, ask, "Has anyone figured out what word we can make with *all* our letters? If so, congratulate them and have one of them make it with the big letters. If not, say something like, "I love it when I stump you. Use all your letters and make _____."

**Step 8**    Once all the words have been made, take the index cards on which you have written the words and place them one at a time (in the same order the children have made them) along the chalk ledge or in the pocket chart. Have children say and spell the words with you as you do this. Use these words for sorting and pointing out patterns. Re-order the words so that patterns are visible.

**Step 9**    To get maximum transfer to reading and writing, have children use the patterns they have sorted to spell a few new words that you say.

**Note:**    Some teachers have chosen to do steps 1–7 on one day and steps 8 and 9 on the following day.

The next method is based on making fun and music part of becoming an effective reader. It is especially suitable for the reluctant and the slow learner.

## SOMETHING JOYFUL (MUSIC)

The charge to do something joyful in class is almost another way of saying that one should provide external motivation to build internal motivation. Music and song offer an easy and proven means of having fun while learning.

There is strong experimental evidence to support the effects of a music-centered, or arts and humanities, curriculum on listening, language awareness, and reading readiness (Eastland, 1980; Taylor, 1981). It has been reported that children taught music on a daily basis scored significantly higher on reading tests than children with no formal exposure to music (McGuire, 1984). However, from a classroom teacher's perspective, the most meaningful research was done by Harp (1988) and Bruno (1992).

Bruno (1985) ties the success of her techniques to the Neurological Impress Method (discussed ahead in the chapter). She now offers these recommendations for combining song and word recognition training (Bruno, 1992):

1. Teach children a "piggyback" song—any popular song with a melody to which other lyrics can be sung.[2]
2. Then teach new words to the same tune (preferably words that are frequently repeated).
3. As children sing the song, write the words on an easel chart as quickly as you can.
4. Point to the words as they sing again.
5. Have individual children point to the words as the class sings (with kindergartners, Bruno actually holds the child's hand and guides the movement and pauses).
6. Take a few minutes each day for singing and pointing.

[2] See Jean Warren's *Piggyback Songs: New Songs Sung to the Tune of Childhood Favorites* (1983), from Totline Press.

**FIGURE 11.3 Piggyback Songs**

Old Ms. Newberg had a class, E-I-E-I-O. And in this class she had some kids E-I-E-I-O.

7. Ask children if they think they can come up and identify a word they know. Have them choose one of three hot-colored, three-sided brackets in large, medium, or small to encompass the chosen word (see Figure 11.3). Some form of bracketing is necessary, Bruno suggests, because identifying a word involves more than just pointing to approximately where it is. She further advises that initially children will isolate longer words and naming terms. It is late in the year before her kindergartners turn to function words like *would, could, will,* and *they* (1992, p. 13).

## NONREGULAR APPROACHES FOR NONREGULAR SETTINGS

In addition to strategies for meeting the needs of all students within the regular classroom setting, there are a number of strategies specially designed for working with special needs students outside the regular classroom. Some simply require an individualized or small-group setting. Others can be used with entire classes but require very specialized materials. Most specialized approaches derive their value from offering a fresh approach to youngsters who are ready to spring back from failure. It is rather like the strategic use of a placebo (a sugar pill) to give a fresh start. For example, you may recall the story from Chapter 1 about some severely disabled (dyslexic) readers who were helped to overcome some of their negative associations with reading simply by using an alternative alphabet (Manzo, 1977a; 1987). There will be occasions when it will occur to a reflective teacher that some "placebo" is needed, largely because it is different and it might raise hope.

Here are some "fresh start" ideas that, for the most part, are outside mainstream teaching. They will not present problems for average functioning children and may be just the ticket for those stuck in a remedial rut. You may need to go to some primary source for more information on these before you can use them.

## McCormick's Multiple-Exposure/Multiple-Context

The M-E/M-C strategy (McCormick, 1990) was developed for severely disabled readers. It provides frequent practice with new words (multiple exposures) but without isolated drill (multiple contexts).

## Steps in Multiple Exposure/Multiple-Context

**Step 1**   Select a high-interest/difficulty-controlled book series.

**Step 2**   In the first remedial session have the student read orally, as a pretest, the first chapter of the preprimer of the selected series. Make note of all words the student does *not* recognize on sight. These words are the instructional content for the next sessions.

**Step 3**   Beginning with the second session, for the first 5–10 minutes, read aloud to the student from good children's literature. This provides exposure to connected text that nonreaders are not yet able to access themselves. The remaining 50 minutes are devoted to exposure to the set of words identified from the chapter. The objective is to expose the student to these words in a variety of contexts, involving:

Games and manipulatives

Contextual activities to promote transfer to real text

Attention to internal features of words

During this process, the teacher visually demonstrates progress by having the student count words learned and record these on a graph or chart. The chapter itself is *not* referred to again until all the words have been mastered.

**Step 4**   When all the words have been mastered, the student rereads the first chapter of the preprimer. At this point, the student should have his or her first experience in successfully reading a complete text.

**Step 5**   The student reads the second chapter as a pretest to target the next set of unknown words. The teacher proceeds with Steps 3 and 4; that is, teaching words to the automatic stage and only then having the student reread the chapter. Steps 2, 3, and 4 are followed with every chapter in the book.

**Step 6**   The student rereads the first book in one sitting—again, a first-time occurrence for nonreaders.

Subsequent Steps: The student progresses through other books in the series in a manner consistent with the previous steps. Learning *rate* should increase as the student moves through the program until it begins to approximate the norm. At that time, the M-E/M-C strategy is abandoned and the student participates in a more typical program of instruction.

## SPECIALIZED METACOGNITIVE AIDS

At-risk students, particularly those who already have fallen more than a year below expected grade level performance, need extra support in becoming strategic readers. Several methods for building metacognitive operations are suggested throughout the text. Box 11.6 provides an additional one in the form of a bookmark that students can be taught to use to think about and "self-fix" their thinking and reading problems as they are encountered.

## FINGER SPELLING WITH THE "MANUAL ALPHABET"

Finger spelling (see Figure 11.4) is used by the hearing impaired to communicate words for which there is no ready sign. Finger spelling has also proven to be quite beneficial for improving word identification and spelling in hearing children as well

---

**BOX 11.6** **Metacognitive Decoding Strategy Bookmarks**

**For Primary Students:**

When I'm reading and I come to a word I don't know, I should:

• read the rest of the sentence.

• think of a word that:

– makes sense in the sentence AND

– has the same beginning letter or letters as the word I don't know.

---

If I still don't know the word, I should look at:

• endings

• word parts

• vowels

If I still don't know the word, I should ask, "Is this word _____ ?" or skip it and just read on.

**For Intermediate Students:**

When I'm reading and I come to a word I don't know, I should:

1. Skip the word and read the rest of the sentence.

2. Think about what word might make sense in the sentence.

3. Look at the beginning letters and try sounding out the word.

4. Try different sounds for vowels.

5. Look for prefixes, suffixes and roots.

6. Use a dictionary, ask, or skip the word and continue reading.

(side 1 of bookmark)          (side 2 of bookmark)

**FIGURE 11.4** **The Manual Alphabet**

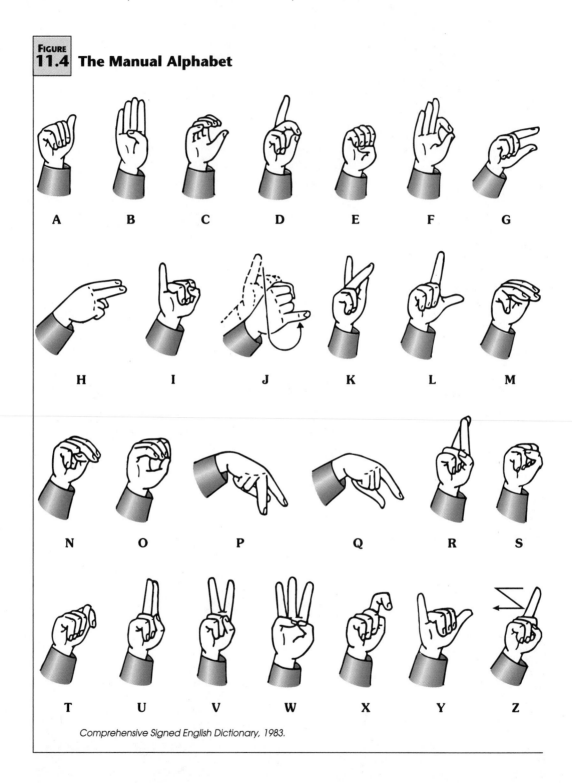

Comprehensive Signed English Dictionary, 1983.

(Andrews, 1988; Isaacson, 1987; Stein, 1982; Wilson, 1984). If you are looking for something different and fresh, try teaching spelling with this tested method.

## VISUAL–AUDITORY–KINESTHETIC-TACTILE (VAKT) METHOD

This method was developed by Helen Keller and her teacher, Anne Sullivan. Keller, blind, deaf, and mute from infancy, was taught by Sullivan to communicate by tapping letters out on her hand. Years later, Keller was able to refine the method with the help of Grace Fernald (Fernald, 1943) into its current form. This is a one-on-one teaching method.

## VAKT STEPS

Step 1   Ask the learner to suggest a word that she or he wishes to learn.

Step 2   The teacher writes the word in large handwriting, speaking the word in a natural way as it is written. (Use a black magic marker or grease pencil.)

Step 3   The learner traces the word with his or her finger while speaking the *whole* word (*not* being permitted to say the individual letters of the word) and being careful to begin and end speech and writing at the same time.

Step 4   The learner does this as often as is needed, until the child feels certain that he or she has learned it.

Step 5   The learner then visualizes it and traces it in the air with his finger.

Step 6   The learner than turns the word card over, takes another piece of paper, and tries to write the word from memory, writing and speaking at the same time.

Step 7   The learner compares this production with the original model.

Step 8   In extraordinary cases, a tray may be filled with moist sand, and the child may be urged to trace the word in the sand.

Step 9   The words taught in this way should be reviewed daily in a short list with other words.

## NEUROLOGICAL IMPRESS METHOD (NIM)

In the Neurological Impress Method (Hecklemann, 1966, 1969), the teacher and student read aloud together from the same material. The idea underlying NIM has been traced back by Pelosi (1982) to Huey, who called it "imitation reading" in his 1908 text.

## STEPS IN THE NEUROLOGICAL IMPRESS METHOD

Step 1   The teacher sits slightly behind the student.

Step 2   The teacher reads into the student's preferred ear. (This is usually the right: it has stronger connections to the left hemisphere, and does not have to cross the sometimes fragile corpus callosum (the hemisphere-connecting fibers) as does sound to the left ear. However, sound to either ear should cross the corpus callosum and give the sensation of the sound to the other ear. If it does not, this can be taken as an indication of a possible neurophysiological problem requiring a referral.)

**Step 3**    The teacher slides a finger under each word being read.

**Step 4**    The teacher first reads in a slightly louder and slightly faster voice than the student, and then with time, lower and slower, and with the student's finger setting the pace.

**Step 5**    The teacher does not attempt to teach word analysis skills at this time.

**Step 6**    The teacher attempts to provide words in advance of the student's need when it is believed that need will slow the student down, even after the shift to student control of pacing and louder oral reading.

Echo reading (Anderson, 1981), a variation on NIM, previously mentioned, has the teacher first read segments of the material to establish cadence and comprehension. On rereading, the student reads in a lower voice, echoing the material.

NIM was designed to improve word recognition and analysis. It seems best suited, however, to increasing fluency and automaticity in response to known words. It probably is best used with students who have very poor word recognition, rather than with those with poor word analysis.

## A WORD ON DYSLEXIA

The term *dyslexia* refers to a reading disability that is both severe and persistent. It affects from 3 to 6 percent of the population. It has no single known cause, nor a single form of expression: It should be thought of as a category of problems, rather than as a specific condition. Most importantly, dyslexia is treatable, and becomes more treatable as we continue to learn more about both the reading process in general and about the physical characteristics and processes of the brain during the reading act.

Contrary to popular belief, dyslexia has very little to do with reading letters or words backwards. These manifestations are largely the same as the errors commonly made by beginning readers; they simply persist in children who might be called "dyslexic" because these children remain in the "early learning" stage for an extended period, thus reflecting the awkward errors of this stage for a longer time.

Until recently, programs for treating dyslexia tended to assume that the causes and the nature of the condition were the same for all, and consequently offered the same treatment to all. Some of these programs were quite unusual, if not radical. In one, for example, children were put through a physical therapy program that replicated the natural developmental process—creeping and then crawling in patterned movements (Delacato, 1959; 1963). Educators should be wary of groups that offer this type of single-treatment program without a thorough preliminary diagnostic analysis of each child. They usually are beneficial for a few, and a waste of time, effort, and money for many.

Boder and Jarrico (1982) developed an assessment model that is based on more current understandings of the reading process and that is linked to differential treatment (Manzo & Manzo, 1993). In simplest terms, this system distinguishes among dyslexic children whose problems result from their inability to make letter-sound connections (about 45% of dyslexic children), those whose problems result from inability to recall whole words (about 10%), and those whose problems result from a combination of both the above problems (about 45%).

An additional consideration in identifying dyslexia has been referred to several times in this text. You may recall the references to a study in which several dyslexic children learned to read quite easily using an alternate alphabet. The diagnostic information collected on those children suggested that the source of their reading problem might have been psychological rather than physiological (Manzo, 1977a). Consequently, remedial efforts addressing the reading problem itself likely would be doomed to failure; a more whole-child approach is called for.

We turn now to another area of very special need—students for whom English is a second language that must be learned while they are attending school. The proportion of these students is expected to continue to grow as America continues to serve as a haven for displaced people from many lands.

## LIMITED ENGLISH PROFICIENCY

Teachers seem to be much more aware of the implications of limited English proficiency in reading than we were a generation ago. Knafle and Geissal (1983) illustrated this in a study that had teachers analyze children's oral reading using an Informal Reading Inventory (described in the next chapter) as a recording system. They found that when children read orally, teachers tended to view dialect variations as "miscues"[3] more so than as errors, so long as the meaning remained intact. Now that more teachers understand this, there still is the issue of what more needs to be done to teach children with limited English proficiency.

Finding the proper thing to do begins with grasping the nature of the problem. For African Americans with limited *standard* English proficiency, it is largely a matter of helping them to remain respectful of the community of language that they live in while helping them to master a more widely used option that will not leave them linguistically isolated. Some of these differences are becoming less pronounced as inner city and rural areas that once were isolated become connected to standard English options through television, radio, magnet school programs, work-related contacts, and the stores and bureaucracies that we all must do business with. It is somewhat different, however, for speakers of other languages, such as Spanish, and foreign-born children. Their first language is not a dialect of English, nor has their culture intermixed with core Anglo-American culture to a great degree.

---

[3] A miscalled word, during oral reading, that does not alter the meaning of the passage and therefore is not interpreted as an "error" in a reading evaluation.

Their language also has entirely different grammatical and sound systems. Ironically, accommodating an entirely new language and cultural milieu can be somewhat less difficult than shifting to one that has a shared base. Many foreign-born children are required to take English in school; however, the native-born tend to think that there is no urgency to master a language that they largely understand and can negotiate when they need to. For both groups, there also is a learning barrier that is technically known as "proactive" inhibition. This means that things previously learned that are close to what one wishes to learn can interfere with and inhibit new learnings. For native dialect speakers this might mean overcoming an ingrained pattern, such as saying "I wants" instead of "I want." Similarly, a German-born youngster learning English needs to learn the English sound of /w/, while overcoming the tendency to make the German /v/ sound for /w/.

Let's see now what can be done to accommodate children from different language and cultural milieus. The guidelines and methods presented ahead are taken largely from summations by Maggart and Zintz (1992) and Early, Cullinan, and associates (1987).

## LIMITED ENGLISH PROFICIENCY GUIDELINES

Basically, children whose first language is not standard English need to be taught to *hear* the segments of sound that are used in English but not in their native language. Before tackling this requirement head-on, however, we shall describe some materials and methods for helping these students in a conventional basal-reading program. The guiding concept in selecting these materials and methods is that Limited English Proficiency (LEP) students, as they sometimes are called, need to be in positive language-learning environments where risk taking is encouraged, teacher expectations remain high, their native language *is* valued, and language is viewed as a cooperative venture between teacher and students. One way to help achieve this is to set up a permanent space in the classroom where students can have access to an abundance of materials that aid vocabulary and concept development.

### LEP Supporting Materials

Material to use with LEP students might include:

1.  Picture files illustrating vocabulary that is developed in reading selections
2.  Read-along tapes for many stories
3.  Tapes of vocabulary words with definitions and sentences to provide opportunities for word practice
4.  Displays of language-experience charts to be used for matching words, phrases, and phonetic elements
5.  Displays of idioms and their meanings to help with concept development and story comprehension
6.  Library books for application of what is being learned to other materials
7.  Tape recorders and blank tapes, for recording students as they read aloud
8.  Materials for journal writing

9. Areas to display student group compositions as well as individual compositions

10. Synonym and antonym charts to help with student writing and vocabulary development

11. A group-developed dictionary for all of the new words learned during the year (a computer with a self-alphabetizing program is very useful in this ongoing activity)

12. Newspapers and magazines to further familiarize students with American idioms, and to be used for finding pictures, names, numbers, and phrases

## LEP Teaching Methods

The following methods can be used with almost any basal or other reading material to further aid second language development:

- Encourage students to comment on reading materials to be read, particularly by trying to predict what the selection in each unit of study might be about. Record students' predictions on a chart. At the end of a unit, encourage students to discuss whether or not their predictions were correct and why.

- Have as many books as possible available for students. Read the descriptions of books to them, encouraging them to select books from this list. In addition, select one book from each unit and read it to students.

- Have a variety of multiethnic literature available, including materials from your students' cultures and some in their languages. Help them to build on their strengths, from a strong base of confidence and self-esteem.

- Exercise materials in any lesson should be read to students and discussed.

- Read poetry aloud to students and discuss. If possible, record the poetry on a tape so students can hear the poet's language again and again.

- Read plays to students before they are asked to take character parts. If possible, provide audio or video recorders so students can practice their parts and hear (and see) themselves before they are asked to read aloud.

- Read postreading questions to students and discuss answers with them before having them write out their own answers.

- Second-language students might have a developmental gap between their ability to read and their ability to write in the second language. These students will benefit by working through stages of the Writing Process as a group activity. After a suitable prewriting activity and/or discussion, students should be asked to talk through the "drafting" stage, while someone records what they say on chart paper. Students then should be asked to reread the composition and make any needed revisions. The recorder should make these revisions while students observe and suggest any editing corrections that need to be made (spelling, usage, punctuation, etc.). Each student should then copy the finished work from the chart, so that they have a sense of ownership. As students gain a sense of confidence in their ability to write, pair students and have them write their compositions together. Move from this procedure to having students write independently.

Now let's turn back to the root problem of learning another language—the problem of unfamiliar phonemic sounds. If you will recall from an earlier chapter, learning to read aids phonemic awareness as much, if not more than phonemic awareness aids learning to read. For this reason, teach LEP children to read in English as soon as possible.

## DECODING STRATEGIES FOR LIMITED ENGLISH PROFICIENCY STUDENTS

Certain English grapheme/phoneme correspondences are particularly difficult for Limited English Proficiency students. The most common of these are presented in chart form in Table 11.1 (p. 476). As a general approach to teaching these "difficult sounds," use the teaching strategies found in the decoding chapter, always beginning with auditory discrimination before moving to auditory/visual association. Use concrete materials (picture and objects) when dealing with phoneme/grapheme correspondences. This practice will not only help "fix" the elements so that they can be heard and visualized, but will increase second language vocabulary acquisition. McCormick's decoding strategy, described earlier in this chapter, is another useful and straightforward approach.

There are certain methods, such as the Lindamoods' (1975) Auditory Discrimination in Depth program, that are especially appropriate for second-language teaching of reading. The Lindamoods' program, for example, gives the teacher labels for talking about troublesome new sounds and to better coach youngsters in making the English-American sound. The sounds /b/ and /p/, for example, are referred to as "lip poppers." In formal linguistics, these would be called *explosives*.

## REINFORCEMENT

Students need a great deal of practice with "difficult sounds." The following is an effective way to provide needed reinforcement. Gather a picture file representative of the difficult sounds. Make a library pocket chart and write a phonetic element in a whole word on the outside of each pocket. Underline the phonetic element. Have students choose a picture from the box, say the picture name, and place the picture in the appropriate pocket chart. Encourage students to use the words in sentences. If students can only name the object, then model sentences for them: "Yes, Sammy, that is a ball. You can play games with the ball." In activities of this kind, it is important to remember that proper pronunciation does not take precedence over clear understanding. If a child mispronounces a word (base for vase), repeat the correct pronunciation: "Yes, but that is a /v/ase."

## RESOURCES FOR WORKING WITH LIMITED ENGLISH PROFICIENCY STUDENTS

There are some obvious problems in working with children who have limited English proficiency, whether they be remedial level readers or solid students from foreign lands. However, there are some ready resources in and about us to draw upon. These are a fitting conclusion to this chapter, since some of these recommendations are applicable to other special needs children:

1. Be respectful of children's cultures and customs.
2. Seek advice and counsel from available specialists and veteran teachers.

3. Let the inevitably humorous miscommunications that arise carry you and the children through the edginess that also is likely to arise in an active classroom.

4. Remind yourself that these children enjoy a certain advantage in speaking more than one language and in knowing another culture.

5. These children can be a valuable resource as representatives from an alternate cultural perspective and as potential teachers of foreign language.

6. If you are proficient in the child's native language, use it to remediate misunderstandings that might be clarified best with a reference to something in the child's native language or culture.

7. Have bilingual students read and write with aides, parents, and former LEP children who speak a student's first language (Freeman & Freeman, 1993).

## LIMITED ENGLISH PROFICIENCY STUDENTS AS RESOURCES

The last point, above, is especially worth considering in our recurring theme of empowering children to be agents of change in their environments as well as being changed by their environments. Picture, for example, a school that has several youngsters from Thailand. These children could be asked if they would like to teach about their language and culture during an occasional activity period. If enough of the other children are interested, this could be done on a scheduled basis. Within one term, children would undoubtedly learn and go home with understandings of aspects of Thai geography, language, religion, political structures, and culture. There also are wonderful books available for children that reflect life and thinking all over the globe (see illustration). All we need is a reason to seek them out. Such learnings might not be in the elementary curriculum guide, but they are enlightening, educational, and enriching in every sense of these words.

For a list of books and magazines of a multiethnic and multilingual nature, see Chapter 13 on classroom and schoolwide programming. The number of these books is growing at a rapid pace. To keep abreast, you will need to contact your resource librarian and local children's bookstores yearly.

*Source: Patrick Owens & Kulaya Campiranonta (1988) Thai Proverbs. Bangkok: Darnsutha Press Co. Ltd.*

## Table 11.1

### Difficult Grapheme/Phoneme Correspondence

| DIFFICULT SOUND | LANGUAGE GROUP FOR WHOM IT TENDS TO BE A PROBLEM | SUGGESTIONS FOR TEACHING |
|---|---|---|
| /b/ as in *bat* (as distinct from /p/ as in *pat* and /d/ as in *dad*) | Chinese, Samoan, Korean | Have student listen to and repeat these words: bat-pat-dad-big-pig-day-bee-pea-deer. Have pictures available to illustrate the words. Mirrors are also useful for helping students differentiate the way these sounds are made by the mouth. |
| /d/ as in *dog* (as distinct from /b/ as in *bed*) | Chinese | Use pictures and related practice using the words: dog-door-donkey-dollar-duck-doctor-doll. |
| /f/ as in *fat* (as distinct from /p/ as in *pat*) | Tagalog, Vietnamese | Use pictures and related practice using the words: fin-fall-fig-fat-feel-fit-fool-four-fast-fan-few-fault-ferry-fine-pin-pail-pig- pat-peel-pit-pool-pour-pan-past-van-vat-veal-view-vast-veil-very-vine. |
| /g/ as in *goat* (as distinct from /k/ as in *coat*) | general | Check students' ability to distinguish these sounds auditorally and to pronounce them correctly: Say a word beginning with one of these sounds, and have the student repeat it. Say word pairs, and ask if the beginning sounds are the same or different. Use word pairs such as: goat/coat; gap/cap; gill/kill; gate/Kate; game/came; goal/coal; good/could. |
| /h/ as in *hot* | Spanish | In Spanish, the letter *h* is silent; hence, students may forget to pronounce this sound. Because the /h/ sound is represented by the letter *j* in Spanish, this letter may be used to spell English words that begin with *h* (*jat* for *hat; jot* for *hot*). Have students repeat words beginning with *h*. Have them repeat the sound they hear at the beginning of words beginning with *h*. Write *h* words on the board, repeating and underlining the h sound. Have students copy the words and illustrate them. The teacher may write a *j* in parentheses in dictated stories as a transition step: ''(J)He put on (j)his (j)hat.'' |
| /j/ as in *jar* (as distinct from /ch/ as in *chest*, and /y/ as in *yam*) | Spanish | In Spanish, the /y/ sound as in *yellow* is often substituted for the /j/ sound. Say words beginning with *j*, and ask students to repeat the words. Provide practice in listening to the sounds, hearing the difference, and using the words in context. Use word pairs such as: Jane/chain; jeep/cheep or cheap; Jerry/cherry; jest/chest; jacks/yellow; jet/yet; jam/yell; job/yes. |

| DIFFICULT SOUND | LANGUAGE GROUP FOR WHOM IT TENDS TO BE A PROBLEM | SUGGESTIONS FOR TEACHING |
|---|---|---|
| /k/ as in *cat* and *king* (as distinct from /g/ as in *go*) | Korean, Samoan, Vietnamese, Thai, Tongan, Indonesian | This sound is especially difficult for speakers of Vietnamese and Thai when it comes at the end of a word. Tell students the /k/ sound can be represented by the letters *k* or *c*. Make 3 × 5 note cards with a *g, k,* or *c* word on one side and a picture on the other side. Have students look at the picture and say the word. Then ask if the word begins with the same or a different sound than another *g, k,* or *c* word. Students can also be asked to write the correct word for the picture on a piece of paper. Use words such as: back-crack-brick-duck-snack-tack-wick-buck-bag-rag-wig-big. |
| /l/ as in *lamp* (as distinct from /n/ and /r/ sounds) | Asian languages | Provide practice through simple repetition, picture cards, and words in context, using words such as: lemon-letter-lion-lamp. |
| /n/ as in *net* (as distinct from /l/ as in *lot*) | Chinese | Provide repetition with words such as: net-night-nest-needle; and word pairs such as not/lot; knee/Lee; knack/lack; knife/life; know/low; knock/lock. |
| /kw/ as in *queen* (as distinct from /w/ as in *wet*) | general | Provide repetition with words such as: queen-quick-quiet-quack-question; and word pairs such as: wit/quit; wick/quick; wake/quake; well/quell; wilt/quilt; will/quill; whack/quack. |
| /p/ as in *pet* (as distinct from /f/ as in *far*) | Tagalog and Vietnamese | Use picture cards of words beginning with *f* and *p*. Have students sort words by beginning sound, using words such as: four-five-fort-fire-frog-pail-pig-pen-pear-people. |
| /r/ as in *ran* (as distinct from /l/ as in *lip*) | Chinese, Japanese, Korean, Vietnamese, Thai | Provide repetition with /l/ words such as lip-lock-lace-leaf-low-lamp; and word pairs such as: list/wrist; long/wrong; lake/rake; lead/read. |
| /v/ as in *vent* (as distinct from /b/ as in *boy*) | Spanish | Have students listen to repeat word pairs such as: van/ban; veil/bail; very/berry; vet/bet; vat/bat. |
| /v/ as in *vent* (as distinct from /f/ as in *far*) | Tagalog, Vietnamese | Have students listen to and repeat word pairs such as: van/fan; veil/fail; vat/fat; veal/feel. |
| /w/ as in *wet* (as distinct from /v/ as in *van* | Chinese, Arabic, German, Samoan, Thai | Have students listen to and repeat word pairs such as: wet/vet; wail/veil; west/vest; went/vent. |

*continued*

## Table 11.1—cont'd

### Difficult Grapheme/Phoneme Correspondence

| DIFFICULT SOUND | LANGUAGE GROUP FOR WHOM IT TENDS TO BE A PROBLEM | SUGGESTIONS FOR TEACHING |
|---|---|---|
| /y/ as in *yam* (as distinct from /j/ as in *jet* | Spanish, Portuguese, Indonesian, Thai | Provide repetition with /y/ words such as: yam-yoyo-yolk-yak-yard-yellow-yawn. |
| /z/ as in *zoo* (as distinct from /s/ as in *soap*) | general | Provide repetition with /z/ words such as: zoo-zebra-zoom-zip-zipper-zero-zone; and word pairs such as: Sue/zoo; sing/zing; sip/zip; see/zee; sink/zinc. |
| final consonants and consonant clusters | Spanish | In Spanish, there are only a few consonants that appear at the ends of words (n, s, z, r, d, l, j), and many Spanish-speaking people tend to drop the final consonant in conversation. Use picture word cards and varied activities to provide practice with words pairs such as rope/robe; ape/ate; add/at; sad/sat; bag/back; wipe/wife; lad/lab; bead/bees; cried/cries. Provide practice with final consonant cluster sounds of /ld/, as in old-gold-cold-sold; /nt/, as in bent-tent-went-spent; /nd/ as in band-wind-pond-spend-find; /ngk/ as in sink-drink-chunk-pink; and /st/ as in west-first-toast-fast-test. |
| initial /s/ and consonant clusters beginning with /s/ as in *school, sleep, star, street* | Spanish | In Spanish, letter clusters beginning with *s* never appear at the beginning of the word. Spanish-speaking students often add /e/ before the /s/ sound; thus, *spot*, for example, is pronounced /espot/. Provide practice with initial *s* and *s* cluster words such as: sleep-spoon-smile-star-skirt-street-screen. |
| /sh/ as in *ship* (as distinct from /ch/ as in *chin*) | Spanish | There is no /sh/ sound in Spanish, and Spanish-speaking students find this sound difficult to distinguish from the /ch/ sound. Provide repetition and practice with word pairs such as: sheet/cheat; Sherry/cherry; ship/chip; shop/chop; shows/chose; sheer/cheer; shoe/chew; shoes/choose; shore/chore. |
| /fr/ as in *frog* (as distinct from /fl/ as in *flat*) | Spanish, Chinese, other Oriental languages | Provide repetition of /fr/ words such as: frog-fruit-friend-front-frozen-fresh. Provide practice distinguishing /fr/ words from /fl/ words such as: float-flower-flag-flat. |
| /tr/ as in *train* | general | Provide repetition with /tr/ words such as: tree-trip-trick-truck-true-treat. |

| DIFFICULT SOUND | LANGUAGE GROUP FOR WHOM IT TENDS TO BE A PROBLEM | SUGGESTIONS FOR TEACHING |
|---|---|---|
| /kr/ as in *cream*, /kl/ as in *clown*, /gl/ as in *glue* | Chinese, Vietnamese | Provide repetition with /kr/ words such as: cry-crab-crack: /kl/ words such as: class-closer-cloth; and /gl/ words such as: glad-glass-glove. |
| short sound of /a/ as in *bat* | general | Short vowel sounds are among the most difficult for LEP students to master. Provide repetition with short /a/ such as bat-cat-hat-pat. |
| short sound of /e/ as in *pen* | general | Provide practice with short /e/ words such as: pen-ten-then-men-hen. |
| short sound of /i/ as in *did* | Spanish, Chinese, Vietnamese, Taglog | LEP students often confuse the short /i/ sound with the long /e/ sound as in *feed*. Provide practice with word pairs such as: seat/sit; hit/heat; green/grin; feet/fit. |
| short sound of /o/ as in *cot* | Spanish, Chinese, Vietnamese, Taglog, Thai | LEP students often confuse this sound with the long /o/ sound in *coat*. Provide practice with word pairs such as: hop/hope; rod/road; tot/tote; not/note; cot/coat. |
| short sound of /u/ as in *umbrella* | general | This is another difficult sound for LEP students because it does not exist in many languages, yet is one of the most common sounds in English. LEP students often confuse this sound with the /a/ as in *bat* and the /e/ as in *bet*. Provide practice with word pairs/groups such as: cup/cap; fun/fan; bug/bag/bet; nut/net/gnat; ran/run. |
| long sound of /a/ as in *race* | Vietnamese, Spanish, Tagalog | These students find it difficult to differentiate the long /a/ sound from the /e/ sound in *pet*. Provide practice with word pairs such as: jail/jell; ball/bell; fail/fell, nail/Nell; sail/sell; tail/tell. |
| long sound of /i/ as in *five* | general | LEP students find it difficult to differentiate the long sound of /i/ from the /a/ sound in *bat*. Provide practice with word pairs such as: pine/pan; bite/bat; like/lack; bike/back; kite/cat; side/sad. |
| long sound of /o/ as in *rope* | general | LEP students find it difficult to differentiate the long sound of /o/ from the /o/ sound in *pot*. Provide practice with word pairs such as: rote/rot; note/not; coat/cot; hope/hop; mope/mop. |

*Adapted from Early et al. (1987). Harcourt, Brace, Jovanovich, pp. T2-T12.*

# **W**here You've Been

### Literacy Provisions for Children with Special Needs

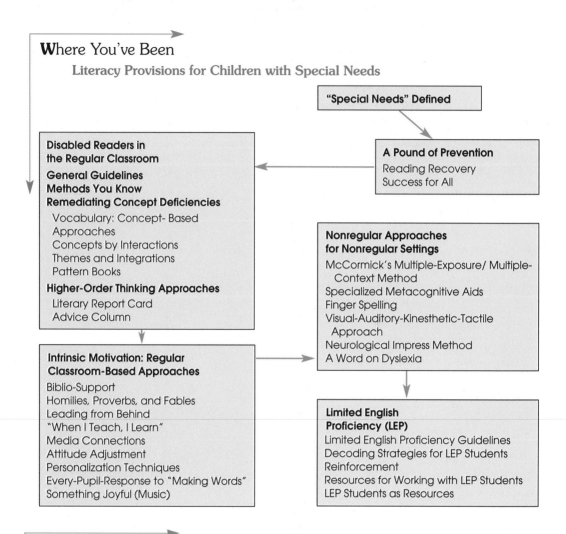

**"Special Needs" Defined**

**Disabled Readers in
the Regular Classroom**

**General Guidelines**
**Methods You Know**
**Remediating Concept Deficiencies**

Vocabulary: Concept- Based
Approaches
Concepts by Interactions
Themes and Integrations
Pattern Books

**Higher-Order Thinking Approaches**

Literary Report Card
Advice Column

**A Pound of Prevention**
Reading Recovery
Success for All

**Nonregular Approaches
for Nonregular Settings**
McCormick's Multiple-Exposure/ Multiple-
Context Method
Specialized Metacognitive Aids
Finger Spelling
Visual-Auditory-Kinesthetic-Tactile
Approach
Neurological Impress Method
A Word on Dyslexia

**Intrinsic Motivation: Regular
Classroom-Based Approaches**
Biblio-Support
Homilies, Proverbs, and Fables
Leading from Behind
"When I Teach, I Learn"
Media Connections
Attitude Adjustment
Personalization Techniques
Every-Pupil-Response to "Making Words"
Something Joyful (Music)

**Limited English
Proficiency (LEP)**
Limited English Proficiency Guidelines
Decoding Strategies for LEP Students
Reinforcement
Resources for Working with LEP Students
LEP Students as Resources

# **W**here You're Going

In the next chapter, you will read about a variety of techniques and tools for assessing student progress in reading. The chapter will assist you in deciding who has special needs, so that you might better aim your decisions about how to provide help. It also will begin to prepare you for the important role of influencing school testing practices.

### *Reflective Inquiries and Activities*

1.  Why do you suppose there likely always will be some few disabled learners, and therefore the need to learn how to help them in a regular classroom setting?

2. Tell about a method that you would add to the "Methods You Know" list (pages 436–438).

3. What's good and reasonable about the "compensation model" for helping disabled readers? What has been learned that has altered the extent to which this model is relied upon for addressing the needs of disabled readers?

4. Tell which two methods, of those listed under intrinsic motivation, are your favorites, and why.

5. Construct a personalization activity for a complex idea, story, or contemporary situation. (For example, the former three political blocs now are more like relatives than combatants. Two of them, the former neutral and soviet blocs, are in very great financial need, and the U.S. and the free world are having their own economic problems. How can this situation and related events be personalized so that children can follow the news and progress with this ongoing problem?)

6. Why is concept-based learning often overlooked in working with remedial level students, and why shouldn't it be?

7. Write a letter to an advice columnist as a child might. Switch with someone and answer their letter while they answer yours. Discuss. (Try writing letters about strange things your teacher does or that you are asked to do in school.)

8. What makes McCormick's approach to word recognition and analysis different from most others?

9. Why might "finger spelling" be an effective teaching tool, other than because it is a fresh idea? (Reread the section on Motor Imaging in the vocabulary chapter for clues.)

10. Identify a child with a certain type of Limited English Proficiency, or from a different but native American cultural and language background. How and what would you address in teaching that child to read standard English?

11. Think of ways other than those mentioned toward the end of the chapter for how foreign-speaking children might be empowered in an English language reading class.

12. How can you know who has special needs? Use this question as a front-end guide to help you peruse the material in the next chapter on assessment.

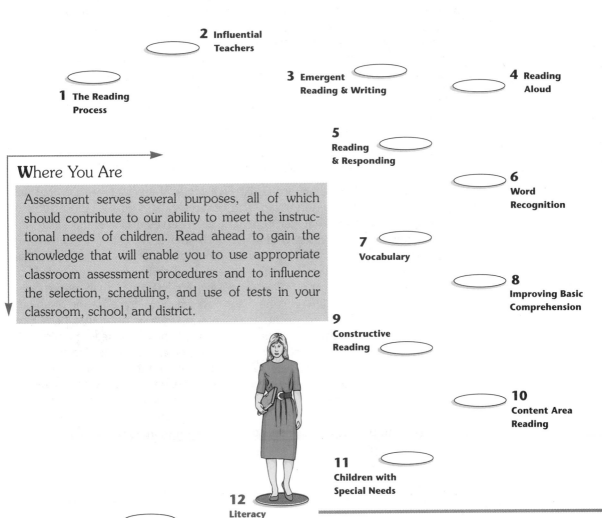

**2** Influential Teachers

**1** The Reading Process

**3** Emergent Reading & Writing

**4** Reading Aloud

**5** Reading & Responding

**6** Word Recognition

**W**here You Are

Assessment serves several purposes, all of which should contribute to our ability to meet the instructional needs of children. Read ahead to gain the knowledge that will enable you to use appropriate classroom assessment procedures and to influence the selection, scheduling, and use of tests in your classroom, school, and district.

**7** Vocabulary

**8** Improving Basic Comprehension

**9** Constructive Reading

**10** Content Area Reading

**11** Children with Special Needs

**12** Literacy Assessment

**13** The Classroom & School Literacy Program

*The examiner pipes and the teacher must dance—and the examiner sticks to the old tune. If educational reformers really wish the dance altered they must turn their attention from the dancers to the musicians.*

H. G. Wells, 1892

## COMPOSING A "NEW TUNE"

As you can see from the 1892 date on the opening quote, educators have long been aware that teaching tends to be reduced to what is tested. If you would be part of a realistic effort to compose a new assessment "tune" to which teachers and children may more willingly dance, it is necessary to know something about the music, the instruments, and the scoring (pardon the puns). It might seem that one would need extensive study in tests and measurements to participate in such a venture, but you do not. You do, however, need to become conversant with the information found in the pages ahead. This information will help you to acquire:

- A basic knowledge of commonly used test instruments and standard assessment procedures
- A sense of the importance of assessing what we believe should be taught
- An appreciation for informal assessment techniques as a means of focusing on objectives that standardized testing does not address adequately

To begin with, you will read about the different *types* of assessment tools that are available: standardized, criterion-based, and observational. None of these tools is appropriate for *all* assessment purposes, but each serves a viable and valid purpose. From this comment, you should infer that in the following pages you will *not* find support for the current tendency toward wholesale criticism and even elimination of formal testing practices. Criticism of this kind neither serves the needs of children nor promotes respect for education. Tests are little more than messengers: we must resist the tendency to shoot the messenger when we don't like the message.

It also should be noted, up front, that the messages are not that bad. Farr (1992), one of the leading authorities in assessment, has repeatedly pointed out that data analyses across the last fifty years have shown very little decline in the reading performance of U.S. students. That is true despite the advent of television and despite the fact that a greater proportion of students being tested in recent years represent groups that were *not tested* in previous years—such as students from educationally depressed circumstances and students who previously would have dropped out of school. Read ahead now to learn more about what constitutes effective and efficient assessment practices.

## ASSESSMENT OPTIONS

Following is a brief summation of the nature, values, and shortfalls of the options available in conducting assessment in literacy, and in most other curriculum areas as well.

### STANDARDIZED TESTS

The term *standardized* means that a test is *norm-referenced* for more meaningful interpretation. When a standardized test such as the Iowa Test of Basic Skills (ITBS) is created, it is given to a large and representative sample of students in order to determine the average number of correct answers students could be expected to make at different age or grade levels. These averages can then be used to interpret the raw scores of students who are given the test in different places and at different times. It is this ability to stretch across place and time that is one of the chief advantages of norm-referenced testing.

Norm-referenced, or standardized, test scores typically are expressed as grade equivalents, percentiles, or stanines. A *grade equivalent* score indicates that a student's raw score is the same as the average score of the sample students in a certain grade level. It is reported in a whole number and a tenth to represent some portion of the year. Thus, 5.5 is equivalent to fifth grade, fifth month of school. A *percentile score* is another way of indicating how a student's raw score relates to those of the sample population. A raw score, for example, may be checked against a table showing that score to be in the 51st percentile. This means that the score is higher than 51 percent of those in the sample group. Finally, there is the *stanine score* (or, standard nine). This score indicates the category of scores in which the student's score falls. A stanine score of six indicates that the student's score fell within the sixth of nine possible segments of scores, with one being low and nine high, and the fifth stanine containing the average raw scores. Most standardized test manuals include conversion tables for translating raw scores into grade equivalent, percentile, and stanine scores. Sometimes special norms are calculated to determine how a given raw score compares with those of students from similar regional, socioeconomic, or ethnic backgrounds.

Two important criteria for evaluating tests are validity and reliability. *Validity* is the extent to which the test measures what it is said to measure; *reliability* is the extent to which the test dependably yields scores that will not vary greatly from one test situation to another. While standardized tests generally have higher levels of validity and reliability than teacher-made tests, they do have some limitations. See Box 12.1 for limitations to keep in mind when interpreting all forms of testing. These cautions should not be taken to mean that the worst will happen in each testing situation, but simply that it *might*.

## CRITERION-REFERENCED TESTS

In contrast to standardized tests, which evaluate students' performance based on that of their peers in a norm group, *criterion-referenced tests* evaluate students' performance based on predefined expectations. "Mastery tests," for example, are a form of criterion-referenced testing. Specific objectives are defined prior to instruction, then taught, and then students are evaluated based on how well they have mastered the predefined objectives. In most cases, criterion-referenced tests are constructed by converting local or state curriculum guides and objectives into test items (Baumann, 1988b). Such tests now are being widely used by various states to ascertain whether a student has achieved certain "minimum competencies." They also are used by state departments to convey clear messages as to what government, business, and society expect schools to accomplish.

In short, unlike standardized tests that attempt to provide a reasonable estimate of a child's relative progress in broad areas of knowledge, criterion-referenced tests

> **BOX 12.1**
>
> ## Limitations and Precautions in Interpreting Test Scores
>
> 1. Tests tend to measure the easy things that usually can be inferred from classwork and simple observation, e.g., general level of comprehension, rate of learning—or IQ, and achievement.
>
> 2. The validity and reliability of an individual student's score cannot always be trusted, since tests usually are based on group norms that can misrepresent an individual's performance; they also can vary widely when individuals are retested with alternate forms of the same instrument, or even with the same test at a different time.
>
> 3. There have been strong objections to the use of grade equivalent scores, which are too often misinterpreted by parents or inexperienced teachers. A grade equivalent score only means that the child answered a particular set of questions about as well as most children in a particular grade. Whether a child's grade equivalent score on a given test is markedly low *or* high, this performance cannot be generalized to other aspects of intellect and social–emotional development. Exercise appropriate caution in referring to these scores.
>
> 4. Most standardized tests tend to provide a measure of a student's highest level of performance, or frustrational level, rather than of instructional or independent levels. To determine a student's instructional reading level from a standardized test score, it generally is necessary to subtract one year from the score; to establish independent level, subtract one and a half to two years. It should also be noted, however, that for some students, such as those with high test anxiety, the standardized test score is likely to be *lower* than their actual functioning levels. In these cases it is necessary to *add to*, rather than subtract from, the standardized score to obtain a better estimate of their actual instructional and independent reading levels.
>
> 5. Very high or low scores on tests can be especially misleading for the fact that standardized scores are not based on "equal interval" scales. In an equal interval scale, such as a basic "percent correct" scale, the number of raw score points between each converted score is equal. For example, on a test with 50 items, the difference between 50 percent correct and 60 percent correct would be the *same number of items* as the difference between 80 percent correct and 90 percent correct: 5 more actual items correct in each case. On a standardized, nonequal interval scale, relatively few items tend to distinguish performance at upper and lower ranges, as compared with the middle ranges. The difference between the 50th *percentile* and the 60th *percentile* might be 10 items, for example, on a test where the difference between the 80th and the 90th *percentile* was 2 items.
>
> 6. Most standardized tests are not of much help in offering insights into how and why someone responded the way they did. Thus, while they offer huge amounts of quantitative information, there is little that is qualitative, and therefore useful in instructional planning.

tend to assess specific, predefined information and skills. Informal tests, the next consideration, also could be considered criterion-based, but tend to have a different purpose and orientation.

## INFORMAL TESTS

There are many types of *informals*. Some are criterion-referenced, and some are even somewhat standardized. Informals like Silvaroli's (1976) Classroom Reading Inventory, however, have one characteristic that distinguishes them from the first two types. They are constructed to bring about focused interaction with a student based either on the actual materials used in class or close facsimiles. More importantly, the *individual* rather than the *group* is the object of the analysis.

While teachers may construct their own informal tests from established guidelines, it usually makes more sense to select one from those that are commercially available. Most commercially prepared informals have a rich history and background of use in clinical and school settings. The use of such informals also permits classroom teachers and resource specialists to be able to communicate better with one another about a student's needs in very specific terms and with some common points of reference.

In sections ahead, you will find guidelines for constructing several types of informal tests, as well as some lists of commercially available versions of these instruments.

## OBSERVATIONAL ASSESSMENT

*Observational assessment* simply is astute watching. It tends to be done in naturalistic settings and in unobtrusive ways (Moore, 1983). Importantly, it permits the teacher to see contextualized "peak performances" (Wood, 1988, p. 440) as well as scores generated in pressurized, decontextualized situations. But, you may ask, is it trustworthy? A study by Monroe, Watson, and Tweddell (1989) reconfirmed that teachers can accurately predict children's IQs, oral comprehension, and reading test scores. Hence, observing, or "kidwatching," as Yetta Goodman (1985) has referred to it, can be a powerful and accurate tool in diagnosis. What is more, because it occurs in conditions that are more representative of typical functioning, it is not closed-ended, or bound to a certain hour or time. Rather, it is open-ended and can continue until the teacher is satisfied that what is being observed is truly characteristic of the child.

There can be problems with free-form observations, however. What the observer "sees" is a function of how we are looking. Jaggar (1985) suggests that teachers should make clear decisions before observing as to what they will attend to, as well as how, when, and where they will do the observing. Checklists and observational schedules help to overcome both of these problems by calling attention to specific behaviors that have been found to be relevant to literacy and learning. Checklists also make it possible for the same person and others to review the observations from more reflective and different perspectives. Sample checklists are provided ahead in the chapter.

Observational systems, or "kidwatching," has grown in popularity in recent years and has become wedded to another popular trend—that of portfolio collection and analysis. As with any procedure, some shortcomings as well as merits have been reported.

## PORTFOLIOS: RATIONALE, FUNCTIONS, PROMISE, PROBLEMS

### Rationale

A portfolio is a collection of works that illustrates skill, range, and progress over time. There are two metaphors for portfolio collection as used in assessing student progress. The first and most popular metaphor is drawn from the use of portfolios in art and resumé preparation. The second we shall refer to as the "investment portfolio" metaphor.

The art and resumé metaphor simply says that artists rely on portfolios to show what they can do and how they have progressed through various stages and periods. A resumé prepared for a job or in consideration of a promotion is based on the same principle—showing where you've been, where you are, and where you could be going. Faced with years of continuous schooling, and with so much of their lives in front of them, students deserve no less.

The investment portfolio metaphor refers to the great potential value of children's, or an individual child's portfolio for revealing how time and effort are being allocated and whether there is visible growth as a result of that allotment. With an investment portfolio, the idea is to be sure that one's money is invested in a diversified way—typically, bonds, stock, property, and cash reserve. In this way, as various markets rise and fall, one can be fairly certain that there will be steady, if modest, growth over time where at least a portion of profits are reinvested. Importantly, however, reallocation may need to be done periodically to meet either: changing personal needs (e.g., the need for a larger investment in housing when raising a family and less later on); or changing environmental conditions that enhance or erode something's value (e.g., silver was $50 an ounce and gold over $800 during the 1980s; now, silver is down to less than $4, and gold is down to less than $365 an ounce). If someone were not monitoring these changing conditions, much of their life savings could have been eroded.

We may not always realize it, but we can and should do something similar in education. One legitimate expectation of parents is that we will educate their children to be job-competitive, which is to say, to have what potential employers may need. At the moment this seems to be greater skill in reading, writing, math, and science. Of course, we must all diversify our time, resources, and instructional allocation to include reasoned proportions of time for such other things as literature, art, music, athletics, and comportment. The purpose of keeping a portfolio of one's readings, writings, art, and so on, is comparable to the purpose of keeping a financial portfolio; that is, to check the level of investment value in each of these areas and to reallocate time and energy as times and expectations change. However, diversification should always be maintained so that needs of the whole child are met and because children must be prepared for many possible futures. People, as well as financial portfolios, must be made "recession-proof," or strong enough to make it through good and bad times. Consider now how portfolios can function to help serve these purposes.

### Student Portfolios

Portfolios for students are based on the simple proposition that students should keep samples of their best work for periodic review. There are two popular types of student portfolios: *show portfolios,* that include only a few selected samples of work, and *working portfolios,* that include a wide array of works in progress (Farr, 1992). Periodically students should be helped to select pieces from their working portfolios to place in their show portfolios. The show portfolio should include the child's best current works, as well as some works that are representative of earlier stages of learning. The teacher's role is largely to serve as a "consultant who helps convince the student that the work should show a variety of materials reflecting the reading–writing–thinking process" (Farr, 1992, p. 35). The process of collecting, reviewing, and maintaining student portfolios tends to create every desirable kind of interaction between teacher and student: diagnostic dialogue, instructional conversation, and a natural therapeutic dialogue.

Student portfolios can include stories, essays, homework assignments, class tests, artistic representations, or even extracurricular productions—anything the student especially values. Bird (1991) suggests that student portfolios should include the following types of entries:

- Quarterly writing samples from a variety of perspectives and across genre: journal writing, personal narrative, fiction, nonfiction, poetry
- Evidence of progress in spelling
- Evidence of progress in comprehension checks and on content tests
- Protocols from informal reading inventories (see ahead)
- Taped oral readings
- Drawings
- Photographs of self, the teacher, or other students
- Periodic anecdotal accounts from teachers

Teacher and student comments and evaluations give the portfolio depth and dimension. Here is a sample teacher-written comment:

> Laura, I agree that 'The Very Special Scooter' is one of the best stories you have written. I especially liked the way you made the scooter come to life for a while and tell the story from its point of view.
>
> Mrs. Francis, 11/10/93

Students can be asked to write short explanations of why they chose certain entries for their show portfolios. For example:

> I like this book report I wrote on *How to Eat Fried Worms*. When I read the book, I kept thinking about how my brother calls me 'wormy' all the time. I wish he would stop it.
>
> Jamie, 10/2/92

> This is a tape recording of me in the spring play. I was the narrator, and I thought I was pretty good. I can listen to it again next year, and see how much I have changed.
>
> Marcus, 5/12/93

The single most important value of portfolio assessment is that it shifts the emphasis away from the errors and false starts children make while acquiring skills. Instead, the emphasis is placed on preserving, and periodically reviewing, completed pieces children value. By offering children authentic reasons to do good work, portfolios build self-esteem and internal motivation. When students initiate, revise, and embellish drafts of their own work, they engage in the important process of acquiring the habits of self-checking and self-correcting. These habits are seldom fostered by the conventional cycle of writing or cramming, and then being criticized and having to gamely accept a grade. The portfolio also is something that the *student* can have control over. Unlike grade books and permanent record files, which children never see, the portfolio collection is kept in an easily accessible part of the room. Maintaining portfolios is something children do for themselves rather than merely for others. As such, the portfolio system helps to build and expand children's interests that lead to further reading (Ediger, 1992). Student portfolios are a key ingredient in a program based on a holistic view of children.

The most serious disadvantage of portfolios is that they can quickly become quite complex—often too complex for their original purposes. Portfolios were originally intended to provide a means of balancing the standardized and/or criterion-referenced assessment scores with a concrete record of a student's actual work. The student portfolio itself, however, is only the raw data on which this balancing assessment may be based. Evaluating this data should be a simple, subjective, and self-evident process. It can, however, be turned into a tedious, objectified, time-consuming one. According to one recent research report, teachers are beginning to view student portfolios as too demanding, and "yet another means of increasing and controlling teachers' work while appearing to empower them" (Gomez, Graue, & Bloch, 1991, p. 621). This is especially regrettable since student portfolios can be quite easy, sensible, and gratifying—for the teacher and the children. See Box 12.2 for a simple checklist that can be used for evaluation of student writing portfolios. For additional information on writing assessment, see ahead in the chapter. For additional theoretical and practical information on portfolio assessment see: Au, Scheu, Kawakami, and Herman (1990); Farr (1992); Glazer (1993); Lucas (1988); Tierney, Carter, and Desai (1991); Valencia (1990); and Wolf (1980).

**Portfolios for Parents**  Flood and Lapp (1989) recommend portfolios for parents. This recommendation reflects sensitivity and insight into the larger issue of how children are perceived by their parents. Schools typically offer parents a picture of their children's progress that is based on what is called "summative evaluations," such as class grades and standardized test scores. Flood and Lapp point out that children operating close to their potentials, but who still have low percentile scores on standardized tests, will appear to parents to be hopelessly "behind" and not making progress. A portfolio assembled for such parents permits the teacher and the child to show that it is largely the child's *pace* that is slower, but that progress may still be occurring. This is a point that the student can benefit from as well. It can be done very simply, by presenting "before and after" examples of writing, types of spelling and vocabulary words being tackled, and representative passages of reading material. These can be charted to further dramatize effort and progress, even while the student's percentile ranking may not have changed markedly (see Figure 12.1, p. 494).

Portfolios for children can be called "My Very Best Work" or "Samples of My Work." They also can include places to record "My Parents' Comments," "My Friends' Comments," and "My Teacher's Comments"—and don't forget

| BOX 12.2 | **Checklist for Evaluating Students' Writing Portfolios** |
|---|---|

*The Writing Process*

1. How often does the writer get ideas for writing
   _____ from the imagination?
   _____ from discussion with others?
   _____ by imitating a book, story, poem, TV show?
   _____ from the teacher's assignments?
   _____ from some other source? (which?)

2. When the writer means to rehearse what will be written, and narrow down the topic, does the writer
   _____ talk to classmates?
   _____ talk to the teacher?
   _____ draw a picture first?
   _____ start writing right away?

3. In drafting a paper, does the writer
   _____ write one draft only?
   _____ invent spellings, use a dictionary, or limit vocabulary to the words he or she can spell?
   _____ scratch out words and lines, and cut and paste?
   _____ seek comments from others about the way the drafting is going?

4. Does the writer revise a paper before it is considered finished/do the drafts
   _____ all look like different papers, new beginnings?
   _____ look like mechanical refinements of earlier drafts?
   _____ interact with and build on the ideas of early drafts?

*The Functions of Writing*

5. What forms of writing has the writer produced?
   _____ stories?
   _____ poems?
   _____ expressive writing (personal experiences and opinions)?
   _____ persuasive writing?
   _____ descriptive writing?
   _____ expository writing (that which explains or gives directions)?

6. What kinds of topics has the writer written about?
   _____ topics about which the writer was an expert?
   _____ topics about which the writer had to learn more before writing?
   _____ topics about things that were present?
   _____ topics about things that were past or absent?
   _____ topics about abstract ideas?

7. What audiences has the writer written for?
   _____ the teacher?
   _____ classmates?
   _____ people known to the child? Whom?
   _____ people unknown to the child? Whom?

---

**BOX 12.2 cont'd**

## Checklist for Evaluating Students' Writing Portfolios

8. In trying to stick to the topic, did the writer

_____    limit the focus of the topic before starting to write?

_____    stick to one thing or ramble?

_____    focus more on the object of the writing or on the writer?

9. In trying to stick to the purpose of writing, does the writer

_____    keep expressing personal feelings, although the topic and purpose suggest doing otherwise?

_____    declare one purpose but pursue another (such as, "The story about . . . " which is expository, not narrative)?

_____    shift from one purpose to another?

10. In trying to meet the audience's need for information

_____    does the writer appear to assume the audience knows and is interested in the author?

_____    is he or she careful to tell the audience things they will need to know in order to understand what is talked about?

_____    does the writer address the same audience throughout?

### Qualities of Writing Style

11. _____    Does the writer use exact, well-chosen words?

12. _____    Does the writer "paint pictures with words" (make the reader see what the writer saw)? Does the writer focus on immediate "here-and-now" images?

13. In regard to the organization of the papers

_____    does the writer keep the focus on one aspect of the topic at a time?

_____    do the papers have identifiable openings?

_____    are the details arranged in a reasonable order and do they relate reasonably to one another?

_____    is there an identifiable ending to the papers?

---

"My Grandparents' Comments." You can bet these will be uplifting for any child. For a commercially prepared portfolio system, see Tierney et al. (1991).

## CHECKLISTS AND SCALES

We rarely see what we are not looking for. Checklists and scales aid "seeing" and anecdotal reporting. They can be simple or complex, but usually require a mere check to indicate that a certain behavior has been, or is being observed. Boxes 12.3 (p. 494), 12.4 (p. 495), and 12.5 (p. 496) offer some fairly comprehensive lists for observing growth in emergent reading, response to literature (oral or written), and of writing development. These were developed by teachers at Blackburn Elementary School, a Pre-K to Grade 2 school in Manatee Country, Florida (as reported in Lamme & Hysmith, 1991).

Hansen (1992) offers a more concise and broader based observation system from her work at Stratham Memorial School, New Hampshire. Hansen's system is shown in Box 12.6 (p. 497).

**BOX
12.2**
cont'd

*Fluency of Writing*

14.   How long are the papers (in words or lines per page)?

15.   What is the average number of words per sentence?

*Mechanics of Writing*

16.   In handwriting, does the writer

_____   have problems forming letters? Which ones?

_____   have problems spacing between letters? Keeping vertical lines parallel? keeping the writing even on the baseline?

_____   write with uniform pressure? in smooth or in jerky lines?

17.   In regard to spelling,

_____   does the writer misspell words in the first draft?

_____   does the writer correct the spellings of many words between the first and later drafts?

_____   what does the writer do when uncertain of how to spell a word?

18.   Does the writer have trouble with standard English usage?

_____   Does the writer write in complete sentences? If not, what are the units of writing like?

_____   Does the writer have problems with punctuation and capitalization?

_____   Are errors made in standard English grammar? If so, describe the errors.

*Enjoying Writing*

19.   _____   Does the writer take pleasure in writing? How do you know?

*C. Temple & J. W. Gillet.* Language Arts: Learning
Processes and Teaching Processes, *2nd ed. Scott Foresman (1989).*

## ANECDOTAL RECORDS

For many years, anecdotal records were the preferred means of gaining insight into students. However, these subjective records came to be replaced by objective test records as testing procedures grew more quantitative than qualitative. Now, as we have begun to see the error in relying on test data alone, anecdotal records are being rediscovered as a valuable means of helping us to keep sight of the larger picture; namely, the pupil, more than just his or her reading progress.

At best, anecdotal records are subjective but unbiased notes written by the teacher to capture the child's typical patterns of behavior, including those that are most characteristic of the student, those that seem to be *out* of character, and those that illustrate the student's response to a certain kind of task or stimuli. In this sense, anecdotal observations are like voice-activated tape recorders that also are smart: They not only know to go on when there is sound, but when the sounds being emitted are potentially meaningful and significant.

FIGURE
12.1 **Charting Children's Growth in Reading: Alternatives to Standardized Tests**

**Charting a Child's Growth in Reading a Single Text**

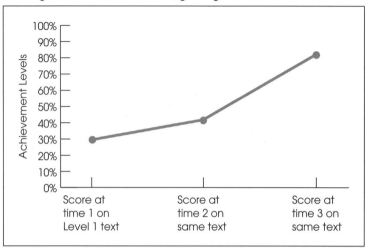

*Flood and Lapp (1989).*

BOX
12.3 **Scale of Emergent Reading**

Level 11:     Child reads fluently from books and other materials.

Level 10:     Child seeks out new sources of information.
              Child voluntarily shares information with other children.

Level 9:      Child uses context clues, sentence structure, structural analysis, and phonic analysis to read new passages.
              Child can read easy books.

Level 8:      Child reads unfamiliar stories haltingly, with little adult assistance.

Level 7:      Child reads familiar stories fluently.

Level 6:      Child reads word-for-word.
              Child recognizes word in a new context.

Level 5:      Child memorizes text and can pretend to "read" story.

Level 4:      Child participates in reading by supplying rhyming words and some predictable text.

Level 3:      Child talks about each picture (not story, really).
              Child pretends to read.
              Child makes up words for pictures.

Level 2:      Child watches pictures as adult reads story.

Level 1:      Child listens to story but is not looking at pages.

*Lamme & Hysmith (1991), p. 632.*

BOX
12.4 **Response to Literature Scale (Oral and Written Responses)**

Level 7:     Child developed criteria to evaluate the book.
*This is a great mystery because I couldn't figure out the answer till the last page and because you really feel like you are there.*

Level 6:     Child generalizes about the book with comments about the theme, type of book, or author's purpose for writing it.
*I guess being a friend means doing something you don't want to do, just to be helpful to someone.*

Level 5:     Child analyzes something about the book: plot, setting, characters, illustrations.
*Ahmed is young to have a responsible job and old to just be learning how to write his name.*

Level 4:     Child relates the book to his or her experiences or to other books.
*I went on a train ride once.*
*Katir Morag reminds me of Sal in* One Morning in Maine.

Level 3:     Child explains *why* he or she likes the book.
*I like it because it was funny.*

Level 2:     Child explains how he or she likes the book.
Child asks you to "read it again."
*It was good.*
*It was OK.*

Level 1:     Child offers no response to literature voluntarily.

NOTE:
Responses are higher when they are child-generated than when they are teacher-assigned.
Responses are higher when they involve emotions.
Responses are higher when they involve taking action as well as discussion.
Responses are higher when they are multidimensional (dramatic, artistic, and action-oriented).
Responses are higher when they lead to further reading.

*Lamme & Hysmith (1991), p. 633.*

Anecdotal records should be brief, factual accounts that more or less speak for themselves. The simplest way to remind yourself to make these is to prepare some index cards, as shown in Figure 12.2 (p. 498), and fill one out on every student at least twice a semester.

Cheek, Flippo, and Lindsey (1989) suggest using the same cards to make brief, unscheduled anecdotal accounts: simply flip over one of the cards, then record and date pertinent comments. For example:

9/15        Joe handed in his first completed assignment this term.

10/10       I hadn't noticed before, but Mark moves his lips and points his finger to keep his place when he reads silently.

For a more compact method of recording anecdotal observations, try the single folder system. Use a plain 8½ × 11-inch folder and 5 × 8-inch file cards: one card

BOX
12.5

## BOX 12.5 | Scale of Writing Development

Level 11:     Child uses a variety of strategies for revision and editing.
              Child uses writing techniques to build suspense, create humor, etc.

Level 10:     Child willingly revises and edits.
              Child writes creatively and imaginatively.
              Child writes original poetry.
              Child writes clearly. The message makes sense.
              Child uses commas, quotation marks, and apostrophes.

Level 9:      Writing includes details or dialogue, a sense of humor or other emotions.
              Child retells a familiar story or follows the pattern of a known story or poem.
              Spelling becomes more conventional.
              Child willingly revises.

Level 8:      Child writes a short story with a beginning, a middle, and an end.
              Child writes for several different purposes (narrative, expository, and persuasive).
              Revision involves adding to the story.
              Child begins to use punctuation.

Level 7:      Child writes the start of a story.
              Child uses both phonics and sight strategies to spell words.
              Child writes several short sentences.

Level 6:      Child invents spellings.
              Story is a single factual statement.
              The message is understandable.

Level 5:      Child labels drawings.
              Letters have some connection to sounds.
              Child writes lists.
              Child separates words with a space or marker.
              Child writes a message.
              Child writes familiar words.

Level 4:      Child repeats message.
              Child has a message concept and tells you what the message is.
              Letters don't match sounds.
              Child writes alphabet letter strings.

Level 3:      Child copies words he or she sees around the room.
              Alphabet letters and mock letters are in a line across the page.

Level 2:      Child writes alphabet and mock letters scattered around the page.
              Child writes mock letters.
              Child pretends to write.

Level 1:      Child attempts to write in scribbles or draws patterns.

*Lamme & Hysmith (1991), p. 631.*

for each student in a class. Tape the first card lengthwise on the bottom left side of the folder. Then tape the next card lengthwise about one half inch higher. Continue taping cards at half-inch intervals up to the top of the left-hand side of the folder, then repeat the process to prepare the right-hand side. When the folder is complete, write each child's name on the visible half-inch border of a card, making an easily visible flip-up card for each child, as shown in Figure 12.3. Informal observa-

---

**BOX 12.6**

## Hansen's Observation Checklist

*Observations About the Student As a Learner:*
*Process Approach to Reading and Writing*

Student: _____     School: _____

Grade: _____     Teacher: _____

| READING                                                    | | | | | | WRITING | | | | | |
|---|---|---|---|---|---|---|---|---|---|---|---|
| **Quarter** | *1* | *2* | *3* | *4* | | **Quarter** | *1* | *2* | *3* | *4* | |
| Initiates Own Reading | | | | | | Initiates Own Writing | | | | | |
| Chooses Reading Materials with Confidence | | | | | | Chooses Writing Topics with Confidence | | | | | |
| Use Appropriate Comprehension Strategies to Develop Meaning | | | | | | Produces Meaningful Writing | | | | | |
| Uses Appropriate Print Cues to Develop Meaning | | | | | | Revises Ideas When Appropriate | | | | | |
| Requests Meaningful Help in Reading | | | | | | Edits when Appropriate (Mechanics) | | | | | |
| Actively Participates in Reading Discussion Groups | | | | | | Requests Meaningful Help in Writing | | | | | |
| Writes Effective Journal Responses to Literature | | | | | | Actively Participates in Writing Conferences | | | | | |
| Shares Own Reading | | | | | | Shares Own Writing | | | | | |

KEY:     ✓ = Demonstrated Most of the Time     X = Demonstrated Some of the Time
         / = Working Toward                     0 = Not Demonstrated

*Hansen (1992), p. 103.*

---

tions can be noted on self-adhesive stickers and affixed to the cards when time permits.

You will find having anecdotal records extremely useful in a wide variety of circumstances. They are useful when you may want to make an entry in a child's dialogue journal or in reviewing portfolios under the teacher's comments. But mostly, they are invaluable to parent–teacher meetings and in staffings with specialists. They're also very impressive. They tend to say, "This teacher cares enough to go the extra mile." One of our university colleagues keeps such records and grades with a picture of each student willing to have one taken with his one-minute camera before class. As a result, he can make recommendations years later, and they are always personal, and often prized. There is something about realizing that someone is watching and keeping account that tends to bring out the best in most of us.

Now let's look at one of the most widely known and used systems for classroom evaluation. It is a form of criterion testing known as the Informal Reading Inventory (IRI). It offers the advantage of being sufficiently well developed and empirically

**Figure 12.2** **Sample Cards: Anecdotal Observation**

---

Date: 10/12

Name: Tom B.

Observer: Sawyer

Place & Situation: Library/Book selection

Observation: Looks around at everyone else, but not at books. Finally picked up a book when he realized that I might be watching him.

Comment: He seems to be more people than task oriented, I've got to try him in different collaborative groups to see where he works best.

---

Name: Nancy K.

Observer: Sawyer

Place & Situation: Class discussion of science selection

Observation: Quick to speak up in science, but says things that are largely irrelevant. Nancy doesn't speak up as quickly in literature discussions, but her responses are more relevant.

Interpretation: When Nancy is uncertain of herself, she gets quite aggressive. I wonder if I should bring this to her attention (?)

---

proven to be used for both diagnostic and gains assessment. In other words, it can be used to ascertain whether gains have been made as a result of the instruction provided. More importantly, it will give this information in fairly specific areas and in ways that are more dependable for tracking individual progress than is provided by standardized tests, and with greater accuracy and precision than can be provided by the "quick" assessment devices described further ahead.

## INFORMAL READING INVENTORY (IRI)

Betts, one of the founders of contemporary reading instruction, is most often credited with the development of IRIs. The idea, simply put, was to see how well the

**FIGURE 12.3**  **Anecdotal Record Folder**

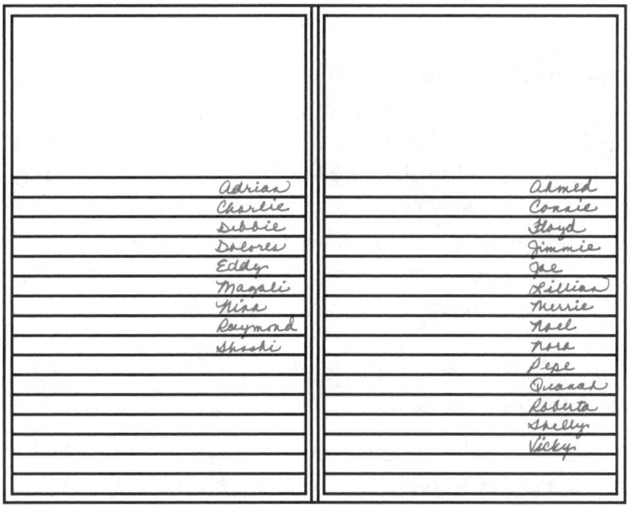

child read and comprehended short selections from basal readers at varying grade levels. To make an informal reading inventory, Betts recommended that the teacher select a few passages from basals at different grade levels and select or write a set of questions to check comprehension at literal and inferential levels (Betts, 1960). It was recommended that a graded word list be used to estimate the appropriate grade level reading passage to use to begin testing. This saves children from being handed a paragraph to read that is far above or below their actual reading levels.

Once these materials had been assembled, the child could be asked to read several of the passages orally, while the teacher made note of any oral reading errors on a separate copy. After each passage, the teacher asked the prepared comprehension questions to assess the child's level of understanding of what he or she read at increasing difficulty levels.

The basic purpose of the IRI was to determine how well the child could be expected to read and comprehend materials of varying difficulty. This was done by establishing four levels:

- **Instructional level.** The level at which the child can most effectively profit from instruction
- **Independent level.** The level at which the child can be expected to read and learn more or less without instructional support
- **Frustration level.** The level at which the child is unlikely to be able to read and comprehend, even with a reasonable level of instructional assistance

- **Listening capacity level.** The level at which the child can *comprehend* material that is read *aloud*, and thus is not affected by his or her limited ability to decode

Information from the IRI could then be used to characterize the child's overall reading in one of three ways:

- **Developmental.** Reading level and listening capacity essentially the same.
- **Corrective.** Reading level approximately 6 months to a year below listening level, and therefore with the child having some deficiencies that needed to be identified but in all probability taken care of within the regular classroom.
- **Remedial.** Reading level more than one and a half years below listening level, and therefore in need of in-class and supplemental, usually outside-of-class, help. This category eventually came to include most all children placed in a regular class who were reading two years below grade level, irrespective of their listening capacity. In other words, an 80 IQ child, whose listening and reading were two years below level, also tended to be treated as if they were remedial level readers for their grade level.

Some systems include an "advanced" category for the child whose reading is a year or more *above* grade level. This designation has also come to include those youngsters whose reading scores exceed their listening scores and IQ estimates, and therefore could be thought of as "overachievers." This seemingly odd designation has turned out to be useful in estimating the difference between youngsters who may be proficient reconstructive readers but not constructive readers, or vice versa (Manzo & Manzo, 1993). This point is explained in more detail further ahead.

Originally constructed by teachers, primarily from available basal materials, IRIs were found to have shortcomings that were more correctable when commercially prepared. Chief among the problems of teacher-prepared IRIs were the following:

1. Readability levels of the excerpts were found to be inaccurate (Bradley & Ames, 1977).
2. Questions often were shown not to be "passage dependent" (Schell, 1991)—meaning that they often could be answered with prior knowledge without reading the passage.
3. When a school changed basals, the predictive or matching value of the IRIs fell off too sharply (Baumann, 1988a,b).
4. Constructing IRIs took an inordinate amount of teacher time and energy.

For these reasons, it generally is more cost-effective to buy one of the several excellent and commercially available IRIs. Several popular IRIs are listed in Box 12.7. Be sure to ask for the latest edition, since they are periodically revised.

## ASSESSING CHILDREN'S ORAL READING

In Betts' original formulation of the Informal Reading Inventory, children's oral reading errors were simply counted and tallied for analysis and interpretation. This was soon challenged, however, as reading came to be better understood as a complex meaning-seeking process, rather than as simple decoding. Goodman (1973a)

BOX
12.7 **Commercially Available IRIs**

Analytical Reading Inventory, 3rd ed. (Woods & Moe, 1985)
Basic Reading Inventory, 2nd ed. (Johns, 1981)
Burns & Roe Informal Reading Inventory (Burns & Roe, 1985)
Classroom Reading Inventory, 5th ed. (Silvaroli, 1986)
The Contemporary Classroom Reading Inventory (Rinsky & deFossard, 1980)
Diagnostic Reading Scales (Spache, 1972)
Diagnostic Reading Inventory (Jacobs & Searfoss, 1979)
Durrell Analysis of Reading Difficulty (Durrell, 1980)
Ekwall Reading Inventory (Ekwall, 1985)
The Informal Reading–Thinking Inventory (Manzo, Manzo, & McKenna, 1995)
Standard Reading Inventory (McCracken, 1966)

developed a system he called "miscue analysis" as a way to better understand and interpret the types of problems children encounter in reading. Miscue analysis is based on the psycholinguistic model of reading, which proposes that reading is a process of making predictions based on minimal clues and continuously checking the "sense" of these predictions. Traditional procedures for recording and scoring IRIs called for recording *every* deviation the reader made from an exact and fluent reading, including repetitions of words or phrases, self-corrections, and lengthy pauses. Goodman proposed that these types of misreadings should *not* be thought of as errors, but merely as "miscues." He felt that repetitions, self-corrections, and pauses should be taken as indications that the reader was trying to make use of available clues to create meaning, rather than simply saying words correctly and in order. Further, miscues could be analyzed to learn more about the *degree* to which the reader is functioning as a meaning maker, rather than simply as a word decoder.

This second level of analysis is based on the premise that readers use different, and increasingly sophisticated *types* of cues as they progress from beginning reading to mature reading. In order of sophistication, these include:

**Orthographic Cues**    At this level, the reader uses individual letters and letter clusters to predict words. Beginning readers have to rely almost exclusively on these cues, making their reading slow and painstaking.

**Syntactic Cues**    At this level, readers have acquired a vocabulary of words they can recognize on sight and are able to use elements of syntax, or sentence structure, to make predictions while reading.

**Semantic Cues**    At the highest level, readers use semantics, or *meaning,* as their primary guide while reading.

To emphasize the importance of interpreting oral reading "errors" as indications of the reader's ability to use these increasingly sophisticated sets of cues, Goodman somewhat tongue-in-cheek has called reading a "psycholinguistic guessing game."

**Using Miscue Analysis versus Simple Error Count to Interpret Oral Reading Performance**

**Student A**

The wasps buzzed around my head, as mad as could be, but they couldn't get through
to sting me.

*(handwritten annotations: wasps, many, there, string)*

**Student B**

The wasps buzzed around my head, as mad as could be, but they couldn't get through
to sting me.

*(handwritten annotations: Fell, hand, cold s.c., wouldn't, in, Steal)*

**Student C**

The wasps buzzed around my head, as mad as could be, but they couldn't get through
to sting me.

*(handwritten annotations: Flew, could not, in, hurt)*

Student A made 4 miscues, not counting repetitions, pauses (including these would make a count of 6 "errors"). The student seems to be using *orthographic* cues alone to predict unknown words: for each of the 4 miscalled words, the student substituted a word that begins with the same letter, and 2 of the 4 substitutions had the same ending letter. None of the substitutions preserved meaning, and only one was a syntactically appropriate substitution.

Student B made 5 miscues, not counting repetitions, pauses and self-corrections (including these would make a count of 8 "errors"). The student seems to be using primarily *semantic* cues: only 2 of the 5 miscalled words began with the same letter as the word in the text, and only one had the same ending letter. Only one of the substitutions preserved meaning, and all were syntactically appropriate substitutions (verbs for verbs, nouns for nouns, etc.)

Student C made 6 miscues, not counting pauses (including this would make a count of 7 "errors"). The two omissions did not alter the meaning, nor did any of the 4 substitutions. The substitutions were syntactically and semantically appropriate substitutions.

Counting "errors" alone, Student C would be judged the poorest reader and Student A the best. Using miscue analysis, the evaluation is reversed.

Figure 12.4 illustrates the process of evaluating miscues in terms of these cue systems, as opposed to interpretation based on simple error count.

Many authorities feel that Goodman's Miscue Analysis is too laborious. Hence, they have continued to use the IRI with some modifications.

## STRUCTURE OF THE **IRI**

An IRI usually is divided into two main parts: Part I consists of graded word lists, and Part II contains graded paragraphs for silent and/or oral reading and/or listening comprehension. Word lists and paragraphs usually start at the preprimer level and extend at least through grade 8 (Harman, 1982). Most commercial IRIs provide the following materials:

**Marking System for Graded Word Lists**

| What to record | What it means |
| --- | --- |
| 1. and  ~~an~~ | (error, same error on second trial) |
| 2. big  + | (correct) |
| 3. can  dk | (don't know - no correction) |
| 4. when  then $^+$ | (error, corrected on next trial) |
| 5. now  o $^+$ | (word skipped, corrected 2nd trial) |

1.   A manual of directions for administering the test, and scoring and interpreting students' performance
2.   Student test materials for Part I—graded word lists; and Part II—graded reading and listening passages
3.   Record forms, for the test administrator, of the graded word lists and graded reading passages
4.   A summary sheet form for recording test results

## ADMINISTRATION OF THE IRI

The graded word lists are administered first. The child's performance on the graded word lists provides an estimate of his or her word recognition abilities, with indications of specific areas of weakness in word recognition. This opening section of the test, as indicated earlier, helps the test administrator to determine the level of difficulty at which to begin the graded paragraphs portion of the test.

### Administering Part I: Graded Word Lists

1.   Establish a comfortable atmosphere and congenial rapport with the student before proceeding with the inventory.
2.   Present the student's copy of the graded word lists. Start at the preprimer level, recording all responses on the record form as illustrated in Figure 12.5 below. When a list has been complete, ask the student to pronounce each word *missed* (e.g., "Tell me number 4 again"). Do not follow this procedure if the list is obviously too difficult.
3.   Discontinue the testing when the student is unable to correct 5 of the 20 words in any list.
4.   Obtain a percent correct score for each list of 20 by totaling the number of correct *and* corrected responses and multiplying by 5.

**FIGURE**
**12.6** **Marking System for Graded Paragraphs**

| _Types of mis-readings_ | _How to mark them_ |
|---|---|
| words pronounced by the teacher | a crowded room |
| words omitted | a (crowded) room |
| words added | a big crowded room |
| words substituted | a crowned crowded room |

**Administering Part II: Graded Paragraphs**

1. For primary students, begin at the highest level at which the child scored 100 percent on the word lists. Older students can be started at the level where the student made the first uncorrected error on the word lists.

2. Ask the student to read "out loud" for you and tell the student that you will ask several questions about what was read after the story is finished. (Many reading professionals now believe that it is best to allow the child to read the passage silently before reading it orally. This reduces miscues, and possible initial misunderstandings, and thus provides a more accurate indication of the child's ability to read for meaning.)

3. Record the four types of misreadings that are counted as errors as shown in Figure 12.6 (Note: certain types of additions, omissions, word endings, and dialect pronunciations may be part of the student's oral language patterns— do not count these as errors.)

4. Count the same error only *once* no matter how many times the error is repeated.

5. Record observations about fluency, word-by-word reading, finger pointing, signs of tension, etc., in the margin or at the bottom of the page.

6. Record hesitations with slashes (He/saw/the//pirate)—one slash per second; record repetitions by underlining repeated words or phrases (one underline for each repetition). Neither hesitations nor repetitions are counted as errors.

7. Errors that are corrected by the child are recorded but *not counted as errors* (see Figure 12.7).

8. Following the oral reading, collect the student booklet and read each comprehension question to the student, recording all responses. If a student's response is the same as the suggested answer (printed on the record form), the answer may simply be underlined. Questions may be rephrased as long as the new wording does not provide additional clues.

| FIGURE 12.7 | **Marking Self-Corrections** |

$$\underset{\text{was}}{(\underline{\text{He}}\ \overset{+}{\text{saw}}\ \underline{a}\ \underline{\text{pig}}.} = \text{"He was a pig...He saw a pig."})$$

9. If a multiple response is required, such as "name two ways .[ . . ]," full credit can be given only if the specified number of correct responses is provided. Such questions may be repeated, and partial credit may be awarded for partial responses.

10. Discontinue testing when the oral reading errors reach frustration level *or the* student attains 50 percent or less in comprehension. Scoring guides are generally provided on the recording booklet.

11. While the basic directions should not be changed, the teacher may reasonably test a level above estimated frustration when the score drops dramatically from one selection to the next, or when the score on the *first* passage is very low (in this case, a passage at a level or two *lower* should be given next).

### Establishing Levels and Interpreting Results

Betts (1946) is said to have first suggested the most popularly used criteria for using student scores on comprehension of grade level reading passages to determine the level at which the student is likely to read at independent, instructional, and frustration levels. His student, Killgallon (1942), conducted a study that focused on the most critical criterion, that for "instructional level." The criteria found in her study for accuracy of words in context was 93.9, very close to the 95 percent level suggested by Betts. The complete Betts–Killgallon criteria are shown in Box 12.8.

Should you wish to construct a conventional IRI, you will want to consider the suggestions in Box 12.9, assembled largely from McKenna (1983) and Valmont (1972). Some of these suggestions need slight modification when constructing an Informal Reading–Thinking Inventory.

## INFORMAL READING–THINKING INVENTORY (IR–TI)

Miscue analysis changed the way reading specialists looked at word recognition behaviors, but comprehension assessment has remained virtually the same since the IRI was first described by Betts in 1936. The Informal Reading–Thinking Inventory (IR–TI) referenced in the chapter on higher-order literacy is one way to enhance the comprehension assessment capacity of the conventional IRI.

The purpose of the IR–TI is to increase attention to higher-order literacy simply by enhancing the conventional IRI format (Manzo & Manzo, 1993). The simple expectation is that if reading assessment included this additional dimension, educators would become more sensitive to it, knowledgeable about it, and committed to

**BOX 12.8** **Betts-Killgallon Criteria for Determining Reading Levels**

I. Independent reading level—easy reading
   A. Word recognition in isolation—90–100% in the "flash" condition
   B. Word recognition in context—99%
   C. Comprehension—90% or better on 10-question inventories, 80% where there are five questions
   D. Freedom from tensions such as frowning, body movements, etc.
   E. Freedom from finger pointing, subvocalization, and/or lip movement
   F. Acceptable reading posture
   G. Oral reading should be rhythmical, in a conversational tone, and with correct interpretation of punctuation
   H. Silent reading comprehension should surpass oral reading comprehension

II. Instructional reading level—guided reading
   A. Word recognition in isolation—75–89% in the "flash" condition
   B. Word recognition in context—95%
   C. Comprehension—a minimum score of 75% (interpreted as 70% on 10-question tests and 60% on 5-question tests)
   D. Freedom from body movements, finger-pointing and/or lip movement
   E. Acceptable reading posture
   F. Oral rereading is mostly rhythmical, conversational, and with correct interpretation of punctuation, and a reasonable eye–voice span
   G. Silent reading can be sustained since word difficulty and concept load are challenging but manageable

III. Frustration level—nonproductive reading
   A. Word recognition in isolation—50% or less in the "flash" condition
   B. Word recognition in context—90% or less
   C. Comprehension—50% or less
   D. Evidence of compensations: finger-pointing, guessing, gross inferencing from graphic clues
   E. Defense mechanisms apparent: withdrawal, crying, attempts at distraction, and/or refusal to read
   F. Oral reading is too poor to permit comprehension and should be discontinued
   G. Lack of enthusiasm, comprehension below oral reading, and disengagement

IV. Listening capacity level—potential to read with understanding
   A. Comprehension—75% or better
   B. Discussion of material parallels the complexity of the selections
   C. Ability to supply information pertinent to the topic from experience
   D. Precise and meaningful use of words—from context of selection
   E. Able to sustain attention to duration of selection

**Suggestions for Constructing and Using Conventional IRIs**

1. Do not assume that the stories in basal readers all represent the assigned readability level. Check readability with one or more readability formulas. (See the last chapter for details on readability formulas.)

2. Make sure the passages in each sequence are from the same general interest area, preferably one of moderate to high interest for both boys and girls of the ages at which the IRI will be given. It is a good idea to ask students individually about their interest in the subjects in the inventory. Make your inquiries prior to a student's reading the passages.

3. In writing questions: (a) state each clearly and simply; (b) limit the number of types; (c) avoid yes/no questions and questions stated in the negative; (d) avoid questions that overlap, or are dependent on one another; (e) begin questions with who, what, when, how, and why; (f) avoid multiple-choice questions.

4. Ensure the passage dependency of literal and inferential questions by "field testing" them on some of your brighter students or by using an adult standard; i.e., would an adult be able to answer this question without reading the passage?

5. Use the Betts criteria, but do not adhere to them too rigidly. Keep these points in mind: (a) in the lower grades, be lenient with the oral accuracy criteria when comprehension is good; (b) always look for signs of actual frustration in the student's behavior; and (c) when comprehension scores are between 65% and 75%, interpret the performance as instructional unless there is evidence of frustration.

6. Do not consider the quality (semantic acceptability) of miscues in obtaining initial scoring levels. However, do consider quality in subjectively evaluating overall patterns once the levels have been determined, concentrating on miscues made at and below the instructional level.

7. If there is a difference between oral and silent comprehension scores, use the higher of the two.

8. For miscue analysis, do not allow students to read passages silently before oral reading. When oral accuracy is at frustration level and silent comprehension is at the instructional level, consider the level as instructional.

9. Don't be afraid to try to assess ability and inclination to read beyond the lines (constructive level) as well as to read the lines (literal level) and between the lines (inferential level). See the formula for the "Information Reading–Thinking Inventory," ahead, for details.

teaching toward it. This impression is given a boost by findings that show that the simple act of altering teachers' questioning also alters their feedback and discussion practices, and that student behavior and learning soon follow (O'Flahavan, Hartman & Pearson, 1988; Ruddell, 1990).

The IR–TI is, like the IRI, an individually administered diagnostic test that can either be purchased or constructed by the teacher. It is designed to assess literal, inferential, and higher-order comprehension, and to elicit information relevant to assessing aspects of language proficiency and personal–social adjustment. Quantitative and qualitative scoring systems are used toward these ends. In general, the IR–TI should be structured as a diagnostic conversation between a teacher and a student. Anything which seriously detracts from this should be set aside, unless the information is crucial at that time. The structure, administration, and interpretation of the IR–TI are identical to the conventional IRI described above, with the following additions:

- In the conventional IRI, the examiner makes a brief statement about the content of each passage before asking the student to read it. In the IR–TI, the examiner asks the student a question designed to elicit relevant background information.

- Following this initial question, the student is asked whether s/he thinks s/he will enjoy reading (or listening to) the remainder of the selection. This permits the teacher and student to judge performance against likely level of interest and motivation.

- In the IR–TI, the *first* question the examiner asks after the student reads a passage is: "How much did you enjoy this (selection/story)?" Answers are given on a 5-point scale from "very little" to "very much."

- In the IR–TI, the student's answers to the IRI-type comprehension questions are evaluated qualitatively. Correct answers can be given extra credit when they are exceptionally full or detailed. Incorrect answers are evaluated as being "congruent" or "incongruent" with the question. This congruency measure can be important: It has been found that remedial students, even those in a one-to-one tutoring situation, answer from 55 to 80 percent of their teacher's questions with totally incongruent, "off the wall" responses (Manzo, 1969a). In other words, they are hardly engaged, and therefore cannot possibly begin to learn. Hence, the congruency score indicates the extent to which a student's listening and interactive comprehension is increasing even though his or her reading scores do not yet reflect this subtle area of growth.

- In the IR–TI, the student is asked how well he or she thinks they answered the IRI-type questions (on a 5-point scale from "poorly" to "very well"). This metacognitive, or "comprehension awareness" (Pressley et al., 1990), measure is later analyzed by comparing the student's judgment of his or her performance with their actual performance on a particular set of questions.

- Following the conventional IRI-type comprehension questions, the IR–TI includes higher-order questions that require reading beyond the lines. The student is asked the metacognitive question of how well he or she thinks they answered these questions as well.

- The IR–TI includes an optional question designed to collect a writing sample based on the reading passage.

- The IRI-type questions on the IR–TI can be used to determine independent, instructional, and frustration levels, following Betts' criteria. However, these scores can also be combined or compared with the scores for the higher-order literacy questions. When these scores are combined, about 45 percent of student rankings tend to change up or down (Ratanakarn, 1992).

- IR–TI selections include excerpts from conventional story and nonfiction prose as well as brief, but complete fables. See the sample IR–TI passage and accompanying questions in Box 12.10.

**Informal Reading–Thinking Inventory Excerpt**

Grade 4
Number of words: 151

### The Shepherd Boy and the Wolf

A shepherd boy was tending his flock near a village, and thought it would be great fun to trick the villagers by pretending that a wolf was attacking the sheep. He shounted out, "Wolf! wolf!" and when the villagers came running up he laughed at them for being so easily tricked. He tried this hoax more than once. Every time the villagers ran to help the boy, they found that they had been tricked again, and there was no wolf at all.

At last, a wolf really did come, and the boy cried, "Wolf, wolf!" as loud as he could, but the people were so used to hearing him call that they took no notice of his cries for help. So the wolf had it all his own way, and killed off many sheep.

The moral of this story is: no one believes a liar, even when he tells the truth.

*Freely adapted from Aesop's Fables (1912).*

### The Shepherd Boy and the Wolf
### (Grade 4)

*Motivation/Schema Activation*

What does a shepherd do? _____

_____

Now you are going to listen to a story about a shepherd boy who got in the habit of telling lies. Then I will ask you some questions about what you have heard and what you thought about it.

(EV)    1.    How much did you enjoy this story? Point to the picture that is closest to the way you feel. *Show student the "rating card" provided with the test materials, reproduced below. Briefly review the meaning of each choice, and circle the number of the student's choice. You may also indicate the "value" of responses by recording a "✓" for any responses that are clearly incongruent, or illogical, or a "+" for any that are exceptionally full or detailed.)*

Explanation (optional)

_____

_____

| very little | little | half & half | much | very much | Value: _____ |
|:---:|:---:|:---:|:---:|:---:|:---|
| **1** | **2** | **3** | **4** | **5** | |

**BOX**
**12.10**
cont'd
## Informal Reading–Thinking Inventory Excerpt

*Reading the Lines*

> *Guidelines for Recording Student Responses:*
> In the "Score" column, record "0" for incorrect or "1" for correct answers, in the "Value" column, record a "✓" for any responses that are clearly incongruent, or illogical, and record a "+" for any responses that are exceptionally full or detailed.

|  |  |  | Score | Value |
|--|--|--|-------|-------|
| (F) | 2. | What was the shepherd boy's job? *(taking care of the sheep)* | ____ | ____ |
| (F) | 3. | What idea did he think of as a way to have fun? *(tricking the villagers by pretending that a wolf was attacking the sheep)* | ____ | ____ |
| (F) | 4. | What did the villagers do when the boy first shouted "wolf"? *(they came running to help)* | ____ | ____ |
| (V) | 5. | What does the word "hoax" mean in this passage? *(a trick or a joke)* | ____ | ____ |

*Reading Between the Lines*          Silent Reading Time: ____ min., ____ sec.

|  |  |  | Score | Value |
|--|--|--|-------|-------|
| (I) | 6. | Did the villagers think that a wolf might harm the sheep? *(yes—that's why they came running when the boy called.)* | ____ | ____ |
| (I) | 7. | Why didn't the villagers come when the wolf was really killing the sheep? *(they couldn't believe the boy when he finally told the truth)* | ____ | ____ |
| (M) | 8. | How well do you think you answered these factual and thought questions? Point to the picture that is closest to the way you think you answered. *(Show student the "rating card," reproduced below. Circle the number of the student's choice. You may also indicate the "value" of responses by recording a "✓" for any responses that are clearly incongruent, or illogical, or a "+" for any that are exceptionally full or detailed.)* |  |  |

Explanation (optional)

_____

_____

| very little | little | half & half | much | very much |
|-------------|--------|-------------|------|-----------|
| 1 | 2 | 3 | 4 | 5 |

Value: _____

**BOX
12.10
cont'd**

### Reading Beyond the Lines

> *Guidelines for Recording Student Responses:*
> In the "Score" column, record "0" for incorrect, "1" for correct answers, or "2" for answers that are correct *and* elaborated upon. In the "Value" column, record a "✓" for any responses that are clearly incongruent, or illogical, and record a "+" for any responses that are exceptionally full or detailed.

(EV)    9.    Tell how much you agree with this statement—*"Trust is more important than fun."*—point to the picture that shows the way you feel:
*(The student's explanation should indicate that fun is important, but trust is more so, and that it is possible to have fun without destroying trust.)*

Explanation (optional)

_____

_____

| very little | little | half & half | much | very much |
|:---:|:---:|:---:|:---:|:---:|
| 1 | 2 | 3 | 4 | 5 |

Value: _____

_____    Score    Value

Score    Value

(AC)    10.    Why is it important not to tell lies?
*(Score any of the following answers correct, as well as any other reasonable answers the student gives.)*    ____    ____

_____    People may not help you when you need it, because they won't know you really do.

_____    People won't believe you.

_____    People won't like you.

_____    Nothing works well when we lose trust in each other.

_____    Other _____

(AC)    11.    This fable is sometimes called "The Boy Who Cried Wolf." Can you see another possible meaning for the term "crying wolf," based on this fable?
*(calling for help when it isn't really needed)*

_____    ____    ____

_____    ____    ____

(M)    12.    How well do you think you answered these related questions? Point to the picture that is closest to the way you think you answered. *(Show student the "rating card," reproduced below. Circle the number of the student's choice. You may also indicate the "value" of responses by recording a "✓" for any responses that are clearly incongruent, or illogical, or a "+" for any that are exceptionally full or detailed.)*

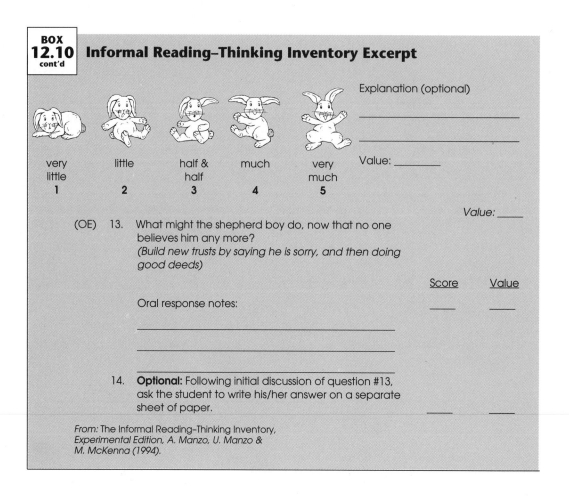

From: The Informal Reading–Thinking Inventory, Experimental Edition, A. Manzo, U. Manzo & M. McKenna (1994).

- A full IR–TI need not be given, nor need the full inventory be given in one sitting. It is OK to establish instructional level with another IRI, or with just the standard word lists and conventional questions of the IR–TI, and then conduct a full inquiry with a passage at the student's instructional level. In other words, it can be used to gather further information on students you suspect of being either *better* than their conventional IRI scores, or those you suspect of being mechanistic thinkers who are functionally *below* their otherwise proficient reading as indicated on a conventional IRI.

The IR–TI could be called a whole-language, whole-person inventory: it attempts to look at the reader as well as his or her reading; it involves reading, listening, speaking, and writing; it invites subjective as well as objective involvement and assessment; and it attempts to connect teacher, students, and textual material. It is a workbench where each of these factors has an opportunity to influence the teacher's understanding of individual children and their respective instructional needs. On a broader scale, the widespread adoption of such a formula could bring about a more tangible and lasting interest in higher-order reading and thinking in the schools.

See now how to assess writing, one of the important entryways to higher-order thinking.

## INFORMAL ASSESSMENT OF WRITING

Writing samples always are one of the more interesting and telling components of a student's portfolio. Nonetheless, there is no agreed-upon way to assess writing. This does not present a serious problem, since most methods tend to correlate with one another to a fair degree. This has led some to recommend that by merely counting the length of each clause, or "T-unit," as Hunt (1965) called them, it would be possible to get a good indication of a student's ability to use complex syntactical structures, as a measure of overall writing expertise. Lundsteen (1979) opposed these counting systems by saying that "It isn't how long you make sentences, but how you make them long."

For this reason, writing is best assessed informally, holistically, and subjectively. This is done by looking at a piece of writing and estimating from your knowledge and experience with children, whether it is "very low," "below average," "average," "above average," or "advanced" for a student's age and grade level. Should you wish to be guided in your judgments to a greater degree of specificity, you may choose to use something like the guide shown in Box 12.11, developed by the State of Missouri for holistic writing evaluation of grade school writing. For assessment of more specific elements of children's writing, you may wish to try the Informal Writing Inventory (Manzo & Manzo, 1993), shown in Figure 12.8. You may use those portions of the inventory that seem appropriate, or administer the entire inventory over a period of several days, so that it is unobtrusively woven into class activities. The IWI provides information that is useful in determining the nature of subsequent instruction and in noting student writing progress over time.

The problem with most systems of evaluating writing is that they tend to treat all elements, from punctuation to content, as having equal importance. Since it is self-evident that this is not the case, it is important to emphasize an "overall" evaluation. This rating will tend to reflect the other item appraisals, but there should be no effort to have it be an average of these. This is the place where the teacher tries to express a sense of where the student is and is likely to be headed. In Figure 12.8, for example, the evaluator felt the need to go to a decimal scale by ranking the overall work as 2.4, meaning below average, but able to construct a story.

For your information, there are standardized measures of writing that have been in use for some time. See Myklebust (1965), Hammill and Larson (1983), and Weiner (1980) for three that have been normed for intermediate and higher grade levels. We are not aware of any that have been normed for the lower grade levels.

Consider now another type of informal assessment tool that can be developed to assess and teach effective use of content area textbooks. This basic formula has been around for many years. We have found examples of it in basal readers dating back to the 1920s. It is still a fresh idea and a clever way to introduce children to textbooks.

---

**BOX 12.11** **Core Competencies for the State of Missouri: Holistic Writing Evaluation**

*Scoring Level Six*

A. FOCUS   Has focus and sense of direction. Responds directly to the topic.
B. ORGANIZATION   Includes logical progression of ideas. Has definite beginning, middle, and end.
C. DEVELOPMENT   Contains specifics to support main ideas.
D. MECHANICS   Has good mechanics, though may have occasional errors.
E. SENTENCE STRUCTURE   Has sentence variety and clarity.
F. DICTION   Includes appropriate vocabulary and diction. Shows vitality of expression.

*Scoring Level Five*

A. FOCUS   Has focus and sense of direction. Remains focused on topic.
B. ORGANIZATION   Shows progression of ideas. Has beginning, middle, and end.
C. DEVELOPMENT   Contains some specifics to support main ideas.
D. MECHANICS   Has good mechanics, but may have some errors.
E. SENTENCE STRUCTURE   Has clear sentences but may lack variety.
F. DICTION   Includes appropriate vocabulary but may lack freshness and variety.

*Scoring Level Four*

A. FOCUS   Has focus and sense of direction but not as evident as at higher levels.
B. ORGANIZATION   Has generally logical progression but may show lapses in coherence and has less fully developed sense of beginning, middle, and end.
C. DEVELOPMENT   Goes beyond a simple listing of activities that relate to the topic. Includes some supporting details but may lack specificity to frame details stated.
D. MECHANICS   Fair to good mechanics.
E. SENTENCE STRUCTURE   Has clear sentences but they may lack variety and complexity.
F. DICTION   Includes appropriate vocabulary but may lack freshness and variety.

*Scoring Level Three*

A. FOCUS   May have sense of direction, but may lack focus. May address the topic only partially.
B. ORGANIZATION   May contain irrelevancies and digressions. May lack beginning, middle, and end.
C. DEVELOPMENT   May have details for support, but may have a listing of activities that relate to the topic with little support.

---

## INFORMAL TEXTBOOK INVENTORY (ITI)

The Informal Textbook Inventory is an open book test constructed by the teacher for a given book. It is *group*-administered and involves assessment and teaching of reading, study, and thinking strategies. Essentially, it asks students to answer an array of questions that help in determining whether they know how to use their textbooks and related resource materials effectively. Any question not answered correctly is taken as an indication of need for additional instructional attention.

**BOX 12.11 cont'd**

### Scoring Level Three

D. MECHANICS   Fair to poor mechanics.

E. SENTENCE STRUCTURE   May have sentences that are fairly clear but sentence structure is likely to be very simple.

F. DICTION   Less sophisticated vocabulary and diction.

### Scoring Level Two

A. FOCUS   May have some focus and sense of direction, or may lack sense of focus altogether. May only partially address topic.

B. ORGANIZATION   May lack coherence. May be characterized by digressions and irrelevancies. May have little sense of beginning, middle, and end.

C. DEVELOPMENT   May have little support or development. Support may be irrelevant. May be a brief list of ideas and consist mainly of sentence patterns such as "He did this. He did that. Then he did this."

D. MECHANICS   Poor to fair mechanics. Often has distracting mechanical errors.

E. SENTENCE STRUCTURE   Immature sentences that lack clarity, complexity and variety. May show lack of sentence boundaries.

F. DICTION   Limited vocabulary and immature diction likely.

### Scoring Level One

A. FOCUS   May possess some focus and sense of direction, or may lack focus altogether. May barely address topic.

B. ORGANIZATION   May lack coherence. May be characterized by digressions and irrelevancies. May have little sense of beginning, middle, or end.

C. DEVELOPMENT   May have little or no development. May be so poorly worded that reader has trouble making sense of what has been written.

D. MECHANICS   Has poor mechanics.

E. SENTENCE STRUCTURE   Immature sentences that may lack clarity and variety. May be a listing of words rather than sentences.

F. DICTION   Limited vocabulary and immature diction. Word order may be tangled; words may be omitted.

Note: Errors in mechanics may lower a paper one to two categories

## Constructing the ITI

### Organization and Structure of the Textbook

- Develop three to five questions that students can answer by referring to *organizational elements* of the text: the index, table of contents, glossary, appendices, or other text sections.
- Develop three to five questions about *how the text is structured*.

*continued on p. 518*

**FIGURE 12.8**

## Informal Writing Inventory: Primer to Fourth Grade (also for upper grade students with more limited skills)

1. Have the student write out his or her own name and address (if able). Rank for:

|  | very low | below average | average | above average | advanced |
|---|---|---|---|---|---|
| A. accuracy | 1 | 2 | 3 | 4 | 5 |
| B. legibility | 1 | 2 | 3 | 4 | 5 |
| C. spelling | 1 | 2 | 3 | 4 | 5 |
| D. placement on page (top left, or center of page is best) | 1 | 2 | 3 | 4 | 5 |
| E. overall | 1 | 2 | 3 | 4 | 5 |
| F. comments _____ | | | | | |

2. Have the student speak or write a description of something that is pictured (see illustration). Record and rank for:

|  | very low | below average | average | above average | advanced |
|---|---|---|---|---|---|
| A. accuracy (details) | 1 | 2 | 3 | 4 | 5 |
| B. reasonable sequence | 1 | 2 | 3 | 4 | 5 |
| C. cogency (lack of irrelevancies) | 1 | 2 | 3 | 4 | 5 |
| D. English usage | 1 | 2 | 3 | 4 | 5 |
| E. overall | 1 | 2 | 3 | 4 | 5 |
| F. comments _____ | | | | | |

3. Invite the student to complete several sentences (see examples). Record and rank for:

|  | very low | below average | average | above average | advanced |
|---|---|---|---|---|---|
| A. relevancy | 1 | 2 | 3 | 4 | 5 |
| B. English usage | 1 | 2 | 3 | 4 | 5 |
| C. comments _____ | | | | | |

---

**Examples**

1. Cats make me . . .

| student response: | relevancy | English usage |
|---|---|---|
| (a) *sneeze and choke* | 5 | 4 |
| (b) *run* | 4 | 3 |

2. I wish that I could . . .

| student response: | relevancy | English usage |
|---|---|---|
| (a) *go with my sister* | 4 | 3 |
| (b) *eat al thats I wanted* | 4 | 2 |

**FIGURE
12.8
cont'd**

## Informal Writing Inventory: Primer to Fourth Grade

*Example*

Name: Lana

Grade: 5

Directions: Describe the drawing below in about 25 words. Make up a title for this descriptive essay.

DESCRIPTION:

One day it was a gril name Jan
She was latte for school She got up
and took a qick bath slipt her
clothes on and took her book to her
friend doght her a cookie Jan said
[gave]
Tankeyou. She was at scool and
her theacher claect the home work:
(collected)            The End

TITLE:  Home work for School

### IWI Profile

A.  accuracy (details)            2
B.  reasonable sequence          3
C.  cogency (lack of irrelevancies)  3
D.  English usage                2
E.  overall                      2. 4
F.  comments: Lana reacted to the picture, rather than *describing* it. Her story was coherent and sequential otherwise, though, strictly speaking, not cogent, since the entire piece is irrelevant. Attention to directions, spelling, and punctuation need some attention. However, there is a definite story line.

## FIGURE 12.8 cont'd   Informal Writing Inventory: Primer to Fourth Grade

4.  Have the student try to fill in a missing word from five sentences read to him. Record and rank for:

|  | very low | below average | average | above average | advanced |
|---|---|---|---|---|---|
| A.  accuracy (allow the student to change his/her mind) | 1 | 2 | 3 | 4 | 5 |
| B.  syntax compatibility | 1 | 2 | 3 | 4 | 5 |
| C.  semantics | 1 | 2 | 3 | 4 | 5 |
| D.  prior knowledge | 4 | 5 | 1 | 2 | 3 |
| E.  comments _____ | | | | | |

---

### Examples

The cat and the _____ were chased off by the store owner.

**Incorrect student answers and evaluations:**

|  | "mouse" | "street" |
|---|---|---|
| accuracy | 2 | 1 |
| syntax compatibility | 5 | 1 |
| semantics | 4 | 2 |
| prior knowledge | 4 | 2 |
| overall | 2 | 1 |

---

**Basic Comprehension**   Select a short portion of the text that contains an *important concept* with supporting details and at least one graph, chart, or picture.

- Develop one or two fill-in or multiple-choice questions that direct students to state or select the *main idea* of the material read.
- Develop three or more fill-in, multiple-choice, or matching questions about *specific factual details* that support the main ideas in the selection.
- Develop three or more fill-in, multiple-choice, or matching questions that direct students to state or select a definition of key *vocabulary* terms used in the selection.
- Develop one or more questions requiring students to state or select an *interpretation of a graph, chart, or picture* that adds information not explicitly stated in the selection.

**Applied Comprehension**   Questions in these sections can be based on the same text selection used above.

- Develop one or more questions requiring students to *draw valid conclusions* based on the information presented.

**FIGURE 12.8 cont'd**

## Informal Writing Inventory: Primer to Fourth Grade

5.  Dictate two to five sentences, repeating each three times. Rate the student's transcription of the sentences for:

| | very low | below average | average | above average | advanced |
|---|---|---|---|---|---|
| A. accuracy | 1 | 2 | 3 | 4 | 5 |
| B. spelling and punctuation | 1 | 2 | 3 | 4 | 5 |
| C. penmanship | 1 | 2 | 3 | 4 | 5 |
| D. comments _____ | | | | | |

6.  Have a student tell you a story for 2 minutes. Offer the student three topic choices, and provide a minimum of 10 minutes for the student to prepare for what they wish to say. Record the story told, and rate for:

| | very low | below average | average | above average | advanced |
|---|---|---|---|---|---|
| A. imagination | 1 | 2 | 3 | 4 | 5 |
| B. sequence | 1 | 2 | 3 | 4 | 5 |
| C. story from (beginning, middle, end) | 1 | 5 | 2 | 3 | 4 |
| D. internal logic (coherence) | 1 | 2 | 3 | 4 | 5 |
| E. overall quality | 1 | 2 | 3 | 4 | 5 |
| F. comments _____ | | | | | |

7.  Read or play back the story (from above) to the child, and ask what, if anything, they might like to revise. Limit the revision period to 10 minutes. Make suggested revisions without unnecessary comments, and rate the revised story for:

| | very low | below average | average | above average | advanced |
|---|---|---|---|---|---|
| A. inclination to correct | 1 | 2 | 3 | 4 | 5 |
| B. quality of corrections | 1 | 2 | 3 | 4 | 5 |
| C. comments _____ | | | | | |

- Develop one or more questions that require students to *evaluate and apply information* from the text in terms of their own experiences, values, and existing knowledge base.

See Box 12.12 for an example of an ITI on an unusual textbook used by the first author when he taught middle school social studies.

### Administering the ITI

Before asking students to tackle the ITI, explain some of its features and purposes. It is not a "test" in the usual sense of the word; every text differs slightly from every other, and this is a way to find out how well students will be able to use this particular text. Also, point out that each student should attempt to complete the

*continued on p. 523*

| BOX 12.12 | **Informal Textbook Inventory** |
| --- | --- |

Social studies text: *New York State in Story,* by Jeanne Schwarz & Minerva Goldberg. (Phoenix, NY: Frank E. Richards, 1962).

### *Organization and Structure of the Text*

#### *Understanding the Textbook Organization*

1. If you wanted to know if your textbook covered the *what, why,* and *who* of New York State government, you would check the:

(x) a. Table of contents

  b. Index

  c. Chapter headings

  d. Publisher

2. Which one of the following would you *first* turn to if you wished to read a book about one of the topics in your text?

  a. Librarian

  b. Table of contents

(x) c. Your teacher

  d. Bibliography

3. Check the following statements by studying the design of this book. If you find a statement to be true, mark it with a plus (+) sign; if false, a minus (−) sign:
   The book has:

(−) a. a very complete bibliography

(+) b. two major parts; really two books in one

(+) c. good charts, pictures, and maps

(+) d. a good description of the authors and their backgrounds

(+) e. a glossary

(+) f. a brief outline of the material covered before each chapter

(+) g. follow-up activities after each chapter

(+) h. a storylike style

(−) i. beautiful color illustrations

(+) j. a comfortable, compact look

(+) k. easily visible printing

#### *Using the Text Organization Effectively*

See how quickly you can answer the following questions using the parts of your book to their best advantage (based on the first half of the book).

4. How long is the term of the Attorney General?

5. (a) What is the meaning of the word *almshouse?*
   (b) Where did you find the answer to 5a?

6. What are the three divisions of Chapter 1?

**BOX 12.12 cont'd**

### Basic Comprehension

#### Comprehending the Main Idea

7. Which of the following best expresses the author's purpose for this brief selection?
    - (a) To show the friendliness of New York people
    - (b) To show the boundaries of New York state
- (x)
    - (c) To show where New York is in relation to the other states and the world
    - (d) To show that New York lies between the parallels of 40–31 and 45 north latitude

#### Noting Supporting Details

8. New York State is bounded by five states, three lakes, three rivers, one foreign country, and one ocean. Name them.

9. New York State most resembles a:
    - (a) hexagon
- (x)
    - (b) triangle
    - (c) circle
    - (d) rectangle

#### Understanding Vocabulary in Context

10. Match the following, based on their use in context:

| Column A | Column B |
|---|---|
| _____ latitude | a. circular lines running east and west around the globe designed to measure distances north and south |
| _____ prime meridian | b. the first line of longitude |
| _____ equator | c. imaginary lines designed to measure distance east and west on the globe |
| _____ longitude | d. a region of a country |
| | e. the center latitudinal line around the earth |

#### Understanding Information Presented in Graphic or Pictorial Form

Study the illustration on page 3 to answer questions 11 and 12 below.

11. The point of this illustration is that:
    - (a) We have neighbors to the north.
    - (b) Different countries are represented by different flags.
- (x)
    - (c) We have good relations with our northern neighbors.
    - (d) People are the same around the world.

12. What symbol in this illustration shows the major difference between the two groups of people shown?
    - (a) people
    - (b) names
- (x)
    - (c) flags
    - (d) boundaries

| BOX 12.12 cont'd | **Informal Textbook Inventory** |

Study the three illustrations on page 2 to answer question number 13 below.

13. What is the major relationship among the three illustrations?

    (a) They are all maps.

(x)  (b) They focus on the relative size and place of New York State.

    (c) They show the size of New York State.

    (d) They show the population density of New York State.

Study the two pictures on page 5, that tell us that New York State has *two* features. They are:

    (a) seashores and rolling hills

(x)  (b) good natural resources

    (c) high population density

    (d) good industry

### Applied Comprehension

**Drawing Conclusions and Critical Thinking**

15. Which of the following is a reasonable conclusion that can be drawn from just pages 3 and 4?

    (a) New Yorkers must be fine people.

(x)  (b) New York must have extremely long boundaries

    (c) New York is probably one of the largest states in the Union

    (d) New York is probably sparsely populated

**Evaluating and Judging**

16. If you were the governor of New York and you wished to raise the educational level of its citizens, which three things would you consider most important to do? Why?

    (a) Build more schools

    (b) Hire more teachers

    (c) Find a new tax source

    (d) Borrow money from the government

    (e) Build more libraries

    (f) Set up adult education courses

    (g) Raise teachers' salaries and attract the best teachers from other states

    (h) Develop a slum-clearing project

    (i) Study the problem more carefully

    (j) Try out different approaches in different parts of the state

**Social Studies: Understanding Diagrams**

17. Below is a circle that represents the earth. Study the key below and mark the spaces with the direction of the arrows in the circle.

*Key*

N = North    NE = Norheast

S = South    NW = Northwest

E = East    SE = Southeast

W = West    SW = Southwest

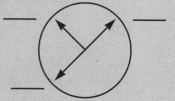

worksheets as thoroughly and accurately as possible, but that all answers will be discussed as a group. Provide adequate time for all students to complete the inventory. It may take two or more 25-minute periods, so you may need to provide an alternate activity for students who finish early.

### Evaluating and Using the Results of the ITI

After all students have finished the ITI's, collect and score the tests. A "total score" need not be recorded on the students' papers, since the purpose of the test is to identify strengths and weaknesses in the various subsections. For diagnostic purposes, any error is taken as a sign of need in that category. Much of the diagnostic value of the inventory comes from the discussion of the items when the tests are returned to students. This discussion can take from one-half to three full class periods, depending on student abilities and the difficulty of the text.

## QUICK ASSESSMENT PROCEDURES

When time and purpose do not justify administering an IRI or ITI, there are several options to consider. Four are detailed here: the "Rule of Thumb," Word List Estimation, the Name Test, and Cloze Passage testing.

### THE "RULE OF THUMB"

The only "material" needed for this simple system is a 100-word passage with a known grade-level difficulty. The student is asked to read the passage aloud while the teacher keeps track of obvious errors, using IRI guidelines to determine what types of misreadings to count as errors. With one hand, out of the student's sight, the teacher raises a finger for each error, ending with the thumb. If one or two fingers are raised, then the material probably is at the student's *independent* reading level. If three or four are used, it is at the student's *instructional* level. If the thumb and more become necessary, the material is becoming to difficult to learn from and probably is at the student's *frustration* level.

Glazer (1984) suggests that *students* be taught the "rule of thumb" as a means of helping themselves to increase metacognitive sensitivity and their ability to select their own reading materials. The same basic procedure can be used in an inverse way to determine the difficulty level of material. See "Estimating Readability" in Chapter 13 for details.

### WORD LIST ESTIMATION

Words lists, you will recall, are used as the first part of an IRI to determine where to begin testing with reading passages. This is because there is a reliably high correlation between recognizing words in isolation and in identifying them in context. This fact makes it possible to infer general reading level quite accurately from sets of carefully selected graded word lists. Some words lists are compiled from basal readers such as Thorndike and Lorge's *The Teacher's Word Book of 30,000 Words* (1944). Others are carefully researched from the responses of children. The best of these is the Dale and O'Rourke list (1976; 1981), which contains more than

**Table 12.1**

### Dale & O'Rourke Word List Excerpt

| GRADE | SCORE | WORD | MEANING |
|-------|-------|------|---------|
| 04 | 87% | bar | piece of soap/candy |
| 06 | 67% | bar | block or barrier |
| 12 | 75% | bar | separate measure |

44,000 words and was used as a guide for controlling the difficulty level of the writing in *The World Book Encyclopedia*. Dale and O'Rourke determined the percent of students who could be expected to know each of the 44,000 words at grades 4, 6, 8, 10, 12, 13, and 16. The word list even provides different grade-level estimates for the same word when it has different meanings (see Table 12.1 for an example).

Although there is a strong *correlation* between reading words from lists and reading words in context, it is also very important to note that these two processes are not identical. At the early stages of reading it can be quite a bit more difficult to read words in isolation than to read them in context. Students will often misread a word from a list that they might easily recognize in context.

Most teachers and reading specialists have a favorite word list. There is no strong evidence, however, that one list is better than another. The San Diego Quick Assessment (LaPray & Ross, 1969) is among the most popular of these lists for elementary school use. It is presented in detail in Box 12.13.

There is one other quick test of decoding ability that is especially worth the notice of teachers of remedial reading since it does a better job of eliciting responses from children who have stopped trying due to excessive failure.

## THE NAME TEST

This quick test, developed by Cunningham (1990), is based on children's ability to decode proper names (see Box 12.14, p. 528). Cunningham found that the use of names has certain advantages over conventional word lists. Names tend to invite better effort from the children. In addition, most names are familiar, and therefore in the child's listening vocabulary. This is important in decoding since it is recognition of having heard a word before that tells us that we probably have pronounced it correctly.

There are no formalized norms yet for the Name Test. The test, however, has been found to be very reliable (.98). Procedures for administering and scoring the Name Test are described below.

### Preparation

1. Type or print legibly the 25 names on a sheet of paper or card stock. Make sure the print size is appropriate for the age or grade level of the students being tested.

2. For students who might perceive reading an entire list of names as being too formidable, type or print the names on index cards so they can be read individually.

3. Prepare a scoring sheet. Do this by typing the list of names in a column and following each name with a blank line to be used for recording a student's responses.

### Administration

1. Administer the Name Test individually. Select a quiet, distraction-free location.

2. Explain to the student that she or he is to pretend to be a teacher who must read a list of names of students in the class. Direct the student to read the names as if taking attendance.

3. Have the student read the entire list. Inform the student that you will not be able to help with difficult names, and encourage him or her to "make a guess if you are not sure." This way you will have sufficient responses for analysis.

4. Write a check on the protocol sheet for each name read correctly. Write phonetic spellings for names that are mispronounced.

### Scoring and Interpreting the Name Test

1. Count a word correct if all syllables are pronounced correctly regardless of where the student places the accent. For example, either Yo'/lan/da or Yo/lan'/da would be acceptable.

2. For words where the vowel pronunciation depends on which syllable the consonant is placed with, count them correct for either pronunciation. For example, either Ho/mer or Hom/er would be acceptable.

3. Count the number of names read correctly and analyze those mispronounced, looking for patterns indicative of decoding strengths and weaknesses.

4. As a benchmark of performance, you can expect the average second-grader to score 23 out of 50.

## CLOZE PASSAGE TESTING

The term "cloze" has come to refer to any activities in which students are asked to fill in missing words in passages. The term was coined by Taylor (1953), who was using this fill-in-the-blanks activity to try to measure the psychological trait of "closure": the tendency to complete missing elements of an incomplete stimulus and recognize it as a meaningful whole. Taylor's cloze test was not a good measure of *closure,* but he did find that it had a strong correlation with reading comprehension. Based on this finding, Bormuth (1965) developed a standardized procedure for constructing and interpreting a cloze test. This Standard Cloze Passage Test can be used to obtain a quick estimate of a student's ability to comprehend material at a given difficulty level. The test norms can be used to interpret each student's performance as independent, instructional, or frustration level for that particular piece of material.

## BOX 12.13   San Diego Quick Assessment

### Preparation

1. Prepare word list cards by typing each of the following lists of words on a large index card. Leave ample space between words so that you can easily point to each word as you administer the test. Type the grade-level designations on the *back* of each card for your reference only. The word card lists can be laminated for durability.

2. Prepare typed word list sheets, with space to write the student's responses beside each word.

### Word Lists

| PREPRIMER | PRIMER | GRADE 1 | GRADE 2 | GRADE 3 |
|---|---|---|---|---|
| see ____ | you ____ | road ____ | our ____ | city ____ |
| play ____ | come ____ | live ____ | please ____ | middle ____ |
| me ____ | not ____ | thank ____ | myself ____ | moment ____ |
| at ____ | with ____ | when ____ | town ____ | frightened ____ |
| run ____ | jump ____ | bigger ____ | early ____ | exclaimed ____ |
| go ____ | help ____ | how ____ | send ____ | several ____ |
| and ____ | is ____ | always ____ | wide ____ | lonely ____ |
| look ____ | work ____ | night ____ | believe ____ | drew ____ |
| can ____ | are ____ | spring ____ | quietly ____ | since ____ |
| here ____ | this ____ | today ____ | carefully ____ | straight ____ |

| GRADE 4 | GRADE 5 | GRADE 6 | GRADE 7 |
|---|---|---|---|
| decided ____ | scanty ____ | bridge ____ | amber ____ |
| served ____ | certainly ____ | commercial ____ | dominion ____ |
| amazed ____ | develop ____ | abolish ____ | sundry ____ |
| silent ____ | considered ____ | trucker ____ | capillary ____ |
| wrecked ____ | discussed ____ | apparatus ____ | impetuous ____ |
| improved ____ | behaved ____ | elementary ____ | blight ____ |
| certainly ____ | splendid ____ | comment ____ | wrest ____ |
| entered ____ | acquainted ____ | necessity ____ | numerate ____ |
| realized ____ | escaped ____ | gallery ____ | daunted ____ |
| interrupted ____ | grim ____ | relativity ____ | condescend ____ |

The cloze format provides an estimate of the child's ability to comprehend a particular piece of material by measuring his or her familiarity with a variable that is strongly related to comprehension: the subtle "language redundancy" patterns in prose (Weaver & Kingston, 1963). A recent study by McKenna and Layton (1990) suggests that the cloze format also is a trustworthy measure of comprehension of a single sentence. For purposes of quick screening, the most reliable and valid results will be obtained when using the Standard Cloze Passage Test in the manner described in Box 12.15. Adaptations of the format, such as varying the length,

BOX
**12.13**
cont'd

| **GRADE 8** | | **GRADE 9** | | **GRADE 10** | | **GRADE 11** | |
|---|---|---|---|---|---|---|---|
| capacious | ____ | conscientious | ____ | zany | ____ | galore | ____ |
| limitation | ____ | isolation | ____ | jerkin | ____ | rotunda | ____ |
| pretext | ____ | molecule | ____ | nausea | ____ | capitalism | ____ |
| intrigue | ____ | ritual | ____ | gratuitous | ____ | prevaricate | ____ |
| delusion | ____ | momentous | ____ | linear | ____ | risible | ____ |
| immaculate | ____ | vulnerable | ____ | inept | ____ | exonerate | ____ |
| ascent | ____ | kinship | ____ | legality | ____ | superannuate | ____ |
| acrid | ____ | conservatism | ____ | aspen | ____ | luxuriate | ____ |
| binocular | ____ | jaunty | ____ | amnesty | ____ | piebald | ____ |
| embankment | ____ | inventive | ____ | barometer | ____ | crunch | |

### Administration

1. Begin with a card that is at least two years below the student's grade placement.
2. Ask the student to read the words aloud. If he or she misreads *any* words on the list, drop to easier lists until the student makes *no* errors. This indicates the base reading level.
3. Write down all incorrect responses, or use diacritical marks on your copy of the test. For example, *lonely* might be read and recorded as *lovely* or *apparatus* as *a-per'-a-tus*.
4. Encourage the students to read words he or she does not know so that you can identify the techniques used for word identification.
5. Have the student read from increasingly difficult lists until he or she misses at least three words on one of the lists.
6. Identify the student's independent, instructional, and frustration levels using the following interpretation criteria:

> **Independent level** = no more than one error on a list
>
> **Instruction level** = two errors on a list
>
> **Frustration level** = three or more errors on a list

using alternative procedures for deleting words, or accepting synonyms, tend to invalidate the scoring criteria.

The issue of accepting or not accepting synonyms has been the subject of a good deal of controversy and research. For informal evaluation, it is informative and interesting to note and analyze the extent to which synonyms and "reasonable guesses" were used. In fact, some studies have shown slightly greater validity and internal consistency when synonyms were accepted in scoring (McKenna, 1976; Porter, 1978; Schoelles, 1971). However, where quick and accurate estimation is

---

**BOX 12.14**   **The Name Test**

| | | | |
|---|---|---|---|
| Jay Conway | _____ | Wendy Swain | _____ |
| Tim Cornell | _____ | Glen Spencer | _____ |
| Chuck Hoke | _____ | Fred Sherwood | _____ |
| Yolanda Clark | _____ | Flo Thornton | _____ |
| Kimberly Blake | _____ | Dee Skidmore | _____ |
| Roberta Slade | _____ | Grace Brewster | _____ |
| Homer Preston | _____ | Ned Westmoreland | _____ |
| Gus Quincy | _____ | Ron Smitherman | _____ |
| Cindy Sampson | _____ | Troy Whitlock | _____ |
| Chester Wright | _____ | Vance Middleton | _____ |
| Ginger Yale | _____ | Zane Anderson | _____ |
| Patrick Tweed | _____ | Bernard Pendergraph | _____ |
| Stanley Shaw | _____ | | |

---

**BOX 12.15**   **Standard Cloze Passage Test**

**Preparation of the Test**

Select a passage of about 300 words from a selection of known difficulty level. Copy the first sentence with no deletions. Then select a word at random in the second sentence. Delete this word and every fifth word thereafter until 50 words have been deleted. Finish the sentence containing the 50th blank, and copy the next sentence with no deletions. The blanks should be typed lines five spaces long, and numbered from 1 to 50. Students record their responses on numbered answer sheets.

**Administration of the Test**

Before giving the test, do several sample cloze-type sentences on the chalkboard or overhead. Demonstrate the task of filling in the blanks with words that make the sentence make sense. Inform students that the task will be difficult, but that 60 percent accuracy is a good score.

**Scoring the Test**

Count the number of actual words filled in correctly. Do not count synonyms (see the discussion above). Multiply this number by 2 (since there are 50 items) to get the percent correct.

**Interpreting the Results**

A score above 60 percent indicates that the material is within the child's independent reading level. Scores between 40 percent and 60 percent indicate that the material is within the child's instructional reading level. Scores below 40 percent tend to indicate that the material is in the child's frustration level. It is best to allow a plus or minus 5 percentage point spread for error of measurement on each of these bands of scores.

concerned, we are inclined to agree with the findings of Henk and Selders (1984), whose research led them to conclude that "there does not seem to be any overt reason to credit synonyms on a cloze test" (1984, p. 286). Counting synonyms makes scoring much more difficult and time consuming and yields very little change in the rank order of performance within a class. More importantly, when synonyms are counted, Bormuth's (1965) criterion for score interpretation cannot be used.

As a test, the cloze task can be quite frustrating for children, since even the best students will make more errors than they are used to. For this reason, it is best to do some cloze-type warmup exercises on the chalkboard before having students tackle a cloze test on their own.

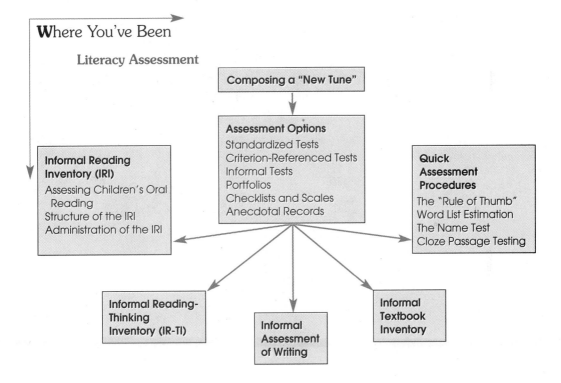

**W**here You've Been

### Literacy Assessment

**Composing a "New Tune"**

**Assessment Options**
Standardized Tests
Criterion-Referenced Tests
Informal Tests
Portfolios
Checklists and Scales
Anecdotal Records

**Informal Reading Inventory (IRI)**
Assessing Children's Oral Reading
Structure of the IRI
Administration of the IRI

**Quick Assessment Procedures**
The "Rule of Thumb"
Word List Estimation
The Name Test
Cloze Passage Testing

**Informal Reading-Thinking Inventory (IR-TI)**

**Informal Assessment of Writing**

**Informal Textbook Inventory**

**W**here You're Going

The next chapter attempts to take a look at the bigger picture, or how to employ all that you've learned up to now so that you can reasonably influence classroom, school, and even district-wide program development and material selections.

## Reflective Inquiries and Activities

1. Talking about tests can be as important as administering them. Write out (or simulate) and then discuss the actual words you would use to do the following:

   (a) Prepare a fourth-grade class to take a standardized battery of tests that will be done over a two- to three-day period.

   (b) Guide fifth-grade youngsters in undertaking an Informal Textbook Inventory in a social studies or science textbook.

   (c) Explain the reading scores below to parents of a 10-year-old child, who is midway through the fourth grade, and has a tested IQ of 110.

   Reading subtest: 4th stanine, Grade equivalent 3.8, Percentile Rank 46

2. There are several ways to determine if a child's oral reading "errors" are of a serious nature. Explain how each of the following would help you to decide how seriously these "errors" should be taken:

   • Doing a qualitative analysis
   • Having the child read silently before orally
   • Checking comprehension against error rate

3. Do you think that you will choose to use portfolios? Why/why not? In what ways or forms?

4. If you use checklists, scales, and anecdotal records, what can you expect to learn from these?

5. Give two reasons for attempting to assess thinking "beyond the lines."

6. Should we trust Betts' criteria for estimating reading levels? After all, they're very old. Explain your answer.

7. Compare the two forms of writing assessment offered in terms of advantages and disadvantages to the classroom teacher.

8. What are the advantages and limitations of cloze passage testing? Include reference to children from language different backgrounds, children who typically are proficient at test taking, and children who are impulsive.

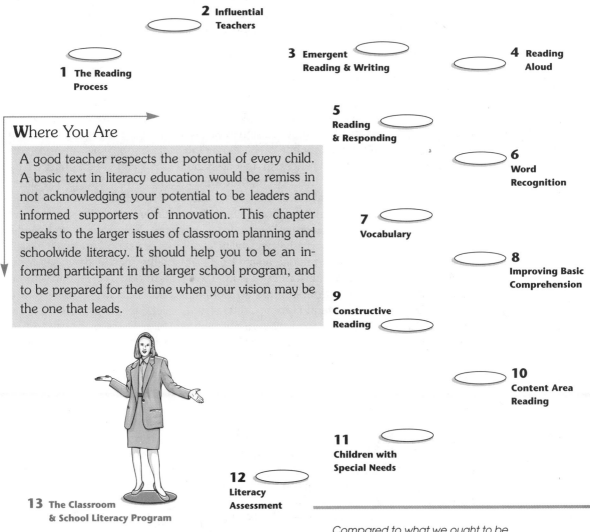

**2** Influential
Teachers

**1** The Reading
Process

**3** Emergent
Reading & Writing

**4** Reading
Aloud

**5**
Reading
& Responding

**6**
Word
Recognition

**W**here You Are

A good teacher respects the potential of every child. A basic text in literacy education would be remiss in not acknowledging your potential to be leaders and informed supporters of innovation. This chapter speaks to the larger issues of classroom planning and schoolwide literacy. It should help you to be an informed participant in the larger school program, and to be prepared for the time when your vision may be the one that leads.

**7**
Vocabulary

**8**
Improving Basic
Comprehension

**9**
Constructive
Reading

**10**
Content Area
Reading

**11**
Children with
Special Needs

**12**
Literacy
Assessment

**13** The Classroom
& School Literacy Program

*Compared to what we ought to be
we are only half awake.*
William James

As an elementary school teacher in training, you probably don't expect anyone to ask you to design a full reading program quite yet. Nonetheless, most of the questions asked in job interviews amount to the same thing. If you have been reading critically and creatively, you probably have collected more ideas than you might immediately realize about designs for classroom and schoolwide literacy programs.

This chapter will further enhance your ability to set up a complete and vital literacy program in your own classroom and to participate as an informed member of the schoolwide literacy program. The chapter includes guidelines for grouping students for classroom instruction, guidelines for selection of instructional materials, and organizational and staffing components of the schoolwide program.

## GROUPING FOR INSTRUCTION

It was only a short time ago that the topic of "ability grouping" would have been a priority in a textbook of this type. Assignment of children to homogeneous ability groups was a central component of basal-reading instruction. This approach to dealing with individual differences in the classroom has been de-emphasized by three recent developments: the movement toward increased use of children's literature in place of "grade-level" texts and supplementary materials; increased advocacy for cooperative learning among students of different ability levels; and increased concern for higher-order literacy for all students. Nonetheless, an issue as sensitive and potentially pervasive as ability grouping does not go away. Even though change is occurring rapidly, ability level remains the most widely used form of grouping (Anderson, Wilkinson, & Mason, 1991). Here now is a brief treatment of some of the views on grouping that an elementary educator needs to be aware of, in order to: (a) understand current attitudes and beliefs; (b) be prepared for the policies you might have to work within; (c) maintain high levels of motivation to learn; and (d) be equipped for the inevitable return of discourse on differences in grouping practices. See Figure 13.1 for a graphic display of some of the most popular grouping patterns.

### ABILITY GROUPING

Grouping children by ability levels is a sort of "middle-of-the-road" solution (Fielding, 1992). It addresses the classroom dilemma of how to teach children of different levels in the same heterogeneous class, rather than creating separate homogeneous tracks, as was popular from the 1930s to the early 1960s. In simple terms, this solution calls for creating three to five homogeneous groups within the class, based on student test scores and teacher judgment. This kind of ability grouping can have a number of negative consequences (Hiebert, 1983; Slavin, 1987). It has even been held to be objectionable by the courts (Moses v. Washington School Board, 1971) on the grounds that its use cannot be justified from educational research (Barr & Dreeben, 1991). A critique of the pros and cons of this type of ability grouping includes the following:

**Pros**

It makes teaching to a heterogeneous group somewhat more manageable.

It results in differential instruction of different groups.

Lessons targeted to small (ability) groups can be the most productive part of the conventional reading program (Anderson, Mason, & Shirley, 1984), at least when there is: (a) an emphasis on meaning more than accurate oral reading; and (b) a high level of student participation. This is related to the finding that children who take an active turn recall more than children who merely follow along while others read (Anderson, Wilkinson, & Mason, 1991).

**Cons**

The nature of the differential instruction can be subtly discriminatory, putting lower readers further and further behind (Shannon, 1985).

The range of abilities within a group have sometimes been found to be so subjective as to be as great as across groups (Barr & Sadow, 1989).

Low groups do too much oral reading and not enough silent reading (Allington, 1983b; Collins, 1986).

Despite grouping to meet ability levels, the relative difficulty level of the material encountered by low-group readers is *greater* than for the high group, hence increasing the probability of errors and frustration (Fielding, 1992).

Feelings of being low-grouped affect children's willingness to read, risk, and learn (Johnston & Winograd, 1985).

There is a disproportionately high placement of culturally and linguistically diverse children in low groups (Fielding, 1992), resulting in a very visible form of segregation.

The groups tend to become rigid, with reassignments occurring only rarely (Allington, 1983b).

## WHOLE-CLASS INSTRUCTION

Whole-class instruction, when simply defined as having the whole class work together on the same material at the same time, is even more problematic than ability grouping. Indeed, it was *because of* the problems inherent in whole-class instruction that ability grouping was developed and gained widespread support.

The biggest problem with whole-class grouping as it is most often practiced is that it ignores individual student differences and tends to reduce everyone in the class to some arbitrary middle ground pace. Even so, lower-ability students begin to fall further and further behind, while higher-ability students are held back. There are other, more subtle objections, including: (a) it can turn *education* into *training;* (b) it reduces teachers to quasi-machines and reduces learning merely to easily measurable products; and (c) poor readers may learn how to read, but they rarely learn to want to read, since with exclusive use of whole-class instruction, they rarely have the opportunity to read anything that is less than tedious for them (remember that,

**FIGURE 13.1** **Grouping Patterns**

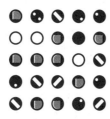

**Whole Group**

All students work from the same materials at the same time.

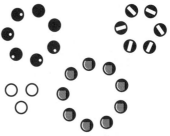

**Ability Groups**

Students of like ability are grouped together. The teacher works with one group at a time while the other groups work on assigned seatwork.

**Cooperative Groups**

Equal sized groups are formed with an intentional mix of ability levels in each group.

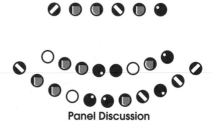

**Panel Discussion**

One group prepares and presents a report, followed by questions from others who have listened.

**Fish Bowl**

One group discusses a topic while the rest of the class sits in a larger outside circle and listens.
(The teacher can be part of either group.)

**Interest Groups**

Groups of various sizes and ability groups are formed based on student interest in aspects of a topic to be explored.

*Concept and some patterns from Fitzgerald (1975).*

by definition, grade-level material will be one to three years above the independent reading level of the lowest 20 percent of an "average" class).

It is frequently assumed that whole-class instruction is supported by a body of research called "time-on-task." The assumption is that if the teacher is spending 100 percent of class time teaching 100 percent of the students, all students will be "on-task" for more time than if the teacher spends on-fifth of class time teaching each of five small groups of students. The research related to time-on-task dates back to a study known as the "Craft Project" (Harris & Server, 1966). This research, however, has more recently been interpreted to mean that learning outcomes can be expected to equal, more or less, the way the teacher budgets class time more so than how the teacher groups the class (Hoffman, 1991).

Whole-class instruction, in sum, is ineffective as a general organizational plan for reading instruction. It is essential to note, however, that there are some instructional strategies that can be used with a whole class that *do* have positive research support when these are used within a larger plan that better meets students' individual needs (Rosenshine & Stevens, 1984). Methods previously discussed, such as the Directed Reading–Thinking Activity and the Guided Reading Procedure, are examples of sound, tested instructional strategies that are appropriate for whole-group instruction.

## LITERATURE-BASED INSTRUCTION WITH FLEXIBLE GROUPING

Currently, the most popular way to deal with the many negative consequences of fixed ability grouping is to seek a balance. The most popular balance chosen is between whole-class instruction based on children's literature that is engaging enough to capture the interest of the most reluctant readers, and provisions for *flexible* groups to ensure that all children experience success (Fielding, 1992). In this system, groups are temporarily convened using a variety of criteria. These include: interest groups, cooperative learning groups, temporary skill or needs-based groups (Hiebert & Colt, 1989; Tunnell & Jacobs, 1989; Zarrillo, 1989), and *some* self-selected, individualized reading.

## SELF-SELECTED OR INDIVIDUALIZED READING

Having each child read at his or her own pace in a literature-based program now has become an integral part of most sensible reading and grouping practices. While no research of which we are aware supports it as the primary way to teach reading, there is a body of research that supports it as a significant part of a core reading program (e.g., Fielding, Wilson, & Anderson, 1986).

The other parts of the grouping picture, as suggested earlier, are coming largely from efforts to promote cooperative learning and higher-order literacy. Concrete examples are given ahead of how these new additions to reading/language arts programming are easing age-old controversies about grouping.

## COOPERATIVE LEARNING GROUPS

The unique concept behind cooperative learning is that it addresses the problem of meeting the needs of varying ability levels by mixing, rather than isolating students of various levels. The primary purpose of cooperative learning is to reinforce and provide for hands-on application of instruction. This is done by following any form of direct instruction with activities designed to be completed by students working together in small, multi-ability level groups. Cooperative learning groups may be temporary, or assembled for longer-term projects. They can be child-selected, teacher-assigned, or interest-groups generated. The idea is to let the task determine the mix. For example, if the project was to write, produce, and sell a book at an upcoming student-made book sale, the task would suggest combining children of different strengths and needs—from writing, to drawing, to manufacturing, to marketing.

Research on cooperative learning (Meloth, 1991; Slavin, 1987; Stevens, Madden, Slavin, & Farnish, 1987) suggests that it is most effective when:

- Student roles are clear.
- Operations are group-oriented and the criterion for group success is satisfactory learning by every member of the group.
- Group activities do not supplant teacher-directed instruction but supplement it.
- Students are expected to explain things to one another, not merely give each other examples (Fielding, 1992).

For specific examples of cooperative learning in action, see Uttero's (1988) cooperative version of the DR–TA (Box 13.1) and Manzo's (1973) Group Reading Activity (Box 13.2). Both of these methods also include attention to higher-order literacy.

## HIGHER-ORDER LITERACY

The value to grouping practices of the new emphasis on higher-order literacy may not be immediately evident, but it is considerable. Basically, the benefit comes from what happens to the "star" system in a class when this new dimension is added to classroom life. When effectiveness in learning is expressed solely in terms of reading the lines and reading between the lines, only a select few youngsters are appreciated for their adeptness. However, when aspects of critical and creative thinking and problem solving are added, other members of the class, possibly including some among the weakest readers, may surface as being astute thinkers and problem-solvers.

What's more, attention to higher-order literacy can be built into most classroom activities without sacrificing attention to traditional learning objectives. For example, the Group Reading Activity attends to conventional reconstructive reading, but also has several aspects of higher-order thinking nested in it. See especially Step 3a, which teaches students to be alert to guiding questions and purposes while reading, and Step 5, which provides children an opportunity to use critical and constructive thinking in the role of responding to the efforts of their peers.

Traditional Language Experience Activities also can be adapted, from the earliest grade levels, to welcome participation by the observant and curious. One systematic way of doing this is by adapting Language Charts to serve as what we have called "Wonder Charts."

**BOX 13.1 Cooperative DR-TA**

### Phase 1: Connection

In this prereading phase, students work cooperatively in small groups to activate and extend their prior knowledge. Sample options include:

1. *Brainstorming:* Students generate ideas related to a few key words provided by the teacher. They do this first in small groups, then as groups to the class.

2. *Semantic Mapping:* The ideas generated in response to the words provided by the teacher are arranged into a semantic map. Each group presents its map on the chalkboard or an overhead.

### Phase 2: Guided Independent Reading

In this phase, activities rather than the teacher guide silent reading. Sample options include:

1. *Guiding Questions:* Students answer questions (either prepared by the teacher or generated by students from previewing the material and formulating questions in groups) during reading.

2. *Outlining:* Students complete partial outlines prepared by the teacher.

3. *Paraphrasing:* Each student paraphrases a section of text. Then the groups coordinate the results to produce a new rendition of the entire selection in their own words.

### Phase 3: Follow-Up

This phase involves summarizing the test preparation. Sample options include:

1. *Summarization:* Students collectively construct a summary from the original text and/or the paraphrased renditions.

2. *Memory Training:* Students apply memory strategies to mastery of the content (see the study skills chapter for examples of these strategies).

3. *Test Making:* Each group constructs a test on the material. Groups can be urged to take one another's tests and then discuss differences in their questions, question types, and answers.

4. *Inferring:* This critical thinking activity encourages students to speculate about the thoughts, motives, and personalities of people connected to the information, including the authors.

5. *Semantic Remapping:* Students construct a postreading semantic map that reflects new information acquired and corrected misconceptions.

*Uttero (1988).*

## Wonder Charts

In a Wonder Chart, a space is provided for youngsters to tell about anything that "wonders" them. It is recorded, by the teacher or the child, and signed by the contributor. Space is provided for illustrating pictures or additional related information. Additional space is provided for "answers"—or explanations, illustrations, pictures, or book titles that relate. In this way children are taught to be question-raisers as well as question-answerers (see Figure 13.2).

BOX
13.2

## Group Reading Activity

**Step 1** The teacher identifies a unit of text to be analyzed. Then the teacher poses a larger question or directive to guide reading and problem solving.
*Examples:* Let's see if we can learn from our textbooks how plants grow. Let's see how our textbook describes the historical events that have come to be called the "Age of Discovery."

**Step 2** The teacher divides the text into subsections of a few pages each and assigns each selection to a small group (five per group is best).

**Step 3** Initially, each group member is required to read silently and record his or her findings and thoughts on the larger directive. A worksheet should be provided with guiding questions such as:

a. What questions does this section answer?

b. Write a statement of the main idea(s) of this section. Support it with direct quotes or paraphrased facts and points found in the text.

c. Comment on the quality of the ideas and supporting statements: Do these seem true? Complete? Biased?

d. What other things, ideas, and facts have you learned in the past that seem to relate strongly to what you have read? (Several illustrations by the teacher over time seem to be necessary before students handle this last question effectively.)

**Step 4** As members of the group become ready—though not before at least 10 to 15 minutes—they should begin to share their individual thoughts with one another and to create a single group rendition on a separate sheet.

**Step 5** As each group becomes ready, a student critic chosen by the teacher from one of the other groups is sent to see and hear the group's collective rendition. He or she is expected to react with constructive criticism: "That sounds fine"; "That doesn't seem to make much sense"; "Perhaps you should have . . ."

**Step 6** The group is permitted time to rework its rendition, drawing on the feedback provided by the student critic.

**Step 7** The teacher consults with each group for a few minutes, helping them resolve remaining conflicts, and then schedules them to present their findings to the class. One of the best ways to learn is to teach.

**Step 8** Each group presents its findings to the class. The class and teacher comment and question during the presentation. The teacher or a designated member of the group lists important findings on the chalkboard.

**Step 9** To build a sense of reading with power and fluency, the class is told to "rapid read" each section covered with an eye toward verifying details and main points.

*Manzo (1973).*

The keenest part of Wonder Chart activities is that they not only broaden the circle of student participants, but tend to include other teachers, library resources, newspapers, magazines, and parents. Every conceivable source of information soon becomes part of this cooperative learning activity. This activity also offers another

FIGURE
**13.2** **Wonder Chart**

| I Wonder | More | Answer | More |
|---|---|---|---|
| I wonder why dogs chase cats? Susie F. | Arf!! Hisss | I read that we really don't know why dogs chase cats. But if cats and dogs are raised together, the dogs won't chase the cats. Tom B. | See: Scholastic Magazine, Feb., 1993 |
| I wonder why cats want to eat birds? Terri K. | | I think just to eat them! Terri K. | I saw this picture in a magazine. It shows what Tom said. Kerrena J. |
| What's a "Governor"? Is he the president? | **News in Brief** Governor Mario Cuomo to Speak | This question would make a good "By Definition" book since there are many meanings for "governor": a head of state, a device to control speed, a slang word in England, a Board of Governors (like a school board). Mrs. Sykes | |

opportunity for teachers to help children bring wonder and learning home to enrich family life:

- "Dad, you're a mechanic, right? Well, we were wondering in school today how a car engine operates. Could you tell me how it works?"
- "Mom, you said that you once worked in a fish canning factory in Seattle. We were wondering today how those little sardines get so neatly into every can."

Another way to promote higher-order literacy in and beyond the classroom is based on using the REAP annotation method, detailed in Chapter 9, in the manner described next.

### Shared Response-to-Text Program

REAP annotations can be used as the basis for creating an environment that is more conducive to reading and writing at all levels of education (Eanet, 1978; Manzo, 1973, 1985; Manzo & Manzo, 1993). It begins at the classroom level simply by storing and making the various types of reader responses to text available to be shared with and possibly reacted to by students. The sharing of summary-type annotations can help weaker readers to better grasp a basic reconstructive message. A critical annotation can impart a fresh insight and deeper meaning, and encourage further constructive reading, thinking, and responding. To broaden the scope of the program, text-responders could include parents, grandparents, community members, and teachers, as well as other students. The creation of cross-generational and cross-cultural conversations among these otherwise seldom interacting groups of individuals not only stirs higher-order thinking in the classroom, but carries this objective out into the community, enriching the writing and thinking of the larger environment in which the school resides. Again children, schools, and libraries can become agents of raising the literacy levels of the host community, not merely depending on it to help them.

Three levels of exchange are possible, each increasingly demanding to implement, but each also yielding higher returns. To establish a classroom, or resource room program, the teacher merely needs some large index cards and a file box. Students are first invited to write annotations, then assisted with editing their work for it to "go public." The best written responses then are stored in the file box under the title of the book or selection to which it is a reaction. Other students then are free to read these or to scan for books and selections they may wish to read, and to guide their pre-, during, or postreading of the material. They then should be encouraged to write a response of their own, of the same or a different type.

Each file card should have an index number and be signed (optional) and dated by the reactor. Selections should be alphabetized, and reaction cards numbered. If a card is permanently removed or lost for any reason, merely invite students to use that card for the next new annotation. Reactions to previous cards should state this fact plainly: "Reaction to Card #10 by George Herman."

The prospect of establishing a response-to-text exchange program at the school or community level is greatly assisted by two new technical innovations. There now are inexpensive personal computers and text scanners (about $300 to $600) that makes it possible to "download" handwritten or typed material into the computer merely by scanning it with a hand-held or full page device. If the original material is written, the scanner will enter the material as a graphic and reproduce it as such. If the original is in print form, it can be entered right into the system's word processing software and be further edited by the teacher and the student. Material can be stored in this way for many years, and turned into hard copy and made available as "reference book" material. It also can be called up on the computer by students and read or printed on an "as needed" basis.

A committee can be formed to select the best annotations for the school- or community-based library system. It should be composed of persons who represent different perspectives. The greatest contribution of a reader response and exchange system is the creation of a literate community of readers and thinkers who are rewarded for their insightful thinking and writing, more so than for their ability merely to respond to "comprehension check" questions. In so doing, the system makes new "stars" of youngsters who think well, not merely recall well. It offers new models of thinking to admire and possibly emulate. In this way, a reader could be influenced by something written by someone, such as their own parent, a generation earlier.

## MATERIALS AND MATERIALS SELECTION

The materials available in a solid literacy program should give the same look and feel of excitement that come with seeing one's first box of crayons. It's true and clear that good teaching can be done with just a few materials; still, there is something about attractive new options, especially once you've mastered the "primary colors," that makes you want to experiment.

Publishing today is more inventive and colorful than ever before. Electronic text and microfiche readers add to the possibilities. The charge accepted by educators to teach *all* children makes these "options" no more optional today than air conditioning, power steering, and power brakes in the family car. They are aids that make it possible for us to do more and to do it efficiently. Consider this partial list of teaching materials and aids that can be found in most modern schools:

- Basal and literature programs
- Supplementary spelling, vocabulary, decoding, and writing programs
- Trade books
- Supplementary materials for teaching thinking (see Box 13.3 for recommendations)
- Reference materials: dictionaries, encyclopedia, atlas, thesaurus
- Content-rich textbooks
- Children's magazines (see Box 13.4, p. 544, for recommendations and sources)
- Pictures, maps, charts
- Worksheets and skillpacks
- Computers with software and printer setups
- File cabinet of favorite "handouts"
- Cable television, videotape player and recorder, and tape library
- Listening and viewing stations with headphones
- Prepared tests

Of these options, the heart of the literacy program today clearly is good literature. Nonetheless, in a recent study by Schell (1990), student teachers reported that many classrooms still rely on kits, worksheets, and skillpacks, and that teacher education programs should offer suggestions as to how to evaluate and use these types of materials.

---

| BOX 13.3 | **Thinking Strategies: Representative Materials** |

*Critical Thinking: Reading, Thinking, and Reasoning Skills* Burgdorf, A., & Wenck, L. S.; Steck-Vaughn Co.; P.O. Box 260115; Austin, TX 78755
*A six-book program for grades 1 through 6 organized around Bloom's taxonomy of thinking.*

*Building Thinking Skills* Edwards, R., & Hill W.; Midwest Publications; P.O. Box 448, Dept. 17; Pacific Grove, CA 93950
*A set of teacher's manuals and separate reproducible activity sheets designed to develop the analysis skills of distinguishing similarities and differences, determining sequence, classifying, and thinking analogously.*

*Primary Thinking Skills* (for Grades K through 2) Edwards, R., & Hill W; Midwest Publications; P.O. Box 448, Dept. 17; Pacific Grove, CA 93950
*A teacher's resource manual which provides detailed lessons involving children in discussion, brainstorming, creative problem solving, and fun physical activities such as drama and interviewing.*

*Breakthroughs: Strategies for Thinking* Jones, B. F., Tinzmann, M., & Thelen, J.; Zaner-Bloser; 1459 King Avenue; P.O. Box 16764; Columbus OH 43216-6764; 800-421-3018
*A grade 1–8 program based on authentic social and personal problems such as waste management, ecology, overpopulation, world economy, and substance abuse.*

*Think: The Magazine on Critical and Creative Thinking.* For teachers in grades K-8; $20 for one year. Sample copies available. ECS Learning Systems, P. O. Box 791437, San Antonio, TX 78279; 800-68-TEACH.

## SUBJECTIVE EVALUATION OF MATERIALS AND LEARNING TASKS

Heeding the request of Schell's student teachers, here are four key terms that can be used to subjectively evaluate kits, worksheets, and skillpacks. Ideas and illustrations are provided further ahead for converting even mediocre materials into more potent ones through reflective use. Think of the evaluative terms below as having the following arithmetic values $-1$, 0, 1, and 2+.

### Counterproductive ($-1$)

Certain tasks and exercises found in materials and in teachers' guides, while well intended, can induce defensive reactions that result in "avoidance" and negative learning outcomes. It is difficult to give examples of this category since it is the context, or the way these materials are presented that determines whether they are productive or counterproductive. However, here are some examples of practices that generally are at risk of becoming counterproductive:

- Whole-class spelling bees and other such highly competitive systems can breed more fear and anxiety about spelling than interest and learning (these may still be held with volunteers, and as a "team sport").
- Materials that have students who are poor readers rely on standard dictionaries to learn new words can be counterproductive, because these students rarely can

read and abstract a contextually appropriate meaning without some further guidance.

- Textual materials that are "inconsiderate," or assume knowledge that students don't have, or simply are too dense, can be frustrating and hence counterproductive (math and science materials are notorious for this, but literature with phonetic dialogue or huge casts of characters and unfamiliar place names can be equally inaccessible).
- Materials with tasks that make little instructional sense can be counterproductive (e.g., "Underline the letters of the alphabet in order as you find them on this page of print until you reach *z*").

Relatively few tasks and materials are counterproductive in and of themselves. Generally the worst that most materials and practices get is described by the next category.

### Perfunctory (0)

These are tasks and activities that are superficial, though largely harmless, except that they may waste valuable instructional time. Many "visual-perceptual" training programs contain tasks that fit in this category. They have students draw lines connecting one thing to another, to improve "eye–hand motor coordination," an operation that has no proven bearing on reading, thinking, or learning (Leibert & Sherk, 1970). Perfunctory tasks are rather like running in place: much activity, lots of sweat, but no progress to speak of.

The next concept-term refers to a category that is a considerable step above this and is characteristic of most materials and school learning tasks.

### Incremental (1)

These are tasks and materials that tend to result in average increments of learning; that is, gains that tend to be small and steady. There are many reading methods and materials that fit this description. They plug along, but often with low student participation, and little to excite pupils to think about and otherwise practice the desired learning objectives outside of the classroom setting. Such materials often lead students through repetitive exercises in a mind-numbing way. They can make a one-hour class feel like two.

Remedial level students are often fed such materials in large doses. This is particularly unfortunate, since these students are characteristically incremental learners to begin with and need something quite active and engaging to help them to continue their self-education.

### Generative (2+)

Generative tasks and activities invite thinking and learning beyond the task itself. They build an orientation toward learning that is reflected in inner rehearsals and in acquisition of *strategies for learning* as well as increments of knowledge. Generative learning, in the language of Rosenblatt (1969), is more transactional—or

---

BOX
**13.4** **Sample Children's Magazines**

The annotations below are abbreviated from *Magazines for Children*, Donald R. Stoll (Ed.). Newark, DE: International Reading Association (co-published with Educational Press Association of America), $3.50.

*Children's Album* (Grades 3–8) emphasizes creative writing and arts and crafts. It features children's original writing and artwork, and includes writing tips, educational puzzles, and seasonal/holiday craft projects. (Children's Album; PO Box 6096; Concord, CA 94520; $12 per year)

*Children's Digest* (Preteens) is a general interest magazine with an emphasis on health. Fiction, nonfiction, poems, activities, cartoons, and puzzles are featured. Each issue also contains jokes, poems, and short stories by readers. (Children's Digest; PO Box 10003; Des Moines, IA 50340; $11.95 per year)

*Children's Magic Window* (Ages 6–12) is a bimonthly general interest magazine. It includes fiction, poetry, articles, games, and activities with a contemporary "real-life" feel. (Children's Magic Window; J Publishing Company; 1008 W. 80 Street; Bloomington, MN 55420; $16.95 per year)

*Cricket: The Magazine for Children* (Ages 6–12) introduces children of all ages to some of the best literature and art from all over the world. *Cricket* seeks to stimulate children's imaginations and their love of reading. (Cricket Magazine; PO Box 51144; Boulder, CO 80321; $22.50 per year)

*Highlights for Children* (Ages 2–12) is a general interest magazine whose motto is "Fun with a Purpose." Each issue has crafts, verses, and thinking features interspersed among short stories and factual articles. (Highlights for Children; PO Box 269; Columbus, OH 43272; $19.95 per year)

*Kid City* (Ages 6–10) is a general interest magazine with an emphasis on reading and writing. It uses themes such as disguise, treasure, flight, and space to interest readers. It features photo essays, fiction, poetry, puzzles, games, and crafts. (Kid City Magazine; PO Box 2924; Boulder, CO 80322; $13.95)

---

process-oriented, than transmissional—or product-oriented. Not only do students learn the information that is put before them, but they learn *how to learn,* and they learn to value and *seek out new opportunities* to learn. In this way generative learning tasks offer the opportunity for students to learn something greater than the simple sum of the individual units of learning. This, of course, is the ultimate purpose of all instruction, and it is assumed to be part of schooling, whether we realize it or not. It is *impossible,* for example, to teach students all the possible combination of ways letters can be pronounced in *every* possible word; therefore, the implicit expectation is that they must leave the classroom and in some way engage letters, words, and print on signs, in names, and on labels in ways that ultimately result in independent learning outside the classroom.

Consider this example of how to potentially convert an incremental activity into a more generative one by attending to the social context of learning. Presume that

**BOX 13.4 cont'd**

*Ranger Rick* (Ages 6–12) is dedicated to helping students gain a greater understanding and appreciaiton of nature. It covers a range of natural history subjects with personalized adventures, animal life histories, fiction, photo/caption stories, how-to articles, jokes and riddles, crafts, plays, and poetry. (Membership Services; National Wildlife Federation; 8925 Leesburg Pike; Vienna, VA 22180; $14 per year)

*Read Magazine* (Grades 6–9) is designed for use in English and reading classes. Every issue contains a play and a short story, word games, logic puzzles, and ideas for student poems. (Read Magazine; Field Publications; PO Box 16630; Columbus, OH 43216; $6.25 for orders of 10 or more)

*Scholastic News* (Grades 1–6) is a weekly classroom newspaper, published in six separate editions for children in grades 1–6. The Teacher's Edition provides background information, discussion questions, activities, skills, reproducibles, and color teaching posters. (Scholastic; PO Box 3710; Jefferson City, MO 65102; $1.95 for grades 1 & 2; $2.25 for grades 3 & 4; $2.50 for grades 5 & 6)

*Skipping Stones: A Multi-Ethnic Children's Forum* (All ages) is a multilingual, environmentally aware magazine designed to let children from diverse backgrounds share their experiences, cultures, languages, and creative expressions. (Skipping Stones; 80574 Hazelton Road; Cottage Grove, OR 97424; $20 per year)

*Stone Soup: The Magazine by Children* (Ages 6–13) is a bimonthly literary magazine publishing fiction, poetry, book reviews, and art by children through age 13. (Stone Soup; PO Box 83; Santa Cruz, CA 95063; $23 per year)

*U*S*Kids* (Ages 5–10) has a "real-world" focus. It includes news, true-life stories, science and nature, activities, and stories. (U*S*Kids; Field Publications; PO Box 16630; Columbus, OH 43216; $18.95 per year)

*Weekly Reader* (Ages Preschool–Grade 6) is a graded series of classroom newspapers. Content includes a main news story dealing with a serious contemporary issue; articles on health, science, and safety; and a reading test. Supplements and other extras are included. (Weekly Reader; Field Publications; PO Box 16630; Columbus, OH 43216; $3.25 per school year)

a small group of students is doing comprehension practice work in SRA's Reading for Understanding Kit (Thurstone, 1969). The instructional task is to select the best word or phrase to complete a sentence or brief paragraph such as shown below.

*Sample (card 08, #5)*
Fixed stars actually move about in space but the ancients who first saw and named them were unable to discern their:

a. arrangements     b. size     c. motion     d. light

(Correct answer is *c. motion;* the key words in the sentence are *move about*)

While students do such exercises, and self-correct them, the teacher usually supervises by walking about and monitoring their work. This typically involves pausing when a student is making errors and helping the student to puzzle out the correct answer.

As described, this is a fairly solid incremental learning activity involving close analytical reading, self-pacing, self-scoring, and teacher monitoring. It is not generative, however, since feedback is shallow, there is no incentive to think deeply, and whenever the teacher stops at a desk, it is like saying that the student has erred. This causes most students to become distracted and to terminate thinking in order to solve the new social problem created by the impression that the teacher only stops to talk to those who are weak and wrong. To overcome this, students typically will quickly (and often mindlessly) select another answer so that, if they guess correctly, the teacher will keep moving.

This incremental lesson can be made more generative in a relatively simple way. The teacher need only be sure that when stopping at a desk he or she asks the student to explain *correct* as well as incorrect responses. This slight adjustment can result in several positive outcomes. First, it relieves the impression that the teacher stops only when errors are being made. Second, it gives students an opportunity to demonstrate competent as well as flawed thinking. Third, it gives the teacher a chance to reinforce and refine solid thinking. Fourth, it develops metacognition by promoting self-examination of one's own thinking and responding (Manzo & Manzo, 1993). In this same vein, DeSanti and Alexander (1986) have found that such self-instructing, self-correcting, and self-pacing materials could be made more potent when the teacher: (a) drew up contracts with students, and (b) held weekly conferences with them.

Just as weaker materials and tasks can be made more effective, usually by adding more instructional conversation, generative ones can be reduced to a countereffective state. Dialogue journals, for example, are inherently generative. They are authentic, personal, and helpful. Nonetheless, if the teacher were to demand that children write extensively in them, and the teacher were to feel *obliged* to respond to every entry, both teacher and students would become overburdened, and that which was fresh and real would have been made stale and sour.

An additional consideration in the selection of classroom materials is the subtle or overt messages about cultural and gender issues that are communicated through the text and/or pictures of the book, workbook, magazine, etc. Here again, your subjective evaluation is called for in evaluating the extent to which instructional materials fairly represent various cultures and avoid gender biases.

## CULTURAL AND GENDER ISSUES IN SELECTION OF MATERIALS

The charge to the teacher, in addressing cultural and gender issues, is a bit trickier than most would have us think. It is to raise cultural awareness while avoiding cultural stereotyping. Classroom teachers Donna Flebbe and Alice Atencio-Howe (1992) offer these "yes/no" questions to guide selection of materials. You are expected to use your judgment in determining when the proportion of negatives exceeds the value of the material.

1.  Is an oversimplified generalization being made about a particular racial group or gender?
2.  Does the information contained in the material carry any derogatory implications?
3.  Do the minority faces in the illustrations look stereotypically alike?
4.  Do the illustrations and text depict minorities in subservient and passive roles?
5.  In the materials, do whites always possess power and leadership?
6.  Do minorities and females function in subservient roles?
7.  Are problems for minority persons always solved by the benevolent intervention of a white person?
8.  Are achievements of girls and women based on intelligence and initiative, or just good looks and their relation to males?
9.  Could the same story be told if gender roles and racial identities were reversed?
10. Does the book portray white as good or black as bad?

For further information on selecting bias-free textbooks and promoting multicultural literature, see these resources:

*Guidelines for Selecting Bias-Free Textbooks and Storybooks* (1980), Council on Interracial Books for Children.

Norton, Donna (1990). Teaching multicultural literature in the reading curriculum. *The Reading Teacher* 44(1), 28–40.

For more general information and guidelines for selecting textbooks, basals, and literature, see Box 13.5. Also, see Box 13.6 for a listing of supplementary multicultural resources and magazines.

The increasing popularity of literature in the classroom is reawakening concern about the need to get children matched to books that will be accessible, in the sense of not too difficult to permit adequate comprehension and positive reading experiences. This is reigniting interest in formulas and methods for approximating "readability," or the difficulty level of text.

## ESTIMATING READABILITY

There are several formulas for asessing the difficulty level, or *readability,* of material. Most rely on measuring simple linguistic variables such as sentence length, number of syllables in words, and number of difficult words (words with a low frequency of occurrence at a grade level). However, none of these formulas, no matter how many variables they take into account, nor how complex the calculations, can yield anything more than a rough estimate of difficulty. Formulas cannot think, but teachers can. Sentences like "To be, or not to be" may be linguistically and syntactically simple, but no teacher would expect a primary school child to even begin to gather in the meaning and significance of that sentence. Materials that have been written to adhere closely to such formulas have been equally unsatisfying in what they have yielded. For example, in the late sixties and early seventies, a social

> **BOX 13.5**
>
> ## Sources of Guidelines for Selecting Reading Materials
>
> "The Eyes of Textbooks Are upon You" (1992) by K. S. Jongsma. *The Reading Teacher*, 46(2), pp. 158–160.
>
> "Guidelines for Judging and Selecting Language Arts Textbooks: A Modest Proposal: Concept Paper No. 1" (1991) by T. Shanahan & L. Knight. Urbana, IL: National Council of Teachers of English.
>
> *A Guide to Selecting Basal Reading Programs* (1986). Center for the Study of Reading. Urbana, IL: Center for the Study of Reading, University of Illinois.
>
> *Language, Authority, and Criticism: Readings on the School Textbook* (1989). S. DeCastell, A. Luke, & C. Luke (Eds.). Philadelphia, PA: Falmer Press, Taylor & Francis.
>
> *Literacy Instruction in Multicultural Settings* (1993), by K. Au. Fort Worth, TX: Harcourt, Brace, Jovanovich.
>
> *Literacy, Textbooks and Ideology: Postwar Literacy Instruction and the Mythology of Dick and Jane* (1988) by A. Luke. Philadelphia, PA: Falmer Press, Taylor & Francis.
>
> *The Politics of the Textbook* (1991). M. W. Apple & L. K. Christian-Smith (Eds.). New York: Routledge.
>
> *Report Card on Basal Readers* (1987) by K. S. Goodman, P. Shannon, Y. S. Freeman, & S. Murphy. Katonah, NY: Richard C. Owen.
>
> *Should Textbooks Challenge Students? The Case for Easier or Harder Books* (1991) by J. S. Chall & S. S. Conard, with S. Harris-Sharples. New York: Teachers College Press.

studies textbook was released by a major publisher that contained the traditional eighth-grade American History curriculum, but "written" at the third- to fifth-grade reader level. This was accomplished by: eliminating many low-frequency words (which often included key concept terms); by writing very short sentences; and, by removing all but the most "relevant" information. The result was a textbook that was terse, ill-connected, and written in completely unnatural language. It was a disaster—it could hardly be read. A similar fate befell the "linguistic readers" written for primary grades that, as indicated in a previous chapter, also were stilted and mindless:

> Matt had a hat.
> Matt had a bat.
> The bat had no hat.
> The hat had no bat.
> But Matt had a hat and a bat.

Since teachers can think and formulas can be useful in screening, consider the following simple means of establishing the readability levels of materials while enhancing your professional judgment of text difficulty and children's capacities:

- Do formula-based readability estimates on a few pieces of material (see Figure 13.3 for the Fry formula).

**BOX 13.6** **Multicultural Resources and Magazines**

**A. General Resources**

Derman-Sparks, L. (1987). *Anti-bias curriculum: Tools for empowering young children.* Washington, DC: National Association for the Education of Young Children.

Everix, N. (1985). *More windows to the world.* (For grades 2–8) Carthage, IL: Good Apple.

Greenberg, P., Ed. *Beginner's bibliography.* (Free list of children's books and magazines for parents and teachers.) National Association for the Education of Young Children; 1509 16th Street NW; Washington, DC 20036; 800-424-2460.

Graeme, J. (1990). *Hand in hand: Multicultural experiences for young children. Teacher's resource book.* (Includes 9 books in English, French, Chinese, and Spanish by Ruth Fahlman, Jocelyn Graeme, & May Henderson; for ages 3–8.). Don Mills, Ontario, Canada and Reading, MA: Addison-Wesley.

Lipson, G. B., & Romatowski, J. A. (1983). *Ethnic pride: Explorations into your ethnic heritage.* (Cultural information, activities, student research; for grades 4–9). Carthage, IL: Good Apple.

**B. Children's Magazines in Foreign Languages (for beginners)**

*Allons!* (text in French) *Bonjour!* (text in French for those with one year of study). *Das Rad* (text in German). *Que Tal* (text in Spanish). All available from Delta Systems Co., 1400 Miller Parkway, McHenry, IL 60050-7030. Subscriptions: 800-323-8270. .

*Skipping Stones: A Multicultural Quarterly Forum.* (Offers prose and poetry in both author's native language and in English; 4 issues a year for $20; for ages 8–14) Available from Aprovecho Institute; P.O. Box 3939; Eugene, OR 97043.

**C. Multicultural Children's Magazines in English**

*Cobblestone: The History Magazine for Young People.* (10 issues a year for $22.95). *Calliope: World History for Young People* (5 issues a year for $17.95). *Faces: The Magazine About People.* (9 issues a year for $21.95). For ages 8–15; available from Cobblestone Publishing, Inc.; 7 School St.; Peterborough, NH 03458; 603-924-7209.

*Daybreak Star Indian Reader.* (8 issues a year for $5.75 to students, $16 to teachers, $24 to libraries). For ages 9–14; available from United Indians of All Tribes Foundation; 1945 Yale Place, E.; Seattle, WA 98102.

*Interracial Books for Children Bulletin.* (8 issues a year for $16 to individuals, $24 to institutions; reviews children's books and activities that fairly portray races, sex, age, cultures, handicaps). Available from P.O. Box 1263; New York, NY 10023.

*Seedling Series: Short Story International.* (4 issues a year for $16; provides insights into many cultures and lifestyles). For ages 9–13; available from International Cultural Exchange; 6 Sheffield Rd.; Great Neck, NY 11020.

*Stone Soup: The Magazine by Children.* (5 issues a year for $23; stories, poems, book reviews, and art by children of different cultures and subcultures). For ages 6–13; available from Children's Art Foundation; P.O. Box 83; Santa Cruz, CA 95063.

- Purchase a computer program that automatically calculates readability estimates from samples typed into the program (the Fry formula is available, for example, from Richard C. Owens Co. of Rhode Island).
- Confirm your findings by using another form of estimation, such as Singer's (1975) SEER method or Carver's Rauding Scales (1974)—*see ahead.*

**Fry Readability Formula for Estimating Readability**

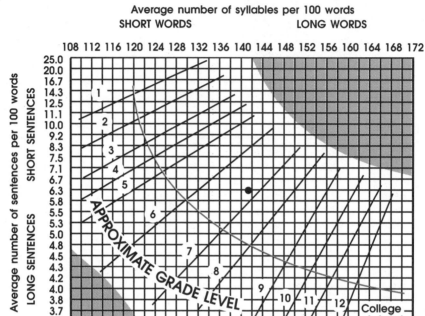

* Keep a confidential record of readability estimates on each book and refer to these when recommending books to children. Don't be afraid to permit a student access to a more difficult book if the child's interest is high.

### Fry Readability Formula

Fry (1968; 1977) developed this formula as a simplification of earlier procedures that required checking each word in a passage against a word list in order to determine the number of "hard words" it contained. In Fry's formula, the total number of *syllables* in each 100-word passage is used as a way to estimate the number of "hard words." Fry also provided a handy chart that could be used instead of a mathematical formula for obtaining the final readability estimate.

To use the Fry formula, follow these simple steps:

* Randomly select three 100-word passages from the book or material to be evaluated.
* Count the number of *sentences* in each passage, and divide by 3 to obtain the average number of sentences in the three passages. Round partial sentences to the nearest tenth. For example:

$$
\begin{array}{rcl}
\text{1st 100 words} & = & 6.6 \text{ sentences} \\
\text{2nd 100 words} & = & 5.5 \text{ sentences} \\
\text{3rd 100 words} & = & \underline{6.8 \text{ sentences}} \\
\text{Total} & = & 18.9 \text{ sentences} \\
& & \underline{\div\ 3} \\
AVERAGE & = & 6.3 \text{ sentences}
\end{array}
$$

- Count the number of *syllables* in each passage, and divide by 3 to obtain the average number of syllables in the three passages. For example:

$$
\begin{array}{rcl}
\text{1st 100 words} & = & 124 \text{ syllables} \\
\text{2nd 100 words} & = & 141 \text{ syllables} \\
\text{3rd 100 words} & = & \underline{158 \text{ syllables}} \\
\text{Total} & = & 423 \text{ syllables} \\
& & \underline{\div\ 3} \\
AVERAGE & = & 141 \text{ syllables}
\end{array}
$$

- Find the point on the graph (Figure 13.3) where the horizontal line for average number of sentences (6.3 in sample above) intersects with the vertical line for average number of syllables (141 in sample above), yielding an estimated readability of seventh grade for the sample.
- If a book or material has a great deal of variability in number of sentences and/or syllables in the three 100-word passages, simply use more than three passages to obtain the average, and note that the book has uneven readability.
- Few books will fall within the gray area on the graph, but if they do, the readability estimates should be considered invalid.

### The SEER Method for Estimating Readability

The Singer Eyeball Estimate of Readability (SEER) is a noncomputational procedure in which the material to be rated is compared with scaled paragraphs of known difficulty level. SEER readability estimates generally are within one grade level of formula estimates, and, after some practice using the scaled paragraphs, take much less time to do (Singer, 1975).

To use SEER, take a passage of about 100 words from the material to be rated. Compare it with a set of scaled paragraphs of known reading level, such as those provided in Box 13.7 below. Determine which scaled paragraph is most like the unknown paragraph. If the unknown paragraph seems to fall between two scaled paragraphs, assign a readability level accordingly. Readability estimates will be more accurate if two or more teacher's ratings are collected and averaged.

### Two Other Quick Methods

There are two other options for estimating readability that you will wish to have in your professional repertoire. These are the Rule of Thumb and the Cloze Passage Test, both described in the chapter on assessment. If you have reliable

BOX
13.7

## Sample SEER Scaled Paragraphs

Readability
Level        Paragraph

1.5    There was something in the pool!
       There it was, in the bright moonlight,
           looking up at him!
       Little Raccoon did not want to show
           he was afraid.
       So he made a face.
       The thing in the pool made a face, too.
       What a mean face it was!
       Little Raccoon turned and ran.
       He ran past Fat Rabbit so fast he
           scared him again.
       He ran and ran and did not stop till
           he saw Big Skunk
       "What is it?
       What is it?" asked Big Skunk
       "There is a big thing in the pool" said
           Little Raccoon.
       "I can't get past it!"

           Source: Lillian Moore, Little
           Raccoon and the Thing in the
           Pool. Pictures by Gioia Flammenghi.
           New York: McGraw-Hill, 1963.

3.0    Mother's clothes go dancing.
       Spring is everywhere!
       Pretty Robin Redbreast
       Laid eggs in her nest.
       Now there are
       Baby birdies three,
       Hungry as can be
       For me to see.
           Up so high
           In the sky
       Sister's swing goes up so high!
           Oh my!
       In the sky,
       Up so high,
       Brother's kite sails in the sky!
           Oh my! Oh my!
       The baby calf goes tripping.
       Spring is in the air!
       Little lambs go skipping.
       Spring is everywhere!
       Pretty flowers blooming gay
       Sister picks a big bouquet!
       Rabbits hopping,
       Long ears flopping.
       Spring is here today.

Readability
Level        Paragraph

       Easter bunny,
       Very funny,
       Pretty eggs will bring
       On Easter . . .

       Source: Lois Lenski, Spring is Here.
       New York: Walck, 1960.

2.5    There was gold dust in the air.
       Gray Burro could almost feel it.
       He could almost taste it.
       He could almost smell it.
       He said, "Well, I don't know.
       Maybe I have found something."
       The burrow's work was not too hard.
       All he had to do was carry bags of
           gold dust from the mine to the
           tramcars.
       The man threw the long stick away.
       He did not need it.
       Gray Burro was a good worker.
       When the other miners saw him they
           said,
       "What a beautiful burro.
       What a strong burro.
       What a willing worker.
       Where did you get him?"

           Source: Ann Nolan Clark, Looking for
           Something. Illustrated by Leo Politi.
           New York: Viking Press, 1952.

3.5    But when he got to the road, he saw
       Dusty coming home. The big dog
       was gone. Dusty looked very brave
       and very proud. His smooth tail was
       still high in the air. His pink tongue
       was showing and he was panting
       from his fight. Tony patted Dusty and
       praised him for saving Kitty. Kitty
       came along the path too. She
       rubbed against Dusty as if she knew
       he had saved her. Just then Tony's
       father drove up in the car. "What's
       all this?" he asked. "Dusty chased a
       big dog that was bothering
       Katherine," Tony said proudly. "He
       DID?" asked his father.

           Source: Irma Black, Dusty and His
           Friends. Pictures by Barbara Latham.
           New York: Holiday House, 1950.

**BOX 13.7 cont'd**

| Readability Level | Paragraph |
|---|---|
| 4.5 | "Then," said he, "dear wife, we can give him life again. But it will cost us both our little sons, whom we must sacrifice." |

The Queen grew pale and sick at heart, but said, "We owe it him, because of his great faithfulness."

Then the King rejoiced because she thought as he did, and he went and unlocked the chest and took out the children and Faithful John, and said, "God be praised, he is delivered and our little sons are ours again."

And he related to her how it had come to pass.

After that they all lived together in happiness to their lives' end.

*Source: Grimm, Jakob L. K., "Faithful John." In Grimms' Fairy Tales. Translated by E. V. Lucas, Lucy Crane, and Marian Edwardes. Illustrated by Fritz Kradel. New York: Grossett and Dunlap, 1945.*

| Readability Level | Paragraph |
|---|---|
| 5.0 | There were always blue and brown denim dresses and suits for every day. The Sunday clothes were more exciting. They were made of nice, dark woolens, and the girls had ruffly white aprons to wear over them. What fun it was to try things on and turn about before the mirror, while Mrs. Hyman, with her mouth full of pins, begged you to stand still! The boys did not enjoy the trying on so much. In fact Tom got all red and cross when he had to be tried on with Katie Hyman sitting by. She scarcely looked up at all, but went on stitching with her yellow curls falling down in front of her face. |

*Source: Carol Ryrie Brink, Caddie Woodlawn. Illustrated by Kate Seredy. New York: Macmillan, 1960.*

| Readability Level | Paragraph |
|---|---|
| 6.0 | "Tom's most well now, and got his bullet around his neck on a watch-guard for a watch, and is always seeing what time it is, and so there ain't nothing more to write about, and I am rotten glad of it, because if I'd a knowed what a trouble it was to make a book I wouldn't a tackled it, and ain't a-going to no more. But I reckon I got to light out for the territory ahead of the rest, because Aunt Sally she's going to adopt me and sivilize me, and I can't stand it. I been there before." |

*Source: Samuel L. Clemens, The Adventures of Huckleberry Finn by Mark Twain (pseud.) Illustrated by Donald McKay. New York: Grossett and Dunlap, 1948.*

| Readability Level | Paragraph |
|---|---|
| 7.0 | "They went down the slope, bellies flat and their bodies almost doubling in two with the urgency of their speed. Behind them came the men, but they were soon left behind. The dogs suddenly swerved, and bayed louder—for they had picked up the trail—the warm scent of new blood. |

Ahead of them Lassie galloped. Twice she halted suddenly and snapped at the flank where the bullet had creased her leg muscles. She could hear the pursuing dogs behind, but she did not increase her pace."

*Source: Eric Knight, Lassie Come Home. Illustrated by Cyrus LeRoy Baldridge. New York: Holt, Rinehart, and Winston, 1940.*

information on the reading levels of your *students*, both of these tools can be used to estimate difficulty level of books. For example, if you know that several of your students are reading on the fourth-grade level, you can use the Rule of Thumb guidelines to test reading materials. Ask these students, individually, to read a

100-word section of a book you wish to evaluate. If the students make three or four errors, the book has about a fourth-grade difficulty level. If they make fewer than three errors, the book is below fourth-grade level, and if they make five or more errors, it is above fourth-grade level.

Similarly, now that you know how to construct, administer, and evaluate a Cloze Passage Test to determine a child's approximate reading level (when the difficulty level of the passage is known), you can invert that system to estimate the difficulty level of books. To evaluate a book or basal material for whole-class use, use a selection from that material to construct a standard Cloze Passage Test. Note the range of students' scores and decide what you would need to provide in the way of instructional support for using that book with that class. Realistically, if less than half of the class scores 40 percent or above on the Cloze Passage Test, it will require more support than you are likely to be able to provide in the regular classroom setting.

The object of all formulas, whether it be the Picture Potency Formula discussed in an earlier chapter, the Fry readability formula, or the SEER system, should be to sharpen the teacher's powers of skillful estimation, reflection, decision making, and problem solving. This combining of technology and human judgment is the essence of professionalism, and, appropriately enough, the pillars of all successful classroom and school programs (see Figure 13.4).

Finally, let's consider *reading technology* as a separate topic. Much has been said about it in various places throughout this text. In all probability, you already know a good deal about it—certainly much more than was popularly known by new teachers only a half-generation ago.

## READING TECHNOLOGY

Most of all the prior technological equipment of the past now is collapsed into microcomputers—devices from rapid reading training machines to "talking type-writers" (an enclosure that contained a keyboard and screen that spoke what was typed, and sold for $44,000 each in the mid-1960s). Today's microcomputers can be used to:

- Quickly and easily spot-check readability levels of materials that are typed or scanned in
- Manage grades and observational information
- Store and generate tests
- Store and show teaching strategies (act as a teleprompter)
- Provide youngsters with a tireless tutor able to provide systematized feedback and automatic adjustments in the difficulty level of practice materials
- Score, collate, and even interpret tests and practice exercises (c.f., McEneany, 1992)
- Provide sound and graphic displays for children that are far more precise and "manipulatable" than conventional print text
- Communicate with other compatible computers and network systems
- Quickly edit and publish student work (see Box 13.8)

FIGURE
13.4 **Pillars of Professionalism**

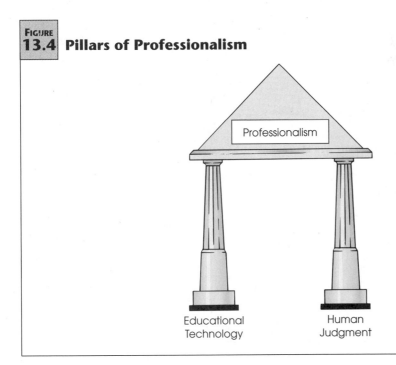

For a vivid example of what microcomputers can do, consider the software program called "Kids Can Read" (see Box 13.9).

Computers are potential marvels that were expected to revolutionize education. While they have not yet quite lived up to their advance billing, and while their promise remains great, there are certain on-going problems. Among the most persistent problems are the following:

- Lack of standardization within the industry (or incompatibility of hardware and software among the major producers)
- Equipment costs that, while forever "coming down," still remain too high for most districts
- Equipment failures and service delays
- Inexperience of most veteran teachers with this equipment—a problem aggravated by the fact that computer companies skipped over the development of software for teachers and went immediately for the larger market of student users
- Complex manuals and unfriendly user systems
- Misguided college courses that stressed computer programming—which only a few could be taught to do, more than computer usage—which almost everyone can easily be taught to do

---

**BOX 13.8**

## Using the Microcomputer Word Processor to Edit and Publish Student Work

In a special writing class, the second author began each session by giving children five minutes to write their responses to a Creative Thinking–Reading Activity (as described in Chapter 9). Students' responses then were compiled, entered into the word processor, edited, printed, and kept in a class notebook that students enjoyed browsing through to see how their classmates had responded. This system has the added benefit of incidentally modeling corrected spelling and phrasing in the edited versions of students' work in the notebook.

In the example below, the CR-TA was: *List all the uses you can think of for a paper grocery sack,* except *for carrying things:*

| | | |
|---|---|---|
| •hair rollers | •make a notepad | •make a paper umbrella |
| •draw on it | •make a pencil holder | •cut out paper animals |
| •make a dollhouse | •make a birthday card | •recycle it |
| •use it to cover a book | •make a costume | •use it to wipe your shoes off |
| •make paperdolls | •make paper mache | •make a kite |
| •make a puppet | •make paper shoes | •make a fan |
| •make a mask | •make a piñata | •make a purse |
| •make posters | •make paper rings | •cut out letters |
| •make a hat or a raincoat | •make paperdoll clothes | •make confetti |
| •make envelopes | •make paper earrings | •make paper animals |
| •make a mat to sit on | •make paper necklaces | •soak up dripping water |

The initial listing, "published" in notebook form, can also serve as a challenge to students. They can be invited to check against the published CT–RA lists, and offer new entries that can be collected and periodically added to the computer-based list for reprinting. Extra incentive can be added to this challenge by adding the name and date of the "creators" of new entries after the original list is published: "Cut it up to use for toilet paper on a camping trip" (Mark Haines, 3/93).

---

- Computer Assisted Instruction (CAI) materials that are little more than print exercises with little of the sophistication and wizardry that computers can provide
- Largely positive, though often confusing, research findings

In the latter category, consider a study by Reinking and Rickman (1990). They investigated whether intermediate grade readers' vocabulary and comprehension would be affected by *three different conditions:*

- A computer screen that provided *optional* help with certain targeted words in a reading passage
- A computer screen which was *mandatory,* in that the youngsters were required to call up the meanings of those same targeted words when encountered in the passage
- *Conventional printed pages* accompanied by a traditional glossary/dictionary containing contextual meanings for the targeted words

**BOX 13.9**    **"Kids Can Read"**

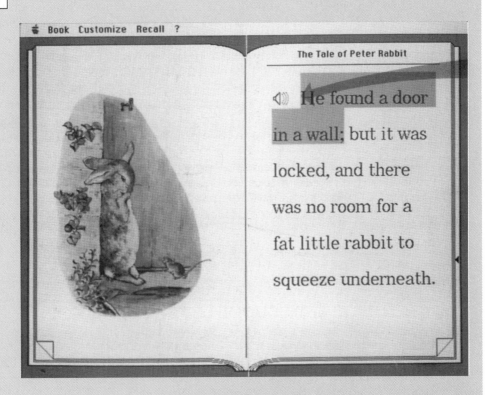

Click, double-click or press & hold on this loudspeaker icon to hear a single sentence or the rest of the Discis Book with music and sound effects. Or perhaps you want a slower reading with a variable time delay between phrases which will aid reader comprehension. As you read, phrase by phrase text highlighting is synchronized with the storytelling for easy following of text.

*Discis Books, Toronto, Ontario, Canada: Discis Knowledge Research, Inc.*
*NYCCPO Box #45099, 5150 Yonge Street.*

A new software series offers books form well-known authors. Pages from the books appear as pages on the screen, with actual text and illustrations. Additionally, real voices, music, and sound effects add life to the pages to create a vivid experience in its own right. The series operates on CD-ROMs.

As the story unfolds, the text is highlighted as it is read. Students can simply click on a word that they cannot decode, and it is pronounced for them.

Titles include *The Tale of Peter Rabbit, The Paper Bag Princess, Mud Puddle, Aesop's Fables,* and some twelve others up to high school and adult levels. These sell for approximately $40 each.

The study revealed that, overall, the two computer-based conditions produced statistically significant gains on vocabulary and comprehension over the conventional printed page. OK, so far so good, computers clearly are better, right? Well, yes and no. The study also revealed that the mandatory assistance condition was significantly better than the optional one. This meant that *every* youngster in the mandatory condition was interrupted in his or her reading by forced loop-outs to vocabulary lessons, something that is less than ideal in reading for meaning. Even more perplexing was this other finding: Subjects in the conventional glossary/dictionary condition freely chose to investigate more words than did those in optional look-up computer conditions. This is another way of saying that these youngsters were, somehow, being more drawn into the important literacy act of building interest in words and in reference materials than were those in the two conditions that showed the greatest amount learned on objective tests. Which is better now?

Obviously, this means that computers are not panaceas (cf., Reinking & Bridwell-Bowles, 1991). It also means that a good deal more research is needed, but that no technology is likely to ever rise above the need for a reflective and adaptive teacher. Of course, this could be said of any approach, method, or material. The next topic is designed to give you a sense of the "bigger picture," which is an essential perspective for a reflective inquirer and adaptive teacher.

## COMPONENTS OF THE SCHOOL LITERACY PROGRAM

Logic and experience suggest that building a quality literacy program for an entire school can be compared to the structural components of the actual school building, as shown in Figure 13.5. Each of these is briefly explained ahead, with examples from the perspectives discussed in previous chapters.

### IDENTIFYING A GUIDING PHILOSOPHY AND RATIONALE

Effective programs rarely just happen; rather, they tend to be built on a guiding philosophy and a well-thought-out rationale. These need to be stated in fairly specific terms if they are to be more than just a paper exercise. The "schools of thought" described in Chapter 2 cover most, though probably not all, of the prevailing philosophies that can serve as the foundation for a schoolwide literacy program. The philosophical bases of the whole child or "new eclectic" philosophy are as follows:

- It invites innovation but is respectful of tradition.
- It lends itself well to collaboration, or at least peaceful co-existence, among groups with different supportable philosophies.
- It is child-centered, and therefore is more likely to be grounded in the needs of the children in a particular school, and less likely to be overly influenced by strong personalities or untested ideas.

Upon taking a teaching position, look through the district and school publications. In most cases, you will find its philosophy quite well stated. Of course, like the "plat-

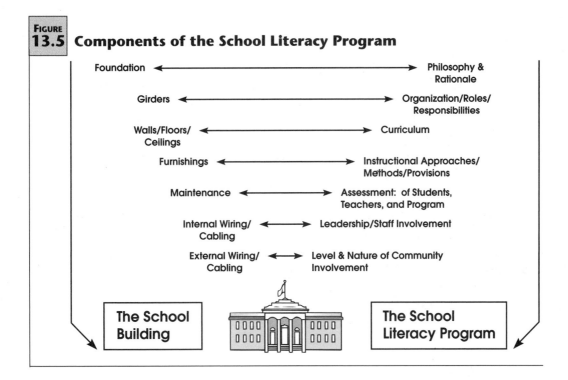

**FIGURE 13.5** **Components of the School Literacy Program**

Foundation ⟷ Philosophy & Rationale

Girders ⟷ Organization/Roles/ Responsibilities

Walls/Floors/ Ceilings ⟷ Curriculum

Furnishings ⟷ Instructional Approaches/ Methods/Provisions

Maintenance ⟷ Assessment: of Students, Teachers, and Program

Internal Wiring/ Cabling ⟷ Leadership/Staff Involvement

External Wiring/ Cabling ⟷ Level & Nature of Community Involvement

**The School Building**

**The School Literacy Program**

forms" of political parties, you might be hard-pressed to find that philosophy implemented. Nonetheless, since these philosophies tend to be well thought out, you would be wise to try to be among those who know the philosophy and who work to implement it. Don't be bashful about saying that you are doing so in your lesson plans—you will be doing the right thing, and impressing your supervisors with your sense of responsibility. Not surprisingly, teachers who show respect for stated policy are more likely to be heeded when suggesting modifications.

## ORGANIZATION, ROLES, AND RESPONSIBILITIES

The assignment of clear roles and responsibilities is essential to translation of program ideals into practice. Following are the most commonly acknowledged responsibilities of the school administrator, reading specialist, and classroom teacher.

### The School Administrator

The school principal has the primary responsibility for initiating and supporting the development and implementation of the goals, objectives, curriculum, and design of the literacy program. In this capacity, the principal is the one to initiate schoolwide survey testing, program evaluation, and on-going literacy-related faculty development programs. Equal to all else, it is the principal's responsibility to cultivate a positive school climate. It is important to note, however, that "a poor climate can inhibit learning, but a positive climate does not guarantee success" (Hoffman, 1991, p. 926).

### The Reading Specialist

As a rule of thumb, an elementary school should have one full-time reading specialist for every 150 students. Reading specialists are expected to serve as resource persons in the development of the goals, objectives, curriculum, and design of the literacy program. They typically are responsible for coordinating and interpreting schoolwide survey testing to assist in the ongoing evaluation of the literacy program, and for administering additional diagnostic tests as needed based on survey tests results and/or referrals. Reading specialists provide ongoing assistance to teachers in a variety of forms: planning in-service activities, evaluating and/or preparing instructional materials, and demonstrating new methods. In addition, they should be responsible for eliciting and coordinating the contributions of other support services such as librarians, counselors, outside consultants, and parents.

### The Classroom Teacher

The ultimate power and responsibility for the overall literacy program rests with the classroom teachers. A vital school literacy program enlists teachers' participation in the development of the goals, objectives, curriculum, design, and evaluation procedures for the schoolwide literacy program. This participation helps to ensure whole-hearted implementation of the program. Teachers' responsibilities in implementing a literacy program include careful planning of what will be taught and how it will be taught, thoughtful monitoring of student progress, and early identification of students with possible reading difficulties. Teachers also are responsible for participating with colleagues in ways that support a shared responsibility for promoting progress in reading and language arts. These interactions include working with other classroom teachers and the reading specialist(s) to evaluate, select, and develop instructional materials and methodology, and to develop appropriate intervention plans for students needing extra assistance. It is not beyond the scope of the classroom teacher to initiate classroom activities that can become school- or district-wide in scope (see the Shared Response-to-Text Program ahead in the chapter as an example).

## CURRICULUM

Curriculum is what is taught and how it is organized or presented. Two popular curriculum options in reading/language arts are:

- A developmental curriculum, or a list of skills and objectives that are sequenced from kindergarten through sixth to eighth grade

- An integrated curriculum, or a structure that may include a list of skills, knowledge areas, and concepts, and occasionally some specific themes that are used to link and deliver integrated reading/language arts and many content area objectives

With respect to the latter option, it should be noted that there is an important difference between theme-driven and concept-driven curricula. In a theme-driven curriculum, themes are selected that opportunistically teach concepts. Such themes can be superficial (e.g., "cats"). In contrast, a concept-driven curriculum attempts to identify important key concepts that teachers agree should be learned at the end of each grade, and then seeks themes that will deliver those concepts in an attractive and engaging package. Box 13.10 provides more details on the process of selection and use of a partial list of curriculum concepts. The examples given are from a K–12 concept curriculum developed by the second author, along with a team of teachers and specialists, over a two-year period. Box 13.11 provides a sample guide for unit planning, using Lambert's (1993) unit on manufacturing to teach the concept of cooperation.

## INSTRUCTIONAL APPROACHES, METHODS, AND PROVISIONS

A solid classroom, school, or district-wide program should reflect its philosophy of instruction by stating compatible instructional approaches and giving examples of fairly *specific* tactics and methods that embody and represent that philosophy. For example:

- *(the teacher)* "I endorse and work out of a child-centered orientation to classroom instruction. I try to use a variety of teaching methods and materials that meet the different interests and needs of varied children and the various and changing needs of each child. I try to plan each day to include some direct teaching, much incidental teaching, some hands-on and cooperative learning, and a good deal of personal communication through writing and oral conferences."
- *(the school)* "This school supports the importance of give and take between teacher and the class. This is exemplified in methods like the ReQuest Procedure, in which students are encouraged to question the teacher about textual material as well as to be questioned (see Appendix ___ for further details)."
- *(the district)* "The district supports school and community cooperation in helping children learn. The Shared Response-to-Text Program exemplifies this commitment." (*See ahead in the chapter for an actual description of this programming idea.*)

In addition to the importance of teaching approaches and methods, there also need to be *provisions* for instruction. This category of programming tends to involve school policy makers, such as the school board, and upper administrators more than classroom teachers. Typically, the schoolwide program should have provisions for:

- Textbook review and adoption
- Purchase of supplementary materials

BOX
13.10 **Concept-Based Interdisciplinary Curriculum**

A. *Identification of Key Concepts for each Grade.* In this project, four concepts—one per quarter—were identified as especially important for children at each grade level. They were selected to be general enough to encompass aspects of most subject areas. Teachers could develop quarterly units around these that were as short as one week or that extended throughout the entire nine weeks of the quarter. The key concepts were further organized into the four "concept domains" shown in the sample below.

**Sample Key Concepts**

Concept Domains:

| Grade | Self-Actualization | Organizing & Expressing Information & Ideas | People & the Environment | Problem-Solving |
|---|---|---|---|---|
| | Quarter 1 | Quarter 2 | Quarter 3 | Quarter 4 |
| K | Self & Family | Sequence | Patterns | Observation |
| 1 | Cooperation | Similarity/Difference | Growth | Measurement |
| 2 | Citizenship | Categorization | Adaptation | Choices |
| 3 | Community | Symbol Systems | Natural Resources | Inference |
| 4 | Point of View | Graphing | Regions | Predication |
| 5 | Propaganda | Cycles | Balance | Interpretation |
| 6 | Freedom | Causality | Consumption | Exploration |
| 7 | Self-Reliance | Contrast | Production | Decision Making |
| 8 | Rights | Aesthetics | Leisure | Goal Setting |

B. *Concept Descriptions and Quarterly Goals.* A brief description of each quarterly concept was written, and basic goals for the unit were articulated. Quarterly goals included multicultural and self-esteem goals as well as knowledge goals.

**Sample Concept Description & Goals**

*Grade 3, Quarter 1: Community*
*Description:*
Natural and/or social communities are groups in which members have common characteristics. The commonalities tend to nurture continuity of the group through changing membership.
*Goals:*
*Multicultural* To understand that human cultures establish and maintain community by keeping their customs alive, and passing them on through the generations.
*Knowledge* To recognize the characteristics that give communities a visible identity.
*Self-Esteem* To recognize the common beliefs and values shared by individuals within a community.

C. *Subject Area Objectives Organized by Quarterly Concepts.* Objectives in each subject area were reviewed by grade level, and organized and/or revised to be as applicable as possible to the four quarterly key concepts for each grade level.

D. *Guides for Unit Planning.* Sample units were available for teachers to use or modify, but teachers were also encouraged to develop their own concept-based interdisciplinary units. See Box 13.10 for a sample planning sheet for developing unit activities.

**BOX 13.11**  **Unit Activity Planning Sheet**

*Sample Unit Activity Planning Sheet*

### Interdisciplinary Lesson Planner

School _____    Grade ___1___    Quarter ___1___
Teacher __(Lambert)_____    Concept __Cooperation_____

Concept Description: _Cooperation is the process of working_
_together in ways and toward ends that are mutually beneficial_

Activity: _Assembly Line Production of Greeting Cards_____

General Description: _Students apply the principles of assembly_
_production to produce greeting cards, learning the benefits of_
_cooperation and division of labor._

Estimated Length of Unit (in days): __10 days_____

Summary of Interdisciplinary Connections (briefly describe
how various subject objectives will be addressed in this activity)

| | |
|---|---|
| Reading reading and following directions; reading and evaluating greeting card messages | Science forming, testing & revising hypotheses about drying times for glues & paints |
| Writing writing directions; writing greeting card messages | Social Studies applying and evaluating the effect of division of labor production |
| Listening listening effectively in whole class and small group discussions & planning meetings | Art evaluating the effect of various design layouts using pictures and print |
| Speaking contributing appropriately in whole-class & small-group discussions & activities | Music evaluating the effect of background music of various kinds during assembly line work |
| Mathematics identifying & communicating with symbols & geometric forms | Physical Education/Health taking safety precautions in cutting, carrying, collating, etc. |

- Acquisition of extensive classroom libraries of trade books
- Audiovisual services
- Teaching assistants/aids
- Consultation with resident and external specialists

- Teacher in-service
- Student needs assessment

Several of these topics are covered ahead. Needs assessment is discussed next.

## NEEDS ASSESSMENT IN THE LITERACY PROGRAM

Once the school literacy program has been defined, it is essential to gather information on how it is being implemented, and the effects it is having on both students and teachers. This type of information should be collected regularly and unobtrusively by the school reading/language arts specialist(s) and cross-verified by an independent "audit" from an outside team of consultants every three to five years. Surveys guided by outside consultants help identify problems that have a way of cropping up in school operations where day-to-day pressures can erode sensitivity to flaws in policy and procedure. Effective businesses routinely budget for such periodic surveys and reviews. It is a fundamental form of quality control.

The school survey should be guided by a comprehensive model that avoids unnecessary disruption of the basic school program. Such disruptions, which are all too common, can be prevented by:

- Using as much existing data as is available from standardized testing
- Collecting data informally and regularly from informal diagnostic-teaching systems and instruments (e.g., IRIs, ITIs, Cloze tests, etc.)
- Using a stratified random sample of students rather than testing all students (typically a random sample of 20 percent of students from different age, grade, and IQ levels, and from different feeder areas, is more than adequate to yield an evaluative picture of a *school's* needs as opposed to those of individual children).

As an aid in determining the types of assessment instruments that should be used, and in structuring data interpretation, we suggest Weiner and Cromer's (1967) "4-D" Diagnostic Model. This model guides assessment into four possible problem areas that can hamper reading and academic success. This broad spectrum model tends to orient assessment and program design toward the whole child rather than segmented skills. The title "4-D" serves to remind schools to include assessment in the categories of: "defects"—IQ and other more or less constitutional factors; "deficits"—analysis of reading skills needs; "disruptions"—emotional interferences; and "differences"—linguistic and cultural incompatibilities with the implicit expectations of schooling. For more precise information on these categories, and some of the informal and formal means by which they may be assessed, see a text on diagnosing reading/literacy needs, such as Baumann (1988b), Harris and Sipay (1990), or Manzo and Manzo (1993).

Another means of encouraging comprehensive assessment of the schoolwide literacy program has been offered recently by Paris and associates (1992). This assessment model covers five phases of assessment:

*Phase 1:* Identifying dimensions of literacy

*Phase 2:* Identifying attributes of literacy dimensions

*Phase 3:* Methods for collecting evidence about literacy proficiency

*Phase 4:* Scoring students' work samples

*Phase 5:* Interpreting and using the data

This assessment model is designed to address "whole literacy" (reading, writing, knowledge about literacy, etc.) through "authentic assessments"—that is, through measures that are grounded in classroom performance. The centerpiece of this assessment model is the identification of specific attributes of the various dimensions of literacy (Phase 2). Paris et al. (1992) developed specific "performance indicators" for seven of these literacy dimensions. See Box 13.12 for one example, and Appendix D for the full listing. Notice how the evaluation scheme implicitly allows for the evaluation of speaking and listening. Because this model is grounded in specific classroom behaviors, it can be used to "help students to engage in monitoring and evaluating their own work, to reflect on their efforts and accomplishments, and to gain insights into the processes of learning that will help them in future tasks" (Tierney, Carter, & Desai, 1991).

In addition to assessing student progress, the school district should periodically survey teachers for their confidential input. This is different from merely involving teachers in authentic literacy assessment. The survey form should allow ample space for open-ended responding. In this way, appropriate authorities can be informed of possible administrative, organizational, and morale problems that may require their attention. Sometimes the smallest glitch can take on irritating and divisive proportions if teachers are aware of it, but administrators appear to be oblivious. Ironically, this step is becoming more important now that schools have been winning greater autonomy from central office control. The break from one source of autocracy can sometimes result in new power brokers taking control, in the form of principals who can come to act like feudal lords and from parent groups who can

---

## BOX 13.12     Sample Performance Indicator

### Reading Is Evaluative

| *Low engagement* | *High engagement* |
|---|---|
| a. Fails to use personal knowledge and experience as a framework for interpreting text | a. Uses prior knowledge and experience to construct meaning |
| b. Is insensitive to the author's style, assumptions, perspective, and claims | b. Is sensitive to, and may even question, the author's style, assumptions, perspective, and claims |
| c. Fails to examine or go beyond a literal account of the ideas in the text | c. Expresses opinions, judgments, or insights about the content of the text |

*Paris, Calfee, Filby, Hiebert, Pearson, Valencia, & Wolf (1992), p. 93.*

make quirky demands that may overly interfere with day-to-day operations. Reports of problems of this type are beginning to build, so we will all need to learn more about how to deal with them. In any case, a yearly survey of teachers, preferably by an independent monitoring committee, should provide a bit of prevention before such matters get out of control. Ideally, a committee of teachers should conduct and oversee this survey. They should be granted some release time and a budget to hire consultants to help with data analysis and interpretation. This may seem costly and excessive, but self-regulation is just as valid an objective for institutions as metacognition is for young learners.

## LEADERSHIP AND STAFF INVOLVEMENT

What is needed in a school leader, whether it be a principal, a reading/language arts coordinator, or a proactive teacher? This question, important as it is, cannot be answered fully, since research has tended to focus largely on designated leaders such as principals. But we can learn from these studies. Accordingly, let's look at a particularly concise summary analysis done by Vogt (1991) of research on effective school principals (Erickson, 1990; Fullan, 1985; Hord & Goldstein, 1982; Paulu, 1989; Vanderpool, 1990; Venezky & Winfield, 1979). Vogt's critique revealed that those who were most successful in implementing positive change were individuals who:

- Bring focus to the change process and tailor efforts to their particular schools
- Maintain open communications, especially by listening to students, faculty, staff, policy makers, and community members
- Encourage and provide staff development for everyone involved, including themselves
- Form instructional leadership teams that encourage collaborative planning and decision making
- Know how to get things done even with limited resources
- Are able to see and articulate a larger picture, and avoid getting bogged-down by details
- Create an atmosphere where ideas can flourish and where reasonable risk taking and initiative are rewarded
- Understand and can tactfully remind everyone that change cannot take place overnight, and that everyone must think constructively as well as critically.

Here are four ways to keep things going and growing. The first, suggested by Vogt (1991) herself, is to get decisions set down on paper. As an example, she offers a detailed "observation guide" for guiding development of an integrated reading/language arts program. This guide, shown in Box 13.13, clearly is the result of many hours of meetings and discussions. A second strategy for keeping a program of change going and growing is to look for and use available resources from the literature of the field—including a school or district's own publications. Everyone seems to agree in principle that we should not have to rediscover the wheel in order

**BOX
13.13**    ## Observation Guide Used to Develop an Integrated Reading/Language Arts Program

### Reading

In this classroom, is the teacher:

- modeling and sharing his/her own joy of reading?
- recommending books of interest to students?
- providing a variety of literature genres (e.g., short stories, novels, poetry, biographies, essays, informational books, magazines, etc.)?
- providing time for daily, self-selected silent reading?
- reading aloud to students on a daily basis?
- requiring a minimum of oral reading practice by the students (and providing silent practice before any oral reading)?
- incorporating thematic units in language arts instruction?
- providing skills (e.g., phonics) instruction for those needing it, not in isolation but within meaningful contexts?
- utilizing a variety of grouping strategies for instruction (e.g., whole class, flexible small groups, partners, cooperative learning groups)?
- providing opportunities for students to read independently and work individually on some tasks?
- utilizing strategies that promote discussion, divergent thinking, and multiple responses?
- assigning reading tasks that promote collaboration and cooperation among students?
- planning reading tasks and strategies that activate and utilize students' prior knowledge before, during, and after reading?
- asking questions that encourage and promote dialogue, inquiry, and critique?
- encouraging a variety of responses to literature and to questions that are asked about the literature?
- collecting portfolio assessment data that is authentic in nature (e.g., transcribed, taped, or analyzed retelling) and selected for inclusion by the student and teacher so that the student, parents, and teacher all are involved in assessing progress?
- using portfolio data to guide instructional decisions and individual instruction?

### Writing

In this classroom, is the teacher:

- modeling and sharing his/her own joy of writing?
- modeling and teaching the stages of the writing process (prewriting, drafting, sharing, revising, editing, publishing)?
- assigning daily writing for a variety of purposes to a variety of audiences?
- encouraging divergent, creative thinking through writing assignments?
- encouraging students to use their writing as a natural response to literature?
- incorporating invented ("temporary") spelling strategies for beginning readers/writers?
- encouraging more mature writers to attempt invented spellings when composing, then assisting them with checking for correct spellings during editing?
- regularly conferring with each student about his/her writing?
- responding to student writing with helpful suggestions, thoughtful comments, and very little "red-marking"?

BOX
**13.13**
cont'd

## Observation Guide Used to Develop an Integrated Reading/Language Arts Program

- promoting student self-assessment and peer conferences for the revision and editing stages?
- displaying and publishing student writing?
- collecting portfolio assessment data that is authentic in nature (e.g., samples of writing in various stages and journal entries) and selected for inclusion by the student and teacher so that the student, parents, and teacher all are involved in assessing progress?
- using portfolio data to guide instructional decisions and individual instruction?

### Listening

In this classroom, is the teacher:

- promoting listening as a means of learning?
- providing opportunities for students to hear other students' responses to literature they have read?
- providing a variety of listening experiences for differing purposes (e.g., "sharing" time, reports, Readers Theatre, students' rehearsed oral reading, etc.)?
- reading aloud to students from narrative and expository text and from poetry selections?
- providing discussion opportunities for students to collaborate, cooperate, and compromise?
- promoting social skills through listening (e.g., providing and maintaining eye contact, paraphrasing to demonstrate understanding, and summarizing what was heard)?

### Speaking

In this classroom, is the teacher:

- providing daily opportunities for structured oral langauge development (e.g., choral reading, speeches, drama, "sharing" time, oral reports, debates, discussion)?
- modeling and teaching correct language usage?
- teaching students to facilitate group discussion?
- modeling and teaching language for a variety of purposes (e.g., informing, persuading, sharing feelings, evaluating, imagining, predicting)?
- using literature and student writing as a source for oral language development?

### General

In this classroom, is the teacher:

- actively observing and noting or recording students' responses and participation during reading/language arts instruction?
- enabling all children to make choices about what they read and write?
- resisting labeling students in terms of ability or achievement?
- communicating to parents the tenets of integrated reading/language arts instruction?
- encouraging parents to read to their children, discuss literature with them, and support and encourage their reading and writing progress?
- providing a structured reading environment where opinion, creative thought, and sharing of ideas are valued?
- celebrating literacy and learning on a daily basis?
- participating in staff development activities and then attempting to implement newly learned ideas?

*Vogt (1991), pp. 208–209.*

to build a cart. Nonetheless, there are file cabinets in most every school that contain valuable but unheeded reports, curriculum guides, and implementation plans. File cabinets are a part of an institution's memory. If they are not consulted, the institution can no more grow in wisdom than can a person who has lost access to past life experience. The novice teacher who is wise enough to access prior efforts can expect to learn a good deal and win some positive attention as a reflective educator.

The third way to keep a program of school revitalization on target is through staff development. There are several excellent staff development models that can be used, depending upon purpose and goals. For example, Gaskins (1988) offers one that focuses on helping teachers adapt to the needs of children with learning problems. Santa (1988) and Tierney et al. (1988) offer programs of change built around teacher-researcher collaboration efforts. These and other options are described in a special monograph of the International Reading Association called *Changing School Reading Programs* (Samuels & Pearson, Eds., 1988: write to IRA; 800 Barksdale Road; Newark, DE 19714). For a more recent model that focuses on comprehension improvement and is especially suitable to inner city circumstances, we recommend the Comprehension and Cognitive Development Program described by George, Moley, and Ogle (1992). The latter is a teacher in-service training model that addresses implementation more than planning. It is based on the finding that before a teacher can be expected to use a relatively simple strategy at a routine level, it takes about 15 to 20 times of seeing the strategy modeled, and 10 to 15 times of practicing it (Joyce & Showers, 1982).

Our own experience as teacher trainers at the pre- and in-service levels suggest that these numbers may be excessive, but perhaps not by much. It clearly takes quite a bit of observation and practice to become proficient at doing anything new. Educators are coming to recognize that in order to think reflectively, teachers need to practice a few methods until they can use them smoothly; that is, until they can pay more attention to the children than to the strategy.

Two of the more interesting and potentially powerful aspects of the George-Moley-Ogle model are its use of teacher portfolios and videotapes on which teachers can rate themselves. Teachers are encouraged to rate themselves on a simple scale in terms of both their knowledge and level of use of each strategy component or instructional interaction activity. The rating system recommended by George (1990) includes four of the levels described in the Concerns-Based Adoption Model developed by Loucks, Newlove, and Hall (1975):

(0) Non-Use

(1) Mechanical Use

(2) Routine Use

(3) Refined Use

Teachers are encouraged to include videotapes and ratings in their professional portfolios. See Box 13.14 for a professional portfolio system designed to help a teacher record and plan an entire professional career in education (Manzo & Manzo, 1990a).

**Professional Portfolio Recorder and Planner**

A Professional Portfolio, begun early in your career, can be an invaluable lifelong resource. To construct the Portfolio, you will need the following materials:

- a 3-ring binder (you may want to begin with a 1" binder, and transfer materials to a larger size binder as your collection grows)
- nine 3-hole punched notebook "pockets" for storing materials in various sections of the portfolio (see below)
- attachable index tabs to mark each section (attach these to the "pockets," since these extend farther than regular-sized sheets)
- the following section descriptions, copied onto separate sheets for insertion into the notebook, between "pockets"

With these simple materials, and a bit of reflection on your past, present, and future, you are ready to assemble a basic Portfolio that will grow with you through your professional career.

*Section I:  Guiding Thoughts*
*In this section, record relevant quotations you run across that strike you as worth remembering, and that can serve to keep your thinking and instructional decision-making on track.*

A.  Thoughts and perspectives on careers in general
   *Examples:*

- Successful careers don't just happen; they are the result of vision, planning, and effort.
- Most successful careers are beset by occasional setbacks. Expect these, and be ready to push on.
- When truth stands in your way, you are headed in the wrong direction.

B.  Thoughts and perspectives on teachers and teaching
   *Examples:*

- The art of teaching is the art of assisting discovery.
- The enthusiastic teacher is a lifelong student.
- The finer the instruction, the more it invites; the poorer it is, the more it compels.

C.  Thoughts and perspectives on schools and schooling
   *Examples:*

- Nowadays, school heads are chosen to *run* a school rather than lead it.
- The school's task is to take a lot of live wires and see that they get well grounded.

*Section II:  Employment Record*
*In this section, keep a running record of both teaching and non-teaching experiences, and store an updated resume.*

A.  Nonteaching job experiences

B.  Educational job experiences

C.  Other
(Pocket: current resume)

**BOX 13.14 cont'd**

*Section III:   Personal History (Birth to High School)*
*In this section, make relevant notes about your family and early school background, and store related documents.*

A.   Family background
B.   Medical/health factors
C.   Social, athletic, religious affiliations
D.   Academic record, K–12
E.   Hobbies and interests
F.   Significant memories
(Pocket: birth certificate, passport, school records, early photos, letters, memorabilia)

*Section IV:   Personal History (Postsecondary)*
*In this section, make notes about your college life and education, and store related documents.*

A.   Academic record (degrees, majors, minors)
B.   Activities (extracurricular, organizational, religious, athletic)
C.   Social life (personal and family)
D.   Intellectual development (books, magazines, ideas)
(Pocket: transcripts, letters of reference, other records)

*Section V:   Material Accounting*
*In this section, keep notes about your financial standing and store related documents.*

A.   Gifts, trusts, support
B.   Income history
C.   Loan history
D.   Assets (stocks, car, furniture, property)
E.   Approximate net worth
F.   Prospects (likely legacies and/or opportunities)
(Pocket: financial records, photos, memorabilia)

*Section VI:   Professional History*
*In this section, make notes about your teaching career, and store related documents.*

A.   Certificates
B.   Evaluations/recommendations
C.   Memorable teachers and colleagues
D.   Teaching experiences: subjects, grade levels, situations
E.   Related nonteaching roles and experiences
F.   Memorable in-service, conferences, sabbaticals
G.   Memorable articles, books, papers
H.   Membership and roles in committees and professional organizations
I.   Grants, travel, awards
J.   Summer activities and employment
(Pocket: teaching certificates, letters, papers or summaries)

---

**BOX
13.14**
cont'd

## Professional Portfolio Recorder & Planner

*Section VII:   Self-Appraisals*
*In this section, keep notes on an ongoing self-assessment, and store related records.*
A.   Attitudes
B.   Interests and abilities
C.   Temperament/personality
D.   Teaching/learning style
E.   Personal assessment of strengths and weaknesses as a person and as a teacher
(Pocket: records)

*Section VIII:   Occasional Notes*
*In this section, make additional notes of memorable events and experiences, and store related records.*
A.   Notes on memorable personal events (marriage, deaths, births, friendships)
B.   Notes on memorable professional experiences (significant mentor relationships, special students)
(Pocket: records)

*Section IX:   Blueprints*
*In this section, keep notes about long-term career plans, and store related documents.*
A.   Personal career goals
B.   Objectives that might contribute to your professional education
         (Pocket: related articles, notes, and documents)

*Section X:   Teaching Competence*
*In this section, keep notes about your experiences in using various teaching approaches and methods, and store related materials.*
A.   Teaching methods you have mastered
B.   Teaching methods you intend to try
(Pocket: related articles and notes on each method)

---

The fourth, though hardly final, way to help keep a staff and program vital is through professional study groups, or peer-led explorations and sharing of information on pertinent works in education and individual teachers' experiences and perspectives on these. Sanacore (1993) makes these critical points about such groups:

- They are designed at a grassroots level, and hence tend to be more relevant to teachers' felt needs.
- Every effort should be made to avoid having the agendas for such meetings dominated by its sponsors, whether this is a school administrator, a teacher's union, or a parent/teacher organization.
- It can be important to find out what other groups are doing and learning. One way to do this is through electronic networking systems, such as one reported by

Watts and Castle in the May, 1992 issue of *Phi Delta Kappan,* called the American National Education Association's School Renewal Network.

One other aspect of staff development and involvement should not be overlooked, although it frequently is. It is the need to arrange symposia, or problem-solving meetings, on troublesome issues and student needs. Focused meetings of this type, with or without invited consultants, can be more pointed than conventional "show and tell" workshops or study groups. The intent of such symposia is not necessarily to *present* fixed solutions, but to challenge teachers to think through problems and possible solutions that could be tried and appraised. Doing this typically involves accessing the available research literature. Symposia of this type tend to invite increased dialogue between university researchers and school-based practitioners. They also can be designed to enhance community involvement, by inviting participation from area professionals and social service agencies. The next section addresses other aspects of community involvement that also have great potential for enhancing the school program.

## LEVEL AND NATURE OF COMMUNITY INVOLVEMENT

Volunteer workers can be a rich resource for school programs. Volunteers can be assigned to help teachers prepare class materials, assemble library resource materials for class projects, and assist in classrooms when children are working on small-group activities. They can help with planning special events such as career days and writing fairs, and even make special presentations to students on places they have been and special interests they pursue. When opening a school to community input however, it is not cynical to take some care that the school does not become a platform for well-intentioned but potentially meddlesome parents and community activists. For example, volunteers need to be told that they do not, and should not, have access to confidential information, especially on children or staff, any more than should volunteer aids in hospitals. It should also be clearly understood by all that while volunteers can and should be included on many planning committees, the final word on all educational decisions rests with the school administrators and faculty. It should also be kept in mind that young and inexperienced teachers will make some mistakes. The presence of community members in the building could serve to draw attention to more of these mistakes than would otherwise be noticed. However, it also can be a "blessing in disguise." When problems that might be hidden are made evident, there is opportunity to address them before they grow worse. Further, the presence of volunteer assistants gives administrators and teachers more time to work on trouble spots.

School/business partnerships are more popular today than ever before, and can be mutually satisfying if not downright remarkable. For an example of the remarkable, consider a recent project initiated by the late Ewing Kaufman, founder of Merriam-Merrill-Dow Pharmaceutical Company and owner of the Kansas City Royals baseball team. Mr. Kaufman has offered to pay full college costs for all students who stay drug-free and graduate from his alma mater, Westport High School of Kansas City, Missouri. The first class to complete four full years in the program

| BOX 13.15 | **School/Business Partnership Activities** |
| --- | --- |

1. Support after-school tutoring and remedial programs
2. Mentor individual students, as in big-brother/big-sister programs
3. Offer part-time work opportunities to youngsters
4. Contribute to classroom and/or school library fund by purchasing titles submitted by the school
5. Offer to pay a portion of consulting costs
6. Provide guest readers, visiting individual classrooms to read aloud a favorite selection from children's literature
7. Sponsor a visiting author of children's books
8. Sponsor fund-raising events, such as bake sales and carnivals

graduated in 1992, with a significant decrease in dropouts and more than double the number of students planning to attend college the next year. School/business partnerships, like individual volunteer programs, need to be structured in advance with both parties agreeing on goals and expectations. This can be initiated by providing interested business representatives with a list of ways that could provide assistance (see Box 13.15).

This kind of up-front planning is the key to successful school/business partnerships. No one gives away large sums of money without the expectation of some form of return. It is good to know from the onset of a relationship what the other parties' interests happen to be, since seemingly common interests almost always diverge at some point. Both business and education, for example, are committed to quality education. However, educators tend to be committed to better schooling for the sake of *individuals,* while the business leaders tend to value educational reform for the purpose of producing a better *workforce,* without excessive tax-funded costs, thus creating a better business climate (Leibert, 1992). Clearly, both business leaders and educators can profit from an on-going dialogue that could lead business to see the world in less "balance sheet and bottom-line" terms, and have educators come to better appreciate how artificial our environment can become when classroom walls are made impermeable to the outside world (Burnett, 1992). Potential misunderstandings are easily minimized. We, as teachers, simply must remember to keep our professional obligations to children as our top priority. This will help us to resist largesse that may come with too many strings attached.

## IN CLOSING

As a final note, it is appropriate to reiterate a theme running throughout this text: Effective education must be a blend of empirically based research, modern technology, human experience, and constant reflection on and concern for the *whole child,* not merely a child's academic progress as measured by standardized tests. As professionals, we must continue to strive to teach and care about objectives that are still difficult to measure. These include values and objectives such as:

- Love of reading and learning
- Respect for others
- Appreciation for tradition
- Ability to accept criticism, and courage to offer it
- Belief in our individual and collective ability to continue to reach constructive solutions thrugh discovery, invention, and creation, rather than muscle, exclusion, and dominance

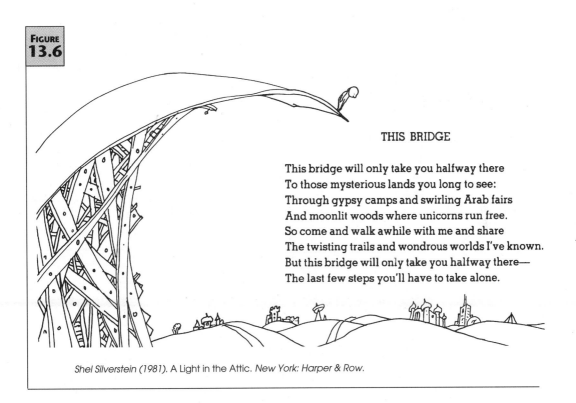

**FIGURE 13.6**

THIS BRIDGE

This bridge will only take you halfway there
To those mysterious lands you long to see:
Through gypsy camps and swirling Arab fairs
And moonlit woods where unicorns run free.
So come and walk awhile with me and share
The twisting trails and wondrous worlds I've known.
But this bridge will only take you halfway there—
The last few steps you'll have to take alone.

*Shel Silverstein (1981).* A Light in the Attic. *New York: Harper & Row.*

This need for reference to our highest values, as well as our research and technology, is the source and foundation of teacher empowerment. Building personal strength in and commitment to each of these needs seems an appropriate and practical way to have strong schools, a strong profession, and literate children.

**W**here You've Been

## The Classroom and School Literacy Program

**Grouping for Instruction**

Ability Grouping
Whole-Class Instruction
Literature-Based Instruction
 with Flexible Grouping
Self-Selected or Individualized
 Reading
Cooperative Learning Groups
Higher-Order Literacy

**Components of the School Literacy Program**

Philosophy and Rationale
Organization, Roles, and
 Responsibilities
Curriculum
Instructional Approaches,
 Methods, and Provisions
Needs Assessment in the
 Literacy Program
Leadership and Staff
 Involvement
Level and Nature of
 Community Involvement

**Materials and Materials Selection**

Subjective Evaluation of
 Materials
Culture and Gender Issues
Estimating Readability
Reading Technology

## *Reflective Inquiries and Activities*

1.  What kind of policies will guide the way you group for instruction? Why?

2.  Set up an operating response to text exchange program for your college class. Note and solve logistical problems. Concentrate your annotations on any or all of the following: sections of the textbook; related articles and studies; children's books.

3.  If readability interests you, try the formula(s) provided on a few self-selected material pieces (see #6 ahead). To learn more about readability, check the indexes of other reading textbooks for the following names of leading readability researchers: Edgar Dale and Jeanne Chall, Rudolph Flesch, George Klare, John Gunning; and from this chapter, Ronald Carver, Edward Fry, John Bormuth, and Harry Singer.

4.  Most schools of education have a section put aside for instructional materials. Go find an instructional material that interests you, write a summary and critique of it, and report your findings to your class. Include an assessment of a few recommended tasks on the counterproductive (−1) to generative (2+) scale described in the chapter. If every class member does one or two such reports, and duplicates these for distribution, you will have a healthy reference collection of materials in use.

5.  As a capstone activity, study the illustration on page 577 and make the following judgments:
    a.  Estimate its readability level.
    b.  How would you prepare children to read orally?

# Animal Tales

**ABOUT THE AUTHOR**  Demi, an award-winning writer and illustrator of children's books, says that "to capture life on paper is magic." Demi's illustrations have been influenced by her studies of art in Mexico and India and by her trips to China.

**SELECTION SUMMARY**  Two fables are retold. In the first, a bear, unaware of some bees, is stung while he is stealing honey. The fable teaches that we often see only what we want to see. In the second fable, a fox tricks a tiger into letting him go. The fable teaches that small creatures must live by their wits.

## Building Background

**Provide background and access prior knowledge about fables.**

Ask children to name other fables they have heard or read. Remind them of the fables "The Tortoise and the Hare" and "The Fox and the Grapes" and the lessons they teach. Tell children that they will read two more fables that teach lessons. Mention that the fables are about a bear, some bees, a tiger, and a fox. Then help children develop a chart telling what these animals look like.

| Bear | Bees | Tiger | Fox |
|------|------|-------|-----|
| large | small | large | bushy tail |
| shaggy coat | wings | black stripes | pointed nose |

**SECOND-LANGUAGE SUPPORT** Explain that bees store honey in something called a honeycomb. Explain that a honeycomb is made of wax and has many small openings. (See Second-Language Support Manual.)

## Strategic Reading

**Help children make predictions and set purposes.**

Ask children to read the titles of both fables and to look at the pictures. Tell them that the bear and the tiger are both looking for something to eat. Ask children what they think will happen.

**STUDENT–SET PURPOSE**  Help children use their predictions to set a purpose for reading "Animal Tales."

**TEACHER–SET PURPOSE**  If children have difficulty setting a purpose, have them read to find out what will happen as the bear and the tiger look for something to eat.

Have children read the fables with their purposes for reading in mind.

*Treasury of Literature, Teacher's Edition.*

*Harcourt Brace Jovanovich 1993. Used by permission.*

   c. Review the "discussion" questions that follow and decide if you think they are adequate. If not, why not?

   d. Rank the overall lesson (as shown) from the introductory remark to the discussion questions, using the subjective concept terms discussed in the chapter.

   e. Is there anything you would change or do differently in using the play to teach youngsters to be strategic readers?

6.  Select one of the components of the school literacy program that particularly strikes your interest, and write/tell about how you see yourself developing further expertise in that area. Consider including the following in your discussion: graduate study; a fresh vision; collaborative research; apprenticeship; reading and independent study.

7.  Begin to fill out the Professional Portfolio Recorder and Planner. See what you have done and accomplished and what you need to attend to. Some of the information categories are quite personal, so you need not record or share these now, but it's not too soon to begin thinking about them. In the financial category, remember to ask about 403b savings plans when you start work. They represent a special opportunity given to us by the government to build financial security, since we don't have the benefits of stock options and profit sharing. You owe it to yourself to learn about these.

Be a great teacher, and have a wonderful career!

# APPENDIXES

## APPENDIX A

---

### PICTURE POTENCY FORMULA (PPF)

Children respond to some pictures much more readily than to others. The Picture Potency Formula (PPF) is a useful means of estimating the language stimulation value inherent in different pictures before planning language arts instruction. It can be used for selecting instructional materials and for planning language development activities for reticent children.

The PPF is not perfect. It does not include *all* factors that might be relevant to the language stimulation value of pictures. In fact, the researchers did not attempt to evaluate each of the many factors that might be involved. Rather, they simply included almost all factors that could be easily observed. The result proved to be a surprisingly valid and reliable instrument.[*]

### CALCULATING A PICTURE POTENCY FORMULA SCORE

There are two steps to calculating the PPF Score. The first step is obtaining raw scores for factors A–J, as described in the PPF worksheet shown in Box A-1. The second step is to convert the raw scores into scaled scores, using the Conversion Chart also shown in Box A-1, and adding the scaled scores to obtain the total score. Picture 1 is scored as an example. To test your understanding of the formula, try scoring Pictures 2 and 3. The language stimulation value of Picture 2 will most likely be a surprise. If you are unconvinced of the validity of the score, give it the final test: Count the total number of sentences and/or questions spoken by children in response to each of the three pictures shown. Our data[*] suggest the following ranges for Total Scaled Score on the Picture Potency formula:

| | | |
|---|---|---|
| 38+ | = | high language stimulation value |
| 32–37 | = | medium high value |
| 28–31 | = | medium low value |
| below 28 | = | low value |

---

[*] Manzo & Legenza (1975b), Legenza & Knafle (1978; 1979), Lengenza (1980), Samson & Wescott (1983).

---

**BOX A.1** **Picture Potency Formula Worksheet and Scaled Score Conversion Chart**

*PPF Worksheet*

| PPF Factors | Raw Score | Scaled Score |
|---|---|---|
| **Factor A. Different Things**   Number of different things in the picture (e.g., people = 1 thing; hills = 1 thing) | ____ | ____ |
| **Factor B. Significant Things**   Number of significant things (e.g., things the picture seems to be mostly *about*) | ____ | ____ |
| **Factor C. Total Things**   Number of things, excluding *only* nondescript things like blades of grass, undifferentiated trees, birds, etc. | ____ | ____ |
| **Factor D. Colors**   Number of different colors | ____ | ____ |
| **Factor E. Action**   Number of actions in progress (a group of people can *all* be engaged in essentially *one* action). | ____ | ____ |
| **Factor F. Children**   Count the number of children present. | ____ | ____ |
| **Factor G. People**   Count the total number of *people* present (count children again). | ____ | ____ |
| **Factor H. Movement**   Count the total number of things with *potential* for movement (other than people), such as cars, motion toys, planes, animals, etc. *Count animals twice:* the heuristic value of animals is strong. | ____ | ____ |
| **Factor I. Size**   Estimate the size of the picture—see Scaled Score Conversion Chart for size categories. | ____ | ____ |
| **Factor J. Empathy**   Assign the picture a value from 1 (low) to 5 (high) for its overall compatibility with the interests and experiences of the children with whom it will be used. Factors such as racial similarities, empathetic quality of the setting (urban, rural, etc.), and familiarity with the event being depicted should be heavily weighted as positive factors. | ____ | ____ |

**Total Scaled Score**   ____

Use the chart to convert the raw score for each factor into a Scaled Score of 1–5:

*Scaled Scores*

| PPF Factors | 0 | 1 | 2 | 3 | 4 | 5 |
|---|---|---|---|---|---|---|
| A. Different Things | (0–1) | (2–5) | (6–8) | (9–12) | (13–19) | (20+) |
| B. Significant Things | (0) | (1) | (2) | (3) | (4–6) | (7+) |
| C. Total Things | (0) | (1–3) | (4–5) | (6–7) | (8–9) | (10+) |
| D. Colors | (0–1) | (2) | (3–5) | (6–7) | (8–9) | (10+) |
| E. Action | (0) | (1) | (2) | (3) | (4) | (5+) |
| F. Children | (0) | (0) | (0) | (1–2) | (3–4) | (5+) |
| G. People | (0) | (0) | (1) | (2) | (3) | (4+) |
| H. Movement | (0) | (1–2) | (3–4) | (5–6) | (7–8) | (9+) |
| I. Size | 2 x 2 or under | 4 x 4 | 5 x 7 | 8 x 10 | 11 x 14 | larger than 11 x 14 |
| J. Empathy | (0) | (1) | (2) | (3) | (4) | (5) |

Use the PPF Worksheet and Conversion Chart to estimate the language stimulation value of Picture 1 below, then match your estimations with those below.

Picture 1: Children on Beach

## PPF Estimation for Picture 1: Children on Beach

| FACTOR | EXPLANATION | RAW SCORE | SCALED SCORE |
|---|---|---|---|
| A. Different Things | animals, sand, people, trees, debris, water, boats, building, helicopter, freight package, cliffs, sky, sun | 13 | 4 |
| B. Significant Things | children & alligator, boat rescue, helicopter, freight package | 4 | 4 |
| C. Total Things | people, lighthouse, thatched house, helicopter, package, cliffs, 2 boats, debris, trees, 2 animals, stick, sand, water, sky, sun | 13 | 5 |
| D. Colors | green, blue, brown, red, yellow, pink, grey | 7 | 3 |
| E. Action | children & alligator, boat rescue, climbing onto boat, helicopter | 4 | 4 |
| F. Children | 2 | 2 | 3 |
| G. People | 13 (including children) | 13 | 5 |
| H. Movement | alligator, spider (double value for alligator & spider), 2 boats, helicopter | 7 | 4 |
| I. Size | 22 × 18 | 5 | 3 |
| J. Empathy | (inner city children in mind) | 3 | 3 |
| | **Total Picture Potency Scaled Score** | | **38** |

Here are two more samples to try. Our estimations are provided on the next page.

Picture 2: Cookie Jar

| FACTORS | RAW SCORES | SCALED SCORES |
|---|---|---|
| A. Different Things | —— | —— |
| B. Significant Things | —— | —— |
| C. Total Things | —— | —— |
| D. Colors | —— | —— |
| E. Action | —— | —— |
| F. Children | —— | —— |
| G. People | —— | —— |
| H. Movement | —— | —— |
| I. Size | —— | —— |
| J. Empathy | —— | —— |

Picture 3: Shoe

| FACTORS | RAW SCORES | SCALED SCORES |
|---|---|---|
| A. Different Things | —— | —— |
| B. Significant Things | —— | —— |
| C. Total Things | —— | —— |
| D. Colors | —— | —— |
| E. Action | —— | —— |
| F. Children | —— | —— |
| G. People | —— | —— |
| H. Movement | —— | —— |
| I. Size | —— | —— |
| J. Empathy | —— | —— |

## PPF Ratings for Pictures 2 and 3

| Factors | Picture 1 Cookie Jar | Picture 2 Shoe |
|---|---|---|
| A. Different Things | 3 | 4 |
| B. Significant Things | 2 | 2 |
| C. Total Things | 5 | 5 |
| D. Colors (actual) | 2 | 4 |
| E. Action | 1 | 5 |
| F. Children | 3 | 5 |
| G. People | 2 | 5 |
| H. Movement | 1 | 3 |
| I. Size | 4 | 4 |
| J. Empathy | 5 | 5 |
| **Total Scaled Score** | **28** | **42** |

# APPENDIX B

## TEACHER'S PRIMER ON PHONICS*

The terms *phonetics* and *phonics* have slightly different meanings. *Phonetics* refers to the science of speech sounds, whereas *phonics* refers to the application of phonetics to word analysis and recognition. The term *phonics* sometimes is used more broadly to refer to all aspects of instruction in word analysis, including structural analysis, syllabication, and rapid recognition of words. Additional key terms are defined below:

**Accented Syllable**  Syllable that receives the greatest stress in a word (di'-gest; char'-ac-ter)

**Breve**  A diacritical mark (ˇ) used to indicate the short sound of a vowel (măd; rĕd)

**Closed Syllables**  A closed syllable ends with a consonant phoneme (sup-pose')

**Consonant Blend**  A combination of two or more consonant phonemes, with each maintaining a distinguishable sound (*bl*ack; *gr*and; co*ld*)

**Diacritical Marks**  A set of marks used to indicate how to pronounce a letter or groups of letters

**Digraph**  A grapheme composed of two letters which represent one phoneme where the speech sound of each is not distinguishable, as in a blend (consonant digraph: *ch*in; *th*ink; vowel digraphs: br*ea*d; g*oo*d)

**Diphthong**  A single vowel phoneme resembling a "glide" from one sound to another (c*oi*n; h*ou*se)

**Grapheme**  The written symbol used to represent a phoneme. It may be composed of one or more letters, and the same grapheme may represent more than one phoneme. (The 26 letters of the alphabet in their various combinations form 251 graphemes that represent from 44 to 46 phonemes.)

**Macon**  A diacritical mark (¯) used to indicate the long (glided) sound of a vowel (cōld). Long vowel sounds make their alphabet names.

**Morpheme**  A letter cluster that carries meaning (non; anti). These are not really relevant to phonics instruction, but for the fact that each is a pronounceable syllable and may even be a word (with*out*; *out*side).

**Open Syllable**  An open syllable ends with a vowel phoneme (fe'-ver). The second syllable in *sup-pose* is not an open syllable because the *e* is silent.

**Phoneme**  The smallest unit of sound which distinguishes one word from another. There are 44–46 phonemes, depending on a few debatable distinctions.

**Schwa**  A vowel sound that is soft, unaccented, and indistinguishable from other vowel sounds. It sounds like the first and last "a" in *America*. The symbol /ə/ is used to represent the sound, as in *cut* which would be shown as (kət) in a typical pronunciation guide.

---

* Assembled from previous works by Cordts (1965), Hull (1976), and Manzo & Manzo (1993).

**Syllable**    The basic unit of pronunciation. There are as many syllables in a word as there are separate vowel sounds; there is only one vowel phoneme in a syllable. The actual pronunciation can vary from syllable to syllable; for example, *differential* is syllabicated dif-fer-en-tial, but it is more frequently pronounced as dif'-ə-ren'-chəl.

## CONSONANT GENERALIZATIONS

1. Consonants tend to represent only one phoneme (for example, *l* almost always represents the /l/ sound in *like*—with notable exceptions below).
2. A phoneme may be represented by more than one consonant letter (*ph* used to represent the /f/ sound in *phoneme*).
3. A consonant blend is made up of two or three consonant letters, each of which retains its own sound (*bl*ack; *sp*ider; co*ld*; *w*e*nt*).
4. A consonant digraph is made up of two consonant letters that represent a single sound (*ch*icken; ele*ph*ant).
5. The letter *c* has no sound of its own. It usually takes the sound of /s/ (known as its "soft" sound), or /k/ (its "hard" sound). When *c* is followed by *a*, *o* or *u*, it usually has the hard sound. When *c* is followed by a consonant, except the digraph *ch*, it has the hard sound.
6. There are several consonant letters that can be silent:

   a. When a double consonant appears in a word, the first is sounded and the second is silent (be*l*l; pu*p*py).
   b. The letters *b* and *p* followed by *t* are silent (de*b*t; recei*p*t).
   c. The letter *b* following *m* is silent (dum*b*; thum*b*).
   d. The letter *c* following *s* is sometimes silent (s*c*ience; s*c*ent).
   e. The letter *g* before *n* is usually silent (*g*naw, *g*nome, si*g*n; but *not* signal).
   f. The letter *h* following a vowel is usually silent (o*h*; e*h*; a*h*).
   g. The letter *k* before n is silent (*k*now; *k*not).
   h. The letter *l* before *d*, *k*, or *m* in some words is silent (cou*l*d, but not co*l*d; wa*l*k, but not po*l*ka; ca*l*m, but not fi*l*m).
   i. The final letter *n* following *m* is usually silent (hym*n*, but not hym*n*al).
   j. The letter *p* before *s*, *n*, or *t* in many words is silent (*p*salm; *p*neumonia; *p*tomaine; but not a*p*t).
   k. The letter *s* in some words is silent (ai*s*le; i*s*land).
   l. The letter *t* in such words as of*t*en and cas*t*le is silent.
   m. The letter *w* before *r* is usually silent (*w*rite; *w*rench).
   n. The letters *gh* in the combination *ght* following a vowel are usually silent (ri*gh*t; ou*gh*t).

## VOWEL GENERALIZATIONS

1. Vowels may represent more than one phoneme: each of the five regular vowels has a short sound and a long sound, as well as other sounds when they occur in diphthongs and vowel digraphs. Each of the five regular vowels also may take the soft schwa sound, as in *America*.
2. A phoneme may be represented by more than one vowel letter (l*oo*k).
3. A letter may represent no phoneme; that is, it may be silent (tak*e*).

4. When a one-syllable word or accented syllable contains two vowels, one of which is a final *e*, the first vowel usually represents its long sound, and the final *e* is silent (rope; cake).

5. A single vowel in an open accented syllable often represents its long sound (ta-ble).

6. A single vowel in a closed accented syllable usually represents its short sound (cab-i-net; dog).

7. When *i* is followed by *gh,* or when *i* or *o* is followed by *ld,* the vowel usually represents its long sound (sigh; gli-de; so-ld).

8. If only the vowel letter in a word or syllable is followed by *r*, the vowel sound will be affected by the *r* (car-ton; sh*i*rt).

9. If the only vowel in a word or syllable is an *a* followed by *l* or *w*, the sound of the *a* is usually that heard in *tall*.

10. When two vowel letters appear together in a one-syllable word or in an accented syllable, the first vowel often has its long sound and the second vowel is silet. This holds true most often for *ai, oa, ee, ey,* and *ay* combinations, or, "When two vowels go walking, the first does the talking" *(sail; boat; feet; say).*

## RULES FOR DIVIDING WORDS INTO SYLLABLES

1. Two identical consonants are divided to form two syllables (lit-tle; bet-ter).

2. The number of vowel *sounds* in a word indicates the number of syllables (*cave*—one vowel sound, *a*, one syllable); *caboose*—four vowels but only two vowel sounds, therefore two syllables—ca-boose).

3. Two unlike consonants generally also are divided to form syllables (mar-ket). *Exceptions:* do not divide between blends and digraphs (be-tween, *not* bet-ween).

4. When the first vowel in a two-syllable word is followed by a single consonant, the consonant usually goes with the second syllable (pa-per).

5. Each small word in a compound word usually is a syllable (cow-poke; horse-fly).

6. Prefixes and suffixes usually form separate syllables (un-pleas-ant; re-pay-ment).

7. When the ending *ed* is preceded by *d* or *t,* the *ed* forms a separate syllable (boast-ed; strand-ed).

## RULES FOR PRONOUNCING WORDS BASED ON SYLLABLES

1. *Le* is pronounced as *ul* when it appears at the end of a word (little; battle).

2. A syllable ending in a vowel often has a long vowel sound (be-tween).

3. When a vowel does not complete a syllable and is followed by two consonants, it has a short sound (ap-ple; pic-nic).

## RULES FOR ACCENTING WORDS

1. When a word contains a prefix or a suffix, the accent usually falls on or within the root word (ex-change').

2. In compound words, the accent usually falls on or within the first word (car'-pool).

3. In a two-syllable word that functions as either a noun or a verb, the accent is usually on the first syllable when the word functions as a noun and on the second syllable when the word functions as a verb (dis'-card [noun]; dis-card' [verb]).

4. When there is a double consonant within a word, the accent usually falls on the syllable that ends with the first letter of the double consonant (bub'-ble).

5. In multisyllabic words ending in *tion,* the primary accent falls on the syllable preceding the *tion* ending (dic-ta'-tion; ju-bi-la'-tion).

6. When the vowel phoneme in the last syllable of a two-syllable word is composed of two vowel letters, that syllable is usually accented (re-coil'; de-tain').

# APPENDIX C*

## VOCABULARY OF SENSES

### THE SENSE OF SOUND: A LIST OF WORDS

| | | | |
|---|---|---|---|
| babble | croon | jangle | quiet |
| bang | crow | jaw | racket |
| bark | crunch | jeer | rant |
| bawl | cry | jingle | rap |
| bay | deaf | knock | rasp |
| beat | deafening | laugh | rattle |
| bell | din | laughter | rave |
| bellow | drawl | lecture | recite |
| blab | drone | lisp | rhythm |
| blabbermouth | drum | listen | ring |
| blare | dumb | loud | ripple |
| blast | eavesdrop | low | roar |
| bleat | echo | melody | roll |
| blubber | fizz | melodious | rumble |
| boom | gab | mew (meow) | rustle |
| bray | gabble | moan | say |
| buzz | giggle | monotone | scream |
| cackle | gobble | monotonous | screech |
| caw | gong | moo | shriek |
| chant | gossip | mum | shrill |
| chat | groan | mumble | shout |
| chatter | growl | murmur | silent |
| cheep | gruff | mute | silence |
| cheer | grumble | mutter | sing |
| chime | grunt | neigh | singsong |
| chirp | gurgle | noise | siren |
| chuckle | harmony | overhear | sizzle |
| clamor | hear | pad | slam |
| clang | hiss | patter | smack |
| clank | hoarse | peal | snarl |
| clink | honk | peep | snort |
| cluck | hoot | pitch | snuffle |
| converse | howl | plunk | song |
| coo | hubbub | pop | sonic boom |
| crackle | hullabaloo | prattle | sound |
| crash | hum | preach | soundless |
| creak | hush | purr | speak |
| croak | jabber | quack | speech |

* From Frazier, A. (1970). Developing a vocabulary of the senses. *Elementary English, 47*(2), 176–187.

## THE SENSE OF SOUND: A LIST OF WORDS

| | | | |
|---|---|---|---|
| speechless | tap | trumpet | whiney |
| splash | tattle | tune | whinny |
| splutter | thud | twang | whisper |
| squall | thump | twitter | whistle |
| squawk | thunder | undertone | whoop |
| squeak | tick | uproar | yap |
| squeal | tinkle | vocal | yell |
| stammer | toll | voice | yelp |
| stereophonic | tom-tom | volume | yip |
| still | tone | wail | yodel |
| strum | tongue-tied | warble | yowl |
| stutter | toot | weep | |
| supersonic | tread | whimper | |
| swish | trill | whine | |

## THE SENSE OF SIGHT: A LIST OF WORDS

| | | | |
|---|---|---|---|
| admire | brunet | flicker | handsome |
| appear | clean | foggy | hazy |
| appearance | clear | freckled | homely |
| array | color | gaudy | hue |
| attractive | colored | gawk | illusion |
| auburn | colorful | gaze | image |
| beautiful | colorless | glance | indistinct |
| beauty | crystal | glare | invisible |
| becoming | dappled | glasses | light |
| binoculars | dark | gleam | look |
| black | darken | gleaming | looking glass |
| blare | dazzle | glimmer | magnify |
| blaze | dazzling | glimpse | microscope |
| blazing | dim | glint | mirage |
| bleached | dingy | glitter | mirror |
| bleary | dirty | glittering | misty |
| blind | discolor | glisten | mottled |
| blindness | discolored | glistening | murky |
| blink | distinct | gloom | nearsighted |
| blond | drab | gloomy | notice |
| blot | dusky | gloss | observe |
| blue | dye | glossy | observant |
| blur | eye | glow | obsever |
| blurred | eyewitness | glowing | observation |
| bright | fade | goggle | ogle |
| brighten | faded | good-looking | orange |
| brightness | faint | gorgeous | pale |
| brilliance | fair | gray | pastel |
| brilliant | farsighted | green | peek |
| brindle | flash | grimy | peep |
| brown | flashy | hallucination | peer |

| | | | |
|---|---|---|---|
| periscope | see | spectacle | transparent |
| perceive | shade | spectator | twinkle |
| perception | shadowy | spectrum | twinkling |
| picture | sharp-sighted | splotched | ugly |
| pigment | sheen | spotted | ugliness |
| pink | sheer | spy | unattractive |
| polished | shimmer | squint | view |
| pretty | shimmering | stain | viewpoint |
| purple | shine | stained | visible |
| radiance | shining | stare | vision |
| radiant | shiny | streak | vista |
| recognize | show | streaked | visual |
| red | showy | stripe | visualize |
| reflect | sight | striped | watch |
| reflection | smeared | sunny | watchful |
| reflector | smudged | survey | well-groomed |
| reveal | soiled | tarnish | white |
| review | sooty | tarnished | witness |
| scan | sparkle | telescope | yellow |
| scene | sparkling | tinge | |
| scrutiny | speckled | tint | |

## THE SENSE OF TOUCH: A LIST OF WORDS

| | | | |
|---|---|---|---|
| alive | feathery | hit | rub |
| blush | feel | hot | sandy |
| blushing | feeling | humid | scratch |
| bristly | feverish | itch | scratchy |
| brush | firm | juicy | sharp |
| bumpy | flabby | jumpy | shiver |
| caress | flat | lifeless | shivering |
| chill | fluffy | light | shivery |
| chilly | flush | limp | shudder |
| coarse | flushed | lukewarm | shuddering |
| cold | fondle | lumpy | shuddery |
| coldness | fumble | massage | shove |
| contact | furry | maul | silky |
| cool | fuzzy | moist | slap |
| crawly | gooey | numb | slick |
| creepy | grab | oily | slimy |
| crisp | grasp | pat | slippery |
| cuddly | grainy | peck | smooth |
| dab | greasy | pet | soft |
| damp | gritty | pinch | solid |
| deadened | gummy | powdery | spongy |
| downy | hairy | prickly | springy |
| dull | handle | pull | squashy |
| dry | hard | push | squeeze |
| dusty | heavy | rough | stiff |

| | | | |
|---|---|---|---|
| sticky | tag | ticklish | vibrate |
| sting | tap | tingle | vibrating |
| stinging | temperature | touch | warm |
| stretchy | tepid | tough | warmth |
| strike | texture | toughtened | wet |
| stroke | thorny | uneven | woolly |
| sweaty | tickle | velvety | |

## THE SENSE OF TASTE: A LIST OF WORDS

| | | | |
|---|---|---|---|
| acid | high-seasoned | seasoned | tangy |
| appetizing | honeyed | seasoning | tart |
| biting | hot | sharp | taste |
| bitter | insipid | sip | tasteless |
| bland | luscious | sour | tasty |
| curdled | mellow | spice | unappetizing |
| delicious | nauseating | spiced | unflavored |
| distasteful | palatable | spicy | unpalatable |
| flavor | peppery | spoiled | unripe |
| flavored | ripe | stale | unseasoned |
| flavorless | rotten | sugary | untainted |
| flavorsome | salty | sweet | vinegary |
| gingery | savor | tainted | yummy |
| green | season | tang | |

## THE SENSE OF SMELL: A LIST OF WORDS

| | | | |
|---|---|---|---|
| aroma | incense | rank | stench |
| aromatic | moldy | reek | stink |
| bouquet | musty | scent | stinky |
| deodorant | odor | scented | strong-scented |
| deodorize | odorless | smell | strong-smelling |
| deodorized | perfume | smelly | sweet-scented |
| deodorizer | perfumed | sniff | sweet-smelling |
| fragrance | pungent | snuff | whiff |
| fragrant | putrid | spice | |
| fumes | rancid | spicy | |

# APPENDIX D*

## PERFORMANCE INDICATORS FOR EACH ATTRIBUTE AND DIMENSION OF LITERACY

### Engagement with Text Through Reading

| LOW ENGAGEMENT | HIGH ENGAGEMENT |
|---|---|
| *Reading Is Constructive* | |
| a. Fails to build on prior knowledge | a. Integrates new ideas with previous knowledge and experiences |
| b. Few inferences or elaborations; literal retelling of text | b. Exhibits within text and beyond text inferences |
| c. Focus is on isolated facts; does not connect text elements | c. Identifies and elaborates plots, themes, or concepts |
| *Reading Is Evaluative* | |
| a. Fails to use personal knowledge and experience as a framework for interpreting text | a. Uses prior knowledge and experience to construct meaning |
| b. Is insensitive to the author's style, assumptions, perspective, and claims | b. Is sensitive to, and may even question, the author's style, assumptions, perspective, and claims. |
| c. Fails to examine or go beyond a literal account of the ideas in the text. | c. Expresses opinions, judgments, or insights about the content of the text |

### Engagement with Text Through Writing

| LOW ENGAGEMENT | HIGH ENGAGEMENT |
|---|---|
| *Writing Is Constructive* | |
| a. Writes disconnected words or phrases with few identifiable features of any genre | a. Writes well-constructed, thematic, cohesive text that is appropriate to the genre |
| b. Fails to use personal knowledge as a base for composing text | b. Draws on personal knowledge and experience in composing text |
| c. Little evidence of voice, personal style, or sense of voice, personal style, and originality | c. Creative writing reveals a strong originality |

* Paris et al. (1992). A framework for authentic literary assessment. The Reading Teacher, 46, (2), 93–95.

### Writing Is Technically Appropriate

a. Writing includes numerous violations of the conventions of spelling, punctuation, and usage

a. Displays developmentally appropriate use of the conventions of spelling, punctuation, and usage

b. Inappropriate or inflexible use of grammatical structure appropriate to the purpose

b. Writing exhibits grammatical structures and genres

c. Limited and contextually inappropriate vocabulary

c. Rich, varied, and appropriate vocabulary

## Knowledge About Literacy

**LOW KNOWLEDGE**                  **HIGH KNOWLEDGE**

### Knowledge About Literacy Conventions and Structures

a. Unaware of the functions of print conventions and punctuation in written communication

a. Understands the functions that print conventions and punctuation play in written communications

b. Unaware of text structures and genres

b. Can identify and use several specific text structures and genres

c. Unaware of the subtleties of language use; does not understand or use connotative meaning, ambiguity, or figurative language

c. Understands that words have multiple meanings; can use and understand ambiguity and figurative language

### Knowledge About Strategies

a. Unaware of the strategies that can be applied while reading and writing

a. Knows strategies that can be applied before, during, and after reading and writing

b. Limited understanding of how strategies can be applied while reading or writing

b. Can explain how strategies are applied or might be used

c. Naive about the value of strategies; does not use strategies selectively

c. Understands how and when strategies can be used and why they are helpful

## Orientation to Literacy

**LOW ORIENTATION**                  **HIGH ORIENTATION**

### Motivation for Reading and Writing

a. Goals for literacy are task completion and extrinsic rewards

a. Goals are intrinsic and mastery oriented

b. Gives up easily in the face of difficulty

b. Persists when confronted with obstacles or difficulties

c. Chooses tasks where success or failure are certain

c. Chooses challenges tasks on the edge of current abilities

*Attitudes About Reading and Writing*

a. Negative attitude about reading and writing

a. Exhibits enthusiasm for reading and writing

b. Exhibits embarrassment, passivity, and insecurity about self as a reader or writer

b. Exhibits pride and confidence about self as a reader or writer

c. View literacy events as under the control of others' contributions

c. Views self as in charge of own literacy and feels others' respect

# Ownership of Literacy

| **LOW OWNERSHIP** | **HIGH OWNERSHIP** |
|---|---|

*Interests and Habits*

a. Expresses little or no preference for topics, genres, and authors

a. Exhibits clear preferences for topics, genres, and authors

b. Avoids reading and writing as free choice

b. Voluntarily selects reading and writing as free-choice activities

c. Does not choose texts to read or topics to write about appropriately

c. Chooses appropriate texts to read and topics for writing

*Self-Assessment of Reading and Writing*

a. Rarely evaluates own work, learning, or progress

a. Frequently assesses own work, learning, and progress

b. Shows little initiative in evaluating own work

b. Takes initiative to review and monitor own performance

c. Uses single, vague, or unclear criteria in assessing own work

c. Employs appropriate criteria to evaluate what has been read or written

# Collaboration

| **LOW COLLABORATION** | **HIGH COLLABORATION** |
|---|---|

a. Little participation with others; engages in isolated activities

a. Frequently engages in collaborative literacy activities

b. Unwilling to engage in the collaborative debate about text meaning

b. Initiates discussion, dialogue, or construction of meaning

c. Reluctant to give or seek help; does not encourage the literacy development of peers

c. Provides positive support, affect, and instructional scaffolding for peers

*Community of Learners*

a. Does not share goals, values, and practices with others

a. Shares goals, values, and practices with others

b. Does not participate, or plays only a limited array of roles, in the learning community

b. Plays a variety of roles (performer, audience member, leader, supporter) within the learning community

c. Is unaware of the contribution others can make to one's own literacy development

c. Values the contributions of others' opinions and help

## Connectedness of the Curriculum

| LOW CONNECTEDNESS | HIGH CONNECTEDNESS |
|---|---|
| *Within School* | |
| a. Views reading and writing as decontextualized activities | a. Understands that reading and writing are tools for learning and personal insight |
| b. Views reading, writing, speaking, and listening as independent of each other | b. Views reading, writing, speaking, and listening as mutually supportive activities |
| c. Sees little relation between reading and writing and other content area | c. Understands that what one learns in reading and writing is useful in other content area |
| *Beyond School* | |
| a. Rarely engages in reading and writing outside of school | a. Reading and writing are part of daily routine activities |
| b. Views the school literacy curriculum as unrelated to one's own life | b. Connects school literacy activities with reading and writing and daily life |
| c. Feels discouraged and unsupported for reading and writing outside of school | c. Feels encouraged and supported to read and write outside of school |

# REFERENCES

**Adams, M. J.** (1990). *Beginning to read: Thinking and learning about print.* Cambridge, MA: MIT Press. **[6]**

**Adler, R.** (1985). Using closed-captioned television in the classroom. In L. Gambrell & E. McLaughlin (Eds.), *New directions in reading: Research and practice* (pp. 11–18). Silver Spring, MD: Yearbook of the State of Maryland International Reading Association. **[11]**

**Afflerback, P.** (1993). Report cards and reading. *The Reading Teacher, 46*(6), 458–465.

**Aiken, E. G., Thomas, G. S., & Shennum, W. A.** (1975). Memory for a lecture: Effects of notes, lecture rate, and information density. *Journal of Educational Psychology, 67,* 439–444. **[10]**

**Al-Hilawani, Y.** (1991). Keyword strategy. *Indiana Reading Quarterly, 23*(4), 21–26. **[8] [10]**

**Allain, V.** (1990). *Teaching as a researching profession: Some initiatives.* Paper presented at the National Conference of the Association of Teacher Educators.

**Allen, I. A.** (1991). Teachers as researchers. *Journal of Reading Education, 17*(2), 24–28. **[2]**

**Allen, R. V.** (1976). *Language experiences in communication.* Boston: Houghton Mifflin. **[2] [6]**

**Allen, R. V., & Allen, C.** (1969). *Teachers' resource book: Language experience in early childhood.* Chicago: Encyclopedia Britannica Educational Corp. **[2]**

**Alley, G., & Deshler, D.** (1980). *Teaching the learning disabled adolescent: Strategies and methods.* Denver, CO: Love. **[8]**

**Allington, R. L.** (1983a). Fluency: The neglected reading goal. *The Reading Teacher, 36,* 556–561. **[6]**

**Allington, R. L.** (1983b). The reading instruction provided readers of differing reading abilities. *Elementary School Journal, 83,* 548–553. **[4] [13]**

**Alvermann, D. E.** (1991). The discussion web: A graphic aid for learning across the curriculum. *The Reading Teacher, 45*(2), 92–99. **[10]**

**Anders, P. L., & Bos, C. S.** (1986). Semantic feature analysis: An interactive strategy for vocabulary and text comprehension. *Journal of Reading, 29,* 610–616.

**Anderson, B.** (1981). The missing ingredient: Fluent oral reading. *Elementary School Journal, 81,* 173–177.

**Anderson, L. M., Evertson, C. M., & Brophy, J. E.** (1979). An experimental study of effective teaching in first-grade reading groups. *Elementary School Journal, 79,* 193–222. **[2]**

**Anderson, R. C., Hiebert, E. H., Scott, J. A., & Wilkinson, I. A.** (1985). *Becoming a nation of readers: The report of the Commission on Reading.* (Contract No. 400-83-0057). Washington, D.C.: National Institute of Education. **[1] [4]**

**Anderson, R. C., Mason, J. M., & Shirley, L.** (1984). The reading group: An experimental investigation of a labyrinth, *Reading Research Quarterly, 20*(1), 6–38. **[13]**

**Anderson, R. C. & Nagy, W. E.** (1989). *Word meanings* (Tech. Rep. No. 485). Cambridge, MA: Bolt, Beranek and Newman. **[7]**

**Anderson, R. C., & Pearson, P. D.** (1984). A schema-theoretic view of basic processes in reading comprehension. In P. D. Pearson, R. Barr, M. L. Kamil, & P. Mosenthal (Eds.), *Handbook of reading research* (pp. 255–291). White Plains, NY: Longman. **[8]**

**Anderson, R. C., Wilkinson, I. A., & Mason, J. M.** (1991). A microanalysis of the small-group, guided reading lesson: Effects of an emphasis on global story meaning. *Reading Research Quarterly, 26*(4), 417–441. **[13]**

**Anderson, V., & Hidi, S.** (1988–1989). Teaching students to summarize. *Educational Leadership, 46,* 26–28. **[8]**

**Andrews, J. F.** (1988). Deaf children's acquisition of prereading skills using the reciprocal teaching procedure. *Exceptional Children, 54,* 349–355. **[11]**

**Ankney, P., & McClurg, P.** (1981). Testing Manzo's guided reading procedure. *The Reading Teacher, 34,* 681–685. **[8]**

**Applebee, A. N.** (1981). *Writing in the secondary school: English and the content areas.* Urbana, IL: National Council of Teachers of English. **[10]**

**Applebee, A. N.** (1986). Problems in process approaches: Toward a reconceptualization of process instruction. In A. R. Petrosky & D. Bartholomae (Eds.), *The teaching of writing.* Eighty-fifth yearbook of the National Society for the Study of Education, Part II (pp. 314–326) Chicago, IL: University of Chicago Press. **[9]**

**Applebee, A. N., Langer, J. A., & Mullis, I.** (1987). *Learning to be literate in America.* Princeton. NJ: National Assessment of Educational Progress. **[9]**

**Armstrong, K.** (1991). *Dynamics of change: Speculation on the forthcoming model of response to literature.* Paper presented at the National Reading Conference, Palm Springs, AZ. **[5]**

**Armstrong, K.** (1992). Dynamics of change: Speculations on the forthcoming model of response to literature (revised and published). In C. Kinzer & D. Leu (Eds.), *Forty-first yearbook of the National Reading Conference* (pp. 275–281). Chicago: National Reading Conference. **[5]**

**Artley, A. S.** (1975). Good teachers of reading—Who are they? *The Reading Teacher, 29,* 26–31. **[4]**

**Aschner, M. J., Gallagher, J. J., Perry, J. M., Afsar, S. S., Jenne, W., & Farr, H.** (1962). *A system for classifying thought processes in the context of classroom verbal interaction.* Champaign: University of Illinois, Institute for Research on Exceptional Children. **[8]**

**Ashton-Warner, S.** (1959). *Spinster.* New York: Simon and Schuster. **[7]**

**Au, K. H., Scheu, J. A., Kawakami, A. J., & Herman, P. A.** (1990). Assessment and accountability in a whole literacy curriculum. *The Reading Teacher, 43*(8), 574–578. **[12]**

**Auckerman, R. C.** (1981). *The basal reader approach to reading.* New York: John Wiley & Sons. **[2]**

**August, D. L., Flavell, J. H., & Clift, R.** (1984). Comparison of comprehension monitoring of skilled and less-skilled readers. *Reading Research Quarterly, 20,* 39–53. **[10]**

**Aulls, M. W.** (1978). *Developmental and remedial reading in the middle grades* (abridged ed.). Boston: Allyn & Bacon. **[8]**

**Aulls, M. W., & Graves, M. F.** (1985). Repeated reading chart. In *Quest, desert magic, Unit 1, Electric butterfly and other stories.* New York: Scholastic. **[6]**

**Austin, M. & Morriston, C.** (1963). *The first R: The Harvard report on reading in one elementary school.* New York: Macmillan. **[10]**

**Babbs, P.** (1983). The effects of instruction in the use of a metacognitive monitoring strategy upon fourth graders' reading comprehension and recall performance. (Doctoral dissertation, Purdue University, West Lafayette, IN). *Dissertation Abstract International, 5,* 44/06A. **[8]**

**Bagley, M. T., & Hess, K.** (1982). *200 ways of using imagery in the classroom.* Woodcliff Lake, NJ: New Dimensions of the 80s. **[8]**

**Baker, L.** (1979a). Comprehension monitoring: Identifying and coping with text confusion. *Journal of Reading Behavior, 11,* 365–374. **[8]**

**Baker, L.** (1979b). *Do I understand or do I not understand: That is the question.* (Reading Education Report No. 10). Washington, DC: National Institute of Education. (ERIC Document Reproduction Service No. EC174 948). **[8]**

**Baker, A., & Green F.** (1986). Listening to children read: The empathetic process. *The Reading Teacher, 39,* 536–543. **[4]**

**Baker, R. L., & Schutz, R. E. (Eds.)** (1972). *Instructional product research.* New York: Van Nostrand.

**Ball, E., & Blachman, B.** (1991). Does phoneme segmentation training in kindergarten make a difference in early word recognition and developmental spelling? *Reading Research Quarterly, 26,* 49–86. **[3]**

**Ballard, R.** (1978). *Talking dictionary.* Ann Arbor, MI: Ulrich's books. **[6]**

**Bandura, A.** (1987). Self-regulation of motivation and action through goal systems. In V. Hamilton, G. H. Bower, & N. H. Frijda (Eds.), *Cognition, motivation, and affect: A cognitive science view* (pp. 412–440). Dordrecht, Neth: Martinus Nijhoff. **[8]**

**Bandura, A., & Walters, R.** (1963). *Social learning and personality development.* New York: Holt, Rinehart and Winston. **[8]**

**Barnes, D.** (1976). *From communication to curriculum.* London: Penguin.

**Barr, R. C.** (1973–1974). Instructional pace differences and their effect on reading acquisition. *Reading Research Quarterly, 9,* 526–554. **[2]**

**Barr, R., & Dreeben, R.** (1991). Grouping students for reading instruction. In R. Barr, M. Kamil, P. Mosenthal, & P. D. Pearson (Eds.), *Handbook of reading research: Volume II* (pp. 885–910). White Plains, NY: Longman. **[13]**

**Barr, R., & Sadow, M.** (1989). Influence of basal programs on fourth-grade reading instruction. *Reading Research Quarterly, 24,* 44–71. **[13]**

**Barron, R.** (1969). The use of vocabulary as an advance organizer. In H. L. Herber & P. L. Sanders (Eds.), *Research in reading in the content area: First report* (pp. 29–39). Syracuse, NY: Syracuse University Reading and Language Arts Center. **[8]**

**Bartlett, F. C.** (1932). *Remembering: A study in experimental and social psychology.* Cambridge, England: Cambridge University Press. **[8]**

**Bates, E.** (1979). *The emergence of symbols.* New York: Academic Press. **[7]**

**Baumann, J. F.** (1984). Implication for reading instruction from the research on teacher and school effectiveness. *Journal of Reading, 28,* 109–115. **[8]**

**Baumann, J. F.** (1988a). Direct instruction reconsidered. *Journal of Reading, 31,* 712–718. **[12]**

**Baumann, J. F.** (1988b). *Reading assessment.* Columbus, OH: Merrill. **[12] [13]**

**Baumann, J. F., & Kameenui, E. J.** (1991). Research on vocabulary instruction: Ode to Voltaire. In J. Flood, J. M. Jensen, D. Lapp, & J. R. Squire (Eds.), *Handbook of research on teaching the English language arts* (pp. 604–632). New York: Macmillan. **[7]**

**Bean, T. W., & Pardi, R.** (1979). A field test of a guided reading strategy. *Journal of Reading, 23,* 144–147. **[8]**

**Bean, T. W., Searles, D., Singer, H., & Cowen, S.** (1987). *Acquiring concepts from biology text: A study of independent generation of procedural knowledge versus the use of text-based procedural knowledge.*

Paper presented at the annual meeting of the National Reading Conference. St. Petersburg, FL.

**Bean, T. W., & Steenwyck, F. C.** (1984). The effect of three forms of summarization instruction on sixth grades' summary writing and comprehension. *Journal of Reading Behavior, 16,* 297–306. **[8]**

**Bean, T., & Zulich, J.** (1989). Using dialogue journals to foster reflective practice with preservice, content-area teachers. *Teacher Education Quarterly, 16*(1), 33–40. **[2]**

**Bear, D. R., & Invernizzi, M.** (1984). Student directed reading groups. *Journal of Reading, 28,* 248–252. **[8]**

**Beck, I. L., & McCaslin, E. S.** (1978). *An analysis of dimensions that effect the development of code-breaking ability in eight beginning reading programs.* Pittsburgh, PA: Learning Research and Development Center, University of Pittsburgh. (ERIC Document Reproduction Service No. ED 155 585). **[6]**

**Beck, I. L., McKeown, M. G., McCaslen, E., & Burkes, A.** (1979). *Instructional dimensions that may affect reading comprehension: Examples from two commercial reading programs.* Pittsburgh, PA: University of Pittsburgh, Learning Research and Development Center. **[8]**

**Beck, I. L., McKeown, M. G., & Omanson, R. C.** (1987). The effects and uses of diverse instructional techniques. In M. G. McKeown, & M. E. Curtis (Eds.), *The nature of vocabulary acquisition* (pp. 147–163). Hillsdale, NJ: Erlbaum. **[7]**

**Beck, I. L., Omanson, R. C., & McKeown, M. G.** (1982). An instructional redesign of reading lessons: Effects on comprehension. *Reading Research Quarterly, 17,* 462–481. **[8]**

**Becker, W. C.** (1977). Teaching reading and language to the disadvantaged—What we have learned from field research. *Harvard Edu-*

*cational Review, 47,* 518–543. **[2] [6]**

**Beers, E. W., & Blachman, B. A.** (1991). Does phoneme awareness training in kindergarten make a difference in early word recognition and developmental spelling? *Reading Research Quarterly, 26,* 49–66. **[11]**

**Bergenske, M. D.** (1987). Humorous homonyms: Using visual clues to teach words that sound the same. *The Reading Teacher, 40*(7), 713–714.

**Bergeron, B.** (1990). What does the term *whole language* mean? Constructing a definition from the literature. *Journal of Reading Behavior, 22*(4), 301–329. **[2]**

**Betts, E. A.** (1936). *The prevention and correction of reading difficulties.* Evanston, IL: Row, Peterson & Co. **[1] [7] [12]**

**Betts, E. A.** (1946). *Foundations of reading instruction.* New York: American Book. **[2] [8] [12]**

**Betts, E.** (1960). *Handbook on corrective reading for the American adventure series.* New York: Row, Peterson & Company. **[12]**

**Bird, L. B.** (1991). Anatomy of a student portfolio. In K. Goodman, L. B. Bird, & Y. Goodman, (Eds.), *The whole language catalog* (p. 262). New York: American School Publishers, MacMillan/McGraw Hill. **[12]**

**Blackwell, D.** (1989). *An ABC Bestiary.* New York: Farrar, Straus. **[9]**

**Blanchard, J.** (1988). Plausible stories: A creative writing and story prediction activity. *Reading Research and Instruction, 28,* 60–65. **[8]**

**Bleich, D.** (1975). *Readings and feelings: An introduction to subjective criticism.* Urbana, IL: National Council of Teachers of English. **[2]**

**Bloom, A.** (1987). *The closing of the American mind.* New York: Simon & Schuster. **[2]**

**Bloom, B. S. (Ed.)** (1956). *Taxonomy of educational objec-*

*tives, Handbook I: Cognitive domain.* New York: David McKay. **[7] [8]**

**Bloom, B. S.** (1971). Mastery learning. In J. H. Block (Ed.), *Mastery learning: Theory and practice* (pp. 47–63). New York: Holt, Rinehart and Winston. **[2]**

**Bloom, B. S.** (1976). *Human characteristics and school learning.* New York: McGraw-Hill. **[1]**

**Bloom, B. S., Hastings, J. T., & Madaus, G. F.** (1971). *Handbook on formative and summative evaluation of student learning.* New York: McGraw-Hill. **[3]**

**Bloomer, R. H., & Norlander, K. A.** (1989). The practice of reading politics: Effects on children with learning problems. In B. Hayes & K. Camperell (Eds.), *Reading researchers, policymakers, and practitioners* (pp. 29–39). Yearbook of the American Reading Forum, Vol. 9. Logan, UT: American Reading Forum. **[3]**

**Bloomer, R. H., Norlander, K. A., & Richard, P. A.** (1991). Short-term memory demands of initial reading curricula: Impact on progress in elementary school reading. In B. L. Hayes & K. Camperell (Eds.), *Literacy: International, national, state, and local* (pp. 187–202). Athens, GA: American Reading Forum. **[6]**

**Bode, B.** (1989). Dialogue journal writing. *The Reading Teacher, 42*(8), 568–571. **[9]**

**Boder, E.** (1972). Developmental dyslexia: a review of prevailing diagnostic criteria. In M. P. Douglass (Ed.), *Claremont Reading Conference thirty-sixth yearbook* (pp. 114–125). Claremont, CA: Claremont University Center.

**Boder, E., & Jarrico, S.** (1982). *The Boder test of reading-spelling patterns.* New York: Grune & Stratton.

**Bohm, D.** (1978). *Wholeness and the implicate order.* London: Ark Paperbacks. **[5]**

**Bohm, D.** (1986). Fragmentation and wholeness. *Forum for corre-*

spondence and contact, *16*, 5–13. **[5]**

**Bohning, G.** (1991a). The ABC's for writing book imitations. *The Florida Reading Quarterly, 28*(2), 17–23. **[3] [9]**

**Bohning, G.** (1991b). Response journals: A professor's perspective. *Journal of Reading Education, 17*(1), 51–56. **[2] [9]**

**Bormuth, J. R.** (1965). Validities of grammatical and semantic classifications of cloze test scores. In J. A. Figurel (Ed.), *Reading and inquiry.* International Reading Association Conference Proceedings, 10, (pp. 283–286). Newark, DE: International Reading Association. **[12]**

**Bormuth, J. R.** (1966). Readability: A new approach. *Reading Research Quarterly, 2*, 5–142. **[13]**

**Bond, G., & Dykstra, R.** (1967). The cooperative research program in first-grade reading instruction. *Reading Research Quarterly, 2*, 5–141. **[2] [6]**

**Botel, M.** (1964). *How to teach reading.* Chicago: Follett. **[6]**

**Bowman, J. D.** (1991). Vocabulary development by "twosies." *Arizona Reading Journal, 19*(2), 66. **[7] [8]**

**Bracey, G. W.** (1987). Measurement-driven education: Catchy phrase, dangerous practice, *Phi Delta Kappan, 68*, 683–686. **[2]**

**Bradley, J. M., & Ames, W. S.** (1977). Readability parameters of basal readers. *Journal of Reading Behavior, 9*, 175–183. **[12]**

**Bradley, L., & Bryant, P.** (1983). Categorizing sounds and learning to read—A causal connection. *Nature, 301*, 419–421. **[3]**

**Bransford, J. D., & Johnson, M. K.** (1972). Contextual prerequisites for understanding: Some investigations of comprehension and recall. *Journal of Verbal Learning and Verbal Behavior, 11*, 717–726. **[8]**

**Bridge, C. A.** (1986). Predictable books for beginning readers and writers. In M. R. Sampson

(Ed.), *The pursuit of literacy* (pp. 110–130). Dubuque, IA: Kendall/Hunt Publishing Company. **[6]**

**Bridge, C. A., Winograd, P. N., & Haley, D.** (1983). Using predictable materials vs. preprimers to teach beginning sight words. *The Reading Teacher, 36*, 884–891. **[6]**

**Bromley, K. D.** (1985). Precis writing and outlining enhance content learning. *The Reading Teacher, 38*, 406–411. **[8]**

**Bromley, K. D., & McKeveny, L.** (1986). Precis writing: Suggestion for instruction in summarizing. *Journal of Reading, 29*(5), 392–95. **[8]**

**Brown, A. L., & Day, J. D.** (1983). Macrorules for summarizing texts: The development of expertise. *Journal of Verbal Learning and Verbal Behavior, 22*(1), 1–14. **[8]**

**Brozo, W. G., Schmlzer, R. V., & Spires, H. A.** (1983). The beneficial effect of chunking on good readers' comprehension of expository prose. *Journal of Reading, 26*, 442–445. **[8]**

**Bruner, J. C.** (1971). *Toward a theory of instruction.* New York: Norton.

**Bruner, J. C.** (1978). The role of dialogue in language acquisition. In A. Sinclair, R. J. Jarvelle, & W.J.M. Leveet (Eds.), *The child's conception of language* (pp. 220–232). New York: Springer. **[2]**

**Bruner, J. C.** (1983). *Child's talk: Learning to use language.* New York: W. W. Norton. **[3]**

**Bruno, M.** (1985). Using the neurological impress technique. *Michigan Reading Journal, 19*(1), 17–18. **[11]**

**Bruno, M.** (1992). Reading in rhythm: Using music to teach literacy. *Michigan Reading Journal, 26*(1), 11–19. **[11]**

**Burnett, R.** (1990). The phonics controversy resurfaces. *Missouri Reader, Spring,* 16–17. **[2]**

**Burnett, R.** (1991). Empowerment: Responding to controversy. *The Missouri Reader, 15*(2), 12–13. **[2] [6]**

**Burnett, R.** (1992). A scores report analysis. *The Missouri Reader, 16*(2), 9. **[13]**

**Burningham, J.** (1976). *The Blanket.* New York: Crowell.

**Burns, P. C., & Roe, B. D.** (1985). *Informal reading inventory* (2nd ed.). Boston: Houghton Mifflin. **[12]**

**Busching, B. A.** (1981). Readers theatre: An education for language and life. *Language Arts, 58*, 330–338. **[4]**

**Butler, A.** (1919). An interview with the editors. *Virginia State Reading Association Journal, 16*. **[11]**

**Byrne, B., Freebody, P., & Gates, A.** (1992). Longitudinal data on the relations of word-reading strategies to comprehension, reading time, and phonemic awareness. *Reading Research Quarterly, 7*(2) 141–151. **[6]**

**Calder, C. R., & Zalatimo, S. D.** (1970). Improving children's ability to follow directions. *The Reading Teacher, 24*, 227–231.

**Cambourne, B.** (1977, August). *Some psycholinguistic dimensions of the silent reading process: A pilot study.* Paper presented at the annual meeting of the Australian Reading Conference, Melbourne. **[8]**

**Camp, D. J.** (1991). 1-2-3 . . . New counting books. *The Florida Reading Quarterly, 27*(3), 13–14. **[4] [5]**

**Camperell, K.** (1982). Vygotsky's theory of intellectual development: The effect of subject-matter instruction on self-regulated cognitive processes. In G. H. McNich (Ed.), *Reading in the disciplines.* Second yearbook of the American Reading Forum (pp. 33–35). Athens, GA: University of Georgia. **[2]**

**Caputo, J.** (1987). *Radical hermeneutics.* Bloomington, IN: Indiana State University Press. **[2]**

**Carbo, M.** (1978). Teaching reading with talking books. *The Reading Teacher, 32,* 267–273. **[8]**

**Carr, E., & Ogle, D.** (1987). K-W-L Plus: A strategy for comprehension and summarization. *Journal of Reading, 30,* 628–629. **[8]**

**Carr, K., & Williams, W.** (1991). Classroom research empowers teachers. *The Missouri Reader, 15*(2), 4–6. **[2]**

**Carroll, J. B.** (1963). A model of school learning. *Teachers college record, 64,* 723–732. **[2]**

**Carroll, J. B., Davies, P., & Richman, B.** (1971). *Word frequency book.* Boston: Houghton Mifflin. **[6]**

**Carver, R. C.** (1974). *Manual for the Rauding Scale Qualification Test.* Kansas City, MO: Revrac Publications. **[13]**

**Carver, R. P.** (1981). *Reading comprehension and Rauding theory.* Springfield, IL: Charles C. Thomas Publishing Co. **[8]**

**Carver, R. P.** (1992). Commentary: Effect of prediction activities, prior knowledge, and text type upon amount comprehended: Using Rauding theory to critique schema theory research. *Reading Research Quarterly, 27*(2), 165–174. **[8]**

**Carver, R. P., & Hoffman, J. V.** (1981). The effect of practice through repeated reading in gains in reading ability using a computer-based instructional system. *Reading Research Quarterly, 16*(3), 374–390. **[6]**

**Casale, U. P.** (1982). Small group approach to the further validation and refinement of a battery for assessing "progress toward reading maturity" (Doctoral dissertation, University of Missouri–Kansas City). *Dissertation Abstract International, 43,* 770A. **[1] [9]**

**Casale, U. P.** (1985). Motor imaging: A reading-vocabulary strategy. *Journal of Reading, 28,* 619–621. **[7]**

**Casale, U. P., & Kelly, B. W.** (1980). Problem-solving approach to study skills (PASS) for students in professional schools. *Journal of Reading, 24,* 232–238. **[10]**

**Casale, U. P., & Manzo, A. V.** (1983). Differential effects of cognitive affective, and proprioceptive approaches on vocabulary acquisition. In G. H. McNinch (Ed.), *Reading research to reading practice.* The third yearbook of the American Reading Forum (pp. 71–73). Athens, GA: American Reading Forum. **[7]**

**Cassidy, J.** (1981, January). Lecture at Benchmark School, Media, Pennsylvania. (As cited by I. W. Gaskins, 1981). **[8]**

**Cazden, C.** (1972). *Child language and education.* New York: Holt, Rinehart and Winston. **[5]**

**Cecil, N. L.** (1990). Where have all the good questions gone? Encouraging creative expression in children. *Contemporary Issues in Reading, 5*(2), 49–53.

**Cell, E.** (1984). *Learning to learn from experience.* Albany, NY: State University of New York Press. **[2]**

**Ceprano, M. A.** (1981). A review of selected research on methods of teaching sight words. *The Reading Teacher, 35,* 314–322. **[2]**

**Chall, J. S.** (1967). *Learning to read: The great debate.* New York: McGraw-Hill **[3] [6]**

**Chall, J. S.** (1983a). *Learning to read: The great debate* (updated edition). New York: McGraw-Hill. **[3] [6] [8]**

**Chall, J. S.** (1983b). Literacy: Trends and explanations. *Educational Researcher, 12*(9), 3–8. **[8]**

**Chall, J. S.** (1983c). *Stages of reading development.* New York: McGraw-Hill. **[13]**

**Chang, S. S., & Raths, J.** (1971). The schools' contribution to the cumulating deficit. *Journal of Educational Research, 64,* 272–276. **[2]**

**Charles, M., Njegovan, G., Triplett, C., & Asberry, G.,** (1990–1991). *Parents assisting children: Helpful hints on ways to help your child with reading while at home.* Illustrated by K. Alexander, M. Hines, & N. Reese. Kansas City, MO: The Steps Program, School District of Kansas City, Missouri. **[3]**

**Cheek, E. H., Jr., Flippo, R., & Lindsey, J. D.** (1989). *Reading for success in elementary schools.* Orlando, FL: Holt, Rinehart and Winston. **[12]**

**Children's non-fiction trade books** (Illustration). Tulsa, OK: EDC Publishing. **[10]**

**Choate, J. S., & Rakes, T. A.** (1987). The structured listening activity: A model for improving listening comprehension. *The Reading Teacher, 41,* 194–200. **[8]**

**Chomsky, C.** (1972). Stages in language development and reading exposure. *Harvard Educational Review, 42,* 1–33. **[5]**

**Chomsky, N.** (1965). *Aspects of a theory of syntax.* Cambridge, MS: MIT Press. **[3]**

**Christie, J. J.** (1992). Environmental print strategies. *Arizona Reading Journal, 20*(2), 123. **[3]**

**Clark, M.** (1976). *Young fluent readers.* London: Heinemann Educational Books. **[6]**

**Clay, M. M.** (1975). *What did I write?* Auckland, New Zeland: Heinemann. **[2] [3]**

**Clay, M. M.** (1982). *Observing young readers.* Exter, NH: Heinemann.

**Clay, M. M.** (1985). *The early detection of reading difficulties* (3rd ed.). Portsmouth, NH: Heinemann. **[6] [11]**

**Clay, M. M.** (1987). Learning to be learning disabled. *New Zealand Journal of Educational Studies, 22,* 155–173. **[1]**

**Clay, M. M.** (1990). *Reading recovery in the United States: Its successes and challenges.* Speech presented at the Annual Meeting of the American Educational Research Association (Boston, MS, April 15–21). **[1]**

**Clay, M. M.** (1991). *Becoming literate: The construction of inner control.* Portsmouth, NH: Heinemann. **[6]**

**Clewell, S. F., & Haidemenos, J.** (1983). Organizational strategies to increase comprehension. *Reading World, 22,* 314–312. **[8] [10]**

**Cline, R. K., & Kretke, G. L.** (1980). An evaluation of long-term sustained silent reading in the junior high school. *Journal of Reading, 23,* 503–506. **[8]**

**Clyde, J. A., & Condon, M. W. F.** (1992). Collaborating in coursework and in classrooms: An alternative for strengthening whole language teacher preparation cultures. In Weaver, C., & Henke, L. (Eds.) *Supporting whole language* (pp. 87–104). Portsmouth, NH: Heinemann.

**Cochran-Smith, M. & Lytle, S.** (1990). Research on teaching and teacher research: The issues that divide. *Educational Researcher, 78,* 12–18.

**Coger, L. I., & White, M. R.** (1982). *Readers theatre handbook: A dramatic approach to literature.* Glenview, IL: Scott, Foresman. **[4]**

**Coleman, S.** (1990). Middle school remedial readers serve as cross-grade tutors. *The Reading Teacher, 43,* 524–525.

**Collins, C.** (1980). Sustained silent reading period: Effect on teacher's behaviors and students' achievement. *Elementary School Journal, 81,* 108–114. **[8]**

**Collins, C.** (1991). Reading instruction that increases thinking abilities. *Journal of Reading, 34*(7), 510–516. **[2] [9]**

**Collins, J.** (1986). Differential instruction in reading groups. In J. Cook-Gumperz (Ed.), *The social construction of literacy* (pp. 94–114). Cambridge: Cambridge University Press. **[13]**

**Collins-Block, C.** (1993). *Teaching the language arts: Expanding thinking through student-centered instruction.* Boston: Allyn & Bacon.

**Colvin-Murphy, C.** (1986). Enhancing critical comprehension of literacy texts through writing.

Paper presented at the National Reading Conference. **[9]**

**Colwell, C. G., Mangano, N. G., Childs, D., & Case, D.** (1986). Cognitive, affective, and behavioral differences between students receiving instruction using alternative lesson formats. *Proceedings from the National Reading and Language Arts Conference.* **[8]**

**Comber, L., & Keeves, J. P.** (1973). *Science education in nineteen countries.* New York: Wiley.

**Combs, W. E.** (1975). *Some further effects and implications of sentence-combining exercises for the secondary language arts curriculum.* Unpublished doctoral dissertation, University of Minnesota. **[9]**

**Commeyras, M.** (1993). Promoting critical thinking through dialogical-thinking reading lessons. *The Reading Teacher, 6,* 486–493.

**Comstock, M.** (1992). Poetry and process: The reading/writing connection. *Language Arts, 69*(4), 261–267. **[9]**

**Condus, M. M., Marshall, K. J., & Miller, S. R.** (1986). Effect of the key-word mnemonic strategy on vocabulary acquisition and maintenance by learning disabled children. *Journal of Learning Disabilities, 19,* 609–613. **[7]**

**Conley, M.** (1984). A teacher's schema for reading instruction. In J. A. Niles & L. A. Harris (Eds.), *Changing perspectives in reading/language processing and instruction.* Thirty-fifth yearbook of the National Reading Conference. Rochester, NY: National Reading Conference.

**Cook, J. E.** (1971). Rhyme time fun. *H.E.L.P. booklet,* 6–7. **[6]**

**Cook, J. E.** (1971). Words! *H.E.L.P. booklet,* 2–5. **[6]**

**Cooter, R. B., & Flynt, E. S.** (1986). *Reading comprehension: Out of the ivory tower and into the classroom.* Unpublished

paper, Northwestern State University, Natchitoches, LA.

**Copeland, K. A.** (1987). *Writing as a means to learn from prose.* Doctoral dissertation, University of Texas at Austin. **[9]**

**Cordts, A. D.** (1965). *Phonics for the reading teacher.* New York: Holt, Rinehart and Winston **[6] [B]**

**Craik, F. M., & Lockhart, R. S.** (1972). Levels of processing: A framework for memory research. *Journal of Verbal Learning and Verbal Behavior, 11,* 671–684. **[10]**

**Cramer, R. L.** (1978). *Writing, reading, and language growth.* Columbus, OH: Charles Merrill. **[9]**

**Crowther, R.** (1977). *The most amazing hide-and-seek alphabet book.* New York: Viking. **[9]**

**Cruickshank, D.** (1985). Uses and benefits of reflective teaching. *Phi Delta Kappan, 66,* 704–706. **[2]**

**Crum, S.** (1991). Going in circles. *The Florida Reading Quarterly, 27*(3), 9–11 **[5]**

**Cullinan, B. E.** (1987a). Inviting readers to literature. In B. E. Cullinan (Ed.), *Children's literature in the reading program* (pp. 2–14). Newark, DE: International Reading Association. **[5]**

**Cullinan, B. E.** (1987b). *Children's literature in the reading program.* Newark, DE: International Reading Association. **[5]**

**Cullinan, B. E.** (1989). *Literature and the child.* San Diego, CA: Harcourt, Brace, Jovanovich. **[5]**

**Cullinan, B. E.** (1992). *Invitation to read: More children's literature in the reading program.* Newark, DE: International Reading Association. **[10]**

**Culver, V. I.** (1975). The guided reading procedure: An experimental analysis of its effectiveness as a technique for improving reading comprehension skills (Doctoral dissertation, University of Missouri, Kansas City). *Disserta-*

tion *Abstracts International, 36,* 7062A. **[8]**

**Culver, V. I., Godfrey, H. C., & Manzo, A. V.** (1972). A partial reanalysis of the validity of the cloze procedure as an appropriate measure of reading comprehension [Research report summary]. *Journal of Reading, 16,* 256–257. **[8]**

**Cunningham, D., & Shablak, S. L.** (1975). Selective reading guide-o-rama: The content teacher's best friend. *Journal of Reading, 18,* 380–82. **[10]**

**Cunningham, J. W.** (1982). Generating interactions between schemata and text. In J. A. Niles & L. A. Harris (Eds.), *New inquiries in reading research and instruction.* The thirty-first yearbook of the National Reading Conference (pp. 42–47). Washington, DC: National Reading Conference. **[8]**

**Cunningham, J. W., Cunningham, P. M., & Arthur, S. V., (Eds.).** (1981). *Middle and secondary school reading.* White Plains, New York: Longman. **[7] [8]**

**Cunningham, J. W., & Tierney, R. J.** (1977). *Comparative analysis of cloze and modified cloze procedures.* Paper presented at the National Reading Conference, New Orleans. **[8]**

**Cunningham, P. M.** (1975). Transferring comprehension from listening to reading. *The Reading Teacher, 29,* 169–172. **[8] [11]**

**Cunningham, P. M.** (1975–1976). Investigating a synthesized theory of mediated word identification. *Reading Research Quarterly, 11,* 127–143. **[6]**

**Cunningham, P. M.** (1978). A compare/contrast theory of mediated word identification. *The Reading Teacher, 32,* 774–778. **[6]**

**Cunningham, P. M.** (1980). Teacher "were," "with," "what," and other four letter words. *The Reading Teacher, 34,* 160–163. **[7]**

**Cunningham, P. M.** (1990). The name test: A quick assessment of decoding ability. *The Reading Teacher, 44*(2), 124–129. **[12]**

**Cunningham, P. M.** (1991). *What kind of phonics instruction will we have?* Keynote address, National Reading Conference, Palm Springs, CA. **[6]**

**Cunningham, P. M., & Cunningham, J. W.** (1992). *The Reading Teacher, 46*(2), 106–115. **[11]**

**Cunningham, P. M., Hall, D. P., & Defer, M.** (1991). Nonability grouped, multilevel instruction: A year in a first-grade classroom. *The Reading Teacher, 44,* 566–571. **[6]**

**Curry, S.** (1992). Parent involvement programs: How can the schools include parents who have difficulty with reading? *Indiana Reading Quarterly, 224*(4), 22–30. **[3]**

**Cutler, R. B., & Truss, C. V.** (1989). Computer aided instruction as a reading motivator. *Reading Improvement, 26* (summer), 103–109.

**Dale, E., & O'Rourke, J.** (1976). *The living word vocabulary.* Elgin, IL: Dome. **[7] [12]**

**Dale, E., & O'Rourke, J.** (1981). *The living word vocabulary* (3rd ed). Chicago: World Book, Inc. **[7] [12]**

**Dana, C.** (1989). Strategy families for disabled readers. *Journal of Reading, 33*(1), 30–35. **[10]**

**Davey, B.** (1983). Think aloud—Modeling the cognitive processes of reading comprehension. *Journal of Reading, 27,* 44–47. **[8]**

**Davey, B.** (1987). Team success: Guided practice in study skills through cooperative research reports. *Journal of Reading, 30,* 701–705. **[8]**

**Davidson, J. L.** (1970). The relationship between teacher's questions and pupils' responses during a directed reading activity and a directed reading thinking activity (Doctoral dissertation, The University of Michigan, Ann Arbor).

*Dissertation Abstracts International, 31,* G273A. **[8]**

**Davis, F. B.** (1944). Fundamental factors of comprehension in reading. *Psychometrika, 31,* 185–187. **[8]**

**Dawson, M., & Newman, G.** (1969). *Oral reading and linguistics,* Book 3, "Loud and clear," (p. 41). Westchester, IL: Benefic Press. **[4]**

**Day, V.** (1963). *Landslide.* New York: Coward McCann. **[10]**

**Debes, J. A.** (1962). A new look at seeing. *Media and Methods, 4,* 26–28. **[7]**

**DeFord, D. E.** (1986). Classroom contexts for literacy learning. In T. E. Raphael (Ed.), *Contexts of school-based literacy* (pp. 163–180). New York: Random House.

**Delacato, C. H.** (1959). *The treatment and prevention of reading problems.* Springfield, IL: Charles C. Thomas.

**Delacato, C. H.** (1963). *The diagnosis and treatment of speech and reading problems.* Springfield, IL: Charles C. Thomas.

**Dellarosia, D.** (1988). A history of thinking. In R. J. Sternberg & E. F. Smith (Eds.). *The psychology of human thought* (pp. 1–18). New York: Cambridge University Press.

**Delpit, L.** (1988). The silence dialogue: Power and pedagogy educating other people's children. *Harvard Educational Review, 56,* 280–298. **[2]**

**Dember, W. N.** (1965). *The psychology of perception.* New York: Holt, Rinehart and Winston. **[3]**

**Dempster, F. K.** (1991). Synthesis of research on review and tests. *Educational Leadership, 48*(7), 71–76. **[8]**

**DeSanti, R. J., & Alexander, D. H.** (1986). Locus of control and reading achievement: Increasing the responsibility and performance of remedial readers. *Journal of Clinical Reading, 2,* 12–14. **[13]**

**Dewitz, P., Carr, E. M., & Patsberg, J. P.** (1987). Effects of inference training on comprehension and comprehension monitoring. *Reading Research Quarterly, 22,* 99–121. **[8]**

**Dillingham, L.** (1991). Critter creations: Empowering students through reading and writing. *The Missouri Reader, 15*(2), 8–10.

**Dolch, E. W.** (1951). *Psychology and teaching of reading.* Champaign, IL: The Gerrard Press. **[6]**

**Dole, J. A., & Smith, E. L.** (1989). Prior knowledge and learning from science text: An instructional study. In S. McCormick & J. Zutell (Eds.), *Cognitive and social perspectives for literacy research and instruction.* Thirty-eighth yearbook of the National Reading Conference (pp. 345–361). Chicago, IL: The National Reading Conference. **[10]**

**Donlan, D** (1975). Teaching word through sense impressions. *Language Arts, 52,* 1090–1093. **[7]**

**Dooling, D. L., & Lachman, R.** (1971). Effects of comprehension on retention of prose. *Journal of Experimental Psychology, 88,* 216–222. **[8]**

**Dowhower, S. L.** (1989). Repeated reading: Research into practice. *The Reading Teacher, 42*(7), 502–507. **[6]**

**Downing, J., and Thomson, D.** (1977). Sex-role stereotypes in learning to read. *Research in the Teaching of English, II,* 149–155. **[4]**

**Drake, S.** (1982). *Creative writing skills,* Grades 2–3. Grand Rapids, MI: Instructional Fair. **[9]**

**Dreher, M. J.** (1990). The role of affect in the reading process. *Literacy: Issues and Practices, 7,* 20–24. **[2]**

**Dreher, M. J., & Gambrell, L. B.** (1985). Teaching children to use a self-questioning strategy for studying expository prose. *Reading Improvement, 22,* 2–7. **[8]**

**Drucker, P.** (1990). An interview with Drucker. *Time,* June 11, 1990. **[2]**

**Drum, Y.** (1992). King Tut revisited. *Ohio Reading Teacher, 26*(4), 25–28. **[11]**

**Duffelmeyer, F. A.** (1980). The influence of experience-based vocabulary instruction on learning word meanings. *Journal of Reading, 24,* 35–40. **[7]**

**Duffelmeyer, F. A., Baum, D. D., & Merkley, D. J.** (1987). Maximizing reader-text confrontation with an extended anticipation guide. *Journal of Reading, 31,* 146–150.

**Duffy, G. G., & Roehler, L. R.** (1987). Improving reading instruction through the use of responsive elaboration. *The Reading Teacher, 40,* 514–520. **[8]**

**Duffy, G. G., Roehler, L. R., & Hermann, B. A.** (1988). Modeling mental processes helps poor readers become strategic readers. *The Reading Teacher, 41,* 762–767. **[8] [9]**

**Duffy, G. G., Roehler, L. R., Sivan, E., Rackliffe, G., Book, C., Meloth, M. S., Vavrus, L. G., Wesselman, R., Putnam, J., & Bassiri, D.** (1987). The effects of explaining the reasoning associated with using reading strategies. *Reading Research Quarterly, 22,* 347–368. **[8]**

**Dunn-Rankin, P.** (1968). The similarity of lower-case letters in the English alphabet. *Journal of Verbal Learning and Verbal Behavior, 7,* 990–995. **[3]**

**Durant, W., & Durant, A.** (1969). *Lessons of history.* New York: Simon & Schuster. **[2]**

**Durkin, D.** (1966). *Children who read early.* New York: Teachers College Press. **[3] [6]**

**Durkin, D.** (1987). *Teaching young children to read* (4th ed). Boston: Allyn & Bacon.

**Durkin, D.** (1989). *Teaching them to read.* Boston: Allyn & Bacon. **[1] [4]**

**Durrell, A., & Sachs M. (Eds.).** (1990). (Illustration). *The big book for peace.* New York: Dutton. **[5]**

**Durrell, D. D.** (1956). *Improving reading interaction.* Orlando, FL: Harcourt Brace Jovanovich. **[10]**

**Durrell, D. D.** (1980). *Durrell analysis of reading difficulty.* New York: The Psychological Corporation. **[12]**

**Eanet, M. G.** (1978). An investigation of the REAP reading/study procedure: Its rationale and efficacy. In P. D. Pearson, & J. Hansen (Eds.), *Reading: Disciplined inquiry in process and practice.* The Twenty-seventh yearbook of the National Reading Conference (pp. 229–232). Clemson, SC: National Reading Conference. **[13]**

**Eanet, M. G.** (1983). Reading/writing: Finding and using the connection. *The Missouri Reader, 8,* 8–9. **[8] [9]**

**Eanet, M. G., & Manzo, A. V.** (1976). REAP—A strategy for improving reading/writing/study skills. *Journal of Reading, 19,* 647–652. **[8] [9]**

**Early, M., Cullinan, B. E., Farr, R. C., Hammond, W. D., Santeusanio, N., & Strickland, D. S.** (1987). *Wishes: Teacher's edition, Part II, Level 4,* HBJ Reading Program. Orlando, FL: Harcourt Brace Jovanovich. **[11]**

**Eastland, J.** (1980). Working with the language deficient child. *Music Educators Journal, 67*(3), 60–65. **[11]**

**Eberdt-Armstrong, K.** (1990). *Research conceptions of adult and college reader response to literature.* Unpublished dissertation, University of British Columbia. **[5]**

**Edelsky, C.** (1992). A talk with Carole Edelsky about politics and literacy. *Language Arts, 69*(5), 324–329. **[2] [7]**

**Eden, C. (Ed.).** (1990). *The glorious abc.* New York: Atheneum. **[9]**

**Ediger, M.** (1991). The affective dimension in reading education. *Journal of Affective Reading Education, 9,* 35–40. **[5]**

**Ediger, M.** (1992). The middle school student and interest in reading. *Journal of Affective Reading Education, 10*(2), 9–13. **[12]**

**Edwards, P. A., & Simpson, L.** (1986). Bibliotheraphy: A strategy for communication between parents and their children. *Journal of Reading, 30,* 110–118.

**Eeds, M.** (1985). Bookwords: Using a beginning word list of high frequency words from children's literature K–3. *The Reading Teacher, 38*(4), 418–423. **[6]**

**Eeds, M.** (1991). The circle of dialogue: Author, student, teacher. Interview with Yvonne Siu-Runyan. *The Colorado Commonwealth, 14*(2), 6–11. **[5]**

**Eeds, M., & Cockrum, W. A.** (1985). Teaching word meanings by expanding schemata *vs.* dictionary work *vs.* reading in context. *Journal of Reading, 28,* 492–497. **[7]**

**Ehlinger, J.** (1988). *The relative merits of characteristics of teacher verbal modeling in influencing comprehension and comprehension monitoring of eighth grade readers.* Paper presented at the National Reading Conference, Tucson, AZ. **[8]**

**Ehlinger, J.** (1989). *Think-aloud: An examination of its transfer to other learning situations.* Paper presented at the thirty-ninth annual meeting of the National Reading Conference Austin, TX. **[8]**

**Ehlinger, J.** (1992). Think-aloud: An examination of its transfer to other learning situations. Paper, National Reading Conference.

**Ehri, L. C.** (1978). Beginning reading from a psycholinguistic perspective: Amalgamation of word identities. In F. B. Murray (Ed.), *The development of the reading process* (pp. 1–33). International Reading Association Monograph No. 3. Newark, DE: International Reading Association. **[6]**

**Ehri, L. C.** (1983). A critique of five studies related to letter-name knowledge and learning to read. In L. M. Gentile, M. L. Kamil, & J. S. Blanchard (Eds.), *Reading research revisited* (pp. 143–153). Columbus, OH: Charles E. Merrill. **[3]**

**Ehri, L. C., & Robbins, C.** (1992). Beginners need some decoding skill to read words by analogy. *Reading Research Quarterly, 27*(1), 12–26. **[6]**

**Ekwall, E.** (1985). *Ekwall reading inventory* (2nd ed.) Boston: Allyn & Bacon.

**Ekwall, E. E., & Shanker, J. L.** (1988). *Diagnosis and remediation of the disabled reader* (3rd ed.). Boston, MA: Allyn & Bacon. **[3] [6] [5]**

**Elley, W., & Mangubhai, F.** (1983). The impact of reading on second language learning. *Reading Research Quarterly, 19,* 53–67. **[8]**

**Elliott, S. N., & Carroll, J. L.** (1980). Strategies to help children remember what they read. *Reading Improvement, 17,* 272–277. **[8] [11]**

**Elly, W. B.** (1989). Vocabulary acquisition from listening to stories. *Reading Research Quarterly 24,* 174–187. **[6]**

***Elson Readers.*** (1909–1931). Glenview, IL: Scott, Foresman. **[2]**

**Engleman, S., & Brener, E. C.** (1983). *Reading mastery I and II: DISTAR reading.* Chicago, IL: Science Research Associates. **[2]**

**Erickson, L. G.** (1990). How improvement teams facilitate school-wide reading reform. *Journal of Reading, 33,* 580–585. **[13]**

**Ericson, B., Hubler, M., Bean, T. W., Smith, C. C., & McKenzie, J. V.** (1987). Increasing critical reading in junior high classrooms. *Journal of Reading, 30,* 430–439. **[9] [10]**

**Erikson, E.** (1965). *The challenge of youth.* New York: Doubleday & Co. **[9]**

**Estes, T. H.** (1990). Ten best ideas for reading teachers. In E. Fry (Ed.), *Ten best ideas for reading teachers* (p. 59). Menlo Park, CA: Addison-Wesley. **[2] [10]**

**Farr, R.** (1992). Putting it all together. Solving the reading assessment puzzle. *The Reading Teacher, 46*(1), 26–37. **[12]**

**Farr, R., & Fay, L.** (1982). Reading trend data in the United States: A mandate for caveats and caution. In G. Austin & H. Garber (Eds.), *The rise and fall of national test scores* (pp. 83–141). New York: The Academic Press. **[12]**

**Farrell, J. F.** (1991). Instructional models for English language arts, K–12. In J. Flood, J. M. Jensen, D. Lapp, & J. R. Squire (Eds.), *Handbook of research on teaching the English language arts* (pp. 63–84). New York: Macmillan. **[2]**

**Farris, P. J., & Kaczmarski, D.** (1988). Whole language: A closer look. *Contemporary Education, 59*(2), 77–81. **[10]**

**Fazzino, M.** (1988). *By definition: Effects on vocabulary acquisition.* Educational specialist degree project, University of Missouri—Kansas City, Kansas City, MO. **[11]**

**Ferguson, A. K., & Kennedy, M.** (1985). P-R-E-V-Teaching predictions and concepts simultaneously. *Reading Horizons, 25,* 194–199.

**Fernald, G. M.** (1943). *Remedial techniques in basic school subjects.* New York: McGraw-Hill. **[6] [11]**

**Ferriero, E., & Teberosky, A.** (1982). *Literacy before schooling.* Exeter, NH: Heinemann. **[3]**

**Fielding, L.** (1992). Grouping patterns for reading instruction. *Iowa Reading Journal, 5*(1), 26–29. **[13]**

**Fielding, L., Wilson, P., & Anderson, R. C.** (1986). A new focus on free reading: The role of trade books in reading instruction. In T. Raphael (Ed.), *The contexts of school-based literacy* (pp.

149–161). New York: Random House. **[13]**

Fisher, C. W., Filby, N. W., Marliave, R., Cahen, L. S., Dishaw, M. M., Moore, J. E., & Berlner, D. C. (1978). *Teaching and learning in the elementary school: A summary of the beginning teacher evaluation study* (BTES), Rep. VII-I. San Francisco: Far West Laboratory for Educational Research and Development. **[2]**

Fitzgerald, J. (1989). Enhancing two related thought processes: Revision in writing and critical reading. *The Reading Teacher, 43*(1), 42–48. **[9]**

Fitzgerald, S. (1975). Teaching discussion skills and attitudes. *Language Arts, 52*(8), 1094–1096. **[13]**

Flavell, J. H. (1981). Cognitive monitoring. In W. P. Dickson (Ed.), *Children's oral communication skills* (pp. 186–254). New York: Academic Press. **[3] [8]**

Flebbe, D., & Atencio-Hower, A. (1992). Cultural awareness is different from cultural stereotyping. *The Colorado Communicator, 16*(1), 10. **[13]**

Flippo, R. F. (1981). Reaction: Effects of listening/reading transfer. In G. H. McNinch (Ed.), *Comprehension: Process and product.* First yearbook of American Reading Forum (pp. 108–110). Athens, GA: University of Georgia. **[8]**

Flood, J., & Lapp, D. (1987). Reading and writing relations: Assumptions and directions. In J. R. Squire (Ed.), *The dynamics of language learning: Research in reading and English* (pp. 9–26). Bloomington, IN: Eric/rcs. **[9]**

Flood, J., & Lapp, D. (1989). Reporting reading progress: A comparison portfolio for parents. *The Reading Teacher, 42*(7), 508–514. **[12]**

Flower, L., & Hayes, J. R. (1981). A cognitive process theory of writing. *College Composition and Communication, 32,* 365–387. **[8] [9]**

Ford, M. P., & Ohlhausen, M. M. (1988). Tips from reading clinicians for coping with disabled readers in regular classrooms. *The Reading Teacher, 42*(1), 18–22. **[11]**

France, M. G., & Meeks, J. W. (1987). Parents who can't read: What the schools can do. *Journal of Reading, 31*(3), 222–227. **[3]**

Frayer, D. A., Fredrick, W. C., & Klausmeier, H. J. (1969). *A schema for testing the level of concept mastery* (Working Paper No. 16). Madison: University of Wisconsin, Wiconsin Research and Development Center for Cognitive Learning. **[7]**

Frazier, A. (1970). Developing a vocabulary of the senses. *Elementary English, 47*(2), 176–184. **[7] [C]**

Freeman, D. E., & Freeman, Y. S. (1993). Strategies for promoting the primary languages of all students. *The Reading Teacher, 46*(7), 552–558. **[11]**

Friedrich, F. J., Schodler, M., & Juola, J. F. (1979). Developmental changes in units of processing in reading. *Journal of Experimental Child Psychology, 28,* 344–358. **[6]**

Frith, U. (1985). Beneath the surface of developmental dyslexia. In K. E. Patterson, K. C. Marshall, & M. Coltheart (Eds.), *Surface dyslexia: Neuropsychological and cognitive studies of phonological reading* (pp. 51–68). Hillsdale, NJ: Erlbaum. **[6]**

Fromm, E. (1941). *Escape from freedom.* New York: Holt, Rinehart and Winston. **[9]**

Fry, E. (1968). A readability formula that saves time. *Journal of Reading, 11,* 513–516, 575–578. **[13]**

Fry, E. (1977). Fry's readability graph: Clarification, validity, and extension to level 17. *Journal of Reading, 21,* 242–252. **[13]**

Fry, E. (1980). The new instant word list. *The reading teacher, 34,* 284–289. **[6]**

Fullan, M. (1985). Change processes and strategies at the local level. *Elementary School Journal, 85*(3), 391–421. **[13]**

Furner, B. A. (1991). Is whole language enough? *Iowa Reading Journal, 4*(3), 12–15. **[5]**

Galda, L. (1982). Playing about a story. Its impact on comprehension. *The Reading Teacher, 36,* 52–58. **[8]**

Galda, L., & West, J. (1993). Giving the gift of words: Reading poetry with children. *The Reading Teacher, 46*(7), 588–594. **[9]**

Gambrell, L. B. (1985). Dialogue journals: Reading-writing interaction. *The Reading Teacher, 38,* 512–515. **[9]**

Gambrell, L. B., & Bales, R. J. (1986). Mental image and the comprehension monitoring performance of fourth- and fifth-grade poor readers. *Reading Research Quarterly, 21,* 454–464. **[8]**

Gambrell, L. B., & Jawitz, P. B. (1993). Mental imagery, text illustrations, and children's story comprehension and recall. *Reading Research Quarterly, 28*(3), 265–276.

Garner, R., Hare, V. C., Alexander, P., Haynes, J., & Winograd, P. (1984). Inducing use of a text lookback strategy among unsuccessful readers. *American Educational Research Journal, 21,* 789–798. **[10]**

Garner, R., & Kraus, C. (1981–1982). Good and poor comprehender differences in knowing and regulating reading behaviors. *Educational Research Quarterly, 6,* 5–12.

Garner, R., & Reis, R. (1981). Monitoring and resolving comprehension obstacles: An investigation of spontaneous text lookbacks among upper-grade good and poor comprehenders. *Reading Research Quarterly, 16,* 569–582.

Garrison, J. W., & Hoskisson, K. (1989). Confirmation bias in predictive reading. *The Reading Teacher, 42*(7), 482–486. **[10]**

Gaskins, I. W. (1981). Reading for learning: Going beyond basals in the elementary grades. *The Reading Teacher, 35*, 323–328. **[8]**

Gaskins, I. W. (1988). Teachers as thinking coaches: Creating strategic learners and problem solvers. *Reading, Writing, and Learning Disabilities, 4*, 35–48. **[2] [6] [13]**

Gaskins, I. W., Downer, M. A., Anderson, R. E., Cunningham, P. M., Gaskins, R. W., & Schommer, M. (1988). A metacognitive approach to phonics: Using what you know to decode what you don't know. *Remedial and Special Education, 9*(1), 36–41. **[6]**

Gaskins, I. W., & Elliot, T. (1991). *Implementing cognitive strategy training across the school.* Media, PA: Brookline Books. **[8]**

Gaskins, R. W., Gaskins, J. C., & Gaskins, I. W. (1991). A decoding program for poor readers *Language Arts, 68*(3), 213–225. **[6]**

Gattegno, C. (1962). *Words in color.* Chicago: Learning Materials. **[11]**

Gauthier, L. R. (1990). Five informal ways to assess students' reading comprehension. *Reading: Exploration and Discovery, 12*, 31–38. **[8]**

Gauthier, L. R. (1991). Using journals for content area comprehension. *Journal of Reading, 34*(6), 491–492. **[9]**

Gawby, G. (1983). Talking books and taped books: Materials for instruction. *The Reading Teacher, 36*, 366–369. **[8]**

Gee, T. C., & Raskow, S. J. (1987). Content reading specialists evaluate teaching practices. *Journal of Reading, 31*, 234–237. **[8]**

Gentile, L. M., & McMillan, M. M. (1978). Humor and the reading program. *Journal of Reading, 21*, 343–347. **[5]**

Gentile, L. M., & McMillan, M. M. (1987a). Stress and reading difficulties: Teaching students self-regulating skills. *The Reading Teacher, 41*, 170–178. **[2]**

Gentile, L. M., & McMillan, M. M. (1987b). *Stress and reading difficulties.* Newark, DE: International Reading Association. **[4]**

Gentile, L. M., & McMillan, M. M. (1990). Literacy through literature: Motivating at risk students to read and write. *Journal of Reading, Writing and Learning Disabilities International, 6*, 383–393. **[9]**

Gentile, L. M., & McMillan, M. M. (1991). Reading, writing and relationships: The challenge of teaching at risk students. *Reading Research and Instruction, 30*(4), 74–81. **[9]**

George, J. E. (1975). *Reading facilitating experience.* Course handout, University of Missouri at Kansas City. **[3]**

George, J. E. (1990). Becoming a successful leader. *Leader.* Newark, DE: International Reading Association. **[13]**

George, J. E., Moley, P., & Ogle, D. S. (1992). CCD: A model comprehension program for changing thinking and instruction. *Journal of Reading, 35*(7), 564–570. **[13]**

Gibson, E., & Levin, H. (1975). *The psychology of reading.* Cambridge, MA: MIT Press. **[6]**

Gilbert, L. C. (1940). Effect on silent reading of attempting to follow oral reading. *Elementary School Journal, 40*, 614–621. **[4]**

Gill, J. T., & Bear, D. R. (1988). No book, whole book, and chapter DR-TAs. *Journal of Reading, 31*, 444–451. **[8]**

Gipe, J. P. (1978–1979). Investigating techniques for teaching word meanings. *Reading Research Quarterly, 14*, 623–644. **[7]**

Glass, G. (1973). *Teaching decoding as separate from reading.* Garden City, NJ: Adelphi University Press. **[6]**

Glass, G. G., & Burton, E. H. (1973). How do they decode? Verbalization and observed behaviors of successful decoders. *Education, 94*, 58–64. **[6]**

Glazer, S. M. (1984). Liberating students to write. *Early years, 15*(1), 67–69. **[12]**

Glazer, S. M. (1990). *Creating readers and writers* (Parent Booklet No. 165). Newark, DE: International Reading Association. **[3]**

Glazer, S. M. (1993). *Portfolios and beyond: Collaborative assessment in reading and writing.* Norwood, MA: Christopher-Gorden. **[12]**

Gleitman, L., & Rozin, P. (1973). Teaching reading by the use of syllabary. *Reading Research Quarterly, 8*, 447–483. **[1] [3]**

Goetz, E. T., Sadoski, M., Olivarez, A., Calero-Breckheimer, A., Garner, P., & Fatemi, Z. (1992). The structure of emotional response in reading a literary text: Quantitative and qualitative analyses. *Reading Research Quarterly, 27*(4), 361–372. **[8]**

Goldenberg, C. (1992). Instructional conversations: Promoting comprehension through discussion. *The Reading Teacher, 46*, 316–326.

Goldstein, D. (1976). Cognitive-linguistic functioning and learning to read in preschoolers. *Journal of Educational Psychology, 68*, 680–688. **[3]**

Gomez, M. L., Graue, M. E., Bloch, M. N. (1991). Reassessing portfolio assessment: Rhetoric and reality. *Language Arts, 68*(8), 620–628. **[12]**

Good, T. L., Grouws, D. A., & Beckerman, T. M. (1978). Curriculum pacing: Some empirical data in mathematics. *Journal of Curriculum Studies, 10*, 75–82. **[2]**

Goodman, K. S. (1967). Reading: A psycholinguistic guessing game. *Journal of the Reading Specialist, 6,* 126–135. **[6]**

Goodman, K. S. (1970). Behind the eye: What happens in reading. In O. S. Hiles (Ed.), *Reading: Process and program* (pp. 94–108). Urbana, IL: National Council of Teachers of English. **[1] [4]**

Goodman, K. S. (1973a). Miscues. Windows on the reading process. In K. S. Goodman (Ed.), *Miscue analysis: Applications to reading instruction* (pp. 3–14). Urbana, IL: National Council of Teachers of English. **[1] [6] [12]**

Goodman, K. S. (1973b). The 13th easy way to make learning to read difficult. *Reading Research Quarterly, 8,* 484–493. **[6]**

Goodman, K. S. (1984). Unity in reading. In A. Purves & O. Niles (Eds.), *Becoming readers in a complex society.* Eighty-third yearbook of the National Society for the Study of Education. Part I (pp. 79–1145). Chicago: University of Chicago Press. **[1]**

Goodman, K. S. (1991). A rebuttal to Priscilla Vail. *Whole language special interest group of IRA newsletter, 3*(2), 4. **[2]**

Goodman, K. S. (1992a). *Unity in reading: Recent thoughts.* Paper presented at International Reading Conference. Orlando, FL.

Goodman, K. S. (1992b). Why whole language is today's agenda in education. *Language Arts, 69*(5), 354–363.

Goodman, K. S., Bird, L. B., & Goodman, Y. M. (Eds.). (1991). *The whole language catalog.* Santa Rosa, CA: American School Publishers: Macmillan/McGraw Hill. **[1] [2]**

Goodman, K., Shannon, P., Freeman, Y. S., & Murphy, S. (1988). *Report card on basal readers.* Katonah, New York: Richard C. Owen. **[2]**

Goodman, Y. (1975). Reading strategy lessons: expanding reading effectiveness. In W. Page (Ed.), *Help for the reading teacher: New directions in research* (pp. 34–41). Urbana, IL: National Council of Teachers of English and Educational Resources Information Center. **[6] [8]**

Goodman, Y. M. (1985). Kidwatching: Observing children in the classroom. In A. Jaggar & M. T. Smith-Burke (Eds.), *Observing the language learner* (pp. 9–18). Newark, DE: International Reading Association. **[12]**

Goodman, Y. M. (1986). Children coming to know literacy. In W. Teale & E. Sulzby (Eds.), *Emergent literacy, writing and reading* (pp. 1–14). Norwood, NJ: Ablex. **[3]**

Goodman, Y. M. (1989). Roots of the whole-language movement. *The Elementary School Journal, 90*(2), 113–127. **[2] [6]**

Goodman, Y. M. (1990). *Kid watching: An alternative to testing* (6th ed.). New York: Macmillan.

Goodman, Y. M. (1990). Phonological priming and orthographic analogy in reading. *Journal of Experimental Child Psychology, 49,* 323–340. **[6]**

Goswami, U. (1990) Phonological priming and orthographic analogy in reading. *Journal of Experimental Child Psychology, 49,* 323–340. **[6]**

Gough, P. B. (1991). (as cited by C. Juel). In R. Barr, M. L. Kamil, P. Mosenthal, & P. D. Pearson (Eds.), *Handbook of reading research* (Vol. II, pp. 768–769). White Plains, New York: Longman. **[6]**

Gough, P. B. Alford, J. A., Jr., & Holly-Wilcox, P. (1981). Words and contexts. In O. J. L. Tzeng & H. Singer (Eds.), *Perception of Print* (pp. 85–102). Hillsdale, NJ: Erlbaum. **[6]**

Gough, P. B., & Cosky, M. J. (1977). One second of reading again. In N. J. Castellan, Jr., D. Pisoni, & G. Potts (Eds.), *Cognitive theory, 2,* 271–288. Hillsdale NJ: Erlbaum. **[1]**

Gough, P. B., & Hillinger, M. D. (1980). Learning to read: An unnatural act. *Bulletin of the Orton Society, 30,* 179–196. **[6]**

Gough, P. B., Juel, C., & Roper-Schneider, D. (1983). A two-stage model of initial reading acquisition. In J. A. Niles & L. A. Harris (Eds.), *Searches for meaning in reading/language processing and instruction* (pp. 207–211). Rochester, New York: National Reading Conference. **[6]**

Graves, D. H. (1983). *Writing: Teachers and children at work.* Portmouth, NH: Heinemann. **[8] [9]**

Graves, M. F. (1986). Vocabulary learning and instruction. In E. Z. Rothkopf & L. C. Ehri (Eds.), *Review of research in education, 13,* 49–89. Washington, DC: American Educational Research Association. **[8]**

Graves, M. F., & Prenn, M. C. (1986). Costs and benefits of various methods of teaching vocabulary. *Journal of Reading, 29*(7), 596–602. **[7]**

Gray, J. (1992). Summary of master's thesis: Reading achievement and autonomy as a function of father-to-son reading. (Under the direction of Jack Graves, California State University—San Bernadino). *The California Reader, 25*(3), 17–19. **[4]**

Gray, W. S. (1925). *Twenty-fourth yearbook of the NSSE, Part I—Report of the National Committee on Reading.* Bloomington, IL: Public School. **[10] [13]**

Gray, W. S. (1925). Summary of investigations related to reading. *Supplementary Educational Monographs, 28.* Chicago: University of Chicago Press. **[10]**

Gray, W. S. (1948). *On their own in reading.* Glenview, IL: Scott, Foresman. **[6] [7] [8] [9] [10]**

Gray, W. S. (1951). *On their own in reading.* Boston: Scott, Foresman. **[10]**

Gray, W. S. (1960). *On their own in reading* (revised ed.). Chicago, IL: Scott, Foresman. **[7]**

Gray, W. S., & Rogers, B. (1956). *Maturity in reading.* Chicago: University of Chicago Press. **[1]**

Green, E. (1972). *An experimental study of sentence-combining to improve written syntactic fluency in fifth grade children.* Unpublished doctoral dissertation, Northern Illinois University. **[9]**

Green, F. (1986). Listening to children read: The empathetic process. *The Reading Teacher, 39,* 536–543.

Greene, F. P. (1979). Radio reading. In C. Pennock (Ed.), *Reading comprehension at four linguistic levels* (pp. 104–107). Newark, DE: International Reading Association. **[4]**

Greenewald, M. J., & Rossing, R. L. (1986). Short-term effects of story grammar and self-monitoring training on children's comprehension. In J. A. Niles, & R. V. Lalik (Eds.), *Solving problems in literacy: Learners, teachers, and researchers* (pp. 210–213). Thirty-fifth yearbook of the National Reading Conference. Rochester, New York: National Reading Conference. **[8]**

Grobler, C.V.E. (1971). Methodology in reading instruction as a controlling variable in the constructive or destructive channeling of aggression. (Doctoral dissertation, University of Delaware, Newark, 1970). *Dissertation Abstracts International, 32,* 6197A. **[8]**

Groff, P. (1991). Word recognition and critical reading. *Journal of Reading, Writing, and Learning Disabilities, 7*(1), 17–31. **[2]**

Gross, D. (1990). *Unlocking and guiding creative potential in writing and problem-solving.* Unpublished Education Specialist Project, University of Missouri-Kansas City.

Guice, B. M. (1969). The use of the cloze procedure for improving reading comprehension of college students. *Journal of Reading Behavior, 1,* 81–92. **[8]**

*Guidelines for Selecting Bias-Free Textbooks and Storybooks.* (1980). Council of Interracial Books for Children. **[13]**

Gunning, R. (1979). Fog index of a passage. *Academic Therapy, 14,* 489–491. **[13]**

Guszak, F. J. (1967). Teacher questioning and reading. *The Reading Teacher, 21,* 227–234. **[8]**

Guthrie, J. T. (1984). Lexical learning. *The Reading Teacher, 37,* 660–662. **[7]**

Guthrie, J. T., Barnham, N. A., Caplan, R. I., & Seifert, M. (1974). The maze technique to assess, monitor reading comprehension. *The Reading Teacher, 28*(2), 161–168. **[8]**

Guzzetti, B. J. (1990). Enhancing comprehension through trade books in high school English classes. *Journal of Reading, 33,* 411–413. **[4] [2]**

Guzzetti, B. J. (1992a). From research to practice: Issues in content reading using text to affect conceptual change in science. *Arizona Reading Journal, 20*(2), 100–101. **[10]**

Guzzetti, B. J. (1992b). Using a literature-based approach to social studies. *Journal of Reading, 36*(2), 114–122. **[10]**

Guzzetti, B. J., Snyder, T. E., & Glass, G. V. (1992). Promoting conceptual change in science: Can texts be used effectively? *Journal of Reading, 35*(8), 642–649. **[10]**

Haas, J. D. (1988). *Futures studies in K–12 curriculum.* Boulder, CO: Social Science Education Consortium. **[9]**

Hafner, E., & Palmer, B. C. (1980). The differential effects of three methods of teaching on the reading comprehension and vocabulary of ninth grade students. *Journal of Educational Research, 74,* 34–37. **[8]**

Haggard, M. R. (1976). *Creative Thinking-Reading Activities (CT-RA) as a means for improving comprehension.* Unpublished doctoral dissertation, University of Missouri—Kansas City, Kansas City, MO.

Haggard, M. R. (1979). Creative thinking-reading activities (CT-RA): Catalysts for creative reading. *Illinois Reading Council Journal, 7,* 5–8.

Haggard, M. R. (1982). The vocabulary self-collection strategy: An active approach to word learning. *Journal of Reading, 27,* 203–207. **[7]**

Haggard, M. R. (1988). Developing critical thinking with the Directed Reading-Thinking Activity. *The Reading Teacher, 41,* 526–535. **[8]**

Hall, D. P., & Cunningham, P. M. (1991). *Reading without ability grouping: Issues in first grade reading instruction.* Paper presented at the National Reading Conference, Palm Springs, CA. **[6]**

Hall, M. (1981). *Teacher reading as a language experience* (3rd ed.). Columbus, OH: Charles C. Merrill. **[6]**

Halliday, M. A. K. (1975). *Learning how to mean: Explorations in the development of language.* London: Edward Arnold. **[7]**

Hamilton, H. (1976). TV tie-ins as a bridge to books. *Language Arts,* (February), 129–130. **[3]**

Hammill, D. D., & Larson, S. C. (1983). *Test of written language (TOWL).* Austin, TX: Pro-Ed.

Hancock, M. R. (1993). Character journals: Initiating involvement and identification through literature. *Journal of Reading, 37*(1), 42–50. **[5]**

Hanf, M. B. (1971). Mapping: A technique for translating reading into thinking. *Journal of Reading, 14,* 225–230, 270. **[8]**

Hanna, G. S., Hodges, R. E., Hanna, J. S., & Rudolph, E. H. (1966). *Phoneme-grapheme correspondence as cues to spelling improvement.* Washington, D.C.: Department of Health, Education, and Welfare, Office of Education.

**Hansen, J.** (1981). The effects of interface training and practice on young children's reading comprehension. *Reading Research Quarterly, 16*(3), 391–417. **[8]**

**Hansen, J.** (1992). The language of challenge: Readers and writers speak their minds. *Language Arts 69*(2), 100–105. **[4] [5] [9] [12]**

**Hansen, J, & Pearson, P. D.** (1983). An instructional study: Improving the inferential comprehension of good and poor fourth-grade readers. *Journal of Educational Psychology, 75,* 821–829. **[8]**

**Hargis, C. H., Terhaar-Yonkers, M., William, P. C., & Reed, M. T.** (1988). Repetition requirements for word recognition. *Journal of Reading, 31*(4), 320–327. **[6]**

**Haring, N. G., Bateman, B., & Carnine, D.** (1977). Direct instruction—DISTAR. In N. G. Haring and B. Bateman (Eds.), *Teaching the learning disabled child* (pp. 165–202). Englewood Cliffs, NJ: Prentice-Hall. **[6]**

**Harman, S.** (1982). Are reversals a symptom of dyslexia? *The Reading Teacher, 35*(4), 424–428. **[12]**

**Harp, B.** (1988). When the principal asks: "Why are your kids singing during reading time?" *The Reading Teacher, 41*(4), 454–457. **[11]**

**Harris, A., & Server, B.** (1966). The CRAFT project: Instructional time in reading research. *Reading Research Quarterly, 2,* 27–56. **[13]**

**Harris, A. J., & Sipay, E. R.** (1975). *How to increase reading ability* (6th ed.). New York: David McKay. **[7]**

**Harris, A. J., & Sipay, E. R.** (1990). *How to increase reading ability: A guide to developmental and remedial methods* (9th ed.). White Plains, New York: Longman. **[1] [6] [13]**

**Harste, J., Burke, C., & Woodward, V.** (1984). *Language stories and literacy lessons.* Portsmouth, NH: Heinemann. **[2] [3]**

**Hayes, D. A.** (1987). The potential for directing study in combined reading and writing activity. *Journal of Reading Behavior, 19*(4), 333–352. **[9]**

**Hayes, D. A.** (1988). *Guided reading and summarizing procedure.* Manuscript, University of Georgia, Athens. **[8]**

**Hayes, D. A.** (1989). Help students GRASP the knack of writing summaries. *Journal of Reading, 33*(2), 96–101. **[9]**

**Hayes, D. A.** (1990). Thinking critically about reading. *Georgia Journal of Reading, 16*(2), 2–5. **[1]**

**Hayes, D. A.** (1991). Passing the torch. *Georgia Journal of Reading, 16*(2), 2. **[1]**

**Hayes, D. A., & Tierney, R. J.** (1982). Developing readers' knowledge through analogy. *Reading Research Quarterly, 17,* 256–280. **[8]**

**Hayes, J. R.** (1989). *Handbook of creativity, assessment, research, and theory.* New York: Plenum. **[9]**

**Haynes, J. E., & Fillmer, H. T.** (1984). Paraphrasing and reading comprehension. *Reading World, 24,* 76–79. **[8]**

**Heaton, M. M., & Lewis, H. B.** (1955). *Reading ladders for human relations* (3rd ed.). Washington, DC: American Council on Education.

**Hebb, D. O.** (1949). *Organization of behavior.* New York: John Wiley & Sons. **[3]**

**Hecklemann, R. G.** (1966). Using the neurological impress remedial technique. *Academic Therapy Quarterly, 1,* 235–239.

**Hecklemann, R. G.** (1969). Neurological impress method of remedial reading instruction. *Academic Therapy Quarterly, 4,* 277–282.

**Heimlich, J. E., & Pittelman, S. D.** (1986). *Semantic mapping: Classroom applications.* Newark, DE: International Reading Association. **[8]**

**Helfeldt, J. P., & Lalik, R.** (1979). Reciprocal student-teacher questioning. In C. Pennock (Ed.), *Reading comprehension at four linguistic levels* (pp. 74–99). Newark, DE: International Reading Association. **[8]**

**Heller, M. F.** (1986). How do you know what you know? Metacognitive modeling in the content areas. *Journal of Reading, 29*(5), 415–422. **[10]**

**Henk, W. A., & King, G. T.** (1984). Helping students follow written directions. In G. H. McNinch (Ed.), *Reading teacher education.* Fourth yearbook of the American Reading Forum (pp. 62–64). Athens, GA: American Reading Forum. **[8]**

**Henk, W. A., & Selders, M. L.** (1984). A test of synonymic scoring of cloze passage. *The Reading Teacher, 38*(3), 282–287. **[12]**

**Hennings, D. G.** (1986). *Teaching the language arts* (3rd ed.) Boston, MA: Houghton Mifflin. **[5]**

**Herber, H. L.** (1978). *Teaching reading in content areas* (2nd ed.). Englewood Cliffs, NJ: Prentice-Hall. **[10]**

**Herman, P. A.** (1985). The effect of repeated readings on reading rate, speech pauses, and word recognition accuracy. *Reading Research Quarterly, 20,* 553–565.

**Hickman, J.** (1983). Classrooms that help children like books. In N. Roser, & M. Frith, (Eds.), *Children's choices: Teaching with books children like* (pp. 1–11). Newark, DE: International Reading Association. **[5]**

**Hiebert, E., & Colt, J.** (1989). Patterns of literature-based instruction. *The Reading Teacher, 43,* 14–20. **[13]**

**Hiebert, J.** (1983). An examination of ability grouping for reading instruction. *Reading Research Quarterly, 18,* 231–255. **[13]**

**Hill, M.** (1991). Writing summaries promotes thinking and learning across the curriculum—but why are they so difficult to write? *Journal of Reading, 34*(7), 536–539. **[8]**

Hirsch, E. D. (1987). *Cultural literacy: What every American needs to know.* Boston: Houghton Mifflin. **[2]**

Hittleman, C. (1984, Spring/Summer). Peer response groups: The writing process in action. *Language Connections: Hofstra University Newsletter,* p. 4. **[9]**

Hoffman, J. (1991). Teacher and school effects in learning to read. In R. Barr, M. Kamil, P. Mosenthal, D. P. Pearson, (Eds.), *Handbook of reading research,* Vol. II (pp. 911–950). White Plains, New York: Longman. **[13]**

Hoffman, J. V. (1977). Intra-Act: A language in the content areas teaching procedure (Doctoral dissertation, University of Missouri-Kansas City). *Dissertation Abstracts International, 38,* 3248A.

Hoffman, J. V. (1985). *The oral recitation lesson: A teacher's guide.* Austin, TX: Academic Consultants. **[4]**

Hoffman, J. V. (1987). Rethinking the role of oral reading in basal instruction. *Elementary School Journal, 87,* 367–374.

Hoffman, J. V. (1992). Leadership in the language arts: Am I whole yet? Are you? *Language Arts, 69*(5), 366–371.

Hohn, W., & Ehri, L. (1983). Do alphabet letters help prereaders acquire phonemic segmentation skill? *Journal of Educational Psychology, 75,* 752–762. **[3]**

Holbrook, H. T. (1988). Sex differences in reading: Nature or nurture. *Journal of Reading, 31*(6), 574–577. **[4] [5]**

Holdaway, D. (1972). Independence in reading: A handbook on individualized procedures. Aukland, New Zealand: Ashton Scholastic. **[3]**

Holdaway, D. (1979). *The foundations of literacy.* New York: Ashton Scholastic. **[6]**

Holly, M. L. (1987). *Keeping a personal-professional journal.* Victoria, Australia: Deakin University Press. **[2]**

Holmes, J. A., & Singer, H. (1961). *The substrata-factor theory: Substrata-factor differences underlying reading ability in known groups.* (Final Report No. 538, SAE 8176) U.S. Office of Education. **[8]**

Holt, S. B., & O'Tuel, F. S. (1989, Winter). The effect of sustained silent reading and writing on achievement and attitudes of 7- and 8-grade students reading two years below level. *Reading Improvement, 26,* 290–298. **[8]**

Hopkins, L. B. (1969). *Books are by people.* New York: Citation. **[4]**

Hopkins, L. B. (1974). *More books by more people.* New York: Citation. **[4]**

Hord, S. M., & Goldstein, M. L. (1982). *What principals do to facilitate change: Their interventions.* Paper presented at the annual meeting of the American Educational Research Association. New York, New York. **[13]**

Hori, A.K.O. (1977). *An investigation of the efficacy of a questioning training procedure on increasing the reading comprehension performance of junior high school learning disabled students.* Unpublished master's thesis, University of Kansas, Lawrence, KS. **[8]**

Hull, M. A. (1976). *Phonics for the teacher of reading* (2nd ed.). Columbus, OH: Charles C. Merrill. **[6] [B]**

Hunt, K. (1965). *Grammatical structures written at three grade levels.* Urbana, IL: National Council of Teachers of English. **[4]**

Hunt, L. (1970). The effect of self-selection, interest, and motivation upon independent, instructional and frustration levels. *The Reading Teacher, 24,* 146–151. **[8]**

Hynd, C. R., & Alvermann, D. E. (1986). The role of refutation text in overcoming difficulty with science concepts. *Journal of Reading, 26,* 440–446. **[8] [10]**

Idol, L. (1987). Group story mapping: A comprehension for both skilled and unskilled readers. *Journal of Learning Disabilities, 20,* 196–205. **[8]**

Ilg, F. (1964). The child from three to eight with implications for reading. *Teaching young children to read.* U.S. Department of Health, Education, and Welfare, OE-30041. Washington, DC: U.S. Government Printing Office. **[3]**

Indrisano, R. (1982). An ecological approach to learning. *Topics in Learning and Learning Disabilities, 1*(Jan), 11–15. **[3]**

Indrisano, R., & Paratore, J. R. (1992). Using literature with readers at risk. In B. E. Cullinan (Ed.), *Invitation to read: More children's literature in the reading program* (pp. 139–149). Newark, DE: International Reading Association. **[10]**

Ingham, J. (1982). *Books and reading development: The Bradford book flood experiment* (2nd ed.). Exeter, NH: Heinemann. **[8]**

Isaacson, A. G. (1987). A fingerspelling approach to spelling. *Academic Therapy, 23,* 89–90. **[11]**

Isakson, M. B. (1992). Learning about reluctant readers through their letters. *Journal of Reading, 34*(8), 632–637. **[9]**

Jacobs, D. H., & Searfoss, L. W. (1979). *Diagnostic reading inventory.* Dubuque, IA: Kendall/Hunt. **[12]**

Jaggar, A. (1985). On observing the language learner: Introduction and overview. In A. Jaggar, & M. T. Smith-Burke (Eds.), *Observing the language learner* (pp. 1–7). Newark, DE: International Reading Association. **[12]**

Jalongo, M. R. (1988). *Young children and picture books: Literature from infancy to six.* Washington, DC: National Association for the Education of Young Children. **[5]**

**Jamar, D., & Morrow, J.** (1991). A literature-based interdisciplinary approach to the teaching of reading, writing, and mathematics. *The Ohio Reading Teacher, 25*(3), 28–35. **[10]**

**Jarrell, R.** (1963). *The bat-poet.* New York: Collier. **[2]**

**Jenkins, J. R., & Larson, K.** (1979). Evaluation error correction procedures for oral reading. *Journal of Special Education, 13*(2), 145–156. **[4]**

**Jenkins, J. R., Larson, K., & Fleisher, L.** (1982). Effects of error correction on word recognition and reading comprehension. *Learning Disability Quarterly, 6*(2), 139–154. **[4]**

**Jett-Simpson, M.** (1981). Writing stories using model structures: The circle story. *Language Arts, 58*(3), 293–300. **[9]**

**Johns, J.** (1982). *Basic reading inventory: Preprimer to grade eight* (2nd ed.). Dubuque, IA: Kendall/Hunt.

**Johnson, D. D., & Pearson, P. D.** (1984). *Teaching reading vocabulary* (2nd ed.). New York: Holt, Rinehart and Winston. **[7]**

**Johnson, D. W., & Johnson, R. T.** (1987). *Learning together and alone: Cooperative, conjunctive, and individualistic learning.* Englewood Cliffs, NJ: Prentice-Hall. **[2]**

**Johnson, T. D., & Louis, D. R.** (1987). *Literacy through literature.* Portsmouth, NH: Heinemann. **[11]**

**Johnston, P., & Winograd, P.** (1985). Passive failure in reading. *Journal of Reading Behavior, 17,* 279–301. **[13]**

**Jones, C.** (1985). *Poetry patterns.* St. Louis, MO: Book Lures. **[7] [9]**

**Jongsma, E.** (1980). *Cloze instruction research: A second look.* Newark, DE: International Reading Association. **[8]**

**Joyce, B., & Showers, B.** (1982). The coaching of teaching. *Educational Leadership, 39,* 4–10. **[13]**

**Juel, C.** (1988). Learning to read and write: A longitudinal study of fifty-four children from first through fourth grades. *Journal of Educational Psychology, 80,* 437–447. **[6]**

**Juel, C.** (1991). Beginning reading. In R. Barr, M. L. Kamil, P. Mosenthal, & P. D. Pearson (Eds.), *Handbook of reading research,* Vol. II (pp. 759–788). White Plains, New York: Longman. **[1] [6]**

**Juel, C., & Roper-Schneider, D.** (1985). The influence of basal readers on first-grade reading. *Reading Research Quarterly, 20,* 134–152. **[1] [6]**

**Kalmbach, J. R.** (1986). Getting at the point of retellings. *Journal of Reading, 29,* 326–333. **[8]**

**Kameenui, E. J., & Shannon, P.** (1988). Point/counterpoint: Direct instruction reconsidered. In J. E. Readence, R. S. Baldwin, J. P. Konopak, & P. R. O'Keefe (Eds.), *Dialogues in literacy research. Thirty-seventh Yearbook of the National Reading Conference* (pp. 35–43). Chicago: National Reading Conference. **[2]**

**Karges-Bone, L.** (1992). Bring on the big books. *The Reading Teacher, 45*(9), 743–744. **[3]**

**Karlin, R.** (1984). *Teaching reading in high school: Improving reading in content area* (4th ed.). New York: Harper & Row. **[10]**

**Kay, L., Young, J. L., & Mottley, R. R.** (1986). Using Manzo's ReQuest model with delinquent adolescents. *Journal of Reading, 29,* 506–510. **[8]**

**Kelly, B. W., & Holmes, J.** (1979). The guided lecture procedure. *Journal of Reading, 22,* 602–604. **[8] [10]**

**Khatena, J.** (1989). Intelligence and creativity to multitalent. *Journal of Creative Behavior, 23*(2), 93–97. **[9]**

**Kierwa, K. A.** (1985). Students' note-taking behaviors and the efficacy of providing the instructor's notes for review. *Contemporary Educational Psychology, 10,* 378–386. **[10]**

**Killgallon, P. A.** (1942). *A study to determine the relationships among certain pupils' adjustments in language situations.* Unpublished doctoral dissertation, Pennsylvania State College. **[12]**

**Kirby, D., & Liner, T.** (1981). *Inside out: Developmental strategies for teaching.* Montclair, NJ: Boynton Cook. **[11]**

**Klausmeier, H. J.** (1992). Concept learning and concept teaching. *Educational Psychologist, 27*(3) 267–286. **[11]**

**Knafle, J. D.** (1989). Sharing books bolsters family bonds. *PTA Today, 14*(5), 24–25. **[3]**

**Knafle, J. D.** (1985). Changing values in children's books. *The Reading Instruction Journal 28*(3), 18–21. **[2]**

**Knafle, J. D., Legenza-Wescott, A., & Passcarella, E. T.** (1988). Assessing values in children's books. *Reading Improvement, 25*(1), 71–81. **[8]**

**Knafle, J. D., & Geissal, M. A.** (1983). Dialect as an influence in attitudes toward oral reading errors. *The Reading Professor, 9* (2 & 3), 1–7. **[11]**

**Knafle, J. D., & Legenza, A.** (1979). Effective components of children's pictures. *Reading Improvement, 16,* 281–283. **[5]**

**Knafle, J. D., Wescott, A. L., & Pascarella, E. T.** (1988). Assessing values in children's books. *Reading Improvement, 25,* 71–81. **[5]**

**Kneller, G. F.** (1965). *The art and science of creativity.* New York: Holt, Rinehart and Winston. **[9]**

**Kohl, H.** (1973). *Reading: How to.* New York: E. P. Dutton & Co. **[2]**

**Kohlberg, L.** (1981). *The philosophy of moral development: Moral stages and the idea of justice.* San Francisco: Harper & Row. **[9]**

**Konopak, B. C., & Williams, N. L.** (1988). Using the key word method to help young readers learn content material. *The Reading Teacher, 41,* 682–687. **[7]**

**Koppman, P.** (1991, Fall). Ideas for working with parents (summarized by Nan Sanborn). *Virginia State Reading Association Newsletter,* p. 9. **[3]**

**Koskinen, P. S., & Blum, I. H.** (1986). Paired repeated reading: A classroom strategy for developing fluent reading. *The Reading Teacher, 40*(1), 70–75. **[2] [4] [6] [8]**

**Koskinen, P. S., Wilson, R. M., Gambrell, L. B., & Jensema, C. J.** (1987). *Using the technology of closed-captioned television to teach reading to handicapped students.* Performance Report, United States Department of Education Grant No. G-00-84-30067. Falls Church, VA: National Captioning Institute. **[11]**

**Koskinen, P. S., Wilson, R. M., Gambrell, L. B., & Neuman, S. B.** (1993). Captioned video and vocabulary learning: An innovative practice in literacy instruction. *The Reading Teacher, 47*(1), 36–43. **[11]**

**Kozliski, E. B.** (1989, Winter). Improving oral reading performance through self-monitoring and strategy training. *Reading Improvement, 26,* 305–314. **[4]**

**Krathwohl, D. R., Bloom, B. S., & Masia, B. B.** (1964). *Taxonomy of educational objectives; the classification of educational goals; handbook 2: Affective domain.* New York: David McKay. **[7]**

**Kuder, S. J.** (1990). Effectiveness of the DISTAR reading program for children with learning disabilities. *Journal of Learning Disabilities, 23,* 69–71. **[2]**

**Kutiper, K., & Wilson, P.** (1993). Updating poetry preferences: A look at the poetry children really like. *The Reading Teacher, 47*(1), 28–35. **[3]**

**Labbo, L. D., & Teale, W. H.** (1990). Cross-age reading: A strategy for helping poor readers. *The Reading Teacher, 43,* 362–369. **[3] [4] [11]**

**LaBerge, D., & Samuels, S. J.** (1974). Toward a theory of automatic information processing in reading. *Cognitive Psychology, 6,* 293–323. **[1] [4] [6] [8]**

**Lach, M. A.** (1993). Humor, literacy, and children's books. *Wisconsin State Reading Association Journal, 37*(1), 41–43. **[5]**

**Lambert, J. C.** (1993). In the classroom: Integrating the content areas to develop reading, writing, thinking activities. *Wisconsin Reading Association Journal, 37*(1), 39–40.

**Lamme, L. L.** (1987). Children's literature: The natural way to learn to read. In B. E. Cullinan (Ed.). *Children's literature in the reading program* (pp. 41–53). Newark, DE: International Reading Association. **[5]**

**Lamme, L. L.** (1989). Authorship: A key facet of whole language. *The Reading Teacher, 42*(9), 704–710. **[9] [10]**

**Lamme, L. L., & Hysmith, C.** (1991). One school's adventure into portfolio assessment. *Language Arts, 68*(8), 629–640. **[12]**

**Langer, J. A.** (1981). From theory to practice: A prereading plan. *Journal of Reading, 25,* 152–156. **[8]**

**Langer, J. A.** (1986a). *Children reading and writing: Structure and strategies.* Norwood, NJ: Ablex. **[9]**

**Langer, J. A.** (1986b). Learning through writing: Study skills in the content areas. *Journal of Reading, 29,* 400–406. **[10]**

**Langer, J. A., & Applebee, A. N.** (1986). Reading and writing instruction: Toward a theory of teaching and learning. In E. Z. Rothkopf (Ed.), *Review Research In Education, 13,* 171–194. **[9]**

**Langer, J. A., & Nicholich, M.** (1981). Prior knowledge and its relationship to comprehension. *Journal of Reading Behavior, 13,* 373–379. **[8]**

**Lapp, D., & Flood, J.** (1992). *Teaching reading to every child*

(3rd ed). New York: Macmillan Publishing Co. **[3] [5] [6] [11]**

**LaPray, M., & Ross, R.** (1969). The graded word list: quick gauge of reading ability. *Journal of Reading, 12*(4), 305–307. **[12]**

**Larking, L.** (1984). ReQuest helps children comprehend: A study. *Australian Journal of Reading, 7,* 135–139. **[8]**

**Larrick, N.** (1987). Keep a poem in your pocket. In Cullinan, B. E. (Ed.), *Children's literature in the reading program* (pp. 20–27). Newark, DE: International Reading Association. **[4]**

**Larson, C., & Dansereau, D.** (1986). Cooperative learning in dyads. *Journal of Reading, 29,* 516–520. **[2]**

**Lauritzen, C.** (1980). Oral literature and the teaching of reading. *The Reading Teacher, 33* (7), 787–790. **[11]**

**Lauritzen, C.** (1982). A modification of repeated readings for group instruction. *The Reading Teacher, 35,* 456–458. **[4] [6]**

**Lawson, R.** (1953). *Mr. Revere and I.* Boston: Little, Brown & Co. **[2]**

**Leedy, L.** (1991) *Messages in the mailbox (or) how to write a letter.* New York: Holiday House. **[3]**

**Legenza, A.** (1978). Inquiry training for reading and learning improvement. *Reading Improvement, 15,* 309–316. **[10]**

**Legenza, A.** (1980). Picture potency formula: Validation study. *Reading Improvement, 17,* 115–116. **[5]**

**Legenza, A., & Knafle, J. D.** (1978). How effective are pictures in basal readers? *The Reading Teacher, 32,* 170–173. **[5] [A]**

**Legenza, A., & Knafle, J. D.** (1979). The effective components of children's pictures. *Reading Improvement, 16,* 281–283. **[5]**

**Leibert, R. E.** (1992). Business-educational partnership. *The Missouri Reader, 61*(2), 5. **[13]**

**Leibert, R. E., & Sherk, J. K., Jr.** (1970). Three Frostig visual perception sub-tests and specific reading tasks for kindergarten, first, and second grade children. *The Reading Teacher, 24*(2), 130–137. **[13]**

Lenahan, A. V. (1992). *Bits and Pieces.* Fairfield, NJ: The Economical Press, Inc. **[11]**

Lesgold, A. M., & Resnick, L. B. (1982). How reading disabilities develop: Perspectives from a longitudinal study. In J. P. Das, R. Mulcahy, & A. E. Wall (Eds.), *Theory and research in learning disability* (pp. 155–187). New York: Plenum. **[6]**

Levesque, J., & Prosser, T. (1991). Partnerships for tomorrow through knowledge and empowerment. *The Missouri Reader, 15*(2), 14–16. **[2]**

Levin, J. R., Morrison, C. R., McGivern, J. E., Mastropieri, M. A., & Scruggs, T. E. (1986). Mnemonic facilitation of text-embedded science facts. *American Educational Research Journal, 23*(3), 489–506. **[7]**

Levin, J. R., & Pressley, M. (1981). Improving children's prose comprehension: Selected strategies that seem to succeed. In C. M. Santa & B. L. Hayes (Eds.), *Children's prose comprehension* (pp. 49–60). Newark, DE: International Reading Association. **[8]**

Lewkowicz, N. K. (1987). On the question of teaching decoding skills to older students. *Journal of Reading, 31,* 50–57. **[6] [8]**

Linn, R. L., Baker, E. L., & Dunbar, S. B., (in press). Complex, performance-based assessment: Expectations and validation criteria. *Educational Researcher.*

Lipka, C., & Gaskill, P. (1992). Literature-based reading instruction: Research and recommendations. *Michigan Reading Journal, 25*(1), 20–31. **[5]**

Lipson, M. Y. (1982). Learning new information from text: The role of prior knowledge and reading ability. *Journal of Reading Behavior, 14,* 243–262. **[1]**

Lipson, M. Y. (1984). Some unexpected issues in prior knowledge

and comprehension. *The Reading Teacher, 37,* 760–764. **[10]**

Lipson, M. Y., & Wixson, K. K. (1991). *Assessment and instruction of reading disability.* New York: HarperCollins. **[8]**

Loban, W. (1963). *The language of elementary school children.* Urbana, IL: National Council of Teachers of English. **[9]**

Loban, W. (1964). *Learning ability: Grades seven, eight, and nine.* Berkeley: University of California. (ERIC Document Reproduction Service No. ED 001 275)

Locke, E. (1977). An empirical study of lecture note taking among college students. *Journal of Educational Research, 71,* 93–99. **[10]**

Loucks, S., Newlove, B. W., & Hall, G. E. (1975). *Measuring levels of use of innovation. A manual for trainers, interviewers, and raters.* Austin, TX: The University of Texas, Research and Development Center for Teacher Education. **[13]**

Lucas, C. K. (1988). Toward ecological evaluation, part one and part two. *The Quarterly of the National Writing Project and the Center for the Study of Writing, 10*(1), 1–7; *10*(2), 4–10. **[12]**

Lundberg, I. (1984). Learning to read. *School Research Newsletter.* Sweden: National Board of Education. **[6]**

Lundberg, I., Frost, J., & Petersen, O. (1988). Effects of an extensive program for stimulating phonological awareness in preschool children. *Reading Research Quarterly, 23,* 263–284. **[3]**

Lundsteen, S. W. (1976). *Children learn to communicate.* Englewood Cliffs, NJ: Prentice-Hall. **[4]**

Lundsteen, S. W. (1979). *Listening: Its impact at all levels on reading and other language arts* (rev. ed.). Urbana, IL: National Council of Teachers of English.

MacGinitie, W. H., & MacGinitie, R. K. (1989). *Gates-*

*MacGinitie's Reading Tests: Manual for scoring and interpretation—level 4* (3rd ed.). Chicago: Riverside.

Machie, B. C. (1982). *The effects of a sentence-combining program on the reading comprehension and written composition of fourth grade students.* Unpublished doctoral dissertation, Hofstra University. **[9]**

Maclay, J. H. (1971). *Readers theatre: Toward a grammar of practice.* New York: Random House. **[4]**

Madden, N. A., Slavin, R. W., Karweit, N. L., Dolan, L., & Wasik, B. A. (1991). Success for all. *Phi Delta Kappan,* 593–599.

Maggart, Z. D., & Zintz, M. V. (1992). *The reading process: The teacher and the learner* 6th ed.), Dubuque, IA: W. C. Brown & Benchmark. **[5] [8] [10] [11]**

Mann, L., & Sabatino, D. A. (1985). *Foundations of cognitive process in remedial and special education.* Rockville, MD: Aspen Publishers. **[10]**

Manning, G. L., & Manning, M. (1984). What models of recreational reading make a difference? *Reading World, 23,* 375–380. **[8]**

Manzo, A. V. (1969a). Improving reading comprehension through reciprocal questioning (Doctoral dissertation, Syracuse University, Syracuse, New York, 1968). *Dissertation Abstracts International, 30,* 5344A. **[2] [8] [12]**

Manzo, A. V. (1969b). The Re-Quest procedure. *Journal of Reading, 13,* 123–126. **[8]**

Manzo, A. V. (1970). CAT—A game for extending vocabulary and knowledge allusions. *Journal of Reading, 13,* 367–369. **[7]**

Manzo, A. V. (1973). CONPASS English: A demonstration project. *Journal of Reading, 16,* 539–545. **[8] [10] [13]**

Manzo, A. V. (1975a). Guided reading procedure. *Journal of Reading, 18,* 287–291. **[2] [8]**

Manzo, A. V. (1977a). Dyslexia as specific psychoneurosis. *Journal of Reading Behavior, 19*(3), 305–308. **[1] [11]**

Manzo, A. V. (1977b). *Recent developments in content area reading.* Keynote address, Missouri Council of Teachers of English, Springfield, MO. **[8]**

Manzo, A. V. (1980). Three "universal" strategies in content area reading and languaging. *Journal of Reading, 24,* 146–149. **[1] [4] [6] [10]**

Manzo, A. V. (1981). The Language Shaping Paradigm (LSP) for improving language, comprehension, and thought. In P. L. Anders (Ed.), *Research on reading in secondary schools: A semi-annual report,* Monograph No. 7 (pp. 54–68). Tucson: University of Arizona, College of Education, Reading Department. **[10]**

Manzo, A. V. (1981b). Using proverbs to teach reading and thinking; or, Com faceva mia nonna (the way my grandmother did it). *The Reading Teacher, 34,* 411–416.

Manzo, A. V. (1983). Subjective approach to vocabulary acquisition (Or, "I think my brother is aboreal!"). *Reading Psychology, 3,* 155–160. **[7]**

Manzo, A. V. (1985). Expansion modules for the ReQuest, CAT, GRP, and REAP reading/study procedures. *Journal of Reading, 28,* 498–502. **[1] [7] [8] [13]**

Manzo, A. V. (1987). Psychologically induced dyslexia and learning disabilities. *The Reading Teacher, 40*(4), 408–413. **[6]**

Manzo, A. V., & Casale, U. P. (1980). The five c's: A problem-solving approach to study skills. *Reading Horizons, 20,* 281–284.

Manzo, A. V., & Casale, U. P. (1981). A multivariate analysis of principle and trace elements in mature reading comprehension. In G. H. McNinch (Ed.), *Comprehension: Process and product.* First yearbook of the American Reading Forum (pp. 76–81). Athens, GA: American Reading Forum. **[1] [9]**

Manzo, A. V., & Casale, U. P. (1983). A preliminary description and factor analysis of a broad spectrum battery for assessing "progress toward reading maturity." *Reading Psychology, 4,* 181–191. **[8]**

Manzo, A. V., & Casale, U. P. (1985). Listen-read-discuss: A content reading heuristic. *Journal of Reading, 28*(8), 732–734. **[8] [10]**

Manzo, A. V. & Garber, K. (in press). In Alan Purves (Ed.), *Encyclopedia of English Studies and Language Arts* **[10]**

Manzo, A. V., Garber, K., & Warm, J. (1992). Dialectical thinking: A generative approach to critical/creative reading. Paper, National Reading Conference, San Antonio, TX.

Manzo, A. V., & Legenza, A. (1975a). Inquiry training for kindergarten children. *Journal of Educational Leadership, 32,* 479–483. **[1] [4] [8] [10]**

Manzo, A. V., & Legenza, A. (1975b). A method for assessing the language stimulation value of pictures. *Language Arts, 52*(8), 1085–1089. **[1] [5] [8]**

Manzo, A. V., & Manzo, U. C. (1985). Listen-read-discuss: A content reading heuristic. *Journal of Reading, 28,* 732–734. **[10]**

Manzo, A. V., & Manzo, U. C. (1987). *Asking, answering, commenting: A participation training strategy.* Paper presented at the annual meeting of the International Reading Association, Anaheim, CA. **[4]**

Manzo, A. V., & Manzo, U. C. (1987b). Using proverbs to diagnose and treat comprehension dysfunctions. *Rhode Island Reading Review, 3*(2), 37–42.

Manzo, A. V., & Manzo, U. C. (1990a). *Content area reading: A heuristic approach.* Columbus, OH: Merrill. **[1] [2] [4] [6] [7] [8] [9] [10] [11]**

Manzo, A. V., & Manzo, U. C. (1990b). Note cue: A comprehension and participation training strategy. *Journal of Reading, 33*(8), 608–611. **[4] [8]**

Manzo, A. V., & Manzo, U. C. (1993). *Literacy disorders: Holistic diagnosis and remediation.* Fort Worth, TX: Harcourt Brace Jovanovich. **[2] [3] [4] [6] [7] [8] [9] [11] [12] [B] [13]**

Manzo, A. V., Manzo, U. C., & McKenna, M. C. (1995). *The informal reading-thinking inventory* Arlington, TX: Harcourt Brace Jovanovich. **[12]**

Manzo, A. V., Manzo, U. C., & Smith, W. (In progress). **[10]**

Manzo, A. V., & Martin, D. (1974). Writing communal poetry. *Journal of Reading, 17*(8), 638–648. **[4] [9]**

Manzo, A. V., & Sherk, J. K. (1971). Some generalization and strategies to guide vocabulary acquisition. *Journal of Reading Behavior, 4*(1), 78–89. **[7]**

Marchbanks, G., & Levin, H. (1965). Cues by which children recognize words. *Journal of Educational Psychology, 56,* 75–81. **[6]**

Maria, K. (1990). *Reading comprehension instruction: Issues and strategies.* Parkton, MD: York Press. **[8]**

Maring, G. H., & Furman, G. (1985). Seven "whole class" strategies to help mainstreamed young people read and listen better in content area classes. *Journal of Reading, 28,* 694–700. **[8] [10]**

Maring, G. H., & Ritson, R. (1980). Reading improvement in the gymnasium. *Journal of Reading, 24,* 27–31. **[8]**

Marsh, G., & Mineo, R. (1977). Training preschool children to recognize phonemes in words. *Journal of Educational Psychology, 69,* 748–753. **[3]**

Marshall, J. D. (1987). The effects of writing on students' understanding of literary texts. *Research in the Teaching of English, 21,* 30–63. **[10]**

Marzano, R. J. (1991). Language, the language arts, and thinking. In J. Flood, J. M. Jensen, D. Lapp,

& J. R. Squire (Eds.), *Handbook of research on teaching the English language arts* (pp. 559–586). New York: MacMillan. **[8]**

Marzano, R. J., & Marzano, J. S. (1988). *A cluster approach to elementary vocabulary instruction.* Newark, DE: International Reading Association. **[7]**

Mason, J. (1980). When do children begin to read: An exploration of four year old children's letter and word reading competencies. *Reading Research Quarterly, 15,* 203–227. **[3]**

Mason, J., Herman, P., & Au, K. (1991). Children's developing knowledge of words. In J. Flood, J. M. Jensen, D. Lapp, & J. R. Squire (Eds.), *Handbook of research on teaching the English language arts* (pp. 721–731). New York: Macmillan. **[8]**

Maw, W., & Maw, E. (1967). Children's curiosity as an aspect of reading comprehension. *The Reading Teacher, 15*(2), 236–240. **[8]**

McCauley, J. K., & McCauley, D. S. (1992). Using choral reading to promote language learning for ESL students, *The Reading Teacher, 45*(7), 526–533. **[4]**

McCormick, S. (1977a). Should you read aloud to your children? *Language Arts, 54,* 143. **[4]**

McCormick, S. (1977b). Choosing books to read to preschool children. *Language Arts, 54,* 545. **[3]**

McCormick, S. (1990, December). *Multiple-exposure/multiple-context longitudinal study of Peter Parsons.* Paper presented at the National Reading Conference. **[8] [6] [11]**

McCoy, K. M., & Pany, D. (1986). Summary and analysis of oral reading corrective feedback research. *The Reading Teacher, 39*(6), 548–545. **[4]**

McCracken, R. A. (1966). *Standard reading inventory.* Klamath Falls, OR: Klamath. **[6] [12]**

McCracken, R. A. (1971). Initiating sustained silent reading. *Jour-*nal of Reading, 14(8), 521–524, 582–583. **[8]**

McCracken, R. A., & McCracken, M. J. (1978). Modeling is the key to sustained silent reading. *The Reading Teacher, 31*(4), 406–408. **[8]**

McEneaney, J. E. (1992). Computer assisted diagnosis in reading: An expert systems approach. *Journal of Reading, 36*(1), 36–47. **[13]**

McEvoy, K., & Homan, S. (1991). How successful are repeated readings? *The Florida Reading Quarterly, 27*(3), 18–21. **[6]**

McEwan, H., & Bull, B. (1991). The pedagogic nature of subject matter knowledge. *American Educational Research Journal. 28,* 316–334. **[9]**

McGee, L. M. (1982). Awareness of text structure: Effects on children's recall of expository text. *Reading Research Quarterly, 17,* 581–590. **[8]**

McGee, L. M., & Richgels, D. J. (1986). Attending to text structure: A comprehension strategy. In E. K. Dishner, T. W. Bean, J. E. Readence, & D. W. Moore (Eds.), *Reading in the content areas: Improving classroom instruction* (2nd ed.), pp. 42–54, Dubuque, IA: Kendall/Hunt. **[8]**

McGuire, F. N. (1984). How arts instruction affects reading and language: Theory and research. *The Reading Teacher, 37*(9), 835–839. **[11]**

McIntyre, J. (1991, June). *The developmental difference: "Skill and will": An investigation into the reported feelings of personal control and competency of community college developmental students.* Presentation to "ABD Club," University of Missouri-Kansas City. **[10]**

McKee, P. (1948). *The teaching of reading in the elementary school.* Boston: Houghton Mifflin. **[1]**

McKee, P., & Durr, W. K. (1966). *Reading: A program of instruction for the elementary* school. Boston: Houghton Mifflin. **[10]**

McKenna, M. C. (1976). Synonymic versus verbatim scoring of the cloze procedure. *Journal of Reading, 20,* 141–143. **[12]**

McKenna, M. C. (1983). Informal reading inventories: A review of the issues. *The Reading Teacher, 36*(7), 670–679. **[12]**

McKenna, M. C., & Layton, K. (1990). Concurrent validity of cloze as a measure of intersentential comprehension. *Journal of Educational Psychology, 82,* 372–377. **[12]**

McKenna, M. C., Robinson, R. D., & Miller, J. W. (1990, April). *Whole language: A research agenda for the nineties.* Paper presented at the American Educational Research Association, Boston. **[2]**

McKenzie, J. V., Ericson, B., & Hunter, L. (1988). *Questions may be an answer.* Manuscript, California State University at Northridge. **[8]**

McKeown, M. G., Beck, I. L., & Worthy, M. J. (1993). Grappling with text ideas: Questioning the author. *The Reading Teacher, 46*(7), 560–566. **[9]**

McMath, J. (1991). Young children. *Shy Charles* and whole language: A vignette. *Ohio Council of the International Reading Association Newsletter, 1*(3), 10–11.

McNeil, J., & Donant, L. (1982). Summarization strategy for improving reading comprehension. In J. A. Niles, & L. A. Harris (Eds.), *New inquiries in reading research and instruction* (pp. 215–219). Rochester, New York: National Reading Conference. **[8]**

Meeks, J. W. (1980). Effects of imbedded aids on prose-related textual material. *Reading World, 19,* 345–351. **[8]**

Meeks, J. W. (1991). Prior knowledge and metacognitive processes of reading comprehension: Applications to mildly retarded readers. In *Advances in mental retarda-*

tion and developmental disabilities, Vol. 4 (pp. 123–144). Lanhen, MD: Jessica Kingley. **[8]**

Meier, D. (1978). Cited in R. J. Trotter, Better learning: Imagine that. *Psychology Today, 19*(4), 22.

Mellon, J. C. (1969). *Transformational sentence-combining*. Urbana, IL: National Council of Teachers of English. **[9]**

Meloth, M. (1991). Enhancing literacy through cooperative learning. In E. Hiebert (Ed.), *Literacy for a diverse society: Perspectives, practices, and policies*, (pp. 172–183). New York: Teachers College Press. **[13]**

Meyer, B. J. F. (1975). *The organization of prose and its effect on memory*. Amsterdam: North-Holland. **[8]**

Meyer, L. A. (1982). The relative effects of word-analysis and word-supply correction procedures with poor readers during word-attack training. *Reading Research Quarterly, 17*(4), 544–555.

Meyer, L. A. (1984). Long-term academic effects of the direct instruction project Follow-through. *Elementary School Journal, 84*, 380–394. **[6]**

Meyer, L. A. Gersten, R. M., & Gutkin, J. (1983). Direct instruction: A project follow-through success story in an inner-city school. *Elementary School Journal, 84*, 241–252. **[2] [6]**

Miller, K. K., & George, J. E. (1992). Expository passage organizers: Models for reading and writing. *Journal of Reading, 35*(5), 372–377. **[8]**

Miller, W. E., & Dollard, J. (1941). *Social learning and imitation*. New Haven, CT: Yale University Press. **[8]**

Monroe, L. B. (1872). Monroe's Readers. In R. C. Aukerman (1981), *The basal reader approach to reading* (p. 7). New York: John Wiley & Sons. **[2]**

Monroe, E. E., Watson, A. R., & Tweddell, D. C. (1989). Relationships among communication apprehension, reading achievement, teacher perceived communication apprehension, and intelligence. *Journal of Reading Education, 15*(1), 10–20. **[12]**

Monson, D., & Sebesta, S. (1991). Reading preferences. In J. Flood, J. M. Jensen, D. Lapp, & J. R. Squire (Eds.), *Handbook of research on teaching the English language arts* (pp. 664–673). New York: Macmillan. **[5]**

Moore, D. W. (1983). A case of naturalistic assessment of reading comprehension. *Language Arts, 60*, 957–969. **[12]**

Moore, D. W. (1987). Vocabulary. In D. E. Alvermann, D. W. Moore, & M. W. Conley (Eds.), *Research within reach: Secondary school reading* (pp. 64–79). Newark, DE: International Reading Association. **[7]**

Moore, D. W., & Readence, J. E. (1980). Processing main ideas through parallel lesson transfer. *Journal of Reading, 23*, 589–593. **[8] [11]**

Moore, M. (1991). Reflective teaching and learning through the use of learning logs. *Journal of Reading Education, 17*(1), 35–49. **[2]**

Mork, T. A. (1972). Sustained silent reading in the classroom. *The Reading Teacher, 25*, 438–441. **[8]**

Morphett, M. V., & Washburne, C. (1931). When should children begin to read? *Elementary School Journal, 31*, 496–503. **[3]**

Morrow, L. M. (1988). Designing the classroom to promote literacy development. In D. S. Strickland, & L. M. Morrow (Eds.), *Emerging literacy: Young children learn to read and write* (pp. 121–134). Newark, DE: International Reading Association. **[5]**

Morrow, L. M. (1989). Creating a bridge to children's literature. In P. Winograd, K. Wixson, & M. Lipson (Eds.), *Improving basal reading instruction* (pp. 210–230). New York: Teacher College Press. **[8]**

Morrow, L. M., & Weinstein, C. S. (1986). Encouraging voluntary reading: The impact of a literature program on children's use of library centers. *Reading Research Quarterly, 21*, 330–346. **[8]**

Murray, D. (1989). *Expecting the unexpected: Teaching myself—and others—to read and write*. Portsmouth, NH: Heinemann. **[9]**

Musgrove, M. (1976). *Ashanti to Zulu: African traditions*. New York: Piper. **[9]**

Muth, K. D. (1987). Teachers' connection questions: Prompting students to organize text ideas. *Journal of Reading, 31*, 254–259. **[8] [10]**

Myklebust, H. R. (1965). *Development and disorders of written languages, Volume one, Picture story language test*. New York: Grune and Stratton.

Nagy, W. E. (1988). *Teaching vocabulary to improve reading comprehension*. Urbana, IL: National Council of Teachers of English.

Nagy, W. E., & Herman, P. A. (1984, October). *Limitations of vocabulary instruction*. Technical Report No. 326. Champaign, IL: Center for the Study of Reading, University of Illinois. **[7]**

National Association for the Education of Young Children. (1986). Position statement on developmentally appropriate practice in programs for 4- and 5-year olds. *Young Children, 41*(6), 20–29. **[3]**

Neal, J. C., & Moore, K. (1991). The very hungry caterpillar meets Beowulf in secondary classrooms. *Journal of Reading, 35*(4), 290–296.

Neal, J., & Vickers, B. (1985, November). *Parental assistance in oral reading*. Interviews at Sycamore Elementary School, Cookeville, TN. **[4]**

Nell, V. (1988). The psychology of reading for pleasure: Needs and gratifications. *Reading Research Quarterly, 23*, 626–633. **[13]**

**Nelson-Herber, J.** (1986). Expanding and refining vocabulary in content areas. *Journal of Reading, 29*, 626–633. **[7]**

**Neubert, G. A., & McNelis, S. J.** (1990). Peer response: Teaching specific revision suggestions. *English Journal, 79*(5), 52–56. **[9]**

**Neuman, S. B., & Koskinen, P. S.** (1992). Captioned television as comprehensible input: Effects of incidental word learning in context for language minority students. *Reading Research Quarterly, 27*, 95–106. **[7] [11]**

**Newell, G.** (1984). Learning from writing in two content areas: A case study/protocol analysis. *Research in the Teaching of English, 18*, 265–287. **[9] [10]**

**Newell, G. E., & Winograd, P.** (1989). The effects of writing on learning from expository text. *Written Communication, 6*(2), 196–217. **[10]**

**Newman, J. M.** (Ed.). (1985). *Whole language; Theory in use.* Portsmouth, NH: Heinemann. **[5]**

**Nichols, N.** (1983). Using prediction to increase content area interest and understanding. *Journal of Reading, 27*, 225–228.

**Nicholson, T., & Hill, D.** (1985). Good readers don't guess—taking another look at the issue of whether children read words better in context or in isolation. *Reading Psychology, 6*, 181–198. **[2]**

**Niles, J., Graham, R., & Winstead, J.** (1977). Teacher feedback as a factor in children's oral reading. *Reading in Virginia, 5*(1), 16–18.

**Norton, D.** (1990). Teaching multicultural literature in the reading curriculum. *The Reading Teacher, 44*(1), 28–40. **[13]**

**Obenchain, A.** (1971). *Effectiveness of the precise essay question in programming the sequential development of written composition skills and the simultaneous development of critical reading skills.* Unpublished master's thesis, George Washington University. **[9]**

**O'Brien, K.** (1992). *The struggle to continue* (Book review of Shannon, P.). *The California Reader, 25*(2), 18–19. **[1]**

**O'Brube, W., Camplese, D., & Sanford, M.** (1987). The use of teletherapy in the mainstream era. In K. VanderMeulen (Ed.), *Reading horizons: Selected readings* (pp. 163–165). Kalamazoo, MI: Western Michigan University. **[11]**

**O'Flahavan, J. F., Hartman, D. K., & Pearson, P. D.** (1988). Teacher questioning and feedback practices: A twenty year perspective. In J. E. Readence & R. S. Baldwin (Eds.), *Dialogue in literacy research.* The thirty-seventh yearbook of the National Reading Conference (pp. 183–208). Chicago, IL: National Reading Conference. **[12]**

**Ogle, D. M.** (1986). K-W-L: A teaching model that develops active reading of expository text. *The Reading Teacher, 39*, 564–570. **[8]**

**Ogle, D. M.** (1989). The know what to know, learn strategy. In K. D. Muth (Ed.), *Children's comprehension of text* (pp. 205–223). Newark, DE: International Reading Association.

**O'Hare, F.** (1973). *Sentence combining: Improving student writing without formal grammar instruction.* Urbana, IL: National Council for Teachers of English. **[9]**

**Ollila, L., & Mayfield, M.** (1992). Home and school together: Helping beginning readers succeed. In J. Samuels, & A. Farstrup (Eds.), *What research has to say about reading instruction* (pp. 17–45). Newark, DE: International Reading Association. **[3]**

**Oppenheim, J., Brenner, B., & Boegehold, B. O.** (1986). *Choosing books for kids.* New York: Ballantine. **[5]**

**O'Shea, L. J., Sindelar, P. T., & O'Shea, D. J.** (1985). The effects of repeated readings and attentional cues on reading fluency and comprehension. *Journal of Reading Behavior, 17*(2), 129–142. **[6]**

**Otte, J. K., Knafle, J. D., & Cramer, E. H.** (1990). Riddles as facilitators of inferred responses. *Journal of Affective Reading Education, 10*, 7–15. **[9]**

**Otto, W.** (1990). Telling stories out of school. *Journal of Reading, 33*(6), 450–452. **[1]**

**Otto, W., Wolf, A., & Elderidge, R.** (1984). Managing instruction. In P. D. Pearson, R. Barr, M. L. Kamil, & P. Mosenthal (Eds.), *Handbook of reading research,* Vol. 1 (pp. 799–878). White Plains, New York: Longman. **[2]**

**Palincsar, A. S., & Brown, A. L.** (1984). Reciprocal teaching of comprehension-fostering and comprehension-monitoring activities. *Cognition and Instruction, 2*, 117–175. **[2] [4] [8]**

**Palincsar, A. S., Brown, A. L., & Martin, S. M.** (1987). Peer interaction in reading comprehension instruction. *Educational Psychologist, 22*, 231–253. **[8]**

**Palmatier, R. A.** (1971). Comparison of four note-taking procedures. *Journal of Reading, 14*, 235–240, 258. **[10]**

**Palmatier, R. A.** (1973). A note-taking system for learning. *Journal of Reading, 17*, 36–39. **[10]**

**Palmatier, R. A., & Bennett, J. M.** (1974). Notetaking habits of college students. *Journal of Reading, 18*, 215–218. **[10]**

**Pany, D., & McCoy, K. M.** (1983). *Effects of corrective feedback on word accuracy and reading comprehension of learning disabled and average readers.* Paper presented at the American Educational Research Association international convention, Montreal, Canada. **[4]**

**Pany, D., McCoy, K. M., & Peter, E.** (1981). Effects of corrective feedback on comprehension skills of remedial students. *Journal of Reading Behavior, 13*(2), 131–43. **[4]**

Paris, S. G. (1986). Teaching children to guide their reading and learning. In T. E. Raphael (Ed.), *The contents of school-based literacy* (pp. 115–130). New York: Random House. **[8]**

Paris, S. G., Calfee, R. C., Filby, N., Hiebert, E. H., Pearson, P. D., Valencia, S. W., & Wolf, K. P. (1992). A framework for authentic literacy assessment. *The Reading Teacher, 46*(2), 88–98. **[2] [13] [D]**

Paris, S. G., Cross, D. R., & Lipson, M. Y. (1984). Informed strategies for learning: A program to improve children's reading awareness and comprehension. *Journal of Educational Psychology, 76,* 1239–1252. **[8]**

Pauk, W. (1974). *How to study in college.* Boston: Houghton Mifflin. **[10]**

Paul, R. W. (1987). Dialogical thinking: Critical thought essential to the acquisition of rational knowledge and passions. In J. B. Baron & R. J. Sternberg, (Eds.), *Teaching thinking skills: Theory and practice* (pp. 127–148). New York: W. H. Freeman.

Pauler, S., & Bodevin, D. (1990). Book-specific response activities: Satisfaction guaranteed. *Georgia Journal of Reading, 16*(2), 30–35. **[10]**

Paulsen, J., & Macken, M. (1978). *Report on the level of achievement in CAI reading programs.* Palo Alto, CA: Computer Curriculum Corporation. **[2]**

Paulu, N. (1989). Principals and school improvement: Sixteen success stories. *NAASP Bulletin, 73*(517), 71–77. **[13]**

Pearson, P. D., & Camperell, K. (1985). Comprehension of text structures. In H. Singer & R. B. Ruddell (Eds.), *Theoretical models and process of reading* (3rd ed., pp. 323–342). Newark, DE: International Reading Association. **[8]**

Pearson, P. D., & Fielding, L. (1991). Comprehension instruction. In R. Barr, M. L. Kamil, P. Mosenthal, & P. D. Pearson (Eds.), *Handbook of reading research,* Vol. II (pp. 815–860). White Plains, New York: Longman. **[1] [2] [8]**

Pearson, P. D., & Gallagher, M. C. (1983). The instruction of reading comprehension. *Contemporary Educational Psychology, 8,* 317–345. **[8]**

Pearson, P. D., & Johnson, D. D. (1978). *Teaching reading and comprehension.* New York: Holt, Rinehart and Winston. **[9]**

Pearson, P. D., Roehler, L. R., Dole, J. A., & Duffy, G. G. (1992). Developing expertise in reading comprehension. In S. J. Samuels & A. E. Farstrup (Eds.), *What research has to say about reading instruction* (2nd ed., pp. 145–199). Newark, DE: International Reading Association. **[8]**

Pellegrini, A. D., & Galda, L. (1982). The effects of thematic fantasy play training on the development of children's story comprehension. *American Educational Research Journal, 19,* 443–452. **[8]**

Pelosi, P. L. (1982). A method for classifying remedial reading techniques. *Reading World, 22,* 119–128.

Penrose, A. M. (1988). *Examining the role of writing in learning factual versus abstract material.* Paper presented at the American Educational Research Association, New Orleans, LA. **[9]**

Pereles, B. (1991). How can parents support their children in reading. *The Missouri Reader, 15*(2), 28–29.

Perfetti, C. A. (1985). *Reading ability.* New York: Oxford University Press. **[1]**

Perfetti, C. A. (1986). Continuities in reading acquisition, reading skill, and reading disability. *Remedial and Special Education, 7*(1), 11–21. **[1]**

Perron, J. D. (1974). *An explanatory approach to extending the syntactic development of fourth grade students through the use of sentence-combining methods.* Unpublished doctoral dissertation, Indiana University.

Petre, R. M. (1970). Quantity, quality, and variety of pupil responses during an open-communication structured group directed-thinking activity and a closed-communication structured group directed reading activity (Doctoral dissertation, University of Delaware, Newark). *Dissertation Abstract International, 31,* 4630A. **[8]**

Petty, W. T. (Ed.). (1967). *Research in oral language.* Urbana, IL: National Council of Teachers of English. **[7]**

Piaget, J. (1959). *The language and thought of the child* (3rd ed.). London: Rontledge & Kegan Paul. **[9]**

Piaget, J. (1963). *The child's conception of the world.* Paterson, NJ: Littlefield Adams. **[2] [7]**

Pierce, K. M. (1991). Empowering readers and writers through knowledge and involvement. *The Missouri Reader, 15*(2), 2. **[2]**

Pincus, A., Geller, E. B., & Stover, E. M. (1986). A technique for using the story schema as a transition to understanding and summarizing event based magazine articles. *Journal of Reading, 30,* 152–158. **[8]**

Pinnell, G. S. (1989). Reading recovery: Helping at-risk children to read. *Elementary School Journal, 90,* 161–82.

Pinnell, G. S. (1990). Success for low achievers through reading recovery. *Educational Leadership, 48*(1) 17–21. **[1]**

Pinnell, G. S. (1992). What is reading recovery? *Arizona Reading Journal, 20*(2), 61–67. **[11]**

Pinnell, G. S., DeFord, D. E., Lyons, C. A., Bryk, A., & Seltzer, M. (1991). *Studying the effectiveness of early intervention approaches for first grade children having difficulty in reading.* Columbus, OH: The Ohio State University, Martha L. King Language and Literacy Center. **[11]**

**Pinnell, G. S., & Jaggar, A. M.** (1991). Oral language: Speaking and listening in the classroom. In J. Flood, J. Jensen, D. Lapp, & J. Squire (Eds.), *Handbook of research on teaching the English language arts* (pp. 691–720). New York: Macmillan. **[3]**

**Pitman, S. J., Mazurkiewicz, A., & Tanzer, H.** (1964). *The handbook on writing and spelling in i/t/a.* New York: i/t/a Publications. **[11]**

**Platts, M.** (1970). Anchor: A handbook of vocabulary discovery techniques for the classroom teacher. Stevensville, MI.: Educational Service Inc. **[7]**

**Pond, M., & Hoch, L.** (1992). Linking children's literature and science activities. *Ohio Reading Teacher, 25*(2), 13–15. **[10]**

**Porter, D.** (1978). Cloze procedure and equivalence. *Language Learning, 28,* 333–341. **[12]**

**Post, A. R.** (1992). The camel caper: An integrated language arts lesson. *Michigan Reading Journal, 25*(2), 29–35. **[10]**

**Post, R. M.** (1974). Readers theatre as a method of teaching literature. *English Journal, 64,* 69–72. **[4]**

**Postman, N., & Weingartner, C.** (1969). *Teaching as a subversive activity.* New York: Delacorte Press.

**Pressley, M.** (1977). Imagery and children's learning: Putting the picture in developmental perspective. *Review of Educational Research, 47,* 585–622.

**Pressley, M., Gaskins, I. W., Wile, D., Cunicelli, E. A., & Sheridan, J.** (1991a). Teaching literacy strategies across the curriculum: A case study at Benchmark School. In J. Zuttell & S. McCormick (Eds.), *Learner factors/teacher factors: Issues in literacy research and instruction* (pp. 219–228). Fortieth yearbook of the National Reading Conference. Chicago, IL: National Reading Conference. **[13]**

**Pressley, M., Gaskins, I. W., Cunicelli, E. A., Burdick, N. J., Schaub-Matt, M., Lee, D. S., & Powell, N.** (1991b). Strategy instruction at Benchmark School: A faculty interview study. *Learning Disabilities Quarterly, 14,* 19–48. **[13]**

**Pressley, M., Ghatala, E., Woloshyn, V., & Pierie, J.** (1990). Sometimes adults miss the main ideas and do not realize it: Confidence in responses to short answers and multiple-choice comprehension questions. *Reading Research Quarterly, 25,* 232–249. **[12]**

**Pressley, M., Johnson, C. J., & Symons, S.** (1987). Elaborating to learn and learning to elaborate. *Journal of Learning Disabilities, 20,* 76–91. **[7]**

**Pressley, M., Levin, J. R., & MacDaniel, M. A.** (1987). Remembering versus inferring what a word means: Mnemonic and contextual approaches. In M. C. McKeown, & M. E. Curtis (Eds.), *The nature of vocabulary acquisition* (pp. 107–129). Hillsdale, NJ: Erlbaum. **[7]**

**Pressley, M., Levin, J. R., & Miller, G. E.** (1981). How does the keyword method affect vocabulary comprehension and usage? *Reading Research Quarterly, 16*(2), 213–225. **[7]**

**Prince, A. T., & Mancus, D. S.** (1987). Enriching comprehension: A schema altered basal reading lesson. *Reading Research and Instruction, 27,* 45–53. **[8]**

***Progressive Teacher.*** (1992). (Illustration). *28*(3), cover page. **[2]**

**Putnam, L., Bader, L., Bean, R.** (1988). Clinic disorders share insights into effective strategies. *Journal of Clinical Reading, 3,* 16–20. **[7]**

**Rapaport, A.** (1950). *Science and the goals of man.* New York: Harper & Brothers. **[7]**

**Raphael, T. E.** (1982). Question-answering strategies for children. *The Reading Teacher, 36*(2), 186–190. **[9]**

**Raphael, T. E.** (1986). Teaching question-answer relationships, revisited. *The Reading Teacher, 39,* 516–522. **[9]**

**Raphael, T. E., & Pearson, P. D.** (1982). *The effect of metacognitive awareness training on children's question answering behavior.* Technical report #238. Urbana, IL: Center for the Study of Reading, University of Illinois. **[9]**

**Raphael, T. E., & Wonnacott, C. A.** (1981). *The effect of metacognitive training on question-answering behavior: Implementation in a fourth grade developmental reading program.* Paper presented at the National Reading Conference, Dallas, TX. **[9]**

**Rasinski, T. V.** (1988). Making repeated readings a functional part of classroom reading instruction. *Reading Horizons, 28,* 250–254. **[6]**

**Rasinski, T. V.** (1989). Fluency for everyone: Incorporating fluency instruction in the classroom. *The Reading Teacher, 42*(9), 690–693 **[6]**

**Ratanakarn, S.** (1992). *A comparison of reader classification by traditional text-dependent measures and by addition of text-independent measures.* Doctoral dissertation. University of Missouri—Kansas City. **[9] [12]**

**Readence, J. E., Baldwin, R. S., & Head, M. H.** (1987). Teaching young readers to interpret metaphors. *The Reading Teacher, 40,* 439–443. **[8]**

**Readence, J. E., Bean, T. W., & Baldwin, R. S.** (1985). *Content area reading: An integrated approach* (2nd ed.). Dubuque, IA: Kendall/Hunt. **[8]**

**Reed, A.J.S.** (1988). *Comics to classics: A parent's guide to books for teens and preteens.* Newark, DE: International Reading Association. **[3] [5]**

**Reed, E. E.** (1968). Improving comprehension through study of syntax and paragraph structure in seventh grade English classes. In J. A. Figurel (Ed.), *Forging ahead* in reading (pp. 575–579). Newark, DE: International Reading Association. **[8]**

Reid, E. R. (1990). Integrating the teaching of literature, comprehension, and composition. *Contemporary Issues in Reading, 5*(2), 61–67. **[9]**

Reinking, D., & Rickman, S. S. (1990). The effects of computer-mediated texts on the vocabulary learning and comprehension of intermediate-grade readers. *Journal of Reading Behavior, 22*(4), 395–411. **[13]**

Reinking, D., & Bridwell-Bowles, L. (1991). Computers in reading and writing. In R. Ball, M. Kamil, P. Mosenthal, & P. D. Pearson (Eds.) *Handbook of reading research,* Vol. II (pp. 310–340). White Plains. New York: Longman. **[13]**

Rentel, V. M. (1971). Concept formation and reading. *Reading World, 11,* 111–119.

Resnick, L. B. (1987). *Education and learning to think* (Report). Washington, DC: National Academy Press.

Reutzel, D. R. (1985). Reconciling schema theory and the basal reading lesson. *The Reading Teacher, 39,* 194–197. **[8]**

Reutzel, D. R. (1991). Understanding and using basal readers effectively. In B. L. Hayes (Ed.), *Effective strategies for teaching reading* (pp. 254–280). New York: Allyn & Bacon. **[8]**

Reutzel, D. R., & Cooter, R. B. (1992). *Teaching children to read: From basals to books.* New York: Merrill/Macmillan **[2] [8]**

Rhodes, L. K. (1981). I can read! Predictable books as resources for reading and writing instruction. *The Reading Teacher, 34*(5), 511–518. **[11]**

Rice, M. J. (1975). How parents may use the physical and cultural environment to teach others. *Journal of Research and Development in Education, 8*(2), 70–82. **[9]**

Richardson, J. S., & Morgan, R. F. (1990). *Reading to learn in the content areas.* Belmont, CA: Wadsworth. **[2]**

Rickards, J. P., & Friedman, F. (1978). The encoding versus the external storage hypothesis in note taking. *Contemporary Educational Psychology, 3,* 136–143. **[10]**

Riesen, A. H. (1949). The development of visual perception in man and chimpanzee. *Science, 106,* 107–108. **[3]**

Riesen, A. H. (1950). Arrested vision. *Scientific American, 183,* 16–19. **[3]**

Rinehart, S. D., Stahl, S. A., & Erickson, L. G. (1986). Some effects of summarization training on reading and studying. *Reading Research Quarterly, 21,* 422–439. **[8]**

Rinsky, L. A., & deFossard, E. (1980). *The contemporary classroom reading inventory.* Dubuque, IA: Gorsuch Scarisbrick. **[12]**

Ripple, R. E. (1989). Creativity: Current perspectives. *Contemporary Educational Psychology, 14*(3), 187–279. **[9]**

Roberts, C. (1956). *Teachers' guide to word attack: A way to better reading.* New York: Harcourt, Brace, & World. **[7]**

Roberts, C. (1988). *Pattern books in the teaching of reading and vocabulary.* Educational Specialist Degree Project, University of Missouri at Kansas City, Kansas City, MO. **[11]**

Roberts, E. E. (1984). *The children's picture book.* Cincinnati, Writer's Digest. **[5]**

Robinson, F. (1946). *Effective study.* New York: Harper Brothers. **[10]**

Robinson, H. A., Faraone, V., Hittleman, D. R., & Unruh, E. (1990). *Reading comprehension instruction 1783–1987.* Newark, DE: International Reading Association. **[8]**

Robinson, S. S., & Dixon, R. G. (1991, December). *The language concepts that low- and middle-class four-year-olds bring to preschool.* Paper presented at the National Reading Conference, Palm Springs, CA. **[3]**

Rongione, L. A. (1972). Bibliotherapy: Its nature and uses. *Catholic Library World, 43,* 495–500. **[11]**

Rosenblatt, L. (1938). *Literature as exploration.* New York: Appleton-Century (1968). New York: Noble and Noble (1970). London: Heinemann (1976). New York: Noble and Noble (1983). **[5]**

Rosenblatt, L. M. (1969). Towards a transactional theory of reading. *Journal of Reading Behavior, 1*(1), 31–49. **[13]**

Rosenblatt, L. (1978). *The reader, the text, the poem.* Carbondale: Southern Illinois University Press. **[5]**

Rosenblatt, L. (1991). Literature—S.O.S.! *Language Arts, 68,* 444–448. **[1] [7]**

Rosenshine, B., & Stevens, R. (1984). Classroom instruction in reading. In P. D. Pearson (Ed.), *Handbook of reading research* (pp. 745–798). White Plains, New York: Longman. **[2] [13]**

Rosenshine, B. V. (1986). Synthesis of research on explicit teaching. *Educational Leadership, 43*(7), 60–69. **[2]**

Roser, N. L., & Hoffman, J. V., with Labbo, L. D., & Farest, C. (1992). Language charts: A record of story time talk. *Language Arts, 69*(1), 44–52. **[5]**

Roshotte, C. A., & Torgensen, J. K. (1985). Repeated reading and reading fluency in learning disabled children. *Reading Research Quarterly, 20,* 180–188. **[6]**

Rosow, L. V. (1991). How schools perpetuate illiteracy. *Educational Leadership, 49*(1), 41–44. **[3]**

Ross, E. P. (1986). Classroom experiments with oral reading. *The Reading Teacher, 40,* 270–275. **[4]**

Rubin, L. J. (1984). *Artistry in teaching.* New York: Random House. **[4] [8]**

**Ruddell, R. B.** (1990). *A study of the effect of reader motivation and comprehension development on students' reading comprehension achievement in influential and non-influential teachers' classrooms.* Paper presented at the annual meeting of the National Reading Conference, Miami, FL. **[12]**

**Ruddell, R. B., Draheim M. E., & Barnes, J.** (1990). A comparative study of the teaching effectiveness of influential and noninfluential teachers and reading comprehension development. In J. Zutell, & S. McCormick (Eds.), *Literacy theory and research: Analyses from multiple paradigms.* The thirty-ninth yearbook of the National Reading Conference (pp. 153–162). Chicago, IL: National Reading Conference. **[2]**

**Ruddell, R. B., & Harris, P.** (1989). A study of the relationship between influential teachers' prior knowledge and beliefs and teaching effectiveness: Developing higher order thinking in content areas. In S. McCormick, & J. Zutell (Eds.), *Cognitive and social perspectives for literacy research and instruction* (pp. 461–472). Chicago, IL: National Reading Conference. **[2]**

**Rumelhart, D. E.** (1977). Toward an interactive model of reading. In S. Dornic (Ed.), *Attention and performance VI: Proceedings of the sixth International Symposium on Attention and Performance.* Stockholm, Sweden, July 28–August 1, 1975 (pp. 573–603). Hillsdale, NJ: Erlbaum Associates. **[1]**

**Rumelhart, D.** (1980). Schemata: The building blocks of cognition. In R. J. Spiro, B. C. Bruce, & W. F. Brewer (Eds.), *Theoretical issues in reading comprehension,* (pp. 33–58). Hillsdale, NJ: Lawrence Erlbaum. **[8]**

**Sadoski, M.** (1983). An exploratory study of the relationships between reported imagery and the comprehension and recall of a story. *Reading Research Quarterly, 19,* 110–123. **[8]**

**Sadoski, M.** (1985). The natural use of imagery in story comprehension and recall: Replication and extension. *Reading Research Quarterly, 20,* 658–667. **[8]**

**Salzer, R. T.** (1991). TAWL Teachers reach for self-help. *Educational Leadership, 49*(3), 66–67. **[2]**

**Sampson, M., Allen, V. R., & Sampson, M. B.** (1991). *Pathways to literacy.* Fort Worth, TX: Holt, Rinehart and Winston. **[2]**

**Samson, K. M., & Wescott, A.** (1983). The use of the picture potency formula in selecting pictures to stimulate stories. *Reading Improvement, 20,* 146–150. **[5]**

**Samuels, S. J.** (1979). The method of repeated readings. *The Reading Teacher, 32,* 403–408. **[2] [6]**

**Samuels, S. J.** (1984). Resolving some theoretical and instructional conflicts of the 1980s. *Reading Research Quarterly, 19*(4), 390–392.

**Samuels, S. J., & Farstrup, A. E.** (1992). *What research has to say about reading instruction* (2nd ed.). Newark, DE: International Reading Association. **[3]**

**Samuels, S. J., & Pearson, P. D.** (Eds.), (1988). *Changing school reading programs.* Newark, DE: International Reading Association. **[13]**

**Samuels, S. J., Schermer, N., & Reinking, D.** (1992). Reading fluency: Techniques for making decoding automatic. In S. J. Samuels, & A. E. Farstrup (Eds.), *What research has to say about reading instruction* (pp. 124–144). Newark, DE: International Reading Association. **[1]**

**Sanacore, J.** (1984). Metacognition and the improvement of reading: Some important links. *Journal of Reading, 27*(8), 706–712. **[8]**

**Sanacore, J.** (1993). Using study groups to create a professional community. *Journal of Reading 37*(1), 62–66. **[13]**

**Sanborn, N.** (1991). Ideas for working with parents. (Summarized from workshop presented by P. Koppman). *Virginia State Reading Association Newsletter, Fall,* (9). **[3]**

**Santa, C.** (1988). Changing teacher behavior in content reading through collaborative research. In S. J. Samuels, & P. D. Pearson (Eds.), *Changing school reading programs* (pp. 185–204). Newark, DE: International Reading Association. **[2] [13]**

**Santa, C. M., & Hayes, B. L.** (Eds.), (1981). *Children's prose comprehension.* Newark, DE: International Reading Association. **[8]**

**Santeusanio, R.** (1967). RAMA: A supplement to the traditional college reading program. *Journal of Reading, 11,* 133–136. **[9] [10]**

**Sapir, E.** (1921). *Language.* New York: Harcourt Brace. **[7]**

**Sawyer, D. J.** (1988). Studies of the effects of teaching auditory segmentation skills within the reading program. In R. L. Masland & M. W. Maland (Eds.), *Prevention of reading failure.* Baltimore, MD: York Press. **[2]**

**Schell, L. M.** (1972). Promising possibilities for improving comprehension. *Journal of Reading, 5,* 415–424. **[8]**

**Schell, L. M.** (1980). Value clarification via basal readers. *Reading Horizons, 20,* 215–220. **[8]**

**Schell, L. M.** (1988). Dilemmas in assessing reading comprehension. *The Reading Teacher, 42,* 12–16. **[8]**

**Schell, L. M.** (1990). Student teachers' perception of basal reader materials and methodology. In B. L. Hayes & K. Camperall (Eds.), *The yearbook of the American Reading Forum* (pp. 105–109). Athens, GA: American Reading Forum. **[13]**

**Schell, L. M.** (1991). In E. Fry (Ed.), *Ten best ideas for reading teachers* (pp. 115–116). Menlo Park, CA: Addison-Wesley. **[12]**

**Schmitt, M. C.** (1988). The effects of an elaborated directed activity on the metacomprehension skills of third graders. In J. E. Readence & R. S. Baldwin (Eds.), *Dialogues in literacy research.* The thirty-seventy yearbook of the National Reading Conference (pp. 167–181). Chicago, IL: National Reading Conference. **[8]**

**Schmitt, M. C., & Baumann, J. F.** (1986). How to incorporate comprehension monitoring strategies into basal reader instruction. *The Reading Teacher, 40,* 28–31. **[8]**

**Schoelles, I.** (1971). *Cloze as a predictor of reading group placement.* Paper presented at the International Reading Association annual convention, Atlantic City, NJ. **[12]**

**Schunk, D. H., & Rice, J. M.** (1987). Enhancing comprehension skill and self-efficacy with strategy value information. *Journal of Reading Behavior, 19,* 285–302. **[8]**

*Science World.* (1989). (Cover page illustration). *46*(6). **[10]**

**Searfoss, L. W., & Readence, J. E.** (1989). *Helping children learn to read* (2nd ed.). Englewood Cliffs, NJ: Prentice-Hall. **[1] [2]**

**Seaton, H. W., & Weilan, O. P.** (1979). *The effects of listening/reading transfer on four measures of reading comprehension.* Paper presented at the Annual Convention of the International Reading Association, Atlanta, GA. **[8]**

**Sebesta, S. L.** (1992). Enriching the arts and humanities. In B. E. Cullinan (Ed.), *Invitation to read: More children's literature in the reading program* (pp. 50–63). Newark, DE: International Reading Association. **[10]**

**Selden, M. V. V.** (1932). *Raum–und Gestaltauffassung bei operierten Blindgeborenen vor und nach der Operation.* Barth, Germany: Leipzig **[3]**

**Shanahan, T.** (1980). The impact of writing instruction on learning to read. *Reading World, 19,* 357–368. **[2]**

**Shanahan, T., & Kamil, M. L.** (1983). A further investigation of sensitivity of cloze and recall to organization. In J. Niles, & L. A. Harris (Eds.), *Search for meaning in reading/language processing instruction* (pp. 123–128). The thirty-second yearbook of the National Reading Conference. Rochester, New York: National Reading Conference. **[8]**

**Shanahan, T., & Lomax, R.** (1986). An analysis and comparison of theoretical models of the reading-writing relationship. *Journal of Educational Psychology, 78,* 116–123. **[9]**

**Shannon, P.** (1985). Reading instruction and social class. *Language Arts, 62*(2), 604–613. **[13]**

**Shannon, P.** (1989). The struggle for control of literacy lessons. *Language Arts, 66*(6), 625–634. **[2]**

**Shannon, P.** (1990). *The struggle to continue: Progressive reading instruction in the United States.* Portsmouth, NH: Heinemann. **[1] [8]**

**Sharan, T., & Sharan, S.** (1987). Training teachers for cooperative learning. *Educational Leadership, 45,* 20–25 **[2]**

**Shaw, P. A.** (1993). Integration of curriculum: A selected review of the literature. *Wisconsin Reading Association Journal, 37*(1), 1–6. **[11]**

**Shearer, B.** (1992). From Dick and Jane to Ken and Yetta: How did we get here? Tracing the roots of whole language. *Wisconsin State Reading Association Journal, 36*(3), 1–5. **[2]**

**Shepherd, D.** (1978). *Comprehensive high school reading methods* (3rd ed.). Columbus, OH: Merrill. **[8]**

**Sherk, J. K.** (1967). *A study of the effects of a program of visual perceptual training on the progress of retarded readers.* Unpublished doctoral dissertation. Syracuse University, Syracuse, New York. **[3]**

**Sherman, E. B.** (1991). Independence avenue. *The Reading Teacher, 45,* 213–220. **[5]**

**Shoop, M. E.** (1986). InQuest: A listening and reading comprehension strategy. *The Reading Teacher, 39*(7), 670–674. **[8] [10]**

**Short, K. G.** (1986). Literacy as collaborative: The role of intertextuality. In J. A. Niles & R. V. Lalik (Eds.), *Solving problems in literacy: Learners, teachers, and researchers* (pp. 227–232). Thirty-fifth yearbook of the National Reading Conference. Rochester, NY: National Reading Conference. **[9]**

**Short, K.** (1990, August–September). Teachers as researchers: Classrooms as communities of inquiry. *Reading Today, 8*(1). **[2]**

**Shuck, J., Ulsh, F., Platt, J. S.** (1983). Parents encourage pupils (PEP): An inner city parent involvement reading project. *The Reading Teacher, 36*(6), 524–528.

**Shugarman, S. L., & Hurst, J. B.** (1986). Purposeful paraphasing: Promoting non-trivial pursuit for meaning. *Journal of Reading, 29,* 396–399. **[8]**

**Siegfried, S.** (1992). Carpe diem. *Language Arts, 69*(4), 284–285. **[9]**

**Silvaroli, N. J.** (1986). *Classroom reading inventory* (3rd ed.). Dubuque, IA: William C. Brown. **[12]**

**Simic, M.** (1991). Why read aloud? *Massachusetts Primer, 20*(3), 6–8. **[4]**

**Simpson, M. L., & Nist, S. L.** (1990). Textbook annotation: An effective and efficient study strategy for college students. *Journal of Reading, 34*(2), 122–129. **[8]**

Singer, H. (1975). The SEER technique: A non-computational procedure for quickly estimating readability level. *Journal of Reading Behavior, 7*(3), 255–267. **[13]**

Singer, H. (1985). Models of reading have direct implications for instruction: The affirmative position. In J. A. Niles & R. V. Lalik (Eds.), *Issues in literacy: A research perspective* (pp. 402–413). Thirty-fourth yearbook of the National Reading Conference. Rochester, NY: The National Reading Conference. **[1]**

Singer, H., & Donlan, D. (1982). Active comprehension: Problem-solving schema with question generation for comprehension of complex short stories. *Reading Research Quarterly, 17*, 166–186. **[8]**

Singer, H., & Donlan, D. (1989). *Reading and learning from text* (2nd ed.). Hillsdale, NJ: Erlbaum Associates. **[13]**

Slavin, R. (1987). Ability grouping and its alternatives: Must we track? *American Educator, 11*(2), 32–36, 37–48. **[13]**

Slavin, R. E. (1987). Ability grouping and student achievement in elementary schools: A best-evidence synthesis. *Review of Educational Research, 57*, 293–336. **[11]**

Slavin, R. E., (1990). Success for all: First-year outcomes of a comprehensive plan for reforming urban education. *American Educational Research Journal, 27*, 255–278. **[11]**

Slavin, R. E., Madden, N. A., & Dolan, L. (1990). Success for all at Buckingham Elementary: First-year evaluation. Baltimore: Center for Research on Effective Schooling for Disadvantaged Students, Johns Hopkins University. **[11]**

Slavin, R. E., & Yampolsky, R. (1991, April). Success for all and the language minority student. Paper presented at the annual meeting of the American Educational Research Association, Chicago. **[11]**

Sloyer, S. (1982). *Readers theatre: Story dramatization in the classroom.* Urbana, IL: National Council for Teachers of English. **[4]**

***Smiles* (Teacher's edition Part I).** (1987). Fort Worth, TX: Harcourt Brace Jovanovich. **[2]**

Smith, F. (1971). *Understanding reading.* New York.: Holt, Rinehart and Winston. **[4]**

Smith, F. (1973). *Psycholinguistics and reading.* New York: Holt, Rinehart and Winston. **[2]**

Smith, F. (1978). *Reading and nonsense.* New York: Teachers College Press. **[1] [10]**

Smith, F. (1981). Demonstrations, engagements, and sensitivity: A revised approach to language learning. *Language Arts, 58*(1), 103–112. **[5]**

Smith, F. (1982). *Writing and the writer.* New York: Holt, Rinehart and Winston. **[2]**

Smith, F. (1984). The creative achievement of literacy. In H. Goelamn, A. Oberg, & F. Smith (Eds.), *Awakening to literacy* (pp. 135–142). Portsmouth, NH: Heinemann. **[9]**

Smith, F. (1985). Demonstrations, engagements, and sensitivity: A revised approach to language learning. In M. R. Sampson, J. H. White, K. M. Feathers, & I. L. Rorie (Eds.), *Literacy and language instruction,* pp. 140–147. Lexington, MA: Ginn Press. **[2]**

Smith, F. (1990). *To think.* New York: Teachers College Press. **[9]**

Soar, R. S. (1973). *Follow-through classroom process measurement and pupil growth.* Gainesville, FL: Education Department of Language and Literacy, University of Florida. **[2]**

Solomon, D., & Kendall, A. J. (1979). *Children in classrooms.* New York: Praeger. **[2]**

Spache, G. D. (1972). *Diagnostic reading scales.* Monterey, CA: CTB/McGraw-Hill. **[12]**

Spears, M., & Gambrell, L. B. (1990). Prediction training and the comprehension and composing performance of fourth-grade students. In J. Zutell, S. McCormick, L.L.A. Caton, & P. O'Keefe (Eds.), *Learner factors/teacher factors: Issues in literacy research and instruction* (pp. 239–245). Fortieth yearbook of the National Reading Conference. Chicago, IL: National Reading Conference.

Spicola, R., Griffin, M., & Stephens, C. (1990). Motivating reluctant readers through literature. *Reading education in Texas: A Yearbook of the Texas State Reading Association of the International Reading Association,* Vol. 6 (pp. 41–47). **[5]**

Spiegel, D. L. (1980a). Desirable teaching behaviors for effective instruction in reading. *The Reading Teacher, 34*(3), 324–330. **[8]**

Spiegel, D. L. (1980b). Adaptations of Manzo's guided reading procedure. *Reading Horizons, 20,* 188–192. **[8]**

Spiegel, D. L., & Fitzgerald, J. (1986). Improving reading comprehension through instruction about story parts. *The Reading Teacher, 39*(7), 676–682. **[8]**

Spires, H. A., & Stone, P. D. (1989). The directed notetaking activity: A self-questioning approach. *Journal of Reading, 33,* 36–39. **[10]**

Spiro, R. J., & Myers, A. (1984). Individual differences and underlying cognitive processes in reading. In P. D. Pearson, R. Barr, M. Kamil, & P. Mosenthal (Eds.), *Handbook of reading research* (pp. 471–501). White Plains, New York: Longman. **[10]**

Stahl, N. A., & Henk, W. A. (1986). Tracing the roots of textbook study systems: An extended historical perspective. In J. A. Niles, & R. V. Lalik (Eds.), *Solving problems in literacy: Learners, teachers, and researchers.* Thirty-fifth yearbook of the National Reading Conference (pp.

366–374). Rochester, New York: National Reading Conference. **[10]**

**Stahl, S. A.** (1986). Three principles of effective vocabulary instruction. *Journal of Reading, 29,* 662–671. **[7]**

**Stahl, S. A.** (1992). Saying the "p" word: Nine guidelines for exemplary phonics instruction. *The Reading Teacher, 45*(8), 618–625. **[6]**

**Stahl, S., & Kapinus, B.** (1991). Possible sentences: Predicting word meanings to teach content area vocabulary. *The Reading Teacher, 45*(1), 36–43. **[7]**

**Stahl, S., & Miller, P.** (1989). Whole language and language experience approaches for beginning reading: A quantitative research synthesis. *Review of Educational Research, 50*(1), 87–117. **[2]**

**Stahl, S. A., & Vancil, S. J.** (1986). Discussion is what makes semantic maps work in vocabulary instruction. *The Reading Teacher, 40,* 62–69. **[7]**

**Stallings, J. A., & Kashowitz, D.** (1974). *Follow-through classroom observation evaluation, 1972–73.* Menlo Park, CA: Stanford Research Institute. **[2]**

**Stanovich, K. E.** (1986a). Cognitive processes and the reading problems of learning disabled children: Evaluating the assumption of specificity. In J. K. Torgesen & B.Y.L. Wong (Eds.), *Psychological and educational perspectives on learning disabilities* (pp. 87–131). New York: Academic Press. **[1]**

**Stanovich, K. E.** (1988). Explaining the difference between dyslexic and garden-variety poor readers: The phonological-core-difference model. *Journal of Learning Disabilities, 21,* 590–612. **[6]**

**Staton, J.** (1980). Writing and counseling: Using a dialogue journal. *Language Arts, 57,* 514–518. **[11]**

**Stauffer, R.** (1969). *Directing reading maturity as a cognitive process.* New York: Harper & Row. **[8]**

**Stauffer, R. G.** (1980). *The language-experience approach to the teaching of reading* (2nd ed). New York: Harper & Row. **[6]**

**Stein, M.** (1982). Finger spelling: A kinesthetic aid to phonetic spelling. *Academic Therapy, 18,* 17–25. **[11]**

**Stevens, K. C.** (1981). Chunking material as an aid to reading comprehension. *Journal of Reading, 25,* 126–129. **[8]**

**Stevens, R., Madden, N., Slavin, R., & Farnish, A.** (1987). Cooperative integrated reading and composition: Two field experiments. *Reading Research Quarterly, 22,* 433–454. **[13]**

**Stewig, J. W.** (1980). *Children and literature.* Boston: Houghton Mifflin. **[5]**

**Stice, C., & Bertrand, N.** (1990, December). *Whole language and at risk children.* Paper presented at the meeting of the American Reading Forum, Sarasota, FL. **[2]**

**Sticht, T. G., Beck, L. J., Hauke, R. N., Kleiman, G. M., & James, J. H.** (1974). *Auding and reading: A developmental model* (Air Force Contract No. F41609-73-C-0025, Project 1121). Alexandria, VA: Human Resources Research Organization. **[8]**

**Stieglitz, E. L., & Stieglitz, V. S.** (1981). SAVOR the word to reinforce vocabulary in the content areas. *Journal of Reading, 25,* 46–51. **[7]**

**Stiles, G.** (1992). Bulletin to the staff: Whole language/whole learning/child centered/integrated. *Language Arts, 69,* 35–36. **[2]**

**Stotsky, G.** (1975). Sentence-combining as a curricular activity: Its effect on written language development and reading comprehension. *Research in the Teaching of English, 9,* 30–71. **[9]**

**Straw, S., & Bogdan, D.** (1990). (Introduction). In *Beyond communication: reading comprehension and criticism.* Montclair, NJ: Boynton Cook. **[5]**

**Straw, S. B., & Schreiner, R.** (1982). The effect of sentence manipulation on subsequent measures of reading and listening. *Reading Research Quarterly, 17,* 339–352. **[9]**

**Strickland, D. S., & Morrow, L. M.** (1988). Creating a print rich environment. *The Reading Teacher, 42*(2), 156–157. **[3]**

**Sulzby, E.** (1985). Children's emergent reading of favorite storybooks: A developmental study. *Reading Research Quarterly, 20*(4), 458–481. **[6]**

**Sulzby, E.** (1989). Assessment of writing and of children's language while writing. In L. Morrow & J. Smith (Eds.), *The role of assessment and measurement in early literacy instruction* (pp. 83–109). Englewood Cliffs, NJ: Prentice-Hall. **[3]**

**Sulzby, E.** (1991). The development of the young child and the emergence of literacy. In J. Flood, J. M. Jensen, D. Lapp, & J. R. Squire (Eds.), *Handbook of research on teaching the English language arts* (pp. 273–285). New York: Macmillan. **[3]**

**Sulzby, E., & Teale, W.** (1991). Emergent literacy. In R. Barr, M. L. Kamil, P. B. Mosenthal, & P. D. Pearson (Eds.), *Handbook of reading research,* Vol. II (pp. 727–757). White Plains, New York: Longman. **[3]**

**Swafford, J.** (1991). A qualitative analysis of changes in student's thinking, text versus demonstration. In J. Zutell, & S. McCormick (Eds.), *Learner factors/teacher factors: Issues in literacy research and instruction* (pp. 255–261). Fortieth yearbook of the National Reading Conference. Chicago, IL: National Reading Conference. **[1] [7] [8] [10]**

**Switzer, S.** (1991). Crosses-curriculum word for the day. *Journal of Reading, 35*(2), 150. **[7]**

**Taba, H.** (1967). *Teachers' handbook for elementary social stud-*

*ies.* Reading, MA: Addison-Wesley. **[7]**

**Taylor, B. M.** (1992). Text structure, comprehension, and recall. In S. J. Samuels & A. E. Farstrup (Eds.), *What research has to say about reading instruction* (2nd ed., pp. 220–235). Newark, DE: International Reading Association. **[8]**

**Taylor, G. C.** (1981). ERIC/RCS report: Music in language arts instruction. *Language Arts, 58,* 363–368. **[11]**

**Taylor, N. E., & Connor, U.** (1982). Silent *vs.* oral reading: The rational instructional use of both processes. *The Reading Teacher, 35,* 440–443. **[4]**

**Taylor, R.** (1992). *Family support of children's reading development in a highly literate society.* Doctoral dissertation. University of Missouri—Kansas City. **[3]**

**Taylor, W.** (1953). "Cloze procedure": A new tool for measuring readability. *Journalism Quarterly, 30,* 415–433. **[12]**

**Tchudi, S. N., & Huerta, M. C.** (1983). *Teaching writing in the content areas: Middle school/junior high.* Washington, DC: National Education Association. **[10]**

**Teachers' choices for 1991.** (1991). *The Reading Teacher, 45,* 213–220. **[5]**

**Temple, C., & Gillet, J. W.** (1989). *Language arts: Learning processes and teaching processes* (2nd ed.). Glenview, IL: Scott Foresman. **[12]**

**Tharp, R. G., & Gallimore, R.** (1989a). *Rousing minds to life: Teaching, learning, and schooling in social context.* New York: Cambridge University Press. **[2] [5] [8]**

**Tharp, R. G., & Gallimore, R.** (1989b). Rousing schools to life. *American Educator, 13*(2), 20–25, 46–52. **[8]**

**Thomas, D. G., & Readence, J. E.** (1988). Effects of differential vocabulary instruction and lesson frameworks on the reading comprehension of primary children. *Reading Research and Instruction, 28,* 1–13.

**Thomas, J. L.** (1988). *Nonprint production for students, teachers, and media specialists* (2nd ed.). Englewood, CO: Libraries Unlimited. **[5]**

**Thompson, R. A.** (1992). A critical perspective on whole language. *Reading Psychology, 13*(2), 131–155. **[2]**

**Thorndike, E.** (1917). Reading as reasoning: A study of mistakes in paragraph reading. *Journal of Educational Psychology, 8*(6), 323–332. **[1] [8] [9]**

**Thorndike, E. L., & Lorge, I.** (1944). *The teacher's word book of 30,000 words.* N.Y.: Teachers College Press. **[12]**

**Thurstone, T.** (1969). *Reading for understanding* (kit). Hempstead, NY: Science Research Associates. **[13]**

**Tierney, R. J., Carter, M. A., & Desai, L. E.** (1991). *Portfolio assessment in the reading-writing classroom.* Norwood, MA: Christopher-Gordon. **[12] [13]**

**Tierney, R. J., & Cunningham, J. W.** (1984). Research on teaching reading comprehension. In P. D. Pearson, R. Barr, M. L. Kamil, & P. Mosenthal (Eds.), *Handbook of reading research* (pp. 609–655). White Plains, New York: Longman. **[8]**

**Tierney, R. J., Readence, J. E., & Dishner, E. K.** (1991). *Reading strategies and practices: A compendium* (2nd ed.). Boston: Allyn and Bacon. **[10]**

**Tierney, R. J., Readence, J. E., & Dishner, E. K.** (1991). *Reading strategies and practices* (3rd ed.). Needham Heights, MA: Allyn and Bacon. **[2] [4] [6] [7] [8] [10]**

**Tierney, R. J., & Shanahan, T.** (1991). Research on the reading-writing relationship: Interactions, transactions, and outcomes. In R. Barr, M. Kamil, P. Mosenthal, & P. D. Pearson (Eds.), *Handbook of reading research,* Vol. II (pp. 246–280). White Plains, New York: Longman. **[10]**

**Tierney, R. J., Soter, A., O'Flahavan, J. F., & McGinley, W.** (1989). The effects of reading and writing upon thinking critically. *Reading Research Quarterly 24,* 134–137. **[9] [10]**

**Tierney, R. J., Tucker, D. L., Gallagher, M. C., Crismore, A., & Pearson, P. D.** (1988). In S. J. Samuels & P. D. Pearson (Eds.), *Changing school reading programs* (pp. 207–226). Newark, DE: International Reading Association. **[13]**

**Tompkins, G. E.** (1992). The scaffolding principle: What to do when the book is too difficult. *The California Reader, 25*(3), 2–4. **[4]**

**Tonjes, M. J., & Zintz, M.** (1987). *Teaching reading, thinking and study skills in content classrooms.* Dubuque, IA: William C. Brown. **[8] [10]**

**Topping, K.** (1987). *Paired reading: A powerful technique for parent use.* The Reading Teacher, 40, 608–614. **[6]**

**Topping, K.** (1989). Peer tutoring and paired reading: Combining two powerful techniques. *The Reading Teacher, 42,* 488–494. **[4]**

**Townsend, B. A.** (1989). Using children's literature to encourage writing. *The Dragon Lode, 7*(1), 1–9. **[9]**

**Trelease, J.** (1982). *The read-aloud handbook.* New York: Penguin Books. **[4]**

**Trelease, J.** (1989). *The new read-aloud handbook.* New York: Penguin Books. **[4]**

**Troyer, S., & Yopp, H.** (1990). Kindergarten teachers' knowledge of emergent literacy concepts. *Reading Improvement, 27*(1), 34–40. **[2]**

**Tunnell, M., & Jacobs, J.** (1989). Using "real" books: Research findings on literature based reading instruction. *The Reading Teacher, 42,* 470–477. **[13]**

**Uhry, J., & Shepherd, M. J.** (1993). Segmentation/spelling instruction as part of a first-grade reading program: Effects on several measures of reading. *Reading Research Quarterly, 28*(3), 219–233. **[2]**

**Uttero, D. A.** (1988). Activating comprehension through cooperating learning. *The Reading Teacher, 41,* 390–395. **[10] [13]**

Vacca, J. L., Vacca, R. T., & Gove, M. K. (1991). *Reading and learning to read* (2nd ed.). New York: HarperCollins. **[4]**

Vacca, R. T., & Linek, W. M. (1992). Writing to learn. In J. W. Irwin & M. A. Doyle (Eds.), *Reading/writing connections: Learning from research* (pp. 145–159). Newark, DE: International Reading Association. **[10]**

Vacca, R. T., & Vacca, J. L. (1986). *Content area reading* (2nd ed.). Boston: Little, Brown. **[10]**

Vail, P. L. (1981). *Clear and lively writing: Language games and activities for everyone.* New York: Walker and Company. **[7]**

Vail, P. (1989). Watch out for the hole in whole language: Keep the wonder, the work, and the welcome. New York: Branch of the Orton Dyslexia Society Newsletter (reprinted in *WLSIG Newsletter, 3*(2), 3–4. **[2]**

Valencia, S. (1990). A portfolio approach to classroom reading assessment: The ways, whats, and hows. *Reading Teacher, 43*(4), 338–380. **[12]**

Valmont, W. J. (1972). Creating questions for informal reading inventories. *The Reading Teacher, 25,* 509–512. **[12]**

Valmont, W. J. (1992). Storyboarding to make videos: An integrated language art activity. *Arizona Reading Journal, 20*(2), 122–123. **[5]**

Vanderpool, M. (1990). Innovations aren't for everyone. *Principal, 69*(4), 38–43. **[13]**

Vaughan, J., & Estes, T. (1986). *Reading and reasoning beyond the primary grades.* Boston: Allyn & Bacon. **[2]**

Veatch, J. (1959). *Individualizing your reading program.* New York: G. P. Putman's & Sons. **[2] [5]**

Veatch, J. (1978). *Reading in the elementary school* (2nd ed.). New York: John Wiley. **[6]**

Veatch, J. (1985). *Reading in the elementary school* (3rd ed) Katonah, NY: Richard C. Owen. **[2]**

Veatch, J., Sawicki, F., Elliott, G., Flake, E., Blakey, J. (1979). Key words to reading: The language experience approach begins. Columbus, OH: Charles E. Merrill. **[2]**

Venezky, R. L. (1967). English orthography: Its graphical structure and its relation to sound. *Reading Research Quarterly, 2*(3), 75–105. **[6]**

Venezky, R., & Winfield, L. (1979). *Schools that succeed beyond expectations in teaching reading.* Newark, DE: University of Delaware. **[13]**

Vogt, M. (1991). An observation guide for supervisors and administrators: Moving toward integrated reading/language arts instruction. *The Reading Teacher, 45*(3), 206–211. **[13]**

Vygotsky, L. S. (1962). *Thought and language.* Cambridge, MA: M. I. T. Press. **[2] [7]**

Vygotsky, L. S. (1978). *Mind in society: The development of higher psychological process.* Cambridge, MA: Harvard University Press. **[2] [7] [8]**

Waern, Y. (1977a). Comprehension and belief structure. *Scandinavian Journal of Psychology, 18,* 266–274. **[8]**

Waern, Y. (1977b). On the relationship between knowledge of the world and comprehension of texts. *Scandinavian Journal of Psychology, 18,* 130–139. **[1]**

Walker, B. J. (1985). Right-brained strategies for teaching comprehension. *Academic Therapy, 21,* 133–141. **[8]**

Walker, B. J. (1993). *Diagnostic teaching of reading: Techniques for instruction and assessment* (2nd ed.). Columbus, OH: Merrill-Macmillan. **[2]**

Walker, D. F., & Schaffarzick, J. (1974). Comparing curricula. *Review of Educational Research, 44,* 83–112. **[2]**

*Ward's rational method in reading.* (1894). (see Aukerman, 1981). **[2]**

Wark, D. M. (1964). Survey Q3R: System or superstition? In D. M.

Wark (Ed.), *College and adult reading.* Third and fourth annual yearbooks of the North Central Reading Association (pp. 161–170). St. Paul: University of Minnesota, Student Counseling Bureau. **[10]**

Warren, J. (1983). *Piggyback songs.* Everett, WA: Totline Press, Warren Publishing House. **[11]**

Watkins, J., McKenna, M., Manzo, A., & Manzo, U. (1995). The effects of the listen-read-discuss procedure on the content learning of high school students. Paper, American Educational Research Association, New Orleans, LA. **[8] [10]**

Watson, D. (1991). Teacher support groups: Reading out, bringing in. In Y. Goodman, W. Hood, & K. Goodman (Eds.), *Organizing for whole language* (pp. 180–188). Portsmouth, NH: Heinemann. **[2]**

Weaver W. W., & Kingston, A. J. (1963). A factor analysis of cloze procedure and other measures of reading and language ability. *Journal of Communication, 13,* 252–261. **[8] [12]**

Weiner, E. (1980). The diagnostic evaluation of writing skills (DEWS): Application of DEWS criteria to writing samples. *Learning Disability Quarterly, 3*(2), 54–59.

Weiner, M., & Cromer, W. (1967). Reading and reading difficulty: A conceptual analysis. *Harvard Educational Review, 37,* 620–643. **[13]**

Wells, D. (1992, February). Teaching about art and artists through children's books. In *Reading excellence through the arts, SIG Newsletter* (pp. 3–4). Newark, DE: International Reading Association. **[5]**

Wells, G. (1990). Creating the conditions to encourage literate thinking. *Educational Leadership, 47*(6), 13–17.

Wertheimer, A. (1974). Story dramatization in the reading center. *English Journal, 64,* 85–87. **[4]**

**West, J., cited in Bohning, G.** (1991). Response journals: A professor's perspective. *Journal of Reading Education, 17*(1), 51–55. **[2]**

**Whimbey, A., & Lochhead, J.** (1980). *Problem-solving and comprehension: A short course in analytic reasoning* (2nd ed.). Philadelphia: The Franklin Institute Press. **[2] [7]**

**Whitehurst, G. J., Falco, F. L., Lonigan, C. J., Fischel, J. E., DeBaryshe, B. D., Valdez-Menchaca, M. C., & Caulfield, M. B.** (1988a). Accelerating language development through picture book reading. *Developmental Psychology, 24*(4), 552–559. **[3] [4] [5] [8]**

**Whitehurst, G. J., Fischel, J. E., Lonigan, C. J., Valdez-Menchaca, M. C., DeBaryshe, B. D., & Caulfield, M. B.** (1988b). Verbal interaction in families of normal and expressive-language-delayed children. *Developmental Psychology, 4*(5), 690–699. **[3] [5] [4] [8]**

**Whitehurst, G. J., & Valdez-Menchaca, M. C.** (1988). What is the role of reinforcement in early language acquisition? *Child Development, 59*(2), 430–440. **[8]**

**Whitmer, J. E.** (1986). Pickles will kill you: Use humorous literature to teach critical reading. *The Reading Teacher, 39*(6), 530–534. **[5]**

**Whittlesea, B.W.A.** (1987). Preservation of specific experiences in the representation of general knowledge. *Journal of Psychology: Learning, Memory, & Cognition, 13,* 3–17. **[6]**

***Whole language.*** (1990). (Illustration). Austin, TX: Steck-Vaughn. **[3]**

**Wiesendanger, K., & Bader, L.** (1987). Teaching easily confused words: Timing makes the difference. *The Reading Teacher, 41*(3), 328–332. **[6]**

**Wilson, R.** (1984). The use of signing and finger spelling to improve spelling performance with hearing children. *Reading Psychology, 5,* 267–273. **[11]**

**Wilson, R. M., & Gambrell, L. B.** (1988). *Reading comprehension in the elementary school.* Boston: Allyn and Bacon. **[8]**

**Wisconsin Department of Public Instruction.** (1986). *A guide to curriculum planning in reading.* **[9]**

**Witty, P. A.** (1985). Rationale for fostering creative reading in the gifted and the creative. In M. Labuda (Ed.), *Creative reading for gifted learners: A design for excellence* (pp. 8–24). Newark, DE: International Reading Association. **[9]**

**Wolf, D. P.** (1980). Portfolio assessment: Sampling student work. *Educational Leadership, 46*(7), 4–10. **[12]**

**Wollman-Bonilla, J. E.** (1989). Reading journals: Invitations to participate in literature. *The Reading Teacher, 43*(2), 112–120. **[9]**

**Wood, K.** (1987). Fostering cooperative learning in middle and secondary level classrooms. *Journal of Reading, 30,* 590–595. **[2]**

**Wood, K. D.** (1988). Guiding students through informational text. *The Reading Teacher, 41,* 912–920. **[12]**

**Wood, K. D., Lapp, D., & Flood, J.** (1992). *Guiding readers through text: A review of study guides.* Newark, DE: International Reading Association. **[10]**

**Wood, K., & Mateja, J.** (1983). Adapting secondary level strategies for use in elementary classrooms. *The Reading Teacher, 36,* 492–496. **[2]**

**Woods, M. L., & Moe, A. J.** (1985). *Analytical reading inventory* (rev. ed.). Columbus, OH: Charles E. Merrill. **[12]**

**Wooten, D. A.** (1992). The magic of Martin. In B. E. Cullinan (Ed.), *Invitation to read: More children's literature in the reading program* (pp. 73–79). Newark, DE: International Reading Association **[10]**

**Wormell, C.** (1990). *An Alphabet of Animals.* New York: Dial. **[9]**

**Yopp, H. K.** (1985). Phoneme segmentation ability: A prerequisite for phonics and sight word achievement in beginning reading? In J. Niles & R. Lalik (Eds.), *Issues in literacy: A research perspective* (pp. 330–336). Rochester, New York: National Reading Conference. **[3]**

**Yopp, H. K.** (1988). The validity and reliability of phonemic awareness tests. *Reading Research Quarterly, 23,* 159–177. **[3]**

**Yopp, H. K.** (1992). Developing phonemic awareness in young children. *The Reading Teacher, 45*(9), 696–703. **[1] [3] [6]**

**Yopp, H. & Ivers, K.** (1988). *Songs and activities for enhancing phonemic awareness.* Unpublished manuscript. **[3]**

**Yopp, H. K., & Singer, H.** (1985). Toward an interactive reading instructional model: Explanation of activation of linguistic awareness and metalinguistic ability in learning to read. In H. Singer & R. Ruddell (Eds.), *Theoretical models and processes of reading* (pp. 275–283). Newark, DE: International Reading Association. **[8]**

**Yopp, H., & Troyer, S.** (1992). *Training phonemic awareness in young children.* Unpublished manuscript. **[3]**

**Yopp, R., & Yopp, H.** (1991). Ten best ideas for reading teachers. In E. Fry (Ed.), *Ten best ideas for reading teachers* (pp. 132–134). New York: Addison-Wesley. **[4]**

**Zarrillo, J.** (1989). Teachers' interpretations of literature-based reading. *The Reading Teacher, 43,* 22–28. **[13]**

**Zifcak, M.** (1977). *Phonological awareness and reading acquisition in first grade children.* Unpublished doctoral dissertation, University of Connecticut. **[3]**

## CHILDREN'S BOOKS CITED

**Adamson, J.** (1960). *Born Free.* New York: Pantheon.

**Addy, S.** (1981). *We Didn't Mean To.* Milwaukee, WI: Raintree.

**Adler, D. A.** (1983). *The Carsick Zebra and Other Animal Riddles.* New York: Holiday.

**Adler, D. A.** (1985). *The Twisted Witch.* New York: Holiday House.

**Adler, D. A.** (1986). *The Purple Turkey and Other Thanksgiving Riddles.* New York: Holiday.

**Ahlbert, J.,** & Ahlberg A. (1981) *Peek-a-Boo!* New York: Viking.

**Alexander, M.** (1970). *Bobo's Dream.* New York: Dial.

**Alexander, M.** (1971). *Nobody Asked Me If I Wanted a Baby Sister.* New York: Dial.

**Alexander, M.** (1981). *When the New Baby Comes, I'm Moving Out.* New York: Dial.

**Aliki.** (1979). *Mummies Made in Egypt.* New York: Crowell.

**Allard, H.** (1974). *The Stupids Step Out.* Illustrated by J. Marshall. Boston: Houghton Mifflin.

**Anno, M.** (1975). *Anno's Alphabet.* New York: Crowell.

**Anno, M.** (1977). *Anno's Counting Book.* New York: Crowell.

**Arrick, F.** (1981). *Chernowitz.* New York: New American Library.

**Aurandt, P.** (1984). *Paul Harvey's "The Rest of the Story."* New York: Bantam.

**Aurandt, P.** (1984). *More of Paul Harvey's "The Rest of the Story."* New York: Bantam.

**Azarian, M.** (1981). *A Farmer's Alphabet.* New Brunswick, NJ: Godine.

**Babbitt, N.** (1975). *Tuck Everlasting.* New York: Farrar, Straus & Giroux.

**Bahr, R.** (1982). *Blizzard at the Zoo.* New York: Lothrup.

**Baldwin, J.** (1974). *If Beale Street Could Talk.* New York: New American Library.

**Banks, L. R.** (1985). *The Indian in the Cupboard,* New York: Doubleday.

**Bannerman, H.** (1923). *Little Black Sambo.* New York: Lippincott.

**Barrett, J.** (1978). *Cloudy with a Chance of Meatballs.* Illustrated by R. Barrett. New York: Aladdin [tall tale].

**Barton, B.** (1986). *Airplanes.* New York: Crowell.

**Barton, B.** (1986). *Trucks.* New York: Crowell.

**Bash, B.** (1989). *Desert Giant: The World of the Saguaro Cactus.* Boston: Little Brown.

**Bauer, C. F.** (1987). *Presenting Reader's Theater: Plays and Poems to Read Aloud.* New York: Wilson.

**Bayer, J.** (1984). *A My Name Is Alice.* New York: Dial.

**Baylor, B.** (1977). *Guess Who My Favorite Person Is.* Illustrated by Robert Andrew Parker. New York: Scribner's.

**Bemelmans, L.** (1939). *Madeline* (reprint, 1962). New York: Viking.

**Bendick, J.** (1989). *Egyptian Tombs.* New York: Franklin Watts.

**Bergman, T.** (1989). *Finding a Common Language: Children Living With Deafness.* Milwaukee: Gareth Stevens.

**Bergman, T.** (1989). *We Laugh, We Love, We Cry: Children Living With Mental Retardation.* Milwaukee, Gareth Stevens.

**Bergman, T.** (1989). *On Our Own Terms: Children Living With Physical Disabilities.* Milwaukee: Gareth Stevens.

**Bergman, T.** (1989). *Seeing in Special Ways: Children Living With Blindness.* Milwaukee: Gareth Stevens.

**Bergman, T.** (1991). *Going Places: Children Living With Cerebral Palsy.* Milwaukee: Gareth Stevens.

**Bethancourt, T. E.** (1992). *The Dog Days of Arthur Cane.* New York: Dell.

**Bishop, C. H.** (1991). *Twenty and Ten.* New York: Puffin.

**Blume, J.** (1972). *It's Not the End of the World.* Scarsdale, NY: Bradbury Press.

**Blume, J.** (1974). *Blubber.* New York: Bradbury Press.

**Blume, J.** (1976). *Tales of a Fourth Grade Nothing.* New York: Dell.

**Blume, J.** (1981). *Tiger Eyes.* New York: Bradbury Press.

**Bonsall, C.** (1974). *And I Mean It, Stanley.* New York: Harper & Row.

**Borland, H.** (1963). *When the Legends Die.* New York: Lippincott.

**Bosse, C.** (1981). *Ganesh.* New York: Crowell.

**Brady, I.** (1976). *Wild Mouse.* New York: Scribner's.

**Branscum, R.** (1986). *The Girl.* New York: Harper & Row.

**Briggs, R.** (1978). *The Snowman.* New York: Random.

**Brink, C. R.** (1990). *Caddie Woodlawn.* New York: Macmillan.

**Brooks, B.** (1986). *Midnight Hour Encores.* New York: Harper & Row.

**Brown, M.** (1947). *Stone Soup.* New York: Scribner's.

**Brown, M.** (1950). *Dick Whittington and His Cat.* New York: Scribner's.

**Brown, M.** (1980). *Finger Rhymes.* New York: Dutton.

**Brown, M.** (1983). *Spooky Riddles.* New York: Beginner.

**Brown, M.** (1985). *Hand Rhymes.* New York: Dutton.

**Brown, M. W.** (1958). *The Dead Bird.* Reading, Mass: Addison-Wesley.

**Brown, M. W.** (1972). *The Runaway Bunny.* Illustrated by Clement Hurd. New York: Harper Collins (first published in 1942, Harper & Row).

**Brown, M. W.** (1988). *Goodnight Moon.* New York: Harper & Row.

**Brown, R.** (1983). *A Dark, Dark Tale.* New York: Scholastic [mystery].

**Bruna, D.** (1968). *A Story to Tell.* New York: Price, Stern.

**Buck, Pearl S.** (1948). *The Big Wave.* New York: Day.

**Bunting, E.** (1988). *How Many Days to America?: A Thanksgiving Story.* New York: Clarion.

**Bunting, E.** (1990). *The Wall.* Illustrated by R. Himler. New York: Clarion.

**Burningham, J.** (1986). *John Burningham's ABC.* New York: Crown.

**Burningham, J.** (1986). *John Burningham's 1 2 3.* New York: Crown.

**Burnett, F. H.** (1989). *The Secret Garden.* Illustrated by Shirley Hughes. New York: Dutton.

**Burton, V. L.** (1939). *Mike Mulligan and His Steam Shovel.* Boston: Houghton Mifflin.

**Butterworth, N.** (1987). *Nice or Nasty: A Book of Opposites.* Boston: Little, Brown.

**Byars, B.** (1970). *The Summer of the Swans.* New York: Viking Press.

**Byars, B. C.** (1977). *The Pinballs.* New York: Harper & Row.

**Calhoun, J.** (1979). *Cross-Country Cat.* New York: Morrow.

**Cameron, A.** (1989). *The Stories Julian Tells.* New York: Knopf.

**Carle, E.** (1969). *The Very Hungry Caterpillar.* Cleveland: Collins World.

**Carle, E.** (1971). *Do You Want to Be My Friend?* New York: Crowell.

**Carle, E.** (1974). *My Very First Book of Shapes.* New York: Crowell.

**Carle, E.** (1977). *The Grouchy Ladybug.* New York: Crowell.

**Carle, E.** (1989). *The Very Busy Spider.* New York: Putnam.

**Carrick, C.** (1976). *The Accident.* New York: Seabury.

**Caseley, J.** (1991). *Harry and Willy and Carrothead.* New York: Greenwillow.

**Caselli, G.** (1992). *Life Through the Ages.* New York: Darling Kindersley.

**Cather, W.** (1918). *My Antonia.* Boston: Houghton Mifflin.

**Cather, W.** (1992). Jack-O-Boy. In *Collected Stories of Willa Cather.* New York: Random House.

**Cavanah, F.** (1959). *Abe Lincoln Grows Up.* Chicago: Rand McNally.

**Cerf, B.** (1959). *Bennett Cerf's Book of Laughs.* New York: Beginner.

**Cerf, B.** (1964). *Bennett Cerf's Book of Animal Riddles.* Illustrated by Roy McKie. New York: Beginner.

**Cerf, B.** (1960). *Bennett Cerf's Book of Riddles.* New York: Beginner.

**Chalofsky, M. S.** (1992). *Changing Places: A Kid's View of Shelter Living.* Mt. Rainier, Maryland: Gryphon House.

**Chambers, C. E.** (1984). *California Gold Rush: Search for Treasure.* (Adventures in frontier America series). Mahwah, NJ: Troll Associates.

**Childress, A.** (1973). *A Hero Ain't Nothin' but a Sandwich.* New York: Coward, McCann, & Geoghegan.

**Childress, A.** (1981). *Rainbow Jordan.* New York: Coward, McCann, & Geoghegan.

**Chorao, K.** (1985). *The Baby's Story Book.* New York: Dutton.

**Ciardi, J.** (1961). *Man Who Sang the Sillies.* New York: Harper & Row.

**Ciardi, J.** (1987). *You Read to Me, I'll Read to You.* Illustrated by Edward Gorey. New York: Harper & Row. (Original work published 1961)

**Cleary, B.** (1965). *The Mouse and the Motorcycle.* Illustrated by Louis Darling. New York: Morrow.

**Cleary, B.** (1983). *Dear Mr. Henshaw.* New York: Morrow.

**Cleary, B.** (1992). *Ramona the Pest.* New York: Avon.

**Cleaver, V., & Cleaver, B.** (1969). *Where the Lilies Bloom.* Philadelphia: Lippincott, New American Library.

**Cleaver, V., & Cleaver, B.** (1973). *Me Too.* Philadelphia: Lippincott.

**Clement, B.** (1980). *Anywhere Else but Here.* New York: Farrar, Straus & Giroux.

**Clements, A.** (1992). *Billy and the Bad Teacher.* Illustrated by Elivia Savadier. Saxonville, MA: Picture Book Studio.

**Clifton, L.** (1976). *Everett Anderson's Friend.* Illustrated by A. Grifalconi. New York: Holt, Rinehart and Winston.

**Cline, S.** (1989). *The Egyptian Cinderella.* New York: Crowell.

**Cobb, V., & Darling, K.** (1980). *Bet You Can't.* New York: Avon Books.

**Coerr, E.** (1988). *Chang's Paper Pony.* New York: Harper & Row.

**Cohen, B.** (1972). *The Carp in the Bathtub.* Illustrated Joan Halpern. New York: Lothrop.

**Cohen, B.** (1983). *Molly's Pilgrim.* New York: Lothrop.

**Cohen, M.** (1983). *See You Tomorrow, Charles.* New York: Greenwillow.

**Cole, W.** (1970). *Oh, How Silly!* Illustrated by Tomi Ungerer. New York: Viking.

**Collier, J. L., & Collier, C.** (1987). *Jump Ship to Freedom.* New York: Dell.

**Collier, J. L., & Collier, C.** (1974). *My Brother Sam Is Dead.* New York: Four Winds Press.

**Collington, P.** (1987). *The Angel and the Soldier Boy.* New York: Knopf.

**Cooney, B.** (1985). *Miss Rumpus.* Puffin Books [flashback].

**Cooper, E.** (1987). Mama Fig's House, from *Smiles,* Harcourt Brace Jovanovich Basal Reader Series, Teacher's Edition, Part I. Orlando, FL: Harcourt Brace Jovanovich.

**Cooper, S.** (1973). *The Dark Is Rising.* Illustrated by Alan Cober. New York: Atheneum.

**Crews, D.** (1980). *Truck.* New York: Greenwillow.

**Crocker, B.** (1988). *Words that Huddle Together.* Adelaide, Australia: Australian Reading Association.

**Crowther, R.** (1978). *The Most Amazing Hide and Seek Alphabet Book.* New York: Viking.

**Curtis, C.** (1978). *Panda.* New York: Delacorte.

**Dacquino, V. T.** (1982). *Kiss the Candy Days Good-bye.* New York: Delacorte Press.

**Dahl, R.** (1988). *Fantastic Mr. Fox.* Illustrated by Tony Ross. New York: Puffin.

**Day, V.** (1963). *Landslide.* New York: Coward McCann.

**DeJong, M.** (1953). *Hurry Home, Candy.* Illustrated by Maurice Sendak. New York: Harper & Row.

**Delaney, A.** (1988). *The Gunnywolf* (pp. 22–25). New York: Harper & Row.

**Delisle, J.** (1991). *Kid Stories.* Minneapolis: Free Spirit.

**dePaola, T.** (1975). *The Cloud Book.* New York: Holiday.

**dePaola, T.** (1978). *Bill and Pete.* New York: G. P. Putnam's.

**dePaola, T.** (1978). *The Clown of God.* New York: Harcourt Brace Jovanovich [linear].

**dePaola, T.** (1978). *Pancakes for Breakfast.* Orlando, FL: Harcourt Brace Jovanovich.

**dePaola, T.** (1979). *Oliver Button Is a Sissy.* San Diego: Harcourt Brace Jovanovich.

**dePaola, T.** (1981). *Now One Foot, Now the Other.* New York: Putnam.

**dePaola, T.** (1983). *The Legend of the Bluebonnet.* New York: Putnam.

**dePaola, T.** (1988). *Tomie dePaola's Book of Poems.* New York: Putnam.

**deRegniers, B. S., Moore, E., White, M. M., & Carr, J.** (Eds.). (1988). *Sing a Song of Popcorn: Every Child's Book of Poems.* Illustrated by Maurice

**Sendak,** Trina Schart Hyman, Arnold Lobel, et al. New York: Scholastic.

**DeVeaux, A.** (1987). *An Enchanted Hair Tale.* New York: Harper & Row.

**Donneley, J.** (1976). *Tut's Mummy Lost . . . and Found.* New York: Random House.

**Doty, R.** (1975). *Q's Are Weird O's.* Garden City, New York: Doubleday.

**Dragonwagon, C.** (1984). *Always, Always.* Illustrated by A. Zeldich. New York: Macmillan.

**Duke, K.** (1983). *The Guinea Pig ABC.* New York: Dutton.

**Dunbar, J.** (1990). *Ten Little Mice.* Illustrated by Maria Majewska. Orlando, FL: Harcourt Brace Jovanovich.

**Dunbar, J., & Dunbar, J.** (1991). *I Want a Blue Banana.* Boston: Houghton Mifflin.

**Dupasquier, P.** (1988). *The Great Escape.* Boston: Houghton Mifflin.

**Durell, A., & Sachs, M.** (1990). *The Big Book for Peace.* New York: E. P. Dutton Children's Books.

**Eastman, P. D.** (1960). *Are You My Mother?* New York: Random House.

**Eckstein, J., & Gleit, J.** (1977). *The Best Joke Book for Kids.* New York: Avon.

**Eckstein, J., & Gleit, J.** (1987). *The Best Joke Book for Kids #2.* New York: Avon.

**Egypt.** *Ranger Rick, 21*(11), 1–11.

**Ehlert, L.** (1989). *Color Zoo.* New York: J. B. Lippincott.

**Ehlert, L.** (1990). *Fish Eyes: A Book You Can Count On.* Orlando, FL: Harcourt Brace Jovanovich.

**Ellison, R.** (1951). *Invisible Man.* New York: Modern Library.

**Emberley, B.** (1967). *Drummer Hoff.* Illustrated by E. Emberley. Englewood Cliffs, NJ: Prentice-Hall.

**Ernst, L. C.** (1986). *Up to Ten and Down Again.* New York: Lothrop, Lee & Shepard.

**Esbensen, B. J.** (1992). *Who Shrank My Grandmother's House? Poems of discovery.* Illustrated by Eric Beddows. New York: HarperCollins.

**Fassler, J.** (1971). *My Grandpa Died Today.* New York: Human Science Press.

**Fast, H.** (1970). *Freedom Road.* New York: Bantam.

**Feelings, M.** (1974). *Mojo Means One.* Illustrated by Tom Feelings. New York: Dial.

**Feelings, T. & M.** (1974). *Jambo Means Hello.* New York: Dial.

**Fisher, A.** (1991). *Always Wondering.* Illustrated by Joan Sandin. New York: HarperCollins.

**Fisher, D. C.** (1987). *Understood Betsy.* New York: Dell.

**Fitzgerald, J. D.** (1967). *The Great Brain.* New York: Viking.

**Flack, M.** (1986). *Ask Mr. Bear.* New York: Macmillan.

**Fleischman, S.** (1963). *By the Great Horn Spoon!* Boston: Little, Brown.

**Foreman, M.** (1978). *Panda's Puzzle.* New York: Bradbury Press.

**Fowke, E.** (Ed.). (1977). *Sally Go Round the Sun; 300 Children's Song, Rhymes, and Games.* Illustrated by Judith Gwyn Brown. New York: Prentice-Hall.

**Fox, M.** (1987). *Hattie and the Fox.* Scarsdale, New York: Bradbury.

**Fox, P.** (1973). *The Slave Dancer.* Scarsdale, New York: Bradbury.

**Freedman, R.** (1984). *Animal Superstars: Biggest, Strongest, Fastest, Smartest.* New York: Prentice Hall.

**French, F.** (1986). *Snow White in New York.* Oxford: Oxford University Press.

**Friedman, I.** (1984). *How My Parents Learned to Eat.* Illustrated by A. Say. Boston: Houghton Mifflin [flashback].

Gag, W. (1928). *Millions of Cats.* New York: Coward, McCann, Geoghegan.

Gage, W. (1977). *Down in the Boondocks.* Greenwillow.

Gaines, E. (1983). *A Gathering of Old Men.* New York: Knopf.

Galdone, P. (1968). *Henny Penny.* New York: Clarion.

Galdone, P. (1970). *The Three Little Pigs.* New York: Clarion.

Gans, R. (1984). *Rock Collecting.* New York: Harper & Row.

Gemming, E. (1974). *Born in a Barn.* New York: Coward, McCann, & Geoghegan.

George, J. (1988). *My Side of the Mountain.* New York: Dutton.

Gibbons, G. (1982). *The Post Office Book: Mail and How It Moves.* New York: Crowell.

Gibbons, G. (1985). *The Milk Makers.* New York: Macmillan.

Giff, P. R. (1980). *Today Was a Terrible Day.* New York: Viking.

Girard, L. W. (1989). *We Adopted You, Benjamin Koo.* Niles, IL: A. Whitman.

Glubok, S. (1968). *Tut-ankh-Amen's Tomb.* New York: Macmillan.

Go Ask Alice. (1971). Englewood Cliffs, NJ: Prentice Hall.

Goble, P. (1990). *Dream Wolf.* New York: Bradbury Press.

Godden, R. (1985). *The Story of Holly and Ivy.* New York: Viking.

Goff, B. (1969). *Where Is Daddy? The Story of Divorce.* Boston: Beacon Press.

Goldin, A. (1989). *Ducks Don't Get Wet.* New York: Crowell.

Goldin, B. D. (1991). *Cakes and Miracles: A Purim Tale.* New York: Viking.

Goodall, J. (1968). *The Adventures of Paddy Pork.* Orlando, FL: Harcourt.

Goodall, J. (1973). *Paddy's Evening Out.* New York: Atheneum.

Goodall, J. (1975). *Creepy Castle.* New York: Atheneum.

Goodall, J. (1982). *Paddy Goes Traveling.* New York: Atheneum.

Goodall, J. (1985). *Paddy to the Rescue.* New York: Atheneum.

Goodall, J. (1988). *Little Red Riding Hood.* New York: Atheneum.

Goudey, A. (1961). *Here Come the Dolphins.* New York: Scribner's.

Graham, A., & Graham, F. (1978). *Whale Watch.* New York: Delacorte.

Grant, N. (1990). *How They Lived: The Egyptians.* New York: Brain Trade.

Green, A. (1957). *Pullett Surprises.* Glenview, IL: Scott Foresman.

Greenberg, J. E. (1986). *Sunny: the Death of a Pet.* New York: F. Watts.

Grillone, L., & Gennaro, J. (1978). *Small Worlds Close Up.* New York: Crown.

Gundersheimer, K. (1984). *1, 2, 3, Play with Me.* New York: Harper & Row.

Gundersheimer, K. (1986). *Colors to Know.* New York: Harper & Row.

Guthrie, D. (1988). *A Rose For Abby.* Nashville: Abingdon Press.

Guy, R. (1973). *The Friends.* New York: Holt, Rinehart and Winston.

Gwynne, F. (1976). *A Chocolate Moose for Dinner.* New York: Windmill Books.

Hague, K. (1986). *Numbears: A Counting Book.* Illustrated by Michael Hague. New York: Holt.

Hahn, M. D. (1988). *December Stillness.* New York: Clarion.

Hall, L. (1981). *The Horse Trader.* New York: Scribner's.

Hall, K., & Eisenberg, L. (1986). *Buggy Riddles.* New York: Dial.

Hamilton, V. (1974). *M. C. Higgins, the Great.* New York: Macmillan.

Hausherr, R. (1985). *My First Kitten.* New York: Four Winds.

Hazen, B. S. (1982). *Very Shy.* New York: Human Sciences.

Hazen, B. S. (1983). *If It Weren't for Benjamin (I'd Always Get to Lick the Icing Spoon).* New York: Human Sciences.

Hawkins, C., & J. (1985). *Old Mother Hubbard.* New York: Putnam.

Heller, R. (1989). *Many Luscious Lollipops.* New York: Grosset & Dunlap.

Henkes, K. (1990). *Julius, the Baby of the World.* New York: Greenwillow.

Herge. (1975). *Tintin in Tibet.* New York: Little Brown.

Hickman, M. W. (1984). *Last Week My Brother Anthony Died.* Nashville: Abingdon Press.

Highwater, J. (1985). *Eyes of Darkness.* New York: Lothrop, Lee & Shephard.

Hill, E. (1980). *Where's Spot?* New York: Putnam's.

Hite, D. (1990). *Demi's Count the Animals 1-2-3.* New York: Grossett & Dunlap.

Hoban, T. (1985). *Is It Larger? Is It Smaller?* New York: Greenwillow.

Hoban, T. (1982). *A, B, See!* New York: Greenwillow.

Hoban, T. (1985). *1, 2, 3.* New York: Greenwillow.

Hoban, T. (1985). *Count and See.* New York: Greenwillow.

Hoban, L. (1976). *Arthur's Pen Pal.* In *Arthur's Prize Reader,* 1978. New York: Harper & Row.

Hodges, M. (1984). *Saint George and the Dragon.* Illustrated by T. S. Hyman. Boston: Little, Brown.

Holm, A. (1990). *North to Freedom.* Orlando, FL: Harcourt Brace Jovanovich.

Hopkins, L. B. (Ed.). (1988). *Side by Side: Poems to Read Together.* Illustrated by Hilary Knight. New York: Simon and Schuster.

Hughes, S. (1985). *An Evening at Alfie's.* New York: Lothrop.

Hughes, S. (1986). *Up and Up.* New York: Lothrop.

**Hughes, S.** (1988). *Moving Molly.* New York: Lothrop.

**Hunter, M.** (1975). *A Stranger Came Ashore.* New York: Harper & Row.

**Hunter, M.** (1985). *Cat Herself.* New York: Harper & Row.

**Hutchins, P.** (1968). *Rosie's Walk.* New York: Macmillan.

**Innocenti, R.** (1985). *Rose Blanche.* Mankato, MN: Creative Education.

**Isadora, R.** (1983). *A City Seen From A to Z.* New York: Greenwillow.

**Isadora, R.** (1984). *I Hear. I See. I Touch.* (set) New York: Viking.

**Janeczko, P.** (1986). *Bridges to Cross.* New York: Macmillan.

**Jaspersohn, W.** (1980). *Bat, Ball, Glove.* Boston: Little, Brown.

**Jenness, A.** (1990). *Families: A Celebration of Diversity.* Boston: Houghton Mifflin.

**Jonas, A.** (1983). *Round Trip.* New York: Greenwillow. [retraceable]

**Jones, A.** (1987). *Street Family: A Novel.* New York: Harper & Row.

**Jordan, M.** (1989). *Losing Uncle Tim.* Niles, IL: A. Whitman.

**Jukes, M.** (1984). *Like Jake and Me.* New York: Knopf.

**Kamerman, S. E.** (1987). *Plays of Black Americans: Episodes from the Black Experience in America,* dramatized for young people. Boston: Plays.

**Katan, N. J.** (1981). *Hieroglyphs: The Writing of Ancient Egypt.* New York: Atheneum.

**Keats, E. J.** (1962). *The Snowy Day.* New York: Viking.

**Keats, E. J.** (1967). *Peter's Chair.* New York: Harper.

**Keeler, S.** (1987). *Passport to China.* Philadelphia: Franklin Watts.

**Keller, C.** (1989). *Tongue Twisters.* New York: Simon & Schuster.

**Kellogg, S.** (1974). *The Mystery of the Missing Red Mitten.* New York: Dial.

**Kellogg, S.** (1985). *Chicken Little.* New York: Morrow.

**The Kids' Question and Answer Book,** by the editors of *Owl* magazine. (1988). New York: Putnam.

**Kightley, R.** (1987). *Opposites.* Boston: Little, Brown.

**Kitamura, S.** (1985). *What's Inside: The Alphabet Book.* New York: Farrar, Straus & Giroux.

**Kitchen, B.** (1984). *Animal Alphabet.* New York: Dial.

**Kitchen, B.** (1987). *Animal Numbers.* New York: Dial.

**Klein, N.** (1974). *Confessions of an Only Child.* New York: Pantheon.

**Kohn, B.** (1974). *What a Funny Thing to Say.* New York: Dial Press.

**Komaiko, L.** (1987). *Annie Bananie.* New York: Harper & Row.

**Konigsburg, E. L.** (1967). *From the Mixed-Up Files of Mrs. Basil E. Frankweiler.* New York: Atheneum.

**Kovalski, M.** (1987). *The Wheels on the Bus.* New York: Little, Brown & Co.

**Krahn, F.** (1977). *The Mystery of the Giant Footprints.* New York: Dutton.

**Krahn, F.** (1982). *Sleep Tight, Alex Pumpernickel.* New York: Little, Brown & Co.

**Krahn, F.** (1985). *Amanda and the Mysterious Carpet.* Boston: Houghton Mifflin.

**Kraus, R.** (1980). *Mert the Blurt.* Illustrated by J. Aruego and A. Dewey. New York: Windmill Books/Simon & Schuster.

**Kübler-Ross, E.** (1982). *Remember the Secret.* Berkeley, CA: Celestial Arts.

**Kuklin, S.** (1986). *Thinking Big: The Story of a Young Dwarf.* New York: Lothrop, Lee & Shepard.

**LaFarge, O.** (1929). *Laughing Boy.* Boston: Houghton Mifflin.

**Lawson, R.** (1953). *Mr. Reeve and I.* Boston: Little, Brown & Co.

**Lawson, R.** (1979). *The Tough Winter.* New York: Puffin Books.

**Lester, H.** (1988). *Tacky the Penguin.* Boston: Houghton Mifflin.

**Levy, E.** (1976). *Lizzie Lies a Lot.* New York: Delacorte.

**Lewis, B. A.** (1992). *Kids with Courage.* Minneapolis: Free Spirit.

**Lewis, C. S.** (1988). *The Lion, the Witch and the Wardrobe.* New York: Macmillan.

**Lilly, K.** (1982). *Animals in the Country.* New York: Simon & Schuster.

**Limburg, P.** (1989). *Weird! The Complete Book of Halloween Words.* Illustrated by B. Lewin. New York: Bradbury Press.

**Litchfield, A. B.** (1984). *Making Room For Uncle Joe.* Niles, IL: A. Whitman.

**Lively, P.** (1985). *Uninvited Ghosts and Other Stories.* Illustrated by John Lawrence. New York: Dutton.

**Livingston, M. C.** (1974). *Listen, Children, Listen.* Orlando, FL: Harcourt Brace Jovanovich.

**Livingston, M. C.** (1992). *I Never Told and Other Poems.* New York: McElderry.

**Lobel, A.** (1970). *Frog and Toad Are Friends.* New York: Harper & Row.

**Lobel, A.** (1972). *Frog and Toad Together.* New York: Harper & Row.

**Lobel, A.** (1975). *Owl at Home.* New York: Harper & Row.

**Lobel, A.** (1976). *Frog and Toad All Year.* New York: Harper & Row.

**Lobel, A.** (1977). *Mouse Soup.* New York: Harper & Row.

**Lobel, A.** (1979). *Days with Frog and Toad.* New York: Harper & Row.

**Lobel, A.** (1982). *Ming Lo Moves the Mountain.* New York: Greenwillow.

**Lobel, A.** (1985). *Whiskers and Rhymes.* New York: Greenwillow.

**Lobel, A.** (1986). *Grasshopper on the Road.* New York: Harper & Row.

**Locker, T.** (1984). *Where the River Begins.* New York: Dial.

**London, J.** (1965). *The Call of the Wild.* New York: Putnam.

**Lord, S.** (1991). *Explorer Books: Mummies.* New York: Trumpet.

**Maccauley, D.** (1975). *Pyramid.* Boston: Houghton Mifflin.

**Maccaulay, D.** (1977). *Castle.* Boston: Houghton Mifflin.

**Maccaulay, D.** (1987). *Why the Chicken Crossed the Road.* Boston: Houghton Mifflin.

**Mann, P.** (1973). *My Dad Lives in a Downtown Hotel.* New York: Doubleday.

**Marshall, J.** (1987). *The Cut-ups Cut Loose.* New York: Viking.

**Martin, A. M.** (1988). *Yours Turly, Shirley.* New York: Holiday House.

**Martin, B., Jr.** (1970a). *Fire! Fire! Said Mrs. McGuire.* New York: Holt, Rinehart and Winston.

**Martin, b., Jr.** (1970b). *Old Devil Wind.* New York: Holt, Rinehart and Winston.

**Martin, B., Jr.** (1970c). *Silly Goose and the Holidays.* New York: Holt, Rinehart and Winston.

**Martin, B., Jr.** (1970d). *Whistle, Mary, Whistle.* New York: Holt, Rinehart and Winston.

**Martin, B.** (1983). *Brown Bear.* New York: Holt, Rinehart and Winston.

**Martin, B., Jr. & Archambault, J.** (1985). *Chicka Chicka Boom Boom.* Illustrated by T. Rand. New York: Simon & Schuster.

**Martin, B., Jr. & Archambault, J.** (1988). *Listen to the Rain.* New York: Henry Holt.

**Maruki.** (1980). *Hiroshima No Pika.* New York: Lothrop, Lee, & Shepard.

**Matsutani, M.** (1968). *The Crane Maiden.* Illustrated by Chihiro Iwasaki. English version by Alvin Tresselt. New York: Parents Magazine Press.

**Matthiesen, T.** (1981). *ABC, an Alphabet Book.* New York: Putnam's.

**Maury, I.** (1976). *My Mother's the Mail Carrier = Mi Mama La Cartera.* New York: Feminist Press.

**Mayer, M.** (1967). *A Boy, a Dog, and a Frog.* New York: Dial.

**Mayer, M.** (1969). *Frog on His Own.* New York: Dial.

**Mayer, M.** (1969). *Frog, Where Are You?* New York: Dial.

**Mayer, M.** (1973). *Frog Goes to Dinner.* New York: Dial.

**Mayer, M.** (1976). *Ah-Choo!* New York: Dial.

**McCloskey, R.** (1948). *Blueberries for Sal.* New York: Viking.

**McCloskey, R.** (1976). *Homer Price.* New York: Puffin.

**McCord, D.** (1986). *One at a Time.* Illustrated by Henry B. Kane. New York: Little Brown.

**McMaster, B.** (1986). *The Haunted Castle: Robena's Rose-Coloured Glasses: Two Children's Plays.* Toronto: Simon and Pierre.

**McMillan, B.** (1983). *Here a Chick, There a Chick.* New York: Lothrop, Lee & Shepard.

**McMillan, B.** (1989). *Spy on Vacation.* New York: Aladdin.

**McNeer, M.** (1950). *The California Gold Rush.* New York: Random House.

**Meddaugh, A.** (1992). *Martha Speaks.* Boston: Houghton Mifflin.

**Millard, A.** (1989). *History Highlights: Pyramids.* New York: Gloucester Press.

**Miller, J.** (1981). *The Farm Alphabet Book.* New York: Scholastic.

**Milton, J.** (1984). *Secrets of the Mummies.* New York: Random House.

**Minarik, E.** (1957). *Little Bear.* New York: Harper & Row.

**Minarik, E.** (1959). *Father Bear Comes Home.* New York: Harper & Row.

**Minarik, E.** (1960). *Little Bear's Friend.* New York: Harper & Row.

**Minarik, E.** (1961). *Little Bear's Visit.* New York: Harper & Row.

**Minarik, E.** (1968). *A Kiss for Little Bear.* New York: Harper & Row.

**Mizumura, K.** (1973). *If I Were a Cricket.* New York: Crowell.

**Momaday, N. S.** (1975). *Owl in the Cedar Tree.* Flagstaff, AZ: Northland Press.

**Mosel, A.** (1968). *Tikki Tikki Tembo.* Holt.

**Munsch, Robert N.** (1986). *The Paper Big Princess.* Toronto: Annick Press.

**Musgrove, M.** (1976). *Ashanti to Zulu.* Illustrated by Leo and Diane Dillon. New York: Dial.

**Nathanson, L.** (1986). *The Trouble with Wednesdays.* New York: Bantam.

**Ness, E.** (1966). *Sam, Bangs and Moonshine.* New York: Holt.

**Neurath, M.** (1964). *They Lived Like This in Ancient Egypt.* New York: Franklin Watts.

**Noble, T. H.** (1984). *The Day Jimmy's Boa Ate the Wash.* New York: Dial.

**Noble, T. H.** (1987). *Meanwhile Back at the Ranch.* Illustrated by T. Ross. New York: Dial.

**Noyes, A.** (1983). *The Highwayman.* Illustrated by C. Keeping. Oxford, England: Oxford University Press.

**Numeroff, L.** (1985). *If You Give a Mouse a Cookie.* Illustrated by R. Bond. New York: Harper & Row.

**O'Brien, R.** (1971). *Mrs. Frisby and the Rats of NIMH.* Illustrated by Zena Bernstein. New York: Atheneum.

**O'Dell, S.** (1976). *Sing Down the Moon.* New York: Dell.

**O'Keefe, S. H.** (1990). *One Hungry Monster: A Counting Book in Rhyme.* Illustrated by Lynn Munsinger. Boston: Little, Brown.

**Omerod, J.** (1985a). *Dad's Back.* New York: Lothrop, Lee & Shepard.

**Omerod, J.** (1985b). *Messy Baby.* New York: Lothrop, Lee & Shepard.

Otey, M. (1990). *Daddy Has a Pair of Striped Shorts*. New York: Farrar.

Owens, M. B. (1988). *A Caribou Alphabet*. Brunswick, ME: Dog Ear Press.

Owens, P., & Campiranonta, K. (1988). *Thai Proverbs*. Bangkok: Darnsutha Press.

Oxenbury, H. (1986). *I Can*. New York: Random House.

Paris, P. (1992). *Amelia Bedelia*. Illustrated by Fritz Seibel. New York: Harper & Row.

Park, B. (1989). *Skinnybones*. New York: Knopf.

Patterson, K. (1977). *Bridge to Terabithia*. New York: Crowell.

Patterson, K. (1978). *The Great Gilly Hopkins*. New York: Crowell.

Pearce, P. (1972). *Beauty and the Beast*. Illustrated by Alan Barnett. New York: Crowell.

Peck, R. (1988). *Princess Ashley*. New York: Dell.

Peck, R. N. (1972). *A Day No Pigs Would Die*. New York: Knopf.

Peppe, R. (1985). *The House That Jack Built*. Delacorte.

Perl, L. (1987). *Mummies, Tombs, and Treasures*. New York: Clarion.

Perrault, C. (1973). *Cinderella*. Illustrated by Errol LeCain. New York: Bradbury Press.

Peterson, J. (1986). *The Littles*. New York: Scholastic.

Phillips, L. (1983). *How Do You Get a Horse Out of the Bathtub?* New York: Viking.

Phillips, L. (1987). *Haunted House Jokes*. New York: Viking.

Piper, W. (1972). *Mother Goose, A Treasury of Best Loved Rhymes*. Illustrated by Tim and Greg Hildebrand. New York: Platt.

Piper, W. (1976). *The Little Engine That Could*. Illustrated by R. Sanderson. New York: Platt.

Pomerantz, C. (1984). *One Duck, Another Duck*. Illustrated by Jose Aruego & Ariane Dewey. New York: Greenwillow.

Pope, J. (1986). *Do Animals Dream?* New York: Viking.

Porte, B. (1983). *Harry's Visit*. Illustrated by Y. Abolafia. New York: Greenwillow.

Porte, B. (1984). *Harry's Dog*. New York: Greenwillow.

Porte, B. (1985). *Harry's Mom*. Illustrated by Y. Abolafia. New York: Greenwillow.

Potok, C. (1967). *The Chosen*. New York: Simon & Schuster.

Potter, B. (1984). *Yours Affectionately, Peter Rabbit*. New York: Warne.

Powell, P. (1984). *Edisto*. New York: Holt, Rinehart and Winston.

Prater, J. (1985). *The Gift*. New York: Viking.

Prelutsky, J. (1976). *Nightmares*. New York: Greenwillow.

Prelutsky, J. (1983). *The Random House Book of Poetry for Children*. Illustrated by Arnold Lobel. New York: Random House.

Prelutsky, J. (1984). *The New Kid on the Block*. New York: Greenwillow.

***Read-Aloud Rhymes for the Very Young***. Collected by Jack Prelutsky. Illustrated by Marc Brown. New York: Knopf.

Price, L. (1990). *Aida*. New York: Gulliver Books.

Pryor, B. (1987). *The House on Maple Street*. Illustrated by B. Peck. New York: Morrow. [flashback]

Quigley, M. (1981). *The Original Colored House of David*. Boston: Houghton Mifflin.

Ramsey, S. (1983). *I Unpacked My Grandmother's Trunk*. New York: Dutton.

Rappaport, D. (1982). *"But She's Still My Grandma!"* New York: Human Sciences.

Rawls, W. (1984). *Where the Red Fern Grows*. New York: Bantam.

Reiff, S. A. (1977). *Secrets of Tut's Tomb and the Pyramids*. Milwaukee: Raintree Children's Books.

Rey, H. A. (1973). *Curious George*. Boston: Houghton Mifflin.

Robart, R. (1986). *The Cake That Mack Ate*. Atlantic.

Roberts, W. D. (1987). *Sugar Isn't Everything: A Support Book in Fiction Form for the Young Diabetic*. New York: Atheneum.

Roberts, W. D. (1988). *Megan's Island*. New York: Atheneum.

Robinson, B. (1972). *The Best Christmas Pageant Ever*. New York: Harper Collins.

Rockwell, A. (1989). *My Spring Robin*. New York: Macmillan.

Rockwell, A., & Rockwell, H. (1979). *The Supermarket*. New York: Macmillan.

Rockwell, T. (1973). *How to Eat Fried Worms*. Illustrated by Emily McCully. New York: F. Watts.

Roffey, M. (1989). *Mealtime and Bathtime*. New York: Four Winds Press.

Rokoff, S. (no date). *Here Is a Cat!* Singapore: Hallmark Children's Editions.

Rosen, L. (1981). *Just Like Everybody Else*. San Diego: Harcourt Brace Jovanovich.

Rosenberg, M. B. (1983). *My Friend Leslie*. New York: Lothrop, Lee & Shepard.

Ruby, L. (1987). *Pig-Out Inn*. Boston: Houghton Mifflin.

Sachar, L. (1985). *Sideways Stories from Wayside School*. New York: Avon.

Sachs, M. (1987). *The Bear's House*. New York: Dutton.

Sargent, S. (1991). *Weird Henry Berg*. New York: Dell.

Schertle, A. (1987). *Jeremy Bean's St. Patrick's Day*. New York: Lothrop, Lee & Shepard.

Schoolcraft, H. R. (1970). *The Ring in the Prairie, A Shawnee Legend*. Edited by John Bierhorst. Illustrated by Leo and Diane Dillon. New York: Dial Press.

Schubert, D. (1987). *Where's My Monkey?* New York: Dial.

Schuchman, J. (1979). *Two Places to Sleep*. Minneapolis: Carolrhoda Books.

Schwartz, A. (1980). *Ten Copycats in a Boat and Other Riddles*. New York: Harper Collins.

Schwartz, A. (1981). *Scary Stories to Tell in the Dark*. Illustrated by Stephen Gammell. New York: Harper Collins.

Schwartz, A. (1986). *More Scary Stories to Tell in the Dark*. New York: Harper Collins.

Schwartz, A. (1988). *Annabelle Swift, Kindergartner*. New York: Orchard.

Schwartz, D. M. (1985). *How Much Is a Million?* Illustrated by Steven Kellogg. New York: Lothrop, Lee & Shepard.

Scott, G. (1981). *Egyptian Boats*. Minneapolis: Carolrhoda Books.

Sebestyen, O. (1983). *Words by Heart*. New York: Bantam.

Sendak, M. (1962). *Chicken Soup with Rice*. New York: Harper.

Sendak, M. (1962). *Pierre*. New York: Harper & Row.

Sendak, M. (1981). *Outside Over There*. New York: Harper & Row.

Sendak, M. (1985). *Where the Wild Things Are*. New York: Harper Collins.

Seuss, D. (1939). *The King's Stilts*. New York: Random House.

Seuss, D. (1960). *Green Eggs and Ham*. New York: Random House.

Seuss, D. (1984). *The Butter Battle Book*. New York: Random House.

Shannon, G. (1992). *Laughing All the Way*. Boston: Houghton Mifflin.

Sharmat, M. W. (1976) *Mooch the Messy*. Illustrated by B. Schecter. New York: Harper & Row.

Sharmat, M. W. (1978). *Mitchell Is Moving*. London: Collier Macmillan.

Sharmat, M. W. (1983). *Frizzy the Fearful*. New York: Holiday House.

Sheppard, J. (1990). *The Right Number of Elephants*. Illustrated by Felicia Bond. New York: Harper & Row.

Shulevitz, U. (1974). *Dawn*. New York: Farrar, Straus & Giroux.

Shulevitz, U. (1978). *The Treasure*. New York: Farrar, Strauss & Giroux.

Shyer, M. F. (1978). *Welcome Home, Jellybean*. New York: Scribner's.

Silverstein, S. (1974). *Where the Sidewalk Ends*. New York: Harper & Row.

Silverstein, S. (1981). *A Light in the Attic*. New York: Harper & Row.

Silverstein, S. (1987). *The Giving Tree*. New York: Harper Collins.

Simon, N. (1979). *We Remember Philip*. Chicago: A. Whitman.

Simon, N. (1986). *The Saddest Time*. Niles, IL: A. Whitman.

Smith, D. B. (1973). *A Taste of Blackberries*. New York: Crowell.

Smith, M. (1989). *Annie & Moon*. Milwaukee: Gareth Stevens.

Sobol, H. L. (1984). *We Don't Look Like Our Mom and Dad*. New York: Coward-McCann.

Spender, S. (1966). *The Magic Flute*. New York: Putnam's.

Sperling, S. (1985). *Murfles and Wink-A-Peeps: Funny Old Words for Kids*. New York: Crown.

Sperry, A. (1990). *Call It Courage*. New York: Macmillan.

Spier, P. (1978). *Oh, Were They Ever Happy!* New York: Doubleday.

Spier, P. (1982). *Peter Spier's Christmas*. New York: Doubleday.

Spier, P. (1982). *Peter Spier's Rain*. New York: Doubleday.

Spier, P. (1986). *Dreams*. New York: Doubleday.

Stanek, M. (1983). *Don't Hurt Me, Mama*. Niles, IL: A. Whitman.

Steig, W. (1976). *Abel's Island*. New York: Farrar, Straus & Giroux.

Steptoe, J. (1981). *Mufaro's Beautiful Daughters: An African Tale*. New York: Scholastic.

Stevens, H. (1987). *Fat Mouse*. New York: Viking.

Stevenson, J. (1980). *All About Bones*. Racine, WI: Western Publishing Company.

Stevenson, J. (1983). *Grandpa's Great City Tour: An Alphabet Book*. New York: Greenwillow.

Stevenson, J. (1984). *Worse Than Willie!* New York: Greenwillow.

Stolz, Mary. (1990). *Storm in the Night*. New York: Harper & Row.

Surat, M. M. (1983). *Angel Child, Dragon Child*. Milwaukee: Raintree.

Swortzell, L. (1985). *Six Plays for Young People from the Federal Theatre Project (1936–39)*. Westport, CT: Greenwood Press.

Tafuri, N. (1986). *Have You Seen My Duckling?* New York: Penguin.

Taylor, M. (1976). *Roll of Thunder Hear My Cry*. New York: Dial.

Taylor, M. (1987). *The Friendship*. New York: Dial.

Taylor, T. (1987). *The Cay*. New York: Doubleday.

*The Teeny Weeny Woman*. (1987). Cleveland, OH: Modern Curriculum Press.

Terban, M. (1989). *Superdupers!: Really Funny Real Words*. New York: Clarion Books.

Tetherington, J. (1986). *Pumpkin Pumpkin*. New York: Greenwillow.

Tetherington, J. (1987). *A Place For Ben*. New York: Greenwillow.

Tompert, A. (1976). *Little Fox Goes to the End of the World*. New York: Crown.

**Tran, K. T.** (1987). *The Little Weaver of Thai-Yen Village = Co Be Tho-Det Lang Thai-Yen*. San Francisco: Children's Book.

**Tremain, R.** (1976). *Fooling Around With Words*. New York: Morrow.

**Turkle, B.** (1976). *Deep in the Forest*. New York: Dutton.

**Turner, A.** (1985). *Dakota Dugout*. Illustrated by R. Himler. New York: Macmillan. [flashback]

**Turner, A.** (1987). *Nettie's Trip South*. Illustrated by R. Himler. New York: Macmillan.

**Unstead, R. J.** (1986). *See Inside: An Egyptian Town*. New York: Warwick Press.

**Van Leeuwen, J.** (1979). *Tales of Oliver Pig*. Illustrated by A. Schweninger. New York: Dial.

**Van Leeuwen, J.** (1983). Tales of *Amanda Pig*. New York: Dial.

**Van Leeuwen, J.** (1985). *More Tales of Amanda Pig*. New York: Dial.

**Varley, S.** (1984). *Badger's Parting Gifts*. New York: Lothrop, Lee & Shepherd.

**Verson Jones, V. S.** (1912). *Aesop's Fables*. New York: Avenel Books.

**Vincent, G.** (1982). *Breakfast Time*. New York: Greenwillow.

**Vincent, G.** (1982). *Ernest and Celestine's Patchwork Quilt*. New York: Greenwillow.

**Viorst, J.** (1987). *Alexander and the Terrible, Horrible, No Good, Very Bad Day*. New York: Macmillan.

**Vipont, E.** (1986). *The Elephant and the Bad Boy*. New York: Putnam.

**Waber, B.** (1973). *Ira Sleeps Over*. Boston: Houghton Mifflin.

**Wadsworth, O. A.** (1985). *Over in the Meadow: A Counting-Out Rhyme*. Illustrated by Mary M. Rae. New York: Viking.

**Wagner, J.** (1972). *J.T.* Photographs by Gordon Parks. New York: Dell.

**Wagner, J.** (1977). *The Bunyuip of Berkeley's Creek*. Illustrated by Ron Brooks. New York: Bradbury Press.

**Walter, M. P.** (1986). *Justin and the Best Biscuits in the World*. New York: Lothrop, Lee & Shepard.

**Ward, C.** (1992). *Cookie's Week*. New York: Putnam.

**Watson, C.** (1982). *Applebet: An ABC*. Illustrated by Wendy Watson. New York: Farrar, Straus & Giroux.

**Weeks, J.** (1977). *The Pyramids*. Minneapolis: Lerner.

**Weiss, L.** (1982). *Chuckie*. New York: Greenwillow.

**Wells, R.** (1973). *Noisy Nora*. New York: Dial.

**Wells, R.** (1979). *Max's Bath. Max's Bedtime. Max's Birthday. Max's Breakfast*. (set) New York: Dial.

**Wells, R.** (1981). *Timothy Goes to School*. New York: Dial.

**Wells, R.** (1984). *My Teacher Sleeps in School*. Illustrated by E. Weiss. New York: Warne.

**White, E. B.** (1952). *Charlotte's Web*. New York: Harper & Row.

**Wildsmith, B.** (1963). *Brian Wildsmith's ABC*. New York: Franklin Watts.

**Wilhelm, H.** (1985). *I'll Always Love You*. New York: Crown.

**Williams, L.** (1986). *The Little Old Lady Who Was Not Afraid of Anything*. New York: Crowell.

**Williams, M.** (1922). *The Velveteen Rabbit*. Illustrated by W. Nicholson. (Reprint). New York: Doubleday.

**Williams, V. B.** (1982). *A Chair For My Mother*. New York: Greenwillow.

**Williams, V. B.** (1983). *Something Special For Me*. New York: Greenwillow.

**Williams, V. B.** (1984). *Music, Music For Everyone*. New York: Greenwillow.

**Wilson, S.** (1985). *Beware the Dragons*. New York: Harper & Row.

**Winter, P.** (1976). *The Bear and the Fly*. New York: Crown.

**Wojciechowska, M.** (1968). *Tuned Out*. New York: Harper & Row.

**Wong, J. S.** (1963). *Fifth Chinese Daughter*. New York: Scholastic.

**Wood, A.** (1984). *The Napping House*. Illustrated by D. Wood. San Diego: Harcourt Brace Jovanovich.

**Yashima, T.** (1955). *Crow Boy*. New York: Viking.

**Yee, W. H.** (1992). *EEK! There's a Mouse in the House*. Boston: Houghton Mifflin.

**Yep, L.** (1977). *Child of the Owl*. New York: Harper & Row.

**Young, E.** (1983). *Up a Tree*. New York: Harper & Row.

**Young, E.** (1984). *The Other Bone*. New York: Harper & Row.

**Zindel, P.** (1984). *Harry & Hortense at Hormone High*. New York: Harper & Row.

**Zion, G.** (1956). *Harry the Dirty Dog*. New York: Harper & Row.

**Zolotow, C.** (1980). *If You Listen*. Illustrated by M. Simont. New York: Harper & Row.

**Zolotow, C.** (1980). *Say It!* Illustrated by James Stevenson. New York: Greenwillow.

# ©COPYRIGHTS AND ACKNOWLEDGMENTS

## PART OPENER PHOTOS

**Part I**    Photo by Skeeter Hagler,
used by courtesy of Harcourt Brace College Publishers

**Part II**    Photo by Jerry White,
used by courtesy of Harcourt Brace School Department

**Part III**    Photo by Mark Cunningham,
used by courtesy of Harcourt Brace School Department

**Part IV**    Photo by Skeeter Hagler,
used by courtesy of Harcourt Brace College Publishers

**Part V**    Photo by Skeeter Hagler,
used by courtesy of Harcourt Brace College Publishers

## ILLUSTRATION CREDITS

6: From McKee, Paul. *The Teaching of Reading in the Elementary School.* Copyright © 1948 by Houghton Mifflin Company. Used with permission.

7: "Comparison of Beginning Reading with Fluent Reading" from Samuels, Schermer, Reinking - "Reading fluency: Techniques for Making Decoding Automatic" in WHAT RESEARCH HAS TO SAY ABOUT READING INSTRUCTION, by Samuels and Farstrup. Reprinted with the permission of the International Reading Association.

17: © Elizabeth Crews

28: Courtesy of Mary Anne Adcock Harris. *"The Progressive Teacher."*

33: © 1993 Boris Drucker and The Cartoon Bank, Inc.

41, 43(4): Excerpts from HARCOURT BRACE SCHOOL PUBLISHERS 1994 K-8 CATALOG by Harcourt Brace & Company, copyright © 1993 by Harcourt Brace & Company, reprinted by permission of the publisher.

61: Copyright © 1990 Steck-Vaughn Company, Austin, Texas. *Whole Language.* Reprinted with permission.

63: © Ulrike Welsch/PhotoEdit

67: © 1993 William Haefeli and The Cartoon Bank, Inc.

76: Selection taken from *The Gunnywolf* by A. Delaney. Copyright © 1988 by A. Delaney. Selection reprinted by permission of Harper-Collins Publishers.

80: © Ulrike Welsch/PhotoEdit

91: "Parents Assisting Children: Helpful hints on ways to help your child with reading while at home" by Charles, M.L., Njegovan, G., Triplett, C., and Asberry, G., illustrated by students of Wheatley School: Kenneth Alexander, Markel Hines and Natasha Reese.

96: Text copyright © 1985 by David A. Adler. Illustrations copyright © 1985 by Victoria Chess. All rights reserved. Reprinted from *The Twisted Witch and Other Spooky Riddles* by permission of Holiday House, Inc.

103: © Elizabeth Crews

111: © James L. Shaffer/PhotoEdit

150: © Elizabeth Crews

155 (2): © 1993, Mary Ann Fittipaldi

156: © Robert E. Daemmrich/Tony Stone Images

156: © 1993, Mary Ann Fittipaldi

168: Reprinted with the permission of the Florida Reading Association.

173: Reprinted with the permission of Bradbury Press, an Affiliate of Macmillan, Inc., from DREAM WOLF by Paul Goble. Copyright © 1990 by Paul Goble.

174: Reprinted with the permission of Teri Sloat.

175: The annotation from "Independence Avenue" from "Teachers Choices 1991," *The Reading Teacher*, Nov. 1991, reprinted with permission of the International Reading Association. Photo of book cover reprinted with permission of the Jewish Publication Society.

206: © Kindra Clineff/The Picture Cube

213: © Elizabeth Crews

229: Reprinted with the permission of Macmillan College Publishing Company from THE STUDY READERS-FIFTH YEAR by Alberta Walker and Mary R. Parkman. Copyright © 1924 by Macmillan College Publishing Company, Inc.

232: © 1993 Frank Cotham and The Cartoon Bank, Inc.

235: Figure from TEACHER'S GUIDE TO WORD ATTACK, A WAY TO BETTER READING by Clyde Roberts, copyright © 1956 by Harcourt Brace and Company and renewed 1984 by Clyde Roberts, reprinted by permission of the publisher.

305: Reprinted with permission of Joan E. Heimlich and the International Reading Association.

329: Question-Answer Relationships reprinted with permission of Taffy Raphael and the International Reading Association.

348: Illustrations based on "The Runaway Bunny" reprinted by permission of the Wisconsin Department of Public Instruction. Illustrations copyright © 1972 by Edith T.

Hurd, Clement Hurd, John Thacher Hurd, and George Hellyer. Selection reprinted by permission of HarperCollins Publishers.

369: Reprinted by permission of the Indiana University Press.

376: Illustration from *Bet You Can't* reprinted by permission of Avon Books.

402: Illustration from *Charlotte's Web* by E.B. White, copyright renewed © 1980 by Garth Williams. Selection reprinted by permission of HarperCollins Publishers.

406: Fig. 10.10 is reprinted with permission of Deborah A. Wooten and the International Reading Association.

410: Reprinted courtesy of NASA.

411(2): Reprinted by permission of the Educational Development Corporation.

475: Reprinted from the cover of *Thai Proverbs*, Darnsutha Press Co., Ltd.

494: Reprinted with permission of the International Reading Association.

534: Grouping patterns from Fitzgerald, S. (1975) "Teaching Discussion Skills and Attributes." *Language Arts, 52* (8), pp. 1094–1096. Reprinted with permission of the National Council of Teachers of English.

550: Adapted from Fry, E. (1977). "Fry's readability graph; Clarification, validity, and extension to level

17." *Journal of Reading*, Vol. 21, pp. 242–252. Reprinted with permission of the International Reading Association.

557: Reprinted by permission of Discus Books.

575: "This Bridge" by Shel Silverstein from A LIGHT IN THE ATTIC. Copyright © 1981 by Evil Eye Music, Inc. Selection reprinted by permission of HarperCollins Publishers.

577: Treasury of Literature, Teachers' Edition. Harcourt Brace Jovanovich 1993. Used by permission.

## LITERARY CREDITS

### Chapter 3
Robinson, S.S., and Dixon, R., (1991). "The language concepts that low- and middle-class four-year-olds bring to preschool." Paper presented at the National Reading Conference, Palm Springs, CA • "Foundations of Emergent Literacy." From HANDBOOK OF READING RESEARCH, Volume II, edited by Rebecca Barr. Michael L. Kamil, Peter Mosenthal, and P. David Pearson. Copyright © 1991 by Longman Publishing Group • Chart-"Should Children Be Allowed to Read Early?" From TEACHING READING TO EVERY CHILD by Diane Lapp and James Flood. Reprinted with the permission of Macmillan College Publishing Company. Copyright © 1992 by Macmillan College Publishing Company, Inc. • From Dorothy Rich, Ed.D., *MegaSkills(r): In School and In Life* (Houghton Mifflin, Revised Edition, 1992). Excerpt from Rosow, La Vergne (1991). "How Schools Perpetuate Illiteracy," *Educational Leadership, 47*(1), 41–44. Reprinted with permission of the Association for Supervision and Curriculum Development and the author. Copyright © 1991 by ASCD. All rights reserved. • "Developing Phonemic Awareness in Young Children." Reprinted by per-

mission of Hallie K. Yopp and the International Reading Association. • "Ideas for Working with Parents." Reprinted with permission from Virginia State Reading Association Newsletter, Fall 1991 • Susan Mandel Glazer (1990). *Creating Readers and Writers. Parent Booklet No. 165.* Newark, DE: International Reading Association.

### Chapter 4
From Robert J. Tierney, John E. Readence, and Ernest K. Dishner. *Reading Strategies and Practices: A Compendium 3/E.* Copyright © 1990 by Allyn and Bacon. Reprinted by permission • Larrick, N. (1987). "Keep a poem in your pocket." In Cullinan, B.E (Ed.), *Children's Literature in the Reading Program.* Newark, DE: International Reading Association, pp. 20–27 • "Benefits of Students' Oral Reading." From Gentile, L., and McMillan, M.M. (1987). *Stress and Reading Difficulties.* Newark, DE: International Reading Association • "Lauritzen's Choral Reading Lesson." Adapted from Carol Lauritzen (1982). "A modification of repeated readings for group instruction." *The Reading Teacher,* 35,456–458. Reprinted with permission of the International Reading Association • Ross's Oral Reading Homework Program.

Reprinted with permission of Elinor P. Ross and the International Reading Association. • "For Diagnostic Information and Corrective Feedback." Adapted from Frank Green (1986). "Listening to Children read: The empathetic process." *The Reading Teacher,* Feb. 1986, Vol. 39, pp. 536–543. Reprinted with permission of the International Reading Association. • "For diagnostic Information and Corrective Feedback." Taken from McCoy, Kathleen M. and Pany, Darlene (1986). "Summary and analysis of oral reading corrective feedback research." *The Reading Teacher,* Feb. 1986, vol. 39, p. 548. Reprinted with permission of the International Reading Association. • "For Weak Readers." From Labbo, L.D., & Teale, W. H. (1990). "Cross-age reading: A strategy for helping poor readers." *The Reading Teacher,* 43, 362–369. Reprinted with permission of the International Reading Association. • Hoffman's Model Oral Recitation Lesson. Reprinted by permission of James Hoffman.

### Chapter 5
"General Sources of Reviews of Children's Books." Reprinted with permission of the publisher, the National Association for the Education of Young Children. • "Developing

# NAME INDEX

# SUBJECT INDEX